James Monroe

Bankers' Code for the Use of National Banks

State Banks, Savings Banks and Private Bankers

James Monroe

Bankers' Code for the Use of National Banks
State Banks, Savings Banks and Private Bankers

ISBN/EAN: 9783337123949

Printed in Europe, USA, Canada, Australia, Japan

Cover: Foto ©Suzi / pixelio.de

More available books at **www.hansebooks.com**

BANKERS' CODE,

FOR THE USE OF

NATIONAL BANKS,

STATE BANKS,

SAVINGS BANKS AND PRIVATE BANKERS.

COMPILED BY

JAMES MONROE.

JULY, 1879.

OFFICE, No. 69 DUANE STREET.

PRICE:

TWO DOLLARS, bound in Cloth; ONE DOLLAR, Paper Cover.

ADDRESS

MONROE & COMPANY, BILL BROKERS,

NEW YORK.

PREFACE.

A READY and trustworthy means of acquiring a knowledge of the established laws relating to Promissory Notes, Bills of Exchange, Checks, Deposits, Collections, Usury, Discounts and other matters connected with the daily transactions of a banker, may not only prevent extended litigation, but will also enable the cautious banker to create a PRACTICAL BASIS OF ACTION, under which his attorney can more effectually DEFEND his rights and PRESERVE HIS INTEREST. If the banker does not conduct his business affairs in conformity with the rules and regulations established by the higher Courts, his attorney, let him be ever so capable and energetic, cannot maintain his rights or preserve those interests which the banker may have neglected or endangered either through carelessness or a want of legal knowledge. The Courts have held that "there is no protection for the rash against the consequences of their imprudent contracts."

JAMES MONROE, EDITOR.

BANKERS' CODE.

ACCEPTANCE.

1. An Acceptance, to be binding, must in every respect meet and correspond with the offer made; neither falling within nor going beyond the terms proposed, but exactly meeting them at all points, and closing with them as they stand. A proposal to accept an offer on terms varying from those proposed amounts to a rejection of the offer, and a substitution of a counter proposition, which cannot become a contract until assented to by the first proposer. The original offer loses its vitality, and is no longer pending between the parties, and becomes an open proposition again only when renewed by the party who first made it. The party submitting a counter proposition, cannot, without the consent of the first proposer, withdraw or abandon the same, and then accept the original offer which he has once rejected. *Fox* v. *Turner*, 1 Bradwell's Ill. App. Rpts. 153.

ACCOUNT STATED.

2. An Account Stated is presumptive evidence only of the balance admitted to be due, and may be corrected for fraud or mistake. On the settlement of accounts, the parties may, by agreement, limit the time within which claim for the correction of mistakes or omissions shall be made; and in such case, evidence of an omitted demand may be excluded, unless proof be made of claim for its allowance within the time agreed upon by the parties. *Vandeveer* v. *Statesir, Adm'r*, 39 N. J. Law, 593.

3. For a period of two years A. kept an account with a bank, for money loaned, checks paid, and credits for deposits and payments; the bank during the time making monthly statements, striking the balance due each month, which was carried forward and charged against A. *Held*, that the monthly balances were not distinct settlements, but that the whole constituted a running account, and was, in effect, but one transaction. *Pickett, et al.,* v. *Merchants' Nat. Bank of Memphis, et al.,* 32 Ark. 346.

AGENCY.

4. The general rule is that the clerks of an agent are not

agents of the principal. *Hope*, v. *Dixon*, 22 Grant's Chancery, Ontario, 439.

5. Payments received by one knowing the agent to be unauthorized to make them, may be recovered by the principal as money wrongfully had and received. *Demarest*, v. *Inhabitants of New Barbadoes*, 40 N. J. Law, 604.

6. Where the acts of the agent will bind the principal, where his representations, declarations and admissions respecting the subject matter will bind the principal, when made at the same time and constituting a part of the *res gestae* *Coyle*. v. *B. & O. R. R. Co.*, 11 W. Va. 94.

7. An agent having special authority to adjust a particular loss cannot, by virtue thereof, adjust a different loss, and whatever he may do with reference to the different loss cannot affect the principal. To find the principal, it must be shown by competent evidence that the agent acted within the scope of his authority. *Hartford Fire Ins. Co.* v. *Smith et al.*, 3 Colo. 422.

8. The employment of an agent by the principal to sell land need not be in writing, but the agent may recover for services rendered in effecting the sale, by virtue of a verbal contract. *Watson* v. *Brightwell*, 60 Ga. 212.

9. Money borrowed by the agent on the credit of the principal, without authority, goes into the principal's business without the latter's knowledge, and the principal has the benefit thereof, yet is not the principal liable therefor to the person of whom it was borrowed, in the absence of a promise to pay. *Spooner* v. *Thompson and wife*, 48 Vt. 259.

10. Authority to make a contract for another is not sufficient to authorize its cancellation or surrender. *Stillwell* v. *Mut. Ins. Co.*, 72 N. Y. App. 385.

10½. One who constitutes another his agent, with full power to manage his mercantile house and to do all acts appertaining to his business, makes himself liable for the value of all goods purchased by the agent in the line of that business. *Schmidt & Zeigler* v. *Sandal et al.* 30 La. 353.

11. Held that the general agent in Canada of a foreign company must be regarded in the same light as the general agent at the head office in the foreign country. *Campbell* v. *National Life Ins. Co.*, 24 Upper Canada Com. Pleas Rpts. 133.

12. Notice to the agent is notice to the principal, if the agent comes to the knowledge of the fact while he is acting for the principal in the course of the very transaction which becomes the subject of the suit. Such knowledge of the agent is imputed to the principal third party who has dealt with the agent in good faith. *Stanly* v. *Chamberlin*, 39 N. J., Law 565.

13. A principal is always bound by the acts and neglects of his agent. And the same rule which applies to a private principal applies to a corporation, whether ordinary or municipal, and, *a fortiori*, to a corporation which can only act by an agent. *City of Petersburg* v. *Appelgarth's* admr. 28 Grattan, Va. 321.

14. An agent's authority, not coupled with an interest, being revocable at the pleasure of the principal, one dealing with such agent after notice of revocation, does so at his peril. *Patton* v. *Coen & Ten Broeke*, 3 Colo. 265.

15. The declarations of one acting as the agent of both parties to a contract, if made within the scope of his authority, are properly receivable in evidence in an action between the parties to the contract. *Schaefer et al.* v. *Gildea et al.* 3 Colo. 15.

16. If the purchaser of property does not know that he is dealing with an agent of the owner, and has not good reason to know it, he is justified in treating the agent as the owner, and payment of the purchase price to him will be a defense to an action by the owner for the amount. *The Eclipse Windmill Co.* v. *Thorron*, 46 Iowa, 181.

17. Where an agent, clothed with power to accept bills, has accepted a bill in the name of his principal, the latter cannot escape liability as acceptor on the ground that he had no interest in the transaction in which the bill was given, and that he had received no consideration, unless he proves that his agent, to the knowledge of the holder of the bill, has abused his power. *Broadway Savings Bank of St. Louis* v. *Edward Vorster et al.*, 30 La. 587.

18. In an action for goods sold and delivered the defence is payment to an agent, the fact that the principal has previously revoked the authority of the agent is not conclusive of plaintiff's right to recover, if the revocation of authority has not been communicated to the defendant, and there is other evidence in the case from which the jury would be authorized in finding that the defendant had reason to suppose that the authority of the agent to receive payment continued. *Parker* v. *Hinckley Locomotive Works*, 122 Mass. 484.

19. One who purchases goods at half their value, he having information from which he may know that the factor with whom he deals is acting without authority, and in fraud of his principal, takes no title thereto, such a purchase being inconsistent with good faith, and void, and the principal may recover the goods from such pretended vendee. *Singer Manufacturing Co.* v. *Hudson*, 4 Mo. Court of Appeals, St. Louis, 145.

20. Where one, without consideration, entrusted an agent with a sum of money to settle a lawsuit between two others, she

has the power of revocation until the settlement is complete, especially if the contract be in writing, and it is therein expressly agreed that the terms of the settlement are to be satisfactory to her in every way, and if not, then the money to be restored to her. *Phillips et al.* v. *Howell*, 60 Ga., 411.

21. Where a party, acting through an agent, loans money on the security of the borrower's mortgage, and the agent, who keeps the note in his possession, pays over from time to time to his principal the accruing interest and parts of the principal of the note received from the maker, finally pays over to the principal the balance due on the note, without stating that he is paying his own money, and without obtaining the consent of his principal to buy, or even intimating that he desired to buy the note, he will not acquire any title to the note ; and the note itself, and the accompanying mortgage, will be deemed extinguished. *Albert G. Brice* v. *John A. Watkins, et al.*, 30 La. 21.

22. Where an agency is continuous and made up of a long series of transactions of the same general character, knowledge acquired by the agent in one or more of the transactions is notice to the agent and the principal, which will affect the latter in any other transaction in which the agent, as such, is engaged and in which the knowledge is material. *Holden* v. *N. Y. and Erie Bank*, 72 N. Y. App. 286.

23. An agent employed in negotiating the sale of a promissory note, making statements regarding the purpose for which the same was executed, such statements will be considered fairly within the scope of his agency and will bind his principal; the general power to negotiate will, by implication, include the power to give such information as would ordinarily be called for. *McBean* v. *Fox, et al.*, 1 Bradwell's Ill. App. Rpts. 177.

24. An agent for the sale of goods, with an interest in the proceeds, is not deprived of the power to sell by the death of the principal. The terms of the agency were that the agent should sell the goods and out of the proceeds pay certain lien and other claims, and apply the balance, first, to the payment of certain notes he held against the principal and return the overplus to the principal. *Held*, that the power was not extinguished by the death of the principal; that the agent had a right to sell, and apply the proceeds as agreed, and to pay his own notes in full, even though the estate was rendered insolvent and other creditors received only a percentage. In this case the notes were delivered by the defendant to the plaintiff, and by her presented to the commissioners. *Held*, that their allowance by the commissioners as a claim against the estate, without the procurement or authority of the defendant, in no way affected his rights. *Merry, admr'x of Patterson* v. *Lynch*, 68 Me. 94.

25. A formal instrument, delegating powers, is ordinarily

subject to a strict interpretation, and the authority is not extended beyond that given in terms, or which is necessary to carry into effect that which is expressly given. *Craighead* v. *Peterson*, 72 N. Y. App. 279.

26. An assignee or trustee cannot speculate with assigned property, save at his own risk. Neither can he engage in business ventures at remote places, and of doubtful results, without rendering himself personally liable for any untoward results. *Stettauer* v. *Carney*, 20 Kansas, 489.

27. W. was the owner (subject to a mortgage) of property which M. wished to buy; R. becoming aware of this, entered into friendly negotiations with both, and bargained with W. to take $3,500, and with M. to give $5,600 for the property; R. concealed this difference from the parties. W. conveyed to M.; on her signing the deed, R.'s attorney paid to her the $3,500 (less the mortgage debt), and on the deed being delivered to M., she (M.) paid to R.'s attorney the $5,600. The facts afterwards coming to the knowledge of W., she filed a bill against R., claiming the balance of the $5,600; and it appearing that in the negotiations he had given W. to understand that he was acting in her interest and had no personal interest of his own, the plaintiff was held entitled to a decree against R. for such balance with interest and costs. There may be an agency, and its duties and liabilities, without express words of appointment or acceptance; and where a party in negotiating between two persons, the one desiring to sell, the other to buy certain land, gave the former to understand that he was acting in her interest, it was held that she was entitled to the full price which he obtained for the land, though it exceeded the amount which he had obtained her consent to accept. In such a case, there being a conflict as to what had passed in the conversations, and no other witness of them being produced, it was held that, all other things being equal, the version of the deceived party should be accepted in preference to that of the other party. *Wright* v. *Rankin*, 18 Grant's Chancery, Ontario, 625.

28. The owner, by delivery of an unendorsed promissory note payable to another, delivered the same for collection to an agent, who, without the knowledge or consent of the owner, delivered the same for collection to a third person, who received knowledge of the rights of such owner. On the trial of an action by such owner against such third person to recover the money so collected by the defendant, wherein the complaint alleged a demand and refusal, the evidence established that the plaintiff, being the owner, by delivery, of an unendorsed promissory note payable to another, delivered the same to an agent for collection; that such agent, without the plaintiff's knowledge or consent, delivered the same for collection to the defendant, without informing him as to the plaintiff's ownership thereof; that the defendant received and collected the same and used the proceeds, believing it to be the property of the payee; and that another agent of the plaintiff, without informing the defendant of his agency or of the plaintiff's rights, demanded of the defendant a settlement. *Held*, that the plaintiff, by suing the defendant, ratified the act of her agent in placing such note in the defendant's hands. *Held*, also, that a demand was necessary, and that a finding that none was properly made will not be disturbed where the evidence in relation thereto is conflicting. *Held*, also that under the averment of the complaint, that demand had been made and refused, evidence of a conversion by the defendant could not be given as an excuse for making no demand. *Kyser* v. *Wells*, 60 Ind. 261.

29. A., who had purchased the bankrupt stock in trade of B., made an agreement with him in writing by which B. was "to do business" at the same shop, as "agent for" A., authorizing B. "to sell the goods now in stock and buy other goods, in order to keep the stock good with the money received, but not to buy on credit without an order in writing" from A., and providing that "if at any time the business is not carried on to the satisfaction" of A., "the store and fixtures, together with all the goods in the store and the books and accounts, shall be turned over, with the keys of the store, to the said" A. B., without an order in writing from A., purchased certain goods on credit of the plaintiff, who was in ignorance of B.'s relation to A., all of which goods went into the stock of the store, to the use and benefit of A. Soon after, A. took possession of all the goods in the shop, including such of those sold by the plaintiff as remained in the stock, and sold them as his own. *Held*, in an action against A. to recover for the goods sold by the plaintiff to B., that the agreement made B. the agent of A. to carry on the shop; that A., by taking and selling a part of the goods, had ratified the act of B. in purchasing on credit without his order; and that the action would lie. *Surtwell* v. *Frost*, 122 Mass. 184.

30. Defendant executed a power of attorney as follows: "To whom it may concern: This is to certify that I hereby authorize H. Loveland, as my agent, to make drafts on me, from time to time, as may be necessary for the purchase of lumber for my account, and to consign the same to the care of P. W. Scribner & Co., Whitehall, N. Y.—A. H. GRISWOLD." *Held*, we think the authority was absolute. The words, "as my agent" do not refer to the form of the contract, but to the capacity in which Loveland acted. If he drew, in fact, as agent, it was not material whether he described himself as such or not; nor was it made material by the power of attorney. So the words "as may be necessary" are not words of condition,

but mean to the extent necessary, and the words "for the purchase of lumber," &c., refer to the business in which the agent is employed, and do not constitute a condition precedent, which a party taking the paper upon the faith of the authority must show has been performed. *Merchants' Bank of Canada* v. *Griswold,* 72 N. Y. App. 472.

There is a distinction, I think, between a conditional authority to draw and a limitation of authority. In the former case the power cannot be exercised at all without showing the performance of the condition; while in the latter it may be exercised, within the limits prescribed, in all the cases where the authority was limited in amount, time and otherwise. (*Barney* v. *Worthington,* 37 N. Y., 112.) In such cases the authority is absolute to draw, within the limit prescribed. In this case the power cannot be said to be general and unlimited. It is restricted to the amount necessary to purchase lumber for the defendant, but within that limit is absolute and unqualified. The agent must determine the necessity of the amount required for the business in which he is engaged, and not the person who parts with his money on the faith of the authority. It was proved on the trial that the money was loaned to be used in that business. The agent, by procuring the discount upon the faith of the power of attorney, represented that it was to be used in the business of the defendant, and that the amount was necessary. *Id.*

As was said in *North River Bank* v. *Aymer* (3 Hill, 267), "The plaintiffs were apprised that Jacob D. Thurber had power to make and endorse notes in the business of the testator, and notes actually made and endorsed by the attorney and purporting to have been so made and endorsed, in conformity with the power, were presented to, and in effect discounted by the plaintiffs. This act was equivalent to an express declaration that the notes were made and endorsed in the business of the testator," and the court held that the principal was bound by these representations. The rule was authoritatively formulated by this court in the Schuyler case (34 N. Y. 30), as follows: "Where the authority of an agent depends upon some fact outside the terms of his power, and which, from its nature, rests peculiarly within his knowledge, the principal is bound by the representations of the agent, although false as to the existence of such fact."

The question then recurs, whether the defendant promised, unconditionally, to accept the drafts. Without elaborating that question, I think it must be regarded as settled in this State that an absolute authority to draw is equivalent to an unconditional promise to pay the draft. (37 N. Y. 112 *supra.* *Ulster Co. Bank* v. *McFarlan,* 5 Hill, 433; S. C., 3 Den. 553; *Bank of Michi-*

gan v. *Ely*, 17 Wend., 510). And this is the natural and necessary implication. *Id.*

The declarations and representations of the agent at the time the draft was discounted are part of the *res gestæ*, and were admissible. (3 Hill, *supra*).

In *Lanusse* v. *Baker*, 3 Wheat. 146, the rule is concisely stated as follows: "When a general authority is given to draw bills from a certain place on account of advances there made, the undertaking is to replace the money at that place." The same principle was reiterated in 6 Peters, 685, and was sanctioned in *First Nat. Bk. of Toledo* v. *Shaw*, 61 N. Y. 293; see also 5 Cl. & Finn. 1. The authority in this case was to draw anywhere, and therefore it was an authority to draw in Canada, and the laws of Canada must govern. *Id.*

31. Power of attorney, authorizing an agent to sue for a specific debt, and to do all in the premises that the principal could do, carries with it the power to make the suit effective by attachment. *De Poret* v. *Gusman*, 30 La. 930.

ASSIGNMENTS.

32. A majority of the creditors of B., an insolvent, signed an agreement with him by which he was to assign all his property for the benefit of the creditors who signed the agreement. The agreement was to be void unless signed by all his creditors. An assignment was duly made, but was not recorded within thirty days. H. and M., creditors who did not sign the agreement, and McF., who did, obtained judgments and levied on and sold the personal estate in the hands of the trustees, under the assignment. There was no evidence that McF. had done anything to estop himself from claiming against the assignment. The court below awarded the fund raised by the sale to H., M. and McF., according to priority. *Held*, not to be error. *Lane's Appeal*, 82 Penn. st. 289.

33. A deed of assignment was made by a firm whose liabilities were $596.41 and whose assets were $614.18, to an assignee in trust for the creditors, which deed contained the following special clause, viz.: "The assignee shall take possession of the property transferred to him, sell and dispose of the same with all reasonable diligence, either at public or private sale, for the best prices that can be obtained therefor, and convert the same into money, *unless the indebtedness of the firm can be paid or settled otherwise by amicable arrangement between the creditors of the firm*," &c., "and out of the proceeds of such sale, *if any be made*," &c. *Held*, that the deed of assignment was void. *Keevil* v. *Donaldson*, 20 Kansas, 165.

34. An assignment for the benefit of creditors vests the title forthwith in the assignee, though ignorant of the assignment. The moment an assignment for the benefit of creditors is placed

by the assignor, or any one interested, in the office of the recorder of deeds of the proper county and within the prescribed time, the beneficial interest of the creditors, the *cestuis que sustent*, is completely vested, and it is totally immaterial when the assignee accepts the trust or whether he ever accepts it. *Mark's Appeal*, 85 Penn. st. 231.

ATTORNEYS.

35. A general retainer does not authorize an attorney to settle or adjust claims, or to alter the terms of a contract made by the client. *Pickett, et al. v. Merchants' Nat. Bank, Memphis, et al.* 32 Ark. 346.

36. An attorney, in fact, can not bind his principal as surety, unless he is specifically authorized to do it. * *State ex rel. Merchant v. Daspit*, 30 La. 112.

37. A stipulation in a promissory note for the payment of a certain sum as attorney's fees, if suit is commenced thereon is valid, and may be enforced in an action on the note. *Danforth v. Charles, et al.*, 1 Bennett's Dakota Reps. 285.

BAILMENT.

38. The finder of a bank note, as against a bailee, without reward, to whom he delivers it to be kept for the finder, has such a possessory interest in the note as entitles him to recover the same of the bailee, on his refusal to redeliver it to the finder upon his request, and in the absence of any claim of the rightful owner made known by him to such bailee. Such bailee is not bound to use as great care and diligence in the keeping of the note as he would be if he were a bailee for compensation ; and if the note was stolen from his possession, he will not be liable for it unless the loss was the result of gross negligence on his part. In such a case, to entitle the plaintiff to recover, he must show that the note was a genuine note and of the value he claimed. *Tancil v. Seaton*, 28 Grattan, (Va.) 601.

39. A man dressed as a police officer told the cashier, in presence of a watchman of the bank, that he had been directed by the lieutenant of the police to warn him that there were "suspicious characters about ;" the cashier told the watchman to admit no one, but he made no inquiry of the lieutenant. After the bank was closed, there then being another watchman there, the first was called from outside by name ; he opened the door ; a man dressed as a policeman and two others in ordinary dress came in ; they overpowered the watchman, took securities, &c., from the vault, including plaintiff's, deposited for safe keeping, and kept as the bank's securities. *Held*, the bank being a voluntary bailee, without reward, the evidence was not sufficient to charge them with negligence. *De Haven v. Kensington Bank*, 81 Penn. st. 95.

40. A bailee, converting goods on which he has bestowed labor and acquired a lien, may, in an action of trover brought by the owner, set up his lien claim in reduction of damages. *Longstreet* v. *Phila.* 39 N. J., Law 63.

41. A receipt, in the words following, imports no legal liability of the signer thereof, and no action can be maintained upon it without evidence *aliunde:* "Received from H. N. Peden one letter envelope, sealed, and said to contain two hundred and ninety dollars." But if it be shown by other evidence that the money was received as a bailment a recovery may be had upon the receipt. And in such case the receipt constitutes a legal liability, and is assignable, under sections 670 and 2228 of the code of 1871. *Hunt & Vaughan* v. *Shackleford*, 55 Miss., 94.

BANKERS.

42. *Bank Stock* assessed under the provisions of the act authorizing the taxation of stockholders of banks (Chap. 761, Laws of 1866), it is the duty of the assessor to deduct from the actual value of each share, a sum bearing the same proportion thereto as the annexed value of the real estate of the bank bears to the actual value of all the capital stock; the words "whole amount of the capital stock," as used in said act, has reference to its value, not to the nominal amount of capital. *People ex rel* v. *Comr's. of Taxes*, 69 N. Y. 91.

43. Article 13 of the State constitution, entitled "Banks and currency," applies to banks of issue, and does not prohibit the legislature from creating banks of deposit and discount. When an incorporation, attempted in good faith under a general incorporation law, by the requisite number of corporators, will be deemed a corporation de facto. *Pape v. Capital Bank*, 20 Kansas, 440.

44. When a bank has become involved and under the general laws it is sought to make the directors and stockholders liable for its debts, proceedings must be in the name of the assignee, and in the Court of Common Pleas of the County in which the bank is located. The liability of the stockholders being secondary cannot be enforced until the assets of the bank, which is the primary debtor, are exhausted. *Mean's Appeal*, 85 Penn. st. 75.

45. The stockholder of a National Bank has legal capacity to sue such corporation for misappropriation of the stockholder's funds, and for other causes. A corporation being a legal entity, as such, distinct from its members, incorporators, or stockholders, it follows that each or all of them may have grievances redressed by actions at law or proceedings in chancery, as any creditor not occupying that relation. *Wilson* v. *First National Bank*, 1 Wyoming S. C. Rps., 108.

46. Money paid to the Cashier of a bank for the use and benefit of the bank, is payment to the bank itself. If such Cashier misapply the funds so received, the bank, as his principal, can maintain an action against him, but not the person paying the money. If the latter suffer injury by reason of such misapplication, his remedy lies against the bank and not against its officer or servant. An agent receiving money from a third person for his principal, if he acted within the scope of his authority, and has the right to receive such payment, is not responsible to the third person; payment to the agent is payment to the principal, who is responsible for the default of the agent. *Wilson* v. *Rogers*, 1 Wyoming Sup. Ct. R. 51.

47. Under the general power of discounting negotiable notes, granted by section 127 of the corporation law to savings associations, such institutions have the power to purchase such notes. *Pape* v. *Capital Bank*, 20 Kansas, 440.

48. Banks organized, prior to the Amendment of General St. c. §13, under the provisions of that chapter had no power to purchase or traffic in promissory notes as choses in action, or as a specie of personal property. The power to carry on the business of banking, by discounting bills, notes, and other evidences of debt, is not within the meaning of that section, a power to buy such securities, but to loan money thereon, with the right to take lawful interest in advance. In First National Bank of Rochester *v.* Pierson, decided September 21, 1877 (to appear in 24 Minn.), the rule laid down in this case was held to apply to National banks. *Farmer's and Mechanic's Bank* v. *Baldwin*, 23 Minn. 198.

49. Under Section 23, Chapter 34, laws of 1876, a private banker is subject to taxation upon the average amount of deposits made by him in his business. *Knox v. Comm'rs of Shawnee Co.*, 20 *Kansas*, 596.

50. I., the President of a National Bank in Nebraska City, obtained from K., in the city of Omaha, his (K.'s) promissory note for the sum of $2,000, payable to I. or order, and payable on demand, for the purpose of purchasing stock in the bank of which he was president. I. procured the note to be discounted by his bank, and had the proceeds thereof placed to his credit therein, and he afterwards drew the same out by checks on the bank. None of the officers of the bank, except the president, were aware of the character of the note, or that it had been given for stock, *held* in an action on the note, that the bank was entitled to recover. *Kennedy* v. *Otoe Co. Nat. Bank*, 7 Neb. 59.

Like other agents, the president of a bank must act within the scope of his authority, in order to bind his principal, unless his acts have been ratified. *Id.*

50½. The word "discount" signifies, "The act of buying a bill of exchange, or promissory note, for a less sum than that which upon its face is payable." *Pape* v. *Capital Bank*, 20 Kansas, 451.

51. *A bank* may maintain an action in its corporate name to recover back a tax illegally assessed and collected against its shares of capital stock, though such stock stands in the names of different individual shareholders. The payment of the illegal portion of the tax being one for which the shareholders were not responsible. *Kimball* v. *Corn Exchange Nat. Bank*, 1 Bradwell's Ill. App. R'pts, 209.

52. The banker having put the money for a check on the counter and the payee having taken it up, the payment is complete though the counting is not finished. *Chambers* v. *Miller*, C. vi. 125; 13 C. B. N. S. 125, (Eng. Com. Law).

53. A country banker receiving a check on another country banker in another town, has until the next day to transmit it for presentment. *Hare* v. *Henty*, C. 65, 10 C. B. N. S. 65, (Eng. Com. Law).

54. A bank discounting a note before its maturity is not chargeable with the knowledge of illegality or want of consideration acquired by one of its directors in other than his official capacity; such director not having acted with the board in making the discount. A director offering a note of which he is owner to the bank of which he is a director, for discount, is regarded in the transaction as a stranger, and the bank is not chargeable with the knowledge of such director of an infirmity or defect in the consideration of the note. P. was a member of the firm of M. & J. S. P., and also a director of the bank of H. He obtained at the bank the discount of a note belonging to the firm, which had been got of the maker by fraud. He had notice, as a member of the firm, of the fraud, before the note was offered for discount, but did not communicate his knowledge to any of the officers of the bank. *Held*, that the knowledge of P. was not, constructively, notice to the bank. *First Nat. Bank of Hightstown* v. *Christopher*, 40 N. J. L. R., 435.

55. Persons who hold stock in pledge, the certificates of which stand on the books of a National Bank in the name of the pledgee, are, in contemplation of the National Banking Act, stockholders, and so long as they thus hold the stock in pledge, are responsible to the creditors of the bank in proportion to the amount so held. But a sale of the stock under an authority conferred by the terms of the pledge, is not obnoxious to the charge of having been done in fraud of creditors, although its leading object and purpose may have been on the part of the pledgee to avoid liability as a stockholder, under the twelfth

section of the National Banking Act, which provides for the personal liability of stockholders of national banks for the debts of the corporation, in proportion to the amount of stock held by them, and enacts that every person becoming a shareholder by transfer, shall succeed to all the rights and liabilities of the prior holder of such shares. *Magruder Receiver v. Colston*, et. al. 44 Md. 349.

55½. The provisions of the act of 1875, in relation to savings banks (§48, chap. 371, laws of 1875), providing that savings banks shall have a preference for moneys deposited over other creditors of an insolvent bank, only applies to deposits made in the ordinary course of business, and subject to the drafts of the depositors, to an amount not exceeding that authorized by §27 of said act. Loans, whether on time or payable on call, are not deposits within the meaning of said provisions. A loan cannot be changed into a deposit by reason of any want of authority in the managers of the savings bank to make the loan, or for the reason that it may have been made in violation of law. *Rosenback v. M. & B. Bank*, 69 N. Y., 358.

56. *A National Bank* has corporate power to enter into an agreement with a customer to exchange for him non-registered U. S. bonds for registered bonds, and it is bound by an agreement to that effect made for a sufficient consideration by its cashier *Yerkes v. National Bank*, 69 N. Y. 382.

57. Where it is sought to hold one who, while president of a bank, loaned moneys of the bank to an irresponsible person, liable for the same on the basis of his representations to the cashier at the time of the loans that he was interested with the borrower, and would see the amounts repaid, it is error to permit the party to testify whether he ever regarded himself as liable; his opinion respecting his legal liability had no bearing on the case. *First National Bank of Sturgis v. Reed*, 36 Mich. 263.

58. A bank president who, while in general charge of the business with the cashier under his authority, has permitted and directed drawing of moneys from the bank without security by one known or supposed to be irresponsible, and with whom he was interested in the business for which the money was obtained, and has requested the cashier not to say anything to the directors about it, is held personally liable to the bank for the moneys thus paid out by him in violation of his trust. *Id.*

59. The fact that the moneys thus drawn out were by the cashier, by direction and on the authority of the president, charged on the books of the bank to the irresponsible borrower, would not necessarily determine the transaction as a loan to him

by the bank; but the bank, in the absence of any act of ratification or acquiescence on its part, would have a right, under the circumstances, to repudiate it a sa transaction with the nominal borrower, and to insist on repayment by its president. *Id.*

60. And such president, if he persuaded the cashier not to make known the facts to the directors, could claim nothing because of the cashier's knowledge; that officer's silence might, under such circumstances, make him accessory to the fraud, but could not tend to excuse the principal. *Id.*

61. The question of the effect to be given to the long silence of the bank directors after the charge to the nominal borrower was entered upon the bank books, is one of ratification, and should be submitted to the jury as such. *Id.*

62. An agent's admissions made after the fact, and entirely unconnected with any act of agency, are not evidence of the fact. *Bowen* v. *School District, etc.*, 36 Mich. 1

63. Proof that a person is clerk for another does not establish his right to receive for his employer payment of demands not shown to have any connection with the business; and evidence simply that payment was made to such clerk of such demands, is not a sufficient showing of agency to receive the same, to authorize evidence of admissions by such clerk of the payment thereof to him. *Id.*

64. The Third National Bank of Baltimore was organized under the National Currency Act of 1864, ch. 106. The firm of W. A. B. & Co., of which W. A. B. was the senior member, was a large customer of the bank through which all the banking business of the firm was transacted, and from which it received accommodations as needed. On the 5th day of February, 1866, the firm was indebted to the bank about $5,000, when the appellee voluntarily proposed to the president of the bank, to deposit with the bank a large amount of bonds, about $37,000, as collateral security for his present and further indebtedness. The terms of the deposit as agreed on between M. Boyd and the president, were dictated by the latter to the discount clerk—and were as follows: "Third National Bank, February 5th, 1866. William A. Boyd has deposited with the Third National Bank of Baltimore, $20,000 in United States 5-20 bonds, and $1,500 5-20 July, 1865; $5,000 Hudson County, New Jersey; $5,000 Town of Saratoga, New York, 7 *per cent.* bonds; $5,000 Stock of Third National Bank of Baltimore, as collateral security for the payment of all obligations of Wm. A. Boyd and Wm. A. Boyd & Co., to the Third National Bank of Baltimore, at present existing, or that may be incurred hereafter, with the understanding that the right to sell the above collaterals in satisfaction of such obligations, is hereby vested in the officers of the Third National Bank. (signed) A. H. Barnitz, Discount

Clerk." "The firm was not indebted to the bank subsequent to July, 1872, when it paid its last indebtedness the bonds were not withdrawn, but left with the defendant, under the original agreement. The bank was robbed and the bonds stolen in the manner described in the testimony, between Saturday evening the 17th, and Monday morning the 19th of August, 1872; the bank was entered by burglars and certain of the bonds were stolen.

By Section 8 of the Act of Congress of 1864, Ch. 106, a bank organized thereunder, is authorized to exercise all such incidental powers as shall be necessary to carry on the business of banking, by discounting promissory notes, drafts, bills of exchange and other evidences of debt; by receiving deposits, by buying and selling exchange, coin and bullion; by loaning money on personal security, and by obtaining, issuing and circulating notes according to the provisions of this Act." In an action by W. A. B. against the bank, to recover the value of the bonds which were stolen, it was *held*, 1st, That the contract entered into by the bank was not a mere gratuitous bailment. 2nd, That the bank had the power to enter into the contract, it being within the terms of the Act of Congress. 3d, That the original contract of bailment being valid and binding, the obligation of the bank for the safe custody of the deposit did not cease when the plaintiff's debt had been paid. 4th, That the defendant was responsible if the bonds were stolen in consequence of its failure to exercise such care and diligence in their custody or keeping as at the time, banks of common prudence in like situation and business, usually bestowed in the custody and keeping of similar property belonging to themselves; that the care and diligence ought to have been such as was properly adapted to the preservation and protection of the property, and should have been proportioned to the consequences likely to arise from any improvidence on the part of the defendant. 5th, That the proper measure of damages was the market value of the bonds at the time they were stolen. Whether due care and diligence have been exercised by a bank in the custody of bonds deposited with it as collateral security, is a question of fact exclusively within the province of the jury to decide. *Third National Bank* v. *Boyd*, 44 Md. 47.

65. One dealing with a corporation in matters not falling within the purview of its delegated powers, is not thereby estopped from pleading its want of authority, to make the contract sought to be enforced against him. *Marion Savings Bank* v. *Dunkin*, 54 Ala. 471.

66. Where, however, the contract is within the delegated powers, one who has dealt with it in its corporate character, is in general estopped from setting up its want of complete organization, according to the provisions of its charter, to defeat the

corporation in the enforcement of the contract he has made with it. *Id.*

67. The accommodation drawee of a bill of exchange, which was discounted by a bank, for the acceptor who procured it to raise money for his own use in that way—the drawer not being aware of this and not being present or participating in the negotiations—is not thereby estopped from denying the proper organization of the banking corporation, when sued by it on the bill. *Id.*

68. Under the provisions of the Revised Code, (Part 2, Title 1, Chapter 1, §§ 1644 *et reg.*) as amended by the act of 1868, "supplementary to the corporation laws of Alabama" a corporation is sufficiently organized to carry on the business of a bank of discount and deposit and loaning money, when the certificate of the associates (properly acknowledged and recorded) for the purpose of carrying on such banking business, shows the name selected by the associates; the town where its business is to be conducted; the amount of capital stock (within the limits prescribed) and the number of shares into which it is divided; the name and place of residence of the stockholders; the shares held by them respectively, and the time when the association is to begin and terminate. The association not claiming the right to issue or circulate its own notes, no deposits of money and transfer of stock to the auditor (under §§1644 and 1646 of the Revised Code) is necessary to authorize it to carry on other banking business. *Marion Savings Bank v. Dunkin*, 54 Ala. 471.

69. The dissolution of a partnership with an individual banker does not relieve the retiring partner from liability for subsequent deposits made, without notice of the dissolution, by one who had been before a depositor. *Howell v. Adams*, 68 N. Y. 314.

70. The liability of the retiring partner is not changed by the fact that the depositor did not know that he was a partner. *Id.*

71. So also, the alteration of a certificate of deposit in respect to the rate of interest, made after the dissolution of the partnership by the partner continuing the business, but before notice to the holder, does not relieve the retiring partner; such holder having the right until notice, to treat the partnership as continuing, the alteration will be deemed to have been authorized. *Id.*

72. Proof of publication of notice of dissolution in newspapers, in the place where the bank was located, unconnected with any evidence that the depositor resided there, or took the papers, is but slight, if any, evidence of notice; and when he testifies that he never saw the notice or heard of the dissolution will not authorize a finding of notice. *Id.*

73. A bank is not liable upon a certificate of deposit until after demand of payment, and therefore, the statute of limitaitons does not begin to run against it until demand is made. *Id.*

74. Where a savings bank is bound by its rules to exercise its best care to prevent fraud, it is not protected by a clause in such rules that a payment to one producing a deposit book shall be deemed good and valid, in case of a payment made by it, merely upon the production of a depositor's book, to one ho has wrongfully obtained possession of and produces it ıder circumstances such as would necessarily excite suspicion ıd inquiry; as where the person who presents the book is of different sex from the depositor. In the absence of any rules sented to by its customers a savings bank is to be governed ʳ the same legal principals which apply to other moneyed stitutions. Where it has prescribed rules to which a deposir has assented, they are the agreement between them, and ⸺ch must conform to them to preserve rights against each other. The by-laws of defendant's, a savings bank, which were printed in its customers' deposit book, contained the following: "The bank will use its *best* efforts to prevent fraud; but all payments made to persons producing the deposit books shall be deemed good and valid payments." It was also worded that drafts might be made personally, or by order in writing of the depositor if the bank have his signature on the signature book. Plaintiff was a depositor, and defendant had his signature in such book. The wife of plaintiff wrongfully obtained possession of his deposit book, which she presented with a forged check or order, for $2,850, and this sum was paid her. In an action to recover the amount the order and the signature book were produced on the trial. Defendants' own officers, as witnesses, stated that there was a difference between the signature to the order, and that in the signature book. They declined to charge that the payment was valid, but left it to the jury to determine whether defendant used its best efforts to prevent fraud. *Held*, That as this Court had not the benefit which the trial Court had of the inspection of the signatures it could not say but that said Court on inspection, discovered such a difference, as with the other circumstances of the case, authorized an inference of negligence and made a submission of the question to the jury proper. Also *held*, that a request to charge that if the defendant exercised ordinary care and diligence, and paid in good faith, it was excused, was properly refused, as defendant had obligated itself to exercise more than ordinary care, *i. e.*, its "best efforts." *Allen* v. *Williamsburgh Savings Bank*, 69 N. Y. 314.

75. A bank which has fraudulently permitted funds on deposit belonging to a trust estate to be transferred to the indi-

vidual account of the trustee, is properly chargeable with interest from time of such transfer. *Holden* v. *N. Y. and Erie Bank*, 72 N. Y. App. 286.

76. A National Bank, the defendant, had in its house certain United States bonds belonging to plaintiff; its cashier in the spring of 1869, for a sufficient consideration, agreed to exchange the same for registered bonds. This the bank neglected to do, and November, 1869, the bonds were stolen. In an action to recover their value, *held*, that defendant was liable. *Yerkes* v. *Nat. Bank of Port Jervis*, 69 N. Y. 382.

77. Where half of bank note sent in payment, other half to ollow, title to note remains in sender. The payment is condiional and inchoate, and therefore revocable. *Smith* v. *Munlay*, C. Vii. 22; 3 E. & E. 22. (Eng. Com. Law.)

BILLS OF EXCHANGE.

78. Bill of Exchange or draft headed "New England Agency of the Pennsylvania Fire Insurance Company," having the words "Foster & Cole, General Agents for the New England States" printed in the margin, and appearing on its face to be drawn upon said insurance company in payment of a claim against it, is the draft of the company, and not of Foster & Cole, although it is signed by them in their own names. *Chipman* v. *Foster*, 119 Mass. 189.

79. Where a bill of exchange was drawn for the sole accommodation of the payees, and accepted by the drawee for the same purpose, and owing to the insolvency of the payees, the acceptor was compelled to pay the bill, and brought an action against the drawers to recover the amount paid; *Held*, that there was no implied obligation on the part of the drawers to reimburse the acceptor. *Barnet* v. *Young*, 29 Ohio 7.

That the drawers and acceptor, as between themselves, in the absence of any understanding to the contrary, were not co-securities for the payers, or liable to contribution. *Id*.

80. Holder cannot sue for original consideration when there has been a failure to stamp foreign bill and a delay of a year. *Pooley* v. *Brown*, C. iii. 565, 11 C. B. N. S. 565, (Eng. Com. Law.)

81. A Bill of Exchange must be payable at all events, not dependent on any contingency, nor payable out of a particular fund; and it should be for the payment of money only, and not for the performance of any act or in the alternative. An instrument drawn for the payment of six hundred dollars, as follows: "Two hundred dollars out of the first estimate or when the first floor joists are in, two hundred dollars when the building is ready for the roof, and two hundred dollars when

the stoops are completed, and charge the same to my account," is not a bill of exchange because payable upon a contingency, and out of a particular fund. Where the payment depends upon a contingency, the happening of the event will not change the character of the instrument. It was not a bill of exchange when made, and would not become such by matter *ex part facto*. *Miller* v. *Excelsior Stone Co.*, 1 Bradwell's Ill. App. Re'pts. 273.

82. An acceptor of a bill of exchange drawn by the purchaser of machinery, cannot by paying the bill before maturity, change the relations of the original parties to it and to each other, and thus cut off the drawer from the defense of failure of consideration, from defects in the machinery so purchased. The acceptor paying before maturity is not a holder for value of the paper, as against the drawer. The liability of the acceptor is to pay according to the terms of the contract. His remedy, is against the drawer, then is for money had and received by him, of which the bill is the evidence. An acceptor, even though he may have been surety for the drawer to the payee for machinery purchased by the drawer, in paying before maturity is subject to any defense which could be made by the maker, if sued by the payee. *Stark* v. *Alford*, 49 Texas, 260.

83. **Draft.**—The possession of the draft by G., the plaintiff's assignee, was presumptive evidence of his ownership; and this presumption was not rebutted by the evidence on the trial. G. was one of the firm of R., B. & Co., upon whose claim the draft was given, and was therefore part owner of the draft when it was given. The paper is produced in Court by the assignee of G., and this *prima facie* establishes the plaintiff's title. *Kidder, Assignee* v. *Norrobin et al*, 72 N. Y. App. 159.

84. In the absence of any express or implied agreement, a party is not compelled to pay a draft drawn on him merely because he has been in the habit of paying similar drafts. *Helm* v. *Meyer, Weis & Co.*, 30 La. 943.

85. Where there is no value or consideration for acceptance it is a good defence in action by drawer or person taking under him. *Vanquelin* v. *Bonard*, C. ix. 341, C.; 15 C. B. N. S. 341 C. (Eng. Com. Law.)

86. **Bill of Exchange.**—Where a draft is drawn in favor of the payee on a certain fund to arise from the sale of property then in the drawee's hands, and the payment of the draft, by its own terms, is postponed to the payment (out of the same fund), of a debt due the drawee, the drawee who has not accepted the draft, is only liable for whatever balance of the fund may remain, after the payment of his own debt. *E. Marqueze & Co.* v. *Fernandez & Co.*, 30 La. 195.

87. A., of St. Louis, being indebted to B., of St. Joseph, requested B. to draw upon him, upon which draft he would

raise the money and remit the proceeds to B. on account of his indebtedness. B. accordingly drew a draft to the order of C., his banker at St. Joseph, upon which C. endorsed "Pay to the order of C.," his banker at St. Joseph, upon which C. endorsed, "Pay to D. or order, for collection for my account." Upon receipt of the draft at St. Louis, A. accepted it, and offered it for discount to plaintiff. By consent of A. and plaintiff, the endorsement was stricken off, and plaintiff then discounted the draft, and A. received and remitted the amount to B. In an action on the draft against B., the drawer, *held*, (1) that plaintiff could not, by parol evidence, show a contract between A. and B. by which the latter was to have the draft discounted on the faith of his name as drawer; (2) that the endorsement, being restrictive, destroyed the negotiability of the draft and operated as a mere power of attorney to the banker at St. Louis to receive the proceeds of the draft for the use of the drawer; (3) that the erasure of the endorsement, without the knowledge or assent of B., destroyed the validity of the draft as to him, and plaintiff, having knowledge of the alteration, was bound to know that such was its effect when he took the draft. *Mechanics' Bank* v. *Valley Packing Co.*, 4 Mo. Ct. Appeals (St. Louis,) 200.

88. When a bill drawn and endorsed in England payable abroad is dishonored by acceptor's non-payment, the holder can recover from endorser the amount of re-exchange and no more. A custom that he is entitled to recover either the re-exchange or the amount he paid for the bill is invalid. *Suse* v. *Pompe*, XCVIII. 538: 8 C. B. N. S. 538. (Eng. Com. Law.)

89. A promise to accept a future bill of exchange, in consideration of money to be advanced thereon by the promisee, is invalid, and an action thereon cannot be maintained against the promissor. *Flato* v. *Mulhall, et al.*, 4 Mo. Ct. Appeals (St. Louis,) 476.

90. Where an accommodation bill is accepted at the request of a third party, who agrees to share any loss, such third party is not discharged by time given acceptor and drawer. *Way* v. *Hearn*, CIII. 774; 11 C. B. N. S. 774. (Eng. Com. Law.)

91. Acceptor who tears the bill in two parts, with the intention of destroying it, is liable to the *bona fide* holder obtaining it from the drawer, who fraudulently joined the pieces in such a way as to look as if the halves had been transmitted by mail. *Ingham* v. *Primrose*, XCVII. 82; 7 C. B. N. S. 82. (Eng. Com. Law.)

BILLS OF LADING.

92. **Bills of Lading** for goods *not actually* put on board, cannot be signed by the master of a ship under his authority

as agent, and therefore the owner of the ship is not responsible to parties taking, or dealing with, or making advances on the faith of such an instrument which is untruthful in this particular. The consignee and every other party thus acting does so *with notice* of this limitation of the power of the master, and acts at his own risk both as respects the fact of shipment and the quantity of cargo purported by a bill of lading to be shipped. Bills of lading are not negotiable in the same sense in which bills of exchange or promissory notes are. They stand in the place of the goods they represent, and delivery or endorsement of them transfers the right of property in the goods, but not in the contract itself, so as to enable the endorsee to maintain at the common law an action on it in his own name. A railroad is not liable for advances made by a commission merchant upon the faith of a bill of lading fraudulently signed by one of its station agents, the goods specified never having been shipped or received at the depot for transportation. *Balto & Ohio R. R. Co.* v. *Wilkens*, 44 Md. 11.

93. **Loss by Innocent Party.**—Where one of two innocent parties must suffer from the wrongful or tortious acts of a third party, the law casts the burden or loss upon him by whose act, omission or negligence such third party was enabled to commit the wrong which occasions the loss. Where the agent of a railroad corporation, engaged as a common carrier, has authority to receive grain for shipment over its road, and issue in the name of the corporation a bill of lading for the consignment, and promise in the bill of lading to deny that it has received the grain mentioned therein, and is liable to the indorsee and assignee for advances made in good faith on the bill of lading. *Wichita Savings Bank* v. *Atchison, Topeka and Santa Fe R. R. Co.*, 20 Kansas, 519.

94. **Bills of Lading** are transferable by indorsement. *Robertson* v. *Stuart*, 68 Me. 61.

BONDS.

95. Generally the term "bond" implies an instrument under seal. The official bond required of a collector of taxes must be a sealed instrument. The words "witness our hands and seals," when no seal is attached, will not make the instrument, though otherwise in proper form, a bond. An instrument, in form a bond, but containing no seal, voluntarily executed and delivered in lieu of a bond and accepted therefor is valid. Its acceptance is a sufficient consideration to cover all official delinquencies in not paying over money actually collected after such acceptance. *Boothbay* v. *Giles*, 68 Me. 160.

96. A married woman cannot bind herself as surety on an official bond. *Hynes* v. *Dickinson*, 32 Ark. 776.

97. A money bond, issued by a body politic, under authority

of law, payable to bearer, has the negotiable quality of ordinary commercial paper, and if, while it is a valid instrument, it reaches the hands of an innocent holder for value before maturity, although he derives his title from a thief, he will be entitled to recover the money due on it. The alteration of the number of a bond, where different bonds of the same series are distinguished alone by the numbers, will render the instrument void in the hands of the person who made the alteration, and also in the hands of those who claim under him. While the alteration of a stolen bond by a thief will avoid it as to him and those who claim under him, it will not impair the rights of the true owner. *Force* v. *Elizabeth*, 28 N. J. Eq. 403.

98. A paper which in the body of it says "as witness my hand and seal," has the word "seal" affixed to the signature of the maker. It is a sealed instrument within the meaning of the statute. Code of 1849, ch. 143, §2 p. 580. *Lewis ex'ors* v. *Overly's adm'r*, 28 Grattan (Va.) 627.

99. A person taking a bond for the future good conduct of an agent already in his employment, must communicate to a surety his knowledge of the past criminal misconduct of such agent in the course of such past employment, in order to make such bond binding. The mere non-communication of such knowledge, irrespective of motive or design, is a fraud in law, which will invalidate the obligation. *Sooy Ads. State of N. J.*, 39 N. J. 135.

100. A bond of indemnity given to an accommodation endorser conditioned upon the payment of certain notes or a single renewal of them, does not cover subsequent renewals. In such case, where the notes were renewed twice to it, by an agreement between them to that effect, is postponed to the lien of a mortgage upon real estate bound by the judgment, given by the defendants in the judgment before the second renewal of one of the notes and on the day of the second renewal of the other. *Appeal of First Nat. Bank*, 82 Penn. st. 488.

101. There can be no innocent holder of paper issued by a municipal corporation without power. *Lindsey* v. *Rottaken*, 32 Ark. 619.

102. Municipal bonds issued without authority, although negotiable in form, are void in the hands of an innocent holder. *Hancock* v. *Chicot Co.*, 32 Ark. 575.

CHATTEL MORTGAGES.

103. A mortgage of a certain described horse, and all other live stock of which the mortgagor may become owner during the year, gives a valid lien upon any horse or other animal which the mortgagor may acquire during the given year, by one or more exchanges of the first mortgaged horse and his successors. *Davis* v. *Marx*, 55 Miss. 376.

104. Where a chattel mortgage fails to duly describe the property, the defect is cured by the subsequent delivery of the property to the mortgagee, as against parties who have not acquired any rights or interest before such delivery. The delivery, in such a case, must be such an actual transfer of the possession and control of the property that, if it was destroyed, the loss would be that of the mortgagee. A constructive possession will not avail. *Parsons Savings Bank* v. *Sargent, et al.*, 20 Kansas, 576.

105. The purchaser of a house and the furniture therein immediately leased the same to the vendor, who remained in possession of the furniture, as lesee, the same never having been out of his possession. *Held*, that, as against creditors of the vendor, the sale of the furniture was void. *Bishop V. O'Connell, et. al.*, 4 Mo. Ct. Appeals (St. Louis, 578.)

106. In a chattel mortgage made by M. & Co., the goods were described as "two sets of blacksmithing and one set of waggon maker's tools complete," &c., "together with all their floating capital stock in trade, to the value of $1,000," &c., "connected with the business they carry on in the said village of Watertown, as wagon and carriage builders, general blacksmiths, &c., under the name and firm of M. & Co. *Held*, an insufficient description as regarded the tools. Per Gwynne J The mortgage clearly could not pass after acquired goods, for though after acquired goods may be affected in equity, it could only be when the mortgage shows an intention to do so. *Mason* v. *Macdonald*, 25 Upper Canada, Com. Pleas Rpts. 435.

107. A mortgage of personal property consisting of goods in a merchant tailoring establishment is void as against creditors, where the mortgagors by the consent of the mortagee continue to carry on business, manufacturing and selling the goods, in the usual course. *City National Bank* v. *Goodrich*, 3 Colo. 139.

108. Husband and wife gave a note and secured it by a mortgage on her furniture. The husband, with money borrowed of his father, paid the note, receiving the papers into his possession. Immediately afterwards and before separation, by arrangement between all parties except the wife (who was not present), the note and mortgage were assigned by the mortgagee to the father. *Held*, that the wife would hold the property clear of the incumbrance by mortgage. The father would have no right in the mortgage by subrogation, being under no obligation to pay it, and having no interest in it when it was paid. *Moody* v. *Moody*, 68 Me. 155.

109. A chattel mortgage is in law a conveyance of the goods and chattels mortgaged, and passes the title of the mortgagor for the purposes for which it was made. The right of a mortgagee, under a mortgage made by a tenant of his

goods and chattels upon the demised premises, is superior to that of a bailiff subsequently seizing them under a warrant to distrain for rent. But a chattel mortgage in this State is regarded as a mere security for the debt, and does not entirely divert the property of the mortgagor. The interest of a mortgagor in the chattels mortgaged is such an interest as may be seized and sold under ordinary process of law against him. *Woodside* v. *Adams*, 40 N. J. L. R. 417.

110. Goods in possession of mortgagee—exemption from seizure under writ of attachment in insolvency. *Held*, that goods and chattels in the possession of a mortgagee of them cannot be seized and sold, and the proceeds paid over to a sheriff acting under a writ of attachment in insolvency against the mortgagor. *Held*, also, that the possession of the defendant to whom such goods had been sent by the plaintiff, the mortgagee, to be sold, and their proceeds paid over to him, was the possession of the mortgagee; and defendant having in such case assented to the seizure by the sheriff, and acting under his directions, sold the goods and paid over the proceeds, was liable to repay them to the mortgagee. *Watson* v. *Henderson, et. al.*, 25 Upper Canada Com. Pleas Rpts. 562.

111. If the holder of a chattel mortgage had taken possession of the chattels under his mortgage, before the judgment creditor recovered his judgment, will not give validity to the mortgage as against the latter, if the mortgage was not filed according to the provisions of the act concerning mortgages, and there were not immediate delivery and continued possession of the goods, according to the provision referred to. A mortgage of after-acquired property can only attach itself to such property in the condition in which it comes to the mortgagor's hands. If it is already subject to mortgages or other liens, the general mortgage does not displace them, though they may be junior in point of time. It only attaches to such interest as the mortgagor acquires. *Williamson* v. *New Jersey R. W. Co.*, 28 N. J. Eq., 277.

112. **Chattel Mortgage.** An immaterial variation between a chattel mortgage and the copy subsequently filed does not invalidate the re-filing. A mistake in the number of the lot where the chattels were, was held to be immaterial under the circumstances. The statement annexed to the affidavit with a copy of the mortgage, did not give distinctly all the information required by the Act, but the affidavit and statement together contained all that was necessary. *Held* sufficient, the statement contained an item of $2.25 as paid for re-filing, which the mortgagee had no right to charge: *Held*, not to vitiate the instrument. A chattel mortgage was given for $1,070; it afterwards appeared that the amount was made up in part of a promissory note made and given by the mortgagee

to the mortgagor at the time of the execution of the mortgage and not paid for some months afterwards. *Held*, that in the absence of fraud the mortgage was valid. *Walker* v. *Niles*, 18 Grant's Chancery, Ontario, 210.

113. The holder of a chattel mortgage agreed to assign his mortgaged interest to a third party who proposed to purchase the chattels of the mortgagor but had no other interest in the mortgage, and who never became the owner of the equity of redemption. The agreement contained the following clause: "In case of failure to pay said notes, or either of them, or the interest, the said party of the first part (the mortgagee) resumes the right to foreclose said mortgage, or take or sell said property, the same to all intents or purposes as if said notes below mentioned were the notes mentioned and specified in said mortgage, and it being the intent hereof to allow said mortgage to remain as security for the payment of the notes below mentioned. *Held*, that this agreement was collateral to the mortgage, and that the payment of one of the notes was not a payment *pro tanto* of the mortgage debt. The mortgagee has previously insured his interests as a mortgagee for $57,000. After a partial payment of $20,000 by the proposed buyer of the property mortgaged there was a loss by fire of $53,000 on the mortgaged property. *Held*, that the insured rights of the mortgagee was not impaired or diminished by such partial payment. The proposed purchaser of the goods mortgaged agreed to keep them insured for the benefit of the mortgagee. This he did not do, and the mortgagee insured his interest as mortgagee in his own name. *Held*, that a liability of the proposed purchaser for the cost of the insurance under his contract with the mortgagee, did not affect the contract between the mortgagee and the insurers. *Haley* v. *Mftrs. Fire and Marine Ins. Co.* 120, Mass. 292.

114. When chattel mortgage was executed it was agreed between the parties that the mortgagor may go on and sell the stock and use the proceeds, generally, in his business, and this ageeement is carried out by permitted sales, the transaction is fraudulent in law as against the creditors of the mortgagor. *Southard* v. *Benner, et. al.*, 72 N. Y., App. 424.

CHECKS.

115. A dishonored check need not be protested to bind the maker. *Henshaw* v. *Root*, 60 Ind. 220.

116. A check on a banker is a negotiable instrument and the endorser is liable to the holder. *Keene* v. *Beard*, XC. VIII. 372; 8 C. B. N. S. 372. (Eng. Com. Law).

117. Where, in an action against a partnership, on a dishonored check, executed in the firm name, the execution of the

check is not denied by plea under oath, and the check is introduced in evidence without objection, the existence of the partnership is thereby admitted. Where, in an action against a partnership, the existence of the partnership may be inferred from the evidence, a finding of that fact will not be disturbed for want of direct evidence thereof. *Henshaw* v. *Root*, 60 Ind. 220.

118. In an action against the maker on a dishonored check, the complaint, setting out a copy thereof, alleged its execution and delivery, its presentation on the day it was issued for payment, its dishonor and notice thereof to the defendant; and that the defendant at the time of its issue had no funds deposited for its payment. *Held*, on demurrer, that the complaint is sufficient. Mere delay in giving notice to maker of the dishonor of his check does not discharge him from liability thereon, but he is entitled to whatever damage he may suffer by reason of such delay. *Henshaw* v. *Root*, 60 Ind. 220.

119. A check may be offered in evidence under the money counts; and if there is no other evidence in the case, it is of itself sufficient to entitle the plaintiffs to recover on those counts; yet it is only *prima facie* evidence of money lent, paid and advanced, or had and received; and where it is proved that no money had come to the hands of defendant, the presumption raised by the check is rebutted, and no recovery can be had on these counts. *Blair & Hoye* v. *Wilson*, 28 Grattan (Va.), 165.

120. The rights of a check-holder and of the bank are fixed when the check is presented for payment, and the bank has no right to pay or satisfy out of the fund thus appropriated other checks or demands subsequently presented, or demands which subsequently accrued to the bank or others; nor can the bank retain the money against the check-holder, under claim of an equitable lien for a debt by the drawer of the check not yet matured. *Zelle et al German Savings Inst.*, 4 Mo. Appeal Reports (St. Louis), 401.

121. Where a check, given in payment of a debt, is dishonored, action need not be brought for such debt, but may be maintained on the check. *Henshaw* v. *Root*, 60 Ind. 220.

122. The holder of a check, by the mere fact of its being drawn in his favor, acquires no right of action in equity, as upon an equitable assignment, against the person upon whom it is drawn. To an action by plaintiffs against defendants for their refusal to pay a check, drawn by plaintiffs and one W. on them, defendants pleaded, on equitable grounds, that before the drawing or presentment of the check in question the plaintiffs and W. had drawn and delivered to various persons certain other checks, amounting in all to the whole of their funds in defendants' hands, which were presented before this check; that neither at the time of the drawing, nor presentment of the

first-drawn checks or the check in question, had defendants more than sufficient funds in their hands to pay the first-drawn checks, as the plaintiff and W. well knew ; and that afterwards, and before the commencement of this action, defendants paid the holders of the first-drawn check the amounts thereof, and thereby paid and disbursed all the plaintiffs' and W.'s moneys in their hands, and afterwards settled with the plaintiff and W. their banking account in full. *Held*, plea bad, for the previous presentment and dishonor of the first-drawn checks not creating any lien on the funds, and it being admitted that at the time of the presentment of the checks in question there were sufficient funds to meet it, such funds were applicable to its payment ; and moreover, it was quite consistent with the plea that at the time of the presentment of the first-drawn checks defendants had no funds to meet them, and that after their dishonor they were placed in funds when the check in question was presented and dishonored, and that the first-drawn checks were then presented a second time and honored. *Caldwell* v. *Merchants' Bank*, 26 Upper Canada Com. Pleas. 294.

123. While the giving of a check by a debtor to a creditor is generally presumed to be only a provisional or conditional payment of the debt for which it was given, yet such check may, by agreement of parties, be given and received in full payment and absolute discharge and satisfaction of the debt; and whether it was so given or received is a question of fact for the jury. *Blair & Hoge* v. *Wilson*, 2 Grattan (Va.), 321.

COMPOSITION.

124. R. holding a promissory note, of which P. was the maker, and L. the endorser, signed a composition deed, whereby the creditors of P. released all claims against him, the deed to be null and void unless signed by all his creditors, and wrote after his name the words, " provided this does not release the endorsers in any manner." In an action against P. by another creditor, who had signed the deed, L.'s name did not appear among the signers of the deed ; but it was agreed that if the signing by R. did not release the endorser, then all the creditors had signed. *Held*—The condition annexed by R. to his signature of the deed of composition was equivalent to a reservation of his rights against Lochman as endorser of the note held by R., and did not prevent his execution of the deed from operating as a release of all his rights against P., the maker of that note, although it could not affect any right of L. against P. *Sohier* v. *Loring*, 6 Cush. 537 ; *Tobey* v. *Ellis*, 114 Mass. 120. But the report expressly states that if this execution of the deed by R. did not release the endorser, all the creditors of P. had signed the composition deed—which, as L.'s name does not appear among the signers of that deed,

necessarily implies that the relation between him and P. was such that he was not a creditor of P., and would, if called upon to pay the note as endorser, have any right to recover against P. The deed of composition having been signed by all the creditors of P. is a bar to this action against him. *Judgment on the verdict for the defendant, Richardson* v. *Pierce,* 119 Mass. 165.

125. An agreement of creditors "to accept seventy-five per cent. of the amount of indebtedness as set against our respective names; said seventy-five per cent. to be paid in two, four and six months, from December 15," the contract to take effect "provided all merchandise indebtedness accept the same settlement," is an agreement on the part of a creditor, who has sold the debtor merchandise to compromise the whole claim set against his name, and rests upon sufficient consideration. *Farrington* v. *Hodgdon,* 119 Mass. 453.

126. Creditors signed an agreement "to accept seventy-five per cent. of the amount of indebtedness as set against our respective names; said seventy-five per cent. to be paid in two, four and six months, from December 15," the contract to take effect "provided all merchandise indebtedness accept the same settlement." A., one of the creditors, held three notes of the debtor, two of which he had previously sold, taken back under false representations by the purchaser, and at the time he signed the above agreement was, with the knowledge of the debtor, endeavoring to force the purchaser to take the notes back, which was done before December 15. *Held,* in an action by A. upon the note not sold, that A. not being in possession, or having control of the two notes sold, the debtor was not obliged as to whom to tender the settlement notes. Held also, as to the note in suit, that the debtor was not obliged to tender a settlement note of seventy-five per cent. on that note after the transfer of the other two notes, which the debtor had paid to the purchaser. *Held,* also, that evidence of conversations, tending to show the understanding of parties as to the notes sold, prior to the execution of the agreement, was not admissible to vary the written contract. *Id.*

127. The creditors of A. and B. by a composition deed agreed to accept from A. and B. "ten per cent. of the amounts due us, and each of us, from said A. and said A. and B. in full settlement and discharge of our debts against them; said ten per cent. to be paid within thirty days." The plaintiff, one of A.'s creditors, who joined in the composition, held a note and account against him, which were then due. He also held another note, which would not become due, until after the expiration of said thirty days, on which A.'s name appeared as endorser. The defendant contends that upon payment of ten per cent. of amounts due, he was entitled to be discharged

from all debts, whether due or not. *Held*, whatever might have been the effect of the deed upon debts, the liability for which was fixed, the character and language of the deed does not indicate that it was intended to be a relinquishment of all liabilities, by reason of which the defendant might afterwards, upon the occurrence of certain events, become chargeable as a debtor. While such a contingent demanded, yet it should appear that they had it in view at the time of executing the deed. *Pierce* v. *Parker*, 4 Met. 80, 89. Here everything points to the opposite conclusion. Before it could be determined whether the defendant would become liable to pay this note, the composition deed would by its terms have been fully executed. There were two claims to which it strictly applied; and the subsequent conduct of the parties, who made no provision for any dividend upon this, tends to show that it was not understood upon either side that this claim was released. *Hamblen* v. *Rartigan*, 119 Mass. 153.

CONTRACTS.

128. A. directs B. to give credit on the application of C. for such goods as the latter may order, and charge to him, as it is immaterial whether A. had any thing further to do with ordering the specific goods, or whether C. is the agent of A. If B., relying on the general direction of A. to deliver goods to C., furnishes goods to C. but gives credit to A., A. is liable whether C. is A.'s agent or not. *Jackson, et. al.* v. *Dodge*, 4 Mo. Ct. Appeals (St. Louis), 567.

129. As a general rule, an action on a contract must be brought in the name of the party having the legal interest therein. A third party may maintain an action in his own name upon a contract made expressly for his benefit where his release would be a sufficient discharge to the promissor, but not where it would leave the promissor liable to an action by the other contracting party. *Kountz* v. *Holthouse*, 85 Penn. St. 235.

130. When the plaintiff in an action on a promissory note avers, in his replication, that the note was given to bind a parol contract for the conveyance of land, to be paid if defendant refused to carry out the bargain, and to be void if the contract was carried out, and that defendant had refused to carry out his part of the contract, it is error to render judgment for defendant on the pleadings. There is nothing illegal, immoral, or unconscionable in such a contract. *Schencko* v. *Meier*, 4 Mo. Ct. Appeals (St. Louis), 566.

131. A contract for the delivery of property being entire, the promissee is not bound to receive a part, though the parties may by consent, sever the contract. In an action upon two due bills payable in specific property, one requiring demand, the other not, and the parties having severed the contract by delivery and receiving part of the property from time to time, *held*, that the plaintiff, to maintain his action, must show a demand and refusal as to the first due bill, and as to the residue remaining undelivered on the second. *Widner* v. *Walsh*, 3 Colo. 548.

132. When one person represents that he owes to the debtor of another a debt of equal amount, substitutes himself in place of the debtor by parol agreement with the creditor, fixes a time for payment, and thus induces the creditor to discharge the debtor and trust exclusively to him, his undertaking to pay is not collateral, but original, and performance may be enforced whether he ever in fact owed anything to the debtor in whose stead he agreed to be bound or not. *Edenfield* v. *Canady*, 60 Ga. 456.

133. It is not a good defence to a promise in writing *under seal*, to pay a sum of money, for value received, that it was voluntary. The Statutes concerning evidence (Rev., p. 380, sec. 16) which permit a defendant to plead and set up fraud in the consideration, and (Rev., p. 387, sec. 52) to show want of sufficient consideration as a defence to a sealed instrument establish new rules of evidence, but were not intended to abolish all distinctions between simple contracts and specialties. *Aller* v. *Aller*, 40 N. J. Law Reports, 447.

134. A planter who has agreed to consign, and pay commission on his entire crop to his factors, in consideration of certain promises and stipulations in his favor made by the factors, is released from his obligation to consign and pay such commission on whatever balance of his crop he may have on hand, when the factors shall fail and refuse to comply with *their* stipulations; more particularly when the failure of the factors to perform their part of the contract, disables the planter from performing his part of it. *Nalle & Cammack* v. *A. L. D. Conrad, et. al.*, 30 La., 503.

135. Defendant signed a written agreement without reading it, and did not contain the contract as in fact made, is no ground for the introduction of parol evidence to vary its terms, etc. It is not the duty of courts to relieve parties from the results of their gross negligence. *Bostwick* v. *Duncan, Johnston & Co.*, 60 Ga. 383.

136. A written contract containing terms not presenting a case of latent ambiguity, are not to be varied by extrinsic and parol evidence, the expression "payable as convenient" cannot reasonably be understood as extended to excuse the defendants in any event, from making any payment at all. It can only mean that some indulgence as to the length of credit was to be allowed to the debtors. The service requested in the contract has been performed and the price agreed upon, as the compensation for that service is yet unpaid, though due and payable. *Black* v. *Bachelder, et. al.*, 120 Mass. 171.

137. When it is attempted to be shown by parol evidence that the operation of a contract was to be limited to a particular time, the evidence thereof must be positive and clear. *Shepler* v. *Scott*, 85 Penn. 329.

138. Written contracts are to be interpreted by the court, and their ambiguities explained by surrounding facts, not by the interpretation of witnesses. *Home Life Ins. Co.* v. *Potter, et. al.*, 4 Mo. Ct. Appeals (St. Louis), 594.

139. Contract signed by one party only, is accepted by the other party, it becomes binding upon both parties, the same as if signed by both. *Brandon Mfg. Co.* v. *Morse*, 48 Vt. 322.

140. Contract in writing for the sale and delivery of a certain quantity of wood at a stipulated price per cord, did not, in terms, fix the time of payment. *Held*, that the law fixed the time as on demand after delivery, and that the fact that the purchaser made voluntary payments to the vendor before delivery, did not vary the contract. *Id.*

141. An assignee of a lease without warranty cannot set up a defect of title in defence to an action upon a note given in consideration of the assignment. In such case the assignee occupies the same position as a purchaser of real estate under a deed of quit claim. *Sanborn* v. *Cree*, 3 Colo. 149.

142. In an action on a contract for the transfer to the plaintiff, by the defendant, of a certain promissory note, an instruction to the jury, that, if such contract was made for a valuable consideration, the transfer should "be made by endorsement, unless a different agreement is made by the parties," and that the burden of proof is upon the defendant to establish the latter agreement, is correct. *Wade* v. *Guppinger*, 60 Ind. 376.

143. Where two parties agree as to what shall be done in case one party fails to perform his part of the contract, and upon such failure the thing agreed upon is done, no action lies for such failure, the contract being discharged by the fulfilment of its terms. *Reel* v. *Ewing*, 4 Mo. Ct. Appeals (St. Louis), 569.

144. The rule which forbids the varying of written instruments by parol proof applies only to the parties to the writing. *Whitney* v. *Cowan*, 55 Miss. 626.

145. In the absence of a stipulation as to the time when an act is contracted to be done, the law allows a reasonable time for its performance. What is reasonable time depends upon the nature and character of the thing to be done, the circumstances of the case, and the difficulties attending its accomplishment. As an abstract question, what is reasonable time may be one of law; but unless the facts are admitted, its determination becomes a mixed question of law and fact. In an action to rescind

a contract, a proffer to perform, made in defence, should show an ability to comply, or a reasonable prospect of being able to do so. *Hart* v. *Bullion*, 48 Texas, 278.

146. Where one brings an action to recover compensation for procuring a sale of real estate under a special contract, it is not necessary to show that he had a license to act as a real estate broker. *Shepler* v. *Scott*, 85 Penn. St. 329.

147. A party may not stand by and see work in the erection of a building progress to completion, and then for the first time object that the work was not done in strict accordance to the plan, refuse payment and charge the builder with the cost of reconstruction. The builder is in such case, entitled to recover what the work is reasonably worth. When work is done under a contract, the terms of the contract should settle the amount to be paid, unless it is shown that in consequence of variations from the plan, the compensation agreed upon should be diminished, and the proper measure of damages in such case is the diminution of the value of the building resulting from the variation. *Schoefer et al.* v. *Gildea, et al.*, 3 Colo. 15.

148. To introduce a new term into a written contract, the evidence of the agreement of the parties to do so must be clear and distinct, and that the contract was executed upon the faith of such collateral agreement. *Railroad Co.* v. *Hodgens*, 85 Penn. st. 501.

149. When the payment of the purchase money is a condition precedent to the delivery of a deed of conveyance, the refusal to pay the whole, or any balance due, leaves the vendor at liberty to rescind the contract. Where the vendor receives part of the purchase money, he must, before seeking relief in a court of equity against the vendee, return, or offer to return, the amount received, with interest. Where A. held title to reality in trust for B., and at B.'s request conveyed to C., the payment of the purchase money being a condition precedent to the delivery of the deed, and the deed having been delivered, without compliance with that condition, *held*, that on refusal of payment, B. had his election either to pursue his remedy at law against C., and thus affirm the contract, or to rescind the contract, and seek equitable relief. *Hamil* v. *Thompson et al.*, 3 Colo. 518.

150. A contract to answer for the debt of another must not only be in writing, but based upon a sufficient consideration. *Langford* v. *Freeman*, 60 Ind. 46.

151. That in consideration of supplies furnished, defendant agreed that crop should belong to claimants; that he would deliver it to them by October 15 thereafter, or, in lieu thereof, pay them $500; that, on failure so to do, he should be considered liable for breach of trust, and they could either take possession of the crop or sue for that amount, with twelve per cent. interest, etc. ; that, in order to secure the fulfilment of the contract, defendant conveyed and delivered to claimants certain personalty, which was, however, to remain in his possession ; that defendant waived homestead and exemption rights, was a mortgage, and did not convey a title. *Lee* v. *Clark, Rosser & Co.*, 60 Ga. 639.

152. Contract founded upon mutual and concurrent promises, afford sufficient legal consideration for the support of each other. *Missiquoi Bank* v. *Sabin*, 48 Vt. 239.

153. The defendant subscribed for shares in a patent right, to be held by him without payment therefor, otherwise than by inducing others to subscribe for shares and give their notes therefor for greatly more than the value of the shares ; the notes afterwards came into his hands by purchase, and were by him negotiated for money, and paid by the makers. *Held*, that these facts would not entitle the makers to maintain an action against him for money had and received. *Lane* v. *Smith*, 68 Me. 178.

154. The maxim, that "the express mention of one thing implies the exclusion of another," is ordinarily used to control, limit, or restrain the otherwise implied effect of an instrument, and not to "annex incidents to written contracts in matters with respect to which they are silent." *Morrow* v. *Morgan*, 48 Texas, 304.

155. If a creditor receives a partial payment before any breach of contract, and agrees to look to another source than the promissor for payment, such new agreement is binding, and the original contract is abandoned or waived; but if such agreement is made only to induce performance, and prevent a breach of the original contract, it is without consideration, and cannot be supported. When a valid contract subsists between the parties, it is competent for them, at any time before its breach, to waive, annul or dissolve the agreement, or to change or modify its terms, and the mutual agreement of the parties is a sufficient consideration. *Burkham* v. *Mastin*, 54 Ala. 123.

156. A **Contract** not under seal, wherein one person makes a promise to another for the benefit of a third person, such third person may maintain an action on it, though the consideration did not move from him. *Price* v. *Trusdell*, 28 N. J. Eq. 200.

157. In a contract for the transportation of freight, it was provided "that in the event of either of the parties failing to comply with the terms of the contract, the party so failing was to pay the other party the sum of one thousand dollars, fixed and settled damages." *Held*, that this was not intended, nor to be construed as meaning a penal sum, but as fixed, settled and

liquidated damages, and the defendant was not permitted to show that the plaintiff had not sustained actual damages to that amount. *Ivinson & Co.* v. *Althorp*, 1 Wyoming S. Ct. Rpts. 71.

158. Where property was sold and delivered to a third person, on the faith of the promise of defendants to accept his draft on them for the purchase money, a specific performance of the contract will be enforced. *Saulsbury, Respers & Co.* v. *Blaudys*, 60 Ga. 646.

159. Where at the execution of a writing a stipulation has been entered into, a condition annexed, or a promise made by word of mouth, upon the faith of which the writing has been executed, parol evidence is admissible, although it may vary and materially change the terms of the contract. In debt upon a bond the defendant offered to prove that the bond was given for unpaid purchase money of a certain lot; that to induce the purchase of said lot, plaintiff verbally agreed that if defendant did not like the property, plaintiff, on request of defendant, would take back the same, and pay defendant a premium and cost of his improvement; that there should be no personal liability by defendant for the purchase-money, and that plaintiff should look solely to the property for payment; that plaintiff was not to part with the bond or mortgage; that when defendant asked that the foregoing agreement should be inserted in the papers being executed, plaintiff said it was unnecessary, that his bond was sufficient, and that defendant has asked plaintiff to take back the property as stipulated, which was refused. The court below rejected these offers. *Held*, that they should have been received. *Greenawalt* v. *Kohne*, 85 Penn. 369.

160. In order to take a parol contract for the sale of land out of the operation of the Statute of frauds its terms must be shown by full, complete, satisfactory and indubitable proof. The evidence must define the boundaries and indicate the quantity of the land. It must fix the amount of the consideration. It must establish the fact that possession was taken in pursuance of the contract, and at or immediately after the time it was made, the fact that the change of possession was notorious, and the fact that it had been exclusive, continuous and maintained. And it must show performance or part performance by the vendee which could not be compensated in damages and such as would make recission inequitable and just. Defendant in ejectment claimed title to land by virtue of a parol sale, possession taken and maintained, improvements, &c. A deed was offered in evidence, signed by plaintiff, which contained a description of the property, and recited the consideration, but which was never delivered to defendant. *Held*, reversing the court below, that the deed, taken in connection with other facts, was sufficient evidence of a parol contract to take

the case out of the operations of the Statute of Frauds. *Hart* v. *Carroll*, 85 Penn. St. 508.

161. A court of equity will not extricate a party from the consequences of his own acts voluntarily committed to carry out an illegal contract relating to the entry of public lands. Generally, those who violate law in their dealings with one another, are left precisely in the same condition they placed themselves. *Ainsworth* v. *Miller*, 20 Kansas, 220.

162. The reduction of an agreement to writing, signed by the parties, is not necessary to its perfection as a contract, unless it clearly appears that the parties intended that it should be complete as a contract, until so written and signed. *Montague et. al.* v. *Weil & Bro.*, 30 La. 50.

163. A promise to pay for property purchased, "out of the proceeds of the first cotton ginned," is evidence conducing to show the time of payment, but does not prove, or tend to prove, that the seller of the property is to look for his pay alone to the profits made in ginning that season. *White* v. *Chaffin*, 32 Ark. 59.

164. When an instrument is prepared by the party to be held liable under it, and it is ambiguous in its terms, that construction is to be adopted which is most favorable to the promissee. *Atlantic Ins. Co.* v. *Manning*, 3 Colo. 224.

165. An act which is forbidden by a statute, or the common law, whether it be *malum in re* or merely *malum prohibitum*, indictable, or only subject to a penalty or forfeiture, cannot be the foundation of a valid contract. *Lindsey* v. *Rottaken*, Collector, 32 Ark. 619.

166. When one party submits a proposal for a contract to another, and the latter's acceptance of the proposal includes a material modification of the proposal, no contract will result until the modification has been acquiesced in by the party making the proposal. *Nicholas Connell* v. *Alexander Hill*, 30 La. 251.

167. Where two contracts between the same parties are distinct and to be performed at different times, the non-performance of the one is no defence to an action on the other. *Turner* v. *Rogers*, 121 Mass. 12.

168. When it clearly appears from the evidence that the intent of parties was to form a written contract, neither party will be bound until the contract has been reduced to writing, and signed by both. No alleged verbal agreement, in such case, can be invoked by either party against the other. *Louisa Fredericks, Tutrix* v. *Robert Fasnacht*, 30 La. 117.

169. Where in a contract to deliver a certain thing, no *time* for the delivery is fixed, the legal implication is that it shall be delivered within a reasonable time from the date of the contract. *Robert H. Bartley* v. *City of New Orleans*, 30 La. 264.

170. Where no fiduciary relation exists between the parties, and they are of legal capacity, however disadvantageous or improvident a contract between them appears, a court of equity will not relieve against it, until the party seeking to avoid it clearly proves that it was the result of fraud, mistake, surprise or undue influence practiced upon him. *Malone* v. *Kelly*, 54. Ala. 532.

171. A contract must be held to have been made when the last act necessary to complete it was done, when no mutual act remains to be performed to entitle either party to enforce it. *Northampton M. L. S. Ins. Co.* v. *Tuttle*, 40 N. J. Law Reports, 476.

172. Contract founded on an act which a statute prohibits under a penalty is void, although the State does not expressly so provide, and the subsequent repeal of the Statute, without any saving clause as to penalties already incurred, will not validate a contract void under the law in existence when the contract was made. *Woods* v. *Armstrong*, 54 Ala. 150.

173. Contract having an unlawful or immoral cause are not merely void themselves, but as a rule, cannot be the basis of any valid auxiliary contract. *Cummings* v. *Saux*, 30 La. 207.

174. Where the evidence shows that the parties intended, originally, that the contract of lease should be reduced to writing, neither will be bound until it is signed by both. *Miguel Avendano* v. *I. W. Arthur & Co.*, 30 La. 316.

175. The written agreement of a debtor who has borrowed certain bonds, to return bonds of the same description, for the same amount, at a certain term, is not a promissory note for the amount of the bonds. The obligations is to return the specific bonds at the time fixed, or pay their value at that time. *Blouin* v. *Liquidators* of *Hart & Hebert*, 30 La. 714.

176. The laws which subsist at the time and place of making of a contract, and where it is to be performed, enter into and form a part of the contract; and that, whether such laws affect its validity, construction, discharge or enforcement. *Roberts' Adm'rs* v. *Cocke, &c.;* also *Murphy* v. *Gaskins' Adm'rs*, 28 Grattan (Va.) 207.

177. A contract is binding when signed by the party making it, though he may use an English translation of a French name, as Seam for Couture, in his signature thereto. *Auger* v. *Couture*, 68 Me. 427.

CONVEYANCE.

178. When land is by one deed conveyed to two or more persons, who contributed to the purchase money in unequal amounts, their share in the property will, in the absence of an agreement to the contrary, be in proportion to their respective contributions. *Shroser* v. *Isaacs*, 28 N. J. Eq. 320.

179. Where the grantor in a deed covenants that he was well seized, etc., and had good right to convey, etc., and then added that he "would warrant and defend the grantee, his heirs and assigns, against all and every person lawfully claiming, or to claim the whole, or any part of the premises, except against the United States." *Held*, that both covenants must be taken and construed together, and that the latter restricted and qualified the first. *Dunn* v. *Dunn*, 3 Colo. 510.

180. Insolvent debtor seeking to prefer certain creditors by mortgage, no ground for equitable relief. *Heidingsfelder et al.* v. *Slade & Etheridge et al.*, 60 Ga. 396.

181. From the mere fact that upon the sale of a piece of property belonging to the wife the husband received the price, it does not necessarily follow that a debt of the latter to the former was intended to be or was created. *Hunt* v. *Spencer*, 20 Kansas, 126.

182. A voluntary conveyance can be sustained, as against existing creditors, only when under all the circumstances of the case the property retained by the grantor furnishes reasonable and adequate provisions for the discharge of his debts. *Id.*

183. A contract for the conveyance of real estate, not in writing, is void by the statute of frauds. When a party to such contract has complied with its conditions, and made all the payments required by its terms, he is entitled to recover back such payments, in case the other party refuses to perform on his part. Nor will it defeat his right of recovery that he is in possession of the premises agreed to be conveyed. *Jellison* v. *Jordan*, 68 Me. 373.

184. Sale of all his landed estate by husband to wife, if *bona fide*, conveys title; *aliter*, if to hinder or defraud creditors, though subsequently perfected by formal conveyance. *Thompson* v. *Feagin*, 60 Ga. 82.

185. A party loses no right by a mere change in the form of his securities, and the holder of a new note, given in exchange for an old one, may attack a conveyance which would be fraudulent as to the old one. *Thomson* v. *Herter*, 55 Miss. 656.

186. A voluntary conveyance from father to son, made by the grantor, with an intent to defraud his subsequent creditors, is void as to such creditors, with either allegation or proof that the grantee participated in that intent when he received or accepted the deed. In such case the intent of the grantor alone determines the validity of the conveyance. *Langton* v. *Harder*, 68 Me. 208.

CORPORATIONS.

187. Liability of Officers and Stockholders.—The personal liability of the officers and stockholders of a corporation for a debt contracted by the corporation is inconsistent with the idea of a body corporate at common law, and can arise only out of some statutory provision. *Salt Lake City Nat. Bank* v. *Hendrickson*, 40 N. J. Law Reports, 52.

188. A creditor of the Eastern Railway Co. held its note, and, as collateral security for the same, three other notes of the corporation, with coupons attached, of a kind regularly quoted in the market, is entitled, under the statutes of 1876, ch. 286, to prove only the amount of the original note against the company. *Third Nat. Bank* v. *Eastern Railroad Co.*, 122 Mass. 240.

189. The defendants were an incorporated company, the capital of which was $30,000, in 100 shares of $300 each, 90 of which had been subscribed for, and paid up in full by duly made calls thereon. Subsequently the defendants employed the plaintiff to take charge of their business, who was appointed president, at a salary of $1,200. He subscribed for seven shares of the unallotted stock, debited himself with the amount thereof, $2,100, in the company's books, and afterwards paid it. Afterwards, desiring to obtain control of the company, he arranged with four of the stockholders for the transfer to him of their stock, but one of them, M., to enable him to remain as a director, was to, and did subscribe for the three remaining shares unallotted. Subsequently the plaintiff wished to withdraw from this arrangement, and the parties agreed to cancel it; but M. was to be relieved of the three shares, and M.'s name was accordingly erased, and the plaintiff's inserted, as subscriber for three shares, the substitution being made either by plaintiff himself, or by the bookkeeper by his direction. It was also arranged between the plaintiff and the other directors that this stock should be entered in the stock-book as paid up in full, but the plaintiff was to be debited with the $900, to be paid out of his salary as president. Accordingly the plaintiff, with his knowledge and assent, was so debited, and from time to time, as his salary became payable, it was set off against it, and a balance afterwards struck in the books on this basis. There was no by-law regulating calls or transfers of stock, and no calls made on the plaintiff for either amounts subscribed by him, and no transfer from M. to plaintiff, except in the manner stated. *Held*, that no transfer was necessary, as the plaintiff's subscription must be held as an original one, nor were any call required, for the plaintiff by his conduct had impliedly agreed that none need be made, and both he and the company were estopped from denying his ownership of the shares. The plaintiff having sued defendant for his salary; *Held*, that defendants were entitled to set off the amount due on his stock. *Held*, also, that they were entitled to have judgment in their favor for the

excess of the set-off over the plaintiff's claim, and that for such purpose no special prayer or conclusion in their plea of set-off was necessary. *Smart* v. *Bowmanville Machine and Implement Co.*, 25 Upper Canada Com. Plea. Repts. 503.

190. The stockholders of a corporation have no right to appropriate any part of its assets to pay salaries due them as officers of the company, or due them on any other account, until all creditors, who are not stockholders, have been paid. *Cochran* v. *Ocean Dry Dock Co.*, 30 La. 1365.

191. No loss suffered by a stockholder, in consequence of a call authorized by the charter of the corporation, made upon each stockholder to pay a proportion of the price due on his stock, will give rise to a claim for damages against the directors of the corporation. *Succession of Woods*, 30 La. 1002.

192. The *bona fide* sale of the stock of an incorporated company, coupled with a power of attorney to the vendee to transfer it on the books of the company, is made complete by the delivery to the vendee of the certificate of stock. It is not necessary to the perfection of the sale, and the consequent protection of the stock from the seizure of the vendor's creditors, that notice of the sale should be served on the corporation, or that an actual transfer of the stock should have been made on its books. *Samuel & A. W. Smith* v. *Crescent City Live Stock Landing and Slaughter House Co.*, 30 La. 1378.

193. Chartered Bank adjudicated a bankrupt, a member of its last active board of directors (the board in existence when the failure occurred and the act of bankruptcy was committed), cannot buy up claims against it at a discount, and entitle himself to credit thereafter at full face value in settlement with creditors on his personal liability as a stockholder. At least this cannot be done so as to defeat the suit of a creditor, who commenced his action before the bought-up claims were actually applied in extinguishment of the stockholder's personal liability, and whilst the stockholder held them, as transferee, open against the bank, he not having surrendered or canceled them until after the action was brought. When a stockholder is sued as such, and he defends on claims against the bank purchased by him, his legal disability as a director to purchase at a discount may be urged by the plaintiff in reply, without any allegation to that effect in the pleadings. *Holland* v. *Heyman & Bro.*, 60 Ga. 174.

194. When the charter of a corporation provides that, in case any subsequent increase of the capital of the concern is authorized, notice of sixty days shall be given of such increase, within which time the stockholders shall have the privilege of taking additional shares, proportioned to the amount of their stock, and that any shares, not taken at the expiration of that time, may be disposed of by the directors for the

benefit of tne association, *Held*, that in order to entitle a stockholder to demand said additional shares, it must appear that he applied for the shares, and paid over or tendered the money necessary to purchase the same before the expiration of the sixty days, or before the expiration of any additional delay, which may have been given by the corporation to enable the stockholders to exercise said privilege. *Mrs. Emily L. Hart et al.* v. *St. Charles Street Railroad Co.*, 30 La. 758.

195. **A Certificate of Stock** accompanied by an irrevocable power of attorney, either filled up or in blank, is in the hands of a third party presumptive evidence of ownership in the holder. And where the party in whose hands the certificate is found is a holder for value, without notice of any intervening equity, his title cannot be impeached. The holder of the certificate may fill up the letter of attorney, execute the power, and thus obtain the legal title to the stock. And such a power is not limited to the person to whom it was first delivered, but enures to each *bona fide* holder into whose hands the certificate and power may pass. Mere knowledge on the part of a purchaser that an executor or administrator is dealing with the assets in a fiduciary capacity, is not enough to raise suspicion or to put the party on inquiry, for the reason that it is to their primary duty to dispose of the assets and settle the estate. A sale and transfer by them is ordinarily in the line of their duty. The common duty of a trustee is not administration or sale, but custody and management for his *cestuis que trust*. *Prall* v. *Tilt*, 28 N. J. Eq. 479.

196. By the Act of 1872, ch. 325, sec. 59, all the stockholders of a corporation are severally and individually liable to the creditors of the corporation of which they are stockholders to an amount equal to any unpaid subscription held by them respectively. If one stockholder is required to pay a debt due by the corporation he is entitled to contribution from all the other stockholders whose subscriptions are unpaid. If any stockholder who has not paid up his subscription claims to be a creditor of the corporation, his unpaid stock is liable for the debt, and he cannot recover from another stockholder the full extent of his claim. Where a stockholder, who is a creditor of the corporation, seeks to recover his debt from another stockholder who has not paid up his subscription, the plaintiff must aver and prove that he has paid up his whole subscription to the stock, and also that the defendant was a stockholder of the corporation *at the time the debt was contracted*, and that he has not paid up his subscription. In an action against a stockholder of a corporation who has not paid up his subscription to recover a debt due by the corporation, wherein the plaintiff declares on a judgment recovered against the corporation as his cause of action, the defendant is entitled to a bill of particulars, in order

that it may be informed whether the debt due by the corporation was contracted at the time the defendant was a stockholder. The judgment is the evidence of the debt due by the corporation, but it does not show *when* the debt was contracted. The date of the debt incurred is a necessary part of the evidence to fix the liability of the stockholder. *Weber* v. *Fickey*, 47 Md. 196.

197. Corporations. A president of a corporation is a trustee, and will not be permitted to create such a relation between himself and the trust property as will make his own interest antagonistic to that of his beneficiary. A president who has voluntarily purchased a small debt against the corporation, will be enjoined from levying an execution for the payment of a balance on the same, where he has already taken valuable property of the corporation in part payment thereof. *Brewster et al.* v. *Stratman et al.*, 4 Mo. Ct. Appeals (St. Louis) 41.

198. Where a corporation is being defrauded by its officers, and by collision the directors refuse to interfere to protect stockholders, or to sue, and will not seek redress in the corporate name, the individual stockholder who seeks relief for himself and others should so frame his bill as to set forth these facts, and should make the directors parties to the bills. *Griffin* v. *St. Louis Wine and Fruit Growers Asso. et al.*, 4 Mo. Ct. Appeals (St. Louis) 595.

199. When it appears that the parties in charge of the property and affairs of a corporation, as liquidators of the same, have been elected as such by the stockholders of the corporation, and their election has not been set aside, and no fear of fraudulent action on their part is alleged, no court is authorized to displace them, and appoint a receiver in their stead. *John F. Follett, et al.* v. *Spencer Field, President, et al.*, 30 La. 161.

200. A legal by-law of a corporation which provides that no shares of its stock shall be transferred on its books, until the certificate thereof has been surrendered to its president, or shown to be lost, is binding on all its stockholders, and their heirs. Before the heirs of a deceased stockholder can compel the corporation to transfer shares, or pay accrued dividends to them, they must comply with the requirements of the by-laws. *State ex rel. Martin et al.* v. *N. O. & Carrollton R. R. Co.*, 30 La. 308.

201. Where the business of a church corporation is required by the articles of incorporation to be conducted by its officers as a board of trustees, the president and secretary have no power to execute a note binding upon the corporation without authority from such board. *Cattron et al.* v. *The First Universal Society of Manchester*, 46 Iowa, 106.

202. Authority conferred by the trustees to erect a church building, however, would carry with it the power to contract debts necessary for that purpose, and notes executed therefor would be valid. *Id.*

203 A corporation having been recognized in the exercise of its corporate functions by legislative enactments, all inquiry into its original organization is precluded. One who deals with a corporation in its corporate capacity cannot afterwards question collaterally the legality of the corporate existence. *Cowell* v. *Colo. Spg's Co.*, 3. Colo. 82.

204. A foreign corporation does not become a domestic corporation by complying with the laws of this State, in pursuance of which a foreign corportion may do business here without liability attaching to the officers, agents and stockholders, upon the contracts of the company. *Cook* v. *Nayer*, 3 Colo. 386.

DAMAGES.

205. Where an examiner of title to real estate gives a certificate of title, he does not thereby become an indemnitor, but he is liable for any mistake arising from want of due care or diligence, or from ignorance of his business. An action for damages against him for false certificate is barred by the Statute of limitations in five years from the delivery of the certificate, and not from the time when it is discovered that the certificate is untrue. *Rankin* v. *Shaeffer, Admr.*, 4 Mo. Ct. Appeals (St. Louis,) 108.

206. Negligence alone is not to be visited with punitive damages ; wilful misconduct, or that entire want of care which would raise the presumption of a conscious indifference to consequences, is necessary to support such damages. *Kansas Pacific R'y Co.* v. *Lundin, Admr.*, 3 Colo. 94.

207. In an action to recover the price of goods sold, the measure of damages is the difference between the value which the article sold would have had in the market at the time of the sale and delivery, if they had corresponded with the guaranty, and their actual value with the defects. *Smith et al.* v. *Mayer et al.*, 3 Colo. 207.

208. If the party who has contracted to deliver a certain thing at a fixed price makes a tender of it at the proper time, and the party who has contracted to receive the thing refuses to receive it, the former may recover from the latter whatever damages are proved to have directly flowed from the latter's breach of contract. *Bartley* v. *City of New Orleans*, 30 La. 264.

209. Recorder of Deeds is liable in damages for a false certificate of researches. The liability of the recorder is to the party who asks and pays for the certificate, not to his assignee or alienee. *Houseman* v. *Girard Building Asso.*, 81 Penn. 256.

DEBTOR AND CREDITOR.

210. Debts. Claims against the estates of decedents, resting on mere oral testimony of declarations and admissions of the decedent are very dangerous, and not to be favored by the Courts. *Pollock* v. *Ray*, 85 Penn. St. 428.

211. Any agreement with one creditor for an advantage to him over other creditors, made to induce him to join in the composition, or required by him as a condition upon which he shall become a party to it, which is not provided for in the composition deed, and is not disclosed to the other creditors, is utterly void, and is incapable of being enforced or confirmed even as against the assenting debtor. A security given in pursuance of such a bargain or a subsequent promise of payment, is equally void with the antecedent agreement; and money paid by the debtor under such an agreement, in excess of the due proportion of such creditor's debt, may be recovered back, unless it be paid under such circumstances as to be regarded in law as a voluntary payment. *Crossley* v. *Moore*, 40 N. J. Law 27.

212. Debtors residing without this State are excluded *ex vi termini* from the operation of the Statute (R. S. p. 418 sec. 103) which provides that "Suits shall be commenced before justices in the township in which the debtor resides." Such non-resident debtors may be sued wherever found. *Wagner et al.* v. *Hallock et al.*, 3 Colo. 176.

213. When a debtor, after being discharged from the obligations of his debts by a deed of composition with his creditors, voluntarily gives a security for a debt from which he is discharged by such composition and which is only due in conscience, such security may be enforced in a court of law. *Crossley* v. *Moore*, 40 N. J. L. R. 27.

DEEDS.

214. In determining the dividing lines between tracts of land, courses, calls and distances, must give way to the marks on the ground, and these marks control as well the description found in the patent as that found in the survey. The deed of the treasurer to the Commissioners of Warren County having been lost, its delivery and contents were properly proved by the books found in custody of the proper officers. *Watson* v. *Jones*, 85 Penn. St. 117.

215. That a deed is ineffectual to convey title as to part of the lands described is of itself no ground for setting aside the deed, nor will a court of equity entertain a bill for compensation or damages, except as incidental to other relief, when there is an adequate remedy at law. *Jaeger* v. *Whitsett*, 3 Colo. 105.

216. A condition in a deed, granting an estate in fee, that intoxicating liquors shall never be manufactured, sold or otherwise disposed of as a beverage in any place of public resort in or upon the premises granted, or upon any part thereof, the grantor reserving the right upon condition broken to declare the deed void, and all right, title and interest in the premises in such event to revert to the grantor, and the grantee consenting to the condition and reservation, held to be a valid condition, binding upon the grantee, not repugnant to the estate granted, and that upon condition broken the grantor might maintain ejectment, upon proof of the breach, without previous entry, demand or notice. *Cowell* v. *Col. Sp'gs Co.* 3 Colo. 82.

217. A deed duly recorded is constructive notice of its existence and contents to all persons claiming what is thereby conveyed under the same grantor by subsequent purchase, but not to other persons. *Gillett et al.* v. *Gaffney et al.*, 3 Colo. 351.

218. The delivery of a deed implies its acceptance by the grantee, in the absence of fraud, artifice, or imposition. *Davenport* v. *Whisler and Shields*, 46 Iowa, 287.

219. By the acceptance of the deed the contract of sale is executed and merged therein; any inconsistencies between its original terms and the deed are in general to be explained by the latter. *Id.*

220. The holder under a quit-claim deed is not entitled to protection, as a *bona fide* purchaser without notice, against outstanding equities. *Springer et. al.* v. *Bartle*, 46 Iowa, 688.

221. Although a deed is *inter partes*, a covenant therein made with a third person may be enforced by such third person by suit, if it clearly appears by the instrument that it was the intention to confer such right. *National Bank at Dover* v. *Segar*, 39 N. J. Law 173.

222. Ordinarily the date of a deed (admitted to have been delivered), is *prima facie* evidence of the time of its delivery, but this presumption may be rebutted by testimony. *Cain* v. *Robinson*, 20 Kansas, 456.

223. In the description in a deed courses and distances must yield to fixed monuments or to any points named which are capable of being certainly ascertained. *Sanders* v. *Eldridge et al.*, 46 Iowa, 34.

224. The recitals in a deed as to the consideration, are not conclusive, but the time and actual consideration may be shown by proof *aliunde*. *Fraley* v. *Bentley et al.*, 1 Bennett's Dakota Rpts. 25.

DEMAND.

225. To enable a party to recover in an action upon a due bill payable in specific property, no time being mentioned, a demand is necessary. Otherwise when time and place are specified. A personal demand elsewhere than at the place designated in a due bill for the delivery of personal property is good, unless met by an offer to pay at the designated place. A right of action, which has accrued by reason of a refusal upon demand to deliver specific articles of property according to contract is waived by a subsequent demand if the party upon whom the demand is made indicates a readiness to deliver according to contract. *Widner* v. *Walsh*, 3 Colo. 548.

226. Where one receives from a municipal corporation warrants drawn upon its treasurer, presentation to that officer, or the allegation in the declaration of facts which will excuse presentation, is necessary before an action can be maintained on the warrants. *City of Central* v. *Wilcoxen*, 3 Colo. 566.

227. A mere demand for the payment of the balance of purchase-money cannot be regarded as an acquiescence in the wrongful delivery of an escrow, and as depriving the vendor of his right to rescind. *Hamill* v. *Thompson et al.*, 3 Colo. 518.

DEPOSITS.

228. In an action against a savings bank, on an account annexed, to recover the amount of a deposit, the book of deposit is admissible in the evidence, at least to show the amount of the plaintiff's money received by the defendant, and it does not appear to have been admitted for any illegal purpose, although the book contained printed conditions of deposit and payment. *Brown* v. *Abington Savings Bank*, 119 Mass. 69.

229. A safe deposit company contracted with a depositor to "keep a constant and adequate guard over and upon the safe" rented by him. A number of bonds deposited therein were found to be missing: *Held*, that the company was bound to make some explanation for the absence of the bonds. *Held*, further, that the question whether the company was guilty of negligence was properly left to the jury. *Safe Deposit Co.* v. *Pollock*, 85 Penn. St. 391.

230. A certificate of deposit, payable on the return thereof properly endorsed, is in legal effect a promissory note, payable on demand; and the principle applicable to such notes should be applied to these certificates. The claim that a certificate of

deposit and a certified check are in legal sense the same thing, are governed by the same rules, and that no mere lapse of time will render such check or certificate past due or dishonored, is held not well founded. Certificates of deposit are not intended for long circulation, or for more than a temporary convenience, and to hold that any ostensibly demand paper could be circulated or used as bank-bills, would be contrary to the general policy of our banking laws. *Tripp* v. *Curlessius*, 36 Mich. 494.

231. A depositor in a savings bank, who is also a debtor to the bank, as a borrower of its funds, cannot, upon the insolvency of the savings bank set-off the amount of his deposit against his indebtedness. *Osborn* v. *Byrne*, 43 Conn. 155.

232. Where, however, a person indebted to a savings bank as a borrower, deposited an amount less than the debt, intending to use the money so deposited for a payment upon the debt, it was held that the amount deposited could be set off against the debt.

233. A savings bank is an agent for the depositors, receiving and loaning their money, and its losses are their losses, and are to be borne by them equally, according to their interest. *Id.*

234. A bank of deposit has no power to apply a money deposit in its possession, belonging to the maker of a promissory note payable at such bank, to the satisfaction of such note, without his consent. *Scott* v. *Shirk*, 60 Ind. 160.

235. When a bank receives deposits it undertakes to pay the depositor's check to the holder, if it has funds of the depositor sufficient to pay the check when presented; and this promise or agreement between the bank and its depositor, implied from the universal usage or custom of the business world enures to the benefit of the holder of the check, and if he presents it to the bank for payment, and payment is refused, the bank having funds of the depositor sufficient to pay it when presented, he may sue and recover of the bank upon the check. *McGrade* v. *German Savings. Int.*, 4 (St. Louis,) Mo. Ct. Appeals, 330.

236. A depository may show by parol evidence that the money deposited with him, and for which he had given his written receipt, was composed of certain bank bills. A depository is not liable for any depreciation in the value of bank bills deposited with him, unless it appears that the depreciation has proceeded from his fault, or has occurred after he was in default to restore the deposit. *Uranie Berard* v. *Vincent Boagni*, 30 La. 1125.

237. Special deposit of bonds was left by a customer with the cashier of a national bank for safe keeping, with the knowledge of its directors, and the bank gave a receipt there-

for. The bonds were subsequently stolen and the bank offered no satisfactory explanation of the manner of the theft. *Held*, that there was sufficient evidence of gross negligence to be submitted to the jury. *Bank* v. *Graham*, 85 Penn. St. 91.

ENDORSERS.

238. The omission to give an endorser notice of the non-payment of previous instalments, as they fell due on a promissory note does not affect his liability for a later instalment, of the non-payment of which he has been duly notified. Notice to the indorser of a promissory note of a demand made upon the maker for an instalment then due and for the interest due upon the note (some of the previous instalments and interest being still unpaid) and of his non-payment, is sufficient to charge the endorser, and is not invalidated by adding that the holder looks to him for the payment of the instalment and of the interest due upon the note. In an action against the indorser of a promissory note to recover an instalment due thereon, it appeared that when previous instalments had become due, of the non-payment of which the indorser had not been duly notified, the indorsee had applied the proceeds of a mortgage, given by the maker to secure the payment of the note, to such instalments. *Held*, that the indorsee had the right so to apply them. *Fitchburg Mutual Fire In. Co.* v. *Davis*, 121 Mass. 121.

239. Where the maker of a promissory note furnishes to the second endorser money to pay the note, a trust is created in favor of the first endorser, as well as the holder, to have the fund applied in payment of the note. Where two persons successively endorse a promissory note for the accommodation of the maker, and the maker furnishes to the second endorser at the time of his endorsement, with the means to pay the note, without the knowledge of the first endorser, the maker and second endorser have a right to subsequently agree that the means shall be applied to another purpose; but if the second endorser promises the first that such means shall be applied to the payment of the note, and thereby induces him to be inactive, which results to his injury, such promise creates an equity in favor of the first endorser which will sustain an action. *Price* v. *Trusdell*, 28 N. J. Eq. 20.

240. The endorsee of a negotiable bill or note, in the absence of proof of fraud, is presumed to be a *bona fide* holder for value—this presumption is not repelled merely by proof that the paper as between the immediate parties was without consideration, and was made, indorsed or accepted by one for the sole accommodation of the other. Where, therefore, in an action by an endorsee before maturity against the acceptors of a bill, the defence was that the acceptance was without consid-

eration of the drawer, and that it was discounted by plaintiffs for the drawer at a usurious rate of interest, *held*, that the burden was upon defendants to show the amount paid by plaintiffs for the bill, and in the absence of any evidence upon the subject, that plaintiffs were entitled to recover. *Harger* v. *Worrall*, 69 N. Y. 370.

241. Notice of dishonor to indorser, certificate of notary, in connection with his testimony that it is genuine, and that, though he has no recollection of the facts stated therein, he is satisfied of their truth, because he would not have certified them had he not been convinced of their truth at the time, admissible to establish, notice, mail used as means of conveying, and it is in evidence that notice did not in fact reach endorser, plaintiff must show that notices were properly directed, stamped, etc. Evidence that notary "served" endorsers with notice "by depositing said notices in the post office, in the city of Atlanta," with no statement as to direction, payment of postage etc., insufficient where endorsers testify that they did not receive notice. *Allen & Co.* v. *Georgia National Bank*, 60 Ga. 347.

242. Agreements of endorsee with a stranger to give time to the acceptor does not discharge the maker. *Frazer* v. *Jordan*, XC. ii. 303; 8 E. & B. 303. (Eng. Com. Law.)

243. That where a party who is a stranger to the note endorses the name before delivery, the law does not define the character of the contract or obligation created by such endorsement, and, therefore, parol evidence will be received to determine what the contract was—whether that of a guarantor or maker—and that the contract may not, because of its ambiguity, be defeated; and whereas, in this case, the law defines the nature of the contract, and the manner in which the endorser may be held by proper legal steps, the court will not receive parol evidence to prove another and different contract from that defined by law. *Id.*; also, *Levering* v. *Washington*, 3 Minn. 323; *Kern* v. *Von Phul*, 7 Minn. 426; *First National Bank* v. *National Marine Bank*, 20 Minn. 63.

244. Where endorsee of a bill of exchange in sets alleges loss in transmission for acceptance, and demand for other sets from prior endorser not immediate as to him, and also alleges the non-delivery by said endorsee and consequent loss, he cannot recover. Such endorsee is bound to apply either to the drawer or his immediate endorser. *Non constat* that if he had applied to them there would have been a loss. *Pinard* v. *Klockmann*, CX. iii. 388; 3 B & S. 388. (Eng. Com. Law.)

245. An endorser of a promissory note, even though it be an accommodation note, is not one; but is a principal debtor if the note be not paid and proper steps have been taken to fix his liability. *Ross* v. *Jones*, 22 Wallace (U. S.) 576.

246. To charge an endorser of a note as maker, it is necessary to show specifically that he put his name upon the back of the note before delivery to the payee. *Best* v. *Hoppie*, 3 Colo. 137.

247. It being necessary for the payee to endorse the note in order to make it negotiable paper, he must be treated as first endorser without regard to the time of his endorsement or the locality of his name, on the note. A second endorser may maintain an action against the first for money paid on the note. *Cogswell* v. *Hayden*, 5 Oregon, 22.

248. The endorser of a promissory note after it falls due, with a contract, and as additional security to prevent legal proceedings from being taken against the payee and endorser, is that of a grantor, and, even if based on a valid consideration, is fatally defective, unless the writing express the consideration. *Crooks* v. *Tully*, 50 Cal. 254.

249. The guarantor of a promissory note is entitled to notice of non-payment. *Id.*

250. Endorsee sold a negotiable promissory note, and endorsed it without recourse. *Held* an implied warranty that the note was valid. *Hannum* v. *Richardson*, 48 Vt. 508.

251. The *Endorser* of a promissory note, though fixed in his liability, by protest, is not entitled, as a creditor, to a share of the estate of the maker under an assignment for the benefit of creditors. Such an endorser is entitled only to be reimbursed payments actually made by him. The holder of the note can claim under the equity of the endorser, out of the assigned estate, only to the amount of payments so made by the endorser. *Farmer's Bank* v. *Gilpin et al.*, 1 Del. Chancery, 409.

252. The names of the payees appeared on the back of a note in the usual position of the first endorser, about three inches from the left end, and that of the defendant in the opposite direction, about the same distance from the right end of the note, so that the latter with reference to the former may be said to have been inverted. *Held*, that this irregular endorsement did not relieve the defendant of liability, as he could have recourse against the payees. *Arnot's Adm'r* v. *Symonds*, 85 Penn. St. 99.

253. Endorsement upon a note, to the effect that the maker may use the principal after maturity by the payment of interest semi-annually, does not release the maker from the obligation of payment. *The Oskaloosa College* v. *Hickok*, 46 Iowa, 237.

254. Upon a failure of the maker to pay the interest according to the terms of the indorsement, the principal of the note became due and payable. The subsequent acceptance of interest would not entitle the maker to an extension of time of payment, the interest thus paid being merely a partial payment of the note. *Id.*

255. A person of unsound mind who signs as surety a note given for an antecedent debt, cannot be held liable thereon even though the person taking the note had no knowledge that the surety's mind was unsound. *Van Patton & Marks* v. *Beals & Hammer*, 46 Iowa, 62.

256. Complaint against two defendants as joint makers of promissory note, payable at any bank in Savannah, one of whom signed on the face and the other on the back, unnecessary, in order to charge the latter, to allege protest and notice. *Hardy* v. *White*, 60 Ga. 454.

257. A party endorsed a negotiable note for $500, for the maker's accommodation. The maker then, by the use of chemicals, rendered the amount of the note invisible, wrote in a larger amount, and procured the note to be discounted at a bank as a note for the larger amount. Before the note came due, the fraud was discovered, and the original writing was restored, and the note duly protested, and an action brought against the indorser, as on a note for the original amount. *Held*, that the endorser was not liable. *Citizens Nat. Bank* v. *Richmond*, 121 Mass. 110.

258. Where a joint and several note, made by the three defendants to the order of plaintiff and another party, was by that party indorsed and transferred to the plaintiff. *Held*, that the plaintiff alone could bring suit on the note, and that the district court did not err in overruling a demurrer to plaintiff's petition, on the ground that "there was a defect of parties plaintiff. *Regan* v. *Jones*, Wyoming S. C. Reps. 210.

259. An endorser of a check given with his knowledge in payment of a gambling debt, who pays the check to the holder upon non-payment by the drawee and protest, cannot recover therefor, from the drawer, or a prior endorser. A. having paid B's gambling debt, A. knowing it to be such debt, gives him no right of action against B. for the amount so paid. *Scollans* v. *Flynn*, 120 Mass. 271.

260. The endorsee of a negotiable note, who takes it discharged of the equities to which it was subject in the hands of the payee, acquires the same right in a mortgage given to secure it, which the payee would have had, if no equities had ever existed against the note. *Linville* v. *Savage*, 58 Mo. 248, *Logan* v. *Smith*, 62 Mo. 455.

261. The transfer of a note received by mortgage carries the mortgage with it, unless the mortgage has been separately extinguished, as by a release for instance. *Id.*

262. The endorser of a note will not be held bound by a fraudulent alteration made subsequently to his endorsement, unless through negligence; the instrument has been so loosely drawn as to easily admit of alteration, and in a matter not calculated to place a man of ordinary prudence on the alert.

But where no blank space was left unfilled, and the rate of interest was, after endorsement and without the knowledge of the endorser, inserted by interlineation in ink of a different color from that employed in the remainder of the note, it was held that the instrument upon its face bore such indications as should have excited suspicion and provoked inquiry; and that under such circumstances the indorser was not bound. *Capital Bank* v. *Armstrong*, 62 Mo. 59.

263. The mere fact that the alteration of a note is not made fraudulently, nor for the purpose of changing its legal effect will not change the rule as to the liability of a prior endorser. *Id.*

264. The defendant in 1867 endorsed the notes of C. for his accommodation to the amount of $7,000, and continued to endorse for him to the same amount, for purposes of renewal or payment, till 1873. In 1869 the plaintiffs, a bank, discounted some of these notes to the amount of $5,000 for C., and continued a line of discount of the same amount and upon the same endorsements till 1873. At this time C., having received from the defendant his endorsement upon a note of $2,000, the note being in all respects complete, fraudulently altered the amount to $5,000, and procured its discount by the plaintiffs, who took it without suspicion, and with the proceeds C. took up his notes at the plaintiffs' bank for $5,000, upon $4,000 of which the defendant was endorser, the bank discounting the note for the purpose of applying the proceeds in that manner. C. had formerly been in the defendants' employment, and had his entire confidence; and the defendant had been in the habit of endorsing paper sent to him for that purpose by C., without making any entry of the transaction, and in several instances had endorsed notes in which the time of payment was left blank. *Held*, That the Court could not, from all these facts, infer an agency on the part of C. under which his act in altering the note would be binding upon the defendant. *Aetna Bank* v. *Winchester*, 43 Conn. 391.

265. That the negotiation of the altered note to the plaintiffs did not render the defendant liable on his endorsement, as an act in the apparent exercise, and within the apparent scope, of an agency on the part of C. *Id.*

266. That the principle that, where one of two innocent persons must suffer by a fraud, he who furnished the means for committing the fraud should bear the loss, had no application to the case, as the defendant, having delivered the note to C. complete, could not be regarded as having furnished him the means of committing the fraud. *Id.*

267. That the rule that holds an endorser liable, although the note is used in a different manner from that intended by him, did not apply, as in such cases the contract is still the genuine contract of the endorser. *Id.*

268. That the defendant was not estopped by the facts from denying his liability upon the endorsement. *Id.*

269. The plaintiffs endorsed a note at the request and for the accommodation of D., which had been made by another person for D.'s accommodation, and which was first endorsed by him. At this time there was an understanding among all the parties that D. was to get the note discounted at a certain bank. He, however, was not able to accomplish this, and, without the knowledge of the plaintiffs, deposited it with the defendant as security for a loan of less amount, with an agreement that he might redeem it on paying the amount loaned, with certain agreed interest. In violation of this agreement the defendant sold the note to a *bona fide* holder for full value; and D. and the maker being insolvent, the plaintiffs were compelled to pay it in an action brought by the plaintiffs for damages caused to them by the fraudulent conduct of the defendant in disposing of the note, in which it was found that he disposed of it to prevent D. from making a set-off of a certain claim which he had against him, it was *held*

(1). That the understanding between the plaintiffs and D., that he would get the note discounted at a certain bank, could not, so long as their endorsement was without condition, affect his right to dispose of the note in any other manner.

(2). That the defendant, having become the lawful holder of the note, had the right, so far as the plaintiffs were concerned, to dispose of it upon any terms that he pleased.

(3). That although in doing so he violated his agreement with D., and might therefore be liable to him in damages, yet the plaintiffs, having been subjected to no liability beyond that which they assumed in endorsing the note—namely, that of having the full amount of the note to pay, if the maker or D. did not pay it, were not injured by his act. *Dawson* v. *Goodyear*, 43 Conn. 548.

GUARANTY.

270. To constitute a valid guaranty, there must be a sufficient consideration, a delivery by the guarantor, an acceptance by the person to whom it is given, a subsequent delivery of goods or other property under and in accordance with its terms, and if it is collateral, request of payment and notice of non-payment. Notice is not necessary when the undertaking is absolute. *Marsh* v. *Putney*, 56 N. H. 34.

271. Where the person, for whose benefit the guaranty is given, becomes insolvent, so that no advantage can arise to the guarantor, notice is unnecessary. *Id.*

272. All promises to answer for the debt or default of a third person must be in writing, whether the promise be made before, at the time, or after the debt or liability is created. In

the absence of words or circumstances showing a contrary intent, the words "we will see the articles paid for," or equivalent words, import a collateral undertaking, and are within the statute of frauds. *Wager et al.* v. *Halleck et al.*, 3 Colo. 176.

273. Where the language of a guaranty addressed to a factor is, "I am willing to go his security for the amount of twenty-five hundred dollars," it is not what is termed a *continuing* guaranty. It only embraces the first $2,500 of money advanced, or goods furnished to the person in whose favor the guaranty is given. The factor thus guaranteed is legally bound to apply to the guaranteed debt, and for the discharge of the guarantor, the first payments received by him from the person in whose favor the guaranty was given. *Ben. Gerson* v. *G. W. & G. M. Hamilton*, 30 La. 737.

274. A., a bank, had discontinued the note of B. for $10,000. C. had deposited with A. for collection a note for $15,000, secured by deed of trust. C. subsequently wrote the president of A. that, having heard that B. "could use advantageously some additional cash over and above the amount already had of your bank," etc., "if your bank will lend to B. $15,000, I shall hold myself responsible for that amount, and will leave with you as collateral security the note and mortgage" * * * "at present in your vault." The proposal contained in his letter was accepted, of which C. had due notice, and B. drew his check on A. for $10,000, and took up his note for $10,000. *Held*, that $15,000 was the amount which C. guaranteed to pay, and not $15,000 in addition to what B. had before received of A.; that the fact that the money was had of A., to whom B. owed a note of $10,000, and that he paid this note out of the $15,000 so advanced, made no difference in his case; and that the terms of the guarantee were complied in his case; and that the terms of the guarantee were complied with by A. A contract of guarantee must be strictly construed, yet must be so construed as to carry into effect the evident intention of the parties, as it is to be gathered from the instrument itself. *Allen, Adm'r*, v. *Central Savings Bank*, 4 Mo. St. Appeals (St. Louis), 66.

275. The guarantor of a note is not discharged from liability by reason of the failure to serve him with notice of non-payment, unless he can show that he suffered detriment thereby. *Rodabaugh* v. *Pitkin*, 46 Iowa, 544.

276. The words "we hereby agree to guaranty the payment to M. H. & Co. for any goods which may be purchased of them by A. W. of Lynn, not, however, binding ourselves to become responsible for a larger sum than five hundred dollars, except by another special agreement. The above guaranty to remain in force until its withdrawal by us." *Held*, that the contract sued on clearly appears upon its face to have been intended to

be a continuing guaranty. The question of fact of extinguishment or discharge has been decided by the court below in favor of plaintiffs. *Melendy et al.* v. *Capen*, 120 Mass. 222. Cases referred to : 1 Met. 24 ; 12 Gray, 447—119 Mass. 435.

277. The words of a guaranty will be read most strongly against the guarantor. *Hoey* v. *Jarman*, 39 N. J. Law, 523.

278. The following instrument, signed by the defendant, was delivered to the plaintiff: "I guarantee the sum of five hundred dollars value in glass shades purchased by my son A. from B. Terms of purchase to be sixty days from date of invoice, and if not paid within ninety days, draft to be drawn on me for the amount." *Held*, that it was not a continuing guaranty. *Held* also, that parol evidence of the previous dealings, or of the dealings contemplated, between the creditor and the principal debtor, or that the grantor had previously agreed to give the plaintiff a guaranty for future advances, and that the goods were sold, relying on such guaranty ; or that the relations of the principal parties were well known to the guarantor, was not admissible to show that the instrument was other than a guaranty of a single transaction. *Boston and Sandwich Glass Co.* v. *Moore*, 119 Mass. 435.

279. An oral guaranty of the payment of the note of a third person, the court held the defendant was doubtless once liable for the goods sold and delivered to him, and upon the due bill which, upon paying part of the price of the goods, he gave to the plaintiffs for the balance ; but upon his procuring and delivering to them the note of Robinson, as the bill of exceptions states, " they at the same time gave up the said due bill to him in settlement," and he orally promised to pay Robinson's note at maturity, if Robinson did not. The claim of the plaintiffs, and the finding of the court did not proceed upon the defendant's liability for goods sold, but solely upon this oral promise of his, thereby necessarily assuming that his previous liability had been settled and discharged by the giving and receiving of the note of Robinson. Upon this state of facts, the only direct liability was that of Robinson upon his note, and the oral promise of the defendant to pay the note, if R. did not, was a collateral promise to pay R.'s debt, and as such within the statute of frauds. *Dows* v. *Swett*, 120 Mass. 322. Cases recited : 3 Met. 396; 106 Mass. 400; 108 Mass. 246; 111 Mass. 501.

280. Defendant gave to C. and D. a separate written agreement to assume at maturity a share of the outstanding notes of R. given for his purchase money. The defendant was jointly interested with Currier & Dean in the purchase of a quarry. Advancements had been made, and expenses incurred by the latter in the purchase and improvement of the same, and part had been sold to one Richmond, and his notes taken in payment. The defendant, in a settlement with Currier & Dean, was charged with his share of the expenses and of the original cost, and credited with the part sold. The balance was paid to him by C. and D., who also gave him the written agreement to pay and save him harmless from an outstanding joint note for the purchase money. The defendant, on his part, at the same time gave C. and D. the written agreement aforesaid with regard to the notes of Richmond, given for his purchase of a part of the quarry. This action is brought on the last named agreement, by the assignees in bankruptcy of Currier and Dean, to recover a balance unpaid on one of the Richmond notes, which became due in 1868. The defendant offered to prove that he had no notice of the non-payment of this note until about the time of the commencemnt of this action, and that for more than two years after the note fell due Richmond was in good credit, and could have paid it, but C. and D. voluntarily gave him time upon it. The court ruled that the evidence would not amount to a defence; and the only question is whether the promise declared on is an original promise of the defendant to pay his own debt, or only a guaranty of the debt of another. In the opinion of the court it is the latter. The fact that the defendant derives benefit from the transaction is not alone enough to make it an original promise, for there must always be some consideration to support a mere collateral undertaking. It is sufficient if the leading object of the contract, as ascertained from the terms of it, is one of suretyship. By these tests it is clear that the defendant's promise in this case was intended to be collateral to the original principal obligation of another. The agreement was a guaranty, and not an original promise. *Davis* v. *Caverly*, 120 Mass. 414, also 98 Mass. 296; 106 Mass. 400; and 118 Mass. 137.

281. Upon assigning a bond and mortgage, the defendant made the following guaranty: "I hereby covenant * * * that, in case of foreclosure and sale of the mortgaged premises in said mortgage, if the proceeds of such sale shall be insufficient to satisfy the same, with the costs of foreclosure, I will pay the amount of such deficiency to the said party of the second part, or its assigns, on demand." *Held*, the fundamental distinction between a guaranty of payment and one of collection is, that in the first case the guarantor undertakes unconditionally that the debtor will pay, and the creditor may, upon default, proceed directly against the guarantor, without taking any steps to collect of the principal debtor, and the omission or neglect to proceed against him is not (except under special circumstances) any defence to the guarantor; while in the second case the undertaking is that if the demand cannot be collected by legal proceedings, the guarantor will pay, and consequently legal proceedings against the principal debtor,

and a failure to collect of him by those means, are conditions precedent to the liability of the guarantor; and to these the law, as established by numerous decisions, attaches the further condition that due diligence be exercised by the creditor in enforcing his legal remedies against the debtor. These rules are well settled, and are not controverted, and the only question is to which class of guaranties the one now before us belongs. It is apparent upon the face of the instrument that the undertaking of the defendant was not an unconditional one that the mortgagor should pay, or that the guarantor would pay on default of the mortgagor, but only that the guarantor would pay in case of a deficiency arising on a foreclosure and sale. The foreclosure and sale were consequently conditions precedent, and the general principle is that whenever a condition precedent is to be performed for the purpose of establishing the liability of a surety or guarantor, such condition must be performed in good faith, and with due diligence. The delay in foreclosing in the present case was fourteen months after the mortgage debt became due. During upward of ten months of this time the property was a sufficient security, but afterward the buildings thereon were destroyed by fire, and the value reduced below the amount of the mortgage debt. It cannot be questioned that this delay was sufficient to constitute *laches*. See *Craig* v. *Parkis* (40 N. Y., 181), a delay of six months in foreclosing a bond and mortgage was held to be *laches*, which discharged a guaranty of its collection. *Mc. Murray et al.* v. *Noyes*, 72 N. Y. App. 523.

INTEREST.

282. Interest in mutual accounts is to be cast on the annual balances. *Davis* v. *Smith*, 48 Vt. 52.

283. Interest on a note payable on demand runs only from demand, or suit brought, and the fact that the note was given for money received at the time it was made does not change the rule. Suit on a note payable on demand may be brought without a previous request for payment, the suit itself being equivalent to a demand. *Hunter* v. *Wood*, 54 Ala. 71.

284. Interest at the rate of only six per cent. can be recovered where no rate of interest is agreed upon between the parties. *Couney* v. *Sheldon*, 1 Bradwell's Ill. App. Rpts. 555.

285. As to parties holding simply the relation of creditor and debtor, compound interest will not be allowed. *Force* v. *Elizabeth*, 28 N. J. Eq. 403.

286. On a note payable on demand, with the rate of interest specified therein, interest is to be computed at such rate till the rendition of verdict, or default. *Colby* v. *Bunker*, 68 Me. 524.

287. As a mere incident, interest on interest is not allowed,

but a promise to pay it is not illegal or without consideration ; and the weight of authority is perhaps in favor of the validity of the promise, at law, whether made at or subsequent to the original contract. *Paulling* v. *Creagh*, 54 Ala. 646.

288. A note bearing interest over ten per cent. per annum, from due until paid, carries the stipulated interest to the date of the judgment, and the judgment bears ten per cent. *Budgett* v. *Jordan*, 32 Ark. 154.

289. A note which contains a stipulation for interest, at the rate of ten per cent., etc., from date, bears six per cent. interest (the legal rate) after maturity, and a judgment thereon should bear six per cent. interest. *Pettigrew* v. *Summers*, 32 Ark. 571.

290. A note which stipulates for interest from date until maturity, at the rate of ten per cent. per annum, bears the statutory rate (six per cent.) after maturity. *Woodruff* v. *Webb*, 32 Ark. 612.

291. Only legal interest will be allowed when a larger interest is not stipulated in writing. *Buckley* v. *Seymour*, 30 La. 1341.

292. On a note payable on demand, with interest at ten per cent., that rate of interest is recoverable up to the date of the verdict, when damages are assessed by a jury, and up to the date of judgment when a default is entered in a suit on the note. *Paine* v. *Caswell*, 68 Me. 80.

293. When a note contains a stipulation for interest, at the rate of ten per cent. per annum until maturity, and two per cent. per month after maturity, the increased interest after maturity cannot be treated as a penalty. When judgment is recovered on a note, the contract is merged in the judgment, and it bears statutory rate of interest. *Miller* v. *Kempner*, 32 Ark. 573.

294. A loan of money was made for two months at two per cent. a month, at the expiration of which time it was contemplated a new arrangement would be made. After the expiration of the two months, no other arrangement having been effected, the court held the lender entitled to claim interest at the rate originally agreed upon, and to sell the notes held by him as security, to repay himself the amount of his claim, subject only to the question whether he had sold the notes for the best price that could be obtained for them ; and as to which the court directed an inquiry by the Master. *O'Connor* v. *Clarke*, 18 Grant, Ontario Chancy. 422.

295. One to whom money is paid, and who receives it believing that it is his due, is not liable for interest upon it before demand made and refusal to pay, nor until he shall have reason to be satisfied that he ought to repay it, and shall know to whom he should pay it. *Ashhurst* v. *Field*, 28 N. J. Eq. 315.

296. Interest on a judgment or debt due is computed up to the time of the first payment, and the payment so made is first applied to discharge the interest, and afterwards, if there is a surplus, it is applied upon the principal, and so *toties quoties*, taking care that the principal thus reduced shall not at any time be suffered to accumulate by the accruing interest. *Davis* v. *Neligh*, 7 Neb. 78.

297. When interest is recoverable merely as damages, an action cannot be maintained for its recovery, after payment of the principal. This, when a bequest or contract is silent as to interest, so that, if it can be recovered at all, it can only be recovered as damages, an action to recover it cannot be maintained after the payment of the principal. *American Bible Soc.* v. *Wells*, 68 Me. 572.

298. In the absence of a written agreement, by the defendant, to pay eight per cent. per annum interest, only legal interest can be recovered. *Bayly & Pond* v. *Stacey & Poland*, 30 La. 1210.

299. The condition of a mortgage, dated June 28, 1871, was that the principal should be paid on April 1st, 1873, "with interest annually on the first day of April in each year." An action was commenced to foreclose the mortgage December 23, 1872, upon the ground of default in the payment of interest alleged to have become due April 1, 1872. *Held*, that by the stipulation as to interest reference was had to, and it was intended to provide for a payment of interest prior to the time when the principal became due, and that plaintiff's claim was well founded. *Cook* v. *Clark*, 68 N. Y. 178.

300. When a party agrees by note to pay a certain sum at the expiration of a year, with interest on it at a rate named, the rate being higher than the customary rate of the State where he lives, and does not pay the note at the expiration of the year, it bears interest, not at the old rate, but at the customary or statute rate. *Burnhisel* v. *Firman*, 22 Wallace (U. S.) 170. If, however, the parties calculate interest, and make a settlement upon the basis of the old rate, and the debtor gives new notes and a mortgage for the whole on that basis, the notes and mortgage are, independently of the Bankrupt Act, and of any statute making such certificates void in toto as usurious, valid securities for the amount which would be due on a calculation properly made. They are bad only for the excess above proper interest. *Id.*

301. Under the provisions of the Banking Act of 1870 (Chap. 163, Laws of 1870), prohibiting banks from charging upon any discount a rate of interest greater than seven per cent., and in case a greater rate of interest has been paid, authorizing a recovery by the party paying it of twice the amount, it is not necessary that the payment should be made in money to subject the receiver to liability. *Nash* v. *White's Bank of Buffalo*, 68 N. Y. 396.

302. When commercial paper is transferred to and discounted by a bank at a greater rate of interest than seven per cent., and the net proceeds, after deducting the interest charged, are credited to the transferrer, this is a payment within the meaning of the statute. The fact that the paper discounted is business paper, so that the purchase thereof is not usurious under the general statutes, does not relieve from liability under said act. *Id.*

LIENS.

303. Judgment entered on an assessment note, under the provisions of the charter of the People's Fire Insurance Company, is not a general judgment which may be enforced against any property of the insurer, but is restricted as a lien to the property insured. *Halfpenny* v. *The People's Fire Ins. Co.*, 85 Penn. st. 48.

304. Where the note or other written obligation of a third person is taken by the vendor of real estate, he thereby waives his equitable lien. *Stevens* v. *Rainwater*, 4 Mo. Court of Appeals (St. Louis), 292.

305. A judgment docketed, but not properly indexed, is a lien upon land in the hands of a subsequent purchaser, without notice. *Old Dominion Granite Co. et al.* v. *Clarke et al.*, 28 Grattan (Va.), 617.

LOANS.

306. Loan by a non-trader to a trader. In 1858, W. D, Sr., opened a credit of $584 in favor of his daughter, J. D. with W. D. & Co., a commercial firm in Montreal, consisting of the appellant and one T. D., W. D. & Co., charging W. D., Sr., and crediting J. D. with the amount. In 1860, W. D., as sole executor of the will of D. D., credited J. D. in the books of W. D. & Co. (appellant at that time being the only member of the firm), with a further sum of $800, the amount of a legacy bequeathed by such will. These entries in the books of W. D. & Co., together with entries of interest in connection with the said items, were continued from year to year. An account current was rendered to J. D., exhibiting details of the indebtedness up to the 31st December, 1861. After 31st December, 1864, the firm of W. D. & Co. consisted of the appellant and his brother, T. D. In December, 1865, another account was rendered to J. D., which showed a balance due her at that time of $1,912,08. The accounts rendered were unsigned, but the record account current was accompanied by a letter, referring to it, written and signed by the appellant. J. D. died, and in a suit brought by G. T,. her husband and universal legatee, to recover the $1,912,08, with interest, from 31st December, 1865: *Held*,

(1). That a loan of moneys, as in this case, by a non-trader to a commercial firm is not a "commercial matter," or a debt of a "commercial nature"; that, therefore, the debt could be prescribed, neither by the lapse of six years under *Consolidated Statutes of Lower Canada*, ch. 67, nor by the lapse of five years under the *Civil Code of Lower Canada*, but only by the proscription of thirty years. *Whishaw* v. *Gilmour*, 15 L. C., R. 177, approved.

(2). That, even if the debt of a commercial nature, the rendering of the account current, accompanied by the letter referring to it, signed by the appellant, would take the case out of the statute.

(3). That the proscription of five years against arrears of interest, under Art. 2250 of the *Civil Code of Lower Canada*, does not apply to a debt the proscription of which was commenced before the code came in force.

(4). That entries in a merchant's books make complete proof against him. *Darling* v. *Brown*, 1 Canada Supreme Co. 360.

MARKET PRICE.

307. The market price of a marketable commodity may be determined as well by offers to sell, made by dealers in the ordinary course of business, as by actual sales; and statements of dealers in answer to inquiries as to price, are competent evidence. *Harrison* v. *Glover*, 72 N. Y. App. 451.

MARRIED WOMEN.

308. In the case of a purchase by a wife during coverture, the burden is upon her to prove distinctly that she paid for the thing purchased with funds not furnished by her husband Evidence that she purchased amounts to nothing, unless it is accompanied by clear and full proof that she paid for it with her own separate funds. In the absence of such proof, the presumption is, that her husband furnished the means of payment. *Rose & Co. et al.* v. *Brown et ux.* 11 W. Va. 122.

309. Under the Statute (Laws 1874, p. 185) a *femme covert* is no longer *sub protestati vivi* in respect to the acquisition, enjoyment, and disposition of real and personal property. She may do with her own property as she will, without reference to any other restraints or disabilities of coverture. She may make conveyance directly to her husband. The removal, in respect to the wife, of a disability that is mutual, and springing from the same source, removes it also as to the husband; and the husband may, acting in his own right, convey to the wife. *Wells* v. *Caywood*, 3 Colo. 487.

310. Separate estate is presumed, in the absence of proof to the contrary, where a married woman signs a note or order for goods or money. *Wilcoxson* v. *State*, 60 Ga., 182.

311. *Married woman* may give a mortgage upon her property to secure the payment of a debt due by her husband; and a mortgage executed by her for such purpose cannot be said to be without consideration. *Comegys* v. *Clarke and Comegys*, 44 Md. 108.

312. Neither the pecuniary embarrassment, nor the actual insolvency of the husband, is any obstacle to a transfer by the husband to the wife, in good faith, for the replacing of her money, or property, used, or alienated by him. *Lehman, Abraham & Co.* v. *Levy*, 30 La. 745.

313. A married woman, in the absence of fraud, or of knowledge thereof on the part of the beneficiaries in a trust deed, given on a *bona fide* consideration, cannot impeach the certificate of the officer taking her privy acknowledgment. *Williams v. Powers*, 48 Texas 141.

MISTAKE.

314. **A Mistake** in facts will always be remedied by the courts as far as can be done consistently with right and justice ; but if the mistake is purely a mistake in law, they will not interfere. *Carpenter* v. *Jones et al., Adm'rs*, 44 Md. 625.

315. A clerical error in entering a consent decree may be corrected by the original draft of the decree, furnished the clerk by the court, on motion at any time, under the provisions of section 5 of chapter 134 of the Code. A consent decree, except where such clerical error has occurred, can never be modified or altered without the consent of parties, not even during the term at which it was entered. *Manion* v. *Fahy*, 11 W. Va. 482.

316. When money is paid under a mutual mistake of law, the mistake of law is. in and of itself, no ground for recovering it back. *Galveston Co.* v. *Gorham*, 49 Texas, 279.

317. Any mistake or misunderstanding between the persons conducting a judicial sale, and intended bidders or parties in interest, by which interests are prejudiced without fault of the injured party or parties, is sufficient cause for refusing confirmation and ordering a re-sale. *Hilleary et al.* v. *Thompson et al.*, 11 W. Va. 113.

MONEY COLLECTED BY AN OFFICER

318. **Money collected** by an officer on legal process, while it remains in his hands is to be regarded as in *custodia legis*, and not the subject of levy or attachment in any form. *Thus*, an

officer, who has collected money on an execution, cannot apply it in satisfaction of another execution, although the latter is against the party for whom the money was collected, and both executions are in the officer's hands for collection at the same time. *Hardy* v. *Tilton*, 68 Me. 195.

MORTGAGES.

319. A tender of the amount due upon a mortgage after condition broken does not discharge the mortgage. A mortgagor cannot maintain a writ of entry against a mortgagee in possession. *Rowell* v. *Mitchell*, 68 Me. 21.

320. A mortgagor of real estate, or the owner of the equity of redemption, has to the day of sale to make payment and release the mortgaged premises from the lien and sale, and the provisions of law require printed notice of the time and place of sale to be given for at least thirty days before any sale can be had. *Blandins, Adm'r*, v. *Wade*, 20 Kansas, 253.

321. A mortgage is not invalidated by a misdescription made by a scrivener, where the premises may be identified by the admission of the parties themselves, by reference thereto in other deeds, and by an actual location thereof by the parties. *Boon* v. *Pierpont*, 28 N. J. Eq. 6.

322. The deed of a married woman is not complete, so as to convey title to land, without the certificate of privy acknowledgment prescribed by the statute; and its absence cannot be supplied by parol evidence. *Looney* v. *Adamson*, 48 Texas, 619.

323. A mortgage containing a clause that the mortgagor shall have possession, without paying rent, of the mortgaged property until a fixed date, is not to be construed thereby to confer the right of possession thereafter to the mortgagee. *Morrow* v. *Morgan*, 48 Texas, 304.

324. A mortgage, primarily without any consideration, given to, secure certain negotiable notes in the hands of any future holder, becomes a valid mortgage in favor of any innocent third person, who may acquire one of the notes before its maturity, and for value. *Billgery* v. *Ferguson*, 30 La. 84.

325. A mortgagee who transfers part of the mortgage debt to another, cannot compete with his transferee for the proceeds of the mortgaged property, where the amount is not sufficient to satisfy both. *Baskdull* v. *Herwig & Smith*, 30 La. 618.

326. An assignee of a mortgage, given to secure the payment of a negotiable note, is held entitled to the same protection that he would have as assignee of the note without the mortgage. *Dutton* v. *Ives*, 5 Mich. 515; also *Helmer* v. *Krolick*, 36 Mich. 371.

327. A stipulation in a mortgage for the payment of reasonable attorney's fees, in case suit is commenced thereon, is

valid, and may be enforced in any action for the foreclosure of the mortgage. *Danforth* v. *Charles et al.* 1 Bennett's Dakota Rpts. 285.

328. A mortgage is binding between the parties to it, whether acknowledged or not. *Lemay* v. *Williams*, 32 Ark. 166.

329. The registry of a judgment against a party will operate as a legal mortgage on all the immovables of that party situate within the parish wherein the judgment is registered, whether the deed to such immovables is recorded or not, and such mortgage is good against everybody that the judgment debtor's title to the immovables is good against. *Logan* v. *Hebert*, 30 La. 727.

330. A mortgage, executed by a tenant in common, of an undivided interest in a specified parcel of land is invalid as against his co-tenants. *Marks* v. *Sewall*, 120 Mass. 174.

331. Mortgage given to secure the payment of a pre-existing debt, the mortgagee cannot claim protection against older equities as a *bona fide* purchaser for a valuable consideration. *Alexander* v. *Caldwell*, 55 Ala. 517.

332. The statute grants no power to an administrator to borrow money upon a mortgage of the real estate of the decedent. Such an act is foreign to the policy and purposes of administration, which aims to close up, not to continue an estate. Such mortgage is without legal authority, and void; and in the absence of fraud, misrepresentation, or mistake, the heirs are not estopped to plead its invalidity by reason of the benefit resulting to them by means of the mortgage. *Black* v. *Dressell's Heirs*, 20 Kansas, 153.

333. Where a mortgagee of chattels, in the absence of an agreement in the mortgage, purchases the property at a mortgage sale, and appropriates it to his own use, he becomes liable for the actual value thereof at the time of the sale, without reference to the amount bid. *Webber* v. *Emmerson*, 3 Colo. 248.

334. A mortgagor of real estate has the right to the possession of the mortgaged property, and to sever and remove timber, wood, sand, earth, coal, stone, or anything else, therefrom, and to sell the same, unless it unreasonably impairs the mortgage security. When it impairs the mortgage security, the remedy of the mortgagee is not at law, but in equity; not replevin to recover the property severed from the realty, but generally injunction, to restrain the commission of waste upon the realty. *Vanderslice* v. *Knapp*, 20 Kansas, 647.

335. An unrecorded mortgage valid as against heirs of mortgagor. A *scire facias* will lie on an unrecorded mortgage. *A. P. Laughlin* v. *Ihmsen*, 85 Penn. St. 364.

336. The assignee of a mortgage is not affected by a collateral agreement between the mortgagor and mortgagee, made at the time of the execution of the mortgage, of which he had no notice, and in a suit upon the mortgage by the assignee said agreement cannot be set up as a defence. *McMasters* v. *Willhelm*, 85 Penn. St. 218.

337. When a party, who was indebted to another, executed a conveyance to secure the indebtedness, and received from the grantee an instrument, binding him to re-convey upon payment of the debt; *held*, that the transaction constituted a mortgage, and that it was not competent for the grantor to insist upon a foreclosure thereof, but that he must pay the amount due before he could ask the cancellation of the conveyance. *White* v. *Lucas*, 46 Iowa, 319.

338. A purchaser from a mortgagor may recover the land mortgaged, in trespass to try title, against parties holding under a foreclosure sale, to which the plaintiff was not a party. Such foreclosure proceedings do not affect the right of a purchaser from a mortgagor prior to the suit for foreclosure, and not made a party to such suit. *Morrow* v. *Morgan*, 48 Texas, 304.

339. In an action to recover upon certain promissory notes, and to foreclose a real estate mortgage given to secure the payment of the notes, where the judgment required the defendant to pay the debt and costs within one day after its rendition, and on default thereof, the clerk is directed to issue a special execution to sell the real estate to satisfy the judgment; *held*, not erroneous because no more time is allowed. The debtor to raise and pay the money prior to the issuance of the special execution. *Blandins, Adm'r,* v. *Wade*, 20 Kansas, 251.

340. The clause in a mortgage, fixing the fees of the creditor's attorney of five per cent. in the event of the non-payment of the debt at its maturity, makes the debtor, on the happening of the event, absolutely liable for that amount; and this liability cannot be affected by the fact the creditor has not really paid, or obligated himself to pay, that amount of attorney's fees. *Renshaw* v. *Richards*, 30 La. 398.

341. A man may make a valid mortgage for the payment of money, without particularly describing the writing which may be evidence of the debt, or without even giving any independent written evidence thereof. But he is not at liberty to subsitute a different condition, by parol evidence, for that which he expressed in his deed. A man may mortgage to an agent in order to procure credit from his principal, and the agent may enforce the mortgage as the trustee of his principal. *Varney* v. *Hawes*. 68 Me. 442.

342. When a mortgagee has, upon demand, rendered a true account of the amount due upon the mortgage, a bill in equity

to redeem cannot be maintained, unless the plaintiff first tender to the mortgagee the amount due, or is prevented from so doing through the fault of the mortgagee. *Dinsmore* v. *Savage*, 68 Me. 191.

343. The same rule as to the necessity of registration, in order to give a priority of title, prevails between different assignees of a mortgage as between grantees under ordinary deeds. A mortgagee assigned the mortgage thus: "I hereby assign to the said (assignee) the within mortgage deed, the debt thereby secured, and all my right, title and interest in the premises therein described." *Held*, that this assignment, having been recorded, transfers the mortgage title as against a prior unrecorded deed of the same land by the mortgagee, unless it is shown that the assignee had actual notice of the prior deed. *Wiley* v. *Williamson*, 68 Me. 71.

344. A mortgagee of real estate, before foreclosure of his lien, even when the mortgagor is insolvent, and the mortgaged premises insufficient to pay the mortgage debt, cannot maintain an action against one who has removed an engine and boiler from the mortgaged premises, and sold them, to recover the value of the property so taken and converted. *Alexander* v. *Shonyo*, 20 Kansas, 705.

345. R. mortgaged to S. certain land, on which was a gristmill, and in which mill were certain fixtures. Afterwards R., for the purpose of defrauding S., severed said mill fixtures from the mill, and sold and delivered them to K., who purchased and received the same for a like purpose. *Held*, that said mill fixtures belonged to R. until he sold them to K., and that they never became the property of S., and that neither S., nor any person claiming under him, can maintain replevin against K. for them. *Vanderslice* v. *Knapp*, 20 Kansas, 647.

346. A mortgage of land to "Pinson, Dillard & Co." is not void for uncertainty, in not giving the surnames of some of the members of the firm, and in omitting the christian names of all of them. And even if the title only vested, by the conveyance, in those whose surnames were mentioned, the mortgage would enure to the benefit of all of the members of the firm, and they might all join in the suit to enforce it. A mortgage given for pre-existing debt is not invalid for want of valuable consideration, as against a prior unrecorded mortgage, where the time of payment of the debt is extended by a note, taken four days before the execution of the mortgage, formed one transaction. *Schumpert* v. *Dillard, Pinson & Co.*, 55 Miss. 348.

347. When a mortgagor conveys real estate, and the conveyance contains a statement that the grantor will assume and pay the note which the mortgage is given to secure, and the grantee accepts the same, and enters into possession of the

premises, he becomes directly and personally liable to the holder of the note and mortgage for the amount due. *Fitzgerald* v. *Barker*, 4 Mo. Court of Appeals (St. Louis), 105.

348. Omitting to name the State, county, and township, in the description of premises in a mortgage, will not invalidate the instrument, where other adequate elements of identification exist; and it is not essential that the property should be so described as to identify it without the aid of extrinsic proofs, but it is always competent to connect the written description with the material subject matter by proof of the surrounding circumstances. Where there are descriptive signs satisfactorily ascertained which designate the thing meant to be granted, the addition of circumstances or accompaniments which are untrue, will not defeat the grant, but they will be rejected. *Slater* v. *Breese*, 36 Mich. 77.

349. A bill in equity alleged that A. purchased an estate with the plaintiff's money, and had it conveyed to his wife, who took it, with notice of the same; that A. and his wife mortgaged the estate to B., who assigned the mortgage to C., both of whom had notice of the resulting trust to the plaintiff. A decree was made that C. assign the mortgage to the plaintiff. *Held*, that an assignment was unnecessary, and would impair the rights of the defendants among themselves; and that the mortgage should be discharged by a deed of release to the plaintiff, or by an entry upon the margin of the record of the mortgage in the registry of deeds. *Harwood* v. *Pearson*, 122 Mass. 425.

350. The unauthorized cancellation of record of a mortgage by the clerk, or register, without the knowledge or consent of the mortgagee, will not affect the rights of the latter under the mortgage, even as against a *bona fide* purchaser of the mortgaged premises, with notice of the mortgage, though he has no notice that the cancellation was unauthorized, and presumed, from the certificate of cancellation, that the lien of the mortgage was extinguished. A mortgage may be assigned by delivery merely. *Harris* v. *Cook.*, 28 N. J. Eq. 345.

351. The holder of two mortgages on the same parcel of land entered to foreclose the first mortgage, but did not enter under the second mortgage. A bill in equity was brought against him to redeem the first mortgage, and in his answer he did not set up the second mortgage. A decree was entered that, on payment of a certain sum, he should release and discharge the mortgaged premises, described in the bill, from the mortgage therein described, and should deliver up possession of the premises. *Held*, on a subsequent bill in equity to obtain the discharge of the second mortgage, that he was not estopped to set up the second mortgage. *Gerrish* v. *Black*, 122 Mass. 76.

352. Mortgage having been made to secure several negotiable notes, and the notes having been passed to several different holders, and one of the holders having obtained a general judgment, and another having foreclosed the mortgage in the name of the mortgagee for his use, a sale of the premises under the general judgment passed the title free from the mortgage lien, the attorney representing the judgment of foreclosure having placed the execution founded thereon in the hands of the officer of the law making the sale, and caused the title, unincumbered, to be sold, and there being no fraud in the sale, and the premises having brought full value, or an amount approximating thereto. The notes not covered by either judgment cannot be enforced against the land, but are thrown, in equity, upon the fund produced by the sale, for their *pro rata* share thereof. *Smith et al.* v. *Bowne et al.*, 60 Ga. 484.

353. Under the Code (§1955) a mortgage must clearly indicate the creation of a lien, and specify the debt to secure which it is given. A deed in fee simple, without condition or defeasance, and a bond for titles from the grantee to the grantor, in which bond the grantee obligates himself to convey the premises to the grantor on the payment of a sum of money, do not separately or together indicate the creation of a mere lien; but the purpose indicated is to divert the grantor of title, and to vest title in the grantee until the payment of the debt. To take a bond for a future conveyance, and then deny that the maker thereof had any estate in the premises at the time he gave the bond, no fraud or mistake being alleged, is idle and inconsistent. If a judgment creditor, whose judgment is junior to an absolute deed made to secure another creditor, can subject the land without redeeming, or offering to redeem, it is because the Registry laws have not been complied with, or else because the debtor having retained possession, the conveyance is to be deemed fraudulent. *Gibson* v. *Hough & Sons*, 60 Ga. 588.

354. A bill of sale whereby a debtor conveys personal property to his creditor as *security*, and which provides that the property shall remain in the debtor's possession, and he have thirty days to redeem by paying the debt, is a mortgage. *Blodgett* v. *Blodgett*, 48 Vt. 32.

A mortgagor of personal property, after condition broken, has an equity of redemption that may be asserted if he brings his bill to redeem within a reasonable time. *Id.*

355. A tender of the amount of the debt after the law day has passed, unaccepted, does not divert the mortgagee of his legal right to the property mortgaged; and Chancery has jurisdiction to decree redemption. *Id.*

356. When the mortgagee disposes of the property, after

tender made, and before final hearing, that an order for its delivery cannot be made, a decree may be entered for the amount of the mortgagor's interest therein. *Id.*

357. While it is not lawful for banking associations, established under the U. S. St. of 1864, c. 106, to purchase, hold, and convey real estate, except in certain specified cases, among these exceptions are included such real estate "as shall be mortgaged to it in good faith by way of security for debts previously contracted; such as shall be conveyed to it in satisfaction of debts previously contracted in the course of its dealings; such as it shall purchase at sales under judgments, decrees, or mortgages held by such associations, or shall purchase to secure debts due to said association."

Under the latter clause, it cannot be deemed that the only authority given to such associations is to purchase only to the exact amount of the debts which may be owing to them, but they are entitled to purchase such real estate as may be necessary in order to secure the debts due to them, so long as the security of such debts is the real object of the purchase. By oral evidence it was proved that a bankrupt applied to the defendant for a loan of a certain sum to enable him, together with his own funds, to take up the mortgage; that the defendant lent him the sum requested ($3,000), upon his verbal promise to assign the mortgage to him to secure the sum lent and certain notes then due ($911) to the defendant by the bankrupt. The claim that this was a loan of money upon real estate security, or a purchase of real estate, is not maintained, when it is found, as a fact, that the inducement to this transaction was the agreement that the mortgage, and the real estate upon which it was secured, should be held for the antecedent debt due the bank. By the assignment in bankruptcy the assignee has succeeded to all the rights of the assignor, Emerson; but his rights here are not superior to those of Emerson. He has come into a Court of Equity to seek its aid in obtaining those rights, and is, therefore, to do what Emerson would have been compelled to do. In order to obtain a decree for the redemption of the mortgage, he must perform the oral agreement that the debt of $911, due the bank, should be paid, as well as pay the balance of the $3,000, which is now due. *Upton, Assignee,* v. *National Bank of South Reading,* 120 Mass. 153.

358. A. executed a mortgage of real estate, with a power of sale, to B., and subsequently conveyed the equity of redemption to C. The mortgage provided that after the expiration of sixty days from the breach of any of the conditions named therein, the mortgagee, or those claiming under him, might sell the premises at public auction, " without further notice or demand, except giving notice " by advertisement for three successive

weeks in a newspaper. Upon breach of condition for non-payment of interest, all the notices by advertisement were duly given, but did not state for what breach of condition the sale was made, and the sale took place as advertised. Before the sale, B. caused to be sent to A., by mail, a copy of the paper containing the advertisement, and A. knew that the interest on the mortgage was in arrears, was informed that it must be paid, and asked where C. was. No formal demand was made upon A. It appeared that A. knew from some source that there was to be a sale of the property, or some interest therein, and, without making proper inquiry, carelessly, but honestly, assumed and believed that it was not to be a sale under the power contained in the mortgage made by him. A. made no effort to escertain the facts, and did not attend the sale, at which the property was sold for less than its value. After the sale, A. offered to redeem the mortgage, and demanded an assignment thereof; was refused, and brought a bill in equity against B. and the purchaser, to redeem. *Held*, that the notices were not required to state for what breach of condition the sale was made; that mere inadequacy of price was not sufficient to invalidate the sale; and that A. could not maintain his bill. *King* v. *Bronson*, 122 Mass. 122.

NEGLIGENCE.

359. An assignee of certificates of shares of stock, who leaves the certificates, with the assignments recorded, in the possession of the assignor, is not thereby guilty of negligence, so as to be estopped to set up his title against a person who claims title to the certificates through an alteration of the assignments by the fraud and forgery of the assignor. *Eaton* v. *Telegraph Co.* 68 Me. 63.

360. One accepting a deed of conveyance of land is bound to exercise ordinary prudence in examining the instrument, and cannot, in a suit against the grantor for alleged defects in the deed, excuse himself for this neglect upon the ground of his confidence in the grantor. *Jaeger* v. *Whitsett*, 3 Colo., 105.

361. The employment of a common carrier is a public employment, and while he may, by special agreement, excuse himself for accidental losses, he is responsible for all damages occasioned by negligence or misfeasance, either of himself or servants, and cannot divest himself of this liability, either by special contract or notice. *Merchants' D. & T. Co.* v. *Cornforth*, 3 Colo. 280.

PARTNERSHIP.

362. A person who permits himself to be held out as a partner is liable as such, whether in fact a partner or not. *Brugman et al.* v. *McGuire et al.* 32 Ark. 733.

363. Accounts between partners are to be adjusted on principles of equity. *Maddox* v. *Stephenson*, 60 Ga. 125.

364. Where one of two partners has advanced to the partnership more than the other, he cannot maintain assumpsit against the other partner for his proportion of it, so long as the partnership debts are not paid. *Mickle* v. *Peet*, 43 Conn. 65.

365. When two or more parties, engaging in a business venture with the understanding that there is to be a communion of profit and loss, will be deemed special partners, and as such, in case of loss, severally liable for their *pro rata* share of such loss. *Stettaner Bros.* v. *Carney & Stevens*, 20 Kansas, 474.

366. Where the evidence shows that the two individual signers of a merely joint note were, at the date of the note, commercial partners, and that the consideration of the note was money borrowed for and used by the partnership, each of the makers will be liable on the note *in solido*. *Mitchell* v. *D. Armond*, 30 La. 396.

367. When one partner in a firm borrows money, representing that it is for the use of the firm, and gives a note of the firm therefor, without the knowledge of his copartners, but appropriates the money to his own use, the firm will be liable, unless the creditor knew, or had reasonable ground to believe, the money was not borrowed for the use of the firm, or the circumstances were such as to put him upon inquiry, and he neglected to inquire. *Wagner* v. *Freschl*, 56 N. H. 495.

368. Real estate held by a commercial firm as partnership assets, upon the dissolution of the partnership, as between the partners, vests in the individual members thereof, as tenants in common. *McGrath v. Sinclair*, 55 Miss. 89.

369. **Power to Dispose of its Property.**—The general creditors of a firm have no lien on its assets, any more than ordinary creditors have upon the property of an individual debtor. And the power of a firm to dispose of its property, all the members co-operating, is as unlimited as that of an individual. *Sehmidlopp* v. *Currie*, 55 Miss. 597.

370. The assignment of its assets for the benefit of its creditors, made by a defunct partnership to an individual member of a new partnership succeeding to the former business of the old concern, will not make the new partnership liable to the defunct partnership for the value of any of its assets, and therefore not amendable to a garnishment at the suit of any creditor of the defunct concern. *Bancker* v. *Harrington & Co. et al.*, 30 La. 136.

371. A creditor of one of the partners of a firm may attach such partner's interest in a specific portion of the stock of goods belonging to the firm, and is not required, in order to render the attachment regular, to take the partner's interest in the entire stock of goods. *Fogg* v. *Lawry*. 68 Me. 78.

372. A promissory note executed in the name of a certain commercial firm, in liquidation, by an agent of one of the former partners, after the dissolution of the firm, is not binding on the former members who have not given any specific authority for the execution of a note. *Dodd, Brown & Co.* v. *John Bishop & Co. et al.*, 30 La. 2nd Book, 1178.

373. A surviving partner is entitled to sue in his representative capacity for the amount due the partnership, and in his own name for the amount due to himself individually. The respective demands may be united in the same action, but should be separately stated. *Quillen* v. *Arnold*, 12 Nevada, 235.

374. Where a loan is made by two members of a commercial firm, in a matter foreign to the business of the firm, and in disregard of the express opposition of the third member, the two members making the loan are justly chargeable with its amount. *David G. Cooke* v. *Hugh and Andrew Allison*. 30 La. 963.

375. Where a creditor of a former commercial firm sues its individual members for goods sold to the firm, and declares in his petition on the itemized account of the goods, and also on a promissory note of the firm, given in liquidation of the account by one not authorized to sign for the firm, he will be entitled to recover for the goods, on the unopposed proof of their sale and delivery. One who acts in such a manner as to induce others to believe that he is a member of a certain partnership, makes himself liable to them as a partner. *Dodd, Brown & Co.* v. *John Bishop & Co. et al.* 30 La. 1178.

376. A party seeking exemption from the liability of a general partner, under the Act of 1874, respecting limited partnerships, must show a strict compliance with the act. The statute does not require that the capital should be paid in cash; but when it is paid in property, it should be so stated, and its cash value given. *Holliday et al.* v. *Union P. & B. Co.* 3 Colo. 342.

377. In an action brought by one member of a partnership to have an accounting with his two partners, and to recover a balance due him, where the referee reports that such plaintiff contributed $663,48 to the capital, and the other two partners $370, and that certain profits were realized from their business, and that by the terms of the partnership the parties were to share equally in the profits thereof, *held*, that each member of the firm, on dissolution of the partnership, is entitled to a return of his capital, and in addition one-third of the profits. *Norman* v. *Conn.* 20 Kansas 159.

378. The individual members of a commercial firm may execute a valid note, and a valid mortgage securing said note on their individual property, in favor of the firm, and any third person acquiring the note from the firm, in good faith, for value, and before maturity, may enforce its payment. *Pike, Brother & Co* v. *Hart & Hebert*, 30 La. 868.

379. **Service upon Member of;**—Service upon one of the firm, after dissolution, confers jurisdiction to render a judgment which may be satisfied out of the partnership property, or the individual property of the member served, but confers no jurisdiction of a partner not served. A judgment having been obtained upon a promissory note, the note became merged in the judgment, and could not afterwards be made a cause of action. *Hartford, Thayer & Co.* v. *Street*, 46 Iowa, 594.

380. When all the partners are in a situation that would authorize their individual creditors to sue out attachments against them respectively, a creditor of the firm may procure an attachment against the partnership, and have the same levied upon the partnership effects. *Starr* v. *Mayer & Co.*, 60 Ga. 546.

381. R. S., c. 82, sec. 87, provides that when the legal representative of a deceased person is a party, he may testify to any facts, legally admissible upon the general rules of evidence, happening before the death of such person. *Held*, that the surviving partner, who gives bond under R. S., c. 69, sec. 2, and is afterwards sued upon a note of the firm, is not, therefore, a representative of his deceased partner, and as such entitled to testify to facts happening before his decease within the provisions of c. 82. *Holmes* v. *Brooks*, 68 Me. 416.

382. Note in renewal of another made by same partner who signed the last, which itself was in renewal of a note by a different firm, of which the signer had been a member, upon plea of *non est factum* by the copartner, *onus* of showing authority to sign is on the plaintiff. *Bryan* v. *Tooke et al.*, 60 Ga. 437.

383. One partner in a mercantile business has power to bind the others by a promissory note given in the usual course of business, and the payee of a note, executed by a partner in the firm name, has the right to presume that it was executed in the usual course of business. *Sherewood* v. *Snow, Foote & Co.*, 46 Iowa, 481.

384. The fact that the partner signed his individual name before signing that of the firm, should be considered by the jury in determining whether or not the payee had reason to know that the consideration was procured for his own individual use. *Id.*

385. The creditors of a corporation selected three of their number, who were elected directors of the company, and charged with the management of its business. *Held*, that they could not be made liable as partners for supplies furnished them and used in the conduct of the corporation business. *Beeson* v. *Lang*, 85 Penn. St. 197.

386. The fact that the owner and shipper of property is doing business in the name of a firm in violation of the provisions of the Act (chap. 281, Laws of 1833), "to prevent persons transacting business under fictitious names," and that the property is marked with the firm name, is no defense to an action by such owner against a railroad corporation for loss of, or damage to the property while in transit. The said act, being highly penal, will not be extended by implication or construction to cases not within the terms of the act fairly interpreted. *Wood* v. *E. R. R. Co.*, 72 N. Y. App. 106.

387. An ordinary partnership cannot be held liable for the individual debt of one of its members because of an agreement to that effect between that member and his creditor, unless it be proved that the member was authorized to make the agreement by his copartners, or that his agreement was ratified by them, or that the partnership was benefited by the transaction. *W. E. Hamilton et al.* v. *Nellie Hodges, Tutrix, et al.*, 30 La. 1290.

388. In a feigned issue to try the right to certain cattle, A. offered evidence that he purchased the cattle through B., who was his agent, in the name of B.; that it was agreed that the latter should butcher and sell the meat, and out of the proceeds return to A. the cost and one-fourth of a cent per pound of dressed meat additional, and that B. should have the balance. Upon this evidence the court granted a nonsuit, on the ground that it did not tend to prove an exclusive ownership in A., but established a partnership. *Held* (reversing the court below), *inter se*, or as to third parties, and that the case should have been submitted to the jury to say what was the actual relation of the parties. *Dale* v. *Peirce*, 85 Penn. St. 474.

389. Partners cannot, during the existence of the partnership, claim individual exemption in partnership property, when taken under legal process for partnership debts. (Overruling in this particular, *Howard* v. *Jones & Starke*, 50 Ala. 67; *Dunklin* v. *Kimball*, 50 Ala. 251; and *Giovanni* v. *First Nat. Bank*, 51 Ala. 177.) *Giovanni* v. *First Nat. Bank*, 55 Ala. 305.

390. Where no other relation exists between the shareholders of a steamboat than that which arises from the joint ownership, they are not partners, nor is their liability to be measured by the rules of law peculiar to the partnership relation. When one of the shareholders sells out his interest in a steamboat, and the bill of sale, in accordance with the Acts of Congress, is duly acknowledged, and recorded, it is valid notice to all parties and subsequent creditors with whom the owners may contract. *Adams* v. *Carroll & Co.*, 85 Penn. St. 209.

391. During the existence of a partnership, which is neither bankrupt nor contemplating bankruptcy, one of the members of the firm may, with the consent of the other partner, or part-

ners, upon a *bona fide* consideration, with no benefit reserved, assign and transfer the assets of the partnership in payment of his individual debt, if no lien has attached to such assets; and such transfer is good against the firm creditors. *Schmidlapp* v. *Currie*, 55 Miss. 597.

392. Where accounts are kept at a bankers by a firm, each partner having a right to draw checks, and also by the individual partners of the firm, it is not the duty of the bankers to inquire into the propriety of any transfer of funds which may be made from and to the different accounts. Upon the death of one partner in the firm having an account at a bankers, the surviving partner has a right to draw checks upon the partnership account. *Backhouse* v. *Charlton*, English Chancery Division, Law Rports, 1878.

393. It is only in equity that separate creditors of a partner are entitled to preference over the creditors of a partnership in the distribution of the separate effects of their debtor. The lien of a subsequent judgment for an individual debt does not take priority over the lien of a judgment first rendered against a debtor upon a partnership debt. *Gillaspy* v. *Peck et al.*, 46 Iowa, 461.

394. In partnership suits the defense of the Statute of Limitations is not available, unless six years have elapsed before the filing of the bill since the dealings of the partners wholly ceased. A partnership was formed between two civil engineers and architects, the profits of which were to be divided in shares of three-fifths and two-fifths. During the continuance of the partnership they invested moneys of the partnership in the purchase of real estate, which resulted in a loss. *Held*, that the loss was to be borne by the partners in the same proportion as they were to share the profits and loss of their other business. *Storm* v. *Cumberland*, 18 Grant's Chancery, Ontario, 245.

395. When a partner fraudulently misappropriates the money of his firm, and purchases, in his own name, real estate and policies of life insurance with firm funds, he will in equity be charged, by construction, as a trustee for the partnership. When all the premiums are paid with partnership moneys, it makes no difference that the fraud doer, in his lifetime, changed the life policies so as to make them payable to his wife. She, having paid no consideration for them, will be charged as a trustee for the firm, and will be permitted to derive no benefit from them. *Shaler* v. *Trowbridge*, 28 N. J. Eq. 595.

396. Acceptance by one partner for separate debt, and not in partnership name—Liability of co-partners. Where the plaintiffs, a bank, discounted a bill, drawn by one partner, and accepted by him in the name of the firm, the manager being aware that it was intended by such partner to reimburse himself for moneys which he alleged that he had advanced to the

firm, and it appeared that such acceptance was unauthorized by the other partners, *Held*, that the bank could not recover against them. The partnership name, when the bill was so drawn and accepted, was J. S. W. & Co., and the acceptance was in the name of W. M. & Co. *Held*, that this also would have been fatal to the plaintiffs' recovery. *Royal Canadian Bank* v. *Wilson, et al.*, 24 Upper Canada Com. Pleas Repts. 3620.

397. Real estate purchased with partnership funds for partnership purposes, and appropriated to partnership uses, is in equity presumed to be partnership property, and it is, under such circumstances, immaterial whether the legal title is taken in the name of a part or all of the partners. Individual real property brought into the partnership by the copartners, at the time of its formation or afterwards, and, by proper agreement of the partners, converted into partnership property, and appropriated to its uses, becomes a portion of the capital stock of the firm, and will be treated in equity as personalty, although standing in the name of an individual partner. *Hoyle* v. *Lowe*, 12 Nevada, 286.

398. **Partnership Property.**—When the property of an insolvent partnership is ordered to be sold, in order to pay the partnership debts, the right of redemption does not exist. *Rhodes* v. *Williams*, 12 Nevada, 20.

399. When a non-resident commercial firm make an agreement with two resident firms, in virtue of which agreement one of the resident firms is to purchase certain merchandise, and ship it in the name of the other, and the other resident firm, with the money of the non-resident firm, is to pay for the merchandise, and each of the resident firms agree to receive, instead of fix sums in payment of their services, certain proportions of the profits to arise from the subsequent sales of the merchandise, and also agree to share in any losses resulting from said sales. *Held*, that such an agreement will not make the said firms commercial partners, even as to third persons, when it appears that they did not *intend* to form a partnership, and that they have not held themselves out to the world as partners. *Chaffraix & Agar* v. *John B. Lafitte & Co.*, 30 La. 631.

400. In 1865, after June 1st, a partner retired, selling out to his co-partner his interest (one-half) in the stock, at cost or invoice prices. The retired partner died; and in October, 1866, administration was granted upon his estate. A suit was commenced against the administrator in August, 1873, by the former partner of the intestate upon a certain award, to which suit the administrator pleaded in January, 1874, among other things, that at the time of the dissolution the stock was worth over $1,500, and that he, the administrator, claimed to be entitled

to one-half thereof, with interest. He neither expressly offered to set off the claim, nor prayed judgment therefor. The action and the plea remained pending until February, 1877, when the action was voluntarily dismissed by the plaintiff therein. The administrator in July thereafter filed the present bill to recover for his intestate's interest in the stock. The bill was barred by the Statute of Limitations, and a demurrer, containing that ground among others, was properly sustained. *Crane* v. *Barry*, 60 Ga. 362.

PAYMENTS.

401. When a payment is made voluntarily on an unfounded demand, or in ignorance of the law or legal circumstances of the case, it cannot be recovered back. Nothing occurring afterwards in the determination of new controversies between other parties can be carried back to affect a transaction which when it took place was fair and just. *Finnell* v. *Brew* 81 Penn. St. 362.

402. When the debts are of like nature, the imputation of payments is made to the debt longest due. *Bloom & Co.* v. *Kern*, 30 La. 1263.

403. Payments made voluntarily by the mortgagee of claims against the estate, which was not necessary for the protection of his own interest in the property, will not entitle him to be subrogated to the rights of the creditors whose liens he discharged. *Bayard et al.*, v. *McGraw*, 1 Bradwell's, Ill. App. Rpts. 134.

404. Partial payments made on a debt past due (Rev. Code, s. 1830) should be applied first to the extinguishment of accrued interest, and only the residue applied to the principal. *Coleman* v. *Smith*, 55 Ala. 369.

405. Payments claimed as credits on a debt, and not allowed when judgment was rendered on it, cannot be recovered back afterwards, without an express promise to repay them. *Turlington* v. *Slaughter*, 54 Ala. 195.

406. Payment of a debt made by giving several notes, and only a part of the notes are paid, the original debt is revived as to the notes unpaid. *Crawford* v. *Roberts*, 50 Cal. 236.

407. The taking of the debtor's acceptances does not operate as payment of the debt in the absence of an agreement that they should be received in payment. *Au Sable River Broom Co.* v. *Sanborn*, 36 Mich. 358.

408. On a suit against six joint and several makers of a note, when some had paid off their shares of principal and interest due at the time paid, by agreement with the payee, the said payments ought to be applied to the *pro rata* of principal as well as interest due by the makers so paying their shares; and that the verdict against all the defendants for the balance, due after said payments are so credited, is legal and valid, and

ought to be upheld, especially where the evidence as to how many of the shares which have been so paid is conflicting, and if some of it was believed by the jury, and the payments had been credited on the note, the verdict would be too large. *Donaldson* v. *Cothran, Adm'r, et al.*, 60 Ga. 603.

409. As a general rule, the premium note of an insurance broker, received by the insurers in payment of a policy for his principal, discharges the principal from liability to the insurers on account of the premium. But if the policy contain a provision that, in case of loss, the amount of the premium note shall be deducted from the insurance, the insured must submit to the deduction, although he has before paid the amount of the premium to the broker. In case of the death and insolvency of the broker, a court of equity will not compel his administrators to sequester for the benefit of the insurers any sum received by them from the insured on account of premiums, if the company hold the broker's note therefor. *Union Ins. Co.* v. *Grant*, 68 Me. 229.

410. The payment of money cannot be made dependent on the performance of a condition by the party to whom it is to be paid, which condition, by its terms, may not be performed until after the date at which the money is to be paid. *Front St. M. & O. R. R. Co.* v. *Butler*, 50 Cal. 574.

411. A legal presumption of payment of a bond, given for the payment of money, does not arise from mere lapse of time, where the bond has not been due for twenty years, before commencement of suit by the recovery of the sum thereby due and payable. If a shorter period, even a single day less than twenty years, has elapsed, the presumption of satisfaction from mere lapse of time does not arise. While the mere lapse of twenty years, without explanatory circumstances, affords a presumption of law that the debt is paid, even though it be due by specialty, still payment may be inferred by the jury from circumstances with the lapse of a shorter period of time than twenty years. *Sadler's Adm'r* v. *Kennedy's Adm'rx*, 11 W. Va. 187.

412. Plea of payment tried by a magistrate, and found for defendants on the evidence, cannot be changed on appeal so as to defeat such defense, by adding *usees* for whom plaintiffs sue. *Cobb et al.* v *Lowry & Co.*, 60 Ga. 637.

413. Where plaintiff held several promissory notes against deceased, all but one being valid, and also held certain shares of mining stock belonging to deceased. *Held*, that, in the absence of any showing to the effect that the deceased ever authorized plaintiff to appropriate the proceeds derived from the sale of such stock toward the discharge of the fraudulent note, the law compelled plaintiff to credit the money on the valid notes. *McCausland* v. *Ralston*, 12 Nevada, 195.

414. Payments made by a debtor, without special instructions as to their imputation, will be imputed in accordance with the tacit agreement of the parties, as disclosed by their dealings and correspondence. A debtor, who receives without objection an account current from his creditor, which imputes payments made by him to the less onerous part of his debt, is held to ratify by his silence the imputation of payment made in the account. *McLear & Kendall* v. *Succession of Hunsicker*, 30 La. 1225.

415. The defendant was indebted to the plaintiff—first, as he was member of a firm, and afterwards individually, and gave his note in payment, taking back this receipt: " Received from F. S. Brewer his 90-day note for $300, to be paid at either bank in Portland." There was a contention on the joint account of the defendants, or on the several account of Brewer. *Held*, that upon this issue it was not error to instruct the jury that the receipt was silent and could have no legitimate bearing one way or the other. *Hunt* v. *Brewer*, 68 Me. 262.

416. A. sent B. to do work for C., and A.'s book-keeper, after the completion of the work, made out, in accordance with his duty, the bill therefor upon one of A.'s printed bill-heads, which he placed in the hands of B., who demanded and received payment for the work from C. Upon the bill-head was printed, in fine type, " All moneys to be paid to the treasurer, and bills to be receipted by him." *Held*, that the bill so made out by their book-keeper, and by him put in the hands of Thayer, and by Thayer shown to the defendant, was sufficient evidence of Thayer's authority to justify the defendant in paying him the amount of the bill, if the defendant acted in good faith, and without having observed the words in fine print at the top of the bill requiring all moneys to be paid to the plaintiff's treasurer. The case was rightly submitted to the jury. *Kinsman* v. *Kershaw*, 119 Mass. 140.

PLEDGES.

417. A Bill of Sale of Goods, absolute in its terms, given to protect the vendee against his liability as surety for the vendor, and to secure a debt of the vendor to the vendee, with a verbal agreement that when the vendee should be relieved from his liability and the debt paid, his interest in the property cease, but with no condition of defeasance in writing, is not a mortgage. As between the parties to the absolute, formal bill of sale, it could not be shown, by proof of a parol defeasance, that the conveyance was a mortgage. *Pennock* v. *McCormick*, 120 Mass., 275.

418. A factor cannot, generally, pledge the goods of his principal for his own liabilities, and is bound to obey the orders of his consignor as to the terms of sale. *Singer Manufacturing Co.* v. *Hudson*, 4 Mo. Ct. Appeals (St. Louis), 145.

419. The fact that the stock of a corporation is only transferable on the books of the company, does not prevent a stockholder from validly *pledging* his stock, by merely delivering to his creditor the certificates of his stock. A transfer of the stock on the books is not necessary to perfect the pledge. *Blonin* v. *Liquidations of Hart & Hebert*, 30 La. 714.

420. A person holding stock in a fiduciary capacity has, *prima facie*, no right to pledge it to secure a debt growing out of an independent transaction unconnected with the trust; and whoever takes it as security for such debt, does it at his own peril. *Prall* v. *Tilt*, 28 N. J. Eq. 479.

421. Where a bailee of goods for safe keeping merely pledges the same with intent to convert the proceeds to his own use, such pledge amounts to larceny by the pledgor, and the pledgee acquires no title as against the owner, though he dealt *bona fide* with the pledgor. *Gottlieb* v. *Hartman*, 3 Colo. 53.

422. When one delivers chattels to another as indemnity for suretyship, the law regards such delivery as a pledge merely. Nor does it alter the case in a Court of Equity that the property is transferred by absolute bill of sale, not even if the contract stipulated that the pledge shall be irredeemable. *Id.*

423. Where the pledgee of a mortgage note, in whose hands it has been placed to secure a debt due him by the pledgor, sells the property mortgaged to secure the note for a sum less than the amount of the note, and immediately re-sells it for a larger sum than that of the note, he becomes liable to the pledgor, not for the price at which the property was re-sold, but merely for the amount of the note. *Mrs. A. R. Richardson* v. *Moses Mann*, 30 La. 1060.

424. A consignee who has made advances on cotton shipped to him, has a right of pledge on it and its proceeds, for the reimbursement of those advances; and until the debt due for those advances is paid, he is not bound to accept or pay any drafts drawn on him by the consignor against said cotton, at or about the time it was shipped, in favor of a third person who had discounted the drafts for the consignor, and thus enabled the latter to buy the cotton shipped to the consignee. *Thos. E. Helm et al.* v. *Meyer, Weis & Co.* 30 La. 943.

425. A pledgee who was surety on a promissory note transferred the property to the payee for the purpose of discharging the debt. *Held*, that the transfer did not change the status of the property, and that the pledgor had the right to redeem, even after the maturity. *Morgan et al.* v. *Dod*, 3 Colo. 551.

426. A pledgee can sell only, and for the purpose of applying the proceeds to the extinguishment of the debt. Such sale must be at public auction, after due notice to the pledgor or owner. *Id.*

427. Where the subject matter of a pledge is divisable, the pledgee has no right to sell more than is necessary to satisfy the debt; and if he does so, is responsible to the pledgor for the damage he may sustain *Fitzgerald* v. *Blocher*, 32 Ark. 742.

428. The acceptance by the pledgor of the surplus arising from an illegal sale of the articles pledged, is no waiver of his rights to damages resulting from the sale. *Id.*

429. Where the pledgor, at the time of making the pledge, waives notice of sale, he cannot, after the sale of the pledged property, complain of a want of notice. *Id.*

430. Where a pledgee of scrip sells more than is necessary to satisfy his debt, and pays the surplus to the pledgor, who buys other scrip to replace what has been sold, the measure of damages is the difference between the price for which the excess sold and that paid by the pledgor to replace it. *Id.*

431. Where one deposits United States "five twenty" bonds for safe keeping with a banking institution, and the cashier of such institution pledges them, the pledgee, acting in good faith, takes a good title; and the recovery of the bonds through the fraud and bad faith of such cashier does not divert the title out of the pledgee and revert it in the depositor. *Ringling* v. *Kohn et al,* 4 Mo. Appeal Reports (St. Louis), 59.

432. There can be no valid pledge of a mortgage, or vendor's privilege, by mere agreement of parties to that effect, unaccompanied by an actual or symbolical delivery of possession. *Sevin & Gourdain, in Liquidation* v. *Theogene Caillonet*, 30 La. 528.

433. The assignee of a note, held as collateral security for a debt due from the assignor, has no power to deal with it, except to accomplish the purpose for which he holds it. He cannot bind the assignor by a contract with the maker for forbearance. His ability to perform such contract is dependant upon the will of the assignor, who may pay his debt and take back the collateral at any time; and, therefore, a promise of the maker to pay a larger interest, in consideration of such forbearance, is without consideration and not binding upon him. *Key* v. *Fielding*, 32 Ark. 56.

434. Such assignee is a trustee for his assignor, and all profit, benefit, or advantage made by him, by his dealing with the note, belongs to the assignor, and not to himself, and must be applied to the satisfaction of the assignor's debt, and the excess, if any, paid to the assignor. *Id.*

435. One to whom a promissory note is pledged as collateral security for a debt, unless specially authorized, cannot sell the same on default, but is bound to collect it at maturity, and apply the proceeds to the debt. *Joliet Iron Co.* v. *Scioto Fire Brick Co.*, 82 Ill. 584.

436. H. & Co. advanced money upon C. O. R. R. Co. stock in good faith, which stock was pledged to them under forged powers of transfer. The railroad company, upon the receipt of the original certificates of stock, in like good faith cancelled them, and issued new ones in the name of H. & Co. *Held*,

(1). That as between H. & Co. and the railroad company [the rights of third parties not being involved] the loss must fall upon H. & Co.

(2). That the fact of the stock issued to H. & Co. having been subsequently sold by them to third parties, did not affect the case, it appearing that the sale was made by H. & Co. with knowledge of the forgery.

(3). That the payment of the dividends on the stock to H. & Co. by the agents of the R. R. Co., after the company was informed of the forgery, had no significance, and could not estop the company, it appearing that they were not paid by the direction of the company, but through the mistake or inadvertence of the agent, in overlooking or failing to observe the directions given by the officers of the company that "they were in litigation, and were not to be paid till ordered by the Court."

(4). That the issuing of the certificates to H. & Co. by the R. R. C., upon the faith of the forged powers of attorney sent them by H. & Co., did not create an estoppel against the company. Declarations to create an estoppel must be made by a party whose duty it is to know and state the truth, and must be relied on by one who has no other means of information, or is justified in relying upon such declarations. *Hambleton & Co. v. Central O. R. R. Co.* 44 Md. 551.

437. A. deposited with B. certain Canada railway bonds as security for a debt. On bill filed by B. for foreclosure or sale, *Held*, that B. was entitled to an order for sale only. Jessel M. R., the plaintiff, is in a position of a mere pledgee at law of certain chattels, and I do not think that a person in that position has the same right of foreclosure as a mortgagee by deposit of the title deeds of land. The principle upon which the Court acts in the latter case is, that in a regular legal mortgage there has been an actual conveyance of the legal ownership, and then the Court has interfered to prevent that from having its full effect; and when the ground of interference is gone, by the non-payment of the debt, the Court simply removes the stop it has itself put on. Then, when there is a deposit of title deeds, the Court treats that as an agreement to execute a legal mortgage, and therefore as carrying with it all the remedies incident to such a mortgage. None of this reasoning applies to a pledge of chattels; the pledgee never had the absolute ownership at law, and his equitable rights cannot exceed his legal title. There will be an order for sale of the bonds by auction, but, as there seems to be a good reason why the plaintiff should not be

forced to part with them, I will give him liberty to bid, he not conducting the sale. *Carter* v. *Wake*, 4 Chancery Division M. R. Feb. 12, 1877, c. 48.

PROTEST.

438. Neither protest, nor notice to the surety of non-payment by his principal, is necessary to bind a surety on a promissory note payable in bank. *Scott* v. *Shirk*, 60 Ind. 160.

439. Where the intention of all parties to an accommodation bill was that it should be met by the last endorser, the previous endorsers cannot be sued unless they have had notice of dishonor. *Turner* v. *Samson*, Queen's Bench, Court of Appeal, 1876, English Reports, 195.

440. Notice to the person named in a will as executor of the non-payment of a promissory note endorsed by his testator, which became payable after the will had been offered for probate, and letters testamentary applied for, and before the executor named declined to accept the trust, is sufficient to charge the estate; but such notice of the non-payment of a note, which matured after the executor had renounced the trust, and a special administrator had been appointed, is not sufficient, although no public notice of the latter's appointment has been ordered or given. *Goodnow* v. *Warren*, 122 Mass. 79.

441. When an endorser of a promissory note dies before the note matures, notice of dishonor to his personal representatives is sufficient to support a claim on the endorsement against his heirs and devisees, without notice to them. Notice served by the notary upon a person in charge of the administrator's usual place of business, is legal service, and its validity is not impaired by the notice not being addressed to the decedent. When the notary knows of the endorser's death, and knows who and where his personal representatives are, a service of notice by mail, addressed to "executors," "administrators," or "personal representatives," is not sufficient. They should be addressed by name, and not by their office merely. *Smalley* v. *Wright*, 40 N. J. L. R. 471.

442. One who is publicly acting as the deputy of a notary, and whose oath of office has been administered by the notary himself, is qualified to make demand of payment, and perform the other functions of a deputy notary. *Buckley* v. *Seymour*, 30 La. 1341.

443. The record of the proceedings of a notary public on the protest of a promissory note, unless verified by his affidavit, is incompetent as evidence; but if no objection be made when it is offered in evidence, the objection cannot be raised on a motion for a new trial, nor on writ of error. *Etheridge* v. *Gallagher*, 55 Miss. 458.

444. In an action against an endorser of a promissory note, proof that notice of protest was duly mailed and directed to him at a certain place, if there be no evidence that it is his place of residence or of business, or his nearest postoffice, or the one where he receives his mail, is not sufficient proof of the notice required. If the endorser had no known place of residence or of business, notice to him was not necessary; but this fact must be shown in evidence. *Id.*

445. Where a note fell due on the 25th of July, 1873, on which day it was duly presented for payment and protested, but the notice of protest, dated on the 26th, incorrectly stated that the note was this day presented and protested. *Held*, that the notice was sufficient, as it did not appear that the endorser was misled by the mistake. *Cassidy* v. *Mansfield*, 24 Upper Canada Com. Pleas Rpts. 383.

446. Two promissory notes, payable at any bank in Boston, were presented when due, one at the North National Bank, the other at the Webster National Bank, and demanded their payment, and the same was refused; the answer to the demand being "No funds," and thereupon the notary mailed to the defendant notices of the demand, non-payment and protest of said promissory notes (which notices, it was agreed, were sufficient in form), addressed to the defendant at Townsend, Mass., where was the principal postoffice in the town in which he lived. It was proved that the endorser usually received his letters at the West Townsend postoffice, and that the plaintiff knew that he lived and that there was a postoffice at West Townsend, and had visited and done business with the endorser there. There was no evidence at the trial that these notices were received by the defendant within three days of the time when they were mailed to him by the notary, or that he otherwise within that time had notice of such demand, non-payment and protest. *Held*, the holder of a promissory note is bound to use reasonable diligence to give the endorser immediate notice of its dishonor. It is *prima facie* sufficient to address the endorser by mail at the town in which he resides, although there are several postoffices in the town, and he receives his letters at one nearer his residence and place of business than the principal postoffice, unless the holder knows, or with reasonable diligence might have known, this fact. *Held*, that the judge, sitting without a jury, was warranted in ruling that the notice was insufficient. *Roberts* v. *Taft*, 120 Mass. 169.

PROMISSORY NOTES.

447. In an action against an endorser of a promissory note, the defendant testified that he said to the plaintiff's agent that he doubted if the maker would pay the note; that he would like to arrange it by giving a new note, making himself prom

isor; if he would make a new note, he would sign it; if he would send up the old note, he would waive demand and notice upon the back of it; and on cross-examination he testified that he did not want to have the note protested; that he wanted to save the expense of demand and notice, and though, if the note was protested, he would have to pay it immediately, and that was the reason why he offered to give a new note. *Held*, that a ruling that, as matter of law, on this evidence the defendant waived demand and notice was incorrect. *Batt* v. *Chase*, 122 Mass. 262.

448. A promissory note made by one member of the firm, in its name, can be enforced against the partnership by the holder thereof, if he has no actual knowledge, suspicion or cause of suspicion, of any fraud upon the partnership in the making of the note. *Blodgett* v. *Weed*, 119 Mass. 215.

449. Possession of a promissory note is *prima facie* evidence that the bank is the owner thereof, and in absence of proof to the contrary is conclusive; and there is no denial of the validity of the note, so it makes no difference to the defendant who holds the note, as long as he owes it to some one. *Fletcher* v. *Fletcher*, 29 Vt. 98.

450. **Action.**—A suit will lie against the administrator of a deceased maker of a promissory note, made jointly by two, during the life of the other maker. *Thompson* v. *Johnson*, 40 N. J. Law. 220.

451. A promissory note payable in bank, endorsed for value, before maturity, in the usual course of business, to a *bona fide* holder, is not subject in his hands to the same defences as a promissory note payable in bank. *Bremmerman* v *Jennings*, 60 Ind. 175.

452. Upon demand and refusal of payment of a promissory note on the last day of grace, a right of action accrues at once to the holder, and the Statute of Limitations begins to run from the date; but if there is no demand, the cause of action does not accrue until the succeeding day. *Holland* v. *Clarke*, 32 Ark. 697.

453. A promissory note of a turnpike company is not void because made before it has filed a copy of its by-laws, as required by statute with the county recorder. *Forbes* v. *San Rufael T. Co* 50 Cal. 340.

454. The makers of a promissory note cannot annul a judgment obtained against them on said note by the administrator of a succession, on the ground that the note did not belong to the succession, or on the ground that the administrator was not qualified to act as such. *Maraist* v. *Guilbeau*, 30 La. 1087.

455. The maker of a promissory note, endorsed in blank, and acquired by the holder before its maturity, cannot resist

the payment of the note on the ground that the holder is not the real owner, unless he alleges and shows that he has good defences or claims against the real owner. An agent, in whose hands a note has been placed for collection, may sue on it in his own name. *George M. Klein* v. *Mrs. Buckner, et al.*, 30 La. 680.

456. Parol evidence of the endorsement of a promissory note, without the production of the note, held inadmissible, though not offered in order to charge the endorser. *De Pusey* v. *Du Pont et al.*, 1 Del. Chancery, 77.

457. Before the maker of a lost note, or mislaid negotiable note, which was transferred before its maturity, can be made to pay it, he is entitled to be indemnified against its subsequent appearance. *Nalle & Cammack* v. *Conrad*, 30 La. 503.

458. Negotiable securities stolen, and afterwards sold by the thief, the owner thereof may follow and claim the proceeds in the hands of the felonious taker, or of his assignee, with notice, and this right continues and attaches to any securities or property in which the proceeds are invested and identified, and the rights of a *bona fide* purchaser do not intervene. The law will raise a trust *in invitum* out of the transaction, in order that the substituted property may be subjected to the purposes of indemnity and recompense. *Newton* v. *Porter*, 69 N. Y. 133.

459. The debtor of a bank, of which A. was cashier, transferred a negotiable note, in payment of his indebtedness, to A. by special endorsement, and thereupon the bank, to enable A. to bring suit thereon, assigned its interest in the note to him. *Held*, that A. might maintain an action on the note in his own name, notwithstanding he may be accountable to the bank for the proceeds when collected. *White, Bonner & Wright* v. *Stanley*, 29 Ohio, 433.

460. Such endorsement and transfer having been made before maturity of the note, the same in the hands of A. is not subject to any defense of which neither he nor the bank had notice at the date of the transfer. *Id.*

461. The signer of a promissory note, which reads that "we promise *in solido*," etc., will be held bound as a solidary debtor on such note, unless he proves that he has been legally released from his obligation. *Wm. H. Boullt* v. *Jerome Sarpy et al.*, 30 La. 494.

462. To defeat the title of an innocent purchaser to a note, on the ground of inadequacy of the price paid for it the inadequacy must be such under the circumstances as to impeach the good faith of the purchase. *Rooker* v. *Rooker*, 29 Ohio, 1.

When the purchaser of such note receives it in part payment, of property sold, his title to the note is not affected by the fact that he retains the title and possession of the property sold as security for the unpaid purchase money. *Id.*

463. A municipal corporation has no power to invest its obligations with the character and incidents of commercial paper, so as to render them unassailable by defenses to which they would be subject in the hands of the immediate parties, unless such power is conferred by legislative authority, either express or clearly implied. *Knapp* v. *Mayor and C. of Hoboken*, 39 N. J. 394.

464. In the case of bills of exchange, promissory notes and other commercial contracts a month is always a calendar month. A note, payable six months after the 30th of May, is due just six calendar months and three days thereafter, the days of grace being included, bringing it to maturity consequently on the 3d of December succeeding. Until that day the endorsers of such paper have not broken their contract by non-payment. *Bank of Tennessee* v. *Alexander, Officer, et al.*, 59 Tenn. 173 (3 Baxter). The demand must be made on the third day of grace, on the second if the third be a holiday. *Id.*

465. The holder of negotiable paper, taking it for good consideration in the usual course of business, without knowledge of facts impeaching its validity, holds it by a good title. It is not enough to defeat his recovery to show that he took it under circumstances that might tend to excite suspicion. *Farrell* v. *Lovett*, 68 Me. 326.

466. In an action against the maker by an endorser of a negotiable promissory note, who purchased the same for a valuable consideration before maturity, and without notice of any fraud or infirmity as between the original parties, the defendant is not liable where it is shown: (1) That at the time of signing and delivering the note he was induced by fraudulent representations as to the character of the paper to believe that he was signing and delivering an instrument other than a promissory note; (2) That his ignorance of the true character of the paper was not attributable in whole or in part to his own negligence in the premises. *De Camp* v. *Hamma*, 29 Ohio, 467.

467. A negotiable promissory note, given for a patent right, without the words "Given for a patent right" inserted therein, as required by No. 68, s. 2, of the Acts of 1872, is good in the hands of a *bona fide* holder for value who takes it before maturity, and without notice of what it was given for. *Pender* v. *Kelley*, 48 Vt. 27.

468. In an action by payee of a joint and several promissory note, payable on demand against a maker, a plea that defendant had signed as accommodation maker, with the following agreement written on note, "This note is to be paid off within three years from date," and that the plaintiff had made no demand, and the note had not been paid within three years, is a bad plea. *Lawrence* v. *Walmsley*, CIX. 797; 12 C. B. N. S. 797 (Eng. Com. Law).

469. Where a negotiable promissory note was made payable upon a condition, and the condition was written below the note on the same piece of paper. *Held*, that the note and condition were parts of a single entire contract, and that the fraudulent removal of the condition, by tearing the paper, was such a material alteration as rendered the note void in the hands of a *bona fide* holder. *Gerrish* v. *Glines*, 56 N. H. 9.

470. An agreement by the endorsee of a promissory note for a definite extension of the time of payment, in consideration of an agreement by the maker to pay a greater rate of interest than that provided for in the note, is binding upon them, and if made without the consent of the endorser, will release him from all liability thereon. *Kittle* v. *Wilson*, 7 Neb. 180.

471. This defense is a legal one, and should be made by the endorser in the action against him on the note; but if he neglects to do so, and suffer judgment to go against him, he cannot afterwards make it available as a ground for enjoining the enforcement of such judgment. *Id.*

472. It is not necessary that any United States internal revenue stamps should be affixed to a note, or a mortgage, in order to make it competent evidence in our State courts. *Pargoud* v. *Richardson*, 30 La. 1286.

473. A promissory note, drawn for a sum certain and made payable to any person, "or order," "or assigns," "or bearer," is negotiable; but if it is payable to a certain person, without words making it payable "to order." "or assigns," "or bearer," it is not a negotiable instrument. *Hosford* v. *Stone*, 6 Neb. 380.

474. Any words in a promissory note, from which it appears that the person making it intended it to be negotiable, will give it a transferable quality; but the words "negotiable and payable without defalcation or discount," do not of themselves make an instrument, otherwise non-negotiable, negotiable. *Id.*

475. Where a note, though negotiable, is payable to order, and unendorsed, and is accidentally destroyed by fire while in the possession of the payee, the payee can maintain an action on such lost instrument without first tendering or giving a bond of indemnity. *Blandin Adm'r* v. *Wade*, 20 Kansas. 251.

476. In a case where a note, framed on a printed blank, was complete at the time it left the hands of the party sought to be charged, but was so printed as to give an apparent authority to fill a blank space, occupying the same position relative to the body of the note that an interest clause usually does, and the space left finished ample room for inserting such clause, and the space was not filled in a way to attract observation, the Court strongly inclined to the opinion that the defendant would be bound to an innocent hold. *Iron Mountain Bank* v. *Murdock*, 62 Mo. 70.

477. Promissory note, given by a vendee for the price of a thing which the vendor assumed to sell, but which never had an existence, are utterly without consideration, and cannot be enforced by the vendor, or by any one who has acquired them after their maturity. *Cummings* v. *Saux*, 30 La. 207.

478. Giving a note for an antecedent debt is not a payment of it, unless the note be received under an express agreement, or under circumstances from which an agreement may be fairly implied to treat it as a payment, or unless payment in fact result from it. *May & Sloan* v. *Gamble*, 14 Fla. 467.

479. An agreement by a debtor and creditor that the creditor will, at a future day, accept new notes and securities in lieu of those held, giving additional time of payment of the indebtedness, cannot be enforced unless some valid consideration be received by, or benefit or advantage has accrued thereby, to the creditor. *Id.*

480. One who has executed a promissory note in error, for a debt not due by her, may legally resist the payment of the note, so long as the note is not in the hands of an innocent third person, who has taken it for value before its maturity. *Bridget Reardon* v. *Daniel Moriarty et al.* 30 La. 120.

481. The maker or indorser of a promissory note cannot, as against an indorser of the same, in this State, for value before maturity and without notice show that the note, although dated in Boston, with intent that it should be a Massachusetts contract, was actually made in New York, and on account of illegal interest, was void under the Usury law of that State. A promissory note, endorsed " L. R., receiver," binds him personally. *Towne* v. *Rice*, 122 Mass. 67.

482. One who is in fact the owner of a note negotiable by endorsement may maintain an action upon it, although no indorsement thereof has been made to him ; and an indorsement subsequent to the commencement of the action, made by the payee, will relate back to and ratify a prior sale of the note made by an agent of such payee. *Weeks* v. *Medler*, 20 Kansas, 57.

483. An instrument which, in its terms and form, is a negotiable promissory note, does not lose that character because it also recites that an additional rate of interest will be paid "after due ;" that the maker has deposited certain certificates as collateral security for the payment of the note, and states the terms upon which they have been deposited and upon which they may be sold by the holder on the non-payment of the note. *Towne* v. *Rice*, 122 Mass., 67.

484. In action on a note and mortgage, when it is admitted that the plaintiff is the holder of the note, which is endorsed in blank by the payee thereof, the law will presume, in the absence

of any evidence to the contrary, that the plaintiff is an innocent and *bona fide* holder for value, and that it was indorsed to him before due. *Acton* v. *Harlan,* 20 Kansas. 452.

485. The title to negotiable paper cannot be defeated by proof of negligence, or want of diligence in inquiring into the title or the equities between the parties thereto. Nothing but fraud will defeat the title thereto. The legal presumption as to an endorsement on negotiable paper is, that it was for value, and for a proper purpose; and where such endorsement purports to be the act of a corporation, through its proper officer, one taking negotiable paper so endorsed, for value, before maturity, is not bound to inquire whether the endorsement was made in the regular course of the business of the corporation, or was for the accommodation of the officer, or was without consideration. *Lafayette Savings Bank* v. *St. Louis Stoneware Co.* 4 Mo. Court of Appeal (St. Louis), 276.

486. When a negotiable promissory note, due sixty days after date, and endorsed by the payee in blank, is put in suit by a third person, the production of the note by the plaintiff, at the trial, is *prima facie* evidence that he acquired it for value before maturity, and without notice of any fact going to defeat its collection. As against him, payment made to payee will not be a defense, without showing that the payee had possession of the note at the time, or was then the owner of it, or for some other reason had a right to receive the money. Generally, payment made to an agent who has parted with possession of the security to his principal, is no discharge. *Paris et al.* v. *Moe, adm'r,* 60 Ga. 90.

487. A promissory note, due from a resident of Colorado to a resident of California, is in no legitimate sense the property of the debtor, and is not subject to taxation under the laws of Colorado (Sess. Laws, 1870, p. 88), although the note is secured by trust deed upon real estate within the jurisdiction of the taxing power. *Com'rs Arapahoe Co.* v. *Cutter,* 3 Colo. 349.

488. When the consideration for a promissory note was expressed in the note to be the stock of a railway corporation, and the directors of the corporation subsequently made an illegal and unauthorized increase in the stock of the company, it was *held* that such illegal increase would constitute a defense to an action upon the note. Following *Merrill* v. *Gamble,* 46 Iowa 615. Ante. *Merrill* v. *Beaver,* 46 Iowa, 646.

489. A note, or other written evidence of indebtedness, payable in *current funds,* is not to be regarded upon its face as negotiable. *Haddock* v. *Woods,* 46 Iowa. 433.

490. In an action upon such paper it is competent to show by parol evidence the peculiar meaning of the term *current funds,* and that the parties understood it to mean money. While the understanding of the parties respecting the condition

of the contract cannot be shown by parol, their understanding of the meaning of the words used therein may be competent. *Id.*

491. This court has repeatedly recognized the rule that an express agreement must be shown to establish the fact that a bill or note of either the debtor or a third person was taken by the creditor in payment of a pre-existing debt. *Brewster* v. *Bours*, 8 Cal. 506; *Griffith* v. *Grogan*, 12 Cal. 320; *Welch* v. *Allington*, 23 Cal. 322; followed in *Brown* v. *Olmsted*, 50 Cal. 162.

492. If the widow is executrix of the estate of the deceased husband, and the estate is community property, so that she has an interest in the same, and she gives her own note for a debt of the deceased husband, which is outlawed, under the mistaken opinion that it is not outlawed, there is a sufficient consideration to support the note. *Mull* v. *Van Trees*, 50 Cal. 547.

493. The party who purchases a promissory note from the payee before it is due, but after the payee has executed to the payor a release of the same, without knowledge of such lease, is a *bona fide* holder, although he purchases for less than the face of the note, and as a speculation, and although by the exercise of a little diligence he might have ascertained that the release had been given. *Schoen* v. *Houghton*, 50 Cal. 528.

494. If one party furnishes another one thousand dollars in money, and such other gives him his note therefor, with the understanding that the payor shall procure third parties to assign to himself certain liens on land claimed by the payee, which liens the payor shall hold for the benefit of the payee in satisfaction of the note, the agreement amounts to an accord and satisfaction, and is a payment of the note. *Treadwell* v. *Himmelmann*, 50 Cal. 9.

495. A contemporaneous written agreement, executed by the payee of a promissory note, showing a contingency upon which the payment of the note is to depend, is admissible in evidence, under the general issue, in an action on the note by an endorser after maturity against the maker. *Munro* v. *King*, 3 Colo. 238.

496. In a suit on a note the affidavit of defence was that it had been given as a donation to a church, on condition that the lot on which it was erected should be conveyed to the church, which had not been done. The suit was by the endorsee; the affidavit averred that defendant "verily believes and expects to prove that the note has been passed by the payee to plaintiffs to avoid making this defence, and that the plaintiffs sold the same to the use of the payee without consideration as between them." *Held* sufficient against the endorsee. *Reznor* v. *Supplee*. 81 Penn. St. 180.

497. Where two or more notes, secured by a single mortgage, fall due at different times, they shall be paid out of the mortgage fund in the order of their maturity, unless a different agreement has been made between the parties, or unless some paramount equity should require a different order of payment. *Richardson* v. *McKim*, 20 Kan. 346–350.

498. The party, who was president and treasurer of a local board of trustees of an insurance company, gave a certificate that the insurance company had on deposit with him a certain number of dollars, and signed it, " H., president and treasurer, local board of trustees." *Held*, that the certificate, in legal effect, was H.'s promissory note, and in a suit at law against him by the insurance company he could show in defence that the contract of which it formed a part was rescinded, or that the contract was of mutual stipulations, and the payee had not performed on his part. *Hart* v. *Life Ass'n*, 54 Ala. 195.

499. The maker of negotiable paper, which is void in the hands of the payee, may, in order to prevent its negotiation, maintain a bill in equity to compel its surrender for cancellation. *Breathuit* v. *Rogers, Adm'r of McLendon*, 32 Ark. 758.

500. A promissory note given by the widow to a creditor of the deceased husband, who does not take it in payment of the debt, and neither lost nor suspended any remedy for its collection, or receipted the account, is without consideration. The fact that there has been no administration, and the widow remains in possession of all the real and personal estate of the husband—the possession not being derived from the creditor—forms no consideration for such a promise. *Watson* v. *Reynolds & Stuckey*, 54 Ala. 191.

501. A promissory note, which is payable "on or before three years from date," is not due until the three years has expired ; and a purchaser for value within that time is entitled to the same protection as if the note was made payable three years from date. *Mallison* v. *Marks*, 31 Mich. 425 ; also *Helmer* v. *Krolick*, 36 Mich. 371.

502. If a promissory note, signed by one member of a partnership in the firm name, is given in payment of debts, some of which were contracted before another member came into the firm, and the rest thereafter, and an action thereon by the payee of the note is defended by such other member alone, the plaintiff, in the absence of evidence of actual fraud on his part, or of knowledge when the party defending entered the partnership, is entitled to recover for such debts covered by the note as were contracted after he became a member. *Gould* v. *Belcher*, 119 Mass. 257.

503. The note sued on having been transferred to plaintiff as collateral security for money loaned before due, it was a *bona fide* holder thereof ; consequently the verdict, finding for

the defendant, on a plea of failure of consideration, was contrary to law. *Exchange Bank* v. *Butner & Edgeworth*, 60 Ga. 654.

504. Three promissory notes, made by the lessee payable to the lessor at different dates, were given to and accepted by him in consideration of the surrender of a lease in a building, which lease provided that, in case of the destruction of the premises by fire, the rent should be suspended or abated. The first two notes were duly paid, and before the last note was due the premises were destroyed by fire. *Held*, that the consideration of the notes given by the lessees was the acceptance by the lessors of the surrender of the lease. After this the defendants had no interest in the real estate, and their liability upon the notes was not affected by the condition of the premises, or by the provisions of the lease, which had ceased to exist. *Brooks* v. *Cutter*, 119 Mass. 132.

505. A protested draft is not an obligation within the meaning of the proviso of the Act of 16th of April, 1850, which declares that the assignees of an insolvent bank " shall receive in payment of debts due to said bank its own notes and obligations and the checks of its depositors at par." *Basehore* v. *Rhodes*, 85 Penn. St. 44.

506. In an action upon a promissory note, in which the declaration alleges that the defendant made the note, and the answer denies this, and alleges an alteration, proof of the defendant's signature is *prima facie* evidence that the whole body of the note written over it is the act of the defendant, but the burden of proof is on the plaintiff to show that the note declared was the note of the defendant. *Simpson* v. *Davis*, 119 Mass. 269.

507. The addition of the name of another joint maker to a note, without the knowledge or consent of the others, is such a material alteration as releases them from liability thereon. The last signer, however, is not released by the discharge of his co-signers, and he is liable for the amount of the note. *Hamilton* v. *Hooper et al.*, 46 Iowa, 515.

508. A promissory note being accepted by the parties, in interest, in payment of a debt, the taking of such note, in pursuance of the agreement, merges the original cause of action in the note, and a recovery, if had at all, must be had upon the note. If such agreement was in fact made, and note given in pursuance thereof, the creditor cannot rescind such contract for the purpose of suing upon the original cause of action by simply returning the note. *Kappes et al.* v. *Geo. E. White*, 1 Bradwell's Ill. App. Rpts. 280.

509. Where a note provided for interest at 10 per cent. per annum, and the mortgage executed to receive it stipulated for "interest at the rate of 10 per cent. per annum, payable an-

nually, according to the terms of the promissory note," *held*, that the mortgage provided for something respecting which the note was silent, and would, therefore, govern. *Dobbins* v. *Parker et ux*, 46 Iowa, 357.

510. Defendants were partners, and K., one of them, furnished money to be used in the partnership business, and took a note therefor, payable to himself, or order, and signed by himself and the other defendants. K.'s wife became the owner of said note, and sent it to plaintiff by K. for collection, and K. indorsed it to plaintiff for collection merely. K. made no defence to the note. *Ormsbee* v. *Kidder et els.* 48 Vt. 361.

511. If the payor of a note conveys land to the holder, by way of security for its payment, and the holder afterwards sells the notes to a third person, and then conveys the land to another person to secure his own debt, these facts do not constitute a defense, if such third person sues the payor to recover on the notes. *Kiel* v. *Reay*, 50 Cal. 61.

512. The omission to insert in a note given for a patent-right the words "Given for a patent-right," inserted therein, as required by statute, does not render the note void. If the patent-right is good and valid, and forms an adequate consideration for the note, the maker cannot defend against a transferee of the note on the ground of the omission of those words. The object of the statute was to prevent the transfer of such notes to innocent and *bona fide* holders. *Streit* v. Waugh, 48 Vt. 298.

513. Nor can the maker defend upon the ground that the plaintiff received the note from another transferee in payment for liquor sold in violation of law. *Id.*

514. It cannot render a purchaser of negotiable paper suspicious that the payee has an interest in getting it off his hands; this fact would not necessarily be known to the purchaser, or influence in any manner his action; and in determining whether a purchaser is entitled to be considered a *bona fide* holder, it is his *bona fides*, and not that of the payee, that is in question. *Helmer* v. *Krolick*, 36 Mich. 371.

515. A promissory note, left blank as to the amount, but perfect in all other particulars, and providing for a certain rate of interest "per annum," was executed by one as principal, and by another as surety, and entrusted by the latter to the former for delivery to the payee; whereupon the payee's agent, with knowledge of the relations of the makers as principal and surety, filled up the blank, and altered the note, by direction of the principal, but without the knowledge or consent of the surety, so as to make it bear interest "after maturity." *Held*, that such alteration relieved the surety from all liability thereon. *Franklin L. Ins. Co.* v. *Courtney*, 60 Ind. 134.

516. On a collateral contract to pay a certain sum per month as interest on a note, if it should not be met at maturity, payee, who has endorsed the note away, cannot recover. *Florence* v. *Drayson*, LXXXVII. 584 ; LC. B. N. S. 584 (Eng. Com. Law).

517. A. being indebted to B., as a surety, in order to enable B.'s agent to raise money, and to obtain further time on the debt to B., made his note to the agent upon an agreement that if he should have to pay the note, the amount paid should be entered as a credit on the debt to B. The agent assigned the note to the plaintiff for value ; after the assignment his agency ceased, and the debt to B. was paid by the principal debtor. *Held*, that at the time of the assignment there was a subsisting consideration, and the subsequent failure of consideration could not affect the right of the plaintiff (the assignee of the note). *Woodruff* v. *Webb*. 32 Ark. 612.

518. Where, by mistake, note at two months, dated January 1st, 1854, instead of January 1st, 1855, and across the face was written, " Due March 4th, 1855," *held*, that the date was 1855, and the memorandum was as if correction of error. *Fitch* v. *Jones*, LXXXV. 238 ; 5 E. & B. 238 (Eng. Com. Law).

519. Negotiable paper, payable at a time certain, is dishonored by mere non-payment at the time, and no one is a *bona fide* holder, without notice, who does not take such paper before maturity. When the time of payment of a negotiable note is extended by agreement, a reference to which is endorsed upon the back, one who takes it after its original maturity will be subject to all equities between the parties. *Dryer* v. *Mercantile Bank*, 4 Mo. Court of Appeals (St. Louis), 598.

520. If A. and B. enter into partnership, and B. is to furnish $1,000 as his part of the capital, and B. hands the money to C. to deliver to A., and A. when he receives it gives C. his promissory note for it, the note is given without consideration. *Ayer* v. *Duncan*, 50 Cal. 325.

521. When the maker of a non-negotiable promissory note is at the maturity thereof bankrupt, the assignee and holder of the note may at once sue the assignor, without waiting for final distribution of the estate of the bankrupt maker, the bankruptcy of the maker being a breach of the implied warranty of the assignor. *Lowenstein* v. *Knopf*, 4 Mo. Ct. Appeals (St. Louis), 594.

522. Where the maker of a promissory note, payable to a certain person or bearer, on being inquired of by a third person to whom the payee had offered after its dishonor to sell it, answered that it was all right, and that he would pay it, and thereupon the purchase was made and the price paid, the maker is estopped from setting up failure or want of consideration, or

any other equity existing between himself and the payee, to an action brought upon the note by the purchaser or his privies *Reedy* v. *Brunner & Co.*, 60 Ga. 107.

523. Where it is claimed by a party defendant that the date of the note in suit is a mistake, and the note on its face is payable six months after date, and such defendant claims that the note was in fact paid when due (which was six months before the date at which it purports to have been executed), the testimony of an endorser of such note that he endorsed such note at the place of its date, in the State of Kansas, at or about the time claimed by the maker as the date of execution, and that he was absent from the State during all the time for a period commencing some three months before the date appearing on the note, and extending some five months beyond such date, is competent as tending to show a mistake in the date of the note *Clary* v. *Smith*, 20 Kansas, 83.

524. In an action upon a negotiable promissory note, it will devolve upon the defendant to show, if he so claims, that the note was fraudulently obtained, or that it was executed without sufficient consideration, or that it has been paid. *Ecton* v *Harlan*, 20 Kansas, 452.

525. Where a person, possessed of the ordinary faculties and ability to read, signs and delivers a negotiable promissory note, without knowing it to be such, but without reading the same, having an opportunity to do so, relying solely upon the representation of the payee that the paper was an instrument other than a note. *Held*, as against a *bona fide* holder before maturity for value, such maker will not be permitted to deny the due execution of the note. *Winchell* v. *Crider*, 29 Ohio, 480

526. A purchaser of negotiable paper is not put upon inquiry by mere knowledge that that the payee is engaged in selling intoxicating liquors, to ascertain whether the consideration of the paper was not the unlawful sale of such liquors *Bottomley* v. *Goldsmith*, 36 Mich. 27 ; also *Paton* v. *Coit*, Mich. 505.

527. In an action against the maker by a *bona fide* endorsee before due, and for value, of a negotiable promissory note, the defendant is liable, if guilty of negligence in the execution thereof, although he did not intend to sign a note, and was induced, through fraudulent representations as to its character, to believe that the instrument executed was one of a different purport. *Ross* v. *Doland*, 29 Ohio, 473.

528. A person, who negligently signs and delivers to another a printed form of a negotiable promissory note, containing blanks, without knowing it to be such, is estopped as against a subsequent *bona fide* holder for value, and before due, from denying authority in the person to whom it was delivered to fill the blanks. *Id.*

529. A petition against several makers of a joint and several note more than fifteen years past due, whereon payments have been made within the time of the statute, but by whom paid not appearing, does not show a statutory bar in favor of any of the defendants. Where the holder of a note past due receives from the principal debtor, without the knowledge of the surety, a sum of money greater than the amount of interest then due, and the amount so received is endorsed on the note as received on account of interest, it not appearing that such endorsement was made by the holder, or that he had knowledge that the same was so made, it is not error to refuse to charge the jury that in law such receipt and endorsement constituted an agreement to extend the time of payment of the note for such period of time as such sum would pay interest. *Vose* v. *Woodford,* 29 Ohio, 245.

530. A. made his promissory note, expressed to be for value received, whereby he promised to pay B. or bearer forty dollars profits, with interest, one year from date. As to A., the note was entirely without consideration, and was obtained from him by fraud. The plaintiff subsequently became the innocent *bona fide* purchaser thereof before maturity. *Held,* that the instrument in the hands of the plaintiff was a valid, negotiable promissory note, and might be recovered; that the word "profits," as to the plaintiff, did not express or suggest a contingency or uncertainty, but an absolute existing fund as the consideration of the promise, and on account of which the money was to be paid, and that the word, as inserted in the note, was not such an apparent defect or infirmity as to put the plaintiff upon inquiry. *Matthews* v. *Crosby,* 56 N. H. 21.

531. In a suit brought against the administrator of a deceased person to recover the amount due upon a promissory note, the defendant should be allowed to allege and prove that the note was made and delivered to plaintiff, without consideration, for the sole purpose of protecting the property of the deceased from his creditors, and that it was agreed between plaintiff and said deceased at the time of the execution of said note that it should be cancelled whenever so desired. *McCausland* v. *Ralston,* 12 Nevada, 195.

532. In an action brought upon a promissory note to recover of one of the endorsers the amount due, the endorser may be declared against as a guarantor, and held liable as such. *Sarbach* v. *Jones,* 20 Kansas, 497.

533. Where a promissory note, obtained from the promisor by fraud, has been transferred to a third party before its maturity, the burden of proof is upon him to show that he purchased it for value in good faith; and to determine this, all the attendant circumstances of the transaction are to be considered. *Sullivan* v. *Langley et al.,* 120 Mass. 437.

534. Good equitable defence by one maker of a promissory note that he was surety for the other, of which the holder had notice at the time the note was made, and that the holder has given principal debtor time, preventing recovery. *Semble*, that the defence would be good, if the holder knew when he gave time that the defendant was surety. *Pooley* v. *Harradine*, XC. 431 ; 7 E. & B. 431 (Eng. Com. Law.).

535. The contract which the law implies from the endorsement of a negotiable note, is as conclusive against parol testimony as though it were written out in full above the endorser's signature. Parol testimony is inadmissible to change a simple, unqualified endorsement, whether in full or in blank, into an endorsement without recourse. *Doolittle* v. *Ferry*, 20 Kansas, 230.

536. Where an insolvent merchant pressed by creditors, nominally sells to his penniless clerk a stock of goods which the clerk and he knows are not paid for, and accepts in payment of the goods a debt for pretended wages he owes the clerk, and the promissory notes of the clerk, the transaction will be considered a fraudulent simulation. *Sattler & Co.* v. *Leonard Marine*, 30 La. 355.

537. Partial *payment* made by one debtor on a note, will not suspend the running of a statute of limitations in favor of the other debtors thereon, although the party paying be the principal debtor, and the others only sureties. *Steele* v. *Souder*, 20 Kansas, 39.

538. A party knowing the signature to a promissory note to be forged, and intending to be bound by it, acknowledges it as his own, assumes the note as his own and is bound by it just as if it had been originally signed by his authority. *Wellington* v. *Jackson*, 121 Mass. 157.

539. Note delared upon last pending action, copy annexed to declaration being still in existence, and produced at the trial, the trial may proceed without establishing a copy in lieu of the lost original, though a plea of *non est factum* be filed. The genuineness of the original, and the correctness of the preserved copy, may be established by parol evidence. *Jernigan Ex'x* v. *Carter*, 60 Ga. 131.

540. Where a promissory note is signed by two, one being surety for the other, with the knowledge of the payee, but without any agreement to that effect between the payee and surety, time given the principal maker is a good defence in an action by payee against the maker who was surety. *Greenough* v. *McClelland*, C. V. 422 ; 2 E. & E. 422. Affirmed C. V. 429; 2 E. & E. 429. (Eng. Com. Law).

541. The alteration of the date of a note by the holder, without the consent and to the prejudice of the maker, is a forgery and renders the note void. *Lemay* v. *Williams*, 32 Ark. 166.

542. A rent note being made payable to bearer, the defendant could not question the plaintiff's title thereto, unless it was shown to be necesary to his defence. A motion for nonsuit, on the ground that the evidence disclosed that the note had been deposited with third persons as collateral security, and the debt was therefore due to them was properly overruled. *Greer* v. *Woolfolk*, 60 Ga. 623.

543. Proof that the consideration of a promissory note upon which suit is brought was the unlawful sale of intoxicating liquors, throws upon the plaintiff the burden of showing that he bought the note in good faith and before it fell due. *Paton* v. *Coit*, 5 Mich. 505.

544. Material alteration, the erasure of the word "surety" after the name of the signers of a note by the payee, before endorsement, is a material alteration discharging the surety, even though the note be transferred for value before maturity. *Lamb* v. *Paine et al.*, 46 Iowa, 550.

545. If a transfer of title in the note without assumption of liability is sought or desired, equally apt and well-known words are at hand. "Without recourse," relieves the indorser. *Doolittle* v. *Ferry*, 20 Kansas, 232.

546. A promissory note of this form: "One year after date we promise to pay to the order of A. B., one thousand dollars, value received," and signed "George Moore, treasurer of Mechanic Falls Dairying Association" is the note of Moore and not of the Association; and it makes no difference that the plural "we" is used instead of "I." *Mellon* v. *Moore*, 68 Me. 390.

547. To pass the legal title by the plaintiff in execution there must be an indorsement or assignment thereof in writing. *Anderson Ex'r* v. *Baker*, 60 Ga. 599.

548. The legal import of a blank endorsement upon a promissory note cannot be varied by parol. *Martin* v. *Cole*, 3 Colo. 113.

549. In a suit by a bank against the maker of a promissory note, a plea of the general issue admits the corporate existence of the bank and its capacity to sue. *Ticonic Bank* v. *Bagley*, 68 Me. 249.

550. The assignment and delivery of a promissory note payable to order, before maturity, without indorsement, gives to the assignee only the rights of the payee, though it may have been taken in good faith and for value. *Allum* v. *Perry*, 68 Me. 232.

551. An averment in a complaint on a promissory note, that a certain sum "*is due*, as principal and interest on said note," is equivalent to an averment that the note remains unpaid. *Downey* v. *Whittenberger*, 60 Ind. 188.

552. A verbal acknowledgment of, and promise to pay a

promissory note, made by one of its solidary makers before its prescription, will interrupt prescription as to all the makers. *Boullt* v. *Sarpy*, 30 La. 494.

553. Forbearance to one maker of a promissory note does not discharge another, who, with knowledge of holder, gave note as accommodation. *Strong* v. *Foster*, lxxxiv. 201; 17 C. B. 201. (Eng. Com. Law).

554. In order to make future services good consideration for a promissory note there must have been a contract for them. *Hulse* v. *Hulse*, lxxxiv. 711; 17 C. B. 711. (Eng. Com. Law).

555. The mortgage note of a wife knowingly received by a creditor of the husband, in satisfaction, or security of the husband's debt, is in the hands of such a creditor, utterly null and void. *Claverie* v. *Gerodias*, 30 La. 291.

556. Note given to creditor to induce him to sign composition deed, consideration illegal. *Clay* v. *Ray*, C.XII. 188; 17 C. B. N. G. 188 (Eng. Com. Law).

557. One who takes a promissory note as collateral security for a debt then created, and on the faith thereof, with notice of no equities, becomes a holder for value. *Logan* v. *Smith*, 62 Mo. 455.

558. B. and C. being indebted to D., B. gave a promissory note to A., the agent of D., in payment thereof. When the note came due it was not paid, and A. agreed to assume the original debt and to transfer the note to C. on C.'s giving his promissory note to A. for the amount of the debt. *Held*, that C.'s note was given for a sufficient consideration. *Turner* v. *Rogers*, 121 Mass. 12.

559. A creditor holding the mortgage note of a third person as collateral security is compelled to credit the debt due him with only the net sum he was legally able to collect on said note. *Blouin* v. *Liquidators of Hart & Hebert*, 30 La. 714.

560. A promissory note, given to one creditor in consideration of an agreement in fraud of the maker's other creditors, is void as between the parties. *Fay* v. *Fay*, 121 Mass. 561.

561. A promissory note is entitled to days of grace, and suit cannot be brought thereon until after they have expired. *McCoy* v. *Babcock*, 1 Bradwells Ill. App. Repts. 414.

562. In a suit on a promissory note by a *bona fide* endorsee for valuable consideration, against the maker, the simple fact that the endorser was at the time of the endorsement indebted to the maker, is no defence. *Price* v. *Keen*, 40 N. J. L. R. 332.

563. A promissory note which has for its consideration the discontinuance by the holder of the note of certain criminal proceedings instituted by him against a party, for obtaining

money under false pretences, is void. *U. Oganne* v. *Abraham Haber*, 30 La. 1384.

564. One who executes a promissory note in the name of another, without authority to do so, becomes personally liable for the amount of the note. *Dodd, Brown & Co.* v. *Bishop & Co.* 30 La. 1178.

565. In an action on a promissory note payable to bearer, by one alleging himself to be the bearer, owner and holder thereof, it is unnecessary to allege delivery. *Block* v. *Duncan*, 60 Ind. 522.

566. In order to recover from the maker of a promissory note, it is not necessary to make a demand at the place of payment designated in the note. *Henry Renshaw* v. *A. Keene Richards*, 30 La. 398.

567. Absolute unconditional promissory note cannot be changed into conditional obligation by parol evidence in absence of fraud, accident, or mistake. *Haley Ex'r* v. *Evans*, 60 Ga. 157. Also, *Brumby et al.* v. *Barnard, Agent*, 60 Ga. 292. Also, *Starr* v. *Mayer & Co.* 60 Ga. 546; and *Wright* v. *Wilson*, 60 Ga. 614.

568. Party taking a promissory note, with notice of fraud before endorsement, cannot recover. Assignee of bill or note without endorsement, takes, subject to all defences. *Whistler* v. *Forster*, 248; CVIII. 14 C. B. N. S. 248 (Eng. Com. Law).

569. Promissory note, in consideration of forbearance to prosecute charge of obtaining money under false pretences, is illegal. *Clubb* v. *Hutson*, CXIV. 414; 18 C. B. N. S. 414 (Eng. Com. Law).

570. One who takes a stolen negotiable instrument *bona fide* and for value is entitled to recover on it, though negligent in availing himself of means of knowledge of bad title. *Raphael* v. *Bank of England*, 84, 161; 17 C. B. 1861 (Eng. Com. Law).

571. The single fact that a promissory note payable to bearer, was transferred to the plaintiff without consideration, or solely to enable him to bring suit upon and collect it, constitutes no defence to the action. *McWilliams* v. *Bridges*, 7 Neb. 419.

572. S. is the owner of the negotiable note of M. for $8,000, which he endorses and deposits with the bank as collateral security for a loan of $4,000, obtained upon the discount by the bank of the note of B. S. sells the note to O. and gives O. an order on the bank to deliver the note to O. On the same day O. presents the order at the bank, and is told that the president of the bank is absent from town. Some days thereafter O. has an interview with the president of the bank, and is then informed that the debt of S. is nearly paid, and that he would deliver the note to O. but for the service of an attachment upon the bank. The debt of S. is afterwards paid in full. Before the sale by S. to O., an attachment has been served upon M. at the suit of a creditor of S.; but of this O. had no notice when he purchased the note. After the sale and notice to the bank by O., an attachment was served upon the bank by another creditor of S. *Held*, the sale by S. to O. is valid, and he is entitled to the note as against the attaching creditors of S. *Blair & Hoge v. Wilson.* 28 Grattan (Va.) 165.

573. An alteration of a promissory note in any material part renders it invalid as against a party not consenting thereto, even in the hands of an innocent purchaser. *Brown v. Straw*, 6 Neb. 536.

574. After an instrument is completed and delivered, no alteration can be made therein, except by consent; an alteration of the date, whether it hasten or delay the time of payment, is a material alteration, and if made without the consent of the party sought to be charged, extinguishes his liability. *Id.*

575. Where a party contracts to pay 18 per cent. interest upon a promissory note at the time of its execution and delivery, the contract will be tainted with usury, although the rate of interest is not expressed in the note. *Keim & Co. v. Avery*, 7 Neb. 54.

A surety may plead a defence to a promissory note that usurious interest was agreed upon by the parties at the time of the execution of the note. *Id.*

576. The defendant being the payee of a negotiable promissory note, upon which his action is brought, his relation is such that he cannot in law be held to be the maker of such note, even though his indorsement was for the purpose of giving credit to the note. *Barnard v. Gaslin*, 23 Minn. 192.

577. That the endorsement by the payee of a negotiable promissory note amounts in law to a contract on the part of such indorser, in which he undertakes to pay the note in case the maker fails to pay at maturity, and of which failure he has due notice; and his liability in this regard cannot be varied or qualified by a parol agreement or understanding simultaneous with that of the endorsement; and hence, parol evidence will not be received to vary this well recognized legal contract. *Id.*

578. G. executed a promissory note to a railway company to aid in the construction of a road between two points named in the note. At the time of its execution it was understood that the note, with others of like purport, if they reached a certain amount, was to be turned over to another company, which was to construct the road; they did not reach the amount, and the road was constructed by plaintiff, who was the assignee of the payee of the note. *Held*, that upon compliance with the other conditions of the note, it was collectible by plaintiff. It being stipulated in the note that the consideration therefor was

to be capital stock of the railway company, which was to be limited to a certain specific amount, an illegal increase thereof would constitute a valid defence to the note. *Merrill v. Gamble*, 46 Iowa, 615.

579. A material alteration in the terms or condition of a note, or o.her commercial paper, made by the holder thereof, with a fraudulent intent, will defeat recovery thereon. *Robinson* v. *Reed et al.*, 46 Iowa, 219.

580. A surety contracts to pay the note, while the guarantor undertakes to pay it upon condition that certain steps are taken, and any writing upon the note, therefore, which seeks to render a guarantor a surety is a material alteration. *Id.*

581. Where the alteration is established, the holder has the burden to show that it was made innocently, for a proper purpose, or by a stranger, and in the absence of such proof it will be presumed to have been fraudulently made. *Id.*

582. The party guilty of the fraudulent alteration cannot by removing it recover the right of action which he has lost by his fraud. *Id.*

583. When a renewal note has been given, with an understanding that the original note shall be surrendered, if the renewal note is not paid at maturity, suit may be commenced thereon ; and the mere fact that the original note had not been surrendered at the commencement of the action is no defence, when it appears that plaintiff has always held possession thereof, that its surrender has never been demanded, and when it is produced on the trial and tendered to defendant. The fact that the defendant, at the maturity of the renewal note, went to the bank, where it was deposited for collection, for the purpose of paying it, and refused to pay because the original note was not there to be surrendered, is no defence to the action, when it is shown that the money was afterwards demanded of him, and that he refused to pay on other grounds, and that plaintiff was at all times ready and willing to surrender the original on payment of the renewal note. *Fleirs et al.* v. *Hellery* 4 Mo. Ct. Appeals (St. Louis), 596.

584. In an action by an endorsee against his endorser on a promissory note, which on its face was executed and payable at a bank in another State, the maker of which was alleged to be a non-resident of this State, all the evidence introduced was the note, the endorsement thereof and a protest. *Held*, on motion for a new trial, that the evidence is insufficient to sustain a verdict for the plaintiff. *Held* also, that the endorsement, in the absence of evidence to the contrary, is presumed to have been made at the time and place of the execution of the note, and that the note and endorsement are governed by the law of that place. *Held* also, it being presumed that the common law prevails in that place, and promissory notes not being governed

at common law by the law merchant, that the note in suit is not so governed. *Held* also, that the statute of such State should be pleaded and proved, as courts of this State do not judicially know the law there in force. *Held* also, that the evidence shows no diligence, and no excuse for a failure to use due diligence in proceeding against the maker necessary to bind the endorser of a note not payable in bank. *Patterson* v. *Carrell*, 60 Ind. 128.

585. It is no defence to a suit against the maker of a negotiable promissory note by a National bank, which has discounted the note for an endorser, that since the commencement of the suit the endorser has paid the bank and taken up the note, and taken an assignment of the suit, and is prosecuting it for his own benefit. Such bank has power to free itself from litigation, and realize its money on a protested note by such an arrangement. Where there is no evidence of fraud or oppression, or any corrupt or improper motive, the owner of endorsed negotiable paper may maintain suit upon it against prior parties in the name of any person or party, capable of giving the defendant a discharge, who will consent to the use of his name for that purpose. It is not essential that a suit upon such paper should be brought or prosecuted in the name of one who has a personal interest in the enforcement of the promise. While the right of the defendant to assert such legal and equitable defences in a suit brought in the name of a nominal plaintiff, as he could maintain were the suit in the name of the real owner, will always be preserved, there being nothing in the case to show that the endorser, or his executor, had he taken up the note at its maturity, could not have maintained an action upon it in his own name. *Held*, that he may lawfully get the benefit of any attachment made by the bank by procuring their consent to the prosecution of the suit in the name of the bank. *Ticonic Bank* v. *Bagley*, 68 Me. 249.

586. Under our Statute the title to a promissory note, whether payable to order or assigns or not, is transferred by endorsement; but the title to a promissory note payable to bearer is vested in each succesive holder by the original promise of the maker to the bearer, and not by the assignment of the promise, Section 2228 of the Code of 1871 construed, which provides that "all promissory notes, and other writings for the payment of money or any other thing, may be assigned by indorsement, whether the same be payable to order or assigns or not; * * * and in all actions on any such assigned promissory note, bill of exchange, or other writing for the payment of money or other thing, the defendant shall be allowed the benefit of all want of lawful consideration, failure of consideration, payments, discounts, and sets-off made, had, or possessed against the same previous to notice of assign-

ment, in the same manner as though the suit had been brought by the obligee or payee." *Held*, (1) that the above statute applies as well to indorsements in blank as to special indorsements; (2) that it refers to assignments made in the due course of business, for value, and before maturity; (3) that it only changes law merchant so far as to allow the the promissee to make any defenses existing before notice of assignment against a remote holder, by indorsement, before maturity, which he could have made against the payee. *Etheridge* v. *Gallagher*, 55 Miss. 458.

587. E. and wife sold a lot to C., and took in payment a promissory note payable to their order, which was transferred by endorsement in blank to W. F. E., and by him transferred for value, after due, to G. A bill was filed by G. to subject the lot sold by E. and wife to C. to the payment of the note held by him, E. and wife filed a cross-bill, alleging that the consideration for which the note was transferred to W. F. E. had failed, and the latter was insolvent, claiming that E. and wife had a superior right to the note, and that the lot should be sold for their benefit. G. demurred to the cross-bill for want of equity, and his demurrer was sustained by the Court. *Held*, that the action of the Court was correct. *Etheridge* v. *Gallagher*, 55 Miss. 458.

588. Our Statute requires those in an action on a promissory note or bill of exchange all the parties thereto resident in the State shall be sued together. If it appears on the face of the declaration that any such party is omitted in the action, the omission may be taken advantage of by demurrer; but if not, it can only be taken advantage of by a plea in abatement. In an action upon a promissory note or bill of exchange, it is too late after trial to object, for the first time, that all the parties were not sued in the same action. *Id*.

589. The defendants were the banker of both the plaintiffs and one E. and E. having given a note payable to the plaintiff at the defendants' bank, the plaintiff, about two weeks before its maturity, left it with the defendants for collection, and to be protested if not paid. On December 4th, the day of its maturity, the ledger keeper debited E.'s account and credited the plaintiff's with the amount of the note, and on the plaintiff calling at the bank next morning, he received his pass-book with an entry crediting him with the amount of the note. Subsequently the manager, on the ground that the entry had been made by the clerk by mistake and without authority—as E.'s account was then overdrawn—caused the entry to be reversed, and refused to pay plaintiff the amount of it. E. stated that he always gave authority to pay each particular note, which he did not do here; and the manager stated that without such authority it was not the custom of the bank to pay any note.

Held, that the plaintiff was entitled to recover the amount of the note from the bank. That by the general law the plaintiff by making the note payable at defendants' bank, authorized them to pay it; and that the act of the ledger keeper in charging it to E.'s account and crediting it to the plaintiff in his account and pass-book, amounted to a payment of the note, and was irrevocable. *Nightingale* v. *City Bank*, 26 Upper Canada Com. Pleas, 74.

590. Promissory note, signed " U. S. Manfg. Co., George H. Fox, treasurer." The plaintiff's case depended entirely on the validity of the promissory note, which Fox had assumed to give in the character and capacity of treasurer of the defendant company. Whether he had authority to do so was a vital question. F. was called by the defendant as a witness, and asked him, against the plaintiff's objection, whether or not he had authority to make this note as treasurer of the company. *Held*, that the question was inadmissible. All that could properly be obtained from him were the facts, by which the inference of authority was to be supported or repelled ; and it was for the counsel to argue, and for the jury to find, under the instructions of the Court, whether the facts so given proved that he had the authority, which he denied. The question is fully discussed in *Short Mountain Coal Co.* v. *Hardy*, 114 Mass. 197. The Court *held*, that a declaration of an agent to a third person is inadmissible in behalf of the principal to prove that the person was not also his agent, or to support the agent's declaration.

591. The drawer of a check made payable to the order of the payee, is not bound by a payment thereof by the bank, upon a forged indorsement of the name of the payee; it is bound, before payment, to ascertain the genuineness of the indorsement. *Welsh* v. *Ger. Am. Bank*, 73 N. Y. Ap. 424.

A depositor owes no duty to a bank requiring him to examine his pass-book, or returned checks, with a view to the detection of forgeries in the indorsements. He has a right to assume that the bank, before paying his checks, will ascertain the genuineness of the endorsement. *Id.*

592. A promissory note, made by one of two members of a firm, in the hands of a *bona fide* holder for value, although not made in the partnership business, and although the other partners did not know of the making of the note. The note is presumptive evidence that it is valid business paper, and was given for a debt due from the makers to the payee. *First National Bank* v. *Morgan*, 73 N. Y. Ap. 593.

593. Where a joint and several promissory note is signed by three persons, as makers, to the signature of the last signer, the word " surety " being added, the presumption is that he is surety for the other two ; this presumption, however, is not conclusive. It may be shown that he was in fact surety for only one, and

that the other signer was also surety. *Sales* v. *Sims*, 73 N. Y. Ap. 552.

594. The possessor of negotiable paper has no better, or other title to the proceeds arising from the sale thereof, than to the paper itself, and if he has no title to the latter, he can be compelled to account to the true owner for the proceeds. *Comstock* v. *Hier*, 73 N. Y. Ap. 269.

Testimony that such person was not an agent, because if the inquiry was whether he had an express authority, it was an inquiry concerning an immaterial matter; and if it was whether he had an implied authority, it was an inquiry as to an inference to be drawn by the jury from the facts in the case. *Providence Tool Co.* v. *United States Mfg. Co.* 120 Mass. 35.

595. On the 9th September, 1875, defendant endorsed a promissory note made by S. & C., bearing that date, and payable to him four months after date at the plaintiffs' branch at Ottawa, but without any amount being filled in. On the same day C. deposited it with the plaintiffs, authorizing them to fill it in for the amount of S. & C.'s then due paper, as also for other paper falling due before the 22d October. On the 21st October the plaintiffs filled in the note for $4,835.84, which included defendants' then due paper, a sum of $2,000 coming due on the following day, and $2.94, the amount of the stamps which were there affixed. The stamps so affixed were sufficient to cover double duty, and were obliterated by writing across them the date on which they were so fixed, namely, 21st October, 1875. *Held*, that defendant, by so endorsing the note, authorized plaintiffs, as *bona fide* holders for value, to fill in the amount, and to affix and cancel the requisite stamps in the mode required by law; and that the note then become a completed note, but speaking from its original date, from which the four months would be counted. By 37 Vic., ch. 47, sec. 3, D., it is provided that in case a bank making or becoming the holder of a note not duly stamped, knowing the same, and not immediately affixing and cancelling the proper stamps, within the meaning of 31 Vic., ch. 9, it should not only forfeit a penalty of $500, but be unable to recover on such note, or make it available for any purpose whatever, and that it should be of no effect in law or equity. *Held*, that the stamps here were not properly cancelled; for if affixed as agents of the makers, which the including them in the amount of the note was evidence of, then, under Sec. 4 of 31 Vic., ch. 9, D., the date of the obliteration must accord with that of the note; whereas, if looked upon as subsequent holders, and as affixing double duty, then, under Sec. 12, as substituted by 37 Vic., ch. 47, sec. 2, the initials or name as well as the date are required. *Semble*, that the privileges accorded by the latter part of this substituted, Sec. 12, to holders, who, from error or mistake, do not at the proper time affix the double duty, does not apply to banks &c. *Le Banque Nationale* v. *Sparks*, 27 Upper Canada Com. Pleas, 320.

596. Plaintiff held a note, whereon N. was principal, and defendants and others were sureties. Plaintiff and N. procured defendant W. to sign another note, agreeing at the time that it should not be used except to take up the former note, nor unless all the signers of the former note signed it. W. was induced by this agreement to sign said last mentioned note, which plaintiff well knew, and also knew that the note was to be presented to defendant S. by N., the principal thereon, with W.'s name on it, as an inducement for him to sign it, and that S. was thereby induced to sign; and plaintiff took the note, knowing S. had been so induced to sign, and advanced money thereon to N., instead of taking it in payment of the former note, as agreed. *Held*, that the defendants' relations as sureties, and said agreement, might be shown by parol, and constituted a defence to the note. *Harrington* v. *Wright et al.*, 48 Vt. 427.

597. The Promissory Note declared on was dated July 1, 1869, for $1,000, payable on demand. The evidence at the trial was that the plaintiff lent the defendant $1,000 in July, in 1868 or 1869, and at the same time received from him a note, which, there being no evidence when it was payable, might be presumed to be payable on demand; and that this note had been lost, and could not be produced. This evidence was sufficient, in the absence of evidence that any other note of this amount was ever given by the defendant to the plaintiff, to identify the note in suit, and to warrant the jury in returning a verdict for the plaintiff, and the court in rendering judgment in her favor upon her filing a sufficient bond of indemnity. The assignment of all the payee's right in the note, without any endorsement, did not prevent the maintenance of an action upon the note in the name of the payee. *Tucker* v. *Tucker*, 119 Mass. 79; also, *Clark* v. *Houghton*, 12 Gray, 38; *Goddard* v. *Sawyer*, 9 Allen, 78; *McGregor* v. *McGregory*, 107 Mass. 543; *Nichols* v. *Allen*, 112 Mass. 23. As to assignment, referred to: *Foss* v. *Nutting*, 14 Gray, 484; *Cook* v. *Fellows*, 1 Johns. 143; *Smalley* v. *Wight*, 44 Maine, 442.

598. In an action on a promissory note against the maker, the defence was that the note in suit was signed by the defendants at the request and for the accommodation of the O. R. Co., the payee, and of W. H. and P., the endorsers, who were officers or stockholders of said company, and that the note had been paid by the endorsers. The evidence tended to show that after the note matured G., acting for the endorsers, made an arrangement with the plaintiff corporation, by which he was to give it their note for the same amount; that he gave it such note, signed by W. H. and P., and the note in the s was delivered to him. The principal question at the trial w whether the new note was given in payment of the note in su or merely as a collateral security for it. Upon this issue t court instructed the jury that, as the transaction took place Connecticut, it was to be governed by the law of that Stat that by that law the giving of a promissory note was not p sumed to be in payment of a preexisting debt, and therefo before they could find for the defendant, they must be satisfi that, by the agreement of the parties, the plaintiff received t new note in payment of the note in suit. *Held* also, the plai tiff, having requested an instruction, that the presumption law is that the holder did not intend to accept the note in pa ment, and to discharge the maker of the note in suit, an unless the jury find that a distinct agreement was made accept the note in payment, they cannot find that it was a cepted in payment, and the instruction being given in substan though not in the words requested, that the plaintiff had ground of exception. *Connecticut Trust Co.* v. *Melendy*, 1 Mass. 449.

599. A promissory note, the following being a copy thereo "$2,268.00. Boston, February 1st, 1872. For value receive I promise to pay to Benjamin B. Newhall, or order, $2,268. in one and a half years, or sooner, at the option of the mo gagor, from this date, with interest, to be paid semi-annual at the rate of seven per cent. per annum during said term, a for such further time as said principal sum, or any part there shall remain unpaid. Secured by mortgage of real estate Boston, Mass., stamped as required by U. S. Internal Reven Laws, to be recorded in Suffolk Registry of Deeds. (E dorsed) Waving demand and notice. Benjamin B. Newhal *Held*, that each of the instruments in suit expresses a prom to pay a certain sum of money in a year and a half from date, " or sooner, at the option of the mortgagor," with intere at a certain rate, " during said term." The principal sum is be paid, either at the time specified, or at any earlier time tl the mortgagor may elect. The interest is to be computed o until the note is paid. Both the time of payment of t principal and the amount of interest are uncertain, and depe upon the election of the mortgagor, who would seem, from t memorandum upon the note itself, to be the maker of the no But if he were a third person, it would not aid the plaint In either alternative the contract, not being a promise to pa fixed sum of money at a definite time, lacks the essent quality of a negotiable promissory note, and cannot be sued such. *Way* v. *Smith*, 111 Mass. 523; *Hubbard* v. *Mosely*, Gray, 170; *Story on Notes*, § 22; *Stults* v. *Silva*, 119 Mass. 1

600. *A promissory note* executed by a married woman in t ordinary form, and perfect in its terms, the fact, that in order

make it binding upon her, the addition of other terms not suggested by the paper itself is required, *i. e.*, an expression of an intent to charge here separate estate, does not justify the payee in making such an addition after delivery of the note and without her knowledge and consent; and if so made it is a material alteration which vitiates the instrument. An authority, however, given by the maker to the payee, to add anything to the note which counsel when consulted may suggest to be needful to make the note "right, legal and proper," is sufficient to authorize such an addition as will make the note legal and binding upon her, and it is not material that she is not advised of the precise terms of the addition.   *Taddiken* v. *Cantrell*, 69 N. Y. 597.

601. *A promissory note* made for the accommodation of the payee, but without restriction as to its use, an endorsee taking in good faith as collateral security for an antecedent debt of the payee and endorser, without other consideration, occupies the position of a holder for value, and can recover thereon against the maker. The precedent debt is a sufficient consideration for the tranfer, and no new consideration need be shown. It is only where the note has been diverted from the purpose for which it was intended, by the payee, or where some other equity exists in favor of the maker, that it is necessary that the holder should have parted with value on the faith of the note, in order to enforce the same.   *Grocers' Bank* v. *Penfield*, 69 N. Y. 502.

602. A promissory note made payable "at any bank" in a specified city, proof of presentation at any bank in such city, and due protest and notice, will bind the endorser. The protest of a note payable "at any bank in Savannah, Georgia," showed that the note was presented for payment "at the Southern Bank of the State of Georgia," but did not expressly state that this bank was in the City of Savannah. The caption showed that the protest was in the City of Savannah, Georgia, and the protest cited that the notary resided in that city. After showing demand and refusal of payment, &c., it concludes: "Thus done and protested in the City of Savannah aforesaid." *Held.* (1.) The protest sufficiently showed that the bank, at which demand was made, was located in the City of Savannah. (2.) Parol proof was admissible, in connection with the protest, to show that a bank of the same name as that mentioned in the protest, was located in the City of Savannah, at the date of the note and its protest.   *Boit & M. McKenzie* v. *Corr*, 54 Ala. 112.

603. In an action on a promissory note by the payee against the maker, on the issue of payment, it appeared by an agreement of even date between the parties, that the maker was to transfer to the payee certain shares of stock in a cor-

poration as security for the payment of the note, and, in case of his failure to pay, the payee was to take the stock in full satisfaction; that, before the note became due, the maker executed an instrument purporting to be a transfer of the stock to the payee, and produced a certificate of stock, which stated that the maker was owner of the stock, and that it was only transferable on the books of the corporation; and that these instruments, together with the original agreement, were deposited by mutual consent with a third person. *Held*, that the transfer and certificate were admissible in evidence; that it was competent for the judge, who tried the case without a jury, to find that the third person held the stock; that the transfer conveyed a title between the parties; and that the maker might testify that he had paid for the stock in full. *Brown* v. *Smith*, 122 Mass. 589.

604. A promissory note in the usual form, with interest coupon notes attached, but containing a clause that if default be made in the payment of any instalment of interest when the same becomes due, and such default shall continue for thirty days, then the principal sum shall, at the election of the holder of said note, become due and payable, such election to be made at any time after said thirty days, without notice, is such an obligation as is denominated in law a promissory note. *Sea* v. *Glover*, 1 Bradwell's Ill. App. Rpts. 335.

In construing the contract of guaranty thereon, it is immaterial whether the instrument is technically a promissory note or not. It is an obligation, the performance of which the guarantor had a right to guarantee, and the undertaking of the guarantee is that the maker of the note shall meet his undertaking according to the terms and spirit of the contract, and on a failure so to do the contract of guaranty is broken, and the liability of the guarantor arises. *Id.*

605. The guarantor is liable on his contract when the holder of the note elects to declare the whole sum due by reason of default in payment of interest, even though the principal sum is not due, by the terms of the note. Bringing suit is sufficient notice of the election of the holder of the note to declare the whole sum due. *Id.*

606. This action was upon a promissory note, made and executed by the S. J. W. and endorsed, among others, by defendants, H. & E., for the accommodation of said corporation, and discounted by plaintiff. The defense was that after the indorsers were duly charged the note was paid by the substitution of a renewal note, not indorsed by the defendants, and the payment of the discount, and when the first renewal note became due, the discounting of another note, to take up the first renewal note, which second renewal note was also without the indorsement of the defendants.

The court found, among other things, in substance, that at, about or shortly after the maturity of the note in suit, the maker, by its treasurer, Bean, presented to the plaintiff another note dated September 19, 1872, and in all other respects precisely like said first note, except the indorsement of the defendants E. & H., and requested the plaintiffs to take the same in renewal of said first note. The plaintiffs refused without the indorsement of E. & H. That thereupon Bean left the second note with the plaintiff, together with a sum which would amount to the discount thereon, saying he would procure E. & H. to call at the plaintiff's bank and endorse the same as they had agreed. That thereupon, and solely in anticipation that said endorsements would be made, the plaintiff's book-keeper entered said second note on the books of the plaintiff. That at or about the maturity of the second note, the same not having been endorsed by E. & H., the said iron works by their treasurer, presented the plaintiff another note dated November 21, 1872, and in all other respects precisely like said second note, and requested the plaintiff to take the same in renewal of said first note. This the plaintiff refused to do, unless the endorsements of said E. & H. were procured thereon. Said Bean therefore took said second note and left said third note with the plaintiff, together with a sum which would amount to the discount thereon, saying, he would have said E. & H. call at the plaintiff's bank and endorse the same, alleging some excuse why they had not already done so. That neither E. nor H. ever called or indorsed said note. That said first note has not been paid or renewed, or the payment thereof extended in any manner. That neither said second or third note was discounted by the plaintiff or taken in renewal of said first note. Court of Appeals, Miller, J. This case involves a question whether there was an extension of the time of payment of the note upon which this action was brought, and a suspension of the right of action on the same, by the substitution of a renewal note became due by the discounting of another note to take up the first renewal note, which also was without the endorsement of the defendants, who have appealed. The judge upon the trial found that the first note was not paid or renewed in any manner, and that neither the second nor third note was discounted by the plaintiff or taken in renewal of the first note. I think that these findings are sufficiently supported by the testimony. The proof shows that when the agent of the iron company presented the first renewal note to be discounted, his proposition was declined upon the distinct ground that the note had not the endorsement of H. &. E. The agent then stated that they were to have been on, and said that they would call in and endorse the notes. The same promise was substantially made upon the presentation of the second renewal note, and excuse given why it had not been done. The payment of the discount, it appears, was made upon the same condition, and the facts in connection with the retaining of the possession of the old note tend to establish an agreement that each of the renewal notes were received, and agreed to be discounted only upon the condition stated. The entry on the books of the plaintiffs shows, on its face, that the renewal notes were discounted, and that both the original and the second note were paid, and is a strong circumstance against the conclusion that the renewal notes were received conditionally; but this fact was subject to be, and as the finding of the judge shows, was explained by evidence to the effect that these entries were made by the book-keeper, and it is claimed in anticipation that the agreement would be perfected by the indorsement of the two defendants named. It must be confessed that the testimony is not very satisfactory; but if we allow full credit to explanation given for the entries made, I do not see why it is not sufficient. Such a state of facts might well exist in entire harmony with the theory that no extension of the time of payment was made, and conceding that such was the case, the finding of the judge would be justified. The counsel for appellants claim that the notes were and must have been received upon some agreement, and that this is expressed in the testimony of the cashier, who, in answer to the question put, How the entries came to be made in the book, answered: Because Bean told him that the indorsers would come in, in a day or two, and indorse. This answer should be considered in connection with all that transpired, and, among other things, with the explanation subsequently given to the effect that the entry was made by the book-keeper, as well as the other circumstances. Certainly the testimony referred to was not entirely conclusive, and was for the judge to pass upon in connection with the other evidence upon the trial. Although the circumstances are quite strong to show that the second and third notes were discounted and the previous note taken up, yet there was an explanation of these facts which, if believed, tended very much to support the finding of the judge; and we are not at liberty to disturb the same. *Auburn City National Bank* v. *Hunsiker et al.* 72 N. Y. App. 252.

607. A party authorized to sell property, in the absence of any express limitation of his powers, is authorized to do any act, or to make any declaration in regard to the property found necessary to make a sale, and usually incidental thereto. This action was brought to have three promissory notes, made by plaintiff payable to his own order, and indorsed by him, declared void for usury, to compel a cancellation thereof, and return of certain stock pledged as collateral, and for an injunction, receiver, &c. The notes were delivered by plaintiff to B. & Co., note brokers in the city of New York, of whom plaintiffs had been in the habit of purchasing commercial paper

to a large amount, and to whom he was indebted upon account, to be sold at a discount of 12 per cent., and the avails to be applied upon plaintiff's account. B. & Co. sold the notes to defendant G. at the rates stated. Prior to the execution by plaintiff of any note, and before B. & Co. had received any authority to sell, G. applied to the latter to purchase notes, saying he desired first-class business paper only. B. & Co. said they would have paper of that kind, and mentioned the plaintiff's name. Shortly after they procured a note from plaintiff, with authority to sell at a discount of 12 per cent., and apply the proceeds to his indebtedness to them. B. & Co. sent this note to G., who purchased it at 12 per cent. *Held*, it cannot be successfully contended that the notes in question had an inception before they were passed to G. The indebtedness to B. & Co. would have been a good consideration for them, and had that been merged in them, and they given as evidence of its existence (*Wilkie* v. *Roosevelt*, 3 Johns. Cases. 66), they would have had an inception prior to the taking of them by G. But they were not given for that indebtedness. They were made for just the purpose for which they were used, to be sold at a discount of 12 per centum per annum. The avails of the sale were to be applied on the indebtedness, and thus only was the indebtedness affected by them. That being so, it is plain that they were taken by G. at a usurious discount; and that they are void, unless Ahern is estopped from setting up the usury. An estoppel arises in such cases when the maker of the note, before the sale of it, has declared to the buyer that it is a business note, and the buyer has so acted thereupon as that he will be harmed if the usury is known. Was Ahern brought within that rule? He did not in person make such declarations. It is claimed that B. & Co. were his agents, and that they made such declarations acting as his agents, and with power to make them. We will first see whether they did so represent, and then whether they had authority so to do; or, if not, whether their act in so doing had been adopted and satisfied by Ahern. *Ahern* v. *Goodspeed*, 72 N. Y. App. 108.

608. The trial Court found that B. & Co. made declaration to G., at the time, and of a purport sufficient to bring them within that rule, and that G. acted upon those declarations. It is manifest that he would be pecuniarily harmed if the usury is shown, and the notes declared void therefor. The plaintiff urges, however, that there was no evidence to sustain the finding above mentioned. The testimony that the declarations were made by B. & C. is sufficient to sustain the finding in its substance, so far as the making is concerned. *G. asked of them for first-class business paper. They said they had a good supply.* They opened their book and began to show their business paper. He said he wanted first-class business paper, secured by collaterals. They told him they had just the notes—some of that class of paper—that is, as I read it, first-class business paper, secured by collaterals. He had before that bought paper of them—impliedly business paper. It is shown that it was accompanied by collaterals. They said that they would have some of that—that is, paper of that character; and then mentioned the name of Ahern. They said that they had some of that kind of paper, and told him about the standing of Ahern. All that had been before declared concerning it still attached to it, and made a part of the continuous transaction. It was taken by G., and sold by B. & C., as the note which was the subject of offer by them, and of consideration by him, and of his and their acts and declaration. It was taken in reliance thereon. Though at the hour, or during the day, of the making of a representation as to property offered for sale, the subsequent vendee, then negotiating for it, or the like of it, does not conclude a bargain for it, if he afterwards, as a continuation of the negotiation, becomes a purchaser, the representations are still a part of the *res gestæ*, and bind the maker of them (see per *Holt, C. J., Lyney* v. *Selby*, 2 La. Raym., 118-20; *Wilmot* v. *Hurd*, 11 Wend., 584). As to the other two notes, the testimony of G. is explicit that B. & C. told him, at the time of sale of them, that they were business paper, and the best kind of business paper. From all that is testified to by G., the inference is easy and natural that he would not have taken the notes, had he not believed that they were business paper, and that he so believed, from what was said and took place between B. & C. and him. *Id*.

609. If B. and Co. were agents of Ahern, with authority to make such declarations, and to do such acts concerning the notes, he also is estopped. B. & C. were not the agents of G. He went to their place of business to buy of them what they had to sell, for themselves or others. They did not own these notes. If they had owned them, the notes would have had an inception in their hands, and a different question would have arisen. So they did not sell them as their own. They sold them for a principal, who could be no other than Ahern. They had been his agents in brokerage, or other pecuniary transactions, for some time. It was from such things that his indebtedness to them grew up. They charged him their commission on the sale of these notes to G., and thus he paid them their hire as his agents. His indebtedness was paid by the sale of these notes, and he received and retained a check of B. & Co. for a balance thereafter due to him from the avails of the sale. *Id*.

610. Here arises an interesting question in the case. When B. & Co. made the representation to G., upon which the first note was taken by him, that note was not in existence, nor had Ahern authorized them to sell a note of his to G. or other person. It is said that they were not then his agents, and that

whatever they said at that time could not affect him. It is not needed that there be an express act of ratification, in order to hold the principal. His subsequent assent may be inferred from circumstances, which the law considered tantamount to an express ratification. And the acts of the principal are to be construed liberally in favor of the adoption of the acts of an agent. (*Codwise* v. *Hacker*, 1 Caines R. 526, per Kent, J. p. 540.) It already appears that Ahern knew that the first note made by him was to be sold by B. & Co. He also knew, as his testimony shows, that it was to be sold in pursuance of a prior negotiation at a discount of twelve *per centum per annum*. He knew that the note was not business paper. He had been a large purchaser of paper of B. & C., hence knew their mode of effecting sales of paper. It is to be inferred that he knew that in the purchase of paper, at a greater rate of discount than seven *per centum per annum*, the buyer usually exacted a representation that the paper sold was business paper, so that he might rely upon the fact, if indeed the paper was such, or upon the estoppel if it was not. *Id.*

611. Ahern adopted the results of B. & Co.'s acts and delarations. He received and has kept the fruits of their action with G. It is a fair inference that he falls within the second branch of the principal, which we have above stated, by which a person ratifies the acts of one acting as his agent, without authority at the time. The maxim is, *omnis ratihabitio retrotrahitur et mandata priori acquiparetur*. Every ratification is retrospective, and is equivalent to a prior command. On this ground the plaintiff Ahern is to be held estopped from setting up usury in the first note. On the ground of a prior authority, he is to be estopped from setting up usury in the other two notes. *Id.*

612. Drafts did not specify any place of payment; they were drawn and discounted in Canada. Defendant pleaded usury. *Held*, that the contract was to be governed by the laws of Canada, not of this State, and as by the laws of Canada usury is not a defence, the plea was not sustainable. *Merchants' Bank of Canada* v. *Griswold*, 72 N. Y. Ap. 472.

613. It appears that the plaintiff's intestate, G., and the defendant lent to one J., the owner of a patent right, $5,000, G. contributing $1,000 and the defendant $4,000. J. gave his note therefor to the defendant, payable in four months, and assigned to him the patent right as collateral security; and also gave him an agreement to convey an interest in the patent right for the benefit of himself and G. It is further agreed that they should be jointly interested in the loan, the collateral security and the agreement to convey an interest in the patent in the proportion of one to four. At the same time the defendant gave the note in suit to G. as evidence of his interest in the

loan and security, with the express agreement that it should not be demanded or paid until the defendant should receive payment of the loan to J. At maturity J. did not pay his note, and with the consent of G. the patent right was sold by the defendant at auction to one T. for an amount equal to the sum, with interest, for which it was held as collateral security ; and, at the request of G., the defendant took T.'s note for the amount, with the agreement that the defendant should hold it as the joint property of himself and G., and that a company should be formed to use and work the patent. This was in effect carrying out and executing the agreement previously made, that defendant should not be called upon to pay his note till J.'s note was paid, by substituting for payment in cash an interest to the same amount in the note given by T. This agreement is not inconsistent with terms of the note. It was made when the note was due, after the sale of the collateral security, when G. had the right to enforce the payment, and when the defendant could have paid it from the proceeds of the sale, instead of taking the note of T. It was a mode of payment agreed upon between the parties. *Ward* v. *Winship*, 12 Mass. 480. The agreement had a sufficient consideration in the fact that the defendant took the note instead of cash at G.'s request. A.'s, an additional agreement, was made at the same time, which was part of the foregoing, as to the use the defendant might make of the note, which he held for their joint benefit. And it was agreed that if the defendant would subscribe to the stock of the company, and pay for the same with the note held for their joint benefit, the note in suit might remain, and the defendant should not be called upon to pay it, until the profits of so much of the stock as equitably represented the amount of the note should be sufficient to pay it. Relying on this agreement, the defendant afterwards subscribed to the s'ock, paid for the same with the note of T., instead of demanding a cash payment from T., and he has never received any profits whatever. G. having agreed to this method of payment, his administratrix cannot recover on this note, in violation of his agreement. *Gleason* v. *Saunders*, 121 Mass. 436.

614. In an action on a non-negotiable promissory note made by the defendant to the plaintiff for $4,000, dated the 7th December, 1872, it appeared that the note when made had no stamps, but that afterwards, in July, 1874, the plaintiff showed the note to her attorney, who informed her that it should have been stamped, and told her to affix stamps for the double duty. Through some misunderstanding she affixed only single stamps ; and afterwards, in September, 1874, she sent the note to the attorney, when he, having discovered this, acting as plaintiff's agent, affixed the required double stamps. *Held*, that the plaintiff was not a "subsequent party to the note," or a "holder without becoming a party," within 33 Vic., ch. 13,

sec. 12, so as to have enabled her to have affixed the double duty, and rendered the note valid, although she might have made it valid by affixing, as agent for the maker, stamps for the single day, when the note was delivered to her. *Escott* v. *Escott*, 22 C. P. 305. Adhered to, and *Wolley* v. *Hunton*, 33 U. C. R. 152, dissented from. *Held*, however, under 37 Vic. ch. 47, sec. 2, that the double stamps affixed to the note in September, after the passage of the Act, by the attorney as plaintiff's agent, rendered the note valid, for that the plaintiff then first acquired knowledge within the Act of stamps being necessary, it being found by the learned Judge that her previous omission to affix them was through error and mistake, and without any intention on her part to violate the law. *House* v. *House*, 24 Upper Canada Com. Pleas Rpts. 526.

615. A. and H., a firm doing business in Hamilton, had a draft for $1,200, accepted by B. at Montreal for their accomodation, falling due on the 27th of April. H., in order to obtain funds to meet it on the 26th of April, procured a draft on B. for $600, to be discounted by the plaintiffs, telling them that it would be accepted, and the proceeds of it were placed to the general credit of the firm. This draft was sent to B. for acceptance, and H. on the same day wrote to him, inclosing the firm's check for $1,200 on the Bank of Montreal, to take up the $1,200 draft, and requested him to accept that for $600. On the 27th B. duly paid the draft for $1,200. On the 28th A. and H. had a difference, and A., hearing from H. that the firm were in difficulties, and that he intended using their funds in paying B. and another person, A. thereupon on the 29th drew out on the check of the firm their balance in plaintiffs' bank, consisting of the proceeds of the draft for $600, of which A. knew nothing, and of other moneys, and handed it to their solicitor for the benefit of the creditors generally. Between the 25th and 29th both the debtor and creditor side of the firm's account had been dealt with, and the balance increased in their favor. H. on the 29th, on hearing what A. had done, wrote to B. that in consequence the check sent him could not be paid, and B. then refused to accept the draft. On the 2d of May the firm became insolvent, and an assignee was appointed, to whom the solicitor handed over the moneys deposited with him. The plaintiffs, however, claimed the amount of the $600 draft, contending that it was only discounted on the faith of its being accepted, and that as one of the partners had caused its non-acceptance by his letter to the drawee, there was a failure of consideration, and that they were, therefore, entitled to follow the money in the assignee's hands; but *held*, that they were not so entitled; that the case was the ordinary one of the discount of a draft on the belief that it would be accepted; and that the money formed part of the firm's general assets and passed to the assignee. *Canadian Bank of Commerce* v. *Davidson*, 25 Upper Canada Com. Pleas Rpts. 537.

616. B. Bros. & Co., carrying on business at Morristown and Syracuse in the State of New York, and also at Brockville in Ontario, and on the 11th October, 1872, at Morristown, signed a promissory note for $500 at three months, payable at a bank at Syracuse to the order of C. F., a sleeping member of the firm, who at that time and until after the maturity of the note resided at Brockville. The note was endorsed by C. F., as also, but merely for the accommodation of the firm, by one H. H. and one A. B., both residents of Syracuse. The note so endorsed was handed to J. W. B., one of the firm, who resided at Brockville, and was there negotiated by him with a person named Harding at a rate exceeding 7 per cent., and Harding sold it to the plaintiff, who also resided in Brockville. The note was left by the plaintiff with a banker at Ogdensburg, N. Y., for collection, and at its maturity H. H. came over to Brockville and saw the plaintiff, who agreed to accept in renewal thereof the joint note of H. H., A. B., and the defendant at six months, which was accordingly made and deposited with the Ogdensburg banker, who then gave up the previous note. *Held*, that the note of the 11th October, 1872, although drawn up and made payable in the State of New York, was in fact made and became a binding contract on all the parties thereto, on its being discounted at Brockville, and must therefore be deemed a Canada contract and governed by our laws; and that therefore the law of New York, which made void any note discounted at a higher rate of interest than 7 per cent., or any note in substitution thereof, did not apply. The plaintiff, therefore, having sued defendant on the last named note, *Held*, that he was entitled to recover. *Cloyes* v. *Chapman*, 27 Upper Canada Com. Pleas, 22.

617. When a vendor, who has executed a deed to the land, assigns a note executed for the purchase money to a firm as collateral security for a claim of a smaller amount, it is competent for the surviving partner of the firm, and the administrator of the vendor, he having died in the mean time, to join as plaintiffs in a proceeding to enforce the vendor's lien. *Reynolds Adm'r et al.* v. *West*, 32 Ark. Reps. 244.

618. A. purchased a tract of land, executed his note for the purchase money and received a bond for title. B., at the request of A., paid the note and the vendor executed a deed to A.; at the same time and as a part of the same transaction, A. made his note to B. for the sum so paid and executed a mortgage on the land to secure it. *Held*, that no new lien was created, there was merely a transfer of the original lien, and a change in the form of the security. *Blevins* v. *Rogers*, 32 Ark. R. 258.

619. The grantor of certain real estate, which was conveyed to the grantee in pursuance of a contract made with the grantor by the agent of the grantee, accepted from the agent, in good faith, as genuine, a false and forged mortgage on such real estate, purporting to have been executed by the grantee, to secure a promissory note of the agent for the unpaid balance of the purchase money. Foreclosure of the mortgage having been defeated on the ground of its forgery, though judgment on such note was rendered against the agent, who was insolvent, the grantor brought an action against the grantee, to enforce a lien against said real estate for such purchase-money. *Held*, on demurrer to evidence tending to establish the foregoing facts, that the plaintiff is entitled to the lien. *Fouch* v. *Wilson*, 60 Ind. 64.

620. Where the purchase-money of land is made payable in several instalments evidenced by promissory notes due at different times, the vendor, being the holder of the notes, may enforce his lien against the land when one or more of such notes have become due, for the payment thereof without waiting till all of the notes have matured. *Furr* v. *Morgan*, 55 Miss. 389.

SALES.

621. A pretended sale by an insolvent debtor to one of his creditors, will be set aside on the petition of any other creditor. *Johnson* v. *Mayer*, 30 La. 1203.

622. Where several distinct articles are bought at the same time for different prices, even if of the same general description, so that a warranty of quality would apply to each, the contract is not entire, but is in effect a separate contract for each article sold, and a right of rescission exists as to each article, if the warranty in regard to it is broken. *Young & Conant Mfg. Co.* v. *Waterfield*, 121 Mass. 91.

623. A delivery of goods by the seller to a carrier, pursuant to the directions of the buyer, is a good delivery to the latter. *Wilcox Silver Plate Co.* v. *Green*, 72 N. Y., App. 17.

624. One who buys property with full knowledge that the title to the same is in dispute, is not an innocent purchaser, and hence he acquires no greater rights than his vendors had. *Joseph V. Ledoux, Adm'r* v. *John C. Burton, Mrs. Ledoux, Intervenor*, 30 La. 576.

625. If an animal has at the time of sale patent defects apparent upon casual inspection or any defect known to the buyer, such defect would not usually be covered by a general warranty. *Hurton* v. *Plato*, 3 Colo. 402.

626. Even when it is shown that the expressed consideration of a transfer does not exist, the contract cannot on that account be invalidated, if the transferee proves that there was another legal, and sufficient consideration. *Brown, Adm'r* v. *Brown*, 30 La. 966.

627. Planter, whether before or after his crop is planted, obtains from a banker an advance of money with which to make it, contracting by parol to deliver at warehouse part of cotton crop of equal value, no price or definite quantity being specified, and dies before any cotton is delivered, sale is incomplete and his title to whole crop remains undiverted. *Lewis* v. *Laftey, et al. Adm'rs,* 60 Ga. 559.

628. Note for fertilizers contained stipulation that unless written notice was given on July 1st, failure of consideration should not be pleaded ; plaintiff setting up such failure, without alleging written notice stipulated for, properly stricken. *Pritchard* v. *Johnson & Calhoun,* 60 Ga. 288.

629. Upon an agreement for the sale of goods, and payment therefor with a satisfactory promissory note, the buyer selected the merchandise, had it weighed, marked with his initials, and placed by itself in the store of the vendor, to be removed upon payment for it, or giving an acceptable note for the amount. The buyer did not comply with these terms, and the vendor refused to allow the buyer to take the goods away until he was paid. Several months thereafter the goods were destroyed by fire. *Held,* that there was no such delivery of the goods as to constitute the vendor a bailee for the purchaser. *Safford* v. *McDonough,* 120 Mass.

630. If the vendee in a contract of sale refuses to receive the article sold, the vendor may sell it at private sale ; and on proving that he thus sold it at its full market price, he may recover from the vendee the difference between that price and the price stipulated in the contract of sale. *Succession of Dougart,* 30 La. 264.

631. A. executed to B. a deed of his property in trust (amongst other things), to convert the same into money. B., under the assumed authority of this deed, mortgaged the property. *Held,* that the mortgage was not authorized by the trust for sale, and was only valid to the extent of B.'s beneficial interest (if any) in the premises. *The Edinburgh Life Ins. Co.* v. *Allen,* 18 Grant's Chancery, Ontario, 425.

632. A defendant cannot resist payment of a demand for the price of goods sold and delivered to him, on the ground that the sale was in fraud of the creditors of the seller. Under our statute of frauds, only pre-existing creditors have the right to object to a sale for that reason. As to them, such sale is voidable at their election, but, as to all others, is valid and obligatory. *Gary, Hudson & Co.* v. *Jacobson,* 55 Miss. 204.

633. A warehouseman sold 3,500 bushels of wheat, part of a larger quantity which he had in store, and gave the purchaser a warehouseman's receipt under the statute, acknowledging that he had received from him that quantity of wheat, to be delivered pursuant to his order, to be endorsed on the receipt. The

3,500 bushels were never separated from the other wheat of the seller. *Held*, by the Court of Appeal (Spragge, C. and Morrison and Gwynne J. J. dissenting), that the purchaser had an insurable interest. *Box* v. *The Provincial Ins. Co.* 18 Grant, Ontario, Chancy. 280.

634. Stipulation that fertilizer is sold under the inspection and analysis of Dr. Means, Inspector at Savannah, and the Department of Agriculture at Atlanta, does not preclude the maker from setting up warranty of quality, and urging failure of consideration, etc. *Austin & Ellis, Agents*, v. *Cox et al.*, 60 Ga. 520.

635. Goods were consigned to A. for sale, who made advances upon them to the consignor, and afterwards sold them to B. under a warranty that they were of a certain quality. The goods did not correspond with the warranty, and B. gave notice thereof to the consignor, and, with his consent, rescinded the sale, but gave no notice to A. *Held*, that A. could not maintain an action against B. for the price of the goods. *Robinson* v. *Talbot*, 121 Mass. 513.

636. Except in a case when there is an express agreement in derogation of the general rule, the sale of goods, produce, or merchandise by weight, tale, or measure, is not perfect, and the goods are not at the risk of the buyer, until they have been weighed, counted, or measured. [The purchaser of goods who has paid their price, knowing them to be damaged when he paid for them, is not thereby estopped from suing for a diminution of price, and damages, when it appears that there was an understanding between him and the seller, at the moment of payment, that his right of reclamation were reserved. A vendor who is ignorant of the vices of the things sold, is liable only for the difference, at the time and place of sale, between the actual value of the thing sold and what it would have been worth if sound, and the expenses connected with the sale. *William S. Peterkin* v. *George Martin*, 30 La. 894.

637. The Court has no authority, on the application of the Sheriff, made after the return-day of the execution, to set aside a sale of personal property regularly and fairly made. A sale is a contract to pass rights of property for money, which the buyers pay, or promise to pay, to the seller for the thing bought and sold; and if the Sheriff gives possession of the property sold, before obtaining the full payment therefor, and the bid was settled by the purchaser in good faith, which is not denied, the right of property passes. When the Sheriff, on his own authority, distributes money levied under several executions before the return-day of the writ, he does it at his own risk. His misapplication of the proceeds cannot destroy the validity of a sale otherwise good. *Mackaness* v. *Long*, 85 Penn. St. 158.

638. By the terms of a sale of goods the buyer was to send

for the goods and take them away. This case was before the Court at a previous stage, 118 Mass. 143. The only additional fact proved at the second trial was, that after the defendant was told that the skins were lying in the doorway, they were pointed out to him, and he passed out of the door where they were lying, and said he would send for them. That there was sufficient evidence of delivery has been conceded throughout this controversy; the question being whether, on the facts reported, there was evidence of acceptance within the statute of frauds. It is enough to say that the additional fact does not necessarily show an acceptance, and the presiding judge could not properly have ruled as requested by the plaintiff; and, having found for the defendant, he must necessarily have found that there was "not such an equivocal act of acceptance as would take the case out of the statute." As it was part of the contract that the defendant should send for the skins, the fact that he said he would do so, when he left the store, does not add to the effect of the evidence. *Knight* v. *Mann*, 120 Mass. 219.

SET-OFF.

639. A cause of action founded upon an implied contract may be the subject of a set-off. *Fanson* v. *Linsley*, 20 Kans. 235.

640. A plea of set-off setting up a promise good in parol, by the common law, need not show a compliance with the requisites of the statute of frauds. The statute prescribes a rule of evidence, and not a rule of pleading. *Lehow* v. *Simonton et al.*, 3 Colo. 346.

641. A surviving partner, in an action against himself to recover a debt which he individually incurred, can set-off a claim of the firm against the plaintiff. The set-off must have been a subsisting right in the defendant at the time the action was commenced. *Johnson* v. *Kaiser*, 40 N. J. 286.

642. Any set-off to a promissory note which would have been good between the original parties, may be pleaded against an endorsee who acquires it after maturity. He takes it subject to any right of set-off which the maker had against any prior holder. *Davis* v. *Neligh*, 7 Neb. 78.

643. Set-off to the maker of a promissory note, who was principal, arising after maturity of the note, does not discharge the other maker who was surety. *Strong* v. *Foster*, LXXXIV. 201; 17 C. B. 201 (Eng. Com. Law).

644. When a promissory note, pleaded as a set-off, shows on its face that it was given for a consideration different from the plaintiff's claim, it carries with it no presumption of a settlement of such claim. *Ross* v. *Boswell*, 60 Ind. 235.

645. A claim arising from a bonus paid on a usurious loan, is

the subject of a set-off, and will be barred, if not presented as a set-off, in a suit that offers an opportunity. *Dey* v. *Jackson*, 39 N. J. Law, 535.

646. In an action arising upon contract, any other cause of action arising also upon contract, and existing at the time of the commencement of the action, is a good counterclaim. *Foulks* v. *Rhodes*, 12 Nevada, 225.

647. A note given by A. to B., and not yet due, cannot, in equity, be set off against a note given by B. to A., upon which A. has brought an action for the benefit of C., to whom he assigned it, although C. knew at the time of the assignment that A. was insolvent, and A. was subsequently declared a bankrupt. *Spaulding* v. *Backus*, 122 Mass. 553.

648. A third party, for whose benefit a simple contract has been entered into for a valuable consideration, moving from the promisee, and upon which the third party might maintain an action against the promisor, such third party may, when sued in assumpsit by the promisor, plead by way of set-off the damages arising from the non-performance of the contract made for his benefit, and if he omits to aver in his plea to whom the promise was made, it will be taken to have been made to the party from whom the consideration proceeded. *Lehow* v. *Simonton et al.*, 3 Colo. 346.

649. In the exercise of its equitable jurisdiction this court has power to order one judgment to be set off against another, where the judgment prayed to be set off may be enforced against the person recovering the judgment to be satisfied by the set-off. The doctrine is a purely equitable one, and will be administered in all cases upon such equitable terms as will promote substantial justice. *Brown ads. Hendrickson*, 39 N. J. Law 239.

650. A counter-claim set up by the defendants in an action can only be maintained when it exists in favor of all the defendants against the plaintiffs, and each and every one of them. Where a note is on its face joint or joint and several, it is conceived that evidence to show that one maker is surety for the other is inadmissible at law if the question arises between the creditor and the surety; but evidence to that effect has been received where the question arises between the principal debtor and the sureties. As between the makers of a promissory note and the holders, all are alike liable, all are principals; but as between themselves, their rights depend upon other questions. *Great West. Ins. Co.* v. *Pierce*, 1 Wyoming S. Ct. Rps. 45.

651. W. purchased of A. a claim against B., pending an action by A. upon the claim. B. had previously purchased a claim against A., and had given notice thereof to A. Suit was brought thereon by B. in the name of the assignor, in which W. appeared as adverse claimant of funds in the hands of B.

summoned as trustee. At the time of his purchase of the first claim W. had no knowledge of the claim against A. against judgment for the plaintiff in the first action. B. purchased this claim after action had been brought by A. against him, so that it could not have been used in set-off in that action, the Statute only permitting demands not negotiable to be so used when a party has become the equitable owner thereof and given notice to the plaintiff before the commencement of his action. Gen. St. c. 130, §5. At the time W. made his purchase he had no knowledge that there was any such claim against A. as that of F. and another. *Ames* v. *Bates.* 119 Mass. 397.

652. In an action against the maker, on a promissory note made payable to bearer, the defendant answered, alleging that he had executed the note in suit to A., in consideration of the assignment to him, by A., of several promissory notes executed to the latter by B. for the purchase-money of certain real estate conveyed by A. to B. by warranty deed; and that B. had been evicted from the possession of part of such land by a purchaser of the same at a sale thereof on decree, to satisfy a mortgage thereon existing at the time of such conveyance; that which eviction was a breach of A.'s warranty, and by reason thereof B. had defeated the collection of a portion of such notes for purchase-money, held by the defendant, prior to any notice to him that the note in suit had been transferred by A. to the plaintiff. *Held*, that an instruction to the jury, stating to them that the consideration of the note in suit was different from that alleged, and testified to, by the defendant is erroneous. *Held*, also, that the allegation of an eviction may be established by showing that the grantee was either turned out of possession by, or was placed in such a situation that to avoid expulsion, he yielded up possession to, or purchased of, a stranger having a paramount title. *Held*, also, that if the defendant had received from B., on such notes for purchase-money, an amount equal to the sum paid therefor by him to A. with interest thereon, the plaintiff should recover; but that, there being no evidence on the point, an ambiguous instruction in relation thereto was erroneous. *Black* v. *Duncan*, 60 Ind. 522.

STATUTE OF LIMITATIONS.

653. The parties to a contract may provide by express stipulation for a shorter limitation to actions thereon than that fixed by the general law. *Wilkinson* v. *Nat. F. Ins. Co.* 72 N. Y. App. 499.

654. Letters written by a partner recognizing the existence of a judgment against the firm, after it is barred by the statute of limitations, will not revive the judgment against him, when he was not originally liable by reason of the dissolution of the

firm before the judgment was rendered. *Harford, Thayer & Co.* v. *Street*, 46 Iowa, 594.

655. Where the party against whom a cause of action exists, by fraud or actual fraudulent concealment prevents the party in whose favor it exists from obtaining knowledge of it, the Statute only commences to run from the time the right of action is discovered, or might by the use of diligence have been discovered. *Findley et al.*, v. *Stewart et al.*, 46 Iowa, 655.

656. Fraud which must have been discovered if reasonable diligence had been exercised, not a good reply to the statute of limitation. *Sutton* v. *Dye*, 60 Ga. 449.

657. A motion to set aside a judgment is barred after the lapse of seven years from its redition. *Cauthorn* v. *Harkness*, 60 Ga. 299.

658. The following writing, addressed to the plaintiffs and signed by the defendant, was offered as evidence of an acknowledgment of the debt sued on, to take the case out of the operation of the statute of limitations: "It will suit my convenience to execute my note for the balance due for rent, payable January 1st, 1877." The court rejected it. *Held*, that the court below properly rejected the writing, as it is too vague and indefinite to prove such acknowledgment. *Trustees, etc.* v. *Gilmer*, 55 Miss. 148.

659. If, at the time when a right of action accrues, there is no one in being to assert it, the statute of limitations will not commence to run until there is some one who has power to sue. *Metcalf* v. *Grover*, 55 Miss. 145.

660. Where a demand is necessary to found an action upon, the demand is barred unless made within the period of the statute of limitations, and the right of action is extinguished by the delay. *Palmer* v. *Palmer*, 36 Mich. 487.

661. Upon all demand paper not excepted by Statute Comp. L. 1871, (§§ 7151), from the provisions of the statute of limitations, the time runs from the beginning, without any special demand, and no one can become a *bona fide* purchaser who does not take it within some reasonably short period; to hold otherwise would enable banks to issue certificates of deposit, of any denomination, for circulation as ordinary bank bills, and with like effect. *Tripp* v. *Curtenius*, 36 Mich. 494.

662. It is questioned whether an administrator of the estate of a deceased person can by any acknowledgment, in writing or otherwise, suspend the running of the statute of limitations against the debt of his intestate. Nor can an administrator, by making payments on a demand of over $50, suspend the running of the statute of limitations against such demand. *Clawson* v. *McCune's Adm'r*, 20 Kansas, 337.

663. An indorsement, in the handwriting of the debtor, but not signed by him, of a payment of part of a promissory note, will not prevent the operation of the statute of limitations, if no money or valuable consideration actually passes between the parties, even if the parties, at the time of the indorsement, orally agree that it shall be deemed to be a payment. *Blanchard* v. *Blanchard*, 122 Mass. 558.

664. The failure of an administrator to sue on, or collect, a note due his intestate until it has become barred by the statute of limitations, does not affect the infant distributees of the estate, but they may bring suit on such note, within the time limited by the Statute after they become of legal age. *Pittman* v. *McClellan*, 55 Miss. 299.

665. Action for recovery of one-half of money expended in purchasing material to build house in joint occupancy of two persons, should be brought as soon as money is expended, and if not brought within four years thereafter, is barred. *Guill* v. *Guill*, 60 Ga. 446.

666. A Statute of Limitations of the *loci contractus* cannot be pleaded in bar in a foreign jurisdiction, where both parties were resident in the *loci contractus* during the whole statutory time, so as to make the bar complete there, unless such statute go to the extinction of the right itself, and not to the remedy only. The rule of the common law is that the limitation of actions depends on the law of the forum, and not on the law of the State or county where the contract was made. A statutory bar of one State cannot be pleaded in another, where the bar only affects the remedy of the contract sued on. If the right of action on a contract has been extinguished by a statute of limitations in another State, where the parties reside, the courts of this State will give effect to that statute in any suit brought in this State on such contract. *Perkins* v. *Guy*, 55 Miss. 153.

667. Mistake of fact induced by attorney of opposite party, in matter easy of verification, no ground to vacate agreement based thereon, on bill filed eight years thereafter. *De Gere* v. *Healy & Berry*, 60 Ga. 391.

667½. Bank bills that ceased to circulate as currency prior to June 1st, 1865, came under the limitation act of 1869. That the bank surrendered its charter in 1877, and its assets were then put by a court of equity in the hands of a receiver, did not disengage the bills from the operation of said act. In distributing the assets between creditors and stockholders, the stockholders can insist on excluding the creditors as to all the demands against the corporation which were barred by the Statute of Limitations prior to the surrender of the charter. *Johnston et al.* v. *Talley et al.*, 60 Ga. 540.

668. Generally limitation laws act only upon remedies, and do not extinguish rights. A surety, therefore, is not absolutely discharged because a suit against him would if brought be barred in the courts of this State by section 2917 of the Code. Were he to subject himself to action in a jurisdiction, and be there sued, the limitation laws of the Code would not avail him, though they had fully run in his favor during his previous residence here. Where principal and surety are both residents of Georgia at the execution of the contract, and the principal afterwards removes to another State, the Statute of Limitations is suspended as to him until his return. (Code, § 2929.) If, before the remedy was barred as to the principal, but after it was barred as to the surety, the latter made a new promise in writing at the instance of the creditor, the new promise is binding, though he made it in ignorance of the true limitation law, believing the remedy not barred as to himself, and though the creditor, in like ignorance and under the same belief, told him it was not barred, and thus influenced his action, there being no fraud or abuse of confidence. *Langston, Adm'r,* v. *Aderhold,* 60 Ga. 376.

SECURITY, SURETY AND SURETIES.

669. A surety's right of action against a co-surety does not accrue until he has paid in excess of his proportionate share of liability. *Magruder* v. *Admire et al.*, 4 Mo. Court of Appeals (St. Louis), 133.

670. In an action for contribution by a surety against one of several co-sureties, the measure of defendant's liability is controlled by the number of his co-sureties who remain solvent. *Id.*

671. Contribution, security on official bond who aids principal in breach, not entitled to from co-security. *Scofield* v. *Gaskill et al.*, 60 Ga. 277 ; also, *Healey, Berry & Co.* v. *Scofield*, 60 Ga. 450.

672. In an action upon an undertaking, the law will not increase or enlarge the terms of the undertaking to the prejudice of its signers, nor create a liability against the sureties which they did not intend to incur, and which is not within the express conditions of the bond. *Hays* v. *Closon*, 20 Kansas, 120.

673. Judgment on replevy bond in attachment, motion to set aside by principal, because of fatal defect on face of affidavit, overruled, not bar to similar motion by surety. *Neal* v. *Gordon*, 60 Ga. 112.

674. A surety for a tenant is not released as to rents subsequently accruing, because of a release, or an extension of the time of payment of rent due. *Coe* v. *Cassidy*, 72 N. Y. App. 134.

675. The promise of a surety assuring the payment of the price of a specific lot of goods to be sold to the principal debtor, is not a continuing guarantee, and hence does not cover other goods subsequently sold to the principal. *Bloom & Co.* v. *Kern*, 30 La. 1263.

676. A valid agreement to give time on a promissory note to the principal, will discharge the surety. *Thompson* v. *Bowne*, 39 N. J. Law, 2.

677. Discharge of the principal discharges the known surety. *Paddleford* v. *Thacher*, 48 Vt. 574.

678. A Surety or creditor has a right to have any collaterals the debtor may have pledged to either for the payment of their debt, at any point in the transaction, applied to the payment of the debt. *Price* v. *Tusdell*, 28 N. J. Eq. 200.

679. Under the law of this State the discharge in bankruptcy of the principal on an appeal bond, will not release the surety on that bond from any obligation he incurred by signing the bond. The surety who pays the debt of his principal is subrogated, by mere operation of law, to all the rights of the creditors. No act of subrogation by the creditor in his favor is required. *Serra e Hijo* v. *Hoffman & Co.*, 30 La. 67.

680. The general rule, that a contract void as to principal, is void also as to surety, does not apply where a person, *sui juris*, guarantees the obligation of, or becomes surety for, a married woman, minor or other person incapable of contracting. *Hicks* v. *Randolph et al.*, 59 Tenn. 352 (3 Baxter).

681. A surety upon a judgment by confession has the right to expect that the judgment will be entered of record within a reasonable time; and he is released from liability by an agreement between the judgment creditor and his principal that the judgment shall not be recorded, in pursuance of which it is not entered of record until after the lapse of an unreasonable time. *Hancock* v. *Wilson*, 46 Iowa, 352.

682. Sureties in a bond given to secure performance by their principal of future mercantile engagements, and in which no period of limitation of liability is fixed, who have notified the obligees that they will no longer be bound for future transactions, are held discharged from liability for transactions thereafter entered upon, where no change in circumstances by the obligees has occurred on the faith of a longer continuance of the suretyship, and they are not prejudiced by such withdrawal. *Jeudevine* v. *Rose*, 36 Mich. 54.

683. In a suit by a bank against a late cashier and the sureties on his official bond, upon the death of the cashier insolvent, the cause will proceed against the sureties, though no administrator of the cashier may have been appointed and made a party defendant. *Farmers' and Mechanics Bank* v. *Polk et al.*, 1 Del. Chancery, 167.

684. Proof of debt in bankrupt court by judgment creditor discharges lien, and endorser is discharged to extent of injury

thereby received. Evidence of older liens sufficient to exhaust all of principal's property, admissible to show that no injury was thereby done to endorser, and if such be the fact, he is not discharged. Surety assenting to application of proceeds of property of principal to junior liens, receiving part himself, not discharged. Nor is endorser discharged, who was also counsel for principal in obstructing collection of debts, by acts which grew out of litigation conducted by such counsel. *Jones* v. *Hawkins*, 60 Ga. 52.

685. In an action by the payee against the estate of a deceased co-surety on a promissory note, the administrator set up as a defence that his decedent's co-surety, within the time necessary for service of process, after the maturity of such note, had executed an assignment for the benefit of his creditors, providing therein that the assignee should complete his trust within three years, to which assignment the plaintiff had assented. *Held*, that such assent and assignment would have been no bar to an action on such note, against such insolvent surety, within three years. *Held* also, that such assent was not necessary to the validity of such assignment. *Held* also, that such assent not having injured the decedent, did not release his estate. *Paul* v. *Logansport Nat. Bank*, 60 Ind. 199.

686. A surety has the right to stand upon the *very terms* of his contract; and if such contract be altered or varied in any material point without his consent, so as to constitute a new agreement varying substantially from the original, he is no longer bound. Any subsequent addition to or deviation from the contract, is such an alteration as will discharge the surety. But if by the terms of the original contract, additions to, or alterations in the work is provided for, or left to the judgment and discretion of the other contracting party, either without limit or within certain limits, then the variation, if within the limits prescribed, is allowed by the contract itself, and the surety cannot complain of a variation which he has agreed to by the original contract. *Wehr* v. *German Lutheran and Ev. Congregation of Baltimore*, 47 Md. 177.

687. When a judgment is rendered against principal and surety, in which the relations of principal and surety are properly certified, the surety cannot thereafter obtain an injunction to stay the levy of an execution upon his property, on the ground that prior to the judgment the creditor agreed with the principal, in consideration of the latter's withdrawing his answer, that he would not attempt to collect the judgment from the principal until he had exhausted the surety's property, nor on the ground that the creditor had delayed issuing execution on the judgment until the principal, who had personal property sufficient to satisfy the judgment, had become insolvent. *Fox* v. *Hudson*, 20 Kansas, 246.

688. When negotiable notes, payable to bearer, are deposited as collateral security for a debt, the creditor is not a mere mortgagee, or lien holder, who, in case of the death of his debtor, must prove up such debt in the Probate Court. He may, after his debt is due, collect and apply the proceeds to his debt. If such notes are uncollectable, and the creditor be driven to treat them as mere personal property pledged to secure the debt, and to invoke the aid of the courts to realize upon the security, then the matter might come within the reach of the Probate laws, and the creditor be compelled to prove his claim, and the securities be administered under the Probate laws. An answer resisting a suit for the possession of negotiable notes in possession of defendant, on the ground that they are held as collateral security, should show the amount of the debt secured by them. *Huyler* v. *Dahoney*, 48 Texas, 234.

689. A person indebted by bond, paid a balance due upon it in notes of an insolvent bank, which was not known, at the time, to have stopped payment. *Held*, not to be a discharge in equity of the debt, but that the creditor might recover the balance due before such payment. *Jefferson et al.* v. *Holland*, 1 Del. Chancery, 116.

690. If the maker of a promissory note, as collateral security for its payment, assigns personal property to the payee, and, as additional security, third persons sign the note as sureties, the liability of the sureties becomes fixed at the time the collateral security is exhausted. *Dussol* v. *Bruguiere*, 50 Cal. 456.

691. The liability of sureties on a promissory note is not discharged by the Statute of Limitations until four years after their liability becomes fixed. *Id*.

692. When several persons are sureties, and all but one pay the whole sum for which all became liable, those who pay may maintain a joint action for contribution against the one who failed to pay his proportion, provided they jointly paid the money. *Id*.

693. If one of several sureties dies, his executor may be joined with a part of the sureties in an action against another for a contribution. *Id*.

694. If one of two sureties dies, and his executor pays all the money for which both became liable, without having the claim allowed in the Probate Court, he, as executor, can recover the demand for a contribution from the other surety. *Id*.

695. A settlement in the Probate Court, by the principal, is binding upon the surety, not because he is a party to the suit, but because it is an act his principal is, by law, required to perform, and is within the condition of the bond. Neither the settlement nor decree determines the fact of suretyship; or, if it once existed, that it continued. *Gravett* v. *Malone*, 54 Ala. 19.

696. In an action on a promissory note, payable in bank, against a principal and surety, wherein judgment by default had been rendered against the principal, the surety thereafter answered, alleging that, though requested by the surety to levy on certain personal property belonging to the principal, the plaintiff had caused the Sheriff to hold the execution without levy, and that the principal had thereafter died insolvent. *Held*, on demurrer, that, even if such answer could be made sufficient, it is insufficient for want of an averment that such property was subject to execution, and of a value sufficient to satisfy the same; it being an answer to but part, though pleaded to the whole, of the complaint. *Scott* v. *Shirk*, 60 Ind. 169.

697. Upon principles of equity, a surety, as between himself and his principal, stands upon a different footing, in some respects, from an ordinary creditor. He is entitled to full indemnity against the consequences of the default of the principal, and is, therefore, entitled to call upon him for reimbursement not only of what he may have been obliged to pay in discharge of the obligation for which he was surety; but also of all reasonable expenses legitimately incurred in consequence of such default, or for his own protection. These do not include expenses incurred in defending himself against the just claim of the creditor, nor remote and consequential damages sustained by the surety, such as sacrifices of property for the purpose of meeting his liability, loss of time, injury to business, expenses incurred in seeking to avoid payment, etc. The cases hold that, on the debt becoming due, the surety may go into equity to compel the principal to pay, and the creditor to receive payment; and that he may also, in equity, compel the creditor to proceed against the principal debtor for the collection of his demand, upon giving security and indemnifying the creditor against delay and expenses. *Thompson* v. *Taylor*, 72 N. Y. App. 32.

698. Facts, and not mere conclusions of law, must be stated in pleadings. Thus, in an action against a surety upon a promissory note, where forbearance to the maker is sought to be interposed; it is not sufficient to cover merely that "for good and sufficient consideration" further time was given. The consideration must be stated.

699. The discharge of a surety upon a promissory note, on the ground of forbearance, may, in an action against the surety, be given in evidence under the general issue. *Winne et al.* v. *Col. Sp'g Co.*, 3 Colo. 155.

700. To exonerate a surety from liability upon the ground of forbearance, the extension must be for a time and upon a consideration binding upon the creditor. *Id.*

701. Limitation laws act upon and do not extinguish rights. Hence, surety is not absolutely discharged because

suit against him would be barred in Courts of this State by sec. 2917 of Code. Foreign jurisdiction, if sued there, limitation laws of this State would not avail him. New promises by surety, after bar as to him, but before bar as to principal, though made in ignorance of true limitation law, believing the remedy not barred as to himself, binding in absence of fraud and abuse of confidence on part of creditor. *Langston Adm'rs* v. *Aderhold*, 60 Ga. 376.

702. N. became surety upon a note of L., and the latter executed a mortgage to secure him against loss by reason of his becoming surety; judgment having been obtained upon the note against both L. and N., and the other property of L. being found insufficient to satisfy the judgment, N. directed the Sheriff to levy upon the property covered by his mortgage, which was accordingly sold to satisfy the judgment. *Held*, that the sale was valid and absolute and that N. could not enforce his mortgage against the property. *Exline* v. *Lowery, et al.*, 46 Iowa, 556.

703. **Collateral Security.** Certain sale notes were deposited with defendants as collateral security for the payment of a note, endorsed by the plaintiff for the accommodation of one M., and discounted by defendants for M. The collaterals were of the same value as the principal note, and were to be paid into the bank and applied on the note, so that when they were paid, the note also was to be paid and the plaintiff's liability to cease. After the principal note became due, defendants denied that they held the sale notes as collaterals and refused to give the plaintiff any information as to what had been paid on them; and the plaintiff then paid the note in full, and demanded an assignment of the collaterals, the plaintiff's payment being made by a part payment in cash and his note for the balance which he paid at maturity. *Held*, that the plaintiff could not maintain trover against defendants for the collaterals; for although, under 26 Vic. Ch. 45, Sec. 2, he was entitled to the immediate possession of them, he had not until assignment any property in them vested in him. *Semble*, that the plaintiff's remedy would be by a special action on the case against defendants for not assigning the notes to him after demand duly made. *Held*, however, that plaintiff was entitled to recover as money had and received to his use, the amount paid to defendants on the collaterals, and that the fact of his only paying part of the principal note in cash and giving his note for the balance did not take away his right. *Semble*, also, that his right would not be affected even if the payment on the collaterals were after his payment. *Cornish* v. *Niagara District Bank*, 24 Upper Canada Com. Pleas Rpts. 262.

TENDER.

704. When the vendee of an animal, after discovering its unsoundness, tenders it back to the vendor, who declines to accept it, the vendee may recover the expenses of keeping over such reasonable time as will be necessary to make a fair sale. *Huston* v. *Plato*, 3 Colo. 402.

705. In order to constitute a legal tender, the money must either be produced and shown to the creditor, or its production expressly or impliedly dispensed with. Where, therefore, to prove a tender of a quarter's rent, for which the defendant had distrained, the evidence showed that the tenant, after refusing to pay some charges and costs which the landlord claimed in addition to the rent, said to the landlord "Here is the rent," which he had, and told the landlord he had, in his right hand, in a desk—but did not produce it or show it to the landlord, who said nothing and left the premises: *Held*, that there was no evidence of a tender, or of a dispensation with a tender. Per Gwynne J.—To divert a landlord of his right to distrain, a strict legal tender must be shown. *Matherson* v. *Kelly*, 24 Up. Canada Com. Pleas Rpts. 598.

706. The payee of an ordinary promissory note, which was not payable at bank, placed the same in a sealed envelope, with other papers, and deposited the same in a bank as a "special deposit." By inadvertence the officers of the bank took the note out of the package, and notified the maker of the time of its maturity, not, however, claiming ownership; whereupon the maker, at its maturity, tendered to the cashier the amount due, which he declined to receive, stating that he was instructed not to receive it, whereupon the maker afterward paid the same to the holder, declining to pay the interest after maturity. *Held*, in an action on the note, for such interest, that such tender was invalid, and that the maker was liable for the interest. *Held*, also, that a court of equity can not supply a defect in a tender, and that it is the duty of the debtor to seek the creditor, and pay the debt, at its maturity. *King* v. *Finch*, 60 Ind. 420.

TRUSTS.

707. Where a trustee is authorized to invest in either of two specified modes, and by mistake invests in neither, the measure of his ability is the loss arising from his not having invested in the less beneficial of the authorized modes. *Patterson* v. *Lailey*, 18 Grants Chancery, Ontario, 13.

708. The purchaser of property at trustee's sale, takes it subject to incumbrances, and is not entitled to any abatement in the price by reason of such incumbrances. *Pickett et al.* v. *Merchants' Nat. Bank of Memphis, et al.*, 32 Ark. 346.

709. A purchaser by quit-claim deed before the maturity of the purchase-money notes, or of any of them, will be considered as holding insubordination to the superior title, dependent upon the payment of the purchase-money, and not adversely to it. While that relation existed between the party in possession and the holder of the purchase-money notes, limitation would not run in favor of such possession. A sale by the holder of such superior title (the original vendor) to another, would be a repudiation of such relation, and from which limitation would run. Until such repudiation by one of the parties, and made known to the others, limitation would not run against the notes, or by three, five or ten years possession of the land, so as to defeat the right of the original vendor to recover the land under his superior title. *Roosevelt et al.* v. *Davis*, 49 Texas, 463.

710. It is the duty of a trustee for sale to use all diligence to obtain the best price; and where a trustee sold property at private sale, without previous advertisement, at a price lower than other persons were willing to give, and did not first communicate with these persons, though informed of offers of the higher price made by them to one of the *cestuis que* trust; the trustee was held responsible for the loss. In such a case the absence of any fraudulent motive in the trustee is no defence, nor is evidence of witnesses that the property was worth no more than the trustee obtained for it. The trustee deposed that he had disbelieved the statement of *cestuis que* trust. *Held*, no excuse for not testing the truth of the statement by reference to the parties. *Graham* v. *Yeomans*, 18 Grant's Chancery, Ontario, 238.

711. A trust fund is traceable into whatever character of property it may be converted, and is still impressed with the trust; and the confusion or mixing of the trust estate with the trustee's own property will not prevent the separation of the former from the latter. Where a guardian buys land with the funds of his ward, though not under the direction, or even by authority of the court, and takes the title in his own name, with the addition, "trustee," he cannot as legal owner convey to a subsequent purchaser a good title to such land, "free from embarrassment and reasonable doubt," notwithstanding the guardian may also have an individual interest in the same; but a purchaser with notice would take the title, subject to the right of the ward to pursue the fund into the land and hold it. *Morrison* v. *Kinston*, 55 Miss. 71.

USURY.

712. Usury is a defence personal to the parties to the contract, or their legal representatives, and cannot be set up by an assignee of the mortgagor, when seeking a redemption. *Mc. Guire* v. *Van Pelt*, 55 Ala. 344.

713. An agent's retention of a percentage as compensation for obtaining a loan on mortgage, without the mortgagee's knowledge, does not constitute usury. *Manning* v. *Young*, 28 N. J. Eq. 568.

714. Money paid usuriously may be recovered. The rule is not changed by the present Usury Act. *Brown* v. *McIntosh*. 39 N. J. Law 22.

715. Notes given in 1876, for excess of interest over seven per cent. upon money loaned in 1873, upon a verbal contract to pay 18 per centum per annum, are without a legal consideration, and no recovery can be had thereon. *Jones* v. *Holcombe*, 60 Ga., 665.

716. In an action upon a note valid upon its face, and calling for only legal interest, the burden of proving payment and usury is upon the defendant. *Lathrop* v. *Davenport*, 20 Kansas, 285.

717. One who comes into a Court of Equity for relief against a usurious contract, will be compelled to pay the principal and legal interest; and if the debt is secured by mortgage, it will stand for the debt and legal interest. *Pickett et al.* v. *Merchants' Nat. Bank of Memphis*, 32 Ark. 346.

718. **Building Societies** are virtually exempted from the operations of the Usury Laws. In mortgages taken by a building society for advances to borrowing members, it is not necessary to express in the instrument how much of the interest reserved is a bonus in respect of the sum advanced, and how much for interest. *The Freehold Permanent Building and Saving Society* v. *Choate*, 18 Grant Ontario Chancery, 412.

719. It is not necessary for a party seeking equitable relief from a usurious contract to show that he has tendered legal interest in addition to the principal of his debt. *Morris* v *Miller et al.* 46 Iowa, 84.

720. Usury may not only be pleaded as a defense, but also may be made the basis of original and affirmative relief. *Id.*

721. M. purchased at judicial sale the property of H. Before the time for redemption expired, B. redeemed it, paying $1,485 for the redemption, and then entered into an agreement with H , whereby, upon the payment to him of $2,000, he should convey the property to H. *Held*, that the transaction between B. and H. constituted a loan, and that the loan is usurious. *Wormley* v. *Hamburg et al.*, 46 Iowa, 144.

722. The defense of usury cannot be set up against a negotiable promissory note while in the hands of an innocent indorsee, who purchased the same before maturity. *Gross* v. *Funk*, 20 Kansas, 653.

723. Where, on a loan of money, the borrower agreed to repay, at a certain time, the amount of the money loaned, with

lawful interest, and further agreed, upon default made in such payment, to perfect and surrender to the lender certain shares of stock pledged as collateral security for the loan, *held*, not to be usurious. *Ramsay* v. *Morrison*, 39 N. J. Law, 591.

724. A sale of cotton at a price beyond its real value to one who re-sold for a less price, will not be denounced as an usurious transaction, unless there was a proposition to the seller to borrow, and negotiations terminating in a sale; or a knowledge of the borrower's necessities, and that he was purchasing at an exorbitant price, to relieve himself by a subsequent sale at a less price; or something showing a design on the part of the vendee to borrow and the vendor to loan money, under device of sale, whereby, under guise of excess of price, usurious interest was reserved. If design existed, it is immaterial in what shape it is veiled. *Barr* v. *Collier*, 54 Ala. 39.

725. When a sale is made under a mortgage, whether the contract was usurious, or not, is immaterial in an inquiry as to the validity of the sale; usury affects only the distribution of the proceeds, not the sale itself. If more than legal interest has been extorted by the mortgagee, the Court, in distributing the proceeds, may direct it to be withheld or refused. *Carroll* v. *Kershner*, 47 Md. 262.

726. Under the Act of February 18, 1848 (S. & C. 744), all payments of usurious interest are to be taken as payments on account of the principal; and where the sureties on a negotiable promissory note, given by way of renewal for money previously loaned, have been compelled to sell such note to an endorsee, who purchased the same *bona fide* before due, they may, under the statute, recover from the payee the amount of usury exacted by him from their principal, which they have been so compelled to pay to the holder by reason of the endorsement of the note. *Kock* v. *Block*, 29 Ohio, 565.

727. The right to borrow money within the prescribed limits, and issue certificates therefor, bearing interest, is conferred by the borough law of the State; and the fact that the bond in this case called for eight per cent. interest, did not invalidate it, and it was only void for the excess over the legal rate of interest. *Parkinson* v. *City of Parker*, 85 Penn. St. 313.

728. A confession of judgment, made for the purpose of aiding in the violation of the Usury law, will be regarded, as between the parties to the usurious contract, void as to the amount in excess of the sum the judgment creditor may lawfully recover. *Mullen et al.* v. *Russell et al.* 46 Iowa, 386.

729. A provision in a note requiring the interest to be paid quarterly, and stipulating that the interest, if not paid when due, shall bear interest at the rate of 10 per cent., does not render the contract usurious. *Ragan* v. *Day et al.* 46 Iowa, 239.

730. The Usury Law of 1862 is constitutional, and a contract made in violation of it will not be enforced. *State* v. *Chapman*, 5 Oregon, 432.

730½. The forfeiture of an usurious debt to the School Fund carries with it the security for the payment of the debt, for the reason that the security is an incident of the debt, and is tainted with the usury. *Id.*

731. The knowingly taking or receiving, by a National Bank, of a greater rate of interest than is allowed by the State in which the bank is located, is, under the Act of Congress, usurious, and the bank incurs the forfeiture of the entire interest. The limitation of two years, contained in the Act, applies alone to proceedings for the recovery of the forfeiture provided for, and not to the defense of usury ; the State Courts have jurisdiction of questions arising under the act. *Pickett et al.* v. *Merchants' Nat. Bank of Memphis et al.*, 32 Ark. 346.

732. That although the Code provides the mode and manner in which a defendant may plead usury, its provisions do not in any manner deprive a party of existing remedies for relief against the payment of illegal interest, even though he may have failed to avail himself of the plea. Such being the law, there is no reason why a party may not except to the confirmation of an award on the ground of usury, even though no such defence was made before the arbitrator. *Woods* v. *Matchett*, 47 Md. 390.

733. Where a loan is effected through an agent, the fact that the amount received by the borrower is less than that advanced by the principal, and specified in the note, does not render it usurious, in the absence of proof that the agent acted for the lender in retaining the sum which is deducted from the note. *Wyllis* v. *Ault et al.* 45 Iowa, 46.

734. A separate note, given by the borrower to the agent for his services in negotiating the loan, will not be tainted with usury where the agent acts for the borrower, and not the lender. *Id.*

735. When usurious interest is carried into a general account, and made part of a sum found due on final settlement, for which a note is executed, it taints the entire contract with usury ; and it matters not that the usurious interest was charged with the tacit consent of the debtor in stating monthly accounts, or by a note substituted for one previously executed. *Pickett* v. *Merchants' Nat. Bank*, 32 Ark. 346.

736. R. S., of 1857, c. 45, relating to usury, was unconditionally repealed by St. of 1870, c. 169, which expressly excepted by the general Repealing Act, c. 174, St. 1870. To a promissory note in which is reserved, and on which was received, excessive interest, given May 13, 1857, while R. S. of 1841, c. 69, was in force, and sued upon August 5, 1874, after

the unconditional repeal of R. S. 1857, c. 45, usury is no defence, and the maker of the note can claim no deductions for excessive interest reserved or paid. *Holmes* v. *French*, 68 Me. 525.

737. The plea of usury is personal, and when a third party assumes the payment of a usurious debt, and gives the creditor an assurance of payment, he can neither dispute with the creditor the validity or the amount of the debt. The consideration passing from the debtor to the party undertaking to pay, is presumed to be adequate to sustain the undertaking; but where the amount of the liability is left for future ascertainment, and there are rights and interests reserved that can only be protected by the party who has contracted to pay the debt, or by the debtor himself, the rule is different, and the defence may be interposed by the third party. *Pickett et al.* v. *Merchants' Nat. Bank*, 32 Ark. 346.

738. J. C. who lived in Ohio, executed his single bill in Ohio, payable to P., and pursuant to a former arrangement with S. C., the brother of J C P., took the single bill to Virginia where he and S. C. lived, and there S. C. signed the bill which was a joint and several obligation, as surety for his brother. The single bill did not specify where it was to be paid, and on its face was to bear interest at eight per cent. per annum from date. By the laws of Ohio the interest was lawful, but by the law then in force in Virginia, December, 1858, a greater rate of interest than six per cent. per annum rendered the contract void. S. C. died, the single bill still being unpaid; suit was brought in Hancock County against the administrator of S. C. to recover the amount thereof; the administrator pleaded usury; the case was tried before the court, in lieu of a jury, and judgment rendered for the amount of the single bill, with eight per cent. interest. *Held*, that if the plea of usury could not have availed the principal obligor in the single bill it would not have been of any avail to the surety, as the surety could not attack the validity of the contract, if the principal could not. That the single bill being executed by the principal in Ohio, and the surrounding circumstances showing it was to be paid there, S. C. in signing it in Virginia as surety, ratified it as an Ohio contract. It being an Ohio contract and valid under the usury laws of that State, the surety although he signed it in Virginia, could not avail himself of a plea of usury thereto. *Pugh* v. *Cameron Adm'r*, 11 W. Va. 523.

739. It is a good defence to an action by a payee against the maker of a promissory note made in New York, payable "on demand with interest," that the payee received it as a substitute for a draft there drawn under an oral agreement, with his knowledge, for more than legal interest, and that the note itself was made under an oral agreement that he should receive the same interest upon it as that received in a certain

other note which was usurious, and the latter note is admissible in evidence to show what that rate was. *Stanton* v. *Demervitt*, 122 Mass. 495.

740. The only question submitted upon the hearing was, whether the defence of usury is established. The mortgagor evidently paid a large commission in the negotiation of the loan of $6,000, and it is probable that he paid a large one on the subsequent loan of $8,000; but it does not appear that Mrs. S., the mortgagee, or B., her agent in making the loans, received or had any benefit from those commissions. The proof that she lent the whole of the $8,000. The defence of usury is not established, and there will be a decree for the complainant accordingly. *Spring, Ex.* v. *Reed, et al.*, 28 N. J. Eq. 345.

741. The answering defendants, by their answer, set up the defence of usury, and they insist that the mortgage in suit is so affected thereby that not only is the whole of the interest forfeited, but the bill must be dismissed, because no interest has ever been recoverable on the mortgage, in consequence of the usury, and therefore, there has been no default; and if no default, the principal is not due, and will not be due until the 1st of July, 1878. The mortgage in suit was given to secure the payment of three several and distinct loans by the mortgagee to the mortgagor, H. On the first of these a premium was taken, but none on either of the others. The second and third loans were neither of them usurious. The first was—to that the forfeiture should be confined. *Crippen* v. *Heermance*, 9 Paige 211. No interest is recoverable in respect to the amount of that mortgage, and the interest received by the mortgagee on the $500 premium must, with the premium be deducted. *Bedle* v. *Wardell*, 10 C. E. Gr. 349. Interest is recoverable on the rest of the amount of the principal, that is, on $2,500. According to the bill, no interest has been paid since the 1st of January, 1875, and the complainant elected that the principal should at once become due, by reason of the default. If, in fact, no interest whatever were recoverable on the mortgage, that fact would not relieve the defendants from the consequences of the default. *The default would still exist, notwithstanding* the fact that the interest is not recoverable by suit. The principal of the mortgage, less the amount of the premium is due. *Mahn* v. *Hussey*, 28 N. J. Eq. 546.

742. The defence, which the petitioner asks an opportunity to set up, is usury. She alleges, in her petition, that the mortgages of the complainant were made in New York upon usurious contracts, and that they are therefore, under the law of that State, absolutely void, and should be decreed to be so in this State. In order to entitle her to the relief which she seeks on this petition she must show that she has an equitable and meritorious defence. *Hooner* v. *Corning, ubi subra*. The *defence of usury under existing law of this State is not unconscientious. Conover* v. *Van Mater,* 3 C. E. Gr. 481. *Wagner* v, *Blanchet,* 12 C. E. Gr. 356. The defence which the petitioner asks leave to interpose against the complainant's mortgage is so. She cannot, therefore, have leave to set it up. *Corning* v. *Ludlum,* 28 N. J. Eq. 398.

743. Wren borrowed money at usurious interest and gave a bond for its payment, on which judgment was entered. He was afterwards adjudged a bankrupt, and his land sold by the assignee subject to the judgment. *Held,* that the purchaser could not have the judgment reduced by the amount of the usury. In the distribution of a fund judgment creditors may attack a judgment collaterally for fraud on them, but not because it is a fraud on the debtor. Payment of usury is not necessarily fraudulent as to creditors. Whenever the usurious contract is intended to defraud creditors, or when the circumstances of the debtor are known to be such, that it can be reasonably presumed that this will be the natural effect, creditors have the right to postpone the excess of interest. *Miner's Trust Co. Bank* v. *Roseberry,* 81 Penn. St. 309.

744. Van Auken gave a note to Everett for $3,340, judgment was entered on it; Everett assigned $2,500 of it to Dunning· on affidavit of Van Auken the judgment was opened and he let into a defence. On the trial he offered to prove that Dunning lent him $2,500 in New York at a rate of interest usurious by the laws of that State; that Van Auken procured the assignment of the judgment as collateral security for the loan, it having been paid by the money borrowed from Dunning. *Held,* that this would be a defence, Dunning was entitled to recover the amount lent and legal interest. The offer not being to show that the contract was void for usury by the laws of New York, the presumption was that they were the same as in Pennsylvania, and the contract was to be treated as void only for the excess of interest. *Van Auken* v. *Dunning,* 81 Penn. St. 464.

745. Where a note which is tainted with usury has been transferred to another without notice, and even where the transferee is not proven to have known of the taint, for a valuable consideration without endorsement and without representation as to legality, no warranty against it will be implied, and an action cannot be sustained against him for loss sustained by the purchaser by reason of the defect; a *scienter* is essential to establish an implied warranty as to the validity of the note. A transfer of this kind implies simply a warranty of title and that the note is genuine. The Court *held* the question whether an action will lie for the loss sustained by the plaintiff by reason of the note being usurious, and the recovery of the amount thereof thereby defeated, has never arisen under the precise

circumstances presented in this case, and demands an examination of the principle applicable to the contract entered into upon the sale of paper of this description, and of the authorities bearing upon the subject. The rule is well settled that generally one who transfers paper by delivery only, incurs none of the liabilities which attach to an endorser, for the reason that the irresistible inference is, that if he transfers it and it is received without his indorsement, that such liabilities did not enter into the bargain or the intention of the parties. This rule, however, is not without exception, and the transferrer of notes or bills by delivery warrants the genuineness of the signatures, and that the title is what it purports to be. If the paper is forged the transferee is liable upon the original consideration which has never been extinguished by the sale. So also, it is laid down by that vendor without endorsement warrants that the paper is an implied warranty that the parties to the paper are under no incapacity to contract, as from infancy or marriage or other disability to contract, and the assignment of a bill or note for a valuable consideration raises an implied warranty that the assignor has done nothing, and will do nothing to prevent the assignee from collecting it. The reason given as to forged paper is that it is nothing, and the one who has transferred it has transferred nothing, and is therefore liable. In Webb v. Odell, 49 N. Y. 583, a recovery for the purchase price was upheld where notes were sold for less than their face, upon a representation that they were business papers, when, in fact, they were accommodation notes, and thus usurious and void in the hands of the vendee. The decision is placed upon the ground that the thing sold differed in substance from what the purchaser was led by the vendee to believe he was buying, and the difference was so substantial and essential in its character as to amount to a failure of consideration. The representation that the notes were business paper was an important fact, and hence the decision does not exactly cover a case where the party transferring had no knowledge of the true character of the paper. In *Ross* v. *Terry*, 63 N. Y. 613, the defendant sold a bond and mortgage to the plaintiff, which was usurious and void. The defendant was personally concerned in the making of them, and in the unlawful acts which vitiated them, and it was held that there was an implied warranty of the validity of the securities. In *Luke* v. *Smith*, 7 Abb. N. S. 106, the defendants, who sold a usurious note to the plaintiff, were held liable upon an implied warranty by defendants on the sale of the note, that there was no legal defense to an action upon it, but it appeared that the defendants were privy to the consideration of the note, and the facts and circumstances under which it was given and transferred. In *Hoe* v. *Sanborn*, 21 N. Y. 552, Selden J., lays down the rule "that whenever an article sold has some latent defect, which is known to the seller, and not to the purchaser, the former is liable for this defect if he fails to discover his knowledge on the subject at the time of the sale. There is no precedent and not a single reported case in the books in favor of the doctrine that where a promissory note is infected with usury, and that fact is unknown to the party who transferred it, that is an implied warranty of the validity of the note. To uphold such a doctrine would be an innovation upon a settled principal of law and the establishing of a new and different rule from that which has governed the sale and transfer of this species of property for a long period of time. *Littauer* v. *Goldman*, 72 N. Y. App. 506.

WARRANTY.

746. The 1st section of the Act of Congress of 1870, ch. 59, establishes the legal rate of interest, in the District of Columbia, at six per cent. Sec. 2 permits parties to stipulate in writing for any rate not exceeding 10 per cent. Sec. 3 forfeits the whole interest under any parol contract providing for a greater rate than six per cent, or written contract stipulating for more than 10 per cent. Sec. 4 provides for the recovery of all the interest paid, when more has been exacted than allowed by the act, provided suit to recover the same be brought within one year after such payment.

In an attachment brought, in Maryland, by K. against E., as a non-resident, E., among other pleas pleaded, was that of set-off ; that the plaintiff was indebted to him for money paid the plaintiff on account of usurious interest ; and proved that he had paid the amount of the set-off to the plaintiff, for usurious interest upon loans made in the District of Columbia, where both parties resided. Said payments were made more than one year, but most of them within three years before the plea filed. *Held* (1.) That a prayer offered by the defendant asserting his right to recover the excess above six per cent. paid by him, but failing to submit to the jury to find that the loan was upon a verbal contract only, was bad. (2.) That the right to recover for the illegal interest, being given by the Act of Congress, must be subject to the terms prescribed by that Act, as to the time within which the right must be asserted. (3.) That the sums paid by the defendant in the District of Columbia, more than one year before the account in bar was filed, could not be abated from the plaintiff's claim. *Eastwood* v. *Kennedy*, 44 Md. 563.

747. A warranty of title is implied in a contract of exchange, the same as in a contract of sale. *Patee* v. *Pelton*, 48 Vt. 182.

748. When goods have been sold with a warranty of quality, and those delivered, though inferior to the stipulation, are retained by the vendee, the latter may either pay the price, and have his action for the breach of warranty, or he may *recoup* his damages in the vendor's action for the price. *Smith et al.* v. *Mayer et al.*, 3 Colo. 207.

749. If the goods delivered to the buyer are inferior in quality to that which was warranted by the vendor, the buyer may refuse to accept the goods, and return them; and while in his charge, or possession, he is certainly not liable for injury to the goods, resulting from no want of due care on his part. *Bigger* v. *Bovard*, 20 Kansas, 204.

750. A vendor impliedly warrants goods sold by him, without any opportunity of inspection on the part of the buyer, to be of a merchantable quality, and reasonably fit for the purpose intended; and if, when the goods are delivered to the buyer, they are unmerchantable and unfit for use, the buyer may return them, without unnecessary delay, and rescind the contract. *Id.*

751. Where the evidence showed, without conflict, that a written warranty was given by vendor to vendee, the latter could not recover for the breach of an additional parol warranty. *Shepherd* v. *Gilroy et al.*, 46 Iowa, 193.

INDEX.

Acceptance—To be binding, must in every respect meet and correspond with the offer made......(Ill.) 1

Account Stated—Is presumptive evidence of the balance admitted to be due. May be corrected for fraud or mistake......(N. J.) 2
For a period of two years, with monthly statements being made by the bank during the time......(Ark.) 3

Agency—The general rule with regard to the clerks of an agent......(Canada) 4
Payments received by one knowing the agent to be unauthorized to make them......(N. J.) 5
Where the acts of the agent will bind the principal......(W. Va.) 6
Having special authority to adjust a particular loss, cannot, by virtue thereof, adjust a different loss......(Col.) 7
Employment to sell land need not be in writing; the agent may recover for services rendered under a verbal contract......(Ga.) 8
Money borrowed by the agent on the credit of the principal without his authority, goes into the principal's business without his knowledge.(Vt.) 9
Authority to make a contract for another, is not sufficient to authorize its cancellation or surrender......(N. Y.) 10
One who constitutes another, with full power to manage his mercantile house, and to do all acts appertaining thereto......(La.) 10½
General agent in Canada of a foreign company, must be regarded in the same light as the general agent at the head office......(Canada) 11
When notice to the agent is notice to the principal......(N. J.) 12
Principal is always bound by the acts and neglects of his agent, and the same rule that applies to a private principal applies to a corporation.(Va.) 13
Authority of agent, not coupled with an interest, being revocable, at the pleasure of the principal......(Colo.) 14
Declarations of one acting as the agent of both parties to a contract..(Colo.) 15
When a purchaser of property does not know that he is dealing with an agent of the owner, and has not good reason to know it......(Iowa) 16
Clothed with power to accept bills for his principal......(La.) 17
Payment to have been made to an agent for goods sold and delivered..(Mass.) 18
Purchasing goods at half their value from an agent, whom he knows is acting without authority......(Mo.) 19
Where, without consideration, one entrusts an agent with money to settle a lawsuit between two others, may revoke any time before a settlement is complete......(Ga.) 20
When the agent loans money for his principal on note and mortgage, and pays from time to time to his principal the interest, and finally the whole loan, without authority to buy said note......(La.) 21
Where an agency is continuous, and made up of a long series of transactions of same general character......(N. Y.) 22
Making statements with regard to a note he has for sale, as agent, concerning the purposes for which the same was executed......(Ill.) 23
For the sale of goods, with an interest in the proceeds, is not deprived of the power to sell by the death of the principal......(Me.) 24
An instrument delegating powers, is ordinarily subject to a strict interpretation......(N. Y.) 25
Assignee or trustee cannot speculate with assigned property......(Kan.) 26
R., an agent, sold property to M. for $5,000, reporting to W. but $3,500 as the price it sold for......(Canada) 27
An unendorsed note, left for collection with an agent, who, without the knowledge or consent of the owner, delivered it for collection to a third person, who collected and retained proceeds......(Ind.) 28
When the purchaser of a bankrupt stock appoints the bankrupt as his agent to sell at same place the stock so bought, and buy other goods to keep up the assortment......(Mass.) 29
Authority to make drafts on principal as may be necessary to purchase lumber, "as my agent"......(N. Y.) 30
Authority to sue for a specific debt......(La.) 31

Assignment—Was made by a firm, authorizing assignee to sell at public or private sale, "unless the indebtedness of the firm can be otherwise settled."......(Kan.) 32
A majority of the creditors of B., an insolvent, signed an agreement with him, by which he was to assign all his property for the benefit of the creditors who signed this agreement......(Penn.) 33
An assignment for the benefit of creditors vests the title forthwith in the assignee, though he is ignorant of the assignment......(Penn.) 34

Attorneys.—A general retainer does not authorize an attorney to settle or adjust claims, or alter contracts....................................(Ark.) 35
In fact, cannot bind his principal as surety, unless specifically authorized.(La.) 36
Stipulation in note for the payment of a certain sum as attorney's fees..(Dakota) 37

Bailment.—The finder of a bank-note as against a bailee without reward, to whom he delivers it to be kept for the finder, has such a possessory interest in the note as entitles him to recover the same of the bailee........(Va.) 38
A man, dressed as a police officer, told the cashier in presence of a watchman of the bank, that he had been directed by the lieutenent of the police to warn him that there were "suspicious characters about".(Penn.) 39
Converting goods on which he has bestowed labor, and acquired a lien thereon..(N. J.) 40
Pledge by bailee of goods left with him for safe-keeping...........(Colo.) 419-420
"Received from H. M. P. one letter envelope, sealed, and said to contain $290," imputes no legal liability of the signor without evidence *aliunde*..(Miss.) 41

Bankers.—Stock assessed under the provisions of the act authorizing the taxation of stockholders of bonds (Chap. 761, Laws of 1866), the assessor must deduct, etc..(N. Y.) 42
Article 13 of the State Constitution, entitled "Banks and Currency," applies to banks of issue, and does not prohibit the Legislature from creating banks of deposit and discount......................................(Kan.) 43
Liabilities of directors and stockholders of insolvent banks..........(Penn.) 44
Stockholders of National banks have legal capacity to sue such corporation for misappropriation of the stockholders' funds, and for other causes..(Wyoming) 45
Money paid to the cashier of a bank for the use and benefit of the bank..(Wyoming) 46
Savings bank's power to discount negotiable notes..................(Kan.) 47
Organized, prior to the amendment of general st. c. § 13, under the provisions of that chapter had no power to purchase or traffic in promissory notes as choses in action ....(Minn.) 48
Private bankers are subject to taxation upon the average amount of deposits..(Kan.) 49
President of a National bank using accommodation paper to pay for capital stock in his bank..(Neb.) 50
Definition of the word "Discount"....................................(Kan.) 50½
Bank can maintain an action in its incorporate name to recover back a tax illegally assessed and collected against its shares of capital stock, though such stock stands in the names of different individual shareholders..(Ill.) 51
When a check is considered paid, although the money is not yet counted by the payee...(Eng.) 52
Country banker receives a check on another country banker..........(Eng.) 53
Bank discounting a note before its maturity, is not chargable with the knowledge of illegality, or want of consideration acquired by one of its directors in other than its official capacity, such director not having acted with the board in making the discount........................(N. J.) 54
Persons who hold stock in pledge, the certificates of which stand on the books of a National bank in the name of the pledgee, are, in contemplation of the National Banking Act, stockholders, and so long as they thus hold the stock in pledge are responsible to the creditors of the bank in proportion to the amount so held....................................(Md.) 55
The preference of Savings banks for moneys deposited, over other creditors of an insolvent bank, only applies to deposits made in the ordinary course of business..(N. Y.) 55½
National banks have corporate power to enter into an agreement with a customer to exchange for him non-registered U. S. bonds for registered bonds...(N. Y.) 56
When president of a bank loans money of the bank to an irresponsible person..(Mich.) 57
When president of a bank permits the drawing of money from the bank without security by a party, in whose business the president is interested..(Mich.) 58
The fact that the money so drawn out by the cashier, and charged on the books to the irresponsible borrower, would not determine the transaction..(Mich.) 59
When the president persuades the cashier not to make koown certain facts to the directors..(Mich.) 60
The effect to be given to the long silence of the directors.........(Mich.) 61
An agent's admission made after the fact, and unconnected with any act of agency..(Mich.) 62
Proof that a person is clerk for another, does not establish his right to receive for his employer payment of demands not shown to have any connection with the business...(Mich.) 63

Deposit of bonds with a National bank, as collateral security for current loans or obligations of over-draft of the depositor to the bank, which bonds were stolen after all such indebtedness had been paid, but the bonds were not withdrawn by the owner........................(Md.) 64
One dealing with a corporation in matters not falling within the purview of its delegated powers......................................(Ala.) 65
When the corporation has not fully completed its corporate character..(Ala.) 66
The accommodation drawer of a bill of exchange, which was discounted by a bank for the acceptor, who procured it to raise money for his own use in that way, the drawee not being aware of this, and not being present or participating in the negotiation..............................(Ala.) 67
When a corporation is duly authorized to do a banking business under the laws of..(Ala.) 68
Dissolution of a partnership with an individual banker, does not relieve the retiring partner from liability for subsequent deposits made, without notice of the dissolution..(N. Y.) 69
The liability is not changed by the fact that the depositor did not know he was a partner...(N. Y.) 70
So also, the alteration of a certificate of deposit in respect to the rate of interest, made after the dissolution, by the continuing partner, but before notice to holder of such dissolution...........'..............(N. Y.) 71
Proof of publication of notice of dissolution in newspaper in the place where the bank was located, unconnected with any evidence that the depositor resided there, or took the paper, is but slight, if any, evidence of notice..(N. Y.) 72
A bank is not liable upon a certificate of deposit until after demand of payment..(N. Y.) 73
When a savings bank is bound by its rules to exercise its best care to prevent fraud, it is not protected by a clause in such rules that a payment to one producing a deposit book shall be deemed good and valid........(N. Y.) 74
A bank which has fraudulently permitted funds on deposit, belonging to a trust estate, to be transferred to the individual account of the trustee...(N. Y.) 75
A National bank agreed, through its cashier, to exchange for a consideration certain U. S. bonds for registered bonds, which the bank neglected to do. The bonds were stolen..(N. Y.) 76
When half of a bank-note is sent in payment, other half to follow, title to note remains in sender...(Eng.) 77
When National banks may take mortgages on real estate............(Mass.) 358

Bills of Exchange—Headed "New England Agency of the Penn. Fire Ins. Co.," have the words "Foster & Cole, General Agents for the New England States" printed in the margin, and appearing on its face to be drawn upon said Co. is the draft of the Co., and not of F. & Co..(Mass.) 78
Drawn for sole accommodation of the payee, and accepted by the drawee for the same purpose, and owing to insolvency of the payees the acceptor was compelled to pay the bill, and he brought suit to recover the amount paid against the drawers.......................................(Ohio) 79
When draft did not specify any place of payment........................ 607
Holder cannot sue for original consideration, where there has been a failure to stamp foreign bill and a delay of a year......................(Eng.) 80
Must be payable at all events, not dependent on any contingency.......(Ill.) 81
An acceptor of a bill of exchange drawn by a purchaser of machinery cannot, by paying the bill before maturity, change the relations of the original parties to it..(Texas) 82
Possession of a draft is presumptive evidence of ownership..........(N. Y.) 83
Habitual payment of a certain party's drafts drawn on him, does not make him liable for such drafts in the absence of an implied or expressed agreement...(La.) 84
Where there is no value or consideration for acceptance, it is a good defence in an action by drawer or person taking under him..............(Eng.) 85
Draft drawn in favor of payee on a certain fund to arise from the sale of property then in drawee's hands..(La.) 86
Draft drawn by A., the creditor, on B., the debtor, in another city, in which debtor was to sell the draft, and remit the proceeds to the creditor in payment of his bill. A. handed the draft to C., his banker at home, who endorsed it to D., or order, for collection. A. and the purchaser of the draft erased C.'s endorsement. See defence...................(Mo.) 87
Bill drawn and endorsed in England, payable abroad, is dishonored by acceptor's non-payment..(Eng.) 88
A promise to accept a future bill of exchange, in consideration of money to be advanced thereon by the promisee..........................(Mo.) 89
Accommodation bill accepted at the request of a third party, who agrees to share any loss..(Eng.) 90
Acceptor, who tears the bill in two parts, with the intention to destroy it, and which the drawer fraudulently joined the pieces, and sold it to an innocent holder...(Eng.) 91
Acceptance of bill by one partner for separate debt, and not in name of the firm..(Canada) 394

Bill of Lading—For goods *not actually* put on board, cannot be signed by the master of a ship as agent. Bills of lading are not negotiable in the same sense in which bills of exchange or promissory notes are............(Md.) 92
Where one of two innocent parties must suffer from the wrongful or tortuous acts of a third party..(Kan.) 93
Are transferable by endorsement..(Me.) 94

Bonds.—The term "bond" implies an instrument under seal. An instrument in form a bond, but containing no seal, voluntarily executed and delivered in lieu of a bond, and accepted therefor, is valid....................(Me.) 95
Married woman cannot bind herself as surety on a bond..............(Ark.) 96
A money bond, issued by a body politic, under authority of law, payable to bearer, has the negotiable quality of ordinary commercial paper, and if, while it is a valid instrument, it reaches the hands of an innocent holder for value before maturity, although his title comes from a thief..(N. J.) 97
A paper, which in the body of it says, "as witness my hand and seal," has the word "seal" affixed to the signature of the maker..............(Va.) 98
Party taking a bond for the future good conduct of an agent already in his employ, must communicate to a surety his knowledge of the past criminal misconduct of such agent.................................(N. J.) 99
Indemnity bond given to an accommodation endorser, conditioned on the payment of certain notes...................................(Penn.) 100
There can be no innocent holder of bonds or paper issued by a municipal corporation without power..................................(Ark.) 101
Municipal bonds although negotiable in form may be void in the hands of an innocent holder..(Ark.) 102

Chattel Mortgages.—A mortgage of a certain described horse, and all other live stock of which the mortgagor may become owner during the year.(Miss.) 103
Defective description; delivery of property to mortgagee...........(Kan.) 104
Mortgage of chattels after condition broken......................(Vt.) 356
Purchaser of a house and the furniture therein immediately leased the same to the vendor..(Mo.) 105
An insufficient description of property mortgaged.............(Canada) 106
Mortgage on stock in store is void as against creditors where the mortgagor by the consent of the mortgagee continue the business.........(Colo.) 107
Note of husband and wife secured by mortgage on wife's furniture, which note was paid by husband who took possession of all the papers, which he afterwards assigned to another..........................(Me.) 108
A chattel mortgage, is in law, a conveyance of the goods and chattels mortgaged..(N. J.) 109
Mortgaged goods in possession of mortgagee....................(Canada) 110
Taking possession before judgment is obtained by other creditors....(N. J.) 111
A mistake or variation in statement in mortgage will not always vitiate the mortgage..(Canada) 112
Bill of sale whereby debtor conveys personal property to his creditor as security..(Vt.) 355
The holder of a chattel mortgage agreed to assign his mortgaged interest to a third party upon conditions subsequent......................(Mass.) 113
When executed it was agreed that the mortgagor might go on and sell stock..(N. J.) 114
Where mortgage disposes of personal property after tender made.....(Vt.) 357

Checks.—A dishonored check need not be protested to bind the maker......(Ind.) 115
A check on a banker is a negotiable instrument...................(Eng.) 116
Check of a firm dishonored, admission of.........................(Ind.) 117
Notice of non-payment of a check. Mere delay in giving notice to the maker does not discharge him from liability....................(Ind.) 118
When a check is considered paid by payee.........................(Eng.) 52
Check may be offered in evidence under the money counts as *prima facie* evidence..(Va.) 119
Rights of a check-holder and of the bank are fixed when the check is presented for payment.......................................(Mo.) 120
Dishonor of a check, action thereon.............................(Ind.) 121
The holder of a check acquires no right of action in equity against the person upon whom it is drawn.................................(Canada.) 122
Giving a check by a debtor to a creditor is generally presumed to be only a provisional or conditional payment.......................(Va.) 123
When drawer is not bound by a payment of check by the bank.....(N. Y.) 589½

Composition Deed signed by R., the holder of a note made by P. and endorsed by L. attaching to his signature "provided this does not release the endorsers in any manner"....................................(Mass.) 124
Agreement of creditors to accept 75 per centum, "provided all merchandize indebtedness accept the same settlement"...................(Mass.) 125
Where one creditor held three notes, two of which he had sold previous to signing the composition....................................(Mass.) 126

INDEX. 153

Agreement to accept ten per centum by a creditor who held a note then due and an account against A., one of the insolvent firm; he also held another note which would not become due until after the time when the ten per cent. should be paid..(Mass.) 127

Contract.—A. directs B. to give credit on the application of C. for such goods as the latter may order, and charge to him, A......................(Mo.) 128
Those only whose release would be a sufficient discharge under a contract have an action thereon ....(Penn.) 129
Note given at time of making a contract to be payable only if the terms of the said contract should not be carried out........................(Mo.) 130
A contract for the delivery of property being entire, the promisee is not bound to receive a part...(Colo.) 131
When one person represents that he owes to the debtor of another a debt of equal amount, substitutes himself in place of the debtor by parol agreement with the creditor..(Ga.) 132
A promise under seal to pay money made voluntary..................(N. J.) 133
A. promises to pay commission to a factor in consideration of certain promises which are not fulfilled.......................................(La.) 134
Signing a written agreement without reading it.....................(Ga.) 135
Written contracts not to be varied by extrinsic and parol evidence...(Mass.) 136
Parol evidence as to the limits of time in a contract must be positive....(Pa.) 137
Written contracts are to be interpreted by the Court..................(Mo.) 138
Contract signed by one party only, and is accepted by the other......(Vt.) 139
Where the time of payment is omitted in the contract................(Vt.) 140
Assignee of a lease without warranty cannot set up a defect in title in defence to an action upon a note given in consideration of the assignment...(Colo.) 141
Contract to transfer a promissory note............................(Ind.) 142
Contract where two parties agree as to what shall be done in case one party fails to perform his part..(Mo.) 143
Application of the rule that forbids the varying of written instruments.(Miss.) 144
In the absence of a stipulation as to the time when an act is contracted to be done...(Texas) 145
Contracts for procuring a sale of real estate, commission thereon....(Penn.) 146
Party may stand by and see work in the erection of a building progress to completion and then for the first time make objections ....(Colo.) 147
To introduce a new term into an executed written contract.........(Penn.) 148
Where the payment of the purchase money is a condition precedent to the delivery of a deed..(Colo.) 149
Contract to answer for the debt of another.........................(Ind.) 150
That in consideration of supplies furnished ....(Ga.) 151
Founded upon mutual and concurrent promises......................(Vt.) 152
What is requisite to a right of action...............................(Me.) 153
The maxim, that "the express mention of one thing implies the exclusion of another"..(Texas) 154
Where a creditor receives a partial payment before any breach of contract, and agrees to look to another source than the promisor..........(Ala.) 155
A contract not under seal, wherein one person makes a promise to another for the benefit of a third.......................................(N. J.) 156
Liquidation and damages..(Wyoming) 157
Property sold on promise of defendants to accept the buyer's draft.....(Ga.) 158
Where a promise has been made upon the faith of which the contract was signed...(Penn.) 159
Parol contract for sale of land...................................(Penn.) 160
Court of equity will not extricate a party from the conseqences of his own acts voluntarily committed to carry out an illegal contract.......(Kan.) 161
The reduction of an agreement to writing, signed by the parties, is not necessary to its perfection as a contract, unless..................(La.) 162
A promise to pay for property purchased, "out of the proceeds of the first cotton ginned"...(Ark.) 163
When a contract has been written by the party to be held liable under it, its terms should be construed favorable to the promisee............(Colo.) 164
An act which is forbidden by a Statute............................(Ark.) 165
One party submits a proposal for a contract to another, and the latter's acceptance of the proposal includes a material modification..........(La.) 166
Two distinct contracts between same parties to be performed at different times..(Mass.) 167
When it appears from the evidence that the interest of parties was to form a written contract...(La.) 168
Where in a contract to deliver a certain thing no time for delivery is fixed..(La.) 169
Where no fiduciary relation exists between the parties, and they are of legal capacity..(Ala.) 170
Where a contract must be held to have been made..................(N. J.) 171
Contract founded on an act which a statute prohibits................(Ala.) 172
Contract having an unlawful or immoral cause......................(La.) 173
A written agreement of a debtor who has borrowed certain bonds, to return bonds of the same description, for the same amount ....(La.) 175

Laws which subsist at the time and place of the making of a contract, and
where it is to be performed................................(Va.) 176
Contract when signed by the use of an English translation of a French name
as Seam for Couture..(Me.) 177

Conveyance.—Where land is by one deed conveyed to two or more persons.(N. J.) 178
Where the grantor in a deed covenants that he was well seized, etc...(Colo.) 179
Insolvent debtor seeking to prefer certain creditors by mortgage.......(Ga.) 180
Voluntary conveyance—husband and wife—creditors of husband....(Kan.) 181
May be sustained as against existing creditors......................(Kan.) 182
Contract for conveyance of real estate...............................(Me.) 183
Sale of all his landed estate by husband to his wife..................(Ga.) 184
Where a new note is taken for an old one a transfer of real estate which
would be fraudulent as to old note may be attached..............(Miss.) 185
A voluntary conveyance from father to son with an intent to defraud his
subsequent creditors..(Me.) 186

Corporations.—Liability of officers and stockholders for a debt contracted by
the corporation...(N. J.) 187
Creditor of a Railway held its note, and as collateral security for the same,
three other notes of the Co., with coupons attached, of a kind regularly
quoted in the market..(Mass.) 188
Stockholders unpaid stock calls—transfers—set-off..................(La.) 189
When stockholders cannot appropriate any part of the Co.'s assets to pay
salaries or any other claim due them from the Co..................(La.) 190
No loss suffered by a stockholder, in consequence of a call authorized by the
charter of a Co. will give rise to a claim for damages ....(La.) 191
Certificate of stock-sale and transfer..................................(La.) 192
A chartered bank adjudicated a bankrupt, members of the board of directors at the time of its suspension cannot buy up claims at a discount
and take full pay from the book assets............................(Ga.) 193
Notice, under the charter of an increase of capital....................(La.) 194
Certificate of stock accompanied by an irrevocable power of attorney..(N. J.) 195
By act of 1872, ch. 325, sec. 59, all the stockholders of a corporation are
severally and individually liable to the creditors of the corporation.(Md.) 196
The president of a Co. is not permitted to create such a relation between
himself and the trust property as will make his own interest antagonistic
to that of his beneficiary..(Mo.) 197
Where a corporation is being defrauded by its officers, and by collusion the
directors refuse to interfere to protect stockholders or to sue, and will
seek redress in the corporate name....... ....(Mo.) 198
When the stockholders have elected a receiver who stands unimpeachable.(La.) 199
A by-law that provides no shares of the stock of the Co. shall be transferred
until the certificate thereof is surrendered as shown to be lost.......(La.) 200
Church corporation, the business of which is enstrusted to a board of trustees,
the president and secretary cannot execute a note binding on the corporation..(Iowa) 201
Authority conferred by said trustees to erect a church building, however,
would carry with it such authority ....(Iowa) 202
Having been recognized in the exercise of its corporate functions by legislative enactments, all inquiry into its original organization is precluded... ....(Colo.) 203
A foreign corporation does not become a domestic one by complying with the
laws of this State...(Colo.) 204

Damages.—Where an examiner of title to real estate gives a certificate of title, he
does not thereby become an indemnitor, but he is liable for any mistake
arising from want of due care..................................(Mo.) 205
Negligence alone is not to be visited with punitive damages, willful misconduct, or that entire want of care which would raise the presumption of
indifference...(Colo.) 206
In an action to recover the price of goods sold, measure of damages...(Colo.) 207
If a party who has contracted to deliver a certain thing at a fixed price
makes a tender of it at the proper time and it is refused...........(La.) 208
Recorder of deeds is liable in damages for a false certificate of research.(Pa.) 209

Debtor and Creditor.—Claims against the estate of decedents, resting on mere
oral testimony..(Penn.) 210
Agreement with one creditor for an advantage to him over other creditors...(N. J.) 211
Non resident debtors..... ....(Colo.) 212
Debtor who is discharged by a deed of composition................(N. J.) 213

Deeds.—In determining dividing lines between tracks of land.............(Pa.) 214
That a deed is ineffectual to convey title as to part of the lands described is
of itself no ground for setting aside the deed................. ...(Colo.) 215

INDEX. 155

Condition in deed, granting land in fee, that intoxicating liquors shall never be manufactured, sold or otherwise disposed of as a beverage, in any place of public resort in or upon the premises granted...........(Colo.) 216
A deed duly recorded is constructive notice of its existence and contents to all persons claiming what is thereby conveyed... ....(Colo.) 217
Delivery and acceptance of a deed ....(La.) 218
By the acceptance of the deed the contract of sale is executed and merged..(La.) 219
Just claim deed—Rights of holder thereof............................(La.) 220
When a third party may sue on deed... ....(N. J.) 221
The date of a deed (admitted to have been delivered) is *prima facie* evidence of the time of its delivery...... ....(Kan.) 222
Description in deeds..(La.) 223
The recitals in a deed as to the consideration.....................(Dakota) 224

Demand.—Where no time is mentioned in a due bill payable in specific property a demand is necessary ....(Colo.) 225
Where one receives from a municipal corporation warrants drawn upon its treasurer, a demand is necessary..........................(Colo.) 226
A mere demand for the payment of the balance of purchase money...(Colo.) 227

Deposits.—In an action against a savings bank, on an account annexed....(Mass.) 228
Responsibility of a safe deposit Co..............................(Penn.) 229
A certificate of deposit payable on the return thereof. ....(Mich.) 230
A depositor in a savings bank, who is also a debtor to the bank as a borrower, when the bank becomes insolvent..............................(Conn.) 231
Where the deposit is less than the debt...........................(Conn.) 232
A savings bank is an agent for the depositors....................(Conn.) 233
A depository may show by parol evidence the money deposited was of certain bank bills..(La.) 236
Special deposit of bonds..(Penn.) 237
Power of bank over its deposits...................................(Ind.) 234
When a bank receives deposits it undertakes to pay the depositor's checks to the holder..(Mo.) 235

Endorsers.—The omission to give an endorser notice of the non-payment..(Mass.) 238
Where the maker of a note furnishes to the second endorser money to pay the note...(N. J.) 239
The endorsee of a negotiable bill or note, in the absence of proof of fraud, is presumed to be the *bona fide* holder for value.................(N. Y.) 240
Notice of protest must be properly directed, stamped, etc......... ....(Ga.) 241
Agreement by endorser with a stranger to give time to the acceptor..(Eng.) 242
Where a stranger to the note endorses the same before delivery.... (Minn.) 243
Where endorsee of a bill of exchange in sets alleges loss in transmission.(Eng.) 244
An endorser of a note, even though it be an accommodation note, is a principal debtor..(U. S.) 245
How an endorser of a note can be changed to a maker...............(Colo.) 246
The payee of a note must endorse it in order to make it negotiable paper, he must be treated as first endorser without regard to the time of his endorsement...(Oregon) 247
Endorser of a note after it falls due is a grantor......................(Cal.) 248
The grantor is entitled to notice..(Cal.) 249
Endorsement without recourse by the one who sells the note...........(Vt.) 250
Endorser of a note, though fixed in his liability by protest, is not entitled as a creditor, to a share of the estate of the maker under an assignment..(Del.) 251
Names of the payees appeared on the back of the note in the usual position of first endorser, about 3 inches from the left end, that of the defendant in the opposite direction about the same distance from the right end...(Penn) 252
Where endorser was induced to sign by fraudulent representations....(Ohio) 464
Note endorsed L. R. receiver................................(Mass.) 479
Endorsement upon a note, that the maker may use the principal after maturity by payment of interest.................. ....(Iowa) 253
Upon failure to pay the interest..................................(Iowa) 254
A person of unsound mind who signs as surety a note given for an antecedent debt..(La.) 255
Two defendants as joint makers, one of whom signed on the face the other on the back...(Ga.) 256
Endorsing, for the maker's accommodation, after which the maker raised the amount of the note by erasing first sum and inserting the larger..(Mass.) 257
When endorser may be declared a guarantor.... ....(Kan.) 530
A joint and several note made by the three defendants to order of plaintiff and another party..(Wyoming) 258
Endorsement of negotiable paper.................................(Kan.) 533
An endorser of a check given with his knowledge in payment of a gambling debt .. ..(Mass.) 259
Endorser of a negotiable note, who takes it discharged of the equities to which it was subject in the hands of payee.........................(Mo.) 260

Transfer of a note secured by mortgage.....................(Mo.) 261
Endorser of a note not held bound by a fraudulent alteration thereof made
  subsequent to his endorsement..............................(Mo.) 262
Although not fraudulently altered the endorser is not liable.........(Mo.) 263
Endorsing for accommodation to a specified amount and continuing to en-
  dorse renewals to same amount.............................(Conn.) 264
Sale of altered note..(Conn.) 265
The rule where one of two innocent parties must suffer by a fraud, he who
  furnished the means for committing the fraud should suffer.....(Conn.) 266
The rule that holds an endorser liable although the note is used in a differ-
  ent manner from that intended..............................(Conn.) 267
Defendant could deny his liability as endorser......................(Conn.) 268
Plaintiff endorsed a note for the accommodation of payee, who obtained the
  note as an accommodation from the maker, which note should be discounted at a certain bank..................................(Conn.) 269
Endorser remote from holder defending for failure of intermediate consideration. Case in judgment....................................(Miss.) 586

Guaranty.—What constitute a valid guaranty..........................(N. H.) 270
The party for whose benefit the guaranty is made, should become insolvent..(N. H.) 271
All promises to answer for the debt or default of a third person must be in
  writing...(Colo.) 272
The language of a guaranty addressed to a factor.....................(La.) 273
A bank discounted the notes of B. for $10,000. C. had deposited with the
  bank for collection a note for $15,000 secured by deed of trust. C. wrote
  the bank that as B. could use some additional cash over the $10,000
  aforesaid that the $15,000 note might be held by the bank as security for
  extra money loaned to B...................................(Mo.) 274
Failure to serve notice of non-payment to guarantor..................(La.) 275
The words "we hereby agree to guaranty the payment to M. H. & Co. for
  any goods which may be purchased of them by A. of Lynn, not however binding ourselves for a larger sum than $500."............(Mass.) 276
A guaranty will be read strongly against the guarantor.............(N. J.) 277
"I guarantee the sum of $500 value in glass shades purchased by my son A.
  from B., terms of purchase to be sixty days from date of invoice, and if
  not paid within 90 days, draft to be drawn on me for the amount."(Mass.) 278
Oral guaranty of the payment of a note of a third person............(Mass.) 279
An agreement to assume at maturity a share of the outstanding notes of R.
  given for his purchase money..............................(Mass.) 280
Upon assigning a bond and mortgage defendant made the following
  guaranty: I hereby covenant that in case of foreclosure and sale of the
  mortgaged premises, if the proceeds of such sale be insufficient to satisfy
  the same, with costs of foreclosure, I will pay the deficiency on demand"...(N. Y.) 281

Interest on mutual accounts...(Vt.) 282
On a note payable on demand..(Ala.) 283
Six per cent. is allowed when no rate is stated.......................(Ill.) 284
When compound interest will not be allowed.........................(N. J.) 285
Rate stated shall be allowed until verdict or default..................(Me.) 286
A promise to pay interest on interest is not illegal....................(Ala.) 287
Ten per centum, stipulated for from due until paid will be allowed until
  maturity and a judgment is obtained thereon............(Ark.) 288, 289, 290
Only legal interest will be allowed when a larger interest is not stipulated.(La.) 291
Mode of computing interest..(Me.) 292
Ten per cent. until maturity and two per cent. per month after cannot be
  treated as a penalty.......................................(Ark.) 293
Loan for two months at two per cent. a month. Same rate allowed after
  due and sale of notes ordered to pay the whole claim.........(Canada) 294
Money paid to a party who receives it believing it his due, when in fact it
  was not..(N. J.) 295
Interest on a judgment is computed up to the time of first payment and the
  payment so made is first applied to pay accrued interest, the surplus
  thereafter, if any, to the principal.........................(Neb.) 296
Where interest is recoverable merely as damages....................(Me.) 297
Only legal interest can be recovered in absence of a written agreement to
  pay more...(La.) 298
Interest payable yearly on a mortgage due near two years after its execution,
  default in payment of interest..............................(N. Y.) 299
Parties agrees to pay a higher rate of interest than is customary in the State
  where he resides..(N. Y.) 300
Banking act 1870, prohibiting a higher rate of interest than 7 per cent.(N. Y.) 301
When commercial paper is discounted in a bank at a greater rate of interest
  than seven per cent.......................................(N. Y.) 302

Liens.—Judgment entered on an assessment note, under provisions of the charter
  of the Peoples' Fire Ins. Co. is not a general judgment or lien.....(Pa.) 303
Where the note or other written obligation of a third person is taken by the
  vendor of real estate......................................(Mo.) 304
A judgment docketed, but not properly indexed......................(Va.) 305

Loans by a non-trader to a trader.................................(Canada) 306

Market Price of a marketable commodity may be determined as well by offers to sell, made by dealers in the ordinary course of business..........(N. Y.) 307

Married Women.—In the case of a purchase by a wife during coverture, the burden is upon her to prove distinctly that she paid for the thing purchased, with funds not furnished by her husband.............. (W. Va.) 308
Under the Laws of 1874, a *femme covert* is no longer *sub protestati viri*, in respect to the acquisition, enjoyment and disposition of real and personal property...(Colo.) 309
Separate estate is presumed in the absence of proof to the contrary....(Ga.) 310
May give a mortgage upon her property to secure the payment of a debt due by her husband...(Md.) 311
Neither embarrassment, nor the actual insolvency of the husband, is any obstacle to transfer by the husband to the wife....................(La.) 312
Married woman impeaching the certificate of the officer taking her acknowledgment...(Texas) 313

Mistake in fact will always be remedied by the courts....................(Md.) 314
A clerical error in entering a consent decree........................(W. Va.) 315
When money is paid under a mutual mistake..........................Texas) 316
Any mistake or misunderstanding between persons conducting a judicial sale..(W. Va.) 317

Money Collected by an officer on legal process as a *custodia legis*........ (Me.) 318

Mortgages.—Tender of the amount due upon a mortgage..................(Me.) 319
Owner of the equity of redemption, has to the day of sale to make payment...(Kan.) 320
Mortgage is not invalidated by a misdescription made by a scrivener.(N. J.) 321
Privy acknowledgement of the wife must be made......................(Texas) 322
A clause giving the mortgagor possession without paying rent....... (Texas) 323
Primarily without any consideration given to secure certain negotiable notes...(La.) 324
A mortgagee who transfers part of the mortgage debt to another....... (La.) 325
An assignee of a mortgage given to secure the payment of a negotiable note...(Mich.) 326
Stipulation in a mortgage for the payment of reasonable attorney's fees in case of suit ....(Dakota) 327
Mortgage is binding between the parties to it whether acknowledged or not..(Ark.) 328
Registry of a judgment against a party will operate as a legal mortgage.(La.) 329
Mortgage executed by a tenant in common............................(Mass.) 330
Given to secure the payment of a pre-existing debt ....(Ala.) 331
Administrator has no power to borrow money upon a mortgage of the real estate of the decedent..(Kan.) 332
Mortgagee of chattels in the absence of an agreement in the mortgage purchases the property at a mortgage sale..........................(Colo.) 333
Rights of mortgagor and of mortgagee..........................(Kan.) 334
An unrecorded mortgage...(Penn.) 335
A collateral agreement between the mortgagor and mortgagee does not affect the assignee of the mortgage.................................(Penn.) 336
Absolute conveyance taking back an agreement to reconvey upon the payment of a certain sum...(Iowa) 337
Purchaser from a mortgagor may recover the land mortgaged, in trespass to try title; against parties holding under a foreclosure sale to which plaintiff was not a party..(Texas) 338
Decree of foreclosure—time of payment.............................(Kan.) 339
A clause in the mortgage fixing the fees of the creditors' attorney of five per cent. in the event of the non-payment of the debt.................(La.) 340
May make a valid mortgage for the payment of money without describing the writing which may be evidence of the debt.....................(Me.) 341
To redeem, after demand of payment a tender must be made..........(Me.) 342
Assignment must be recorded the same as the grants are made........(Me.) 343
Remover of part of property mortgaged to another the remainder being insufficient to pay, on sale, the mortgage debt....................(Kan.) 344
Where fixtures are severed from the realty mortgaged, by the owner.(Kan.) 345
A mortgage to the firm name omitting some of the surnames of the firm...(Miss.) 346
When the mortgagee agrees to pay the note secured by the mortgage and enters into possession of the premises................................(Mo.) 347
Omitting the name of State, County and Township in the description of premises mortgaged...(Mich.) 348
When A. purchased an estate with B.'s money and had it conveyed to his wife, who took it with notice of the same.........................(Mass.) 349
Unauthorized cancellation of record of a mortgage by the clerk or register...(N. J.) 350
Holder of two mortgages on the same parcel of land, entered to foreclose one of them...(Mass.) 351

Mortgage given to secure several negotiable notes, and the notes having been assigned to several different holders..........................(Ga.)	352
Mortgage must clearly indicate the creation of a lien, and specify the debt to secure which it was given...(Ga.)	353
Bill of sale whereby a debtor conveys personal property to his creditor as security...(Vt.)	354
Mortgage of personal property after condition broken..................(Vt.)	355
Where mortgagee disposes of the property after tender made and before hearing that an order for its delivery cannot be made..............(Vt.)	356
When national banks may take real estate mortgages..............(Mass.)	357
Mortgage with a power of sale to B., and afterwards mortgagor conveyed the equity of redemption to C...(Mass.)	358

Negligence.—An assignee of certificates of stock, who leaves the certificates, with the assignments recorded, in the possession of the assignor. ...(Me.) 359
One receiving conveyance of land is bound to exercise ordinary prudence...(Colo.) 360
Employment of a common carrier..(Colo.) 361

Partnership.—One who permits himself to be held out as a partner........(Ark.) 362
Accounts between partners..(Ga.) 363
Where one of two partners has advanced to the firm more money than the other...(Conn.) 364
Commission of profit and loss make special partners ....(Kan.) 365
Where joint signers of a note are commercial partners................(La.) 366
One partner borrowing money representing that it is for the firm for which he gave the firms' note without the knowledge of his partners and used the money for his own use...(N. H.) 367
Real estate held by a commercial firm as partnership assets............(Miss.) 368
Power to dispose of partnership property.......................................(Miss.) 369
Assignment of partnership property for benefit of its creditors..........(La.) 370
Enforcement of individual debts against a firm's assets...............(Me.) 371
Note executed in firm name in liquidation, by an agent of one of the former partners..(La.) 372
Surviving partner may sue for the amount due his late firm ......(Nevada) 373
Loan made by two members of a commercial firm in a matter foreign to the business...(La.) 374
Suit by a creditor of a former firm against the individual members of new firm for itemized account and also on a note of the firm, given in liquidation of the account by one not authorized to sign for the firm....(La.) 375
Exemption from the liability of a general partner under the act of 1874, respecting limited partnerships...(Colo.) 376
Action brought by one partner to have an accounting with his two partners, and to recover a balance due him ....(Kan.) 377
Individual members of a commercial firm may execute a valid note on their individual property in favor of the firm.......................................(La.) 378
Service upon one member of the firm, after dissolution, confers jurisdiction to render a judgment which may be satisfied out of the partnership property..(Iowa) 379
Where all the partners are in a situation to sue out attachments against them respectively..(Ga.) 380
Surviving partner who gives bond under R. S. C. 69, sec. 2, and is afterwards sued upon a note of the firm, is not, therefore, a representative of his deceased partner and as such entitled to testify, etc..................(Me.) 381
Note in renewal of another made by same partner who signed the last, which, itself, was in renewal of a note by a different firm of which signer had been a member..(Ga.) 382
Authority of one partner to bind the others..................................(Iowa) 383
When the partner who signs the note signs his individual name before that of the firm..(Iowa) 384
Creditors of a corporation selected three of their number to act as directors of the Co. and charged with the management of the business....(Penn.) 385
Owner and shipper of property doing business under name of a firm when there is no other connected with him.......................................(N. Y.) 386
Ordinary partnership cannot be held liable for the individual debt of one of its members...(La.) 387
A. claimed that B. was his agent only, and not a partner, although he was to have a portion of the proceeds of their products.................(Penn.) 388
Partners, during the partnership, cannot claim individual exceptions in partnership property when taken under legal process....................(Ala.) 389
Promissory note signed by one partner for his own benefit..........(N. Y.) 589½
Where no other relation exists between the shareholders of a steamboat than that which arises from joint ownership, they are not partners...(Penn.) 390
When one of the partners of a firm may transfer the assets of the partnership in payment of his individual debt.......................(Miss.) 391
Partners and bankers, accounts of individual partners and of firm....(Eng.) 392
In equity only, are the separate creditors of a partner entitled to a preference over the creditors of the partnership.................................(Ia.) 393

Statute of Limitations. Division of losses......................(Canada)	394
Where a partner fraudulently misappropriates the money of his firm..(N. J.)	395
Acceptance of bill by one partner for separate debt, and not in name of firm. Liability of co-partners...............................(Canada)	396
Real estate purchased with firm funds for firm purposes..........(Nevada)	397
Partnership property of insolvent firm when sold to pay firm debts no right of redemption exists..........................Nevada)	398
Non-resident commercial firm make an agreement with two resident firms to purchase certain merchandise......................(La.)	399
Statute of limitations as running against estate of a deceased partner who previous to his death had retired from the firm...............(Ga.)	400
Payments made voluntarily on an unfounded demand or in ignorance of the law...(Penn.)	401
Where the debts are of like nature the imputation of payments........ (La.)	402
Payment made voluntary by the mortgagee of claims against the estate, which was not necessary for his protection...................(Ill.)	403
Partial payments made on a debt past due......................(Ala.)	404
Payments claimed as credits on a debt.......................(Ala.)	405
Payment of a debt by giving several notes and only a part of them are paid..(Cal.)	406
Taking the acceptance of the debtor............................(Mich.)	407
Where some had paid their share in a suit against six joint and several makers of a note......................................(Ga.)	408
Payment by an insurance broker.................................(Me.)	409
Payment of money cannot be made dependent on the performance of a condition by the party to whom it is to be paid...............(Cal.)	410
Legal presumption of payment of a bond, given for the payment of money, does not arise from mere lapse of time....................(W. Va.)	411
Plea of payment before a magistrate and found for defendant......(Ga.)	412
When plaintiff held several notes against the deceased............(Nevada)	413
Made by a debtor without special instructions as to their importation...(La.)	414
Defendant was indebted to plaintiff, first, as he was member of a firm and afterwards individually...............................(Me.)	415
A. sent to do work for C. and A.'s bookkeeper made out a bill for the work, when finished, which was given to B. who demanded the money from C. and received it, etc..................................(Mass.)	416
Pledges.—A bill of sale of goods, absolute in its terms, given to protect the vendee against his liability as security for the vendor.............(Mass.)	417
Factor cannot, generally, pledge the goods of his principal for his own liability..(Mo.)	418
Stock of a corporation which is only transferable on the books of the Co. can be pledged validly by delivery to the creditor of certificate.....(La.)	419
Stock held in a fiduciary capacity, has *prima facie*, no right to pledge it to secure a debt growing out of an independent transaction.........(N. J.)	420
Bailee who pledges goods, left with him for safe keeping and converts the proceeds to his own use..............................(Colo.)	421
The delivery of chattels to another as indemnity for suretyship.......(Colo.)	422
Pledgee of a mortgage of note in whose hands it has been placed to secure a debt due him by the pledgor, sells the property mortgaged to secure the note for a less sum than the amount of the note and immediately sells it for a larger sum....................................(La.)	423
A consignee who has made advances on cotton shipped to him has a right of pledge on it, and its proceeds; for the re-imbursement of those advances..(La.)	424
Pledgee was security on a promissory note, transferred the property to the payee for the discharge of the debt......................(Col.)	425
Pledgee can sell only, and for the purpose of applying proceeds to extinguish the debt......................................(Colo.)	426
Where the subject matter of a pledge is divisable...................(Ark.)	427
Acceptance by the pledgor of the surplus arising from an illegal sale..(Ark.)	428
Waiver of notice of sale...(Ark.)	429
Measure of damages for illegal sale................................(Ark.)	430
Deposit of U. S. 5-20 bonds with a bank for safe keeping and the cashier pledges them.......................................(Mo.)	431
No valid pledge of a mortgage, or vendor's privilege can be made by mere agreement of parties..................................(La.)	432
Authority of pledgor of note-forbearance, etc.....................(Ark.)	433
Where assignee is a trustee for his assignor.......................(Ark.)	434
One to whom a promissory note is pledged as collateral security for a debt..(Ill.)	435
Loan on pledged stock, the assignment of which was forged........(Md.)	436
Pledge of certain Canada Railway bonds as security for a debt......(Canada)	437
Protest may not be in some cases necessary........................(Ind.)	438
Where last endorser is expected by all parties to pay the bill........(Eng.)	439
Notice, to the person named in a will as executor, of the non-payment of a note endorsed by his testator.........................(Mass.)	440

Where endorser dies before the note comes due......................(N. J.) 441
Notice from a deputy Notary Public.............................(La.) 442
Record of the proceedings of a notary public on the protest of a note.(Miss.) 443
Proof of notice of protest in an action against endorser.............(Miss.) 444
Note fell due on 25th July, on which day it was duly presented for payment and protested, but notice of protest was dated on the 26th......(Canada) 445
Two notes payable at any bank in Boston........................(Mass.) 446

Promissory Notes.—Where the endorser offered to give a new note at the maturity of first note..(Mass.) 447
Note made in name of firm by one partner and held by an innocent holder..(Mass.) 448
Possession of a note is *prima facie* evidence that the bank is the owner thereof...(Vt.) 449
Suit against administrator of a deceased joint maker of a note........(N. J.) 450
Note payable in bank endorsed for value before maturity ....(Ind.) 451
Upon demand and refusal of payment of a note on last day of grace....(Ark.) 452
Note of a turnpike company......................................(Cal.) 453
Because a note did not belong to a succession or that the administrator was not qualified to act cannot be used to annul a judgment on said note.(La.) 454
Note endorsed in blank and acquired by the holder before maturity...(La.) 455
Parol evidence of the endorsement of a note ....(Del.) 456
Lost note, which was transferred before its maturity.................(La.) 457
Negotiable securities stolen and afterwards sold by the thief........(N. Y.) 458
Note transferred by its debtor to a bank, in payment of his indebtedness and the bank transferred it to A. its cashier for him to sue on it...(Ohio) 459
Note being transferred before maturity, A. is not subject to any defence of which neither he nor the bank had notice.......................(Ohio) 460
Signer of a note which reads that " we promise *in solido,*" etc..........(La.) 461
To defeat the title of an innocent purchaser to a note, on the ground of inadequacy of the price paid for it............................(Ohio) 462
Municipal corporation has no power to invest its obligations except by act of the legislature..(N. J.) 463
In case of notes, bills, etc., a month is always a calender month......(Tenn.) 464
Innocent holder of a note...(Me.) 465
Where endorser was induced to endorse by fraudulent representation.(Ohio.) 466
Note given for patent-right without the words inserted "Given for a patent rights"..(Vt.) 467
Action by payee of a joint and several note payable on demand against a maker, wherein the maker pleads that he signed as accommodation maker..(Eng.) 468
Note made payable upon a condition which was written below the note on the same piece of paper......................................(N. H.) 469
Agreement by the endorser of a note for a definite extension of time, the maker agreeing to pay a greater rate of interest.............(Neb.) 470, 471
U. S. Stamps on a note..(La.) 472
Note made payable to any person "or order," "or assigns," "or bearer"..(Neb.) 473
Any words in a note from which it appears that the maker intended it to be negotiable will give it a transferable quality...................(Neb.) 474
Note payable to order but has not been endorsed, and which is accidentally burned while in the possession of the payee.....................(Kan.) 475
Where a note framed on a printed blank, was complete at the time it left the party sought to be charged, but was so printed as to give an apparent authority to fill a blank.....................................(Mo.) 476
Note given for the price of a thing which the vendor assumed to sell, but which never had an existence................................(La.) 477
Giving a note for an antecedent debt is not necessarily a payment of it...(Fla.) 478, 479
Note executed in error, for a debt not due by the maker..............(La.) 480
Note though dated in Boston, was actually made in New York......(Mass.) 481
Owner of a note negotiable by endorsement may maintain an action although no endorsement has been made to him........................(Kan.) 482
That an additional rate of interest will be paid "after due" does not vitiate the negotiability of a note..................................(Mass.) 483
Action on a note and mortgage where it is admitted that the plaintiff is the holder of the note......................................(Kan.) 484
Title to negotiable paper cannot be defeated by proof of negligence or want of diligence in enquiring into the title or the equities between the parties thereto..(Mo.) 584
Note of firm made by one partner and disposed of for his own benefit...(N. Y.) 591
Note, endorsed in blank by the payee, in the possession of a third party, who produces it at the trial is *prima facie* evidence that he acquired the same before maturity without notice.........................(Ga.) 486
Note due from resident of Colo. to a resident of Cal. is not subject to taxation in Colo..(Colo.) 487
Where consideration is expressed in a note to be stock in a Railway Co...(Iowa) 488

INDEX.

Note or other written evidence of debt, payable in *current funds*..(La.)	489, 490
Payment by a note of a pre-existing debt must be accompanied by an agreement to accept the same as such payment............................Cal.)	491
Note signed by three persons as makers, one of whom write surety after his name...(N. Y.)	593
Where a widow, who is executrix of the estate of the deceased husband, and the estate is community property, and she gives her note for a debt of her deceased husband, which is outlawed, supposing it was not....(Cal.)	492
Rights of possession of negotiable paper...............................(N. V.)	594
Party purchasing a note from the payee before it is due, but after the payee has executed to the payor a release ....(Cal.)	493
What may be considered an accord and satisfaction and payment of a note..(Cal.)	494
Comtemporaneous written agreement executed by the payee of a note showing a contingency upon which the payment of the note is to depend..(Colo.)	495
As defence in a suit on a note it was claimed that the note was donated to a church on condition that the lot on which it was erected should be conveyed to the church..(Penn.)	496
Two or more notes secured by a single mortgage fall due at different times, shall be paid, etc.......................................(Kan.)	497
President of an Ins. Co. gave a certificate that the Co. had on deposit a certain number of dollars and signed it " H. president and treasurer, local board of trustees"...(Ala.)	498
Negotiable paper which is void in the hands of the payee.........(Ark.)	499
Note given by the widow to a creditor of the deceased husband, who does not take it in payment of the debt.......................(Ala.)	500
Note payable on or before three years from date, is not due until the three years has expired...(Mich.)	501
Note given by one member of a firm in its name, in payment of debts, some of which were contracted before another member came into the firm..(Mass.)	502
Suit on a note transferred to plaintiff as collateral security for money loaned before due..(Ga.)	503
Notes made by the lessee payable to the lessor at different dates were given to and accepted by him in consideration of the surrender of a lease in which it was provided that in case of fire rent should be suspended..(Mass.)	504
A protested draft offered in payment of a debt due to an insolvent bank..(Penn.)	505
Where defendant alleges an alteration.............................(Mass.)	506
The addition of the name of another joint maker to a note without the knowledge or consent of the others......................................(Ia.)	507
Acceptance of a note in payment of a debt........................(Ill.)	508
Where the note and mortgage provide for ten per cent. per annum......(Ia.)	509
One of two partners loaned money to the firm for which he took the firm's note signed by both partners..............................(Vt.)	510
Maker of a note conveys land to the holder, by way of security for its payment, and the holder afterwards sells the note to a third person and the land to another..(Cal.)	511
Omitting to insert the words " given for a patent-right "...............(Vt.)	512
Note received for liquor sold in violation of law.....................(Vt.)	513
The payee of a note being anxious to get it off his hands is not considered suspicious..(Mich.)	514
Note left blank as to the amount but perfect in all other particulars, executed by one as principal and another as surety and entrusted to the former for delivery to payee...(Ind.)	515
Collateral contract to pay a certain sum per month as interest on a note, and the payee soon after sells the note...............................(Eng.)	516
A., being indebted to B., as surety, in order to enable B.'s agent to raise money, and to obtain further time on debt to B. made his note to the agent of B..(Ark.)	517
By mistake a note at two months was dated Jan, 1st, 1854, instead of Jan. 1st, 1855, and across the face was written "due March 4th, 1855 ".(Eng.)	518
Negotiable paper payable at a time certain is dishonored by non-payment at the time..(Mo.)	519
A. and B. enter into partnership, and B. is to furnish $1,000 as his part, which he hands to C. to deliver to A., and A. when he receives it gives C. his note therefor..(Cal.)	520
Where the maker of a non-negotiable note is, at the maturity thereof, bankrupt..(Mo.)	521
Where maker of a note payable to a certain person or bearer, on being enquired of by a third person to whom the payee had offered, after its dishonor to sell it, answered that it was all right................(Ga.)	522
Where it is claimed that the date of a note in suit is a mistake, and the note on its face is payable six months after date.......................(Kan.)	523
When it is claimed the note was fraudulently obtained..............(Kan.)	524
When a person who can read, signs and delivers a negotiable note without knowing it to be such....................................(Ohio)	525

Purchaser of paper is not put upon inquiry by mere knowledge that the payee is engaged in selling liquor....................(Mich.) 526
Maker of note is liable to endorsee before due and for value, if guilty of negligence in the execution thereof....................(Ohio) 527
He who negligently signs, and delivers to another, a printed form of a negotiable note containing blanks, without knowing it.........(Ohio) 528
Petition against several makers of a joint and several note more than 15 years past due....................(Ohio) 529
Note pleaded as a set-off shows on its face that it was for sufficient consideration....................(Ind.) 639
Note in which it is expressed to be for value received payable to B. or bearer. As to maker the note was entirely without consideration and was obtained from him by fraud....................(N. H.) 530
Note given to hinder, delay and defraud the makers' creditors.....(Nevada) 531
When endorser may be declared a guarantor....................(Kan.) 532
Where a note, obtained from the possessor by fraud, has been transferred to a third party....................(Mass.) 533
Good equitable defence by one maker of a note that he was surety for the other....................(Eng.) 534
Endorsement of negotiable paper....................(Kan.) 535
Sale of his stock of goods by an insolvent merchant to his penniless clerk, accepting said clerk's note therefor....................(La.) 536
Limitation of action—partial payment....................(Kan.) 537
Party knowing the signature to a note to be forged, yet acknowledges it as his own....................(Mass.) 538
Note declared upon lost pending action....................(Ga.) 539
Note signed by two, one being surety for the other, with the knowledge of the payee but without any agreement to that effect between payee and surety....................(Eng.) 540
Alteration of the date of a note without consent and to prejudice of maker....................(Ark.) 541
Defence of note payable to bearer that the note had been deposited with third person as collateral security....................(Ga.) 542
Proof that the consideration of a note upon which suit is brought was the unlawful sale of liquor....................(Mich.) 543
Material alteration by the erasure of the word "surety" on a note....(Ia.) 544
Where transfer of title in note without liability....................(La.) 545
Note signed by "George Moore, treasurer of M. F. D. Asso."........(Me.) 546
Endorsement is necessary to pass title by plaintiff in execution........(Ga.) 547
Legal import of a blank endorsement upon a note....................(Colo.) 548
Plea of general issue by a bank against the maker of a note...........(Me.) 549
Assignment and delivery of a note payable to order before maturity, without endorsement....................(Me.) 550
Averment in a complaint on a note, that a certain sum "is due as principal and interest on said note"....................(Ind.) 551
Verbal acknowledgment of, and promise to pay a note made by one of its solidary makers....................(La.) 552
Forbearance to one maker of a note....................(Eng.) 553
Future services as a consideration of note....................(Eng.) 554
Mortgage note of a wife knowingly received by a creditor of the husband....................(La.) 555
Note given creditor to induce him to sign composition..............(Eng.) 556
Note given as collateral security for a debt then created, with notice of no equities....................(Mo.) 557
B. and C. owing D. for which B. gave a note to A., the agent of D. at maturity the note was not paid. A. agreed to assume the original debt and to transfer note to C. on C.'s giving his own note to A......(Mass.) 558
Creditor holding mortgage note of a third person as collateral security.(La.) 559
Note given to one creditor, in fraud of the maker's other creditors....(Mass.) 560
Note entitled to days of grace....................(Ill.) 561
Where the endorser was indebted to maker when he endorsed........(N. J) 562
Note given in consideration of certain criminal proceedings being discontinued....................(La.) 563
Executing a note in the name of another without authority to do so....(La.) 564
Suit on note payable to bearer....................(Ind.) 565
When demand not necessary for payment of a note at place designated in note....................(La.) 566
Unconditional note cannot be changed into conditional one by parol evidence....................(Ga.) 567
Taking note with notice of fraud before endorsement.............. (Eng.) 568
Note given for forbearance to prosecute....................(Eng.) 569
One who takes a stolen negotiable instrument *bona fide* and for value....................(Eng.) 570
Note payable to bearer transferred to plaintiff solely to enable him to bring suit on it....................(Neb.) 571
Negotiable note endorsed and deposited with the bank as collateral security by S. for a loan of half its amount. Sometime after S. sells note to O. and gives him an order for it on the bank....................(Va.) 572
Alteration of a note in any material part....................(Neb.) 573

Note completed and delivered, no alteration thereafter can be made except by consent ....(Neb.)	574
Agreement to pay 18 per cent. interest on a note at the time of its execution is usury..(Neb.)	575
Payee of a negotiable note cannot be held as a maker thereof, although his endorsement was for the purpose of giving it credit..........(Minn.)	576, 577
Any set-off to note which would have been good between the original parties, may be pleaded against an endorsee.............................(Neb.)	637
Set-off to the maker of a note, who was principal, arising after maturity of the note..(Eng.)	638
Note given to Railway Co. to aid in construction of a road between two points named in the note, with proviso that others give their individual notes to a certain amount, but which were never obtained..........(Ia.)	578
Material alteration of a note made by holder............................(Ia.)	579
Surety contracts to pay note, while the guarantor undertakes to pay it upon condition, to alter the note as to make a guarantor a surety........(Ia.)	580
Such alteration without proof to the contrary, will be presumed fraudulent ....(Ia.)	581
Cannot recover right of action by removing the alteration..............(Ia.)	582
Renewal given with understanding that the original note shall be surrendered...(Mo.)	583
Note payable at a bank in another State................................(Ind.)	584
In suit against the maker it is no defence to, that since the commencement of suit the endorser has paid the plaintiff and taken up the note and taken an assignment of the suit......................................(Me.)	585
Under our State the title to a note whether payable to order or assigns or not, is transferable by indorsement.................................(Miss.)	586
Endorser remote from holder defending for failure of intermediate consideration. Case in judgment..(Miss.)	587
Failure to sue all the parties to a note................................(Miss.)	588
Note payable at a bank of both maker and payee, credit given to payee in pass-book, right to revoke..(Canada)	589
Note made by one of two parties in hands of *bona fide* holder........(N. Y.)	592
Joint and several note signed by three persons........................(N. Y.)	593
Possessor of negotiable, no better title to proceeds than to paper.....(N. Y.)	594
Note signed "United States Mf'g. Co., George H. Fox, treasurer," (see Paragraph after No. 594)...(Mass.)	590
Note endorsed in blank, etc..(Canada)	595
Suit on a note whereon N. was principal and defendants and others were sureties. Plaintiff and N. induced defendant to sign another note to be used in taking up the former note. After getting new note signed plaintiff bought it of N., advancing money thereon................(Vt.)	596
Note payable on demand given instead of a note issued previously and alleged to have been lost..(Mass.)	597
Action on a note against the maker, the defence was that the note in suit was signed by the defendant at the request and for the recommendation of the O. R. Co...(Mass.)	598
Note as follows, "$2,268.00. Boston, February 1st, 18.2. For value received I promise to pay to B. B. N., or order, $2,268.00 in one and a half years, or sooner at the option of the mortgagor, from this date, with interest to be paid semi-annually at the rate of seven per cent. per annum during said term, for such further time as said principal sum or any part thereof shall remain unpaid;" endorsed "waving demand and notice". (Mass.)	599
Note executed by a married woman, omitting essential statement therein. ....(N. Y.)	600
Note made for accommodation of payee, but without restriction as to its use...(N. Y.)	601
Note made payable at any bank in a specified city......................(Ala.)	602
Maker, on delivery of the note was to transfer to payee certain stock as security for the payment of the note, and, in case of his failure to pay, the payee was to take the stock in full satisfaction..................(Mass.)	603
Note, with interest coupons attached, but containing a clause that if interest is not paid, etc., principal shall be due........................(Ill.)	604, 605
Note containing stipulation that unless notice was given on July 1st, failure of consideration should not be pleaded....................(Ga.)	623
Note endorsed and when due a new note given, with promise that the endorsers would come in and endorse but did not..................(N. Y.)	606
Power to sell property, in the absence of any expressed limitation, is authorized to do any act or to make any declaration in regard to the property found necessary to make a sale. Action brought to have three notes declared void for usury.......................(N. Y.) 608, 609, 610,	611
Where draft did not specify any place of payment. Plea of usury...(N. Y.)	612
Note given between two parties in the purchase of a patent right, etc..(Mass.)	613
Note given without stamps, only part of which were put on, some afterwards by holder..(Canada)	614
Part payment of a draft by drawing and discounting another...(Canada)	615
Note given by a firm in N. Y. to a silent partner in Canada, but payable in N. Y., the Canada partner sold the note in Canada at a higher rate of	

discount than 7 per cent.; was the note subject to N. Y. usury laws.........(Cana.)	616
Note given for the purchase money for land assigned by the vendor of the land to a firm as collateral security for a claim of a smaller amount (Ark.	617
A. purchased a tract of land, executed his note for the purchase money and received a bond for title. B., at request of A. paid the note and vendor executed a deed to A. who at same time made his note to B, for the sum so paid and gave him a mortgage on the land...........(Ark.)	618
Acceptance of vendor of land of a forged mortgage to secure the payment of a note of the agent............(Ind.)	619
Purchase money of land is payable in several instalments evidenced by notes due at different times, holder may enforce his lien against the land when one or more of such notes come due..........(Miss.)	620
Sale.—Pretended sale by an insolvent debtor to one of his creditors.....(La.)	621
Where several distinct articles are bought at same time for different prices......(Mass.)	622
Delivery of goods by a seller to a carrier...........(N. Y.)	623
Buying property with full knowledge that the title to the same is in dispute.....(La.)	624
Defect of an animal apparent upon casual inspection.........(Colo.)	625
When it is shown that the expressed consideration of a transfer does not exist......(La.)	626
Advances on a growing crop..........(Ga.)	627
Note for fertilizers contained stipulation that unless notice was given on July 1st, failure of consideration should not be pleaded.........(Ga.)	628
Goods sold selected by buyer weighed, marked with initials of buyer and placed by itself in store of vendor to be removed upon payment for it or giving an acceptable note for the amount. Goods were destroyed by fire in vendor's store........(Mass.)	629
Where vendee in a contract of sale refuses to receive the article sold....(La.)	630
Trustee to whom property is entrusted for sale mortgages the same.........(Canada)	631
Defendant cannot resist payment of a demand for price of goods sold and delivered to him, on the ground that the sale was in fraud of the creditors of seller.......(Miss.)	632
A warehouseman sold part of a larger quantity which he had in store and gave the purchaser a warehouse receipt under the statute, without separating the wheat. Insurance interest..........(Canada)	633
Warranty with sale........(Ga.)	634
Goods consigned to A. for sale who made advances on them to consignor......(Mass.)	635
Except in cases where there is an express agreement, goods are not at the risk of the buyer until they have been weighed, counted or measured.....(La.)	636
Cannot set aside a sheriff sale after the return day of the execution..(Penn.)	637
By terms of sale of goods, the buyer was to send for them......(Mass.)	638
Set-off—Implied contract..........(Kan.)	639
Plea of set-off, setting up a promise good in parole, by the common law........(Colo.)	640
Surviving partner, in an action against himself to recover a debt which he individually incurred.........(N. J.)	641
Any set-off to a note which would have been good between the original parties, may be pleaded against an endorsee.......(Neb.)	642
Set-off to the maker of a note, who was principal, arising after maturity of note........(Eng.)	643
Note pleaded as a set-off shows on its face that it was given for a different consideration........(Ind.)	644
A claim arising from a bonus paid on a usurious loan.....(N. J.)	645
Action arising upon contract..........(Nevada)	646
Note given by A. to B. and not yet due, cannot, in equity, be set-off against a note given by B. to A. upon which A. has brought an action...(Mass.)	647
A third party, for whose benefit a simple contract has been entered into for a valuable consideration moving from the promises, and upon which third party might maintain an action against the promisor......(Colo.)	648
When one judgment can be set-off against another...........(N. J.)	649
Counter-claim set up by the defendants in an action can only be maintained where it exists in favor of all the defendants...........(Wyoming)	650
W. purchased of A. a claim against B., pending an action by A. upon the claim. B. had previously purchased a claim against A., and had given notice thereof to A..........(Mass.)	651
Set-off—Failure of consideration. Eviction—Measure of damages....(Ind.)	652
Statute of Limitations.—Parties to a contract may provide by express stipulation for a shorter limitation to actions........(N. Y.)	653
Letters of a partner recognizing the existence of a judgment against the firm, after it is barred by the statute....(Iowa)	654
Where the party, against whom a cause of action exists, by fraud or actual fraudulent concealment, prevents the party in whose favor it exists from obtaining knowledge of it........(Iowa)	655

INDEX.   165

Fraud which must have been discovered if reasonable diligence had been
    exercised...(Ga.)   656
When a motion to set aside a judgment is barred......................(Ga.)   657
"It will suit my convenience to execute my note for the balance due for
    rent, payable January 1st, 1877." The above was offered in evidence as
    an acknowledge of the debt...(Miss.)   658
If, at the time when a right of action accrues, there is no one in being to
    assert it...(Miss.)   659
When a demand is necessary to found an action........................(Mich.) 660
Upon all demand paper not excepted by statute from the provisions of the
    Statute of Limitations...(Mich.) 661
Debt of intestate—The acknowledgment of administrator...............(Kan.)   662
Endorsement in handwriting of the debtor, but not signed by him, of a part
    payment of a note, will not prevent the operation of the statute..(Mass.)   663
Failure of an administrator to sue on, or collect, a note due his intestate
    until it is has become barred by statute.........................(Miss.)   664
Action for recovery of one-half of money expended in buying material for a
    house in joint occupancy..(Ga.)   665
The Statute of Limitations cannot be pleaded in bar in a foreign juris-
    diction..(Miss.) 666
Mistake of fact induced by attorney of opposite party................(Ga.)   667
Bank bill that ceased to circulate as currency prior to June 1st, 1855...(Ga.) 667½
Generally limitation laws act only upon remedies, and do not extinguish
    rights..(Ga.)   668

Security, Surety and Sureties.—Surety's right of action does not accrue
    until he has paid in excess of his proportion.....................(Mo.) 669-670
Security on official bond aids principal in breach....................(Ga.)   671
In action upon an undertaking, the law will not increase or enlarge the terms
    of the undertaking to the prejudice of its signers................(Kan.)   672
Judgment on replevy bond in attachment...............................(Ga.)   673
For a tenant is not released as to rents subsequently accruing.......(N. Y.) 674
Promise of a surety assuring the payment of the price of a specific lot of
    goods..(La.)   675
Valid agreement to give time on a note to the principal..............(N. J.) 676
Discharge of principal discharges the known surety....................(Vt.)   677
Liability of surety on judgment by confession........................(Iowa)   681
Bond given to secure performance by their principal of future mercantile
    engagements...(Mich.) 682
Suit by a bank against a late cashier and the sureties on his official bond.(Del.) 683
Surety or creditor has a right to have any collaterals the debtor may have
    pledged to either for payment......................................(N. J.)   678
Discharge in bankruptcy of the principal will not release surety......(La.)   679
Rule that a contract void as to principal is void also as to surety, does not
    apply always..(Tenn.) 680
Proof of debt in bankruptcy court by judgment creditor discharges lien, and
    endorser is discharged to extent of inquiry thereby................(Ga.)   684
Agreement by co-surety for benefit of creditor. Assent of payee....(Ind.)   685
Surety has the right to stand upon the very terms of his contract...(Md.)   686
Delay of creditor...(Kan.)   687
Where negotiable notes, payable to bearer, are deposited as collateral
    security for a debt..(Texas)   688
Person indebted by bond paid a balance due on it in notes of an insolvent
    bank, which was not known at the time.............................(Del.)   689
When personal property is assigned to payee as security by maker of a note,
    and as additional security, third persons sign the note as securities.(Cal.) 690
When several persons are securities, and all but one pay the whole sum.(Cal.) 691
If one of several sureties dies......................................(Cal.)   692
If one of two sureties dies, and his executor pays all the money for which he
    became liable..(Cal.) 693-694
A settlement in the probate court by the principal, is binding upon the
    surety..(Ala.) 695
Judgment against principal. Negligence in issuing execution........(Ind.)   696
Upon principles of equity, a surety, as between himself and his principal,
    stands upon a different footing, in some respects, from an ordinary
    creditor...(N. V.) 697-698
In an action against a surety upon a note, when forbearance to the maker is
    sought to be interposed, it is not sufficient to aver merely that "for good
    and sufficient consideration."....................................(Colo.) 698-699
To release surety by granting forbearance, it must be given for a time and
    upon a consideration..(Colo.) 700
Suit against surety in a foreign note is not subject to Statute of Limitations
    in this State..(Ga.)   701
L. became surety on a note for S., and received a mortgage as security
    against loss...(Iowa) 702
Notes deposited with defendants as collateral security for the payment of a
    note, endorsed by the plaintiffs for the accommodation of M., and dis-
    counted by defendants...(Canada) 703

Tender.—Tender made of an animal to vendor because of its unsoundness.(Colo.) 704
Evidence of or dispensation with....................................(Canada) 705
Demand of payment by, and tender of one unauthorized—Equity.....(Ind.)   706

Trusts.—When trustee is authorized to invest in either of two specific modes(Canada) 707
Purchaser of property at trustee's sale.....(Ark.) 708
Purchaser of quit-claim deed before the maturity of the purchase-money notes, or any of them.....(Texas) 709
Trustee selling trust property at less price than other persons are willing to give.....(Canada) 710
When guardian buys land with the funds of his ward, and take the title in his own name.....(Miss.) 711

Usury—Is a defence personal to the parties to the contract, or their legal representatives.....(Ala.) 712
Agent's retention of a percentage as compensation without the mortgagee's knowledge.....(N. J.) 713
Money paid usuriously may be recovered. Rule not changed by present usury act.....(N. J.) 714
Notes given in 1876 for excess of interest in 1873.....(Ga.) 715
Note valid on its face, and calling for only legal interest.....(Kan.) 716
Even in a charge of usury the principal and legal interest must be paid.(Ark.) 717
Building societies are virtually exempt from the operations of the usury laws.....Canada) 718
Need not show that legal interest has been tendered, in an action...(Iowa) 719-720
M. bought at judicial sale the property of H. Before the time for redemption expired B. redeemed it, paying $1,485, and agreed to convey it to H. upon his payment of $2,000.....(Iowa) 721
Note in the hands of an innocent holder not subject to usury.....(Kan.) 722
A. agreed, on a loan of money, to pay the lender at a certain time, with legal interest, and not paid then, he would surrender to the lender certain shares of stock pledged as collateral thereto on this loan.....(N. J.) 723
Sale of cotton at a price beyond its real value to one who sold it for a less price.....(Ala.) 724
Sale made under a mortgage, whether the contract is usurious or not, is immaterial.....(Md.) 725
All payments of usurious interest are to be taken as payments on account of the principal.....(Ohio) 726
To borrow money, and issue certificates therefor bearing interest, is conferred by the borough law of the State, and although interest allowed is in excess of legal rate, it does not invalidate the certificates. Is only void for excess.....(Pa.) 727
Confession of judgment, made for the purpose of aiding in violating the usury laws.....(Iowa) 728
Quarterly payments. Interest upon unpaid interest.....(Iowa) 729
The usury law of 1862 is constitutional, and a contract made in violation of it will not be enforced.....(Oregon) 730-730½
The knowingly taking or receiving, by a national bank, of a greater rate of interest than is allowed by the State in which the bank is located..(Ark.) 731
That although the Code provides the mode and manner in which a defendant may plead usury, its provisions do not in any manner deprive a party of existing remedies for relief.....(Md.) 732
When a loan is effected through an agent.....(Ia.) 733-734
When usurious interest is carried into a general account.....(Ark.) 735
R. S. of 1857, c. 45, relating to usury, was unconditionally repealed by st. of 1870, c. 169.....(Mc.) 736
Plea of usury is personal.....(Ark.) 737
Bill executed in Ohio by one party, and in Virginia by another, thus making a joint bill. No place of payment indicated. On its face was to bear 8 per cent. interest.....(W. Va.) 738
Note made in New York on demand, with interest, and given to payee as a substitute for a draft then drawn under an oral agreement, with his knowledge, for more than legal interest, and on the note itself it agreed orally to pay same interest.....(Mass.) 739
Only question, was the defence of usury established.....(N. J.) 740
Defence of usury against a morgage.....(N. J.) 741
Defence set up that the mortgages were made in New York, and are subject to the laws of that State.....(N. J.) 742
Judgment entered on a bond given for money loaned at usurious rate of interest.....(Penn.) 743
E. obtained judgment on a note against V., afterward E. assigned $2,500 of it to D. On affidavit V. opened the judgment, and offered to prove that D. loaned him (V.) $2,500 in New York at usurious rate of interest..(Pa.) 744
Where a note tainted with usury has been transferred to another without notice.....(N. Y.) 745
Legal rate of interest in District of Columbia.....(Md.) 746

Warranty of title is implied in a contract of exchange same as in a contract of sale.....(Vt.) 747
Goods sold with a warranty of quality, and those delivered, though inferior, are retained by the vendee.....(Colo.) 748
Vendee can refuse to receive goods because they are inferior, and is not liable for injury while in his charge, if due care of them has been taken by him.....(Kan.) 749
Breach—return of goods.....(Kan.) 750
Cannot recover on an additional parole warranty.....(Ia.) 751

"THE FINANCIAL SITUATION"

CONSIDERED IN A PAPER

SUBMITTED TO THE

Committee on Banking and Currency

OF THE

House of Representatives,

BY A

MERCHANT OF PHILADELPHIA.

"The Resumption Act of January 14, 1875, a Charter without limit; the Law Indestructible by Legislation."

WASHINGTON, D. C.:
J. E. Beardsley, Printer, 479 Penna. Avenue.

1877.

Mr. JOSEPH C. GRUBB, of the Philadelphia Board of Trade, said:

Mr. Chairman and Gentlemen: In the half-hour of your time that I will occupy, I shall discuss the financial situation from a business stand-point. All that I know of the question has been gathered by observation as a merchant and from the traditions of an occupation that was established at the foundation of the general government, and has come from father to son down to the present time. Chiefly, I shall try to show, that the resumption act, for the repeal of which a bill is now before Congress, is a charter, the fourth of the kind that Congress has enacted, and that it is indestructible by legislation; the right to repeal is not in the power of Congress, and that while it is not imperfect, it is yet still incomplete. Further, I hope to show, if I have the ability, that it may by supplementary legislation secure the object for which the law was framed.

The law itself, which was enacted January 14, 1875, and is known as the resumption act, unmistakably declares, in effect, that the national circulation, after January 1, 1879, shall consist of coin and national bank notes redeemable in coin. It was a notice to the authorities to substitute, at that date, this currency for the legal tender notes. The law was wise in every sense in which it can be regarded. It is, without doubt, a binding contract between the people, the national banks, and the Government. It is a precept to the people and a mandate to the banks. It is one and the same with the colonial charter granted in 1781, to the Bank of North America by the Continental Congress. This bank rescued the colonies from the Continental money and supplied a solvent paper circulation in its stead; it still survives in all the vigor of its primitive days, now close upon its centennial year, a marvel of successful usefulness.

The act is one and the same with the law incorporating the bank of 1791 that succeeded it, which gave a lead and a consistence to the debts of the war for independence, and also with the bank charter of 1816, which followed and reconstructed the finances after the war ending in 1815; this bank, with the two former, discharged in full the debts incurred in both wars, the Government, in addition, by their frugal management being enabled to divide a large surplus with the several States. The city of my residence was the seat of these institutions, and it is known that in the administration of their affairs covering a period of sixty years, not a cent was lost to any one.

I affirm that the resumption law is the same with these several charters, that its powers are corporate and that in its legal proportions it is in all respects the same. I claim that the act repeals the legal tender clause of the law of 1862, and that the circulating notes, commonly known as greenbacks, issued under it, become portable bonds without the legal tender clause, from the first day of January, 1879. Maintained at par with coin of gold from that date, they remain a legal tender; but how, it may be asked, can they continue to be a legal tender, when their par in coin is not maintained and they are, as they may be under protest for non-payment. Would not the coin in hand and held for their redemption, then become a sum which the holders of the notes would be entitled to as a distributive share? It seems to me the act of resumption fixing a day for their payment in coin lifts them to the dignity of unchallenged constitutional money. If I am right the taxes now levied on the capital and deposits of the national banks by the Revised Statutes, are abolished from the same date, January 1, 1879, the right of State taxation only remaining; also that the law requiring reserves in lawful money is repealed after that date.

Mr. Chairman and Gentlemen, there can be no resumption otherwise than through a bank parlor. Such an authority at the head of the national banks and acting as a directory is the only road, and it is the beaten track. It is not the business of a Secretary of the Treasury; all he can do is to improve income and regulate expenditure, so as to make both ends meet. Resumption is the special duty of those who are friends of stable credit, and who are conversant with the science of money and exchange, of those who have the opportunity to handle and control the results of industry, and of traffic, international, national and individual, in their form of commercial equivalents. This means banking, reformed and perfected, with its precedents, its local knowledge, its traditional means, its organized connections, and it offers the sole means of restoration. There are in each of the chief commercial nations to be found men of calm judgment, a family of regulars, with habits in striking contrast to the feverish bustle of the commercial and trading world about them. The one stable, unchanging institution will there be found in which they are cradled. The public capital and private fortunes joined to the supreme authority, is intrusted to their vigilance and their skill. They receive all values and emit but one. They interpret and enforce the laws of trade with incomparable faithfulness. Until we are willing to accept such a central system of control there will be no settlement of our business or of our financial difficulties. Finance without such an authority as a court of last resort, is nothing less than lynch law. At present *our* institution is an army of volunteers, wings without a centre, clamorous and undisciplined, a misty multitude of people, of every variety of character and of all shades of opinion.

I have said the resumption act is *only* incomplete, and that it is not imperfect. It is just possible that it went far enough at the time of its adoption. Three years have passed since its introduction into Congress, and one year yet remains as the limit of the law; thus we are near the appointed time when its details should be perfected. In my judgment, these centre in a tariff judiciously imposed, and in the adjustment of our various legal dollars by a dollar of standard value.

This may not be the place, nor, perhaps, the time to discuss the details; yet, speaking for myself only—for I have consulted no one, neither am I authorized to speak for any one—I will state what, in my opinion, the terms might be. If Congress would stipulate by an enabling act that the corporate powers conferred by the resumption law, shall be an uninterrupted succession for a term of thirty years, and agree that the national banks in that time shall enjoy exemption from all taxation by the general government, and that State taxation shall be restrained within certain limits if Congress will, in that period, direct the accounting officers of the Government to deposit daily the receipts from custom duties and internal revenues and from all other sources into the national banks, the banks, on their part might, I think, in return agree to receive in exchange for the four hundred millions of gold loans; which amount it is estimated the national banks hold, a fifty year lawful money loan, similar to the Pacific currency sixes, and within the five succeeding years in addition, as the agent of the Government, fund all the remaining part of the national debt, which has matured, or shall become payable in that time, in a similar loan, the interest to be paid at three stated periods within each year, at the rate of four and a half per cent. per annum. They might also agree to pay, as the disbursing agents of the Government, all its current outlays, including the coupon and registered interest on the national debt, at the option of the holder in coin, or in paper with the premium added, so long as there shall be a premium, and contribute their stock of gold, now amounting to a round sum of twenty-five millions, to the common fund of coin, without receiving premium or interest for it. The fiscal service remaining to the treasury would be

First, The holding of such an amount of the loan, thus consolidated, as, in the opinion of Congress, would be a sufficient guarantee fund for the faithful performance of the trust of resuming and maintaining specie payments.

Second, The care and issue of the national circulation.
Third. The custody of the coin at designated centres.

Resumption will be found to be a question of economy and savings—the annual supply of home-grown bullion being a reserve.

If such an arrangement, as a plan of adjustment, should find favor, the Government, the banks and the business interests, might properly agree upon and present the details for the consideration of Congress. In this moment of supreme anxiety and apprehension, both sides can afford to be liberal.

There are some conclusions in the theory and practice of finance that are held as fixed by the men with whom my lot is cast—the middlemen, or factors between the producer and consumer, and which are the settled convictions of the class. The costliest standard is looked upon as the best standard and the cheapest, for the reason that the largest superstructure of credit can be erected upon it.

If Congress confers authority to print or to coin legal dollars, all agree that their value should be measured by a denominator or legal standard, or that they should be called by some other name.

The tariff question is a side issue. It is considered—and all experience points in the one direction, which is that a national standard of value is in its nature a tariff of itself; at the same time an intolerant protection may produce the same effect as too much paper money.

It is generally believed to be far more essential that the assets of the saving banks we already have, should be made solvent, than that a law establishing a postal saving bank should be enacted at this time.

The "talk on change" is, there are no soundings, no bottom. The wilt, shrink and sap is eating into the very marrow of the securities, which are the chief elements of our permanent success. The debtors are deluded with the hope of getting out of their embarrassments by throwing their burthens upon others through another debauch of paper money, or, what is the same thing, the kindred dodge of cheap coin ; the same issue through all history. There is the usual denunciatory talk, mainly in single instances, of subsidized presses and the like, and a desire for cheap money, but when that man's paper is extended he is docile and his voice is stilled. The commerce of the country asks, with Secretary Sherman, that coin shall be held for its proper commercial uses by arresting its export.

The national banking system, as far as it goes, is regarded with unusual favor, and banks as being well conducted. The currency of sound trade is a natural volume following successful business. There will be just as much of it as industry can create.

The clearest-headed men think you cannot arbitrarily or safely fund a single dollar of the legal tenders, (except by redeeming it in coin on the instant) until production supplies its equivalent as a means of barter or export. The legal tenders represent supplies furnished in the rebellion, but not paid for, and they survive the transaction. They will be all right in a perfected money system. Good book-keeping will find the proper place for them at the proper time.

I feel I have reached the limit of my privilege and I dare say of your patience, yet there is still something more to say ; I shall try to make it as brief as possible.

I shall barely lift the veil that covers the occurrences after the abandonment of the first national system in 1833, and the period subsequent to it. The removal of the public deposits and their transfer to the State banks, the distress that followed, the directions from the United States Treasurer to the State banks to loan liberally that it might be mitigated, the excessive issues of printed money in response, the bursting of the paper balloon and the crash of credit in 1837, the chaos of values and wreck of fortunes that came after it. There were tramps in those days, and for a time I was one of them. Then the restoration wrought by the tariff of 1842;

its threatened repeal in 1846, and the lower rates imposed by the tariff enacted in that year ; then the support derived as an offset, from the discovery of gold in 1847 in California, and from the food supplied to Ireland in the famine of the same year, the support these afforded to industry, and after that the incline downward until 1857, then again another panic. The rally of credit between that time and 1862, the issue of the legal tenders, the constant additions to them of various forms of irredeemable credit, the riotous living that followed, the crash of 1873, and that was the finish. Inflation would inflate no longer. I verily believe if there had been a central bank proportioned to the needs of all these years, our sufferings would have been limited to our own improvidences.

The Hon. E. G. Spaulding, the author himself of the legal tender act, has said, " the Bank of England is a striking example of the combined power of public authority and private influence in sustaining the credit of a government. We may safely profit by the example. Notwithstanding it is a bank of circulation, deposit and discount, it has thus far disbursed the public money without the loss of a single dollar entrusted to it. " Had such a bank," Mr. Spaulding continues, "been in full operation at the commemcement of the rebellion, it would probably have been unnecessary to have issued the Government greenbacks."

This recital of the past revives some recollections of the times of forty-five years ago. It was my privilege, by association and in the avenues of trade, to some extent, to meet the men of that period. They were of solid demeanor and frugal lives. There was but one money then. It harvested the crops, followed the flag to the extremities of the earth, and it exacted from other nations the duty of propping their own credit without drawing our substance from us for this purpose. Especially I recollect the demeanor of the men in charge of the bank, men who had been associates of Hamilton, Gallatin, of Marshall and Jay, and who upheld, as it came to them in its lineal descent, the solvent standard dollar; and their companions Sargent, Binney, Ingersoll, and Randall, their legal counsel; the latter, the respected father of the present Speaker of the House of Representatives. They received the imperious edicts of President Jackson as a grevious personal insult, as an unmitigated slander, and so it proved itself, the official records of the Treasury showing, in its final settlement in 1856, that instead of the Government losing it realized a clear profit from the operations of the bank of more than six millions of dollars.

It was remarked of British rule, by one of the foremost of English Statesmen, that he attributed the prosperity of England, in a great degree, to a characteristic of its people, that that country at the proper time generally retraced its steps, and it has been said that a free people always has just as good a Government as it deserves to have, and no better.

You, gentlemen, have this example to consider. All eyes are turned toward Washington. Honest money is the desired of the Nation. A solvent dollar is a providential and a beneficent fact, since it is of the plan in gaining over to civilization the peoples of the earth and thus it is a divine decree.

The political hero is he, who, when others have crumbled stands firm till a new order of things has built itself around him, who will show a way out and beyond where others can only see written, " No Thoroughfare."

Coin values have been reached, in many cases have been passed, and they are still falling through space. Our paper circulation is losing its supporting power, and is no longer a prop. My duty is done in asking that you will apply the proper remedy before all respect is lost for the means of accomplishing it.

I thank you, gentlemen, for your patience and considerate attention.

MR. GRUBB, being interrogated, said:

The Silver Bill will be the subject of another paper, if it is agreeable, at a future time. This, however, may be said now. If the resumption act *is* a charter and enacts that coin of gold, as a single standard or its equivalent, is to be the national circulation after January 1, 1879,—and it seems clearly to do this,—then it is too late to reopen the compact that another standard, and of less value, may be injected into it from without. The resumption law plainly defines the Public-Debt Act of March, 1869, to mean *coin of gold*, and settles the question. Silver is its associate, and will be interchangeable just so long as it possesses the same value, that is, the same market value. The intention of the resumption act manifestly is, to so blend and merge the stock in money of the people, the Government, and the National Banks, that an unassailable value as a standard may be drawn from its concealment. It is unfortunate for those who regard themselves as the special friends of silver, at this time, that they have treated it as a question of finance instead of as a matter of coinage.

WASHINGTON, D. C., *December* 14, 1877.

EXTRA SESSION OF THE 46TH CONGRESS.

SPEECHES

OF

HON. JAMES A. GARFIELD,
OF OHIO,

IN THE

HOUSE OF REPRESENTATIVES,

AT

THE EXTRA SESSION, MARCH 18 TO JULY 1, 1879.

WASHINGTON.
1879.

CONTENTS.

I.

	Page.
THE APPROPRIATION BILLS:	
1. Opening the debate on the first Army bill—Revolution in Congress	3
2. Closing the debate on the first Army bill	13
3. On the legislative appropriation bill—National elections should be protected by national authority	17
4. On the second Army appropriation bill	21
5. On the judicial appropriation bill	25
6. On the judicial appropriation bill—Nullification	31

II.

Defense of the Union soldiers of the seceded States. 35

III.

1. Resumption and the currency—The reserves for redemption of public obligations must be maintained 37
2. The new silver bill 40

IV.

The Mississippi River an object of national care 42

V.

The revived doctrine of State sovereignty 44

VI.

Greek and Democratic panics 53

I.

THE APPROPRIATION BILLS.

1. FIRST ARMY BILL.

REVOLUTION IN CONGRESS.

SATURDAY, *March* 29, 1879.

The House being in Committee of the Whole, and having under consideration the bill (H. R. No. 1) making appropriations for the support of the Army for the fiscal year ending June 30, 1880, and for other purposes—

Mr. GARFIELD said:

Mr. CHAIRMAN: I have no hope of being able to convey to the members of this House my own conviction of the very great gravity and solemnity of the crisis which this decision of the Chair and of the Committee of the Whole has brought upon this country. I wish I could be proved a false prophet in reference to the result of this action. I wish I could be overwhelmed with the proof that I am utterly mistaken in my views. But no view I have ever taken has entered more deeply and more seriously into my conviction than this, that the House has to-day resolved to enter upon a revolution against the Constitution and Government of the United States. I do not know that this intention exists in the minds of half the Representatives who occupy the other side of this Hall. I hope it does not. I am ready to believe it does not exist to any great extent. But I affirm that the consequence of the programme just adopted, if persisted in, will be nothing less than the total subversion of this government.

THE QUESTION STATED.

Let me in the outset state, as carefully as I may, the precise situation. At the last session, all our ordinary legislative work was done in accordance with the usages of the House and Senate, except as to two bills. Two of the twelve great appropriation bills for the support of the government were agreed to in both Houses as to every matter of detail concerning the appropriations proper. We were assured by the committees of conference in both bodies that there would be no difficulty in adjusting all differences in reference to the amount of money to be appropriated and the objects of its appropriation. But the House of Representatives proposed three measures of distinctly independent legislation; one upon the Army appropriation bill, and two upon the legislative appropriation bill. The three grouped together are briefly these: First, the substantial modification of certain sections of the law relating to the use of the Army; second, the repeal of the jurors' test oath; and third, the repeal of the laws regulating elections of members of Congress.

These three propositions of legislation were insisted upon by the House; but the Senate refused to adopt them. So far it was an ordinary proceeding, one which occurs frequently in all legislative bodies.

The Senate said to us through their conferees, "We are ready to pass the appropriation bills; but we are unwilling to pass as riders the three legislative measures you ask us to pass." Thereupon the House, through its conference committee, made the following declaration—and in order that I may do exact justice, I read from the speech of the distinguished Senator from Kentucky [Mr. Beck], on the report of the conference committee:

> The Democratic conferees on the part of the House seem determined that unless those rights were secured to the people—

alluding to the three points I have named—

> in the bill sent to the Senate, they would refuse, under their constitutional right, to make appropriations to carry on the government, if the dominant majority in the Senate insisted upon the maintenance of these laws and *refused to consent* to their repeal.

Then, after stating that if the position they had taken compelled an extra session, the new Congress would offer the repealing bills separately, and forecasting what would happen when the new House should be under no necessity of coercing the Senate, he said:

> If, however, the President of the United States, in the exercise of the power vested in him, should see fit to veto the bills thus presented to him, * * * then I have no doubt those same amendments will be again made part of the appropriation bills, and it will be for the President to determine whether he will block the wheels of government and refuse to accept necessary appropriations rather than allow the representatives of the people to repeal odious laws which they regard as subversive of their rights and privileges. * * * Whether that course is right or wrong, it will be adopted, and I have no doubt adhered to, no matter what happens with the appropriation bills.

That was the proposition made by the Democracy in Congress at the close of the Congress now dead.

Another distinguished Senator [Mr. Thurman]—and I may properly refer to Senators of a Congress not now in existence—reviewing the situation, declared, in still more succinct terms:

> We claim the right, which the House of Commons in England established after two centuries of contest, to say that we will not grant the money of the people unless there is a redress of grievances.

These propositions were repeated with various degrees of vehemence by the majority in the House.

The majority in the Senate and the minority on this floor expressed the deepest anxiety to avoid an extra session and to avert the catastrophe thus threatened—the stoppage of the government. They pointed out the danger to the country and its business interests of an extra session of Congress, and expressed their willingness to consent to any compromise consistent with their views of duty which should be offered—not in the way of coercion but in the way of fair adjustment—and asked to be met in a spirit of just accommodation on the other side. Unfortunately no spirit of adjustment was manifested in reply to their advances. And now the new Congress is assembled; and after ten days of caucus deliberation, the House of Representatives has resolved, substantially, to reaffirm the positions of its predecessors, except that the suggestion of Senator Beck to offer the independent legislation in a separate bill has been abandoned. By a construction of the rules of the House far more violent than any heretofore given, a part of this independent legislation is placed on the pending bill for the support of the Army; and this House has determined to begin its career by the extremest form of coercive legislation.

In my remarks to-day I shall confine myself almost exclusively to the one phase of the controversy presented in this bill.

Mr. ATKINS. Will the honorable gentleman allow me to interrupt him a moment?

Mr. GARFIELD. With pleasure.

Mr. ATKINS. Do I understand you to state that in the conference committee no proposition was made other than the one suggested in the legislation proposed to be attached to the bill by the House conferees?

Mr. GARFIELD. I did not undertake to state what was done in conference except as reported by Senator Beck, for I was not a member of the committee.

Mr. ATKINS. I thought you did.

Mr. GARFIELD. No; I only declared what was proposed on the floor of the House and Senate.

Mt. ATKINS. With the gentleman's permission I will state that the proposition the House made in conference committee was substantially the proposition now before the House and here offered to be attached to these bills.

Mr. GARFIELD. I take it for granted that what my friend on the other side says is strictly true; but not even that proposition was reported to either House.

The question, Mr. Chairman, may be asked, why make any special resistance to the clauses of legislation in this bill which a good many gentlemen on this side declared at the last session they cared but little about, and regarded as of very little practical importance, because for years there had been no actual use for any part of these laws, and they had no expectation there would be any? It may be asked, why make any controversy on either side? So far as we are concerned, Mr. Chairman, I desire to say this: we recognize the other side as accomplished parliamentarians and strategists, who have adopted with skill and adroitness their plan of assault. You have placed in the front, one of the least objectionable of your measures; but your whole programme has been announced, and we reply to your whole order of battle. The logic of your position compels us to meet you as promptly on the skirmish line as afterward when our entrenchments are assailed; and, therefore, at the outset, we plant our case upon the general ground upon which we have chosen to defend it.

THE VOLUNTARY POWERS OF THE GOVERNMENT.

And here, sir, I wish to make a brief digression, in which I hope no gentleman will consider my discussion as controversial or personal. I had occasion, at a late hour of the last Congress, to say something on what may be called the voluntary element in our institutions. I spoke of the distribution of the powers of government. First, to the nation; second, to the States; and, third, the reservation of power to the people themselves.

I called attention to the fact that under our form of government the most precious rights that men can possess on this earth.are not delegated to the nation nor to the States, but are reserved to the third estate—the people themselves. I called attention to the interesting fact that lately the chancellor of the German Empire made the declaration that it was the chief object of the existence of the German Government to defend and maintain the religion of Jesus Christ—an object in reference to which our Congress is absolutely forbidden by the Constitutiou to legislate at all. Congress can establish no religion; indeed, can make no law respecting it, because in the view of our fathers—the founders of our government—religion was too precious a right to intrust ts interests by delegation to any government. Its maintenance was eft to the voluntary action of the people themselves.

In continuation of that thought, I wish now to speak of the voluntary element inside our government—a topic that I have not heard discussed, but one which appears to me of vital importance in any comprehensive view of our institutions.

Mr. Chairman, viewed from the stand-point of a foreigner, our government may be said to be the feeblest on the earth. From our stand-point, and with our experience, it is the mightiest. But why would a foreigner call it the feeblest? He can point out a half dozen ways in which it can be destroyed without violence. Of course, all governments may be overturned by the sword; but there are several ways in which ours may be annihilated without the firing of a gun.

For example, if the people of the United States should say we will elect no Representative to the House of Representatives—of course this is a violent supposition—but suppose they do not, is there any remedy? Does our Constitution provide any remedy whatever? In two years there would be no House of Representatives; of course no support of the government, and no government. Suppose, again, the States should say, through their legislatures, we will elect no Senators. Such abstention alone would absolutely destroy this government; and our system provides no process of compulsion to prevent it.

Again, suppose the two Houses were assembled in their usual order, and a majority of one in this body or in the Senate, should firmly band themselves together and say we will vote to adjourn the moment the hour of meeting arrives, and continue so to vote at every session during our two years of existence; the government would perish; and there is no provision of the Constitution to prevent it. Or, again if a majority of one in either body should declare that they would vote down, and did vote down, every bill to support the government by appropriations, can you find in the whole range of our judicial or our executive authority any remedy whatever? A Senator or a member of this House is free, and may vote "No" on every proposition. Nothing but his oath and his honor restrains him. Not so with executive and judicial officers. They have no power to destroy this government. Let them travel an inch beyond the line of the law, and they fall within the power of impeachment. But against the people who create Representatives, against the legislatures who create Senators, against Senators and Representatives in these Halls, there is no power of impeachment; there is no remedy, if by abstention or by adverse votes they refuse to support the government.

At a first view, it would seem strange that a body of men so wise as our fathers were should have left a whole side of their fabric open to these deadly assaults; but on a closer view of the case their wisdom will appear. What was their reliance? This: the sovereign of this nation, the God-crowned and Heaven-anointed sovereign, in whom resides "the State's collected will," and to whom we all owe allegiance, is the people themselves. Inspired by love of country and by a deep sense of obligation to perform every public duty, being themselves the creators of all the agencies and forces to execute their own will, and choosing from themselves their representatives to express that will in the forms of law, it would have been like a suggestion of suicide to assume that any of these great voluntary powers would be turned against the life of the government. Public opinion—that great ocean of thought from whose level all heights and all depths are measured—was trusted as a power amply able, and always willing, to guard all the approaches on that side of the Constitution from any assault on the life of the nation.

Up to this hour our sovereign has never failed us. There has never been such a refusal to exercise those primary functions of sovereignty as either to endanger or cripple the government; nor have the majority of the representatives of that sovereign in either House of Congress ever before announced their purpose to use their voluntary powers for its destruction. And now, for the first time in our history, and I will add for the first time for at least two centuries in the history of any English-speaking nation, it is suggested and threatened that these voluntary powers of Congress shall be used for the destruction of the government. I want it distinctly understood that the proposition which I read at the beginning of my remarks, and which is the programme announced to the American people to-day, is this: That if this House cannot have its own way in certain matters not connected with appropriations, it will so use, or refrain from using, its voluntary powers as to destroy the government.

Now, Mr. Chairman, it has been said on the other side, that when a demand for the redress of grievances is made, the authority that runs the risk of stopping and destroying the government is the one that resists the redress. Not so. If gentlemen will do me the honor to follow my thought for a moment more, I trust I will make this denial good.

FREE CONSENT THE BASIS OF OUR LAWS.

Our theory of law is free consent. That is the granite foundation of our whole superstructure. Nothing in this republic can be law without consent—the free consent of the House, the free consent of the Senate, the free consent of the Executive, or, if he refuse it, the free consent of two-thirds of these bodies. Will any man deny that? Will any man challenge a line of the statement that free consent is the foundation of all our institutions? And yet the programme announced two weeks ago was that, if the Senate refused to consent to the demand of the House, the government should stop. And the proposition was then, and the programme is now, that, although there is not a Senate to be coerced, there is still a third independent branch in the legislative power of the government whose consent is to be coerced at the peril of the destruction of this government; that is, if the President, in the discharge of his duty, shall exercise his plain Constitutional right to refuse his consent to this proposed legislation, the Congress will so use its voluntary powers as to destroy the government. This is the proposition which we confront; and we denounce it as revolution.

It makes no difference, Mr. Chairman, what the issue is. If it were the simplest and most inoffensive proposition in the world, yet if you demand, as a measure of coercion, that it shall be adopted against the free consent prescribed in the Constitution, every fair-minded man in America is bound to resist you as much as though his own life depended upon his resistance.

Let it be understood that I am not arguing the merits of any one of the three amendments. I am discussing the proposed method of legislation; and I declare that it is against the Constitution of our country. It is revolutionary to the core, and is destructive of the fundamental principle of American liberty, the free consent of all the powers that unite to make laws.

In opening this debate I challenge all comers to show a single instance in our history where this consent has been thus coerced. This is the great, the paramount issue which dwarfs all others into insignificance.

THE ORIGIN OF THE LAW SOUGHT TO BE MODIFIED.

I now turn aside, for a moment, from the line of my argument to say that it is not a little surprising that our friends on the other side should have gone into this great contest on so weak a cause as the one embraced in the pending amendment to this bill.

Victor Hugo said, in his description of the battle of Waterloo, that the struggle of the two armies was like the wrestling of two giants, when a chip under the heel of one might determine the victory. It may be that this amendment is the chip under your heel, or it may be that it is the chip on our shoulder. As a chip, it is of small account to you or to us; but when it represents the integrity of the Constitution and is assailed by revolution, we fight for it as for a Kohinoor of purest water. [Applause.]

The distinguished and venerable gentleman from Georgia [Mr. Stephens] spoke of this law, which is sought to be repealed, as "odious and dangerous." It has been denounced as a piece of partisan war legislation to enable the Army to control elections.

Do gentlemen know its history? Do they know whereof they affirm? Who made this law which is denounced as so great an offense as to justify the destruction of the government rather than let it remain on the statute-book? Its first draft was introduced into the Senate by a prominent Democrat from the State of Kentucky, Mr. Powell, who made an able speech in its favor. It was reported against by a Republican committee of that body, whose printed report I hold in my hand. It encountered weeks of debate, was amended and passed, and then came into the House. Every Democrat present in the Senate voted for it on its final passage. Every Senator who voted against it was a Republican. No Democrat voted against it. Who were the Democrats that voted for it? Let me read some of the names: Hendricks, of Indiana; Davis, of Kentucky; Johnson, of Maryland; McDougall, of California; Powell, of Kentucky; Richardson, of Illinois, and Saulsbury, of Delaware. Of Republican Senators thirteen voted against it; only ten voted for it.

The bill then came to the House of Representatives and was put upon its passage here. How did the vote stand in this body? Every Democrat present at the time in the House of Representatives of the Thirty-eighth Congress, voted for it. The total vote in its favor in the House was 113; and of these 58 were Democrats. And who were they? The magnates of the party. The distinguished Speaker of this House, Mr. Samuel J. Randall, voted for it. The distinguished chairman of the Committee of Ways and Means of the last House, Mr. Fernando Wood, voted for it. The distinguished member from my own State who now holds a seat in the other end of the Capitol, Mr. George H. Pendleton, voted for it. Messrs. Cox and Coffroth, Kernan and Morrison, who are still in Congress, voted for it. Every Democrat of conspicuous name and fame in that House voted for the bill, and not one against it. There were but few Republicans who voted against it. I was one of the few. Thaddeus Stevens and Judge Kelley voted against it.

What was the controversy? What was the object of the bill? It was alleged by Democrats that in those days of war there were interferences with the proper freedom of elections in the border States. We denied the charge; but lest there might be some infraction of the freedom of elections, many Republicans, unwilling that there should be even the semblance of interference with that freedom, voted for it. This law is an expression of their purpose that the Army should not be used at any election except for the purpose of keeping the peace.

Those Republicans who voted against it did so on the ground that there was no cause for such legislation; that it was a slander upon the government and the Army to say that they were interfering with the proper freedom of elections. I was among that number——

Mr. CARLISLE. Will the gentleman allow me to ask him a question?

Mr. GARFIELD. Certainly

Mr. CARLISLE. I ask if the Democrats in the Senate and House of Representatives did not vote for that proposition because it came in the form of a substitute for another proposition that was still more objectionable?

Mr. GARFIELD. The gentleman is quite mistaken. The original bill was introduced by a gentleman from Kentucky, Mr. Powell; it was amended in its course through the Senate; but the votes to which I have referred were the final votes on its passage after all the amendments had been made; and, what was more, a Republican Senator moved to reconsider it, hoping that he might thereby kill it. And after several days' delay and debate it was again passed, every Democrat again voting for it. In the House there was no debate, and therefore no expression of the reasons why anybody voted for it. Each man voted according to his convictions, I suppose.

Mr. STEPHENS. Will the gentleman yield to me?

Mr. GARFIELD. I yield to the venerable gentleman from Georgia for a question.

Mr. STEPHENS. I simply ask if the country is likely to be revolutionized and the government destroyed by the repealing a law that the gentleman himself voted against? [Laughter on the Democratic side.]

Mr. GARFIELD. I think not. That is not the element of revolution, as I will show the gentleman. The proposition now is, that after fourteen years have passed, and not one petition from one American citizen has come to us asking that this law be repealed, while not one memorial has found its way to our desks complaining of the law, so far as I have heard, the Democratic Representatives declare that if they are not permitted to force upon another house and upon the Executive, against their consent, the repeal of a law that Democrats made, this refusal will be considered a sufficient ground for starving this government to death. That is the proposition which we denounce as revolution. [Applause on the Republican side.]

Mr. FERNANDO WOOD. I desire to ask the gentleman from Ohio a question.

Mr. GARFIELD. Certainly.

Mr. FERNADO WOOD. Before he leaves that part of his remarks to which the gentleman from Kentucky [Mr. Carlisle] has referred, I desire to ask the gentleman whether he wishes to make the impression upon the House that the bill introduced by Senator Powell, of Kentucky, and which resulted finally in the law of 1865, was the bill that passed the Senate, that passed the House, and for which he says the present Speaker of this House and myself voted?

Mr. GARFIELD. I have not intimated that there were no amendments. On the contrary I have said that it was amended in the Senate. One amendment permitted the use of the Army to repel armed enemies of the United States from the polls.

Mr. FERNANDO WOOD. So far as I am personally concerned, I deny that I ever voted for a bill except as a substitute for a more pernicious and objectionable measure. [Much laughter on the Republican side.]

Mr. GARFIELD. What I have said is a matter of record. And I say again the gentleman voted for this law; and every Democrat in the Senate and in the House who voted at all, voted for this law just as it now stands; and without their votes it could not have passed. No amendments whatever were offered in the House, and there was no other bill on the subject before the House.

Mr. FERNANDO WOOD. I desire to submit another question to my friend.

Mr. GARFIELD. Certainly.

Mr. FERNANDO WOOD. It is whether, in 1865, at the time of the passage of this law, when the war had not really subsided, whether there was not in a portion of this country a condition of things rendering it almost impossible to exercise the elective franchise unless there was some degree of military interference? [Great laughter.] And further, whether, after the experience of fourteen years since the war has subsided, that gentleman is yet prepared to continue a war measure in a time of profound peace in this country?

Mr. GARFIELD. No doubt the patriotic gentleman from New York [Mr. Fernando Wood] took all these things into consideration when he voted for this law; and I may have been unpatriotic in voting against it at that time; but he and I must stand by our records, as they were made.

THE NEW REBELLION.

Let it be understood that I am not discussing the merits of this law. I have merely turned aside from the line of my argument to show the inconsistency of the other side in proposing to stop the government if they cannot force the repeal of a law which they themselves made. I am discussing a method of revolution against the Constitution now proposed by this House, and to that issue I hold gentlemen in this debate, and challenge them to reply.

And now, Mr. Chairman, I ask the forbearance of gentlemen on the other side while I offer a suggestion, which I make with reluctance. They will bear me witness that I have, in many ways, shown my desire that the wounds of the war should be healed; that the grass which has grown green over the graves of the dead of both armies might symbolize the returning spring of friendship and peace between citizens who were lately in arms against each other.

But I am compelled, by the conduct of the other side, to refer to a chapter of our recent history. The last act of Democratic domination in this Capitol, eighteen years ago, was striking and dramatic, perhaps heroic. Then the Democratic party said to the Republicans, "If you elect the man of your choice as President of the United States we will shoot your government to death"; but the people of this country, refusing to be coerced by threats or violence, voted as they pleased, and lawfully elected Abraham Lincoln as President of the United States.

Then your leaders, though holding a majority in the other branch of Congress, were heroic enough to withdraw from their seats and fling down the gage of mortal battle. We called it rebellion; but we recognized it as courageous and manly to avow your purpose, take all the risks, and fight it out in the open field. Notwithstanding your utmost efforts to destroy it, the government was saved. Year by year, since the war ended, those who resisted you have come to believe that you have finally renounced your purpose to destroy, and are willing to maintain the government. In that belief you have been permitted to return to power in the two Houses.

To-day, after eighteen years of defeat, the book of your domination is again opened, and your first act awakens every unhappy memory, and threatens to destroy the confidence which your professions of patriotism inspired. You turned down a leaf of the history that recorded your last act of power in 1861, and you have now signalized your return to power by beginning a second chapter at the same page, not this time by a heroic act that declares war on the battle-field, but you say, if all the legislative powers of the government do not consent to let you tear certain laws out of the statute-book, you will not shoot our government to death as you tried to do in the first chapter, but you declare that if we do not consent against our will, if you cannot coerce an independent branch of this government, against its will, to allow you to tear from the statute-books some laws put there by the will of the people, you will starve the government to death. [Great applause on the Republican side.]

Between death on the field and death by starvation, I do not know that the American people will see any great difference. The end, if successfully reached, would be death in either case. Gentlemen, you have it in your power to kill this government; you have it in your power, by withholding these two bills, to smite the nerve-centers of our Constitution with the paralysis of death; and you have declared your purpose to do this, if you cannot break down that fundamental principle of free consent which, up to this, hour has always ruled in the legislation of this government.

Mr. DAVIS, of North Carolina. Will the gentleman allow me to ask him a question?

Mr. GARFIELD. Certainly.

Mr. DAVIS, of North Carolina. Do I understand the gentleman to say that the refusal to permit the Army at the polls will be the death of this government? [Derisive cries of "Oh!" "Oh!" on the Republican side.] That is the logic of the gentleman's argument, if it means anything. But we say that it will be the preservation of this government to keep the military power from destroying liberty at the polls.

Mr. GARFIELD. I have too much respect for the intellect of the gentleman from North Carolina to believe that he thinks that is my argument. He does not say he thinks so. On the contrary, I am sure that every clear-minded man on this floor knows that such is not my argument. The position on the other side is simply this: that unless some independent branch of the legislative power of this government is forced against its will to vote for or to approve what it does not freely consent to, you will use the voluntary power in your hands to starve the government to death.

Mr. DAVIS, of North Carolina. Will the gentleman permit me to ask him another question? Do I understand him to assume that we are forcing some branch of the government to do what it does not wish to do? How do we know that, or how does the gentleman know it? Does the gentleman, when he speaks of "the government," mean to say that it is not the government of the majority, or does he assume that the majority is on his side?

Mr. GARFIELD. I am perfectly protected against the suggestion of the gentleman. I read in the outset declarations of leading members of his party in both branches of Congress asserting this programme and declaring the intention of carrying it through to the end, in spite of the Senate and in spite of an Executive veto, which they anticipate. The method here proposed invites, possibly compels, a veto.

COERCION OF THE PRESIDENT.

Touching this question of executive action, I remind the gentleman that in 1856 the national Democratic convention, in session at Cincinnati, and still later, the national Democratic convention of 1860, affirmed the right of the veto as one of the sacred rights guaranteed by our government. Here is the resolution:

That we are decidedly opposed to taking from the President the qualified veto power by which he is enabled, under restrictions and responsibilities amply sufficient to guard the public interests, to suspend the passage of a bill whose merits cannot secure the approval of two-thirds of the Senate and House of Representatives until the judgment of the people can be obtained thereon.

The doctrine is that any measure which cannot be passed over a veto by a two-thirds vote has no right to become a law, and the only mode of redress is an appeal to the people at the next election. That has been the Democratic doctrine from the earliest days, notably so from Jackson's time until now.

In leaving this topic, let me ask what would you have said if, in 1861, the Democratic members of the Senate, being then a majority of that body, instead of taking the heroic course and going out to battle, had simply said, "We will put on an appropriation bill an amendment declaring the right of any State to secede from the Union at pleasure, and forbidding the President or any officer of the Army or Navy of the United States from interfering with any State in its work of secession?" Suppose they had said to the President, "Unless you consent to the incorporation of this provision in an appropriation bill we will refuse supplies to the government." Perhaps they could then have killed the government by starvation; but even in the madness of that hour the leaders of rebellion did not think it worthy their manhood to put their fight on that dishonorable ground. They planted themselves on the higher plane of battle and fought it out to defeat.

Now, by a method which the wildest secessionist scorned to adopt, it is proposed to make this new assault upon the life of the republic.

Gentlemen, we have calmly surveyed this new field of conflict; we have tried to count the cost of the struggle, as we did that of 1861 before we took up your gage of battle. Though no human foresight could forecast the awful loss of blood and treasure, yet in the name of liberty and union we accepted the issue and fought it out to the end. We made the appeal to our august sovereign, to the omnipotent public opinion of America, to determine whether the Union should perish at your hands. You know the result. And now lawfully, in the exercise of our right as Representatives, we take up the gage you have this day thrown down, and appeal again to our common sovereign to determine whether you shall be permitted to destroy the principle of free consent in legislation under the threat of starving the government to death.

We are ready to pass these bills for the support of the government at any hour when you will offer them in the ordinary way, by the methods prescribed by the Constitution. If you offer those other propositions of legislation as separate measures we will meet you in the fraternal spirit of fair debate and will discuss their merits. Some of your measures many of us will vote for in separate bills. But you shall not coerce any independent branch of this government, even by the threat of starvation, to consent to surrender its lawful powers until the question has been appealed to the sovereign and decided in your favor. On this ground we plant ourselves, and here we will stand to the end.

PROTECTION OF THE NATIONAL BALLOT-BOX REFUSED.

Let it be remembered that the avowed object of this new revolution is to destroy all the defenses which the nation has placed around its ballot-box to guard the fountain of its own life. You say that the United States shall not employ even its civil power to keep peace at the polls. You say that the marshals shall have no power either to arrest rioters or criminals who seek to destroy the freedom and purity of the ballot-box.

I remind you that you have not always shown this great zeal in keeping the civil officers of the general government out of the States. Only six years before the war, your law authorized marshals of the United

States to enter all our hamlets and households to hunt for fugitive slaves. Not only that, it empowered the marshals to summon the *posse comitatus*, to command all bystanders to join in the chase and aid in remanding to eternal bondage the fleeing slave. And your Democratic Attorney-General, in his opinion published in 1854, declared that the marshal of the United States might summon to his aid the whole able-bodied force of his precinct, all bystanders, including not only the citizens generally, "but any and all organized armed forces, whether militia of the State, or officers, soldiers, sailors, and marines of the United States," to join in the chase and hunt down the fugitive. Now, gentlemen, if, for the purpose of making eternal slavery the lot of an American, you could send your marshals, summon your *posse*, and use the armed force of the United States, with what face or grace can you tell us that this government cannot lawfully employ the same marshals with their armed *posse* of citizens, to maintain the purity of our own elections and keep the peace at our own polls. You have made the issue and we have accepted it. In the name of the Constitution and on behalf of good government and public justice, we make the appeal to our common sovereign.

For the present I refrain from discussing the merits of the election laws. I have sought only to state the first fundamental ground of our opposition to this revolutionary method of legislation by coercion. [Great applause.]

Mr. SPARKS. Before the gentleman from Ohio takes his seat I hope he will give to the House the name of the Attorney-General of the United States to whom he referred.

Mr. GARFIELD. I refer to Caleb Cushing, the Democratic Attorney-General of President Pierce.

2. CLOSE OF DEBATE ON FIRST ARMY BILL.

At the conclusion of the general debate on the sixth section of the Army appropriation bill, Friday, April 4, 1879, Mr. Garfield said:

Mr. CHAIRMAN: During the last four days, some fifteen or twenty gentlemen have paid their special attention to the argument I made last Saturday, and have announced its complete demolition. Now that the general debate has closed, I will notice the principal points of attack by which this work of destruction has been accomplished.

In the first place, every man, save one, who has replied to me, has alleged that I held it was revolutionary to place this general legislation upon an appropriation bill. One gentleman went so far as to fill a page of the Record with citations from the Congressional Globe and the Congressional Record to show that for many years riders had been placed upon appropriation bills. If gentlemen find any pleasure in setting up a man of straw and knocking it down again, they have enjoyed themselves.

I never claimed that it was either revolutionary or unconstitutional for this House to put a rider on an appropriation bill. No man on this side of the House has claimed that. The most that has been said is that it is considered a bad parliamentary practice; and all parties in this country have said that repeatedly.

The gentleman from Kentucky [Mr. Blackburn] evidently thought he was making a telling point against me when he cited the fact that, in 1872, I insisted upon the adoption of a conference report on an approriation bill that had a rider on it; and he alleged that I said it was revolutionary for his party to resist it. Let me refresh his memory. I said then and I say now that it was revolutionary for the minority party to refuse to let the appropriation bill be voted on. For four days they said we should not vote at all on the sundry civil appropriation bill because there was a rider on it, put there not by the House but by the Senate.

I was sorry the rider was put on, and moved to non-concur in the amendments when they came to the House. But when the minority on this floor said that we should not act on the bill at all, because the rider was put upon it, I said and now say it was unjustifiable parliamentary obstruction. We do not filibuster. We do not struggle to prevent a vote on this bill. I will be loyal to the House of which I am a member, and maintain now, as I did then, the right of the majority to bring an appropriation bill to a vote.

You have a right—however unwise and indecent it may be as a matter of parliamentary practice—you have a perfect right to put this rider on this bill and pass it. When you send it to the Senate, that body has a perfect right to pass it. It is your constitutional right and theirs to pass it; for the free consent of each body is the basis of the law-making power.

When it goes to the President of the United States, it is his constitutional right to approve it; and if he does, it will then be a law, which you and I must obey. But it is equally his constitutional right to disapprove it; and should he do so, then, gentlemen, unless two-thirds of this body and two-thirds of the Senate pass it, notwithstanding the objections of the President, it is not only not your right to make it a law, but it will be the flattest violation of the Constitution, the sheerest usurpation of power to attempt to make it a law in any other way. Without these conditions you cannot make it a law.

What, then, is the proposition you have offered? You say that there are certain odious laws that you want to take off the statute-book. I say repeal them, if you can do so constitutionally. But you declare that you will compel consent to your will by refusing the necessary support—not to the President, not to any man—but to the government itself. This proposition I denounce as revolution, and no man has responded to the charge either by argument or denial.

No member on this side brought the question into this chamber. The issue was not raised by us. Who brought it here? The proclamation of your caucus, the declaration of your conference committees. They announced it in the last House as their programme. They said you would combine these measures of legislation together and send them to the President in a separate bill, and if he did not approve them you would never vote the supplies for the government.

You threatened the President in advance before you allowed him an opportunity to say yes or no. You entered this Hall fulminating threats against him in a high-sounding proclamation. You " thundered in the index." It remains to be seen whether, in the body of your work, and in its concluding paragraphs, your thunder will be as terrible as it was in the opening chapter. By adopting the programme of the last House you have made it your own; but you have put the measures in their most offensive form by tacking them all to the two great appropriation bills.

Another equally groundless charge against me and my associates, is that we have threatened your bills with an executive veto. I repel the charge as wholly untrue in fact. I said nothing that can be tortured into such a threat. It would be indecent on my part; it would be indecent for any of us even to speak of what the executive intends to do;

for none of us have the right to know. But you, in advance, proclaimed to the country and to him that if he dares to exercise his constitutional right of refusing his consent, you will refuse to vote the supplies for the government; in other words, you will starve it to death. That is the proposition we have debated.

My distinguished friend from Virginia [Mr. Tucker], who has come nearer meeting this case with argument than any other man on that side, has made a point which I respect as an evidence of the gallantry of his intellect. He says that under our Constitution we can vote supplies to the Army but for two years; that we may impose conditions upon our supplies, and if these be refused the Army ceases to exist after the 30th of June next. In short, that the annual Army bill is the act of reconstituting the Army. He is mistaken in one vital point. The Army is an organization created by general laws; and so far as the creation of officers and grades is concerned, it is independent of the appropriation bills. The supplies, of course, come through appropriation bills. I grant that that if supplies are refused to the Army, it must perish of inanition. It becomes a skeleton; but its anatomy was created by general law, and it would remain a skeleton, your monument of starvation. The gentleman from Virginia says, "Unless you let us append a condition which we regard a redress of grievances, we will let the Army be annihilated on the 30th day of next June, by withholding supplies." That is legitimate argument; that is a frank declaration of your policy. Let us examine the proposition. What is the "grievance" of which the gentleman complains? He uses the word "grievance" in the old English sense, as though the King were thrusting himself in the way of the nation by making a war contrary to the nation's wish. But his "grievance" is a law of the land—a law made by the representatives of the people—by all the forms of consent known to the Constitution. It is his "grievance" that he cannot get rid of this law by the ordinary and Constitutional method of repeal. [Applause.] When he can get rid of any law by the union of all· consents required to make or unmake a law, he gets rid of it lawfully, whether it be a grievance or a blessing. But his method is first to call a law a "grievance," and then try to get rid of it in defiance of the processes which the Constitution prescribes for the law-making power of the nation. I denounce his method as unconstitutional and revolutionary, and one that will result in far greater evil than that of which he complains.

If he goes to the American people with the proposition to annihilate our Army on the 30th day of June next, unless the President, contrary to his conscience, contrary to his sense of duty, shall sign whatever Congress may send him——

[Here the hammer fell.]

Mr. KEIFER obtained the floor, and yielded his time to Mr. GARFIELD.

Mr. GARFIELD. I say, if the gentleman from Virginia puts that proposition before the American people, we will debate it in the forum of every patriotic heart and will abide the result. If the party which, after eighteen years' banishment from power, has come back, as the gentleman from Kentucky [Mr. Blackburn] said yesterday, to its "birthright of power," or "heritage," as it is recorded in the Record of this morning, is to signalize its return by striking down the gallant and faithful Army of the United States, the people of this country will not be slow to understand that there are reminiscences of that Army which these gentlemen would willingly forget, by burying both the Army and the memories of its great service to the Union in one grave. [Applause.]

We do not seek to revive the unhappy memories of the war; but we are unwilling to see the Army perish at the hands of Congress, even if its continued existence should occasionally awaken the memory of its former glories.

Now, let it be understood once for all, that we do not deny, we have never denied your right to make such rules for this House as you please. Under those rules, as you make or construe them, you may put all your legislation upon these bills as "riders." But we say that, whatever your rules may be, you must make or repeal a law in accordance with the Constitution, by the triple consent to which I referred the other day, or you must do it by violence.

Now, as my friend from Connecticut [Mr. Hawley] well said, if you can elect a President and a Congress in 1880, you have only to wait two years, and you have the three consents. You can then, without revolution, tear down this statute and all the rest. You can follow out the programme which some of your members have suggested, and tear out one by one the records of the last eighteen years. Some of them are glorious with the unquenchable light of liberty; some of them stand as the noblest trophies of freedom. With full power in your hands, you can destroy them. But we ask you to restrain your rage against them until you have the lawful power to smite them down.

My friend from Virginia, whom I know to be a master and lover of mathematics, has formulated his argument into an equation: "Right equals duty plus power." Now, I say to the gentleman that his sense of duty resides in his own breast; but power, the other factor of the second member of his equation, must be found, not in his conciousness, but in the Constitution of the United States. His notions of duty lead him to tear down the laws which the Republic enacted to protect the purity of national elections and to use such force as may be necessary to keep the peace while the national voice is finding expression at the polls. That, I say, is his notion of duty, of which he is sole arbiter; but when he comes to superadd power, in order to complete his "right" as a legislator, I hope he will not evoke that power out of his conciousness, but will seek for it in the great charter, the Constitution of the United States. According to his own algebra, he must have both these elements before he can claim the "right" to overturn these laws which he denounces as grievances.

Now, Mr. Chairman, let me add a word in conclusion, lest I may be misunderstood. I said last session, and I have said since, that if you want this whole statute concerning the use of the Army at the polls torn from your books, I will help you to do it. If you will offer a naked proposition to repeal those two sections of the Revised Statutes named in the sixth section of this bill, I will vote with you. But you do not ask a repeal of those sections. Why? They impose restrictions upon the use of the Army, limiting its functions and punishing its officers for any infraction of these limitations; but you seek to strike out a negative clause, thereby making new and affirmative legislation of the most sweeping and dangerous character.

Your proposed modification of the law affects not the Army alone, but the whole civil power of the United States. "Civil officers" are included in these sections; and if the proposed amendment be adopted, you deny, to every civil officer of the United States, any power whatever to summon the armed posse to help him enforce the processes of the law. If you pass the section in that form, you impose restrictions upon the civil authorities of the United States never before proposed in any Congress by any legislator since this government began. I say, therefore, in the shape you propose this, it is much the worst of all your "riders." In the beginning of this contest we understood that you desired only to get the Army away from the polls. As that would still leave the civil officers full power to keep the peace at the polls, I thought it was the least important and the least dangerous of your demands; but as you have put it here, it is the most dangerous. If you re-enact it in the shape presented, it becomes a later law than the supervisors and marshals law, and *pro tanto* repeals the latter. As it stands now in the statute-book, it is the earlier statute, and is *pro tanto* itself repealed by the marshals law of 1871, and is therefore harmless so far as it relates to civil officers. But if you put it in here, you deny the power of the marshals of the United States to perform their duties whenever a riot may require the use of an armed posse.

The gentleman from Maryland [Mr. McLane] said, the other day, there was nothing in the Constitution which empowered any officer of the United States to keep the peace in the States. A single sentence, Mr. Chairman, before your hammer falls. I ask that gentleman to tell us whether the United States has no power to keep the peace in the great post-office in Baltimore City, so that the postmaster may attend to his duties; whether we have not the power to keep the peace along the line of every railroad that carries our mails, or where any post-rider of the "star service" carries the mail on his saddle; whether we have not the right, if need be, to line the post-road with troops, and to bring the guns of the Navy to bear to protect any custom-house or light-house of the United States? And yet, if the gentleman's theory be correct, we cannot enforce a single civil process of this government by the aid of an armed posse without making it a penitentiary offense on the part of the officer who does it. [Applause on the Republican side.]

3. LEGISLATIVE APPROPRIATION BILL.

NATIONAL ELECTIONS SHOULD BE PROTECTED BY NATIONAL AUTHORITY.

The House, being in Committee of the Whole on the state of the Union, and having under consideration the legislative appropriation bill, on the 26th of April, 1879—

Mr. GARFIELD said: Mr. Chairman, I move as an amendment to the pending bill to strike out lines 2006 to 2064 inclusive, commencing with the proviso.

I had intended to speak somewhat elaborately upon this bill, but I have preferred to give way for the sake of allowing those who had not spoken an opportunity to be heard.

I would not rise now to ask the attention of the House at all but for the sake of correcting a few plain misapprehensions and evasions in this debate. The gentleman who has just taken his seat, [Mr. Ewing] has said that I have led in an attempt to raise sectional feeling in the North against the patriotic people of the South. It is the old and absurd cry of a sectional North and a national South; that is, the thirty million people of the North, and their Representatives, of whom he is one, are sectional, passionate, unkind; and the fifteen million of "national-minded and patriotic" people of the South are suffering from the narrow and unjust sectionalism of the thirty million among whom my colleague and I live!

The gentleman reminds me of what he was pleased to call a patriotic sentiment of mine, uttered at the last session of Congress, when I said what I am glad to have remembered, that in my judgment the man or political party who sought to raise sectional issues and revive the unhappy passions that ought to sleep in the graves of our dead on both sides was not patriotic, nor would he find an echo to his sentiments in the hearts of the best people of this country. I said that deliberately, with all the meaning that the words import.

The blindness that leads my colleague to call two-thirds of this nation sectional, also leads him to think my denunciation of those who reawaken old sectional strife can apply only to Republicans. Let him not forget the origin of the present controversy. Who raised this unhappy issue? Did any Republican begin it? Was it not brought here by the predetermined caucus action of the Democractic party? Was it not embodied in the declaration of your Senators and members that if you could not force certain acts of legislation upon the statute-book you would never grant supplies for the support of the government? That was the party and that was the act which raised this controversy, involving an issue never raised before in this nation; and, because we meet it and denounce it, you declare that those who stand by orderly and constitutional methods are sectional, and you who make the innovation are national!

Gentlemen, I took upon myself a very grave responsibility in the opening of this debate when I quoted the declarations of leading members on the other side and said that the programme was revolution and, if not abandoned, would result in the destruction of this government. I declared that you had entered upon a scheme which if persisted in would starve the government to death. I say that I took a great risk when I made this charge against you as a party. I put myself in your power, gentlemen. If I had misconceived your purposes and misrepresented your motives, it was in your power to prove me a false accuser. It was in your power to ruin me in the estimation of fair-minded, patriotic men, by the utterance of one sentence. The humblest or the greatest of you could have overwhelmed me with shame and confusion in one short sentence. You could have said, "We wish to pass our measures of legislation in reference to elections, juries, and the use of the Army; and we will if we can do so constitutionally; but if we cannot get these measures in accordance with the Constitution, we will pass the appropriation bills like loyal Representatives; and then go home and appeal to the people."

If any man, speaking for the majority, had made that declaration, uttered that sentence, he would have ruined me in the estimation of fair-minded men, and set me down as a false accuser and slanderer. Forty-five of you have spoken. Forty-five of you have deluged the ear of this country with debate; but that sentence has not been spoken by any one of you. On the contrary, by your silence, as well as by your affirmation, you have made my accusation overwhelmingly true.

And there I leave that controversy. The assaults upon my speech have been, from the beginning to the end, evasions of the issue. What have you said? Not less than thirty of you, in spite of my plain and emphatic declarations to the contrary, have insisted that I said it was revolutionary to put a rider on an appropriation bill, a thing that no man on this side of the House has said. You were guilty, gentlemen, and in this I include the gentleman from Pennsylvania [Mr. Kelley], of what Sidney Smith once called "an indecent exposure of your intellects."

Mr. KELLEY. Did I misunderstand you when I said that your speech which lay before me had the title of "Revolution in Congress," and said if the gentleman believed that doctrine now he had undergone a mental revolution?

Mr. GARFIELD. The gentleman should not confine his reading to the title. If he had read my speech as well as its title, he would have read that in 1872, in the debate to which he referred, the Democratic party on this floor said we should not consider an appropriation bill at all. I said to them, "You have a right to vote against it; you have a right to filibuster to get a chance to speak on it if need be; but when you say that the majority shall not act on an appropriation bill at all, because there is a rider on it, that is parliamentary revolution"; and so I say to-day, and the gentleman quoted that as though it were inconsistent with my present position, which is as that of 1872, that to refuse to act on the appropriations is revolutionary. In 1872 the Democracy said the appropriation bill should not be acted on at all because a rider was on it. Now they say the appropriation bills shall not be acted upon at all unless there are "riders" on them. I resisted their position then, and I resist it now.

There is another point which I must touch to show the evasions which have been resorted to in this debate. The other side seeks to go before the country on pleas like this which stands as the heading of the speech of the distinguished gentleman from Virginia [Mr. Tucker]: "Elections by the people must be free from the power and presence of the standing Army." They seek to make the people believe that Democrats in Congress are struggling to get the bayonets away from the breasts of the voters, and that we are striving to keep the Army at the polls. The Democratic press is everywhere stating the issue in this way, that the Republicans are defending an odious law, enacted amid the passions of the war, to authorize the use of the Army at State elections.

Now, "mark how plain a tale shall put that down." On this side, this proposition was made: If you find fault with the law of 1865 we will help you repeal it altogether. On the motion of the distinguished gentleman from Michigan, [Mr. Conger] every Republican on this floor who voted at all, when the Army bill was here, voted to repeal *in toto* the law of 1865, which you complained of to the people as putting the bayonets at the breasts of the voters; and every Democrat, who sits here and voted at all, voted "No." You would not repeal the law, but you told the people we were trying to keep it on the statute-books, and you were trying to get it off.

Now, Mr. Chairman, our vote on that subject has put us beyond all cavil on this high and unassailable ground. We are willing and we have voted to repeal the whole of that law, and we even went so far as to put that repeal on the Army bill, and you voted against it. Now, never again go to the people and say you tried to repeal the odious law of 1865 and the Republicans would not let you.

My colleague [Mr. Ewing], who has just taken his seat, says that the sections sought to be repealed by the bill now before us, authorize unwarrantable and unconstitutional interference with elections in the States. He says that the supervisors and marshals are intruders at the election of Congressmen; that they have no constitutional right to be there, even as witnesses. Gentlemen, I never believed in State rights to the extent you did and do; but there is one thing concerning which I have always thought that the States came very near being sovereign. I suppose that all our States claim the right to have a legislature of two houses, each house with a right to make its own rules, sit in its own separate chamber, pass measures according to its own rules, and regulate the conduct of its own clerks. Yet, gentlemen, if you will read from sections 14 to 19 of the Revised Statutes, you will find that the following has been done: The supreme power of the United States, by force of national law, has gone into the legislature of every State in this Union, and said to them, "There is a certain Tuesday, the second Tuesday after you have organized, when you shall not fix your own time of meeting; when you shall not even adjourn over. You shall meet at twelve o'clock. When you meet you shall not vote by ballot; you shall vote *viva voce*. Your clerk shall call the roll. You shall vote for a Senator." The law prescribes how the clerks of both houses shall make the entries in their journals. If there is no election, the clerk shall certify it; and then this national authority says: "If there is no election by the separate vote of the two houses the second day, I take your two houses and consolidate them into one. I abolish the distinction between senator and representative, put them into one hall and hold them in joint session from day to day, and they shall vote as one body until a Senator is elected."

Who does all that to State legislatures? It is done by a law of the United States passed in July, 1866; and no Democrat has denounced it as unconstitutional; no State legislature has made any opposition to it; and every one of the seventy-six Senators now at the other end of this Capitol, holds his seat in pursuance of the operation of that law.

Now, if we do all that unchallenged to the legislature of a sovereign State, who will say that we cannot go among our own citizens and supervise and protect our own ballot-boxes where men are to be elected to seats on this floor? Your constitutional question is given away when you admit the supervisions there, as you do in this bill; still more decisively it is given away by the universal acquiescence in the law for electing Senators.

The great danger which threatens this country is, that our sovereign may be dethroned or destroyed by corruption. In any monarchy of the world, if the sovereign be slain or become lunatic, it is easy to put another in his place, for the sovereign is a person. But our sovereign is the whole body of voters. If you kill or corrupt or render lunatic our sovereign, there is no successor, no regent to take his place. The source of our sovereign's supreme danger, the point where his life is vulnerable, is at the ballot-box, where his will is declared; and if we cannot stand by that cradle of our sovereign's heir-apparent and protect it to the uttermost against all assassins and assailants, we have no government and no safety for the future. [Applause.]

Mr. EWING. I hope the House will allow me to ask the gentleman a question and him to reply. I ask the gentleman, may we therefore authorize United States supervisors to inspect the officers of the house and senate of each State as to the manner of election when electing a United States Senator, and appoint marshals to back up the supervisors, and send out the Army to back up the marshals?

Mr. GARFIELD. Not at all. The gentleman from New Jersey [Mr. ROBESON] answered that by anticipation.

Our Constitution adopted the legislatures of the States as our agents to elect Senators at the times and in the manner which Congress may by law direct. They were adopted as bodies organized under State laws.

For the election of Representatives to this House, we may set up all our own machinery if we please. We may adopt the State machinery, and superadd our own national superintendence and safeguards; and the safeguards which have already been established we will maintain and defend. [Applause.]

4. SECOND ARMY APPROPRIATION BILL.

The House being in Committee of the Whole on the State of the Union, on the second Army appropriation bill, June 11, 1879—

Mr. GARFIELD said: Permit me, Mr. Chairman, to recount, ver briefly, the steps which have been taken in regard to this Army appropriation bill in connection with the legislative bill. At the close of the last session, those two bills were prevented from passing, upon the alleged ground that there were three grievances in the form of laws which gentlemen on the other side said must be redressed by repeal before they would vote the appropriations necessary to carry on the government. One grievance was set forth in a vague general charge, but not well founded, that there was a law upon the statute-book that authorized military interference with elections. The second was that the jurors' test oath, made necessary by the war, was now a hardship and a grievance. The third was that the several sections of the law relating to supervisors and marshals at national elections were a grievance which must be removed by repeal. And we were told, in the most unequivocal language, by the Democratic leaders in both Houses, that the $45,000,000 needed for the maintenance of the civil and military functions of the government should never be appropriated until these statutes were repealed.

In response to these demands, we declared our willingness on this side of the House, first, to pass a bill which the Senate, a Republican Senate, sent to us repealing that section of the statute which prescribed a test oath for jurors. We were ready then, we are ready now, to pass that bill just as the Senate sent it to us at the last session. Second, we said then, we have frequently repeated the offer this session, and we say now, that we have never voted for a law to make use of the Army to run elections. We have said repeatedly that there never was in this country and there is not now such a law; and we do not desire such a law or such a practice; and that, if any act was needed to prevent the running of elections by bayonets, we were ready to help prevent it. These two propositions we offered at the close of the last session, in order to remove any real or apparent ground of complaint on those two scores, provided that on the other side, the third demand, namely, the repeal of the laws relating to supervisors and marshals, should be abandoned.

These offers were rejected with arrogant contempt; and the extra session was forced upon the country. A struggle of nearly three months has followed. Nearly all the legislative appropriations have now passed this House without conditions or change of the laws.

With this general review I shall now confine my remarks wholly to the history of the Army appropriation bill. Soon after this session began, we were tendered an Army bill that had in it not a repeal of the law of 1865, alleged to be an offense—not that; for we tendered that, and 109 Republicans voted to repeal it, and not one Republican voted against the repeal while every Democrat in this House voted against its repeal. Instead of a repeal, it was proposed so to modify the law of 1865 as to enlarge its restrictions beyond the Army and Navy and make it a crime, punishable by imprisonment or fine, for any civil officer of the United States to employ any armed force, soldiers or citizens, to keep the peace at the national elections. In other words, we were tendered a proposition which swept the whole circle of the civil powers with its prohibitions, and prevented the civil authorities of the nation from preserving the peace at the elections of our national legislature or protecting supervisors in the execution of their duties.

That assault upon the law we resisted as one man. But while we resisted, we protested that we were not and never had been advocates of running elections by bayonets.

Though that bill, with its revolutionary menance, passed both Houses, it was wrecked upon the rock of the Constitution, and went down, leaving not a spar afloat on the face of the political waters.

A MEMBER. It met with a veto.

Mr. GARFIELD. Yes; it met the veto with which the Constitution had wisely armed our Chief Magistrate. Then came the second chapter. A short bill of six or eight lines was introduced, not merely repealing the military provisions of the law of 1865, but in effect declaring that the Army of the United States should not be used to enforce any of the laws of the Union anywhere, at any time when an election was being held. We pointed out the fact that the bill would smite with paralysis the executive authority of the nation during two, three, five, ten, or possibly a hundred days of every year; that under its provisions even the property of the nation could not be protected from destruction at any place where any election was being held. This violent measure was also passed by the solid Democratic vote of both Houses; but, like its predecessor, it ran against the rock of the Constitution and went to the bottom [applause on the Republican side], and only bubbles mark the spot where it went down.

And now we have before us another bill making appropriations for the support of the Army. Before considering its other provisions, I turn aside to congratulate the country and the Army that so many gentlemen on both sides have finally consented to strike out the ninth section, which would have proved a hardship to the meritorious officers of the Army by stopping promotions for an indefinite period; and I tender my compliments and thanks to the distinguished gentleman from Virginia [Mr. Johnston] who made the motion. The country and the Army will not forget it. I believe the appropriations made in this bill are sufficient for the support of our military establishment, and no laws in reference to which there is any controversy are repealed by it.

This brings me to the consideration of the only provision about which there is any question. It is the sixth section, and I will read it:

SEC. 6. That no money appropriated in this act is appropriated or shall be paid for the subsistence, equipment, transportation, or compensation of any portion of the Army of the United States to be used as a police force to keep the peace at the polls at any election held within any State.

My first observation is, that this section does not profess to repeal, and does not repeal, any law of the United States. There is not now and, so far as I know, there never was on our statute-book a law which authorized the use of the Army "as a police force" at the polls; and even if this section were a repealing clause, there is nothing on which it can operate as a repeal.

But whatever the section means, it is in the form of a limitation for the coming year upon the objects to which the appropriations are to be applied. It is declared that this money is not "appropriated for the subsistence, &c., of any portion of the Army to be used as a police force to keep the peace at the polls." I affirm, without fear of successful contradiction, that this limited and indirect prohibition does not apply to any law or to any practice known in this country.

Mr. HAWLEY. Not since the Kansas troubles.

Mr. GARFIELD. Certainly not since the Kansas troubles. And, furthermore, I do not know of a man in this House who is in favor of using the Army of the United States as an ordinary police force to run elections. [Applause on the Democratic side and counter-cheers on the Republican side.] There are, I believe, about forty thousand polling-places in the United States. If our Army roster was full—officers, soldiers and camp followers—we would not have over twenty-five thousand in all. And if there were a law for using the Army as a police force at the polls, we should have about three-fourths of one soldier to each polling place.

Now, if anybody proposes to deploy our Army in that way I do not know where the lunatic lives. I speak for myself, and of course for everybody who thinks as I do, and for nobody else. We hold two things: first, that we will not, if we can help it, let vital and righteous laws be repealed or nullified as the condition of getting an appropriation to support the government. We have resisted, and will resist to the end, all such measures. And, in the second place, even under the pressure of party feeling and party opposition, we will do no act and cast no vote that will place us really or apparently in any attitude inconsistent with the old and recognized principles and traditions of English and American liberty, namely, that civil, not military, force is the usual, the safe, the American method of keeping peace at the polls.

That no one may misunderstand me, let me put the case thus: Suppose some one should offer the following as a substitute for this section:

Be it enacted, &c., That it shall be lawful for the President of the United States to use the Army or any portion of it as a police force to keep the peace at the polls at any election held within any State.

Is there a man in this House that would vote to make that a part of our law? If there be one, let him speak. [A pause.]

Mr. FINLEY. Did not the gentleman vote for a proposition substantially that?

Mr. GARFIELD. Never in my life, nor anything like it.

Mr. FINLEY. The vote of the gentleman last session was precisely that in effect.

Mr. GARFIELD. The gentleman is utterly mistaken. Now, if no one would vote to enact into law the thing which this section says is not appropriated for, how can any one hold that the section prohibits anything that ought to be done?

I say, for one, that in so far as this section indicates the relation between the civil and military arm of the government in the conduct of elections it meets my cordial concurrence; and a vote for the section will put at rest the reckless and false charge that this side of the House desire to run elections by bayonets.

I admit, as my friend from Indiana [Mr. Baker] has said, that the section is mere surplusage. It does not repeal or change any existing law; but if its framers think that by offering it they expect to gain a party advantage by getting me, or those with whom I act, to cast a vote that implies that the Army ought to be used as an ordinary police at elections they are greatly mistaken; for they have set a very open trap, baited with a very small piece of very poor cheese.

Now, Mr. Chairman, a word further in reference to the language of the section. Some gentlemen may be troubled about the scope and meaning of the words "to be used as a police force." Let me recall a little history. When flagrant war was raging, when eleven States were banded against the Union to destroy it, and the theater of war pread over five or six States that adhered to the Union, there was in fact military interference at the elections; it was the military interference of the armed enemies of the United States.

I once voted at an election where there was very serious military interference. In the autumn of 1862 under the heights of Missionary Ridge, near the city of Chattanooga, when 5,000 Ohio soldiers under the laws of that State were permitted to vote, I in company with my comrades voted for a governor of Ohio.

While we were voting, the shells from the batteries of armed enemies of the United States were bursting over our heads, and some of our voters were killed while in the exercise of their right of suffrage as citizens of Ohio. That was the only military interference with elections that I ever witnessed. [Applause on the Republican side.] Now, it was to prevent that kind of military interference that the armies of the United States in time of war kept off the armed enemies of the United States in the State of Kentucky and in other border States while elections were being held there. And in order that, in the performance of that necessary duty, they might not interfere with the freedom of elections and the right of citizens, the act of February, 1865, was passed while our guns were yet smoking and while we were yet in line of battle. Even in that act it was provided, under the severest penalties of criminal law, that no officer, civil, military, or naval, should interfere with the right of any man to vote, or should undertake to prescribe qualifications for a voter.

Now, I say that the act of 1865 was in the interest of civil liberty, restraining our armies from doing any wrong or committing any outrage. And in that act there occurs for the first time in the history of our legislation connected with the Army the expression "to keep the peace at the polls." And even there it is used for the purpose of saying that the law does not make it a crime punishable by imprisonment and fine for an officer of the government to "keep the peace at the polls" or to repel the armed enemies of the United States. Nothing in that law refers to the use of the Army as an ordinary police force. The marshals and their deputies are the police force of the United States. Our Army is governed by the rules and articles of war, and is always used as an army when it is ordered to execute the laws.

The proposition to use our Army as a police, to send the soldiers out and station them one by one at the polls to run the elections as a police, is a fiction so absurd that I trust no man on this side of the House will give the least color to the assumption that he favors it by holding that this sixth section repeals, suspends, or modifies any existing statute.

Mr. WILLIAMS, of Wisconsin. Will my distinguished friend allow me to submit to him one question, which he will understand I put in the utmost good faith.

Mr. GARFIELD. Certainly.

Mr. WILLIAMS, of Wisconsin. It is this: Are you now in favor of using any portion of the Army of the United States at any time, under any circumstances, in any emergency, to keep the peace at the polls?

Mr. GARFIELD. Not in the sense of using that Army as an ordinary police force.

Mr. WILLIAMS, of Wisconsin. In any form or manner?

Mr. CARLISLE. This section does not refer to the use of the Army as an ordinary police force. I do not mean as an ordinary civil police, but in any form whatever. Is the gentleman in favor of using the Army in any form whatever to keep the peace at the polls?

Mr. GARFIELD. I am in favor of using the Army and the Navy and all the militia of the United States to enforce the laws of the United

States, any one of them and all of them, everywhere, and at all times when the civil force is inadequate, but not until then.

Mr. WILLIAMS, of Wisconsin. Including the keeping of the peace at the polls. [Laughter on the Democratic side.]

Mr. GARFIELD. If there be any law that authorizes the President to use the Army as an ordinary police force for that purpose I am in favor of enforcing it.

Mr. WILLIAMS, of Wisconsin. Does my friend think that we have that law, or does he think that we do not have it?

Mr. GARFIELD. I think we have not; that we never have had it, and that we never ought to have it. The marshals and their deputies are our police.

Under our laws, at the present moment, we have the amplest power to add deputy marshals and assistant marshals in any number that may be needed to keep the peace at the polls, and those marshals may summon the posse, the armed posse of all faithful citizens who will obey the orders of the marshals and keep the peace at the polls. This is the traditional law of English-speaking people.

Now, if my friend from Wisconsin [Mr. Williams] will remember, it was distinctly provided in the law of last year that the Army of the United States should not be used as a part of the *posse comitatus* in any case except where the law expressly provided that it should be so used. Therefore, in the presence of that restrictive legislation, passed almost unanimously by a Republican Senate—although I and my friend voted against it in the House; yet it was finally concurred in without a division—in the presence of that restrictive legislation, I say there is no law in the United States to which this sixth section can attach itself, either as a repealing or as a modifying clause.

Therefore I say in conclusion that whatever use may be made of this section as party literature, it is evident to me that, in the judgment of lawyers and courts and executive officers of the government, it will be regarded merely and only a stump speech, changing no law and having no legal effect whatever. I shall vote for the bill.

---

5. JUDICIAL APPROPRIATION BILL.

The House being in Committee of the Whole House on the state of the Union on the judicial appropriation bill, June 10, 1879—

Mr. GARFIELD said: Mr. Chairman, those provisions of this bill which itemize the expenses of the courts, are in the right direction, the direction of economy and a prudent regard for the safe disbursement of the public funds. I welcome them in this respect as in pursuance of a policy which we ought always to approve.

In so far as the bill creates unnecessary deficiencies, as has been stated by the gentleman from New York [Mr. Hiscock], it is objectionable. The fair and manly course for the House to pursue is to appropriate what is fully adequate, and no more, to meet the expenses of the current fiscal year. The opposite course has been frequently pursued by political parties; but, in the long run, it has been found to be wise to make an apparent reduction of expenditures knowing that the supplies withheld must be made up by subsequent deficiency bills. There is no real gain to any party in the long run; and it is a bad way to manage the fiscal affairs of the government. I hope, therefore, whatever amendment this bill may need in that respect will be made, and that the full amount required for the actual service of the year will be added.

In reference to the two clauses which have been referred to by the gentleman from New York, and which are found on pages 2 and 3 of the bill (which I have a copy of only by borrowing it from a member of the committee), I will make a few observations. It is not a valid objection against the passage of an appropriation bill that it does not embrace all the objects for which appropriations should be made. We cannot justly vote against appropriations which are proper in themselves merely because the amounts are not large enough.

But there is a clause at the end of the first section which is something more than a mere omission to make a necessary appropriation; I read it: "No part of the money hereby appropriated is appropriated to pay any salaries, compensations, fees, expenses, under or in virtue of title 26 of the Revised Statutes." It is fair to inquire whether those statutes do not command the executive officers of the government to perform some positive duty, and whether by this clause we are not only neglecting to appropriate, but are virtually nullifying the law by preventing its enforcement. If the clause which I have read stood alone, it would be less objectionable; but taken in connection with the second section, which I will read presently, it amounts to a legislative prohibition, for one year, to enforce the provisions of title 26. The sections of that title are the laws which this House and the Senate have vainly tried to repeal, but have found they have not the constitutional power to do so. We were told, in the outset, that these laws should be repealed or no appropriations would be made. But it has been demonstrated to the most unobservant, that the present Congress is powerless to repeal these laws, and the attempt has been wisely abandoned. The chief amounts needed for the support of the civil departments were appropriated in the bill which we passed yesterday, with no provision for repealing or modifying the law; but now the Committee on Appropriations propose a bill by which, for the coming year, these laws shall be not repealed, but not enforced—nullified.

Now, gentlemen, that is only an indirect way of doing temporarily, for one year, what you have no constitutional authority to do absolutely and permanently. This provision ought to be stricken out. As I have already intimated, the clause to which I have referred draws its evil inspiration from the provisions of the second section, which I will now read:

That the sums appropriated in this act for the persons and public service embraced in its provisions are in full for such persons and public service for the fiscal year ending June 30, 1880; and no department or officer of the government shall, during said fiscal year, make any contract or incur any liability for the future payment of money until an appropriation sufficient to meet such contract or pay such liability shall have first been made by law.

Now, Mr. Chairman, let us consider the effect of this section upon existing law.

Mr. COX. I desire to ask the gentleman whether what he has just read is not substantially the law now?

Mr. GARFIELD. My remarks will soon answer the gentleman. In 1870, in order to prevent the extravagant use of the public money, Congress passed a law restricting the expenditures for any one year to the appropriations made for that year; that is, if the appropriations made for the year were not sufficient, a deficiency must be asked for. Unexpended balances, remaining from previous years, could not be applied to meet deficiencies. This was a wise provision. Then it was found that there was a tendency to incur obligations by making contracts, such as for the rent of buildings, the lease extending over a series of years ahead. Thus obligations were incurred for which no appropriations of money had been made. To check that tendency, section 3679 of the Revised Statutes was enacted in these words:

> No department of the government shall expend, in any one fiscal year, any sum in excess of appropriations made by Congress for that fiscal year, or involve the government in any contract for the future payment of money in excess of such appropriations.

Now, *in pari materia*, as part of the same general prohibition, gentlemen will find, in section 3732, this enactment:

> No contract or purchase on behalf of the United States shall be made, unless the same is authorized by law or is under an appropriation adequate to its fulfillment, except—

But here is an important exception that gentlemen appear to have overlooked, and it answers the question of the gentleman from New York [Mr. Cox]—

> Except in the War and Navy Departments, for clothing, subsistence, forage, fuel, quarters, or transportation; which, however, shall not exceed the necessities of the current year.

Perhaps this section may throw a little side-light on another bill which is shortly to be before us in regard to feeding, clothing, and transporting the Army. Under the laws as they now stand, if Congress neglects to pass the regular appropriation bills, or if the appropriations run out, still the Army is to be fed and not starved, clothed and not left naked, transported to points of danger and not left idle and useless. So also with the Navy. But here is a section which, for one year, nullifies section 3732, for it makes no exception.

Mr. CARLISLE. Did not the act of 1870 repeal all that?

Mr. GARFIELD. No, sir.

Mr. CARLISLE. Why not?

Mr. GARFIELD. Because of the exception which I have just read with reference to the Army and the Navy, which has never been construed as repealed.

Mr. CARLISLE. You have read the exceptions in the act of 1861; but the act of 1870, a later statute, contained no exceptions whatever.

Mr. GARFIELD. I have read to the gentleman from the Revised Statutes now in force two exceptions which must be construed together; one does not repeal the other.

Mr. CARLISLE. How did that provision get there?

Mr. GARFIELD. It is enough for me to know that this is the law. Both sections have been adopted by Congress in the revision of 1874. But this is not all. Besides nullifying the exceptions of that section for the coming year, there is imported into this second section of the bill a new term. Before this, outside of these exceptions, a department could not make a contract, a written contract, binding the government to pay money for an object for which no appropriation had been made.

That was wise and judicious, for it prevented the departments from entering into large schemes that bound the government in advance of the action of Congress. But here is another expression not known in our existing statutes:

> No department or officer of the government shall * * * make any contract *or incur any liability.*

Here is a provision which   ich broader than any that can be found in the statutes, as eve   wyer will concede. "Incur liability." What does that mean?   uppose the President of the United States should think it important to send a minister extraordinary to some foreign court, being authorized thereto by the Constitution, and in an emergency should send him. Would he incur liability? Certainly. Suppose he had been ordered by Congress to do it. Suppose it was made mandatory under the law, but there happened to be no special appropriation for it, and he should make the appointment. Would he "incur liability" for which an appropriation had not first been made? Suppose it should so happen that a new judicial district had been created by act of Congress, and the President should be ordered by the law to appoint a judge, but there happened to be no appropriation for the salary of the judge. The President in appointing that judge according to law incurs a liability for the government to pay the salary. In short, any executive act of his which by law he is commanded to perform, he is here forbidden to perform, during the coming year, because in doing so he incurs a liability for which an appropriation has not been specially made in advance.

The object of this legislation is plain. During the coming year there is to be an election for members of Congress in the State of California, and one in the Westchester district of New York to fill a vacancy; and this legislation is leveled at these elections, so that neither the courts nor the United States marshals shall appoint deputy marshals to act as official witnesses or to keep the peace at those elections, in order that the United States may be properly and lawfully present at the creation of its own legislators. This legislation is an attempt to defeat and cripple the power of the United States to be present at those two elections which are to be held during the coming summer. It is an attempt to accomplish by indirection what cannot be done by an open and plain repeal.

Now, Mr. Chairman, as we have successfully resisted the repeal of righteous laws, in spite of the threat that the appropriations would be refused, none the less will we resist their nullification. The chapter of forced repeal seems to have been closed. Gentlemen have abandoned it. But the chapter of nullifying laws is now opened. Again we stand upon the unassailable proposition that not only shall these just laws remain upon the statute-book, but that they shall be executed.

If you do not appropriate the money we cannot help ourselves. We are powerless to appropriate it without your aid. You are the majority; but not by our consent shall you nullify a law which the Constitution does not permit you to repeal. I will now hear the gentleman from Illinois.

Mr. SPRINGER. I rose to ask the gentleman the question whether it was not within the province of a majority of this House and of the Senate to withhold appropriations for any purpose that they might desire.

Mr. GARFIELD. Oh, yes.

Mr. SPRINGER. What complaint, then, have you to make against the majority of this House and of the other House for refusing appropriations for objects which they deem subversive of the rights and liberties of the people?

Mr. GARFIELD. I answer the gentleman from Illinois by a quotation from the distinguished gentleman from Virginia [Mr. Tucker], who is not now here. He defined right to be equal to power plus duty. Now you have the power to withhold appropriations for executing the laws, but have you the right? Your power and your duty put together constitute your right in the best sense of the word. Of course you are your own judges of duty. But we are all here, Mr. Chairman, under the solemn obligation of an oath. We are all sworn before the Searcher of all hearts that we will well and faithfully perform the duties of Representatives under the Constitution. And the Constitution makes it our duty to appropriate the necessary means to enforce the laws. The Constitution provides that the judges, the President, and other officers shall receive a fixed compensation at stated times, and this can only be done by our being faithful to our oaths.

Will the gentleman deny that we are under a solemn obligation to make all the appropriations necessary to carry on the government and execute the laws of the United States? If any gentlemen here see fit to neglect that high duty and violate that great obligation, they must answer to their own constituents, to their consciences, and to God. But, as for me, I hold that to appropriate the money required by the law is my duty; and my vote shall be for the appropriations under the laws as they are, and not coupled with acts which nullify or obstruct them.

There have come into our Treasury during the last year $235,000,000. Every dollar of that money came from the people under the sanction of laws which were passed for the express purpose of raising money for the support of the government. That money is in the Treasury for that purpose; and we are the trustees of that fund under the law and the Constitution. The people paid it without imposing any conditions; they paid it, under the laws as they now exist, to support the government.

Now, therefore, if we, the trustees of that great fund, step in between those for whom we hold the trust and the execution of the trust, and say we will not apply this money according to the laws under which we received it, but will impose conditions of our own different from those under which they paid it, are we not betrayers of a trust, and violators of the Constitution?

During the debate on the second section of the bill, the same day, Mr. GARFIELD said:

Mr. Chairman, I move to amend by striking out in line 6, section 2, the words "or incur any liability." I do that because it will leave the statutes on the subject plain and unambiguous. If these words are out, the remainder of the provision is not unlike what is now in the law, and I think there would be no ambiguity in the section; but if these words be retained, no man can know precisely what he may or may not do without violating the law.

I do not myself think that, strictly and properly construed, this section suspends a number of sections of the Revised Statutes which some gentlemen may think are temporarily repealed; but with these words here they leave an uncertainty hanging over many sections of the Revised Statutes as to what constitutes incurring liability.

I can conceive such a thing as this: The President may appoint a man and may say to him, "Go and do this duty; the law authorizes me to appoint you. You may never receive any pay. You will never receive any unless Congress appropriates it hereafter." Possibly the President would not thereby incur any liability. I presume, when election day comes, the judges can appoint supervisors and the marshals can appoint assistant marshals in the same way. There is certainly nothing here which prevents them from doing their duty; and if they are told at the time of their appointment that they never can have any pay from the government unless Congress should thereafter appropriate it, query, whether any liability has been incurred. I rather think not.

Mr. SPRINGER. I should think there had been.

Mr. GARFIELD. I think not. The liability spoken of here is certainly a pecuniary one. But if the gentleman thinks there is liability, it proves the necessity of making the language clear, which certainly will be done by striking out the words which render it doubtful. [Cries on the Democratic side of "Vote!" "Vote!"] Not quite yet.

Now, if gentlemen have put these words in here to suit two views of this case, so that they can say to one class of their friends, "We have done it," and to others who do not think they ought to have done it, "We have not done it", I say if they have had a double purpose in view, these words are well chosen. But if they have a plain, frank, manly purpose in view, that everybody can understand, they should leave these words out. I think, therefore, for the honor of the House and for the clearness and definiteness of the statutes, these words ought to come out; and in the interest of good legislation I make the motion to strike them out.

Mr. COX. I understand my friend from Ohio to say that he believes United States supervisors and others will be appointed.

Mr. GARFIELD. I did not say they would be, but perhaps they can be——

Mr. COX. That the President and the judges would appoint them under this clause if passed—that they would be appointed.

Mr. GARFIELD. The gentleman will understand I am merely saying if it should be done and they were told they never could have any pay until Congress subsequently appropriated the money—I refer to deputy marshals—I doubt whether that would constitute under this section an incurred liability.

In the debate on the third section, the same day—

Mr. GARFIELD said:
I offer the following amendment:

In line 16, after the word "citizen," insert the words "of good standing"; and strike out all after the word "held," in line 17, down to and including the word "belong," in line 19; so that it will read:

"Which commissioner shall be a citizen of good standing residing in the district in which such court is held."

This will strike out the words:

And a well-known member of the principal political party opposed to that to which the clerk may belong.

I offer this amendment because I am unwilling, if I can prevent it, to allow a statute to pass this House, which, for the first time in the history of this government, injects party politics into our jury laws. The words "political parties" are unknown in our Constitution. There is not a word in the Constitution that indicates such a creation as a political party.

Political parties are probably necessary in all free governments; but there has been one place in the whole circle of our judicial system into which hitherto the word party has never found its place as a part of the law. Our goddess of justice, so far as persons are concerned, is painted blind; but so far as the objects and essence of justice are concerned, she sees the whole world.

Now it is proposed, most unwisely, and I think for the first time in our history, (and I beg the lawyers and judges who sit before me to think of this,) to put into the jury-boxes a man recognized as a political partisan, and then another beside him recognized as belonging to another political party, to administer justice. One is to do Democratic justice, another Republican justice, another Greenback justice, and so on to the end of the chapter.

If that phrase be planted in our law no man can tell the bitter, bad fruits that it may produce in the future of our jurisprudence.

Let us, gentlemen, have one place where, as lawyers and citizens seeking their rights, there shall be no such thing as politics recognized, but where equal and exact justice will be meted out to all men.

Now, the gentleman from Iowa [Mr. WEAVER] proposed, a little while ago, what was entirely proper, that it should not be confined to two political parties. There may be two, three, four, or five parties—there are perhaps that many in the country—and if you let the idea of party politics get into the law of juries at all, you ought to go through the whole list of parties, to be just or fair.

Let me ask how many clerks of national courts there are whose politics you can really ascertain without an inquest? There are a great many of these clerks who have held their positions during the lives of half a dozen political parties, and who have no political partisanship in them, and who make it a part of their daily bread to keep out of politics. Some of these clerks were in office before the Republican party was born, and do not know to which party they belong. Now, in order to execute this proposed law, you must find out what their political opinions are; you must, in fact, make them partisan before you can appoint a commissioner or impanel a jury.

I beg gentlemen to let this amendment of mine pass, in the interest of law and justice. I hope that the fact that we have been looking into each other's faces and fighting a political battle, has not put the majority into such an attitude that they will reject everything proposed by me or my associates. I should be glad for the sake of justice to see the House agree to this amendment.

In reply to Mr. McMahon, Mr. GARFIELD said:

Mr. Chairman, the gentleman has referred to the electoral commission. He will remember that there was not, in that law, a word which referred to one political party or the other. It was the sense of decency and fair play between the two parties which, after the law was passed, led them voluntarily to put men of both parties upon that commission. The Republican Senate put upon it a fair share of Democrats, and the Democratic House put upon it a proper share of Republicans. But the law said not a word about selecting men from opposite political parties to serve upon the commission. The law was just as this law ought to be—free from the recognition of party politics.

---

6. JUDICIAL APPROPRIATION BILL.

NULLIFICATION.

The House having under consideration the conference report of the two Houses on the judicial appropriation bill, June 19, 1879—

Mr. GARFIELD said: Mr. Speaker, we do not insist that this House is obliged to vote all the money which some of us may think necessary or any given purpose. If the majority offer to appropriate for a particular purpose a part only of the money needed, we would not be justified in voting against the bill merely because the amount is insufficient, for it might be your purpose to supply the deficiency hereafter. But it is certainly an objectionable mode of legislation so to cut down the appropriation bills as to make a deficiency inevitable. This bill is open to that objection; it does not appropriate enough; for it wholly omits a part of the usual supplies. But that objection alone would not prevent this side from voting for it.

The feature of the bill which is most objectionable, and to which we do not and cannot agree, has been well stated by my colleague [Mr. Monroe]. The bill goes beyond appropriations, and proposes by law to lay hold of the executive department of this government and affirmatively prevent its officers from enforcing certain laws of the land. That is the attempt which we resist and shall continue to resist. The objectionable provision is now made definite and unmistakable in this conference report. The language of the clause as it first passed the House was somewhat vague, but here it is plain, and we perfectly understand its import. If any doubt remained, my colleague who presented the report [Mr. McMahon] removed it, by declaring the purpose of the clause. The issue is narrowed down to this: The gentleman tells us that he and his associates are determined that there shall be appointed no marshals, deputy marshals, or assistant marshals to execute the laws of the Union, as embodied in title 26 of the Revised Statutes; that they have devised and agreed on this clause in the conference between the two Houses so as to prevent the enforcement of that part of the existing law. This makes a sharp issue which everybody can understand.

Now, assuming that the gentlemen on the other side do not like these provisions of law relating to elections (and we understand that to be their unanimous sentiment), they ought to propose amendments to them. My colleague who presents this report says that the law has been used for partisan purposes; that marshals, deputy marshals, and assistant marshals have been appointed merely to advocate and advance the political interest of one party at the elections. If that be so, it is a just criticism of the law, and an amendment ought to be offered to correct such an abuse. If my colleague will offer an amendment, or allow us to offer an amendment, so as to put the appointment of deputy and assistant marshals who are to serve in connection with Congressional elections on the same basis as the appointment of supervisors—that is, that they shall be appointed by the courts, and shall be chosen in equal numbers from the different political parties—we will aid him, and the abuse of which he complains can be corrected. But that is not in the line of the gentleman's purpose nor that of his party. They do wish not to better the law, but to annul it. They do not wish the law executed, so long as they have not the power to make the appointments and execute it in their own way.

Recent events have shown them that they cannot repeal these statutes. In the present situation of parties and opinions in Congress it is impossible to repeal them. Those who wish to repeal them have not the constitutional majority to do so. They can no more remove them from the statute-book than they can enact a law without a majority of votes. In short, they have not the constitutional majority to repeal these laws. Not being able constitutionally to repeal them, gentlemen on the other side say, "We will prevent their enforcement." And, in attempting this, they attack the government in a very vital part. They know that the whole country, without regard to party, needs to have the courts of the United States open to all suitors. They know that ustice ought to be administered in every district and circuit court of the United States.

They know that United States prisoners are locked up, some under sentence of our courts, others awaiting trial; and that the Constitution provides that all who are held under charges shall have a speedy trial. The great duty, the imperative obligation, to provide for the speedy and prompt administration of justice rests upon members of Congress, Republicans and Democrats alike. But the majority of this House have segregated from all the other appropriations of the year this one for the judicial expenses of the government, and now offer an appropriation of two and a half millions of dollars, and say, not to us alone, but through us to the nation and to all the officers of the nation, that this money of the people, which has been paid into the National Treasury for the very purpose of maintaining the courts, shall not be used for that purpose, only on condition that the Democratic party shall be permitted to couple with it a provision that certain laws of the land which they cannot repeal shall not be enforced; nay, more, that for the coming year these laws shall be nullified. In short, we are told that we must submit to the nullification of the election laws, or the courts of the United States shall be closed, the prisoners awaiting trial shall be discharged or shall be held untried, against the constitutional provision in their behalf, and that no provision shall be made even to feed them. It is to be made unlawful to try them, unlawful to keep them, and it is unlawful to discharge them. With these hard conditions you have fettered the appropriations, the use of which reaches to the very vitals of national justice. You say, "Take these appropriations coupled with the nullification of certain laws, or you shall not have them at all."

Gentlemen, we earnestly desire to go home. We have borne the burden of this long, weary, and profitless session until we are anxious to go to our homes and rest and give the country rest. But we cannot, even under the persuasive heat of the dog-star and the pressure of this weary and distasteful work, accept the dishonor which this bill offers. It is a moral bribe to us to consent to the nullification of laws which you seek not to improve but to destroy. We cannot, we will not, consent.

You have retained in this bill a clause which, if it becomes a law, will place the President of the United States between two fires—the fire of this law if he disobeys it, and the fire of Heaven if he violates his oath by obeying it.

Mr. McMAHON. Will my colleague allow me to ask him how the President is at all interfered with?

Mr. GARFIELD. I will answer. The President has taken an oath that he will see to it that the laws be faithfully executed. You do not repeal the election laws, but you make it impossible for him to execute them without violating another. You seek to place him in reach of your impeachment on the one hand or, on the other, compel him to neglect his duty and violate his oath. We have no legal or moral right to put the Chief Executive in such an attitude. The wisdom of the Old Testament proverb, "in vain is the net spread in the sight of any bird," may be fitly applied in this case. I do not see that there is the slightest probability you can catch a bird in this net.

Mr. HOUSE. Do I understand the gentleman from Ohio as threatening us with another veto?

Mr. Speaker, we have heard of war and rumors of war in another quarter; but this House, this body, whose members come directly from the people—the only real sovereigns in this country—has not only not come to blows, but so far as I know have not come to threats.

Mr. HOUSE. The gentleman talks about blows.

Mr. GARFIELD. I say, neither blows nor threats. I am certainly indulging in no threats. I only say you offer a bill for the approval of the Executive which if he approves puts him in a position where he will be involved in a conflict between the Constitution and the law you make.

Mr. HOUSE. What a very frank answer.

Mr. GARFIELD. It is both frank and just. I appeal to you, gentlemen, whether this kind of legislation meets the approval of your best judgment.

Now, I had some hope, when we were told yesterday by my colleague [Mr. McMahon] that the amendment which had come from the Senate was left open so as to enable the conference committee to soften the asperities of this bill—I had some hope that we should see our way through the entanglement by finding a bill which gentlemen on this side could support, and that we might then adjourn, shake hands, and go home. But I am compelled for the present to bid farewell to that pleasing prospect. WE STAY. [Applause from the Republican side.]

II.
DEFENSE OF UNION SOLDIERS OF THE SECEDED STATES.

The Committee of the Whole on the state of the Union having under consideration a proposition to abolish the Southern Claims Commission, April 15, 1879—

Mr. GARFIELD said: Mr. Chairman, the general doctrine of belligerency in a territorial war is one of course understood by everybody to include technically as enemies, all of the inhabitants of the hostile territory. That doctrine is recognized by lawyers everywhere. But nobody, so far as I know, unless it be the gentleman from Wisconsin, has ever denied that, during our late war and since, the Supreme Court has repeatedly determined that the question of loyalty could not be raised against a claimant, if a pardon had been granted him by the President or Congress; that by a pardon disloyalty is wiped out, so far as his legal rights before the court are concerned. This is an answer to all that has been said on that point.

The gentleman from Wisconsin [Mr. Bragg] agrees with me that the amendment of the gentleman from Tennessee [Mr. Young] ought not to be adopted. He thinks, however, that the Southern Claims Commission ought to be abolished, because he says it was a mistake from the first to pay any loyal claims from the South. On that point I take issue with him; and I wish to refer to some official statistics which I prepared at the last session, in view of a statement then made and now repeated in this debate. It was said by the gentleman from Louisiana [Mr. Ellis] that 99 per cent. of all the people of the seceded States were disloyal, in our sense of that word; that almost every Southern man who amounted to anything belonged to that category. I desire to traverse that proposition by some facts. Leaving out of view all the border States, do gentlemen know that there were, from the States that went into secession and rebellion, military organizations amounting to fifty regiments and seven companies of white men who were regularly mustered into our Army and who fought bravely under our flag? I have the official record in my hand. Passing to the border Southern States, which did not secede, but whose people were divided, do gentlemen know that in the State of Kentucky alone more white soldiers fought under our flag than Napoleon took into the battle of Waterloo? more than all the allied armies which Wellington commanded at that battle? Do they not know that Missouri furnished one hundred and eighteen regiments of white soldiers to the Union Army; that the Southern States furnished one hundred and eighty-six thousand colored troops to the Union Army, and that of these ninety thousand were from the States which seceded, and twenty thousand from the State of Kentucky? I say that from the States that seceded and went into the rebellion 50,700 white soldiers fought in our ranks and under our flag. And this statement does not include the thousands of individual men who came into our lines, and joined Northern regiments. To say that these men were enemies and had no legal rights, and that the government should not pay them or their families all proper claims for supplies and other property taken from them by the government they were defending, is a proposition I had hoped no man on either side of this House would make; and I am glad to know that the gentlemen who fought against us in the field do not make it.

Not one of them has yet indorsed it. It remains for one of our own soldiers, the gentleman from Wisconsin [Mr. Bragg], to say that there ought to be nothing paid to any man, however loyal, if he came from the South. I am sure that even this House, consisting so largely of Confederate soldiers, will denounce this proposition as in the highest degree inequitable and unjust. Let the Southern Claims Commission continue until it has acted on the cases now before it, and then let us muster it out; for the cases not already presented are barred by the statute of limitation. Let us not enlarge the claim business, but let us complete it; and most of all, let us not so change the law as to abolish the distinction between loyal and disloyal claims, making the latter payable, which the law has never done.

III.
1. RESUMPTION AND THE CURRENCY.

The Committee of the Whole on the state of the Union having under consideration an amendment to use the reserve provided by law for the redemption of fractional currency, April 10, 1879—

Mr. GARFIELD said:

Mr. Chairman, my colleague [Mr. McMahon] has gone into the whole merits of this question on the point of order. I shall only follow his example to a very small extent. The attempt of my colleague, in the speech he has just made, to set himself, in contrast with me and many others on this side, as the special champion and friend of the soldier, is quite too thin a disguise to deceive anybody. He will remember, as will the House, that this side tried, again and again, to pass a measure authorizing the Secretary of the Treasury to extend the sales of 4 per cent. bonds sufficient to cover this whole case. We brought the House to a vote on that proposition at least twice at the last session, and but for the resistance on the other side it would have prevailed, and the soldiers would have been paid. The responsibility for not paying them rests with those who resisted that measure, not with those who proposed it. We have been selling these 4 per cent. bonds to assure resumption; and that is the law. I think it might fairly be the law that they should be issued to provide for payment of soldiers' pensions.

There is another thing which, perhaps, my colleague did not remember. Under a law of last session we issued bonds to the extent of a quarter of a million of dollars to endow a private institution for the blind, in one of the States of this Union, the endowment being $10,000 a year; and to keep it out of the power of Congress to repeal the act the bonds thus issued were made a part of the permanent debt of the United States, in order to endow an institution in a State—an institution not national in its character. But gentlemen are unwilling to increase the 4 per cent. bonded debt of the United States to pay pensions of our soldiers already provided by law.

Now, I have simply made the point of order, that is all; and no man can torture anything I have said on this point of order into an unwillingness that the soldiers shall have their pensions, or that all necessary legislation shall be had to make the payment prompt and full to secure all their rights. It is altogether too late in the day to tell the soldiers that gentlemen on this side who have remembered them in a thousand ways (my colleague, to say the least, has not remembered them in more) are not their friends.

I made this point (and I have no concealments about it) because I look upon this amendment as the entering wedge to a general purpose to break down the system of reserves on which the maintenance of resumption depends.

Mr. McMAHON. My colleague will permit me to ask him how the issue of $10,000,000 of the $346,000,000 authorized by law is going to break down the specie reserve which amounts to $236,000,000?

Mr. GARFIELD. That is what I am about to tell the gentleman. I say, at the outset, that our whole body of legislation relating to resumption makes together a connected chain; and

> Whichever link you strike,
> Tenth or ten thousandth, breaks the chain alike.

Such legislation as this tends at least to weaken that chain. Now, my colleague, whose financial knowledge would not have been doubted if he had not made this speech, amazed me very much by saying that the subsidiary coinage and the subsidiary currency are no part of the general problem of resumption. Why, does he not know perfectly well that the subsidiary currency in the form of these scrip notes or in coin goes to make up the volume of our circulating medium just as much as greenbacks, just as much as gold? The great currency question embraces everything that circulates as money; and it will not do to say that the subsidiary coinage has nothing to do with the general proposition. It has very much to do with it. Subsidiary currency in any form circulates far more rapidly than dollar bills, and dollar bills more rapidly than five-dollar bills, and these more rapidly than tens. Just in proportion to the smallness of the denomination of the bill is its circulation rapid. Here was a proposition to hasten the issue of subsidiary coin. As the law first stood, the silver could only be issued on the presentation of the scrip, the silver being paid in exchange therefor. In order to facilitate the process, Congress provided that, as there was a rush to make the exchange, people might deposit greenbacks and receive silver coin in place of it, but that the greenbacks thus deposited should be held to redeem according to law the scrip as it might come in. This reserve, therefore, of which my colleague speaks, is a reserve laid away as a provision against the demand for the scrip, in place of which the silver coin has already been issued.

MR. WARNER. Will my friend permit me to ask him a question?

Mr. GARFIELD. Certainly.

Mr. WARNER. Is it not perfectly well understood that the fractional currency, against which I understand it is claimed this $10,000,000 is held, is now out of existence, or at least that only a small part of it remains for redemption?

Mr. GARFIELD. I will answer my colleague. Estimates have been made on that subject. All agree that a certain portion of the scrip is probably destroyed, and will never be presented for redemption. What that proportion is nobody knows. The amount, however, of any circulating medium which is actually destroyed, is much smaller than people suppose. I will give a single instance. There is a bank in my district which was in actual operation nearly fifty years, under the State laws, and when the new banking system was adopted, it undertook to wind up its old business; that is, being solvent, to redeem all its old bills. They have gone on redeeming and redeeming, and the last time I talked with the cashier he told me that less than two per cent. of the whole issue, covering a period of forty years of State banking, was still out; and even then almost every week, fifteen, twenty, or thirty dollars of old bills came back; showing that the destruction of outstanding circulating paper money is far less than the people suppose.

Now, the highest estimate which has been made is that perhaps $10,000,000 of the fractional scrip is destroyed and will never come in. And here is outstanding at least $15,000,000 not yet brought in. I saw the papers yesterday of a single party who took $6,000 of this scrip to the Treasury. We have sometimes six, eight, or ten thousand dollars a day brought in. The time will doubtless come when it will be safe to reduce this reserve, leaving enough to cover what is outstanding and will not come in, and let the rest go into circulation. But to say now that the whole $10,000,000 shall go into circulation, leaving none to protect this issue, is to break down one of the stated reserves of the government to meet its obligations.

Mr. McMAHON. Will the gentleman from Ohio allow me to put a question to him?

Mr. GARFIELD. Certainly.

Mr. McMAHON. Under the specie-resumption law—and I do not wish to argue, I only want to state it—under the specie-resumption law the Secretary of the Treasury was ordered to redeem fractional currency in silver coin. Now, in July, 1876, we authorized him to pay out $10,000,000 of silver coin and to take in $10,000,000 of greenbacks. We authorized him to redeem this fractional currency outstanding in greenbacks, and he has never done it.

Mr. GARFIELD. How does my colleague know that?

Mr. McMAHON. I say it because the debt statement shows it; I have it here, and I read on page 4 of the Treasury report, currency assets, "United States notes, special fund for redemption of fractional currency, $10,000,000." Now it never was in contemplation of the gentlemen who passed that law in 1876 that when that $10,000,000 was taken in it should be kept. That was a little private scheme of contraction of Mr. Sherman himself. Our order to him was to pay out in redemption of fractional currency. Instead of that he is redeeming constantly in silver coin and keeping the $10,000,000 in.

Mr. GARFIELD. I will answer my colleague. I am not responsible for the Secretary's execution of his duty under that law. But I should say if I were the Secretary I would be bound by the law and by the reason of the case to hold a sufficient amount of that fund for the ample protection of all the outstanding scrip which would be likely to come in. Perhaps the Secretary has kept more than is needed; and if he has, it is perfectly proper for Congress to ascertain, after a fair examination, how much of that he can spare, and then let it out. I will agree to that at any time. But my colleague adopts no such method; he says simply let it all go, and he proposes to make this sweeping change of law and give up the whole reserve for that purpose, and therefore to that extent, or at least to some extent, breaks over the line of our reserves.

Now I have said all I desire to say on that subject except a single word in conclusion. My colleague pained me by a single expression in his speech. Nothing has ever occurred between him and me which entitles either of us to say discourteous and indecent things about the other; and when my colleague said that though I owed more allegiance to the soldier than perhaps to any other class, yet that I appeared to act as though I owed my chief allegiance to Wall street, he said what he had no more right to say, either as a matter of fact or a matter of fair inference, than I would have a right to say he owes his chief allegiance to the groggeries and whisky-shops of Dayton; and as I would not say that, I do not think he was entitled to say the other.

Mr. McMAHON. In answer to the gentleman I say this: I have followed with interest the public career of the gentleman, and if in all the discussions which have ever taken place in this House or this country on financial questions he can show one vote or one speech that was not based upon the idea of speedy resumption, no matter at what cost to the great mass of the people, even when his own party separated from him upon that question in the Forty-third Congress, when he was in a minority in his own party upon this question—if he can show one vote which he ever cast in favor of what was regarded then by the majority of his own party in the West as the interest of the people on this question, I will take my statement back. That is all that it covered.

Mr. GARFIELD. I will relieve my colleague upon that point. He could not certainly praise me any more according to my notions of legislative praise than to say what he has said. If I ever did cast a vote that was not in favor of the resumption of specie payments, that was not against all schemes to delay and prevent it, I cast a vote that my conscience and my judgment disapproved of. [Applause.] And I venture to say I have cast as many votes as any man on this floor against Wall street and the business of gold-gambling which has been destroyed by resumption; that gold-gambling in Wall street which locked up one hundred millions of the business capital of this country for fifteen years, away from all profitable investment, and converted Wall street into a hell of gamblers with the business of this country up and down. And if every vote of mine in favor of honest money has not been a blow at gambling in Wall street, then it has not had the effect I intended.

Mr. BRIGHT. I desire to ask the gentleman from Ohio a question. Have not the operations of Wall street been simply transferred to the Treasury of the United States?

Mr. GARFIELD. In answer to the gentleman from Tennessee, I will say that I hope there has been enough of the gold and silver in this country that had hitherto been lodged in Wall street for gold-gambling purposes transferred to the Treasury of the United States to break down the bulls and bears of Wall street permanently, and to maintain the supremacy of honest money. [Applause.]

2. THE NEW SILVER BILL.

The House having under consideration a bill to authorize the unlimited coinage of silver, and to give the profits thereof to the owners of bullion, May 17, 1879—

Mr. GARFIELD said:

Mr. Speaker, we have probably never legislated on any question the influence of which reaches further, both territorially and in time, and touches more interests, more vital interests, than are touched by this and similar bills. No man can doubt that within recent years, and notably within recent months, the leading thinkers of the civilized world have become alarmed at the attitude of the two precious metals in relation to each other; and many leading thinkers are becoming clearly of the opinion that by some wise, judicious arrangement both the precious metals must be kept in service for the currency of the world. And this opinion has been very rapidly gaining ground within the last six months, to such an extent that England, which for more than half a century has stoutly adhered to the single gold standard, is now seriously meditating how she may harnsss both these metals to the monetary car of the world. And yet, outside of this Capitol, I do not this day know of a single great and recognized advocate of bi-metallic money who regards it prudent or safe for any nation largely to increase the coinage standard of silver coin at the present time beyond the limits fixed by existing laws. France and the states of the Latin Union, that have long believed in bi-metallism, maintained it against all comers and have done all in their power to advocate it throughout the world, dare not coin a single silver coin and have not done so since 1874. The most strenuous advocates of bi-metallism in those countries say it would be ruinous to bi-metallism for France or the Latin Union to coin any more silver at present. The remaining stock of German silver now for sale, amounting to from forty to seventy-five millions of dollars, is a standing menace to the exchanges and silver coinage of Europe. One month ago the leading financial journal of London proposed that the Bank of England buy one-half of the German surplus and hold it five years on' condition that the German Government shall hold the other half off the market. The time is ripe for some wise and prudent arrangement among the nations to save silver from a disastrous break-down.

Yet we, who during the past two years, have coined far more silver dollars than we ever before coined since the foundation of the government—ten times as many as we coined during half a century of our national life—are to-day ignoring and defying the enlightened, universal opinion of bi-metallists, and saying that the United States, singlehanded and alone, can enter the field and settle the mighty issue alone. We are justifying the old proverb that "Fools rush in where angels fear to tread."

It is sheer madness, Mr. Speaker. I once saw a dog on a great stack of hay that had been floated out into the wild, overflowed stream of a river, with its stack-pen and foundation still holding together, but ready to be wrecked. For a little while the animal appeared to be perfectly happy. His hay-stack was there and the pen around it, and he seemed to think the world bright, and his happiness secure, while the sunshine fell softly on his head and his hay. But by and by, he began to discover that the house and the barn and their surroundings were not all there as they were when he went to sleep the night before; and he began to see that he could not command all the prospect and peacefully dominate the scene as he had done before. So with this House. We assume to manage this mighty question which has been launched on the wild current that sweeps over the whole world, and we bark from our legislative hay-stacks, as though we commanded the whole world. [Applause.] In the name of common sense and sanity, let us take some account of the flood; let us understand that a deluge means something, and try, if we can, to get our bearings before we undertake to settle the affairs of all mankind by a vote of this House.

To-day we are coining one-third of all the silver that is being coined in the round world. China is coining another third; and all other nations are using the remaing one-third for subsidiary coin. And if we want to take rank with China and part company with all of the civilized nations of the Western World, let us pass this bill, and then "bay the moon" as we float down the whirling channel to take our place among the silver monometallists of Asia.

What this country needs above all other things, is that this Congress shall pass the appropriation bills, adjourn, and go home [applause on the Republican side], and let the forces of business and good order and brotherhood, working in their natural and orderly way, bring us into light and stability and peace. And we want time to adjust this great international question. Now, while I am speaking, the Administration is opening negotiations with all the western nations, to see if there cannot be some international arrangement whereby this question of bi-metallism may be wisely settled. We tried it by international monetary conference. It was a preliminary reconnaissance, and——

[Here the hammer fell.]

IV.

THE MISSISSIPPI RIVER AN OBJECT OF NATIONAL CARE.

The House having under consideration a bill to provide for a commission to survey the Mississippi River, June 21, 1879—

Mr. GARFIELD said:

Mr. Speaker, I should oppose this bill, very decidedly, if it committed us at this time to any plan or theory of managing the Mississippi River; and I think the remarks of the gentleman from Indiana [Mr. Baker], warning us against committal in any such direction, are wise. But I have looked the bill over with what care I could, and it does not seem to me that by its passage we commit ourselves to anything further than the purpose to obtain accurate official information touching the present condition and needs of this great stream. I admit that we have already had examinations and explorations of the Mississippi, some of them scientific and very valuable; but everybody will concede that one important experiment has been made, in recent years, which, though against the opinion of the majority of engineers, has proven apparently a great success: I mean the jetty system at the mouth of that river. I say "apparently," because it is possible that in the long run it may not prove a success; but at the present moment it appears to be a great and striking success in the management of the mouths of that river. If it prove to be permanently so, all our calculations and, indeed, all our theories concerning the improvement and management of other portions of that river need to be reconsidered in view of the new light that the jetty system will throw upon the question. Hence a proposition to turn on the light, to get information, and to get it from the best scientific advisers that we can call to our aid, is a step in the right direction. I have always favored measures which will result in giving us information upon all questions about which we are called upon to legislate. What shall be done with this knowledge when it comes, will be for our successors to say. We do not commit ourselves or them to any scheme at this time. But for myself, I believe that one of the grandest of our material national interests—one that is national in the largest material sense of that word—is the Mississippi River and its navigable tributaries. It is the most gigantic single natural feature of our continent, far transcending the glory of the ancient Nile or of any other river on the earth. The statesmanship of America must grapple the problem of this mighty stream. It is too vast for any State to handle; too much for any authority less than that of the nation itself to manage. And I believe the time will come when the liberal-minded statesmanship of this country will devise a wise and comprehensive system, that will harness the powers of this great river to the material interests of America, so that not only all the people who live on its banks and the banks of its confluents, but all the citizens of the republic, whether dwellers in the central valley or on the slope of either ocean, will recognize the importance of preserving and perfecting this great natural and material bond of national union between the North and the South—a bond to be so strengthened by commerce and intercourse that it can never be severed. [Applause.]

One of our early Presidents went so far as even to exceed his early preconceived opinions of the constitutional power of the Executive, in order to buy from France a mighty empire to be added to the Union; and he did it for this reason chiefly, that the young Republic could not permanently endure as a nation without owning and controlling the mouths of the Mississippi. Nearly the whole continent west of that river was bought, to make the Union perpetual by bringing every foot of the shore of the Mississippi under our flag. If I did not think it almost unworthy of so great a theme, I would say that if there had been no patriotic impulse higher than any consideration of material welfare which moved twenty millions of Americans to resist the attempt to break the Union in pieces, and impelled them to hold it together by all the cost of blood and treasure that our late war required, if there had been no higher national sentiment inspiring them, the immense material stake which the people of the great North and West and center of this country had in the free use of that river from its sources to its mouth, that their commerce might go southward to the sea under the one flag, unvexed by conflicting nationalities, this material stake alone would have made all the people of the upper valley of the Mississippi resist to the last the dismemberment of the Union.

This great river, which our fathers made such sacrifices to acquire, and which the present generation made so much costlier sacrifices to redeem from disunion and to hold within the grasp of the nation, we have held, not in obedience to mere sentiment alone, not with a view of keeping it as a vast and worthless waste of water, but to utilize it by making it the servant of all the people of this country. How shall we utilize it, unless at some time, and in some wise way, we bridle it by the skill of man and make it subservient to the interests of commerce?

Now, Mr. Speaker and gentlemen of the House, there is another reason why I am in favor of this measure. I rejoice in any occasion which enables Representatives from the North and from the South to unite in an unpartisan effort to promote a great national interest. [Applause.] Such an occasion is good for us both. And when we can do it without the sacrifice of our convictions, and can benefit millions of our fellow-citizens, and thereby strengthen the bonds of the Union, we ought to do it with rejoicing; for, in so doing, we shall inspire our people with larger and more generous views, and help to confirm for them and for our posterity to our latest generations, the indissoluble Union and the permanent grandeur of this Republic. I shall vote for this bill. [Applause on both sides of the House.]

V.
THE REVIVED DOCTRINE OF STATE SOVEREIGNTY.

The House being in Committee of the Whole on the marshals' appropriation bill June 27, 1879—

Mr. GARFIELD said:

Mr. Chairman, "to this favor" it has come at last. The great fleet that set out on the 18th of March, with all its freightage and armament, is so shattered that now all the valuables it carried are embarked in this little craft, to meet whatever fate the sea and the storm may offer. This little bill contains the residuum of almost everything that has been the subject of controversy at the present session. I will not discuss it in detail, but will speak only of its central feature, and especially of the opinions which the discussion of that feature has brought to the surface during the present session. The majority in this Congress have adopted what I consider very extreme and dangerous opinions on certain important constitutional questions. They have not only drifted back to their old attitude on the subject of State sovereignty, but they have pushed that doctrine much further than most of their predecessors ever went before, except during the period immediately preceding the late war.

So extreme are some of these utterances, that nothing short of actual quotations from the Record will do their authors justice. I therefore shall read several extracts from debates at the present session of Congress, and group them in the order of the topics discussed.

Senator Wallace (Congressional Record, June 3, pages 3 and 5) says:

The Federal Government has no voters; it can make none, it can constitutionally control none. * * * When it asserts the power to create and hold "*national elections*" or to regulate the conduct of the voter *on election day*, or to maintain *equal suffrage*, it tramples under foot the very basis of the Federal system and seeks to build a consolidated government from a democratic republic. This is the plain purpose of the men now in control of the Federal Government, and to this end the teachings of leading Republicans now are shaped.

* * * * *

There are no national voters. Voters who vote for national Representatives are qualified by State constitutions and State laws, and national citizenship is not required of a voter of the State by any provision of the Federal Constitution nor in practice.

* * * * *

If there be such a thing, then, as a "national election," it wants the first element of an election—a national voter. The Federal Government, or (if it suits our friends on the other side better) the nation, has no voters. It cannot create them, it cannot qualify them.

Representative Clark, of Missouri (Record, April 26, page 60), says:

The United States has no voters.

Senator Maxey, Texas (Record, April 21, page 72), says:

It follows as surely as "grass grows and water runs" that, under our Constitution, the entire control of elections must be under the State whose voters assemble; whose right to vote is not drawn from the Constitution of the United States, but existed and was freely exercised long before its adoption.

Senator Williams, Kentucky (Record, April 25, page 8), says:

The legislatures of the States and the people of the several districts are the constituency of Senators and Representatives in Congress. They receive their commissions from the governor, and when they resign (which is very seldom) they send their resignations to the governor and not to the President. They are State officers and not Federal officers.

Senator Whyte (Record, May 21, page 14) says:

There are no elections of United States officers and no voters of the United States. The voters are voters of the States, they are the people of the States, and their members of the House of Representatives are chosen by the electors of the States to represent the people of the States, whose agents they are.

Mr. McLANE. Do I understand him to say that the Government of the United States has the right to keep the peace anywhere within a State? Do I understand him to say that there is any "peace of the United States" at all recognized by the Supreme Court of the United States?

Mr. ROBESON. Certainly I do.—(Record, April 4, page 14.)

Mr. McLANE (RECORD, April 4, page 15) says:

I believe that the provision of law which we are about to repeal is unconstitutional; that is to say, that it is unconstitutional for the United States to "keep the peace" anywhere in the States, either at the polls or elsewhere; and if it were constitutional, I believe in common with gentlemen on this side of the House that it would be highly inexpedient to exercise that power.

* * * * * *

When that law used the phrase "to keep the peace" it could only mean the peace of the States.

* * * * * *

It is not a possible thing to have a breach of the United States peace at the polls.

Senator Whyte (Record, May 21, page 18) says:

Sovereignty is lodged with the States, where it had its home long before the Constitution was created. The Constitution is the creature of that sovereignty. The Federal Government has no inherent sovereignty. All its sovereign powers are drawn from the States.

The States were in existence long before the Union, and the latter took its birth from their power.

* * * * * *

The State governments are supreme by inherent power originally conceded to them by the people as to the control of local legislation and administration. The Federal Government has no part or lot in this vast mass of inherent sovereign power, and its interference therewith is utterly unwarrantable.

Senator Wallace (Record, June 3, pp. 3 and 4) says:

Thus we have every branch of the Federal Government, House, Senate, the executive and judiciary departments, standing upon the State governments, and all resting finally upon the people of the States, qualified as voters by State constitutions and State laws.

Senator Whyte (Record, May 21, p. 15) says:

No, Mr. President; it never was declared that we were a nation.

* * * * * *

In the formation and adoption of the Constitution the States were the factors.

These are the declarations of seven distinguished members of the present Congress. The doctrines set forth in the above quotations may be fairly regarded as the doctrines of the Democracy as represented in this Capitol.

Let me summarize them: First, there are no national elections; second, the United States has no voters; third, the States have the exclusive right to control all elections of members of Congress; fourth, the Senators and Representatives in Congress are State officers, or, as they have been called during the present session, "embassadors" or "agents" of the State; fifth, the United States has no authority to keep the peace anywhere within a State, and, in fact, has no peace to keep; sixth, the United States is not a nation endowed with sovereign power, but is a confederacy of States; seventh, the States are sovereignties possessing inherent supreme powers; they are older than the Union, and as independent sovereignties the State governments created the Union and determined and limited the powers of the General Government.

These declarations embody the sum total of the constitutional doctrines which the Democracy has avowed during this extra session of Congress. They form a body of doctrines which I do not hesitate to say are more extreme than was ever before held on this subject, except perhaps at the very crisis of secession and rebellion.

And they have not been put forth as abstract theories of government. True to the logic of their convictions, the majority have sought to put them in practice by affirmative acts of legislation.

Let me enumerate these attempts. First, they have denounced as unconstitutional all attempts of the United States to supervise, regulate, or protect national elections, and have tried to repeal all laws on the national statute-book enacted for that purpose. Second, following the advice given by Calhoun in his political testament to his party, they have tried to repeal all those portions of the venerated judiciary act of 1789, the act of 1833 against nullification, the act of 1861, and the acts amendatory thereof, which provide for carrying to the Supreme Court of the United States all controversies that relate to the duties and authority of any officer acting under the Constitution and laws of the United States.

Third. They have attempted to prevent the President from enforcing the laws of the Union, by refusing necessary supplies and by forbidding the use of the Army to suppress violent resistance to the laws, by which, if they had succeeded, they would have left the citizens and the authorities of the States free to obey or disobey the laws of the Union as they might choose.

This, I believe, Mr. Chairman, is a fair summary both of the principles and the attempted practice to which the majority of this House has treated the country during the extra session.

Before quitting this topic, it is worth while to notice the fact that the attempt made in one of the bills now pending in this House, to curtail the jurisdiction of the national courts, is in the direct line of the teachings of John C. Calhoun. In his "Discourse on the Constitution and Government of the United States," published by authority of the Legislature of South Carolina in 1851, he sets forth at great length the doctrine that ours is not a national government, but a confederacy of sovereign States, and then proceeds to point out what he considers the dangerous departures which the government has made from his theory of the Constitution.

The first and most dangerous of these departures he declares to be the adoption of the twenty-fifth section of the judiciary act of 1789, by which appeals were authorized from the judgments of the supreme courts of the States to the Supreme Court of the United States. He declares that section of the act unconstitutional, because it makes the supreme court of a "sovereign" State subordinate to the judicial power of the United States; and he recommends his followers never to rest until they have repealed, not only that section, but also what he calls the still more dangerous law of 1833, which forbids the courts of the States to sit in judgment on the acts of an officer of the United States done in pursuance of national law. The present Congress has won the unenviable distinction of making the first attempt, since the death of Calhoun, to revive and put in practice his disorganizing and destructive theory of government.

Firmly believing that these doctrines and attempted practice of the present Congress are erroneous and pernicious, I will state briefly the counter-propositions:

I affirm: First, that the Constitution of the United States was not created by the government, of the States, but was ordained and established by the only sovereign in this country—the common superior of both the States and the nation—the people themselves; second, that the United States is a nation, having a government whose powers, as defined and limited by the Constitution, operate upon all the States in their corporate capacity and upon all the people; third, that by its legislative, executive, and judicial authority, the nation is armed with adequate power to enforce all the provisions of the Constitution against all opposition of individuals or of States, at all times and all places within the Union.

These are broad propositions; and I take the few minutes remaining to defend them. The constitutional history of this country, or rather the history of sovereignty and government in this country, is comprised in four sharply defined epochs—

First. Prior to the 4th day of July, 1776, sovereignty, so far as it can be affirmed of this country, was lodged in the Crown of Great Britain. Every member of every colony (the colonists were not citizens but subjects) drew his legal rights from the Crown of Great Britain. "Every acre of land in this country was then held mediately or immediately by grants from that Crown," and "all the civil authority then existing or exercised here, flowed from the head of the British Empire."

Second. On the 4th day of July, 1776, the people of these colonies, asserting their natural inherent right as sovereigns, withdrew the sovereignty from the Crown of Great Britain and reserved it to themselves. In so far as they delegated this national authority at all, they delegated it to the Continental Congress assembled at Philadelphia. That Congress, by general consent, became the supreme government of this country—executive, judicial, and legislative in one. During the whole of its existence it wielded the supreme power of the new nation.

Third. On the 1st day of March, 1781, the same sovereign power, the people, withdrew the authority from the Continental Congress and lodged it, so far as they lodged it at all, with the Confederation, which, though a league of States, was declared to be a perpetual union.

Fourth. When at last our fathers found the confederation too weak and inefficient for the purposes of a great nation, they abolished it and lodged the national authority, enlarged and strengthened by new powers, in the Constitution of the United States, where, in spite of all assaults, it still remains. All these great acts were done by the only sovereign in this Republic, the people themselves.

That no one may charge that I pervert history to sustain my own theories, I call attention to the fact that not one of the colonies declared itself free and independent. Neither Virginia nor Massachusetts threw off its allegiance to the British Crown as a colony. The great declaration was made not even by all the colonies as colonies, but it was made in the name and by authority of "all the good people of the colonies" as one people.

Let me fortify this position by a great name that will shine forever in the constellation of our Southern sky—the name of Charles Coatsworth Pinckney, of South Carolina. He was a leading member of the constitutional convention of 1787, and also a member of the convention of South Carolina which ratified the Constitution. In that latter convention the doctrine of State sovereignty found a few champions; and their attempt to prevent the adoption of the Constitution, because it established a supreme national government, was rebuked by him in these memorable words. I quote from his speech as recorded in Elliott's Debates:

> This admirable manifesto, which for importance of matter and elegance of composition stands unrivaled, sufficiently confutes the honorable gentleman's doctrine of the individual sovereignty and independence of the several States. In that declaration the several States are not even enumerated, but after reciting, in nervous language and with convincing arguments, our right to independence and the tyranny which compelled us to assert it, the declaration is made in the following words: "We, therefore, the representatives of the United States of America, in general congress assembled, appealing to the Supreme Judge of the world for the rectitude of our intentions, do, in the name, and by the authority of the good people of these colonies, solemnly publish and declare that these united colonies are, and of right ought to be, free and independent States."
> The separate independence and individual sovereignty of the several States were never thought of by the enlightened band of patriots who framed this declaration. The several States are not even mentioned by name in any part of it, as if it was intended to impress this maxim on America, that our freedom and independence arose from our union, and that without it we could neither be free nor independent. Let us, then, consider all attempts to weaken this union by maintaining that each is separately and individually independent as a species of political heresy, which can never benefit us, but may bring on us the most serious distresses.

For a further and equally powerful vindication of the same view I refer to the Commentaries of Justice Story, vol. 1, p. 197.

In this same connection, and as a pertinent and effective response to the Democratic doctrines under review, I quote from the first annual message of Abraham Lincoln, than whom no man of our generation studied the origin of the Union more profoundly. He said:

> Our States have neither more nor less power than that reserved to them in the Union by the Constitution, no one of them ever having been a State *out* of the Union. The original ones passed into the Union even *before* they cast off their British colonial dependence, and the new ones each came into the Union directly from a condition of dependence, excepting Texas. And even Texas, in its temporary independence, was never designated a State. The new ones only took the designation of States on coming into the Union, while that name was first adopted for the old ones by the Declaration of Independence. Therein the "united colonies" were declared to be "free and independent States;" but, even then, the object plainly was not to declare their independence of *one another*, or of the *Union*, but directly the contrary, as their mutual pledge and their mutual action before, at the time, and afterward abundantly show.
>
> *   *   *   *   *   *   *
>
> The States have their status in the Union, and they have no other legal status. If they break from this, they can only do so against law and by revolution. The Union, and not themselves separately, procured their independence and their liberty. By conquest or purchase, the Union gave each of them whatever of independence and liberty it has. The Union is older than any of the States, and in fact it created them as States. Originally some dependent colonies made the Union, and in turn the Union threw off their old dependence for them and made them States, such as they are. Not one of them ever had a State constitution independent of the Union. Of course it is not forgotten that all the new States framed their constitutions before they entered the Union; nevertheless, dependent upon and preparatory to coming into the Union.

In further enforcement of the doctrine that the State governments were not the sovereigns who created this government, I refer to the great decision of the Supreme Court of the United States in the case of Chisholm *vs.* The State of Georgia, reported in 2 Dallas, a decision replete with the most enlightened national spirit, in which the court stamps with its indignant condemnation the notion that the State of Georgia was "sovereign" in any sense that made it independent of or superior to the nation.

Mr. Justice Wilson said:

> As a judge of this court I know, and can decide upon the knowledge, that the citizens of Georgia, when they acted upon the large scale of the Union as a part of the "people of the United States," did not surrender the supreme or sovereign power to

that State; but, as to the purposes of the Union, retained it to themselves. As to the purposes of the Union, therefore, Georgia is not a sovereign State.

*　　　*　　　*　　　*　　　*　　　*

Whoever considers in a combined and comprehensive view the general texture of the Constitution will be satisfied that the people of the United States intended to form themselves into a nation for national purposes. They instituted for such purposes a national government, complete in all its parts, with powers legislative, executive, and judiciary, and in all those powers extending over the whole nation. Is it congruous that, with regard to such purposes, any man or body of men, any person, natural or artificial, should be permitted to claim successfully an entire exemption from the jurisdiction of the national government?

Mr. Chairman, the dogma of State sovereignty which has reawakened to such vigorous life in this chamber, has borne such bitter fruits and entailed such suffering upon our people that it deserves more particular notice. It should be noticed that the word " sovereignty " cannot befitly applied to any government in this country. It is not found in our Constitution. It is a feudal word, born of the despotism of the middle ages, and was unknown even in imperial Rome. A " sovereign " is a person, a prince who has subjects that owe him allegiance. There is no one paramount sovereign in the United States. There is no person here who holds any title or authority whatever, except the official authority given him by law. Americans are not subjects, but citizens. Our only sovereign is the whole people. To talk about the " inherent sovereignty " of a corporation—an artificial person—is to talk nonsense; and we ought to reform our habit of speech on that subject.

But what do gentlemen mean when they tell us that a State is sovereign? What does sovereignty mean, in its accepted use, but a political corporation having no superior? Is a State of this Union such a corporation? Let us test it by a few examples drawn from the Constitution. No State of this Union can make war or conclude a peace. Without the consent of Congress it cannot raise or support an army or a navy. It cannot make a treaty with a foreign power, nor enter into any agreement or compact with another State. It cannot levy imposts or duties on imports or exports. It cannot coin money. It cannot regulate commerce. It cannot authorize a single ship to go into commission ·anywhere on the high seas; if it should, that ship would be seized as a pirate or confiscated by the laws of the United States. A State cannot emit bills of credit. It can enact no law which makes anything but gold and silver a legal tender. It has no flag except the flag of the Union. And there are many other subjects on which the States are forbidden by the Constitution to legislate.

How much inherent sovereignty is left in a corporation which is thus shorn of all these great attributes of sovereignty?

But this is not all. The Supreme Court of the United States may declare null and void any law or any clause of the constitution of a State which happens to be in conflict with the Constitution and laws of the United States. Again, the States appear as plaintiffs and defendants before the Supreme Court of the United States. They may sue each other; and, until the eleventh amendment was adopted, a citizen might sue a State. These " sovereigns " may all be summoned before their common superior to be judged. And yet they are endowed with supreme inherent sovereignty?

Again, the government of a State may be absolutely abolished by Congress, in case it is not republican in form. And finally, to cap the climax of this absurd pretension, every right possessed by one of these " sovereign " States, every inherent sovereign right except the single right to equal representation in the Senate, may be taken away, without its consent, by the vote of two-thirds of Congress and three-fourths of the States. But, in spite of all these disabilities, we hear them paraded as independent, sovereign States, the creators of the Union and the dictators of its powers. How inherently "sovereign" must be that State west of the Mississippi which the nation bought and paid for with the public money, and permitted to come into the Union a half century after the Constitution was adopted! And yet we are told that the States are inherently sovereign and created the national government.

Read a long line of luminous decisions of the Supreme Court. Take the life of Chief Justice Marshall, that great judge, who found the Constitution paper and made it a power, who found it a skeleton and clothed it with flesh and blood. By his wisdom and genius he made it the potent and beneficent instrument for the government of a great nation. Everywhere he repelled the insidious and dangerous heresy of the sovereignty of the States in the sense in which it has been used in these debates.

Half a century ago, this heresy threatened the stability of the nation. The eloquence of Webster and his compeers and the patriotism and high courage of Andrew Jackson resisted and for a time destroyed its power; but it continued to live as the evil genius, the incarnate devil, of America; and in 1861 it was the fatal phantom that lured eleven millions of our people into rebellion against their government. Hundreds of thousands of those who took up arms against the Union, stubbornly resisted all inducements to that fatal step until they were summoned by the authority of their States.

The dogma of State sovereignty in alliance with chattel slavery finally made its appeal to that court of last resort where the laws are silent and where kings and nations appear in arms for judgment. In that awful court of war two questions were tried. Shall slavery live? And is a State so sovereign that it may nullify the laws and destroy the Union? Those two questions were tried on the thousand battle-fields of the war; and if war ever "legislates," as a leading Democrat of Ohio once wisely affirmed, then our war legislated finally upon those subjects, and determined, beyond all controversy, that slavery should never again live in this Republic, and that there is not sovereignty enough in any State to authorize its people either to destroy the Union or nullify its laws.

I am unwilling to believe that any considerable number of Americans will ever again push that doctrine to the same extreme; and yet, in these summer months of 1879, in the Congress of the reunited nation, we find the majority drifting fast and far in the wrong direction, by reasserting much of that doctrine which the war ought to have settled forever. And what is more lamentable, such declarations as those which I read at the outset are finding their echoes in many portions of the country which was lately the theater of war. No one can read the proceedings at certain recent celebrations, without observing the growing determination to assert that the men who fought against the Union were not engaged in treasonable conspiracy against the nation, but that they did right to fight for their States, and that, in the long run, the lost cause will be victorious. These indications are filling the people with anxiety and indignation; and they are beginning to inquire whether the war has really settled these great questions.

I remind gentlemen on the other side that we have not ourselves revived these issues. We had hoped they were settled beyond recall, and that peace and friendship might be fully restored to our people.

But the truth requires me to say that there is one indispensable ground of agreement on which alone we can stand together, and it is this: The war for the Union was right, everlastingly right [applause]; and the war against the Union was wrong, forever wrong. However honest and sincere individuals may have been, the secession was none the less rebellion and treason. We defend the States in the exercise of their many and important rights, and we defend with equal zeal the rights of the United States. The rights and authority of both were received from the people—the only source of inherent power.

We insist not only that this is a nation, but that the power of the government, within its own prescribed sphere, operates directly upon the States and upon all the people. We insist that our laws shall be construed by our own courts and enforced by our Executive. Any theory which is inconsistent with this doctrine we will resist to the end.

Applying these reflections to the subject of national elections embraced in this bill, I remind gentlemen that this is a national House of Representatives. The people of my Congressional district have a right to know that a man elected in New York City is elected honestly and lawfully; for he joins in making laws for forty-five millions of people. Every citizen of the United States has an interest and a right in every election within the republic where national representatives are chosen. We insist that these laws relating to our national elections shall be enforced, not nullified; shall remain on the statute-books, and not be repealed; and that the just and legal supervision of these elections ought never again to be surrendered by the Government of the United States. By our consent it never shall be surrendered. [Applause.]

Now, Mr. Chairman, this bill is about to be launched upon its stormy passage. It goes not into unknown waters; for its fellows have been wrecked in the same sea. Its short, disastrous, and, I may add, ignoble voyage is likely to be straight to the bottom. [Applause.]

In reply to Mr. Hurd, same day, Mr. GARFIELD said:

Mr. CHAIRMAN. Two points were made by my colleague from Ohio [Mr. Hurd] to which I desire to call attention. To strengthen his position, that the United States has no voters, he has quoted, as other gentlemen have quoted, the case of Minor *vs.* Happersett, 21 Wallace, page 170.

The question before the court in that case was, whether a provision in the State constitution which confines the right of voting to *male* citizens of the United States is a violation of the fourteenth amendment of the Constitution. The court decided that it was not; and, in delivering his opinion the Chief Justice took occasion to say that "the United States has no voters in the States, of its own creation." Now, all the gentlemen on the other side who have quoted this decision, have left out the words "*of its own creation*," which makes a very essential difference. The Constitution of the United States declares who shall vote for members of Congress, and it adopts the great body of voters whose qualifications may be or have been prescribed by the laws of the States. The power of *adoption* is no less a great governmental power than the power of *creation*.

But the second point to which I wish to refer, and which has been made by several gentlemen, and very markedly by my colleague [Mr. Hurd], is this: He says that the contemporaneous construction of that clause of the Constitution which provides that Congress may at any time make or alter the regulations in regard to the time, place, and manner of holding elections, has determined that Congress can never exercise that right so long as the States make provisions for it. So long as the States do not neglect or refuse to act, or are not prevented by rebellion or war from acting, it was their exclusive right to control the subject. That is what my colleague says. That is what is said in the Record of June 3 by a distinguished member of the Senate.

Now, mark how plain a tale shall put that down.

On the 21st day of August, 1789, in the first House of Representatives that ever met, Mr. Burke, a member from South Carolina, offered the following as one of the amendments to the Constitution. I will read it:

Congress shall not alter, modify, or interfere in the times, places, or manner of holding elections of Senators or Representatives, except when any State shall refuse or neglect, or be unable by invasion or rebellion, to make such elections.

That was the very proposition which my colleague says is the meaning of the Constitution as it now stands. This amendment was offered in a House of Representatives nearly one-half of whose membership was made up of men who were in the convention that framed the Constitution. That amendment was debated; and I hold in my hand the brief record of the debate. Fisher Ames, of Massachusetts, approving of the clause as it now stands, said:

He thought this one of the most justifiable of all the powers of Congress. It was essential to a body representing the whole community that they should have power to regulate their own elections, in order to secure a representation from every part, and prevent any improper regulations, calculated to answer party purposes only. It is a solecism in politics to let others judge for them, and is a departure from the principles upon which the Constitution was founded. * * * He thought no legislature was without the power to determine the mode of its own appointment; * * * that such an amendment as was now proposed would alter the Constitution; it would vest the supreme authority in places where it was never contemplated.

Mr. Madison was willing to make every amendment that was required by the States which did not tend to destroy the principles and efficacy of the Constitution; he conceived that the proposed amendment would have that tendency; he was therefore opposed to it.

Mr. Sherman observed that the convention was very unanimous in passing this clause; that it was an important provision, and if it was resigned it would tend to subvert the government.

Mr. Goodhue hoped the amendment never would obtain. * * * Now, rather than this amendment should take effect, he would vote against all that had been agreed to. His greatest apprehensions were that the State governments would oppose and thwart the general one to such a degree as finally to overturn it. Now, to guard against this evil, he wished the Federal government to possess every power necessary to its existence.

After a full debate, in which the doctrine of State rights was completely overwhelmed so far as this subject was concerned, the vote was taken, and 23 voted in favor of the amendment and 28 voted against it. It did not get even a majority, much less a two-thirds vote, in the House; and it never was called up in the Senate at all.

Now, who were the men that voted against it? Let me read some of their honored names; Fisher Ames, of Massachusetts; Charles Carroll, of Carrollton; Clymer, of Pennsylvania, whose distinguished descendant is a member of this House; Fitzsimmons, of Pennsylvania; Muhlenberg, of Pennsylvania, who was Speaker of the first House of Representatives; Lee and Madison, of Virginia; Trumbull and Sherman, of Connecticut—all those great names are recorded against the very construction of the Constitution which my colleague defends as the correct interpretation of the existing clause on that subject. That is all I desire to say.

VI.

ANCIENT AND MODERN PANICS.

After the journal was read, July 1, 1879, several gentlemen made personal explanations as follows:

Mr. ELLIS. I rise to a question of personal privilege.

The SPEAKER. How much time does the gentleman desire?

Mr. ELLIS. Only time enough to have read by the Clerk the article which I send to the desk, and to say that it is false.

Mr. GARFIELD. I think we had better have this thing out, now that it has been started. I hope the article will be read.

The Clerk read as follows:

THE CONGRESSIONAL MUDDLE—GOSSIP AT THE CAPITOL ABOUT AN ALLEGED BARGAIN.

It is rumored at the Capitol to-day, and generally believed, that if Congress adjourns at four o'clock on Monday without providing for the pay of United States marshals, the President will forthwith issue his proclamation for an extra session of Congress to assemble on Tuesday next. The President will veto the bill which was the product of the last Democratic caucus. It is believed, and is common talk at the Capitol, that in view of some arrangement made with about fourteen Southern Democrats, the end will be that a bill for the pay of the marshals will be passed without any riders. Western Democrats say boldly that General Garfield made a trade with certain Southern Congressmen whereby in consideration of the Republicans allowing the bill to provide for the Mississippi River commission to be passed, those Congressmen pledged their votes to help the passage of all of the appropriation bills before Congress finally adjourned. "Why," said a Western Democrat to-day, "the trade is as plain as the nose on a man's face. President Hayes knows that through sharp practices of General Garfield and other Republican leaders the Democrats are divided, and that if he keeps on pressing Congress he can eventually dictate any terms he wants. He proposes, therefore, to take advantage of it, and hence will not permit Congress to go away until he gets all of the necessary supplies to carry on the government without restrictions of any kind." To-day there is a good deal of talk among the Western men, who say that while they are certain that a few Southern men have made a trade, and mean to sell their Northern allies out, that it may be the goods cannot be delivered. They declare with all the vehemence of language that they will filibuster against the passage of any other bill for the support of the marshals than the one which will be sent to the President and which will be vetoed. McMahon, of Ohio, has even gone so far as to serve notice on certain Southern leaders that hereafter he will not vote for any bill looking to improvements in the South, as a distinctive proposition. The votes which it is claimed the Administration has secured through General Garfield's diplomacy are all of the Louisiana delegation, three from South Carolina, three from Georgia, and two from Alabama.

Mr. ELLIS. Mr. Speaker, life is too short generally to stop to kick at every cur that barks about our heels. I usually take no notice of falsehoods published about me in the papers; and I would not do so on this occasion, but counseling with some friends, gentlemen of more age and experience than myself, they think that some notice should be taken of this article. I take no further notice of it than upon my own behalf, and on behalf of my colleagues who are also assailed in the article, to pronounce it unqualifiedly, deliberately, willfully false in every particular.

Mr. EVINS. Mr. Speaker, it was not the intention of any member of the South Carolina delegation to take any notice of this article; but, inasmuch as it has been read, all we have to say is that it is unqualifiedly false; there is not a word of truth in it.

Mr. ACKLEN. I think it is in order for the gentleman from Ohio [Mr. Garfield] to rise to a personal explanation. [Laughter.]

Mr. GARFIELD. Mr. Speaker, I do not rise to a personal explanation, but to respond to the inquiry of the gentleman from Louisiana [Mr. Acklen]. I happened to be re-reading the other day that interesting old history of Xenophon in which he describes the retreat of the ten thousand Greeks. A little incident recorded in that work will illustrate the subject which gentlemen are discussing. One night there suddenly sprang up in the Grecian camp without apparent cause what is known as an army panic.

The SPEAKER. Does the gentleman rise to a personal explanation? [Laughter.]

Mr. GARFIELD. Oh, no, sir; I am only answering a question. All at once the veteran Greeks appeared to be seized with consternation, and began to flee in all directions. Clearchus, an unscrupulous but adroit general, appreciating the danger of the situation, with ready invention ordered his trumpeter to announce throughout the camp in a loud voice that Clearchus offered a thousand talents of silver as a reward to any one who should discover who it was that let the ass loose among the armor. [Laughter.] He invented this clever device to stay the panic. The lie was successful; and the fleeing Greeks returned with laughter to their tents.

Now, I take it that some shrewd but unscrupulous Democratic leader of the House, fearing that by a stroke of good sense some of his party, and especially some from the South, were going to be patriotic enough to put through the necessary appropriations for the support of the government—fearing, in short, a panic in the party camp—got up this fiction of a trade, in order to bring back all his soldiers to their tents. Who represents Clearchus, and who the ass in this new retreat, gentlemen must judge for themselves. But the whole story is an absurd fiction, which ought to disturb no one.

o

SUSPENSION AND RESUMPTION

OF

SPECIE PAYMENTS

ADDRESS

OF

Hon. JAS. A. GARFIELD,

DELIVERED AT

Chicago, Ill., Jan. 2d, 1879.

CHICAGO, ILL.
PUBLISHED BY THE HONEST MONEY LEAGUE OF THE NORTHWEST.
1879.

INVITATION.

OFFICE OF THE HONEST MONEY LEAGUE OF THE NORTHWEST,
CHICAGO, ILL., December 20, 1878.

To the Hon. James A. Garfield:

DEAR SIR—Having been appointed at a recent meeting of the Executive Committee of the Honest Money League of the Northwest to make arrangements to celebrate the event of the resumption of specie payments by a public meeting in the city of Chicago, we beg to invite you to address the gentlemen of the Honest Money League, whom we represent, and other citizens of Chicago and the Northwest, at such time after January 1, 1879, as may be most agreeable to yourself.

We remain, very truly and respectfully yours,

M. L. SCUDDER, JR.,
THOMAS A. BONES,   } Committee.
THOMAS M. NICHOL,

ACCEPTANCE.

WASHINGTON, D. C., December 23, 1878.

M. L. Scudder, Thomas A. Bones and Thomas M. Nichol, Executive Committee Honest Money League:

GENTLEMEN—I am in receipt of your favor of the 20th instant, inviting me to address a meeting of the Honest Money League of the Northwest, to be called for the celebration of the "resumption of specie payments." I take pleasure in accepting your invitation, and will suggest the evening of January 2, 1879, if agreeable to you.

Very respectfully, your obedient servant,

J. A. GARFIELD.

SUSPENSION AND RESUMPTION
— OF —
SPECIE PAYMENTS.

Mr. Chairman and Fellow Citizens:

The Resumption of Specie Payments closes the most memorable epoch of our history, since the birth of the Union. Eighteen hundred-sixty-one and eighteen hundred-seventy-nine, are the opposite shores of that turbulent sea, whose storms so seriously threatened, with shipwreck, the prosperity, the honor, and the life of the Nation. But the horrors and dangers of the middle passage have, at last, been mastered; and, out of the night and tempest, the Republic has landed on the shore of this new year, bringing with it union and liberty, honor and peace.

We have met to-night to celebrate the close of the war. Battles are never the end of war; for the dead must be buried and the cost of the conflict must be be paid.

The union men of eighteen hundred-sixty-one enlisted for the *whole* war. They served on the field of battle until the last rebel flag went down in surrender; they served in the field of legislation, and at the bollot box, until the last slave was free and the last of the seceding states re-entered the circle of the Union; they served in the public councils until the perils of our foreign relations were ended by honorable arbitration; they have served during the fierce trials of the public faith; and they will not be mustered out until the equal rights of all citizens are acknowledged and secured; until the pension of the last disabled soldier of the Union is faithfully paid, and the last war obligation of the government is honorably redeemed.

If the Resumption now declared by law be maintained against all assaults then, indeed, so far as our finances are concerned, the war for the Union is ended; the victory is complete.

Will our great sovereign, the people of all these States, make the decree irreversible? Will Resumption be maintained?

Believing that, in the long run, the matured and deliberate judgement of this nation is honest and intelligent, I answer, "yes," it will be maintained; and for two reasons. First, because national honesty, good government, and the prosperity of all our people demand it; and Second, because we are able to maintain it. The defence of these positions will be the theme of this address.

PUBLIC FAITH—THE BASIS OF PROSPERITY.

To the thoughtful business men assembled here to-night, whose genius and industry have made this city the great commercial centre of the northwest, I need not argue the proposition that the sanctity of contracts is the foundation of all industrial posperity. In the complex and delicately adjusted relations of modern society, confidence in promises lawfully made is the life-blood of trade and commerce. It is the vital air which labor breathes. It is the light which shines on the pathway of prosperity. The betrayal of one great business trust by a single private citizen may beggar a thousand families, and paralyze the industry of half a city.

An act of bad faith on the part of a State or municipal corporation, like poison in the blood, will transmit its curse to succeeding generations. Examples of this are not wanting. An eminent citizen of Mississippi, a gentleman of national reputation, recently declined an important and honorable business mission to Europe, in behalf of the Southern Board of Trade, on the ground that his usefulness would be seriously impaired by the fact that Europeans still charge Mississippi with financial bad faith in her legislation of 1851. Thus, a single act of repudiation has cast its blighting shadow across a quarter of a century, still clouds the prosperity of a great State, and cripples the influence of its worthiest citizens.

But bad faith on the part of an individual, a city, or even a State, is a small evil in comparison with the calamities which follow bad faith on the part of a sovereign government. The United States is still a debtor nation, mainly, it is true, a debtor to our own people, but also, to a great extent, a debtor to the people of other nations. We are still in the market, soliciting loans with which to re-fund our great debt at a lower rate of interest. Every dollar thus re-funded reduces the annual burden of interest; and, to that extent, the government ceases to be a competitor of private citizens in securing loans. Any act of bad faith, therefore, tends to prevent refunding, tends to prevent the reduction of the public burdens, and keeps up the rate of interest, both public and private.

Our bonds have become the basis of private interests, involving hundreds of millions of dollars. The vast aggregate of investments by people of small means in savings banks, in fire, marine, and life insurance and the estates of thousands of widows and orphans depend largely for their value upon the security and steady value of government obligations; and any law or policy which tends to depreciate these obligations, is communicated through all the channels of private business, carrying loss and disaster to millions of citizens.

THE CURRENCY AND THE PUBLIC FAITH.

At the risk of repeating what may be familiar to every one, let us consider the relation of the greenback to the public faith. Whatever new theories of currency may have sprung up since 1862, it will not be denied as a fact of history and law that, the greenback was a loan without interest, forced upon the people by the overmastering necessities of the war. Its issue as a legal tender for private debts was acknowledged at the time, to be an act of doubtful constitutionality, and justified only on the plea of inexorable necessity. The measure was adopted with great hesitation, by a small majority, and against the protest and warning of many able and patriotic Senators and Representatives. The law was acknowledged by its supporters, to be a radical departure from the traditions, the theory and practice of our government. Its strongest supporters acknowledged the great danger of the experiment, and threw around it every safeguard against the evils it would inflict. They embodied in the law, and stamped upon the face of every greenback, this solemn promise: "The United States will pay." They provided a method by which the notes should be funded and ultimately redeemed. They did not propose to create a permanent system of paper money. They declared that the measure was to be a temporary one—the "Medicine of the Constitution, and not its daily bread." They aserted, again and again, that the money of the constitution was *coin*, not paper. The greenback itself, was a promise to pay coin; but the date of payment was not fixed. It was a government due-bill; and the only excuse in morals or in law for not paying it on demand, was inability to pay. The moment the government was able to pay, refusal became dishonor and reproduced its injustice in every business interest—public and private.

But the unredeemed greenback produced evils far greater than those which resulted from the ordinary refusal to pay a debt. Besides being a debt, it was a legal tender currency, and its excessive volume expelled real money from all the channels of internal trade, destroyed the old measure of value, and substituted in its place a standard whose value fluctuated every day and every hour during the seventeen years of suspension. On account of its twofold character as debt and currency, the value of the greenback was changed by every military and political event which affected the fortunes of the war. The march of a hostile army to the near neighborhood of the national capitol, in 1864, reduced the market value of the greenback forty per cent. in a single week. The same year a futile attempt of Congress to abolish the premium on gold, by a penal law, caused an equally violent fluctuation. At first the greenback was received at par with coin; but later every increase of issue reduced its market value. In 1864 the volume was increased one hundred and ninety millions, and the coin value of the whole mass became one hundred and seventy-five millions less than before the increase.

Through a series of innumerable and fitful fluctuations, it fell from par to thirty-eight cents on the dollar, reaching its lowest point on the fifth of July, 1864. By a series of changes. equally irregular, it has returned through an ascending scale of fifteen years, to par.

No arithmetic can compute the injustice and loss which these fluctuations have inflicted upon the people and business of this country. The chief mischief, resulted from two unequal and varying qualities of the greenback as a currency: Its debt-paying and its purchasing power. The first was arbitrarily fixed by Congress at one hundred cents on the dollar; but the second was controlled by laws which no human legislation can set aside—the laws of value; and the value of the greenback as a purchasing power suffered all the changes of the market.

In July, 1864, a citizen who had loaned his neighbor a hundred dollars in coin three years before, was compelled by law to accept as a discharge of the debt a handful of paper notes which he could purchase for thirty-eight dollars in coin. That is, the same note which paid a debt of one hundred cents, would buy in the market only thirty-eight cents worth of merchandise, valued in real money. This difference between its debt-paying power and its purchasing power, carried confusion and injustice into every department of business.

During the whole period of decline, the creditor was wronged by underpayment; and during the whole period of appreciation, the debtor was wronged by being compelled to make overpayment.

During the seventeen years of suspension the payment of every debt inflicted a wrong, either upon the creditor or the debtor; and thus the whole machinery of credit was converted into an engine of injustice. This will always happen when the two functions of currency are of unequal value.

THE MISTAKE OF 1865.

The first great opportunity for putting an end to these evils occurred soon after the close of the war. Probably at no other time in our history was the *per capita* average of private indebtedness so small as in 1865. Private debts had been paid—in depreciated paper; the government had become the great borrower; and had loaned nearly all the surplus capital of the country.

Two millions of hardy, enterprising men had just been mustered out of the lately hostile armies, and were ready again to become producers of wealth. It was a matter of the utmost importance that the fruits of their labor should be safe when earned, and that ventures in business should be made as free as possible from violent artificial fluctuations. The volume of currency then outstanding was nearly four times as great as had ever existed at any one time before the war. It amounted to nearly eight hundred millions of paper obligations, in various forms, endowed with the quality of legal tender. Even in the midst of the war, this volume was known to be far to great for financial safety. But on the return of peace, when the government ceased to be a great consumer and the payments from the treasury were reduced sixty per cent. in a single year, it was almost universally admitted that the volume of currency was greatly in excess of the legitimate wants of business.

Under the combined influence of this expanded volume of depreciated currency, and the enormous expenditures of the government, prices had risen to an average of ninety per cent. above those of 1859-61. They could not continue to rise without great danger to trade, and still greater danger to the interests of labor. We had a surplus revenue of a hundred millions per annum, and were abundantly able to retire, gradually, the excess of legal-tender notes, and thus bring the business of the country safely down from the dangerous height to which war and inflation had carried it.

Congress should not have compelled the new and aspiring industries of peace to put to sea in a crazy craft which was all sail and no anchor. The government had itself produced the condition in which business was placed; and to withdraw from its interference, to undo the mischief it had caused by allowing business to be governed by the natural laws of trade was the immediate and imperative duty of Congress.

This situation was clearly and ably portrayed by Secretary McCulloch, in his annual report of December 1865. He demonstrated the fact that we then stood at the parting of the ways, that one path if followed with wisdom and courage, would lead down from the dangerous heights of war prices to the safe level of solid values and steady business; that the other would lead through increased speculation and still greater expansion of credits, to inevitable and measureless disaster.

Studied by the light of subsequent experience, the Secretary's warnings now read like prophecy. At first, his policy was generally approved. In December 1865, the House of Representatives, with but six dissenting votes, pledged itself to early resumption by reducing the surplus volume of currency. Early in 1866, a bill was prepared which armed the Secretary with the requisite authority. But before the debate closed, many began to shrink from the responsibility of applying so heroic a remedy. Though approving resumption, and admitting the necessity of reducing the volume of currency, they hesitated to adopt any measure which would reduced prices and for the time being check the activity of trade. The dangers of inaction and delay were clearly pointed out in debate. The citizens of Chicago are not likely to forget the clearness and boldness with which the Hon. John Wentworth, then a member of the House, predicted the evils which inaction in timid and half way measures would involve. Late in the session, the bill was passed by a close vote; but the powers conferred upon the Secretary were so restricted that before the remedy could be fairly applied, the era of wild speculation had begun, and the current was soon too strong to be restricted. In less than two years, Congress over-riding the President, prohibited the further retirement of United States notes; and all attempts to resume Specie payments and return to solid values, were, for the time, virtually abandoned.

The high prices of all home products, measured, as they were by the standard of depreciated currency, made it impossible for our manufacturers to sell their wares in any foreign market. Our exports fell off beyond all precedent. Besides the breadstuffs, which Europe could not buy elsewhere, and the bullion dug from our mines, which was virtually banished by our laws, hardly a product of American industry crossed the ocean. At the same time ours was the most tempting market in the world for the sale of foreign merchandise. We were paying the highest prices known in modern times. A flood of foreign fabrics poured in upon us, and the great balance against us was paid in bonds of the nation, of the States, and of municipal and private corporations, bonds bearing the highest rate of coin interest. It is estimated that during the seven years which preceded the panic of 1873, not less than one thousand millions of American bonds were sold abroad. Pay day was pushed out of sight. The present possession of this vast inflow of borrowed capital led its holders to seek everywhere for investment. The surplus revenues of the National Treasury were applied to extensive and extravagant public works. National, State, municipal, and private credit was devoted to the building of railroads and to magnificent enterprises which fired the imagination of our people, and filled them with crazy enthusiasm.

The saddest and most curious phenomenon of that period, and one which the historian will some day record, was the delusion that we were then in the midst of great prosperity. Visions of wealth danced before the imaginations of enterprising men, and they ventured everything in the wild and exhilirating chase. They reveled in the light of a conflagration which was consuming their wealth, and called it the sunshine of prosperity. They lost sight of the only safe road, the old, hard, rough road, upon whose finger post is written: "In the sweat of thy face shalt thou earn thy bread." The delusion calls to mind the remark of Secretary Chase, that, "an irredeemable legal tender note was the devil made manifest in paper."

COMMERCIAL GAMBLING.

The fluctuations between the debt-paying and the purchasing power of our currency, created the new trade of gold gambling. The Gold Exchange and the Gold Clearing House, of New York, will be remembered in history as the Germans remember the robber castles of the Rhine, whose brigand chiefs levied black-mail upon every passer by. It was a business that never added a farthing to the national wealth, but in which everything gained by one was lost by another. It was simply betting on what the difference between coin and paper would be, and then employing every device to win the bet by increasing the fluctuation. In New York alone, for many years, a daily average of sixty millions of capital was withdrawn from industry and invested in this reckless business. Its fascination spread to all parts of the country. Each day some lucky gambler grew suddenly rich by the ruin of another. If these losses had been confined to the gamblers alone, the evils of the gold-room would have been less serious. But all our people who were engaged in honest industry, all producers and consumers of wealth, were made its victims. The great conspiracy of 1869, which culminated in "Black Friday," involved in ruin thousands of firms who were following legitimate business. As all our foreign trade was measured by the coin standard, the business of every importer and exporter of merchandise was at the mercy of the "bulls" and "bears" of the gold-room — whose chief effort was, by fair means or foul, to create sudden changes in the price of gold.

To insure himself against this additional risk, the importer was compelled to increase his prices. The increase was charged over to the jobber, and again to the retail dealer, until at last, its dead weight fell upon the consumer of the goods. The exporter could protect himself against loss only by paying lower prices for products to be sent abroad, and so the whole enormous cost of seventeen years of gold gambling has been paid out of the earnings of the American people. But gambling was not confined to gold. The habit engendered by a fluctuating currency which led men to sell what they did not own, and borrow what they sold was carried into every department of trade. Bright, ambitious young men, lured from the farm and workshop, sought their fortunes in the seductive chances of the stock board, or in the mysteries of "options," sales and "corners" in wheat. The population of many agricultural districts actually decreased. The cities and manufacturing centres were overcrowded. Some leading industries, notably railroad building and iron making, were greatly overdone. As speculation increased and credits expanded, the cry was raised that there was not currency enough, that the small measure of contraction, effected by Secretary McCullough, had destroyed the peoples' money and crippled their business. It was the drunkard's cry for more rum to steady his nerves, already shattered by drink.

THE CRASH.

Nothing could resist the downward tendency; and the wild dance went on, until, at last, when no more could be borrowed, the inevitable pay-day came, and with it the deluge of 1873. The vast fabric of municipal and private debt, tottered and fell, involving in general ruin; the industries of our people. We have no means of knowing the aggregate of that enormous indebtedness; but we may judge something of its magnitude by a simple example. If the statistics can be trusted, the municipal debts of a hundred and twenty-six Chief Cities of the Union increased two hundred per cent. in ten years, and amounted, in 1876, to six hundred and forty-four million dollars; and private debts had increased in proportion. While the catastrophe might have been prevented in 1865, it was now too late to avert the blow or mitigate its severity.

With such conditions, the crash was inevitable. Its details of loss and suffering need not be recounted.

LOSSES OF LABOR.

It brought innumerable bankruptcies and losses to capitalists on every hand; but in the whole sad chapter of calamities, the laborers of our country have been the greatest sufferers. If the employer grew suddenly rich by speculation, during the period of expansion, his workmen did not share his riches; but, when he suffered the destruction of his business, by the crash, they shared the disaster by losing the opportunity to work.

During the period of expansion, the wages of labor were somewhat increased, but the cost of living increased still more. When prices declined, wages were the first to fall. The capitalist can take advantage of the market. If he has anything to buy, he is not compelled to buy it to-day, he can wait for lower prices. If he has anything to sell, he is not compelled to sell at once, but can wait on the market and sell at the best advantage. Not so with the laboring man. He goes into the market with just one thing to sell—his day's work. He must sell it to-day, at to-day's prices, or it will be wholly lost. What he needs to buy, he must buy when necessity compels him. Fluctuation in the standard of values is his worst enemy. It strikes him both ways, and strikes him hard. Therefore, of all men in the world, the laboring man most need a steady market and an unvarying standard of value. When he has earned his wages, he wants to be paid in currency that will keep over night; that will be worth as much when he uses it as it was when he received it. I make this plea for the laboring man, not on his account alone, but on account of our national prosperity as well.

The hand of labor has built this great metropolis, has created its wealth, and to-day supports its half million of people. Within the memory of men who have hardly passed the meridien of life, Chicago was an Indian trading post, which sheltered only a dozen white families. In less than half a life time, the magical power of labor has made this city what we see it to-day. In our country there is no need of a conflict between capital and labor; for capital is only another name for accumulated labor. Every industrious and intelligent working-man looks forward to the day when his earnings will make him a capitalist. There is no barrier of caste to prevent his rising to the highest place of honor and wealth. He asks no special privilege from the government; but he does ask that the law shall not rob him of employment, nor destroy his earnings by making them the sport of the gold-room, the foot ball of speculation.

RECOVERY.

If the foregoing analysis is correct, it must be seen that depreciated and fluctuating currency has been the chief cause of our recent disasters; and this view accords with all experience, at home and abroad.

The same story has been reported in every language, and in every nation. Recovery from such disasters has come in only one way, by economy, reduction of credits, and a return to the basis of real money. By these means, and in the midst of great suffering, our people have been slowly making their way out of the ruins. The illusion of the seven years which preceded the crash have been rudely dispelled, and we have been brought face to face with realities. It has been a period of adjustment and payment. Prices have settled back to the old peace level; the wrecks have been gradually cleared away; the revival has begun. The products of our labor are again finding their way to the markets of the world. During the last three years, in our foreign trade, we have sold six hundred millions more than we have bought; and the balance in our favor is increasing. Less than two hundred millions of our national bonds are now held in Europe, and more than two thirds of them are long bonds at low interest. The favorable balance of trade has made ressumption comparitively easy.

RESUMPTION ACT OF 1875.

Four years ago Congress saw another opportunity to place the business of the country again on a stable foundation. The law of 1874 fixed the date when the promise of the war should be redeemed. It was a great act of National faith, too long delayed, but made doubly necessary by the sufferings of our people. The effort to keep this promise has been fiercely resisted at every stage. Orators, in Congress and out of Congress, have demonstrated, to their own satisfaction, that resumption was impossible, and the demonstration has been repeated even as late as two months ago.

Corbett, the great English pamphleteer, declared, in 1816, that Resumption in England was impossible; and he publicly offered himself to be broiled on a gridiron on the day when cash payments should be resumed. For years he kept the picture of a gridiron at the head of his paper, to remind his readers of his prophecy. We too, have our gridiron prophets; but all their predictions have failed.

Against determined opposition and repeated prophecies of evil, Resumption has come; and it has come to stay. As I said in the outset, it will stay, because it ought to stay, and because we are able to maintain it. In anticipation of its coming, the business of the country has gradually adjusted itself to the coin standard. Every legitimate enterprise will be benefited by resumption, and all classes of the community will rejoice in it, except the gold-gamblers and their associates, whose craft it has destroyed; and except, also, those political prophets, whose occupation is gone, by the explosion of their theories and the failure of their predictions.

RESUMPTION A SUCCESS.

That Resumption can now be maintained, intelligent men no longer doubt.

There are locked up in the vaults of the Treasury, to-day, one hundred and forty millions of coin, with no other demand upon it than the maintainance of the greenback at par. All experience declares that this reserve is amply sufficient to maintain Resumption. Should it prove insufficient, the Secretary of the Treasury has both the authority and the ability to increase it.

The people will have no motive to demand any great amount of coin; for paper at par is more convenient than gold or silver. The banks are bound, both by law and their own interests, to aid in maintaining resumption. The amount of National bonds now held abroad is too small to enable foreign creditors to drain us of our coin. If necessary, we can sell to Europe more of our four per cent. bonds than she can send home of our six per cents.

HOW RESUMPTION MAY BE DEFEATED.

But we must not assume that all danger is past. Resumption can be defeated in one of two ways: *First*, by great and unexpected calamity, like war, or the general failure of our crops, which should turn the balance of trade against us; or, *Second*, by the hostile legislation of Congress. The probability of the former is too remote to be seriously considered; the danger of the latter must be prevented by the intelligence and vigilance of our people.

Though the opposition to Resumption has shown great strength in Congress, even down to a very recent date, yet, now that par has been reached, I do not believe it will be longer assailed by direct legislation. The instinct of self-preservation will probably lead politicians to abandon such efforts. The real danger lies in indirect assaults, which may be made in several ways. If the expenditures of the government should be increased by large appropriations for the various schemes which are urged upon Congress, so as to produce a deficit in the revenues, rather than levy additional taxes, Congress will be tempted to issue more greenbacks, and carry expansion to a point at which Resumption will break down. Rigorous economy, and a persistent maintainance of revenue sufficient for necessary current expenses, and for the sinking fund, will be our safeguard in this direction.

THE BANK QUESTION.

The most dangerous, indirect assult upon Resumption is the attempt to abolish the national banks and substitute additional greenbacks in place of bank notes. This effort will call to its support the sentiment which, to some extent, prevails against moneyed corporations. Should the attempt succeed, it will inevitably result in suspension of specie payments. While the Treasury, aided by the banks can now easily maintain at par the outstanding volume of greenbacks, resumption would unquestionably break down, if the volume were increased three hundred and twenty millions. We must debate the bank question with our eyes open to the certainty of this result. And this ought to be decisive against the measure. But besides destroying resumption, it would be a most radical and dangerous revolution in our system of government. During the period of war and reconstruction, many good-people were alarmed at the tendency to centralize power at Washington; but the proposition we are now considering would result in a centralization of power without a parallel in our history. Before the war, except for the purpose of furnishing small change in the form of subsidiary and token coinage, it was never so much as suggested that the government had any right to become the proprietory manufacturer of money. It was the acknowledged duty of Congress to declare the value of coins and to coin the bullion of private citizens which might be brought to the mint for that purpose; but it had no authority to determine volume of currency or to regulate its distribution.

The substitution of greenbacks for national bank notes is proposed on the theory that the treasury should be converted into a work shop for the manufacture and sale of money; that not only its quality but its quantity and distribution shall depend solely upon the will of Congress.

To force a citizen into the army, and put him in the front of battle without his consent, was thought by many a violent invasion of private rights; but Congress to assume the power to raise, or depress all prices, to change the value of every purchase, and of every private contract, would be a usurpation of power the most despotic and dangerous ever proposed to Americans.

CURRENCY TO MEET THE WANTS OF TRADE.

We are told that the people demand a volume of currency sufficient for the wants of trade. So they do. But what man or set of men is wise enough to measure these wants, and declare the exact volume of currency that will meet them.

Suppose a hundred wise men of New York should take the contract of housing, clothing, feeding, and supplying the wants of the million people who live on Manhattan Island. Remember that all nations are placed under contribution to supply that city. The ships of every sea are landing at her docks the products of every clime. Railway trains from every quarter of the Union are pouring in their contributions. Millions of people in various parts of the world are at work creating the merchandise which the city needs. Hundreds of thousands of her own people are busy preparing these products for her use. Is it possible to conceive that the wit of man is able to devise any artificial system by which the infinite daily wants of New York shall be accurately measured and constantly and promptly supplied? Extend the scheme till it shall embrace the whole Union, with its forty-five millions of people. Is any Congress wise enough to measure all this vast business and to determine in advance just how much currency is needed to transact it? To propose it is to ask impossibilities; and yet, by the operation of laws higher and more potent than human legislation, all this is silently and perfectly accomplished. Millions of men, acting without concert, each working for his own interest in obedience to the great law of demand and supply, house, clothe, feed and transport the people of the United States, and carry on their manifold enterprises with perfect harmony and regularity. Any attempt of Congress to adjust the volume of currency to the wants of trade by arbitrary legislation is doomed to certain and disastrous failure.

The national banking sytem is that part of our financial machinery, by which, the volume of paper currency may increase or diminish in obedience to the laws of trade. If the volume becomes excessive, their notes are returned to the banks to be issued again, when increasing business requires them. The abolition of the national banks means the destruction of this indispensible self-adjusting principle of our currency system.

Surely, intelligent men do not suppose we can get on without a banking system of some kind. The bank is the chief instrument of modern exchange. It is as necessary to trade as the railroad is to transportation. It brings the borrower and lender together, and renders available for the uses of industry, the loanable capital of the community. Ninety per cent. of all our trade is carried on by means of the bank credits, in the form of drafts, checks and commercial bills, and only ten per cent. by the actual use of money which has become the small change of commerce. The vast mass of deposits and bank credits is now subjected to searching national inspection. If the power to issue notes be taken from the banks they will have no inducement to remain under such scrutiny. We shall go back to the wretched system of State banks and private broker shops, and create three hundred and twenty millions more of paper currency, which will escape all taxation.

On every principle of public policy the attempt should be resisted. It ought not to succeed, and I do not believe it can succeed. To make resumption sure, we should insist that our present currency and coinage laws shall remain for the present unchanged. Whether we can safely allow the Government to keep $340,000,000 of currency in circulation, and to that extent make the treasury a bank of issue, remains to be tested by experience. For myself, I doubt its wisdom as a permanent policy. But let the experiment be fairly tried.

Later on, some modification may be needed in our coinage law. If other nations persist in their refusal to restore silver to its old place of honor, as a part of the world's coinage, if the principle of bi-metallic currency should be practically abandoned by other nations who have long maintained it, we may, by and by, encounter serious difficulties, as our coinage of silver increases. I do not believe that our people will allow either metal to drive the other out of circulation. In some wise and just way they will meet and avert the danger when it comes.

EFFECTS OF RESUMPTION.

Successful Resumption will greatly aid in bringing into the murky sky of our politics, what the signal service people call "clearing weather." It puts an end to a score of controversies which have long vexed the public mind, and wrought mischief to business. It ends the angry contention over the difference between the money of the bond-holder and the money of the plow-holder. It relieves enterprising congressmen of the necessity of introducing twenty-five or thirty bills a session to furnish the people with cheap money, to prevent gold-gambling, and to make custom duties payable in greenbacks. It will dismiss to the limbo of things forgotten, such Utopian schemes as a currency based upon the magic circle of inter-convertability of two different forms of irredeemable paper, and the schemes of a currency "based on the public faith," and secured by "all the resources of the nation" in general, but upon no particular part of them. We shall still hear echoes of the old conflict, such as "the barbarism and cowardice of gold and silver," and the virtues of "fiat money;" but the theories which gave them birth will linger among us like belated ghosts, and soon find rest in the political grave of dead issues. All these will take their places in history alongside of the resolution of Varsittart, in 1811, that "British paper had not fallen but gold had risen in value," and the declaration of Castlereagh, in the House of Commons, that "the money 'standard is a sense of value in reference to currency as compared with 'commodities," and the opinion of another member, who declared that 'the standard is neither gold nor silver, but *something set up in the imagina-* '*tion to be regulated by public opinion.*"

When we have fully awakened from these vague dreams, public opinion will resume its old channels, and the wisdom and experience of the fathers of our constitution will again be acknowledged and followed.

We shall agree, as our fathers did, that the yard stick shall have length, the pound must have weight, and the dollar must have value in itself, and that neither length, nor weight, nor value can be created by the fiat of law. Congress relieved of the arduous task of regulating and managing all the business of our people, will address itself to the humbler but more important work of preserving the public peace, and managing wisely the revenues and expenditures of the government. Industry will no longer wait for the legislature to discover easy roads to sudden wealth, but will begin again to rely upon labor and frugality as the only certain road to riches. Prosperity, which has long been waiting. is now ready to come. If we do not rudely repulse her she will soon revisit our people, and will stay until another periodical craze shall drive her away.

THE TRIAL OF THE CONSTITUTION.

During the whole period which Resumption closes, our Constitution has been on trial for its life. When the greatest rebellion the world has ever known assailed it, the believers in governments founded on hereditary right, or on sheer force, told us that the bubble of Republican Government was about to burst. They did not understand the resources of a government based on the national will. They did not understand that in our Constitution the greatest powers—rights too precious to be delegated to the Congress or to the States—are reserved to the people themselves.

In the supreme moment of our peril, these voluntary powers were displayed in unsurpassed majesty and strength, on a thousand battle-fields, and they preserved the Republic from overthrow. Many feared that in the great struggle to save the Union, personal liberty, freedom of opinion, and respect for law, would be lost. But, outside of the actual theatre of military operations, the orderly course of justice was undisturbed. The rights of persons and property were almost everywhere sacredly preserved.

During the great conflict between Great Britain and the first Napoleon, though no hostile army landed on her territory, yet in England itself, as we are told by one of her eminent historians, the ordinary course of law was suspended, opinion was gagged, the right of public meeting was curtailed, Government indictmrnts for libel and trials for constructive treason were numerous, and other measures were adopted far more repressive than any which prevailed here during the great war on our own soil and among our own citizens. Professor Goldwin Smith has noted with admiration the behavior of our people during the crisis. He says: "History can

"scarcely supply a parallel to this perfect reliance of a Government on
"its moral strength and the unconstrained loyalty of its people. The sec-
"cond election of Lincoln took place at the acme of excitement,. when
"every other family had a member in the field for the Union, or in a sol-
"dier's grave. Yet there was not only perfect order maintained without
"any intervention of the police, but perfect respect for every right, not
"only of voting, speaking and writing, but of public demonstration..
"What government in Europe could safely have allowed sympathy with a
"great rebellion to hang out its banner in all the streets? Never to be
"forgotten, either, are those predictions of military usurpation and sabre
"rule as the sure result of civil war, uttered with exhultation by enemies,
"with sorrow by friends, warranted by the experience of history, but belied
"by the Republican loyalty of the generals and the imediate return of the
"armies to civil life."

This testimony from an eminent foreigner is as important as it is just. The people passed cheerfully and joyfully from the ambition and glories of war to the humbler walks of peace. And finally, notwithstanding the confusion of public opinion, caused by great suffering, the public faith has been preserved, and the national character greatly strengthened.

Reviewing the whole period, we have a right to say that the wisdom of our institutions has been vindicated, and our confidence in their stability has been strengthened. Legislation has been directed more and more to the enlargement of private rights and the promotion of the interests of labor. It has been devoted not to the glory of a dynasty, but to the welfare of a people. Slavery, with the aristocracy of caste which it engendered, and the degradation of labor which it produced, has disappeared. Without undue exultation, we may declare that the bells of the new year

>   Ring out a slowly dying cause,
>   And ancient forms of party strife;
>   Ring in the nobler modes of life,
>   With sweeter manners, purer laws.

We have learned the great lesson, applicable alike to nations and to men:

>   Self-knowledge, self-reverence, self-control—
>   These three alone lead life to sovereign power.

46TH CONGRESS, } HOUSE OF REPRESENTATIVES. { MIS. DOC.
1st Session. } { No. 11.

UNLIMITED COINAGE OF SILVER AND THE TRADE-DOLLAR.

MINUTES

OF A

CONFERENCE BETWEEN THE COMMITTEE ON COINAGE, WEIGHTS AND MEASURES OF THE HOUSE OF REPRESENTATIVES, AND THE SECRETARY OF THE TREASURY AND THE DIRECTOR OF THE MINT.

MAY 1, 1879.—Recommitted to the Committee on Coinage, Weights, and Measures and ordered to be printed.

NOTES OF A CONFERENCE BETWEEN THE COMMITTEE ON COINAGE, WEIGHTS, AND MEASURES AND SECRETARY SHERMAN AND DIRECTOR OF THE MINT BURCHARD.

WASHINGTON, *April 26, 1879.*

The CHAIRMAN. Before proceeding to the main subject of this conference, I wish to ask some questions in relation to the trade-dollar. Can you give us, Mr. Secretary, a correct statement or estimate of the number of trade-dollars now in the United States?

Secretary SHERMAN. I can state that the amount of trade-dollars that have been coined is $35,959,300. The amount of them exported, as shown by the statistics we have, partly estimated but nearly accurate, may be said to be about twenty-nine million dollars. These are about the figures that were given in my annual report in December last, and I believe they are as nearly accurate as possible. This would leave in the country between six and seven millions of trade-dollars.

Mr. CLAFLIN. Is there any evidence that any of those have been taken up, used as bullion, or in any other way?

Secretary SHERMAN. We have no evidence on that point. It is hardly probable, however, that they would be, because bullion has been cheaper all the time than trade-dollars.

The CHAIRMAN. Is there any serious objection to taking up those trade-dollars and giving standard silver dollars for them and then recoining them—never issuing them again?

Secretary SHERMAN. I think the objections are very serious. There are three radical objections, any one of which, I think, ought to prevent the government from taking that course. First, it would be a discrimination against our own miners in the price of silver bullion and in favor of the holders of these dollars in China. At least from twenty-six to twenty-eight millions of these trade-dollars are held in China as bullion. The trade-dollars were coined as bullion and sold as bullion, for private parties, for private profit, and the government had no connection with them except to charge the actual cost to the owners of the bullion. They had a limited legal-tender quality until July 22, 1876, but they did not get into circulation in this country until October, 1876; so that every trade-dollar that is now in circulation in this country was put in circulation at a time when it was not a legal tender, but simply represented 420 grains of standard silver. If we should now make it exchangeable for the standard silver dollar, and equal to the gold dollar, it would be worth for that purpose 14 or 15 cents more than it is worth as bullion, and the owners of this bullion in China, or the purchasers of those coins for the purpose of bringing them here, would get the benefit of that difference. We can buy the same amount of silver bullion from our own miners to-day for four or five millions of dollars less than we can get this bullion in China, if the proposed measure should become a law. That is the first objection.

Mr. WARNER. Would that objection, however, lie if silver was admitted to free or unlimited coinage in the United States?

Secretary SHERMAN. No; if silver coinage is made free at the rate of 16 of silver to 1 of gold we shall have a mono-metallic system of silver coinage excluding gold from circulation. Then, as a matter of course, the objection would cease; then the trade-dollar would be worth more than the standard dollar. That is, if you adopt the bullion value of silver as the sole standard in this country, then it makes no difference what is done with the trade-dollar; but as long as you maintain the gold standard or the present standard based upon the gold coin of $25\frac{8}{10}$ grains, the introduction of the trade-dollar, either as a coin or as the equal of the standard dollar, will be a discrimination in favor of the owners of this silver bullion in China and against our own miners to the extent that I have stated.

Mr. WARNER. That is, while silver is coined under existing law and regulations?

Secretary SHERMAN. Certainly. The chairman did not ask me about my view in regard to the question of bi-metallic or mono-metallic money.

The CHAIRMAN. Suppose we change our system in relation to the coinage of silver and make it unrestricted, so that the government will not purchase bullion at all; suppose that the system of purchasing bullion for coin is abrogated and the unlimited coinage of silver is introduced, then ought not the trade-dollar and the legal-tender standard dollar to be interchangeable?

Secretary SHERMAN. If Congress should finally determine to adopt the silver standard——

The CHAIRMAN. The double standard?

Secretary SHERMAN. Yes; the free coinage of both gold and silver upon the present ratios. If that is to be adopted, then the proposition is not objectionable; but that brings up at once the great question whether that ought to be done.

The CHAIRMAN. That is the point we have before us, and I understand that in case we do that, your opinion is that then the trade-dollar and the standard silver dollar ought to be interchangeable.

Secretary SHERMAN. Yes; but in case you should do that, no man of ordinary sagacity would surrender a trade-dollar for the standard dollar; he would want to receive the difference between them. You would not be able to get the trade-dollar exchanged for the standard dollar, because the trade-dollar contains 420 grains of silver, while the standard dollar contains only $412\frac{1}{2}$.

The CHAIRMAN. Then you would not be bothered with the recoining?

Secretary SHERMAN. No. The trade-dollar would be, as the old Mexican dollar was formerly, a little more valuable than our standard dollar.

Mr. WARNER. It would simply go to the mint as bullion?

Secretary SHERMAN. Hardly; it would not be exchanged on an equality with the standard dollar.

The CHAIRMAN. What amount of standard silver dollars coined since the act of last year are now in circulation?

Secretary SHERMAN. According to latest returns received at the department there have been coined of these dollars $30,542,950. We have now on hand $22,887,695; leaving $7,655,255 of those dollars in circulation.

The CHAIRMAN. How many coin certificates have been issued under the act of 1878?

Secretary SHERMAN. An amount of $10,437,000. Nearly all our silver bullion is purchased by silver certificates, but then they are at once returned to the Treasury.

The CHAIRMAN. I understand you to say that there are very few of them out now?

Secretary SHERMAN. Very few. They are at once converted. They come right back.

Mr. WARNER. They come back in payment of duties.

Secretary SHERMAN. Largely in payment of bonds, and also for the payment of duties. The whole amount outstanding now is only $176,330.

The CHAIRMAN. In connection with the sales of bonds that have been made lately?

Secretary SHERMAN. Yes; lately and all along.

The CHAIRMAN. What would be the objection to issuing coin certificates down to denominations of fives, and threes, and twos, and ones, and halves and quarters for change?

Secretary SHERMAN. The objection to issuing coin certificates while you have legal-tender notes outstanding is that the coin certificates, of whatever denomination they may be, will not circulate while the legal-tender notes are outstanding. Until the 1st of January the coin certificates had the advantage over the legal-tender notes, because they were receivable for bonds, for customs duties, and for all purposes, and therefore they had a special value or use which the legal-tender notes had not; but now the legal-tender notes are, in effect, a coin certificate, and may be used for all purposes. There is now no occasion for coin certificates, which come back into the Treasury.

Mr. VANCE. Then can they not be put out again?

Secretary SHERMAN. They can, but we have "greenbacks," which we are bound to keep in circulation, and which fill all the channels of circulation, under existing law. It would be difficult to keep the two forms of currency afloat at the same time. If either were taken away, then the other would fill the channels of circulation.

Mr. WARNER. Is there any objection to those certificates if persons holding bullion or coin prefer the certificates to handling the coin or bullion, even though the certificates may come back, as coin would, in payment of duties to the government?

The CHAIRMAN. The question I meant to ask is this: Is there any practical objection to issuing coin certificates, if persons prefer them, so as to get rid of these fractional silver dollars; in other words, is there any objection to having coin certificates ready to exchange with any persons who prefer them, down to the denominations of fives, ones, halves, and quarters?

Secretary SHERMAN. If you issue them in small sums there is the same objection that was made always to the fractional currency, that it was very perishable and very costly, and a great loss to the people on account of its being so perishable.

The CHAIRMAN. Would they be more perishable, or a greater loss to the government, or more costly after the plates are made, than the coin itself is? Is not the waste and abrasion of the coin itself quite as great as that of the fractional currency?

Secretary SHERMAN. Experience shows that it is not. The fractional currency was found to last only about fifteen or eighteen months, while silver coin lasts in circulation about twenty-three years, and gold coin about fifty years. The actual cost of the fractional currency in the last year or two before it was abandoned was shown to be about three per cent. per annum, and that currency perished in about fifteen or eighteen months on an average.

The CHAIRMAN. But you would have the plates, so that there would be no cost in replacing it except for the paper?

Secretary SHERMAN. Yes; but on ten-cent and twenty-five cent currency the cost, even of a million, is considerable.

The CHAIRMAN. I would not have the denominations go below twenty-five cents. You speak of gold coin wearing fifty years, and silver coin a much less time; how do you account for that?

Secretary SHERMAN. That, I suppose, is because the gold coin passes through fewer hands.

The CHAIRMAN. We had a statement here the other day about a double-eagle which was weighed in the Treasury Department and found to have lost seven grains.

Secretary SHERMAN. It must have undergone pretty rapid and extensive usage.

The CHAIRMAN. Mr. Riggs, I understand, says that his loss is immense on gold coin because the Treasury will not take it from him except by weight, and his loss thereby is several per cent.

Secretary SHERMAN. There are statistical tables in the reports of the Director of the Mint which show very accurately the amount of abrasion of different coins. Gold coin, from the fact that it does not circulate so freely, lasts longer than any other.

The CHAIRMAN. I understand your answer to my question to amount to this: that there is no practical objection to issuing these coin certificates except the increased cost.

Secretary SHERMAN. As to the fractional notes the objection is one of cost and wear and tear. Another objection is this: I think the instinctive desire of men generally, especially laboring men, is to handle the coin itself. I think this desire is better gratified by the sense of touch in handling coin than in handling paper.

The CHAIRMAN. My question does not go to that extent, because it leaves it optional with people to have the one or the other as they prefer. Is there any practical objection to the government being ready to issue these certificates if the holders of coin or bullion shall so desire?

Secretary SHERMAN. I do not think that the double system is wise. If you adopt the one you should reject the other. The double system puts us to the great expense of maintaining mints to supply the coin, and also the Bureau of Engraving and Printing to supply the paper. In my judgment it is better to have either the one or the other, not both. Many very intelligent people, bankers as well as others, do, I know, prefer small fractional currency to silver currency.

There is another grave objection to the issue of coin certificates, that they will inevitably replace and destroy the legal-tender notes, or compel the suspension of specie payments on such notes. In case of the slightest suspicion or doubt of the ability to maintain redemption, or in case brokers or bankers choose for speculative purposes to make gold scarce, they may, without cost or trouble, or without handling the coin, present legal-tender notes to the Treasury and demand coin, and turn over the coin for certificates. Upon issuing the certificates the Treasury must keep the full amount of coin for the payment of the certificates, thus reducing the coin reserve for the payment of United States notes, and throwing upon the Treasury the risk and expense of keeping the coin for private and perhaps hostile purposes. It was this very danger that induced me to decline in December last to issue any more gold certificates. One protection to the Treasury is the inconvenience to which the parties presenting the coins would be put in receiving and hoarding them, but if the issue of certificates is made mandatory, a few active brokers might convert all the coin in the Treasury into certificates, and leave no means with which to redeem United States notes. I can see no public interest that would be promoted by a mandatory issue of coin certificates in exchange for gold or silver bullion, and if they are issued without an actual deposit of coin, to be held for their redemption, they are only another form of United States notes.

The CHAIRMAN. One other question. What do you think of having ingots of gold or silver, say silver, of the value of $100, assayed, refined, and stamped, for purposes of exchange, instead of coin? Do you or not think that such ingots would answer the purpose of a medium of exchange with other countries, to be used instead of coin in settling balances—I mean ingots of pure silver or gold? Dr. Linderman made the suggestion to us last year, and that is why I want to get your views on the subject now. If that were done, there would be no drain from abroad upon our coinage. These ingots would be resorted to instead.

Secretary SHERMAN. We have ingots of gold and silver now. In the assay office in New York you will see great ingots of gold and silver of various denominations and values, with the values stamped upon them, just as you suggest.

The CHAIRMAN. But they are not of the same denominations as the coin?

Secretary SHERMAN. No.

The CHAIRMAN. The suggestion was to have them of the same denominations, and to have them all alike, fine ingots of silver of $100 each, with $100 worth of silver in them, measured by our standard dollar. Dr. Linderman's idea was that those ingots would be used in commerce, for the purposes I have suggested, without a resort to coin.

Secretary SHERMAN. That is rather a question of convenience. It is to provide coin of the denomination of $100 or ten eagles.

The CHAIRMAN. The idea was, I believe, that when those ingots went abroad the foreign mints would not be troubled with our alloy, because the ingot would be pure silver.

Secretary SHERMAN. Well, that is a technical question which I do not pretend to know much about—whether it is better to export silver in the pure state or not. Most of the bullion in the mint and at the assay office is gold or silver with a shade of alloy; then when coined they add the proper alloy to conform to the law of the country.

The CHAIRMAN. I will put the same question to Mr. Burchard, the Director of the Mint, whether he has given any attention to that point.

Mr. BURCHARD. I have not, particularly. The question of stamping a value upon silver bars has not been raised or considered since I have had charge of the Mint Bureau.

The CHAIRMAN. I wish, Mr. Secretary, that you and Mr. Burchard, when the notes of this conference are submitted to you, will add anything that may occur to you in the mean time upon this point.

Mr. BURCHARD. A person bringing silver bullion now to the Mint and desiring to have it converted into fine bars is entitled to have that done, and to have fine silver bars delivered to him in lieu of the bullion. The value is not stamped upon such silver bars but simply the weight and fineness. That is now the the course of business at the coinage mints and at New York assay-office.

Mr. WARNER. And the only limit under the law now is that nothing shall be stamped less than five ounces; which would be a very small bar of silver.

Mr. VANCE. What is the trade-dollar worth at the Treasury now, Mr. Secretary? At what rate do you receive it in place of bullion?

Secretary SHERMAN. We are not authorized to receive it at all except as bullion; the bullion value is now 85.8. The commercial value among the brokers is 98.75. We would buy it as bullion, if it was offered, at one cent under the market rate, because we buy at one cent less than the bullion value when offered in small lots, but in large lots we buy at the market rate for bullion.

Mr. VANCE. What is the probable amount of the fractional coin now in circulation.

Secretary SHERMAN. The exact amount of fractional silver in circulation cannot be given. Of the amount which has been paid out since January 1, 1875, there is now outstanding $41,485,438.56, and the amount now on hand at the several mints and Assistant Treasurer's Offices, is $6,598,492.44.

Mr. FISHER. To pursue the inquiry of the chairman a step further: What would you think of the idea of the issuance of silver certificates of the denominations of one dollar and two dollars? There is a scarcity of legal-tender notes of those denominations in the country.

Secretary SHERMAN. I think that the objections to issuing silver certificates or gold certificates of any denominations while United States notes are in circulation are very clear. As to the scarcity of United States notes of small denominations, that is simply because persons who come to the Treasury for money will not take them. We issue ones and twos freely, but hardly anybody wants them. Any one who chooses can come to the Treasury with a draft for $100 or $1,000, and get every dollar of it in one-dollar notes if he wishes.

Mr. FISHER. Can that be done now?

Secretary SHERMAN. Certainly, and it could always be done. I know that a stringency does occur in some localities, because the great transactions with the government require large sums of money, and people prefer notes of larger denominations because it is easier to carry large sums of money in that form. Always, since I have been in the department, I have taken great pains to distribute ones and twos, and any person receiving money can get any number of them he wishes to carry away at any time.

Mr. FISHER. In my section of Pennsylvania we have been suffering from a scarcity of those small notes. You have spoken of people preferring coin to paper; now, our people consider the silver dollar a nuisance.

Secretary SHERMAN. I think the silver dollar is rather too large for change. I was speaking rather of the subsidiary coinage. But so far as the one and two dollar notes are concerned, I am very glad to state and to have it generally known, that anybody can get as many of them

UNLIMITED COINAGE OF SILVER AND TRADE DOLLAR. 7

at the Treasury as he wants, either in payment of drafts or in exchange for larger sums.

Mr. FISHER. I have heard it said that the Treasury took in the smaller notes and issued only the larger ones, and I am glad to know from the Secretary that we can get the smaller denominations.

Secretary SHERMAN. I have endeavored to promote the circulation of the ones and twos in every way that I could.

Mr. CLAFLIN. The difficulty in keeping the smal llegal-tender notes in circulation is that the banks, having to keep a reserve, gather up the legal tenders and do not pay them out, but put them in the Treasury. That is because they do not issue ones and twos of their own. If they issued ones and twos of their own, the legal-tenders would be freely circulated, but as it is, the tendency must be for them to go into the bank reserves.

The CHAIRMAN. But why don't they pay them out?

Mr. CLAFLIN. Because they have to keep from 10 to 25 per cent. reserve, and they do not want to go and get gold and silver and pay out the 1's and 2's; they prefer to hold the small notes for their reserve. That is the difficulty.

Mr. FISHER. That is not the difficulty with us. The difficulty in our section is that the 1's and 2's have been worn out and have gone in for redemption, and we have not received others of the same small denominations to supply their places.

Mr. CLAFLIN. That is, your bank-notes, 1's and 2's, that were in circulation, have gone home, and the department has sent back $5 notes, or notes of some other larger denomination in place of the 1's and 2's.

Mr. FISHER. Then it is only a question of time when they will all go out of circulation.

Mr. CLAFLIN. It is only a question of time in regard to the 1's and 2's.

Secretary SHERMAN. There never was more than between five and six millions of small bank-notes in circulation, while we have from forty to fifty millions of small United States notes in circulation.

Mr. CLAFLIN. But those are all held by the banks; they are not in circulation.

Secretary SHERMAN. We give 1's and 2's for 5's, 10's, and 100's, and pay them out when called for.

Mr. CLAFLIN. But the natural result is that they are held by the banks for reserves.

Mr. WARNER. Has there been, then, within the last year, or since the act of May 31, 1878, any absolute contraction in the amount of 1 and 2 dollar legal-tender notes in circulation? Is the amount absolutely any less now than a year ago?

Secretary SHERMAN. In answer to that I will give you a table, showing the exact amount of 1's and 2's out May 31, 1878, and at the present date.

Date.	Denomination.	Amount.	Date.	Denomination.	Amount.
May 31, 1878	Ones	$21,576,728 80	Apr. 26, 1879	Ones	$18,953,172 80
May 31, 1878	Twos	21,601,458 20	Apr. 26, 1879	Twos	18,871,394 20

Mr. WILLIS. Mr. Secretary, in answer to the first question which was put to you by the Chairman you said that there were three objections to the recoinage of the trade-dollar. You stated one, and were interrupted before you had completed the statement of those objections. I should be very glad to have you now state the other two.

Secretary SHERMAN. The second objection is that it would bring us abruptly to the single silver standard. The few millions of trade-dollars now in circulation are very unpopular and cause the demand to Congress to get rid of them. If you now make them lawful money, or authorize them to be converted at par into lawful money, the largest part of the 30 millions exported will be presented for redemption in the standard silver dollars. If you force the standard silver dollars into circulation, I know by experience they will at once come back for taxes and bonds, and as often as reissued will come back until we will be driven to hoard them in our vaults, or they will drag our paper money down to the market value of silver bullion and will expel gold. This will create wide and sweeping changes in contracts. For forty years all contracts have been based upon gold coin, except since the issue of legal-tender notes. Now these are at par with gold coin, and thus far we have maintained our silver coin at the same standard because the amount was limited and the supply mainly in the Treasury. The addition of 30 millions of trade-dollars to our active circulation, together with the continued coinage of two millions a month of standard dollars, would soon force into use the silver dollar as the sole standard of value for all paper money and for all contracts. If this is to be done it should be directly by free coinage, when all silver bullion would have an equal chance and not by discriminating in favor of bullion in a trade-dollar, every one of which now in circulation in this country is a fraud upon the law. My view of this trade-dollar was given last year in a letter which was published, and was bettere xpressed than I can in this conversation. If you will allow me I will hand it to the reporter.

TREASURY DEPARTMENT,
OFFICE OF THE SECRETARY,
Washington, D. C., September 3, 1878.

SIR: I hasten to fulfill the promise I made you that upon my return to the department I would write you fully concerning the issue of the trade-dollar and the present depreciation in its value.

The coinage of this dollar was authorized by the coinage act of February 12, 1873, in words as follows:

"That any owner of silver bullion may deposit the same at any mint to be formed into bars or into dollars of the weight of four hundred and twenty grains troy, designated in this act as trade-dollars, * * * and the charges for converting standard silver into trade-dollars, for melting and refining, when bullion is below standard, for toughening when metals are contained in it which render it unfit for coinage, for copper used for alloy, when the bullion is above standard, for separating the gold and silver when these metals exist together in the bullion, and for the preparation of bars, shall be fixed from time to time by the Director [of the Mint], with the concurrence of the Secretary of the Treasury, so as to equal, but not exceed, in their judgment, the actual average cost to each mint and assay office of the material, labor, wastage, and use of machinery employed in each of the cases aforementioned."

As its name indicates, the purpose of this coin was for *trade*, not for circulation, though by classifying it with other silver coins the law made it a legal tender to the amount of five (5) dollars in any one payment.

At the time of the passage of the act the actual value of this dollar, including the charge of 1¼ cents for coinage, was a little more than $1.04 in gold.

Under such circumstances there could be no object for the owner to put the coins into circulation, and consequently they were exported mostly to China, where, from lack of a circulating medium, these pieces, convenient in size, and bearing the guarantee of a great government as to their weight and fineness, obtained an extensive circulation, and created a market for the silver of the Pacific States, as intended by the act.

After a few months, however, an unforeseen depreciation in the value of silver bullion occurred, and in the early part of 1876 this depreciation reached such a point that one dollar in gold would purchase more than the necessary amount of silver for a trade-dollar and pay for its coinage.

Under such conditions dealers in bullion found a profit in putting trade-dollars into circulation at par in the Pacific States, where the currency was upon a gold basis, but the coin being a legal tender for only five (5) dollars, its circulation was necessarily limited in amount as well as restricted in locality.

The people of the Pacific States, however, objected to its use at all for circulation, and the attention of Congress having been called to the matter, on the 8th of May, 1876, Hon. Samuel J. Randall, of Pennsylvania, introduced into the House a bill the third section of which repealed the legal-tender quality of these coins.

On the 10th of June following, Hon. S. S. Cox, of New York, reported the measure to the House, urging its adoption.

No objection was raised, and it became a law July 22, 1876, without modification or an opposing voice or vote in either House, and is as follows:

"That the trade-dollar shall not hereafter be a legal tender; and the Secretary of the Treasury is hereby authorized to limit, from time to time, the coinage thereof to such an amount as he may deem sufficient to meet the export demand for the same."

Up to that time (excepting a few days), and for several months thereafter, the trade-dollar cost more than a paper currency dollar, and consequently none of the coins got into circulation in other than the Pacific States.

Owing to the appreciation of the paper currency, however, in the fall of 1877 the trade-dollar became of less value than the paper dollar, and in December of that year a large number of them were put into circulation, at their face value, at a profit to the owners of the bullion.

Apprehensive of such misuse of the coins, on the 15th of October in that year I ordered the discontinuance of their coinage at the mint at Philadelphia, and four days later at the other mints. Meanwhile the Department, in reply to numerous inquiries, had uniformly stated that the trade-dollar possessed only a commercial value depending upon the price of silver bullion.

It will be seen that the coins were put into circulation months after the passage of the act taking from them their legal-tender character, and mainly after their coinage had ceased.

But in their use as money the department has never had any interest or derived any profit. For the expense of their coinage the owner of the bullion reimbursed the government, and this ended the connection of the government with the transaction. At no time and on no account have they ever been received, or paid out, by the Treasury, and it is a cause of regret that so many of our people should have accepted them at their face value, thus enabling their owners to put them into circulation at a considerable profit.

Under date of July 25, 1878, the Director of the Mint published tables from which the value of these coins can he ascertained and the terms on which they are received at the mints. He does not advise any one to dispose of them at such rates. The law under which the department buys bullion with which to coin the standard silver dollar requires the same to be bought at the market price, and it can purchase trade-dollars only as bullion. Possibly in time these coins will find a ready market in China at nearly or quite their face value, for circulation as coin.

In this connection permit me to correct any misapprehension as to the purpose and effect of the Director's circular. As early as August 24, 1876, the department informed an inquirer that the trade-dollar had only a bullion value, and this information has been repeated scores of times, and published by the press throughout the country. To avoid the labor of preparing manuscript letters, the Director embodied the information in a circular, adding thereto tables for the computation of such value. There was no new decision involved in the circular, though possibly its publication may have hastened the depreciation of the coins to their true value—an event which was inevitable, and could not have been much longer delayed.

Very respectfully,

JOHN SHERMAN,
Secretary.

O. H. BOOTH, Esq.,
Mansfield, Ohio.

The third objection to monetizing the trade-dollar is, that it would seriously impair the public credit, and delay, if not defeat, the important refunding operations that ought to occur two years hence, when 800 millions of United States bonds will become redeemable at the pleasure of the government. In January last, after resumption was accomplished, it became very easy to sell our 4 per cent. bonds. We sold nearly as many in the month of January as we did in two years before. I can assure you that if the public mind had been convinced that the trade-dollar was to be monetized, and that the government would adopt the single silver standard, we could not have accomplished the refunding of the 5-20s and 10-40s. The forbearance of Congress at the last session greatly aided the Treasury Department. The shadow of this fear was the only restraining motive in refunding. If by 1881 the measures proposed shall have been adopted, it will not, in my opinion, be possible to sell 4 per cent. bonds at par. But if let alone, the whole 800 millions may be funded at 4 per cent. or less. Public credit is exceedingly sensitive. Gold was the standard coin in contemplation when all the bonds were issued. To take advantage of the unforeseen fall of silver bullion to issue a silver coin worth only 85 per cent. of gold coin would excite distrust and fear. To advance public credit you must do all or more than was expected by your creditor when your securities were issued, and you get the full benefit of this in lower rates of interest and improving credit.

My general answer to your question as to the trade-dollar is that this coin ought to be left precisely where it is, a piece of silver bullion containing 420 grains of standard silver, issued for the benefit of merchants, at their cost and for their benefit, for exportation; that every one of them now in circulation is there by an evasion of the law. They were issued after they ceased to be a legal tender for any amount, and their circulation should be discouraged and refused by every citizen. If they are now monetized it will be a discrimination of full .15 per cent. against our miners of silver who have bullion to sell and in favor of the Chinese and of our own merchants, who, by buying up this form of silver bullion in China for 85 cents, can sell it to the government for a dollar. The proposition if adopted would suddenly change our standard of values from gold to silver, and would seriously impair our public credit and our ability to reduce the interest of the public debt.

If, however, it is deemed politic to redeem the trade-dollar and get it out of the way, the better course would be to authorize its purchase as bullion, at a slight advance over other forms of bullion, to be paid for with lawful money, or by the sale of bonds. This would soon retire those in this country without tempting their importation from China. The public would soon understand that they were not lawful money, and this would stop their circulation.

Mr. WARNER. I understood you to say, Mr. Secretary, in connection with the trade-dollar, that you regarded it as stamped bullion rather than as United States coin. The language of the law is: "The silver coins of the United States shall be a trade-dollar, a half-dollar," and so on. Is there any objection to so amending that section as to strike out the words "trade-dollar"?

Secretary SHERMAN. No. I think that the best way to dispose of the trade-dollar is to just let it alone as so much bullion, and to coin no more. I know the origin of it. It was issued simply for the convenience of merchants of California, to give them a market for their silver. It was stamped a trade-dollar, but neither that nor any other silver dollar was put in circulation in this country until three years afterward. I think its limited legal-tender quality was given it on the revision of the statutes, but afterward was taken away.

Mr. WARNER. This language that I have read is in the coinage bill of 1873.

Secretary SHERMAN. Then it was grouped with other silver coins as a legal tender for five dollars. The trade-dollar was coined at the expense of the depositor of the silver, for his benefit, and without any profit to the United States.

Mr. WARNER. Is there any longer any object in coining that piece at all for private parties?

Secretary SHERMAN. No, sir; and I should refuse to do it now if such an application were made.

Mr. WARNER. Is it not true that the owner of the bullion really gets no more for his bullion when it is divided into pieces of 420 grains each than he would get if it were divided into pieces of 412½ grains? Was there ever any gain to the owner in having it coined?

Secretary SHERMAN. Yes; there was an advantage to him from 1873 up to the time when the trade-dollar fell below the market value of gold coin.

Mr. WARNER. But could he get any more per ounce for his silver? A bar of silver containing 100 ounces will make 114 trade-dollars, or 116 standard dollars. The owner of the bar could get no more per ounce for his silver when divided into pieces of 420 grains than when divided into pieces of 412½ grains each, could he?

Secretary SHERMAN. Yes, in China he could get more. The Mexican dollar was formerly the only dollar that got a foothold in China. The Chinese would not take our old American dollar of 412½ grains, because it was less valuable than the Mexican dollar, and therefore the trade-dollar was coined, containing 420 grains, so as to make it better than the Mexican dollar, and thus win its way into circulation in China. That was the object.

Mr. DE LA MATYR. It was rather as money than as bullion.

Secretary SHERMAN. It was bullion put into a form more valuable or more acceptable to the Chinese.

Mr. WARNER. But is it not true that we got no more per ounce for our silver in the end?

Secretary SHERMAN. The government did not get any more.

Mr. WARNER. Neither did the bullion-dealer.

Secretary SHERMAN. But he got a market for his silver. They would take it in this form when they would not take it in the form of our old dollar.

Mr. WARNER. But at the time when the trade-dollar was adopted we stopped the coinage of the standard dollar. It was done in the very same act. Now, my point is this, that when our standard dollar would not pass in China and Japan at the same value as the Mexican dollar, the reason was simply because it contained a little less silver; but would it not pass for its bullion-value, the same as all coins pass for in foreign countries?

Secretary SHERMAN. No; at that time the silver dollar did not pass anywhere except for exportation to China or India. Several millions of the old standard dollars were sent to China but they were objected to by the Chinese, and therefore the merchants of California, who wanted to make their silver bullion available, got Congress to order the coinage of this trade-dollar which could be exported successfully.

Mr. WARNER. Then you think that by dividing 100 ounces of silver into pieces of 420 grains each the bullion-dealer did get more per ounce for his silver than he would have got for it in pieces of 412½ grains each?

Secretary SHERMAN. He did in China; he did not here. He did in China because they liked the form of the coin; just as a person is willing to pay more for one piece of calico than for another of the same material because he likes the pattern.

Mr. CLAFLIN. Did not the bullion men obtain more use for their bullion in this form than they could in the ordinary form?

Secretary SHERMAN. They did.

Mr. FISHER. They had a commodity to sell, and by getting it coined into trade-dollars they put it in a form to suit their customers.

Secretary SHERMAN. Yes.

Mr. WARNER. But it comes right back to this point, that if you divide up 100 ounces of silver into pieces of 420 grains each you get more per ounce for your silver than if it were divided into pieces of 412½ grains. Now, would that be the case in England or France?

Secretary SHERMAN. No; but we did not send them to England or France at that time.

Mr. WARNER. But when we export coin don't all foreign countries assay it and determine its value according to the quantity of metal that it actually contains?

Secretary SHERMAN. All European countries do and Japan does now; but in China they took the coin of a foreign nation and circulated it. They put a kind of stamp upon it, which did not impair its value at all, but served to naturalize it, as we might say, and then they circulated it.

Mr. WARNER. Our trade-dollar is unlike any other coin issued by any country. It has a little more value than the Japanese yen, and it has a little more value than the Mexican silver dollar.

Secretary SHERMAN. Yes, it has a little more value than the Mexican silver dollar. I do not know that any other coin contains just the same amount of bullion. None of the trade-dollars have been issued lately, and none can be issued now.

Mr. WARNER. Then I understand that you think there is no objection to striking out the trade-dollar from our coinage?

Secretary SHERMAN. Not the slightest. I am in favor of that course. In October, 1877, I issued an order, under the authority which the law gave me, stopping the coinage of the trade-dollar. The reason was that at that time, by the gradual depreciation of silver, the gold value of the trade-dollar was less than par, and there was no demand for it for exportation.

Mr. CLAFLIN. The law gave you power to stop the coinage of the trade-dollar?

Secretary SHERMAN. The law leaves it discretionary with the Secretary of the Treasury.

Mr. CLAFLIN. So that if a demand for them should spring up, you could issue them again?

Secretary SHERMAN. Yes; the amount to be issued is left discretionary with the department.

Mr. CLAFLIN. And if a man now should ask you for trade-dollars, you would not make them unless you had evidence that he wanted to send them abroad?

Secretary SHERMAN. No; the language of the law is that they are to be coined for exportation only.

Mr. WARNER. The present language of the statute is, "The silver coins of the United States shall be a trade-dollar," &c.

Secretary SHERMAN. Yes; but the act of July 22, 1876, authorizes the Secretary to limit the coinage of the trade-dollars to such an amount as he may deem sufficient to meet the export demand for them.

Mr. WARNER. I wish to call your attention now, Mr. Secretary, to section 3511 of the Revised Statutes, which is section 1 of the bill now before this committee. The law as it now stands leaves out the word "unit," which, I believe, up to 1873, always followed both the gold and silver coins, and substitutes the words "which at the standard weight of 25.8 grains shall be the unit of value." That you understand, I suppose, as changing the standard from both metals to gold alone.

Secretary SHERMAN. I think that your insertion in this bill of the words "or unit" is substantially the same as the language of the original section. But that is a matter of criticism.

UNLIMITED COINAGE OF SILVER AND TRADE DOLLAR. 13

Mr. WARNER. The language now is "which at the standard weight of 25.8 grains shall be *the* unit of value.

Secretary SHERMAN. Well, I think that is substantially the same. There can be but one unit. If you mean the word unit in its singular sense you can have only one.

Mr. WARNER. But a silver dollar may be a unit as well as a gold dollar?

Secretary SHERMAN. Yes, you might make it "units," in the plural.

Mr. WARNER. But a silver dollar may be a unit as well as a gold dollar, may it not? Whether both the units are of the same value or not, is another question.

Secretary SHERMAN. That is a question which I suppose I need not discuss here.

The CHAIRMAN. Mr. Warner's idea is that this legislation, making the gold dollar the unit of value, was the turning point in our monetary system.

Mr. WARNER. Before that the standard rested upon both metals, or either, alternately, if they varied in value.

The CHAIRMAN. One was not made the unit of value to the exclusion of the other; but when this change was made silver was demonetized, and that was the turning point in our monetary system.

Secretary SHERMAN. I would suggest to Mr. Warner that he had better say "a unit." But what you want to get at is my opinion as to whether we should have a single or a double standard.

Mr. WARNER. Yes, we will come to that later; but, at this point, I want to ask another question. Gold dollars, I believe, are now recoined, or it is the law that they shall be if they fall in weight more than one-half per cent. below the standard fixed by law and the limit of tolerance.

Secretary SHERMAN. Yes, the law provides for recoinage in such cases.

Mr. WARNER. What limit of tolerance would you advise for silver coins? I will ask the Director of the Mint the same question.

Secretary SHERMAN. I have no very accurate knowledge about these technical questions; and I think you can get that information better by asking the assayer or some of the technical officers of the mint, than you can from us.

Mr. WARNER. The States of the Latin Union make it one per cent. Should that be adopted here with reference to the silver dollar if it is proposed to coin silver dollars unlimitedly?

Secretary SHERMAN. Our coinage is thought to be the best in the world now, because our limit of tolerance is very low, and the actual tolerance is very slight. At least that has been claimed for our coinage. But Mr. Robert Patterson, of Philadelphia, formerly superintendent of the mint, or Mr. Snowden, the present superintendent, can give you more definite information on that subject than I can.

Mr. WARNER. The most important feature of this bill is, of course, in section 3, proposing to change section 3520 of the Revised Statutes, which now reads as follows: "Any owner of silver bullion may deposit the same at any mint, to be formed into bars or into dollars of the weight of 420 grains Troy, designated in this act as trade-dollars."

Secretary SHERMAN. I suppose you would rather have me state my view as to whether or not we should have a double or single standard?

Mr. WARNER. Yes, your view in regard to restoring silver to unlimited coinage.

Secretary SHERMAN. It would be a great object of national desire if we could restore silver and gold to free coinage; but it is one of the most difficult and delicate financial operations that you can propose.

It has been more debated than almost any other question in the whole range of financial discussion. My idea is that you cannot do it; that it is not possible to do it, and that this law would not do it, unless you make the ratio of the two metals as fixed by the law correspond as nearly as may be to the market value of the two coins.

Mr. WARNER. Do you think that practicable? Is the market value, under the present coinage laws of Europe, so stable that it would be possible for one country alone to do that?

Secretary SHERMAN. I will come to that in a moment. It is undoubtedly an important point. Now the attempt to make common or free coinage of the two metals, when there is a wide divergence between the legal ratio and the market ratio, has utterly failed in the past in many countries and in different ages. It is no use to try to do it. You cannot do it. The inevitable result will be that the cheaper bullion will fill all the channels of circulation, and that instead of a bi-metallic money of two metals you will have a mono-metallic money of the cheapest. That is an axiom, which it is hardly worth while to discuss because it has been proved so many times.

Now let me go a step farther. If the effect of this law would be to bring silver and gold to the relative standard that you propose, it would be a great object of desire, and nobody would be more in favor of it than myself, but I am sure (expressing an opinion pretty strongly) that the only effects of its adoption would be to bring upon us the surplus silver of other nations, of Germany and of France, where there is supposed to be four hundred million of dollars of silver, and also to relieve England from her embarrassments about India; and that our gold would flow from us until we would be practically and substantially at the single silver standard upon its bullion value.

Mr. WARNER. Upon that point I would like to ask you how, under this bill, which proposes the unlimited coinage of silver, silver bullion of other countries would come here any more than it does now. Will an ounce of silver bullion, or a pound or a ton, exchange for any more of our commodities after being coined under the provisions of this bill than now; and if not, why would it come here then any more than it does now?

Secretary SHERMAN. Because silver being the cheaper metal, all the balances of trade will be met and all commodities bought from this country will be paid for in that coin which is the cheaper, and the result would be that gold would be as thoroughly demonetized as silver was demonetized from 1834 until 1873.

Mr. WARNER. Would that change the value of silver bullion as compared with commodities in the United States?

Secretary SHERMAN. No, but it would reduce the value of the silver dollar as compared with our commodities.

Mr. WARNER. Then why would silver come here in the form of bullion from other countries any more after being coined than it does now?

Secretary SHERMAN. Simply because foreign nations would pay for all they bought of us in the cheaper coin, and all our values would come to be measured by the standard silver dollar, $412\frac{1}{2}$ grains of silver bullion. Now they are measured by 25.8 grains of gold, but if you adopt the double standard it means the single standard of the cheaper metal, because in the nature of things you cannot maintain two standards unless you have two equivalent values. Mr. Warner's object is all right, and I agree with him perfectly in desiring it, but I believe that any attempt to attain it by depending upon the present ratio of 16 to 1 would be as futile as the attempt of King Canute to check the ebb and flow of the sea. It is one of those operations of nature which human government cannot control. But if this government would adopt the standard or relation between the two metals which conforms as nearly as may be—you cannot come to it exactly—but as nearly as may be to the relative value of the two metals, then I believe it would be a very great object of desire, because then, if the surplus silver of the world came to us, we would get it at its market value and not at an exaggerated value. The fixed ratio resulting from this action would probably prove to be a close approximation to the market ratio for a considerable period of time. If you approximate the true relation within one or two cents, it may prove for perhaps a hundred years about the true ratio between silver and gold. In France the ratio of $15\frac{1}{2}$ to 1 adopted in 1803 was very near the market rates for a long time.

If this government is now to adopt a ratio which will fulfill these conditions, the present market values of the two metals will have to be taken as the basis.

Mr. CLAFLIN. Do you mean our government alone or the commercial nations acting together?

Secretary SHERMAN. That is a question. Just now there is evidently a strong desire in several nations to adopt a new relation. Great Britain is threatened with great disasters from different standards in England and India. Among French statesmen there is a desire for a readjustment of this question, and I believe that if we hold firmly to our present position of a limited coinage of silver, or if we adopt the present market value of gold and silver as our ratio, we will bring the other nations to adopt that ratio. The conference that was had last summer really produced a great deal of good.

Mr. WARNER. Do you think that if we should adopt the market ratio of London to-day, there is any more probability that other nations will come to us at that ratio, or as great a probability, as there would be if we should adopt the ratio of $15\frac{1}{2}$ to 1, the ratio now existing between most of the silver and gold coin of Europe?

Secretary SHERMAN. The trouble is that the ratio of $15\frac{1}{2}$ to 1 is not the true ratio between the two metals, owing to two or three causes.

Mr. WARNER. Is not the change caused mainly by the recent German and the American laws, and the suspension of silver coinage in Europe?

Secretary SHERMAN. No; it is caused mainly by the falling off of the enormous drain of silver to India and China, by the increased production of silver, and the estimated enormous yields that are to come in a few years from the mines that are now being developed in our Western country, and also by the action of the German and the French Governments in limiting the coinage of silver. The English first commenced this in 1815; then came the action of France and other nations in the formation of the Latin Union, and then the action of the German Government, and our own coinage act in 1873.

Mr. WARNER. But is it not true that in the early part of this century the proportion of the production of silver to gold was much greater than the present proportion?

Secretary SHERMAN. Yes, that is true; but the aggregate of exchanges as well as values have enormously changed since then. The nominal prices of things now, except in cases where human devices have cheapened commodities by facilitating their production, are two or three times as great as they were in the beginning of this century. The use of gold to settle balances of trade has enormously increased.

Mr. WARNER. To recur to the opinion which you have expressed that under free coinage we should be put at a disadvantage in our trade with other countries, or be liable to have our commodities taken from us at less value than we are getting for them now: do you really think that that would be the case? Would our people part with more commodities for the same weight of silver under free coinage than they do now?

Secretary SHERMAN. No; but we would be reduced to a single silver standard instead of what we have now—a single gold standard—and we would gain nothing. We are now competing successfully with foreign nations on the gold standard, but we would then be competing at the disadvantage of having an inferior metallic standard.

Mr. CLAFLIN. And would not that single standard be changing constantly in comparison with the gold standard of Europe, just as our currency has been?

Secretary SHERMAN. Yes.

Mr. WARNER. Is it not a fact that the value of gold now, under the German law demonetizing silver and under our law of 1873 and under the laws of other States in Europe suspending the coinage of silver—is it not the fact that under these laws the value of an ounce of gold is very different from what it would have been if those laws had never been passed? And if that be true, then, by those laws (including our own law) has not the value of gold as a standard been changed?

Secretary SHERMAN. I do not think that our law has had the slightest effect in that respect. At the time the law was passed there were no silver dollars in circulation. But all the causes that I have mentioned have contributed to disturb the former relation between gold and silver. If you ask me whether that has not been injurious, and has not contributed to raise the relative price of gold, I say, frankly, yes; but how can we single-handed help it? We can only conform the law to existing facts. In adopting a new ratio we only do what has been done many times—what our ancestors did; we must weigh and adjust carefully the present relative value of the two metals. Between the time of the framing of the Constitution and the passage of the act of 1792 experiments of the most delicate character were carried on at different places for the purpose of ascertaining the real comparative value of the two metals, and when Hamilton ascertained that, he fixed the coinage ratio at precisely the market ratio. He said that it was important to maintain the two metals in circulation, but that it could be done only by adopting the market value as the legal ratio, and in this way the ratio was fixed at 15 to 1. On the same basis the French, a little later, fixed it at 15½ to 1. This divergence left the silver here and gold went abroad. We tried to correct this in 1834 by making the ratio 16 to 1, and then the silver disappeared and gold came into circulation here.

Mr. WARNER. But is it not true that what you call the market value depends very largely upon the laws of the different States establishing the ratios?

Secretary SHERMAN. It depends somewhat upon those laws, but laws must recognize facts; natural facts are never controlled by laws. Law cannot give value to a grain of sand.

Mr. WARNER. But if the laws of different countries give greater use to one metal and less to another, then do they not contribute directly to determining the relative market value of the two?

Secretary SHERMAN. If the passage of laws was the sole operating cause of the present divergence of market value from the old ratio, then the re-enactment of the old laws might restore the old ratio; but it is only one and the least of several causes, and therefore you must examine the other causes and establish your new ratio so as to get at the market value irrespective of all laws. Your laws must recognize market values, for they cannot control them.

Mr. WARNER. Suppose we should establish the market ratio to-day, and to-morrow or next month France should demonetize silver and offer her stock on the market, and call for gold to take its place in the currency of France, where would the American ratio be then?

Secretary SHERMAN. My answer to that is that I would wait in patience and expectancy until France and England ask us, as I believe they will within two years from this time, to join them in making a new ratio; or, if we are compelled to make a new ratio, it should be such a one as will not induce other nations to send to us the depreciated metal at above its market value as bullion. We are strong, but we are not strong enough to make 16 ounces of silver equal to 1 ounce of gold. The inevitable result of such an attempt would be that we would lose our gold and have a single standard of silver coin. If, on the contrary, we adopt a ratio of about 18 to 1, other nations would not bear the loss of a sale at that rate of their silver coin. The true way is to wait, using silver at the present ratio only to the extent that is demanded for convenient use, and no more.

Mr. WARNER. Under existing laws, must it not follow as a necessary consequence that gold will still further appreciate as compared with property and commodities generally? From the very nature of things, must it not be so, and, consequently, will we not be subject to a constant appreciation of gold under our standard if we leave it as it is?

Secretary SHERMAN. My impression is that commercial exchanges being conducted, as they are now, very largely by paper money or public securities, there will not be any further appreciation; but that is a matter of which you, gentlemen, can judge as well as I. Now, I wish to say this: All our Treasury operations, which have been very heavy during the last few months, have been conducted without the use of gold or silver. At the end of the first fifteen days in April, after we had paid out about $80,000,000 for called bonds, I made inquiry to ascertain how we had paid it, and whether we had used coin, and it turned out that no coin whatever had been used. Sixty-five millions of the amount was paid by exchanges of bonds for bonds, and the remaining fifteen millions by drafts which were paid through the clearing-house.

Mr. WARNER. Between countries only balances are at any time paid in money, I believe, but nevertheless you do not mean to intimate, I suppose, that if half of the metallic money was destroyed prices would not be affected?

Secretary SHERMAN. No.

Mr. DE LA MATYR. Our bonds that are out we have contracted to pay in coin, and our silver was coined at its present value. Now, do we not appreciate the bonds when we appreciate the value of the coin in which we agreed to pay them?

Secretary SHERMAN. Our bonds were sold at a time when the gold unit was, as it still is, the standard of value. The silver coin has not for nearly forty years been the standard, but, on account of the limited amount now in circulation, has been lifted up to the gold value, in spite of its market depreciation. It would seem to me that after we have brought our paper, our bonds, and our silver up to the gold basis, the better way is to adhere to it rather than to take advantage of the depreciation of silver to pay in a coin of less market value than was received for our bonds.

Mr. DE LA MATYR. You think it would be dishonest and a measure of repudiation to do otherwise?

Secretary SHERMAN. I do not like to use the word dishonest, because I know a great many honest men who do not think that such a measure would be dishonest; but I am quite satisfied that it would be very bad public policy, and that if we should adopt it we would suffer terribly in consequence, not only in public credit but in actual loss of trade and money.

Mr. WARNER. The Secretary has expressed the opinion here that unlimited coinage of silver would operate to expel gold from the country. The question I want to ask is whether, under the present law requiring the coinage of not less than two millions of silver a month, the same effect will not be produced in a somewhat longer time, and whether to avoid this result it will not become necessary at no distant day to change the present law, and whether the Secretary would not recommend a change?

Secretary SHERMAN. I do recommend a change of the present law. I think with you that the coinage of silver dollars at the rate of two millions a month would finally (it might take three or four or five years) so load us down with depreciated silver coin that, by the necessities of the government, it will be forced into circulation and be depreciated to its bullion value; but I take it that the good sense of Congress, enlightened as it will be by public discussion, will find some solution of this silver question. My hope is that you will suspend the coinage of the silver dollar, which now the people refuse to take, or at once return to the Treasury when issued, and await a negotiation for a new ratio; or, if that is deemed unadvisable, that it will increase the weight of the silver dollar so as to make it fairly equal in market value to the gold dollar. Then I would be willing to take the risk of the free coinage of both metals.

Mr. CLAFLIN. But as you purchase on bullion value now, the government would not suffer except by the loss of interest, unless there was still further depreciation.

Secretary SHERMAN. No.

Mr. WOOD. What would be the effect of passing this bill, in your opinion, Mr. Secretary?

Secretary SHERMAN. I think I have already answered that. I think the effect would be to bring us to the single silver standard and the expulsion of gold.

Mr. WARNER. The coinage of our silver dollar has really the same effect upon gold, has it not, that an increase of two millions a month of legal-tender notes would have?

Secretary SHERMAN. No; because we cannot get the silver dollars into circulation. We have tried it in every way, but we cannot succeed.

Mr. VANCE. Can't you pay them out for bonds?

Secretary SHERMAN. There would be no object in that. They would come right back.

Mr. WARNER. But with unlimited coinage the government would not have that question to meet at all.

Secretary SHERMAN. No.

Mr. WARNER. It would simply be with the public to say whether they would have the silver or not.

Secretary SHERMAN. O, if Congress says so, we can make the public take the silver.

Mr. WARNER. But under unlimited coinage the government would have nothing to do with putting coins into circulation?

Secretary SHERMAN. No; but there would be no gold coin at all; not a dollar.

Mr. WARNER. But that you have stated will sooner or later be the result under the present law.

Adjourned.

APPENDIX.

MONETARY CONVENTION CONCLUDED DECEMBER 23, 1865, BETWEEN FRANCE, BELGIUM, ITALY, AND SWITZERLAND. RATIFIED AT PARIS JULY 23, 1866.

[Translated by Mrs. A. J. Warner.]

His Majesty the Emperor of France, His Majesty King of Belgium His Majesty King of Italy, and the Swiss Confederation, equally desirous of establishing a more perfect harmony in their monetary legislation to remedy the inconveniences which proceed from the diversity of standard in their silver money of account in the business transactions between the inhabitants of their respective States and for the furtherance of a uniformity of weights, measures, and coins, have determined to conclude a convention for this purpose, and have appointed commissioners, with full powers, as follows:

[Here follow the names of the commissioners, with their titles:]

Who, after exhibiting their respective credentials, and finding them in good and due form, concurred in the following articles:

ART. 1. France, Belgium, Italy, and Switzerland are constituted a State of Union in relation to the weight, fineness, model, and circulation of their gold and silver coins.

Nothing is changed at present in the legislation respecting debased money in any of the four States.

ART. 2. The high contracting parties agree neither to coin nor allow to be coined, with their imprint, any gold coins excepting pieces of a hundred francs, of fifty francs, of twenty francs, of ten francs, and of five francs, fixed as to weight, fineness, tolerance, and diameter as follows:

Kind of pieces.		Weight.		Fineness.		Diameter.
		Correct weight.	Tolerance of weight.	Fineness.	Tolerance of fineness.	
	Francs.	*Grammes.*	*Thousandths.*	*Thousandths.*	*Thousandths.*	*Millimetres.*
Gold	100	32, 258. 06	1	900	2	35
	50	16, 129. 03				28
	20	6, 451. 61	2			21
	10	3, 225. 80				19
	5	1, 612. 90	3			17

They shall receive without distinction into their public treasuries the pieces of gold coined according to the preceding conditions in either of the four States, with the right, however, to refuse those pieces where weight is reduced by wear one-half per cent. below the tolerance indicated above, or from which the imprint has disappeared.

ART. 3. The contracting governments bind themselves neither to fabricate, nor permit to be fabricated, any silver coins excepting pieces of five francs, in weight, fineness, tolerance, and diameter set out below:

Kind of piece.	Weight.		Fineness.		Diameter.
	Correct weight.	Tolerance of weight.	Fineness.	Tolerance of fineness.	
	Francs.	*Grammes.*	*Thousandths.*	*Thousandths.*	*Thousandths.*	*Millimetres.*
Silver................ 5	25	3	900	2	37

They shall reciprocally receive the said pieces in their public banks under the right to exclude those of which the weight has been reduced by wear one per cent. below the tolerance indicated above, or from which the imprint has disappeared.

ART. 4. The contracting parties shall hereafter fabricate only pieces of silver of two francs, of one franc, of fifty centimes, and of twenty centimes, under the conditions of weight, of fineness, of tolerance, and diameter determined below.

Kind of pieces.		Weight.		Fineness.		Diameter.
		Correct weight.	Tolerance of weight.	Fineness.	Tolerance of fineness.	
	Francs. Centimes.	*Grammes.*	*Thousandths.*	*Thousandths.*	*Thousandths.*	*Millimetres.*
Silver.........	2 00	10 00	5	835	3	27
	1 00	5 00				23
	0 50	2 50	7			18
	0 20	1 00	10			16

Those pieces must be recoined by the governments which issue them when they become reduced by wear five per cent. below the tolerance indicated above, or whenever the imprint shall have disappeared.

ART. 5. The pieces of silver of two francs, of one franc, of fifty centimes, and of twenty centimes, coined under conditions differing from those indicated in the preceding article, must be retired from circulation before January 1, 1869.

The time is extended until January 1, 1878, for the pieces of two francs and of one franc, put in circulation in Switzerland by virtue of the law of January 31, 1860.

ART. 6. The pieces of silver fabricated under the conditions of Article 4 shall be legal tender between private persons of the State which has coined them up to the sum of fifty francs for each payment.

The State that puts them into circulation shall receive them from citizens without limitation of quantity.

ART. 7. The public treasuries of each of the four countries shall receive the silver pieces coined by any of the other contracting States, conformably to Article 4, up to the amount of one hundred francs for each payment made to the said treasuries.

The Governments of Belgium, of France, and of Italy shall receive upon the same terms, until January 1, 1878, the Swiss pieces of two francs and of one franc emitted in virtue of the law of January 31, 1860, and which during the same period are similar in all respects to the pieces coined under the conditions of Article 4. The whole is subject to the provision relative to wear given in Article 4.

ART. 8. Each of the contracting governments pledges itself to take from private parties or from the public banks of the other States the money of account of silver which has been put in circulation, and to exchange it for an equal value of legal-tender money (pieces of gold or of silver five-francs) with the condition that the sum presented for exchange shall not be less than one hundred francs.

This obligation shall continue two years after the expiration of the present treaty.

ART. 9. The high contracting parties shall put in circulation coins of silver of two francs, of one franc, of fifty centimes, and of twenty centimes, coined under the conditions given by Article 4 to the amount only of six francs for each inhabitant.

The quantity shall be determined by taking the last census made in each country and the presumed increase of population until the expiration of the present treaty.

Table for the various States.

France	239,000,000 francs.
Belgium	32,000,000 francs.
Italy	141,000,000 francs.
Switzerland	17,000,000 francs.

There shall be deducted from the foregoing sums, which the governments have a right to coin, the sums already in circulation:

For France, in virtue of the law of May 25, 1864, in pieces of fifty centimes and twenty centimes, about sixteen millions.

For Italy, in virtue of the law of August 24, 1862, in pieces of two francs, one franc, fifty centimes, and twenty centimes, about one hundred millions.

For Switzerland, in virtue of the decree of January 31, 1860, in pieces of two francs and one franc, about ten million five hundred thousand francs.

ART. 10. The date of the coinage shall be inscribed upon the pieces of gold and silver coined hereafter in the four States.

ART. 11. The contracting governments shall communicate annually the proportion of their circulation of gold and silver, the account of redemption and recoinage of their gold and silver money, the account of the redemption and recoining of their old coins, and the whole situation, and all the administrative documents relating to money.

They shall give an impartial account of all the facts which concern the mutual circulation of their gold and silver coins.

ART. 12. The right to join the present convention is reserved for any other State which may accept the obligations and adopt the monetary system of the Union, as far as concerns their gold and silver coins.

ART. 13. The execution of the mutual obligations included in the present convention, as far as may be, is subject to the methods and regulations established by the laws of the contracting States, which are considered to promote the fulfillment, and which shall cause it to be carried into effect with the least possible delay.

ART. 14. The present convention shall remain in force until January 1, 1880.

If one year previous to that time no notice has been given, it shall remain binding by right for a further period of fifteen years, and so continue for periods of fifteen years, except notice be given.

ART. 15. The present convention shall be confirmed and the ratification shall be exchanged at Paris within six months, or earlier, if possible.

22   UNLIMITED COINAGE OF SILVER AND TRADE DOLLAR.

In proof of which the respective commissioners have signed the present convention and affixed their seals.
Done and four copies made at Paris, December 23, 1865.
For France:
              E. DE PARIEU.
              PELOUZE.
For Belgium:
              FORTAMPS.
              A. KREGLINGER.
For Italy:
              ARTOM.
              PRATOLONGO.
For Switzerland:
              KERN.
              FEER HERZOG.

MANIFESTO RELATIVE TO THE COINAGE OF SILVER DURING THE YEAR 1876, IN SWITZERLAND, BELGIUM, FRANCE, ITALY, AND GREECE.

[Translated by James Gilmore for the Cincinnati Commercial.]

The undersigned, delegates of the Governments of Switzerland, of France, of Italy, and of Greece, in conference assembled, in conformity with Article 5 of the Monetary Manifesto of February 5, 1875, and regularly authorized for this purpose, have decided on the following plans, subject to the approval of their respective governments:

ARTICLE 1. The contracting governments agree, for the year 1876, neither to coin nor allow to be coined any five-franc pieces, according to conditions determined by Article 3 of the compact of December 23, 1865, excepting for an amount not exceeding the sum of 120,000,000 of francs, fixed by Article 1 of the supplementary compact of January 31, 1874.

ART. 2. The said sum of 120,000,000 francs is distributed as follows:

                             Francs.
1. For Belgium 10,800,000
  France 54,000,000
  Italy 36,000,000
  Switzerland 7,200,000

2. As to Greece, which acquiesced in the compact of December 23, 1865, by a manifesto of the 26th of September, 1868, the complement fixed for this government, in proportion to that of the other contracting powers, is fixed at the sum of 3,600,000 francs.

3. Beyond the complement fixed in the paragraph preceding, the Government of Greece is exceptionally authorized to cause to be coined and to put into circulation, on her territory, during the year 1876, a sum of 8,400,000 francs in silver pieces of five francs, said sum being intended to facilitate the withdrawal of the different coins at present circulating, and to substitute for the same five-franc pieces, according to the conditions determined by the compact of 1865.

ART. 3. Are deducted from the complements fixed in the first paragraph of the preceding article the silver coin certificates delivered up to this date, according to the conditions determined by Article 6 of the manifesto of February 5, 1875.

Is likewise deducted from the total sum of 12,000,000 of francs assigned to Greece, by paragraph 2 and 3 of the preceding article, the sum of 2,500,000f. which the Government of Greece had been authorized to cause to be coined in 1876 as equivalent of the silver coin certificates which the other contracting governments have been allowed to issue against silver bullion.

ART. 4. A new monetary conference will be held at Paris in the month of January, 1877, between the delegates of the contracting governments.

ART. 5. Until after the meeting of the conference referred to in the preceding article, there shall be delivered no silver coin certificates for the year 1877, except for a sum not exceeding the half of the complements fixed by the paragraphs 1 and 2 of the Article 2 of the present manifesto.

ART. 6. The Article 11 of the compact of the 23d December, 1865, in regard to the exchange of correspondence touching monetary facts and documents, is completed by the following arrangement:

The contracting governments will give to each other, mutually, advice of any facts which may reach their knowledge on the subject of adulteration and counterfeiting of their gold and silver coins in the countries belonging or not belonging to the Monetary Union, especially in regard to the processes employed, prosecutions brought, and the suppressions arrived at. They will confer with each other on the measures to be taken in common in order to prevent the adulterations and counterfeits, cause the same to be suppressed in all places where they have been manufactured, and hinder the repetition of the same."

ART. 7. The present manifesto will be in force from the moment that notice thereof shall have been made, in accordance with the special laws of each one of the five governments.

In faith of which the respective delegates have signed the present manifesto, and have thereto placed the seals of their respective States. Done and five copies made at Paris, 3d February, 1876.

For Switzerland,
     KERN,
     FEER-HERZOG.

For Belgium,
     AD LAINCTELETTE,
     BN. DE PITTEURS HIEGARTS.

For France,
     DUMAS,
     DE SOUBEYRAN,
     CH. JAGERSCHMIDT.

For Italy,
     C. BARALIS,
     RESSMAN.

For Greece,
     N. S. DELYANNI.

RENEWAL OF THE LATIN UNION.

By GEORGE WALKER.

[From the Bankers' Magazine for January, 1879.]

The Paris Journal des Debats, of November 18th, contains an article, by Baron Jules de Reinach, on the new treaty which has been agreed upon by the representatives of Belgium, France, Greece, Italy, and Switzerland, by which the so-called Latin Union is continued in existence until the 1st of January, 1886. The conference held at Paris for this purpose closed its eleventh and last session on the 5th of November. The unprecedented number of its sittings indicates that its discussions were more than usually interesting. M. de Reinach describes the conference as differing essentially from that of 1865. The latter was, in a strict sense, a monetary conference, in which no questions of principle were put forward or debated. Its sole object was to assimilate the coins of several contiguous countries, so as to give them an international circulation and a legal-tender character within the territory of the treaty-making States. The conference of 1878 was of quite another character; it was a politico-economical conference, and the president, who is also one of the presiding officers of the Paris Society of Political Economists, might well have imagined himself at one of the monthly meetings of that body.

The precise nature of these economical discussions can only be conjectured until the publication of the *procès-verbaux*, which will probably not take place till the action of the conference has been submitted to the legislatures of the several contracting states and confirmed by them. M. Léon Say has already brought a bill into the French Chambers to ratify the treaty, but the full particulars of the measure, as reported by him, have not reached us. Meanwhile the article of M. de Reinach may be looked upon as semi-official, in view of the well-known intimacy existing between him and the finance minister and the confidential position which he occupies towards the financial administration of France.

The treaty of 1865 was to expire in January, 1880, provided a year's notice to terminate it was given by one of the signatories; otherwise it was to remain in force for fifteen years longer. Rather than remain bound together for so many years by a convention, the operation of which had essentially changed since it was entered into, the contracting States would have abrogated it altogether. Switzerland, therefore, which more than any other country has been dissatisfied with the treaty since the silver agitation began, acting on her own behalf, and doubtless at the desire of all her associates, gave the notice which was necessary to terminate the Union in January, 1880.

This being done, the question was whether to draw up an entirely new treaty or to amend the old one. M. Leon Say proposed the latter plan, and it was adopted. One of the most important new questions to be considered was as to the steps to be taken to wind up the treaty (*liquider la situation*) when the term of it shall have expired; and another and more immediately pressing one was how to deal with Italy and Greece, States which are under a suspension of specie payments, and to provide against the possible contingency of other States falling into the same difficulty. The treaty of 1865 did not provide for such a state of things, inasmuch as Italy did not suspend till May, 1866, and Greece, which joined the Union in 1868, was then a specie-paying country. As the case now stands, paper money has driven coin out of Italy, and the greater part, both of its full-valued silver five-franc pieces and of its divisionary token money have taken refuge in France, Belgium, and Switzerland. For all beneficial purposes to her associates, Italy would be better out of the union than in it.

The excessive accumulation of silver coin in certain parts of the union, and particularly at the Bank of France, is an evil mainly due to the currency system of Italy. The Italian plenipotentiaries admitted this fact, and declared the determination of their government to relieve the situation by a return to specie payments at the earliest day possible. On the 7th of September, 1878, there were in circulation in Italy paper notes of the denominations of $\frac{1}{2}$, 1, and 2 francs to the amount of 112,000,000 of francs ($22,500,000), and the maximum emission of such notes authorized was 135,000,000 ($27,000,000). The total authorized issue of all denominations of paper money is fixed by royal decree of

February 26, 1876, at 1 milliard ($200,000,000). These are denominated *consortial* notes, and are issued by the six associated banks on the deposit by the government with them of its bonds to that amount. There are, besides, bank notes not so secured, but the latter are not a legal tender.

The Italian Government having declared its willingness to suppress its notes of smaller denominations than 5 francs, the other contracting States have agreed to assist the operation by withdrawing from circulation, and refusing to take at their public treasuries, the silver divisionary coins of Italy. The arrangements for accomplishing these ends were made the subject of article 8 of the treaty, the essential provisions of which will be presently stated. By the treaty of 1865, the amount of divisionary coins permitted to each of the contracting nations was 6 francs a head of their population. By the latest census returns, this allowance gives to Belgium 33,000,000 of francs; to France and Algeria 240,000,000; to Greece 10,500,000; to Italy 170,000,000, and to Switzerland 18,000,000. Italy, however, owing to the loss of her small coins since the suspension of specie payments, has replaced them to such an extent by small notes that the aggregate sum of her divisionary money, coin and notes, now amounts to 270,000,000 of francs, or 100,000,000 in excess of her allotted quota. The whole of this excess is supposed to be in the other countries of the Union, France being understood to have about 87,000,000 and the other States 13,000,000. It will be impossible to drive these small coins back to Italy so long as the other countries continue to give them currency; and, on the other hand, Italy cannot suppress her small notes until she has coins to put in place of them. Article 8 of the treaty, therefore, makes the following provisions:

It should be premised that each of the contracting States has agreed to redeem its divisionary coins, when presented in sums of not less than 100 francs, either in gold money or in silver 5-franc pieces. This obligation is to continue for one year after the termination of the treaty. By article 8 the other States have agreed not to receive Italian divisionary coins after January 1, 1880. France is to gather up these coins and deliver them to Italy, which is to pay cash to the other States for all received from them up to 13,000,000 of francs. The French contingent of 87,000,000 is to be paid—17,000,000 in cash, and the balance in three annual installments—in 1881, 1882, and 1883, with 3 per cent. interest on the deferred payments; all above 100,000,000 is to be paid for in cash. The small notes which Italy engages to retire are not to be reissued. After the resumption of specie payment in Italy, her small coins will be again received by the other powers as heretofore.

Greece has coined silver *drachmas* under the treaty of 1865, and a considerable number of them now circulate in France, Belgium, and Switzerland. They have increased in those countries since legal-tender paper has taken the place of metallic money in Greece. The delegate of the Hellenic Government explained to the Conference that during the last year a loan had been contracted with the National Bank of Greece and the Ionian Bank, by which the privilege of legal-tender had been conceded to their notes so long as the loan remained unpaid. The actual amount of such notes issued is 73,000,000 ($14,600,000), and the maximum authorized 78,000,000 ($15,000,000). The two banks have a specie reserve of about 16,000,000, or more than 20 per cent. Before the suspension of specie payments there were about 45,000,000 of notes in circulation, the lowest denomination being of 10 francs. The Greek Government is very anxious to resume specie payments, and will attempt to accomplish it by a credit operation, but it is not able to enter into any engagement with the other powers on the subject, nor to fix any date at which resumption can be accomplished.

The gold coins of the several States are to continue, as heretofore, of the denomination of 100, 50, 20, 10, and 5 francs, but the coinage of gold 5-franc pieces remains provisionally suspended. This suspension is owing to the too rapid abrasion of those coins. Experiments made in 1868 showed that gold 20-franc pieces used themselves up in about forty years, 10-franc pieces in twenty years, and 5-franc pieces in eight years.

Both gold and silver 5-franc pieces are to be admitted into the public treasuries of the contracting governments without distinction. The Bank of France and the National Bank of Belgium have come into this arrangement by agreement, during the full term of the treaty, to receive those coins at their counters. Although the legal tender of the larger foreign coins seems not to be explicitly imposed on individuals, they will not hesitate to ratify it in fact, as the action of their respective governments and banks leaves no motives to private persons for refusing them. Token coins (those of less than 5 francs) are declared a legal tender in payments of not more than 50 francs.

The coinage of silver 5-franc pieces is provisionally suspended, and cannot be resumed except by the unanimous consent of the contracting States. This agreement is also made applicable to the year 1879—the last year of the old treaty. An exception has, however, been made in favor of Italy, which is to be allowed to coin 20,000,000 of francs. Though not so expressed in the treaty, it is understood that this contingent is allowed to Italy to enable her to replace her old silver coins with 5-franc pieces. Even if she should elect to buy new silver of Germany for the whole amount, rather than melt down the coins of the Bourbon dynasties, no objection would probably be made, as the quantity of silver pressing upon the market would be thereby measurably reduced.

As already stated, the new treaty is to remain in force from January 1, 1880, to January 1, 1886. If, one year prior to the latter date, no notice shall have been given to dissolve it, it is to be continued thereafter from year to year.

Although no other provisions were made in the treaty respecting legal-tender paper in circulation in Italy and Greece than those under article 8, it was nevertheless agreed to be proper to insert in the *procès verbaux* of the Conference certain declarations on that subject. Belgium, accordingly, declared that, if in future either of the States should establish the *cours forcé*, or should render the consequences of it more onerous to other States by increasing the issues of legal-tender paper, the Belgian Government would admit that the other States might take any measures proper to protect themselves. The Belgian delegate further declared that a State which should be forced to suspend specie payments should not be allowed to recover its liberty of action towards the other States of the Union, even after the treaty had expired, until it had relieved its associates from any burdens which such a state of things might have imposed on them. It is to be hoped that these cautionary declarations will never need to be acted on, and the considerable period fixed for the duration of the treaty will, in all probability, enable the States now under suspension to bring themselves into line, so that its indefinite prolongation may not be imperiled.

Baron de Reinach concludes his article, of which the foregoing is a summary, with the following passage:

"If we now cast our eyes over the labors of the Conference, we cannot but felicitate ourselves on the results arrived at, in view of the different ways in which the monetary question is looked at by the contracting

States. Switzerland and Belgium do not conceal their sympathies for the single gold standard; France is bimetallic; but before pronouncing upon the propriety of continuing the coinage of silver 5-franc pieces, which is, nevertheless, reserved in the treaty, she desires to know the results of the monetary laws recently enacted in America. In this state of things it was necessary, as far as possible, to relieve the present situation, which might become embarrassing by reason of the liquidation which would have to be made at the end of the next year, when the treaty of 1865 would expire. To assist Italy, therefore, to establish her metallic circulation, was not only a proof of sympathy given to that State, but it was also an act of good policy on the part of the other contracting parties. If they had precipitated matters by not renewing the treaty, Italy alone would have profited by it.

"Thus, although there was a difference of opinion between the contracting parties on the theoretical side of the monetary question, the Latin Union has been renewed and consolidated. Both governments and people will, without any doubt, learn with satisfaction that the five nations are to continue to be united by the bond of a common monetary circulation; and it is to be hoped that this union established between them in respect to money will continue to exercise a happy influence on their political and business relations."

It is not the purpose of the present article to make any lengthened comments on the new Latin treaty as it bears upon the United States. It cannot, however, be overlooked, that the clause which suspends the coinage of silver for seven years longer, is likely to have a most important influence on the future monetary system of this country. For the largest part of the decade which is now opening, and which is so full of promise in all its material aspects, we shall be the only silver-coining country of the civilized world. There can be little doubt that this will make us a silver country, almost as absolutely as India and China are silver countries, unless the restrictions imposed by the silver bill of last winter are rigidly adhered to—that is, a coinage limited to two millions a month, with all the resulting profit reserved to the Federal Government. This is not such a double standard as the silver party bargained for, nor is it such a bimetallism as those who favor an international system desire to secure. No party will be satisfied with it, and further legislation, either forward or backward, seems to us, imperatively necessary. If we go forward, and open the mints to free coinage, all our gold will leave us, and we shall elect to become a silver country pure and simple, which is just what Mr. Goschen desires. If we go backward and repeal the silver bill, making silver token-money only, with, perhaps, a large field given to it by a liberal legal-tender clause, we shall force England, Germany, and the Latin Union to face the situation, and to share with us the perils and inconveniences which a scramble for gold will certainly entail. In that scramble the United States would stand a better chance to come out unscathed than any other nation. This is the course recommended by M. Cernuschi, and we incline to think that it promises the earliest and most substantial victory to the bimetallic cause.

o

INTERVIEW

OF THE

COMMITTEE ON FINANCE

OF THE

UNITED STATES SENATE

WITH THE

HON. JOHN SHERMAN,
SECRETARY OF THE TREASURY,

IN REGARD TO THE

REPEAL OF THE RESUMPTION ACT.

WASHINGTON:
GOVERNMENT PRINTING OFFICE.
1878.

INTERVIEW

OF THE

COMMITTEE ON FINANCE WITH THE HON. JOHN SHERMAN SECRETARY OF THE TREASURY,

IN REGARD TO

THE REPEAL OF THE RESUMPTION ACT.

UNITED STATES SENATE,
COMMITTEE ON FINANCE,
March 19, 1878.

The CHAIRMAN. Mr. Secretary, I have jotted down a few general questions and some in detail, which I propose to ask you, and I suppose that other members of the committee may have questions which they may desire to ask at a later period, but I will ask some general questions in order that you may make a statement, if you choose, with more freedom than you can by going into smaller details at the commencement.

First, ought the resumption act, in your opinion, to be repealed; and, if not, why not?

Secretary SHERMAN. That question, as you say, is very general, and it is rather a legislative than an executive question, but I have no objection to answering. I think that the resumption act ought not to be repealed; that it was a declaration of public policy, commenced with the act of February, 1862, repeated by Congress several times, notably in 1866, notably again in 1869, and again by the passage of the resumption act, that we would, as soon as practicable, redeem any United States notes which were presented for redemption, in gold and silver coin; that this is the declared public policy of this country, and it ought to be adhered to; and now I am fully convinced that we are able to do what we have so often promised to do, and ought to do. Beside this, several States have, by their legislation, indicated a purpose to conform their laws to ours.

Senator BAYARD. Which States besides New York?

Secretary SHERMAN. Well, Massachusetts to some limited extent, but I don't know how far; and many corporations and many individuals have made their contracts upon the basis of resumption in 1879. The whole country seems to have settled down to the conviction that we can resume, and that business has adapted itself, and contracts have been made with that view. So far as any suffering from resumption, or preparation for resumption is concerned, we have already suffered, and now to go backwards would be only to invite suffering again. It strikes me therefore that it is better to go ahead, and that to retrace the policy of resumption now would separate the metals from our currency, and we would have to go through the same trouble again. It would be an evidence of national weakness. The struggle between metallic money as the basis of paper money and irredeemable paper money, must be made some time, and I think we had better complete it now. Therefore I say, in regard to your question—although it is a legislative question for you gentlemen to answer, and not for me—I think we ought to adhere to the policy of resumption and complete it.

The CHAIRMAN. Do you think resumption is practicable under the present law? You have partially anticipated that question, but still I ask it.

Secretary SHERMAN. That is a question very much of figures, and, supposing that it would be the principal one I would have to answer, I have brought quite a number of documents here which I will give you, and they will speak better than I can. The best evidence that we are able to resume on the 1st of January next is the progress that has already been made. When the resumption act passed the premium on gold was about ten and one-half per cent. Since that time it has been reduced to a nominal rate. It is now a little over one. Since that time we have accumulated in preparation for resumption a large sum of gold. I have taken some pains to get the figures which I will give you now. They are accurate, so that you may have the exact condition of the Treasury. This is the statement of the Treasurer, made yesterday:

TREASURY OF THE UNITED STATES,
Washington, March 18, 1878.

SIR: In accordance with your request I have the honor to state the amount of gold and silver in the Treasury on the 28th ultimo, the date of the last debt-statement, which is as follows, viz:

Gold coin	$117,151,455 62	
Gold bullion	7,937,300 21	
		$125,088,755 93
Less amount to credit of disbursing-officers and outstanding checks	6,189,626 60	
Gold-certificates actually outstanding	44,498,500 00	
Called bonds and interest	6,818,677 29	
Interest due and unpaid	4,909,705 21	
		62,416,509 10
Available gold coin and bullion		62,672,246 83
Available silver coin, fractional		5,972,895 42
Available silver bullion		3,130,718 31
Total available gold and silver		71,775,860 56

The amount of gold coin in the Treasury is $117,151,455.62; the amount of gold bullion is $7,937,300.31, making an aggregate of gold coin and gold bullion, $125,088,755.93. That is, however, subject to a deduction of the following items:

First. Outstanding checks to officers, $6,189,626.60. Although that is really money in the Treasury, yet it is drawn for and not paid.

The CHAIRMAN. Doesn't that always happen?

Secretary SHERMAN. It always happens that some money is drawn upon and not paid, and this item is always large.

Senator BAYARD. You spoke of gold bullion; that is the property of individuals, is it not?

Secretary SHERMAN. All that is government property.

Senator BAYARD. Where does the government get gold bullion?

Secretary SHERMAN. We buy it, or receive it on deposit, or melt foreign coins into bullion, and coin it as needed. We receive it just like gold coin, but not much of it in comparison with the coin received.

Second. Then there are gold-certificates outstanding, $44,498,500, for gold deposited by banks and individuals.

Third. Called bonds and interest, $6,818,677.29. That amount is always large, and has reached eighteen millions.

Fourth. Interest due and unpaid, $4,909,705.21. That makes $62,416,509.10 gold subject to demand, or about one-half the supply on hand, leaving available gold coin and bullion, against which there is no demand liability, $62,672,246.83. Then there is silver fractional coin, $5,972,895.42; silver bullion, $3,130,718.41. I can say, though, if this statement was made up to date the silver bullion would be a good deal larger. We have bought lately. The total available gold and silver over and above demand liablities is $71,775,860.56.

Of the items that are counted here and deducted from gold, about $20,000,000 are practically available for resumption, because the outstanding drafts and the called bonds and interest due and unpaid, although due, yet the amount actually in the Treasury is generally about the same. It is remarkable that so much money is left after it is due. Bonds that are due and not presented, and interest that is due for years, are left in government custody without being drawn. Of the amount of gold certificates issued: the law authorizes 20 per cent. more certificates to be issued than the amount of gold or gold bullion deposited, although that power has never been exercised, at least not within my recollection; not certainly within my term.

Senator FERRY. You spoke of the $44,000,000 of gold certificates; is that about the annual outstanding average?

Secretary SHERMAN. No; it is more than the average.

Senator FERRY. What is the average for ten years back?

Secretary SHERMAN. Thirty to forty millions.

The CHAIRMAN. It is $34,000,000 or $35,000,000.

Secretary SHERMAN. The amount of gold now on deposit is very large. For the reasons I have stated the amount of gold and silver coin and bullion available for resumption in a business sense is about ninety millions, but the actual gold and silver bullion and coin in the Treasury over and above all demand liabilities is $71,775,860.56.

Senator JONES. Could the amount of subsidiary coin which you speak of as being on hand be counted as in any way assisting resumption?

Secretary SHERMAN. I think so, because it is exchanged for United States notes or fractional currency, and can be paid out for current debts.

Senator JONES. I thought you could only exchange it for fractional currency?

Secretary SHERMAN. Probably there is enough silver coin on hand to redeem all the balance of the fractional currency.

The CHAIRMAN. That is, the Secretary thinks some fractional currency has been lost?

Secretary SHERMAN. Now, in regard to another point pertinent to your question, we have, in the process of preparation for resumption, reduced the volume of United States notes. The precise figures are familiar to you. The amount was $382,000,000 at the time of the passage of the resumption act, and the amount now is $348,618,024. Again, the amount of outstanding bank-notes has been reduced. On December 31, 1875, the amount was $346,479,756; on December 31, 1877, $321,672,505, and on February 28, 1878, the amount of bank-notes outstanding was $321,989,991; but the amount of bank-notes of banks in existence, not in process of liquidation, was $299,240,475, and the difference between these two sums being the notes of banks in process of liquidation, although the notes are in circulation, yet an equal amount of greenbacks are in the Treasury as a special deposit to redeem them.

Senator KERNAN. They make part of the $348,000,000 legal-tender notes?

Secretary SHERMAN. Yes; as many of the legal-tender notes are held in the Treasury as there are bank-notes in process of redemption.

Senator FERRY. Then really there should be but $299,000,000 of national-bank notes outstanding.

Secretary SHERMAN. If you count the whole greenbacks as outstanding there would be $299,000,000 national-bank notes. Then it must be remembered that United States notes have been in circulation since 1862, and bank-notes since 1864, and that large sums are lost or destroyed. This diminishes to some extent the amount outstanding— how much, I don't know. You can judge as well as I.

The following statement shows, by months, the issue of silver coin, and the reduction of fractional currency under the act of April 19, 1876 (19 Statutes, 33), from April 20, 1876, to February 28, 1878, viz:

Months.	Fractional currency redeemed.	Total silver payments.
April, 1876	$648, 698 00	$648, 698 00
May, 1876	3, 500, 565 18	6, 740, 066 11
June, 1876	2, 912, 878 91	3, 608, 333 86
July, 1876	1, 543, 715 00	1, 593, 228 80
August, 1876	1, 547, 568 94	4, 015, 295 56
September, 1876	1, 496, 895 83	3, 079, 335 25
October, 1876	1, 302, 937 57	2, 411, 734 58
November, 1876	1, 146, 969 07	1, 606, 407 81
December, 1876	1, 060, 302 53	1, 659, 718 99
January, 1877	923, 639 31	1, 776, 056 82
February, 1877	990, 146 79	1, 565, 732 51
March, 1877	993, 908 27	1, 239, 012 92
April, 1877	1, 253, 936 56	1, 253, 936 55
May, 1877	979, 645 29	979, 645 29
June, 1877	803, 792 89	911, 590 42
July, 1877	616, 801 45	616, 446 67
August, 1877	612, 221 50	716, 775 07
September, 1877	385, 472 12	955, 522 37
October, 1877	434, 067 61	1, 043, 168 41
November, 1877	309, 554 14	709, 662 26
December, 1877	276, 911 62	703, 089 93
January, 1878	292, 189 18	225, 106 00
February, 1878	281, 221 58	220, 718 49
Total	24, 318, 039 31	38, 479, 308 68

Below is given the total amount of fractional notes outstanding, by issues, on the 16th instant:

First issue	$4, 291, 074 82
Second issue	3, 114, 104 26
Third issue	3, 018, 941 52
Fourth issue (first series)	3, 008, 423 44
Fourth issue (second series)	737, 939 15
Fourth issue (third series)	414, 407 70
Fifth issue	2, 524, 824 73
Total	17, 109, 715 62

The average monthly reduction of outstanding fractional currency, estimated upon the basis of the redemptions of the past four months, is $290,000.

Senator JONES. How many millions, then, of legal-tenders do you estimate as being in circulation now, outside of what you hold to redeem the notes of banks in process of liquidation?

Secretary SHERMAN. I should think $320,000,000; deducting those that may have been lost or destroyed and those held for the outstanding bank-notes, making the aggregate of bank-notes and greenbacks about $643,000,000. As a matter of course, that is a mere estimate.

Senator ALLISON. It would be about $341,000,000, according to your statement; that is, exclusive of fractional currency.

Secretary SHERMAN. Of the first, second, and third issues the amount outstanding is over $10,000,000, and comparatively none of it is presented for redemption. Of the first issue of fractional currency only $3.54 was presented last month for redemption. Of the second issue, only $3.93. Of the third issue, $4,854.62, with $3,018,941.62 outstanding. Of the first series of the fourth issue, $26,540.52 was redeemed, with $3,008,423.44 outstanding. Of the fifth issue, the amount outstanding was $2,524,854.73, and the amount presented for redemption was $205,912.76; so that practically we may say the first three issues have been redeemed, although it appears on our books and statements as outstanding. The balance of the fourth and fifth issues probably would not exceed five or six millions; so that the silver on hand will redeem every dollar of this, in all human probability. It is coming in at about $250,000 a month.

Senator BAYARD. You believe that of the outstanding currency not more than one-third will ever be presented for redemption?

Senator JONES. I should not think it would be a matter of much moment. If the whole $17,000,000 should come in, silver could be got.

Secretary SHERMAN. There would be no trouble about that.

Senator DAWES. Do you redeem it in dollars or in fractional currency?

Secretary SHERMAN. We redeem it in silver money. We give fractional silver, because that is the law.

To repeat the general result of our preparations for resumption, we have already practically abolished the premium on gold; we have reduced the amount of United States notes and the amount of national-bank notes outstanding; we have paid off, practically, the fractional currency, and now we have a very remarkable circumstance in our favor. The balance of trade is in our favor to the amount of $160,000,000 a year, bringing silver and gold and bonds back to us. In the last three years the balance of trade in our favor is $414,034,666. I bring you this statement because I thought you might deem it important to have actual figures about the state of our trade. The table showing details I will leave with you.

Senator ALLISON. That is up to January 1?

Secretary SHERMAN. Yes, sir; the calendar year. For the year 1875 it was $64,201,852, for the year 1876 it was $185,202,605, and for 1877 $164,630,209, making $414,034,666, and the last few months have been as favorable as any.

Senator JONES. Do you understand that as meaning any particular change in the gold drift of the world, or is not that balance of trade met by the interest due by private corporations, cities, and States, and debts of every description? Do you think that it means a gold balance to anything like that extent?

Secretary SHERMAN. I think it is rather a payment of debts. The excess of exports over imports must come back in some form, and mostly in debts paid, private debts, corporation debts, and national debts. The drift this way of government bonds has been large during the last year. I have noticed this especially in the last few weeks, and recently the drift has been very large.

Senator BAYARD. They have taken that means of paying off the balance?

Secretary SHERMAN. Yes.

Senator DAWES. You think instead of gold they send our bonds?

Senator JONES. What I was getting at is, could they send very much gold?

Secretary SHERMAN. We have got both gold and silver from England, but we must do it as Lincoln said, "unbeknownst to them." It must come by the natural currents of trade. To attempt to bring by any artificial movements large sums of gold to this country would be to create alarm. All last summer and fall the accumulation was from five to eight millions of dollars each month. Some of that came from our own mines and some of it from abroad, but we accumulated it without any perceptible injury to anybody.

Now, in general answer to your question, I do express my opinion, officially and persoually, that, for the reasons I have given, we can resume on the 1st of January next, under the basis of the existing law.

The CHAIRMAN. What effect has the silver bill had or is likely to have upon resumption?

Secretary SHERMAN. I do not want to tread on delicate ground in answering that question, Mr. Chairman. I shall have to confess that I have been mistaken myself. Now as to the silver bill, I have watched its operation very closely. I think the silver bill has had some adverse effects and it has had some favorable effects on the question of resumption. Perhaps the best way for me to proceed would be to state the adverse effects first. It has undoubtedly stopped refunding operations. Since the agitation of the silver question, I have not been able largely to sell bonds, although I have made every effort to do so.

Senator JONES. At what date was the last bond sold?

Secretary SHERMAN. We are selling bonds all the time.

Senator JONES. I mean the refunding of the bonds into four per cents?

Secretary SHERMAN. The 16th of October was the time when the last of the popular loan was paid for, and we had then a call ready to issue of $10,000,000, and the associates, as they had a right to do, withdrew the call. The sales from the 1st of September, 1876, to the 15th of October, 1877, were about $275,000,000. We sold $200,000,000 four and a half per cents, and then we sold $75,000,000 four per cent. bonds.

Senator ALLISON. About a year or eleven months.

Secretary SHERMAN. Since October last we have sold four millions, and perhaps now the sales have gone up to between four and five millions of four per cent. bonds.

Now, another adverse effect the silver bill has had is to stop the accumulation of coin. Since the 1st of January, we have accumulated no coin except for coin-certificates, and except the balance of revenue over expenditure; the revenues in coin being more than enough to pay the interest of the debt and coin liabilities, we accumulate some coin.

Another effect that the silver bill has had is to cause the return of our bonds from Europe. Although the movement of our bonds in this direction has been pretty steady for more than a year, yet it is latterly largely increased; how much I am not prepared to say.

On the other hand, I will give the favorable effects. In the first place, the silver bill satisfied a strong public demand for bi-metallic money, and that demand is, no doubt, largely sectional. No doubt there is a difference of opinion between the West and South and the East on this subject, but the desire for remonetization of silver was almost universal. In a government like ours it is always good to obey the popular current, and that has been done, I think, by the passage of the silver bill. Resumption can be maintained more easily upon a double standard than upon a single standard. The bulky character of silver would prevent payments in it, while gold, being more portable, would be more freely demanded, and I think resumption can be maintained with a less amount of silver than of gold alone.

Senator BAYARD. You are speaking of resumption upon the basis of silver, or of silver and gold?

Secretary SHERMAN. Yes, sir; I think it can be maintained better upon a bi-metallic, or alternative standard, than upon a single one, and with less accumulation of gold. In this way remonetization of silver would rather aid resumption. The bonds that have been returned from Europe have been readily absorbed—remarkably so. The recent returns in New York show the amount of bonds absorbed in this country is at least a million and a quarter a day. We have sold scarcely any from the Treasury since that time. This shows the confidence of the people in our securities, and their rapid absorption will tend to check the European scare.

Senator VOORHEES. That shows, Mr. Secretary, that this cry of alarm in New York was unfounded. Then this capital seeks our bonds when this bi-metallic basis is declared?

Secretary SHERMAN. Yes; many circumstances favor this. The demand for bonds extends to the West and to the banks.

Senator DAWES. Inasmuch as funding at a lower rate is stopped, there is a greater demand for this higher rate of interest bonds that come back. The banks seek these bonds, thinking they will not be called in.

Secretary SHERMAN. The bonds that come back are 4 and $4\frac{1}{2}$ per cents largely, and their prices are well maintained. They are quoted every day at par. When I the other day felt the market to see whether there was any demand for $4\frac{1}{2}$ per cent. bonds, I had no difficulty in getting bids for them above par in large quantities.

Senator FERRY. Would there be any difficulty in disposing of the 4 per cents now?

Secretary SHERMAN. Yes; I am trying to sell them, and the sales are increasing.

Senator BAYARD. I understand that there could be a ready sale for $4\frac{1}{2}$ per cent. bonds.

Secretary SHERMAN. I have no doubt we can sell $4\frac{1}{2}$ per cent., and I think within a month we can sell all we want of 4 per cent. bonds to carry out the resumption law, for I would not accumulate more than five millions a month, and that largely in silver and gold bullion. There is no special necessity to force the bond market in order to maintain resumption. We now have seventy-one to ninety millions of dollars on hand, and every one can measure how much more will be necessary to maintain resumption. If the sale of bonds was ever so free I would not accumulate more than five millions of dollars a month of both metals, and all sales beyond that should be applied for refunding 6 per cent. bonds.

Senator ALLISON. Do you think that you can add largely to the stock of coin in this country by your process of adding to your reserves $5,000,000 per month? That is to say, will you accumulate from other countries, or simply draw into the Treasury the accumulations already existing in our own country?

Secretary SHERMAN. I am glad you mentioned that point. Although since the 1st of January last we have accumulated no coin in the Treasury, the amount that we had prior to that accumulated per month has since then gone into the banks; the banks have already accumulated more than five millions of gold since the first of January.

Senator MORRILL. They have increased their reserves by the amount of five millions, gold, per month?

Secretary SHERMAN. Here is a statement which shows the aggregate amount of specie held by the banks of the United States during the several periods therein mentioned. Now, in the United States there have been no statements of national banks since December last, but they have in the city of New York a weekly statement of the clearing-house. This shows the amount at the beginning of every week from January 5, 1878. On that day the amount was $21,884,100; that has increased in amount until March 16, 1878, when it reached $34,551,000, a difference of about thirteen millions, which is just about five millions per month increase. So that this accumulation of coin has gone on in the banks since it stopped in the Treasury.

Senator FERRY. Then if you embrace the accumulation in the banks and Treasury, it has been progressing gradually at the rate of about five millions per month?

Secretary SHERMAN. Yes, sir; more than that. In New York alone the accumulation is five millions per month, but in Boston and Philadelphia it is also going on.

Senator FERRY. What, in your judgment, is the accumulation in both the banks and the Treasury per month in amount?

Secretary SHERMAN. I should think it to be between five and ten millions dollars per month.

Senator ALLISON. Do you think that this bank accumulation, from the 1st January to the 16th March, is gathered both from this country and to the same extent from other countries?

Secretary SHERMAN. Undoubtedly.

Senator JONES. Have we any record of the imports of coin?

Secretary SHERMAN. Certainly. And in this statement of our exports and imports you will find the amount stated exactly.

Senator DAWES. Is the import of coin eliminated by itself?

Secretary SHERMAN. Yes, sir.

Senator BAYARD. Does it show where the coin comes from?

Secretary SHERMAN. It can be ascertained. In giving an answer to Mr. Morrill's question, as to the general effect of the silver bill, I would not like to give a positive opinion. I do not think, taking it altogether, that it is an obstacle in the way of resumption. It has operated in some respects adversely, and in some respects favorably, but, on the whole, I do not think it should discourage us from resumption, or from carrying out our general policy.

Senator JONES. Then, in its effect upon the return of the vast amount of bonds you refer to, would there not be an element of strength added in favor of resumption in that the interest on these bonds returned would not be a constant drain upon the country?

Secretary SHERMAN. Undoubtedly.

Senator JONES. Would the fact that they come back enable us to maintain resumption much easier?

Secretary SHERMAN. Undoubtedly. The fact that we have paid four hundred and fourteen millions of debt in foreign countries is favorable. There is another point in this connection. It seems to me that it is not necessary to determine this question now, because a sufficient time has not elapsed to enable us to determine the effect of the silver bill, and you had better let things run along and see its effect. It may be that its effect will be such that all will favor resumption and that resumption will come without effort. The passage of this bill can have no effect until January next, and it may be that before that time all will agree that it ought or ought not to be repealed. As you have this measure in the Senate you can control it by a majority vote of the Senate at any time. Why not let it stay here?

Senator VOORHEES. Did I understand you to say that you would undertake to maintain resumption with ninety millions of coin reserve?

Secretary SHERMAN. No, sir; I would undertake to resume upon the power afforded by the present law, by going on and doing what I did last summer.

Senator VOORHEES. How much surplus did you say you had on hand?

Secretary SHERMAN. I have now seventy-one millions.

Senator VOORHEES. Then you say that you would be willing to undertake resumption under the existing laws by the 1st of next January. Now, with the aid of the silver bill and the coinage, what amount of coin would you expect to have on hand, with which to undertake resumption at that time?

Secretary SHERMAN. I would accumulate about five millions per month of both metals from the 1st of April to the 1st of January, which would be forty-five millions; and, if the market is favorable, I think I would try to make good the loss that I have suffered by not accumulating in January, February, and March of the present year. I think I could in this way accumulate fifty or sixty millions.

Senator VOORHEES. That would give you one hundred and fifty millions.

Secretary SHERMAN. Not so much; nor do I think it is necessary to have so much.

Senator JONES. And does that look to eliminating the legal-tender function on the 1st of January next?

Secretary SHERMAN. No, I think not, sir; I am in favor of maintaining the legal-tender currency; but that is in controversy.

Senator KERNAN. You thought that you could practically redeem all that would be presented?

Secretary SHERMAN. I have no doubt of my power to reissue, up to three hundred millions of legal-tenders.

Senator JONES. I have an idea that would make a good deal of difference.

Senator VOORHEES. Have you spoken of the capacity of the present coinage?

Secretary SHERMAN. No, sir.

Senator FERRY. Then, on the question of resumption, your view is that, with ninety millions on hand, and the accumulation of sixty millions more, or even forty millions—which would be one hundred and thirty millions—you would be willing to commence the resumption of the present volume of the currency, both national and bank?

Secretary SHERMAN. O, yes. The banks must look out for themselves.

Senator BAYARD. I would like to ask you if the condition of the country will sustain this resumption with this very large accumulation of gold by the banks in New York; and if they will not have a tendency to continue to increase their reserve, as they find the Treasury running in the same direction?

Secretary SHERMAN. The national banks will take care of themselves.

Senator BAYARD. I am speaking not only as to their self-preservation, but as to the country at large; with the Treasury continuing this policy of resumption and accumulating, as you think you can, about five millions per month, for the next ten months, and the ninety millions you already have, giving you one hundred and forty millions, and the banks, since the 1st of January, of their own motion and for their own safety, making an accumulation of five millions a month of coin, I say will they not rather continue that, so that that reserve of coin will be increased by the banks, and at the same time the Treasury would not be retarded by it? In other words, it will make the coin reserve of the country still greater by January, 1879, should the banks pursue this policy.

Secretary SHERMAN. Yes, sir; and besides that I ought to say that the banks are exceptionably strong; the reserves in the banks now are very large. Their liabilities have been reduced upon deposits about sixty millions within the last year. While their reserves are $220,979,426 in currency, the legal reserve required is only $136,694,239, so that they have upward of $84,000,000 in excess of legal requirements.

Senator JONES. Suppose there should come at the period of resumption a great dearth of gold; would not the national banks retire their currency, rather than redeem it with gold?

Senator MORRILL. I desire to ask you whether you have any anticipation that in the course of events, as they are now tending, resumption will take place prior to 1st January, without your interfering at all?

Secretary SHERMAN. I would not like to answer that.

Senator MORRILL. I will now ask you this question: How can the policy of resumption be aided by Congress?

Secretary SHERMAN. I am very willing to answer that, although I think it is a legislative question. I think that you can aid resumption very much if you will allow me to receive United States notes in payment of bonds, as the Senate has already expressed a willingness to do, and if the House would concur with them—if I could sell 4 per cent. bonds for currency, and then reissue the currency in the purchase of 6 per cent. bonds, it would be an aid to resumption.

Senator BAYARD. What would you do with the proceeds of the sale of these bonds?

Secretary SHERMAN. I would use them in the purchase of outstanding bonds. All I would have to do would be to pay the difference between the greenback and gold, but that would only be paying 1 per cent. premium. I have a right to call the bonds, and I could use the currency in their payment by giving $1.01 for the bond in currency, the difference between currency and gold at the present time.

Senator BAYARD. You can sell your 4 per cent. bonds at par in currency and you can then use the currency to redeem the higher-rate bonds.

Senator JONES. How would that aid resumption?

Secretary SHERMAN. By repealing the discrimination that is now made against the legal-tender note in payment of bonds. The bond issued would be a coin bond.

Senator JONES. Let me see if I understand you. Is your idea this, that if you were permitted to sell 4 per cent. bonds for currency it would raise the value of currency?

Secretary SHERMAN. It would.

Senator JONES. And in that respect would aid you in resumption; it would extinguish to a certain degree the premium between gold and currency?

Secretary SHERMAN. Yes, sir. The people want these bonds, and we expect to sell them at home. If the people could buy these bonds at par in currency, the money they own, you could sell more bonds, because that 1¼ per cent. premium deters them.

Senator VOORHEES. In other words, I buy a 4 per cent. bond and you agree to pay it in gold or silver, and you take in payment for it, from me, currency.

Senator MORRILL. But he issues a bond at 4 per cent. instead of four and a half or five.

Senator FERRY. You would substantially recognize currency, then, as equal to coin?

Secretary SHERMAN. I think it makes it so.

Senator VOORHEES. Why could not the government receive its customs duties in currency?

Secretary SHERMAN. I will answer that in a moment, if you please.

Senator DAWES. Is not the general essence of what you have just said, in regard to selling bonds for currency, what you have heretofore introduced in the Senate, and which has been before the House Committee of Ways and Means?

Secretary SHERMAN. Yes, sir. Always, until 1866, when Mr. McCulloch adopted his policy, bonds were issued in exchange for currency, and we never asked gold for them.

Senator VOORHEES. Then you propose, when you get currency for the bonds, to reissue the currency?

Secretary SHERMAN. Yes, sir; and buy at once the other bonds, paying in currency the market-price in gold.

Senator FERRY. The process is to retire the higher-rate-interest bonds and to put out the lower-rate bond?

Secretary SHERMAN. Yes, sir; the saving in the difference of interest in six months would cover the extra amount paid as difference between currency and coin. I think another aid to resumption is very desirable. If you could make it clear by legislative enactment that the Secretary has the power to reissue United States notes after the 1st of January to the amount of $300,000,000, that would relieve the people and relieve the whole country from the fear which they have that the greenback currency is to be entirely destroyed. If we are to attempt on the 1st of January to pay off all these greenbacks as presented and to destroy them, I have my doubts of our ability. I think the law is perfectly clear now as to the power to reissue up to three hundred millions currency.

Senator ALLISON. But you think it ought to be on the contract?

Secretary SHERMAN. I think it ought to be plainly expressed in the law. I think the passage of some such bill as Mr. Wallace has introduced and the Senate passed, with some amendments I would suggest to it, or rather the one that Mr. Burchard introduced, and recently reported by Mr. Robbins of North Carolina.

Senator DAWES. Is the Burchard bill and the Robbins bill the same?

Secretary SHERMAN. Mr. Robbins's bill is the same with modificatins made at different stages. I think the passage of that bill would aid me greatly, because that would enable me to sell bonds to all classes of the people.

Senator DAWES. You would get a new market for the bonds?

Secretary SHERMAN. I think that some such law as that would be very good.

Senator BAYARD. A long bond for a small amount?

Senator DAWES. Yes.

Secretary SHERMAN. Another thing I would recommend, and this is in answer to Mr. Voorhees. I would on the first of October next receive

United States notes in payment for duties, and yet provide for the interest on bonds in coin—in other words, I would assume on the first of October next that our notes were as good as gold and silver, and would receive them as such.

Senator MORRILL. Can you do that in the face of the solemn pledge on the statute-book?

Secretary SHERMAN. Yes, if we mean to redeem the notes on the 1st of January next; and I would show my confidence by doing it beforehand. The Secretary has the legal right now to prepay, to anticipate payment of the interest on the public debt, one year. If the note is the practical equivalent of coin it will be received as coin for interest, and we should take it as coin for duties. If we lose a fraction of one per cent. it is a small matter. I think an act of courage of that kind would be very beneficial.

Senator DAWES. If there was a difference between the value of greenbacks and coin you would be obliged to make it up.

Secretary SHERMAN. Certainly. I would show my faith in our promise. We promised to redeem these notes on the 1st of January. Now we show our willingness to carry out the promise by receiving these notes a little before that date.

Senator BAYARD. What becomes of your law of 1862?

Secretary SHERMAN. It does not abrogate it.

Senator BAYARD. I think that declared that the duties should be made payable in coin, and they were specially pledged to this end.

Secretary SHERMAN, I know; but we pay the interest in coin.

Senator BAYARD. I know you pay the interest, but the underlying idea, to a certain class, has been to pay these duties in Treasury notes. If these were not redeemable, to do this would be a violation of that solemn pledge.

Senator ALLISON. If we do the thing as the Secretary says——

Senator BAYARD. Whenever they are paid, undoubtedly; but you still have your public stipulation that you are to pay your duties in a certain measure or material commodity, or what you please to call it, and you say, "No; we will pay them by another form of indebtedness."

Senator ALLISON. What is that pledge? It is that these duties shall be set apart for interest. Now the duties amount annually to certainly twenty or thirty millions more than the annual interest. Therefore, if that fund is still set apart for the payment of the interest, it certainly can be used for that purpose although there is a difference of, say, 1½ per cent. between the material received and the material with which the interest is paid.

Secretary SHERMAN. I want to state to Mr. Bayard that we are receiving customs now in a form of paper money. Our duties, nearly all of them, are paid in certificates of money; we pay out these certificates and we pay but coin.

Senator BAYARD. The certificates actually represent gold, otherwise there would be a breach of contract. Instead of taking gold we take certificates of deposit.

Secretary SHERMAN. We receive greenbacks in the same way as gold certificates, payable after three months after the 1st of October next.

Senator BAYARD. I understand that is so, and I agree with you that whenever a greenback is equivalent to a certificate of deposit for gold, then it is a mere convertibility of terms.

Secretary SHERMAN. That is precisely what I would make it.

Senator ALLISON. That is rather an interesting statement. I would like to have you elaborate that as to what the gold operations of the Treasury are.

Secretary SHERMAN. I asked Mr. Gilfillan this question and told him to put his answer in writing as to what proportion of our bonds and our interest is now paid in gold coin. I was surprised to see so little of it paid in coin. Most of it is paid in certificates.

TREASURY OF THE UNITED STATES,
Washington, March 18, 1878.

SIR: As to what proportion of interest and principal of the national debt is paid by check or in gold certificates, it may be said that all interest on $407,842,050, registered principal of the 5 per cent., 4½ per cent., and 4 per cent. funded loans, is now paid by coin checks, and while there is no record showing how other registered and coupon interest is paid, there is no doubt that, so far as the denominations of gold certificates will permit—the lowest being $100—payments of interest are made at the principal offices in gold certificates. Should denominations convenient for the purpose be issued, very little actual coin would be used in making the interest payments. The principal and accrued interest of all bonds redeemed at maturity or under the call of the Secretary are paid by coin check. The amount of payments by check of the principal of bonds during the fiscal year ended June 30, 1877, was $127,124,450.

Very respectfully,

JAS. GILFILLAN,
Treasurer United States.

Hon. JOHN SHERMAN,
Secretary of the Treasury.

The CHAIRMAN. These certificates of deposit are precisely the same as gold.

Senator BAYARD. It represents an absolute metal at a place whence it can be taken on the presentation of the check.

Senator KERNAN. They can at their option go and get the gold on them.

Senator FERRY. The Secretary stands upon the presumption assured by these facts, that on the first of January there is no question that he can on the volume now out resume, and as respects the greenbacks, it is simply a difference of form between them and certificates of coin, and, therefore, he says he would be ready on the first of October to receive the greenbacks in payment of duties, because he has or will have coin enough to meet maturing interest and resume.

Secretary SHERMAN. I never would receive the greenback for customs duties until I knew it was as good as coin, and I would be willing to run the risk of anticipating that for three months if that would help the matter.

Senator VOORHEES. Suppose the result of such action would be to close the gap between the paper and coin or would help to do it?

Secretary SHERMAN. I say it would help. If you gentlemen will feel your way clear to allow my receiving the United States notes in payment of bonds, and will make it clear that I won't be compelled to redeem all the United States notes that come in after the first of January next; and if you think, under the circumstances, I would be strong enough to receive these notes on the first of October, I should be willing to guarantee the resumption. I think for us to go backward over all of this long, weary agony and struggle toward resumption would be a sign of national weakness and do the nation great harm, do our credit harm, and bring injury upon us all.

Senator BAYARD. Suppose that on the first of October the premium between gold and paper has passed away and gold has come to par, and you can use it as you would paper, and that is your agreement to receive that at the custom-house, where will your supply of gold be found in case you are called upon for actual exchange in payment of your notes?

Secretary SHERMAN. We have the large revenue of gold and silver. We have the incoming notes, which will then be as good as coin to pay out. And if need be, we could sell our bonds. I do not think it would be difficult to supply the quantity of coin required.

Senator JONES. Couldn't you buy gold with the notes?

Senator FERRY. Would there be any difficulty in purchasing gold when there would be less demand for it? There being no active demand for it, you would be able to purchase gold as the single purchaser much easier than you do now with numerous competitors in the market?

Secretary SHERMAN. As a matter of course there is some risk in resuming, and we have got to take that risk. If we take it on the first of January, we have got to strengthen ourselves as much as possible, but the risk is greatly exaggerated. Some future Congress will have to provide for exigencies that may arise from financial panics or adverse trade, by authorizing a temporary suspension of specie payment or a temporary issue of notes, as is done by the Bank of England.

Senator JONES. If greenbacks are made a legal tender, I don't see why you require the law. If you didn't have the gold to redeem them, people would simply go right on, and you couldn't pay it out.

The CHAIRMAN. What is your opinion as to the amount of gold and silver coin outside of the Treasury, estimated to be in the hands of the people of the country?

Secretary SHERMAN. I thought you would probably ask me that question, and I have got a statement from Mr. E. B. Elliott, of the Treasury, giving the amount of gold and silver on hand. It is a mere estimate. Mr. Elliott estimates it now, the first of March, at $280,000,000. Doctor Lindermann last October estimated it at $260,000,000, of which $200,000,000 was gold, showing a small increase.

Senator JONES. Does this give the localities where that gold is to be found?

Secretary SHERMAN. Mr. Elliott had that all figured out in another statement. This is the aggregate.

The CHAIRMAN. What effect would a repeal of the resumption act have upon the relations of the currency, legal tenders, and our coin, gold and silver? Would not a repeal of the resumption act cause a fall of paper below gold and silver?

Secretary SHERMAN. I have no doubt of that. I think a repeal of the resumption act would at once cause a widening between coin and paper money, depending entirely upon the confidence the people at large would have in the ultimate redemption of paper, but I don't want to enter on this delicate ground.

The CHAIRMAN. I would like to know whether there is any general feeling among business men in favor of a repeal of the resumption act since the passage of the silver bill; that is, whether it is the opinion of the business men that a repeal of the resumption act will give greater confidence in the future?

Secretary SHERMAN. I do not think there is. There was a strong feeling in favor of remonetization of the silver, founded, I think, upon the mistaken idea that somebody or other had been guilty of demonetizing silver for a bad purpose, and we know very well that at the time this was done the silver dollar was worth more than the gold dollar. I believe the public mind is prepared now to settle down to resumption— that is, in the equivalency of the coin to paper money.

Senator BAYARD. You speak of resumption upon a bi metallic basis being easier. Do you make that proposition irrespective of the readjustment of the relative values of the two metals as we have declared them?

Secretary SHERMAN. I think so. Our mere right to pay in silver would deter a great many people from presenting notes for redemption who would readily do so if they could get the lighter and more portable coin in exchange. Besides, gold coin can be exported while silver coin could not be exported, because its market value is less than its coin value.

Senator BAYARD. I understand that it works practically very well. So long as the silver is less in value than the paper you will have no trouble in redeeming your paper. When a paper dollar is worth 98 cents nobody is going to take it to the Treasury and get 92 cents in silver; but what are you to do as your silver coin is minted? By the 1st of July next or the 1st of January next you have eighteen or twenty millions of silver dollars which are in circulation and payable for duties, and how long do you suppose this short supply of silver and your control of it by your coinage will keep it equivalent to gold—when one is worth ten cents less than the other?

Secretary SHERMAN. Just so long as it can be used for anything that gold is used for. It will be worth in this country the par of gold until it becomes so abundant and bulky that people will become tired of carrying it about; but in our country that can be avoided by depositing it for coin certificates.

Senator BAYARD. Do you suppose it is possible to retain in this country these two moneys, one of gold and one of silver, at the ratio you have adjusted them of 16 to 1, when their market value is different?

Secretary SHERMAN. I think we can do it until the amount of silver gets to be somewhere between $50,000,000 and $100,000,000.

Senator BAYARD. That would take you about one and a half or two years?

Secretary SHERMAN. Yes; but that is a question of opinion. Let me give you the basis of that opinion. In England they maintain over $100,000,000 of silver at par with gold.

Senator BAYARD. They do it by limiting its legal tender.

Secretary SHERMAN. Then in France they maintain a much larger amount.

Senator JONES. How much silver is circulating at a parity with gold in France?

Secretary SHERMAN. Between two and three hundred millions, perhaps more than that. You know better about their statistics than I do, but it is very large.

Senator JONES. Within a very small fraction of the amount of gold.

Senator KERNAN. About how much silver should there be in the country to have a fair supply of coin to pay all the duties?

Secretary SHERMAN. That is a doubtful question. If the coin is convertible into coin certificates I think $10,000,000 or $20,000,000 will do it.

Senator KERNAN. If there were $20,000,000 in coin certificates in existence they would probably pay the duties, would they not?

Secretary SHERMAN. I think so.

Senator ALLISON. You stated that most of these transactions relating to gold are conducted in certificates. Why is that?

Secretary SHERMAN. Because gold is unhandy and risky to carry. At the custom-houses they prefer to send certificates to pay duties, because certificates can be easily handled.

Senator BAYARD. These certificates represent that amount of gold, and are payable on demand to bearer?

Secretary SHERMAN. Yes; they are payable on demand.

Senator JONES. I understand that the bulkiness would not have any more effect on the silver than on the gold.

Senator VOORHEES. There is a committee of very prominent men of my State in the city, and I agreed to ask the Secretary a question. Our folks are very anxious to have a mint established at Indianapolis, and they wanted me to ask the Secretary about the capacity of the present mints. How much can be coined now by the present capacity of the mints.

Secretary SHERMAN. I received this morning a letter from Dr. Linderman upon this subject, which I will be very happy to read:

THE MINT OF THE UNITED STATES AT PHILADELPHIA, PA.,
March 18, 1878.

DEAR SIR: This mint is coining silver dollars at the rate of about $55,000 per working day.

The dies are not working satisfactorily. Some of them sink and others crack. I have been, since my arrival here, examining the matter and trying to remedy the defect. It appears to be mostly caused by inferior steel. A new *obverse* hub has been prepared, and a new *reverse* hub is in course of preparation and will be finished by Wednesday. The first two hubs prepared sunk somewhat, and the working dies made from them were not as perfect as they should be. I have decided *not* to send any dies for the dollar to the Western mints until they can be prepared with the new hubs. The experience of the mint for many years has been that much difficulty attends the striking of all large-sized coins from new devices, and that occasionally defective steel is encountered, no matter how much care is taken in the selection. I expect all these difficulties to be fully overcome by about the 1st proximo, after which the capacity of this mint will be brought up to 75,000 silver dollars per working day.

I deem it prudent to remain here until the new hubs have both been finished (day after to-morrow).

The newspaper cry about the "English design" and "English engraver" is all nonsense. The regular engraver of the mint is an Englishman, and the design which he prepared took *two* strokes of a powerful screw or medal press to bring up the devices, and particularly the eagle. The present silver dollar has one very important advantage over the trade-dollar as well as the old silver dollar, and that is that the *border* is so arranged as to fully protect the devices from coming together when piled one upon another. In this way only can undue abrasion be prevented, and that is what I have had in view in the preparation of new devices for nearly two years past. We shall fully succeed, but in the mean time must take the raps of all the wise and knowing ones in the land.

Truly, your friend,

H. R. LINDERMAN.

Hon. JOHN SHERMAN:

Secretary SHERMAN. The San Francisco mint, it is thought, can coin about $100,000 a day. We think it better to run these two large mints to their fullest capacity on the silver dollar and stop issuing the trade-dollars. Perhaps we shall issue trade-dollars from Carson; but at any rate these two mints furnish enough, so that I do not really think a new mint necessary.

Senator ALLISON. The Philadelphia mint, at $75,000 each working-day, would issue about $1,800,000 a month, and the San Francisco mint, at $100,000 a day, would issue $2,400,000 a month, aggregating $4,400,000 a month.

Senator VOORHEES. You would not be prepared to recommend the establishment of the mint under the present circumstances?

Secretary SHERMAN. No; it would take two years to make a mint.

Senator ALLISON. In the event of a change in the balance of trade, so that our imports shall exceed our exports, beginning, say, July 1 and continuing to the end of the year, what probable effect would that have upon your ability to resume; or have you any machinery by which you can counteract any such influence that might happen temporarily during this interval?

Secretary SHERMAN. If the current of trade should be against us, it is pretty difficult to answer. If we had power to raise the rate of interest, we might check it. I do not know that the government would be much affected by the balance of trade, and I think we could go on. It would undoubtedly be harder upon the people.

The CHAIRMAN. Suppose there should or should not be a European war; would either have any effect?

Secretary SHERMAN. All such circumstances would have an effect upon merchants.

Senator FERRY. There is one point; you state that the greenbacks and United States notes amount to $348,000,000, but aside from the reserves there are really in circulation about $320,000,000.

Secretary SHERMAN. I mean we are holding greenbacks in lieu of notes of suspended banks, so that really there are in circulation only about $320,000,000.

Senator FERRY. Now, you state that with $140,000,000 gold reserve you would be willing to hold $300,000,000 as a part of the currency, and meet resumption on that basis. Now, I desire to ask if, with the contraction as it is going on, it would be any obstacle to resumption even if the outstanding circulation should be $320,000,000 on the first of January next?

Secretary SHERMAN. I think the $20,000,000 would be provided for by the increase of bank-notes.

Senator FERRY. Without any direct further contraction than under the present resumption act?

Secretary SHERMAN. The present resumption act would be sufficient. I would not by myself provide for and direct contraction of the currency except what is done under the act.

The CHAIRMAN. Don't you believe there will an expansion come upon us naturally or by action of the Treasury Department on the 1st of January? Will there not be more money in actual circulation after that period?

Secretary SHERMAN. I think and hope so.

Senator FERRY. Would not that produce a healthier condition?

Secretary SHERMAN. Yes, sir.

Senator BAYARD. What would be the effect, in your opinion, of a declaration that $300,000,000 of Treasury notes might be reissued as a minimum and as a maximum, to be supported by a retention by law of $100,000,000 of gold in the Treasury?

Secretary SHERMAN. That would be very beneficial, because I think the fear about that $300,000,000 would be overcome.

Senator KERNAN. And your opinion is that authority to reissue the legal-tender notes should be expressly given by law.

Secretary SHERMAN. I think that authority to reissue, unquestioned and undoubted, would take away the fears of all classes of people: First, those in favor of inflation, who do not want the greenback destroyed; then in the Eastern States, where they think we ought to retire the greenbacks and issue bank-notes instead, and believe that we are bound under existing law to pay the whole of the $300,000,000. And that we are not prepared to do.

Senator ALLISON. In other words, you think we cannot come to and maintain specie payments without the power to reissue?

Secretary SHERMAN. I do not think we can.

APPENDIX.

Comparison of condition of the Treasury March 1, 1877, and March 1, 1878.

Balances.	1877.	1878.
Currency	$9,122,874 05	$2,690,765 52
Special fund for the redemption of fractional currency		10,000,000 00
Special deposit of legal tenders for redemption of certificates of deposit	34,445,000 00	28,555,000 00
Coin	90,263,771 44	131,318,156 33
Coin certificates	52,146,700 00	48,456,000 00
Coin, less coin certificates	38,117,071 44	82,862,156 33
Outstanding called bonds	7,826,550 00	6,475,650 00
Other outstanding coin liabilities	9,070,572 41	5,539,020 57
Outstanding legal tenders	354,239,484 00	348,618,024 00
Outstanding fractional currency	24,434,420 35	17,190,698 14
Outstanding silver coin	28,683,170 01	38,489,490 94
Total debt, less cash in Treasury	2,088,781,143 04	2,042,037,129 08
Reduction of debt for February	2,070,429 06	2,230,237 18
Reduction of debt since July 1	10,658,201 95	18,121,094 18
Market value of gold	104 87	101 87
Imports (12 months ending January 31)	422,943,252 00	477,712,900 00
Exports (12 months ending January 31)	603,418,793 00	622,167,514 00

TREASURY DEPARTMENT,
 Warrant Division.

Statement of outstanding coin and currency certificates at end of each quarter from October 1, 1872, to January 1, 1878.

	Coin certificates.	Currency certificates.
October 1, 1872	25,792,760	15,630,000
January 1, 1873	23,263,000	25,370,000
April 1, 1873	24,141,000	24,450,000
July 1, 1873	39,460,000	31,730,000
October 1, 1873	33,935,400	11,250,000
January 1, 1874	37,543,300	36,720,000
April 1, 1874	37,045,000	51,720,000
July 1, 1874	22,825,100	58,760,000
October 1, 1874	26,415,600	56,350,000
January 1, 1875	23,540,600	41,200,000
April 1, 1875	24,191,900	43,045,000
July 1, 1875	21,796,300	58,415,000
October 1, 1875	11,645,200	60,660,000
January 1, 1876	31,198,300	35,175,000
April 1, 1876	32,337,600	34,230,000
July 1, 1876	28,681,400	32,840,000
October 1, 1876	29,777,900	34,520,000
January 1, 1877	47,280,000	31,000,000
April 1, 1877	48,279,400	35,155,000
July 1, 1877	41,572,600	54,930,000
October 1, 1877	37,997,500	43,110,000
January 1, 1878	33,424,900	32,830,000

Reduction of United States notes, by months, from March 1, 1875, to March 1, 1878.

	Outstanding.	Reduction each month.	Total reduction.
March 1, 1875	$382,000,000		
April 1, 1875	379,226,900	$2,773,100	
May 1, 1875	378,051,760	1,175,140	
June 1, 1875	377,064,000	987,760	
July 1, 1875	375,771,580	1,292,420	
August 1, 1875	374,755,108	1,016,472	
September 1, 1875	374,245,708	509,400	
October 1, 1875	373,941,124	304,584	
November 1, 1875	373,236,244	704,880	
December 1, 1875	372,471,772	764,472	
January 1, 1876	371,827,220	644,552	
February 1, 1876	371,273,140	554,080	
March 1, 1876	370,943,392	329,748	
April 1, 1876	370,755,248	188,144	
May 1, 1876	370,527,876	227,372	
June 1, 1876	370,123,668	404,208	
July 1, 1876	369,772,284	351,384	
August 1, 1876	369,619,228	153,056	
September 1, 1876	369,334,604	244,624	
October 1, 1876	368,494,740	839,864	
November 1, 1876	367,535,716	959,024	
December 1, 1876	366,911,000	624,716	
January 1, 1877	366,055,084	855,916	
February 1, 1877	364,984,812	1,070,272	
March 1, 1877	364,239,484	745,328	
April 1, 1877	362,656,204	1,583,280	
May 1, 1877	361,494,404	1,161,800	
June 1, 1877	360,412,580	1,081,824	
July 1, 1877	359,764,332	648,248	
August 1, 1877	359,094,220	670,112	
September 1, 1877	357,976,164	1,118,056	
October 1, 1877	356,914,932	1,061,232	
November 1, 1877	354,490,892	2,424,040	
December 1, 1877	351,340,288	3,150,604	
January 1, 1878	349,943,776	1,396,512	
February 1, 1878	349,110,424	833,352	
March 1, 1878	348,618,024	492,400	$33,381,976

TREASURY DEPARTMENT,
OFFICE OF COMPTROLLER OF THE CURRENCY,
Washington, February 16, 1878.

[Number of banks, 2,074.]

Abstract of reports made to the Comptroller of the Currency, showing the condition of the national banks in the United States, including national gold banks, at the close of business on Friday, the 28th day of December, 1877.

RESOURCES.		LIABILITIES.	
Loans and discounts	$878,055,305 95	Capital stock paid in	$477,128,771 00
Overdrafts	3,801,438 92	Surplus fund	121,618,435 32
U. S. bonds to secure circulation	343,869,550 00	Other undivided profits	51,530,910 18
U. S bonds to secure deposits	13,538,000 00	*National-bank notes outstanding	299,240,475 00
U. S. bonds on hand	28,479,800 00	State-bank notes outstanding	470,540 00
Other stocks, bonds, and mortgages	39,169,491 03	Dividends unpaid	1,401,178 34
Due from approved reserve agents	75,960,087 27	Individual deposits	604,512,514 52
Due from other national banks	44,123,924 97	U. S. deposits	6,529,031 09
Due from State banks and bankers	11,479,945 65	Deposits of U. S. disbursing officers	3,780,759 43
Real estate, furniture, and fixtures	45,511,932 25	Due to other national banks	115,773,660 58
Current expenses	8,958,903 60	Due to State banks and bankers	44,807,958 79
Premiums paid	8,841,839 09	Notes and bills rediscounted	4,604,784 51
Checks and other cash items	10,265,059 49	Bills payable	5,843,107 02
Exchanges for clearing-house	64,664,415 01		
Bills of other national banks	20,312,682 00		
Fractional currency	778,084 78		
Specie, viz: Gold coin $5,506,556 39, Silver coin 4,300,274 31, U. S. gold certificates 23,100,920 00	32,907,750 70		
Legal-tender notes	70,568,248 00		
U. S. certificates of deposit for legal-tender notes	26,515,000 00		
Five per cent. redemption fund with Treasurer	15,028,340 14		
Due from Treasurer other than redemption fund	1,465,236 94		
Aggregate	1,737,295,145 79	Aggregate	1,737,295,145 79

* The amount of circulation outstanding at the date named, as shown by the books of this office, was $321,672,205; which amount includes the notes of insolvent banks, of those in voluntary liquidation, and of those which have deposited legal-tender notes under the act of June 20, 1874, for the purpose of retiring their circulation.

JOHN JAY KNOX,
Comptroller of the Currency.

21

Lawful-money reserve of the national banks, as shown by their reports to the Comptroller of the Currency, in 1877.

Date.	Number of banks.	Deposits.	Reserve required.	Reserve held.	Classification of reserve held.								
					Specie.			Legal-tender.			Due from reserve-agents.	Redemption-fund.	Aggregate.
					Coin.	United States coin-certificates.	Total.	United States certificates.	Notes.	Total.			
1877.													
Jan. 20	2,083	$721,209,793	$150,440,232	$251,188,995	$10,597,487	$39,111,780	$49,709,267	$25,470,000	$72,669,710	$98,159,710	$88,698,309	$14,631,709	$251,188,995
Apr. 14	2,073	696,283,138	144,725,891	231,223,371	10,070,458	16,999,580	27,070,038	32,100,000	72,351,573	104,451,573	64,942,718	14,759,042	231,223,371
June 22	2,078	769,646,876	161,325,637	240,514,815	9,156,476	12,179,520	21,335,996	44,420,000	78,004,396	122,414,396	82,132,100	14,612,133	240,514,815
Oct. 1	2,080	689,124,748	138,343,154	210,768,270	8,570,360	14,088,460	22,658,820	33,410,000	66,920,664	100,330,664	73,294,133	14,494,633	210,768,270
Dec. 28	2,074	682,332,485	136,694,239	220,979,426	9,806,631	22,100,980	32,907,751	26,515,000	70,568,248	97,083,248	75,960,087	15,028,340	220,979,426

TREASURY DEPARTMENT, OFFICE OF COMPTROLLER OF THE CURRENCY.
Washington, March 15, 1878.

Additional circulation under act of January 14, 1875.

	1875.	1876.	1877.	1878.
January	$537,580	$702,370	$1,337,840	$1,041,690
February	1,062,440	329,385	931,660	615,500
March	1,956,580	322,380	1,979,100	
April	1,390,200	225,815	1,452,250	
May	1,237,500	476,560	1,352,280	
June	1,735,525	485,670	810,310	
July	1,151,140	144,880	837,640	
August	626,960	360,100	1,397,570	
September	520,650	1,045,510	1,326,540	
October	768,100	1,198,780	3,030,050	
November	981,010	780,895	3,938,255	
December	821,220	1,069,895	1,745,640	
Total	12,788,905	7,142,240	20,139,135	1,657,190

	December 31.	December 31.	December 31.	February 28.
Legal-tender notes outstanding	371,827,220	366,055,084	349,943,776	348,618,024

Total outstanding circulation of national-bank notes at the following dates, viz:

	December 31, 1875.	December 31, 1876.	December 31, 1877.	February 28, 1878.
Currency banks	$344,391,896	$319,498,216	$320,240,385	$320,557,871
Gold banks	2,087,860	2,097,390	1,432,120	1,432,120
Total	346,479,756	321,595,606	321,672,505	321,989,991

Total outstanding circulation of national banks in operation as shown by their reports at the following dates:

	December 17, 1875.	December 22, 1876.	December 28, 1877.
Including gold banks	$314,979,451	$292,011,575	$290,240,475

Specie held by the national banks, as shown by their reports to the Comptroller of the Currency, and in New York City by their statements to the clearing-house.

UNITED STATES.

Date.	Coin.	United States coin-certificates.	Total.
June 30, 1876	$6,455,237 42	$18,764,320 00	$25,219,557 42
December 22, 1876	8,484,367 89	24,515,280 00	32,999,647 89
June 22, 1877	9,156,476 06	12,179,520 00	21,335,996 06
December 28, 1877	9,806,830 70	23,100,920 00	32,907,750 70

NEW YORK CITY.

Date	Coin	U.S. coin-certificates	Total
June 30, 1876	$1,214,522 92	$16,872,780 00	$18,087,302 92
December 22, 1876	1,434,701 83	21,602,900 00	23,037,601 83
June 22, 1877	1,423,258 17	10,324,320 00	11,747,578 17
December 28, 1877	1,955,746 20	19,119,080 00	21,074,826 20

NEW YORK CITY—WEEKLY STATEMENTS TO THE CLEARING-HOUSE.

Week ending—	Amount.
January 5, 1878	$21,884,100
January 12, 1878	23,904,000
January 19, 1878	24,974,400
January 26, 1878	26,452,400
February 2, 1878	27,085,800
February 9, 1878	28,133,300
February 16, 1878	29,391,900
February 23, 1878	28,902,200
March 2, 1878	29,384,000
March 9, 1878	32,932,900
March 16, 1878	34,551,000

During last year the United States accumulated coin; during this year the banks have done so.

CURRENCY VALUE OF GOLD.

Table showing the value in currency of one hundred dollars in gold in the New York market, by months, quarter-years, half-years, calendar years, and fiscal years, from January 1, 1862, to February 28, 1878, both inclusive.

[Prepared by E. B. Elliott, United States Treasury.]

Periods.	1862.	1863.	1864.	1865.	1866.	1867.	1868.	1869.	1870.	1871.	1872.	1873.	1874.	1875.	1876.	1877.	1878.
January	102.5	145.1	155.5	216.2	140.1	134.6	138.5	135.0	121.3	110.7	109.1	112.7	111.4	112.5	112.8	106.3	102.1
February	103.5	160.5	158.6	205.5	134.4	137.4	141.4	134.4	119.5	111.5	110.3	114.1	112.3	114.5	113.4	105.4	102
March	101.8	154.5	164.9	173.8	130.5	135	139.5	131.3	112.6	111	110.1	115.5	112.1	115.5	114.3	104.8	
April	101.5	151.5	172.7	148.5	127.3	135.0	138.7	132.9	113.1	110.6	111.1	117.8	113.4	114.8	113.0	106.2	
May	103.3	148.9	176.3	135.6	131.8	137	139.6	139.5	114.7	111.5	113.7	117.7	112.4	115.8	112.6	106.9	
June	106.5	144.5	210.7	140	140.7	137.5	140.1	138.1	112.9	112.4	113.9	116.5	112.8	117	112.5	105.4	
July	115.5	130.6	258.1	142.1	151.6	139.4	142.7	136.1	122.9	112.4	114.3	115.5	110	114.8	111.9	105.4	
August	114.5	125.8	254.1	143.5	148.1	140.4	143.5	134.2	116.8	112.4	114.4	115.4	109.7	113.5	111.5	105	
September	118.5	134.2	222.5	143.9	145.3	143.5	143.6	130.8	117.9	114.5	113.5	112.7	110	115.5	111.2	103.3	
October	128.5	147.7	207.2	145.5	148.3	143.5	143.1	130.2	114.8	113.2	113.2	108.9	110	114.4	110	103	
November	131.1	148.0	223.2	147	142.8	139.6	134.4	130.2	111.4	111.2	113.9	108.6	110.9	114.7	109.1	102.8	
December	132.3	151.1	227.5	146.2	136.7	134.8	135.2	121.5	110.7	109.3	112.2	110	111.7	113.9	107.9	102.8	
First quarter-year	102.6	153.4	159	198.5	134.3	135.7	139.8	133.8	117.8	111.1	109.8	114.1	111.9	114.2	113.5	105.5	
Second quarter-year	103.8	148.3	186.6	141.4	135.9	136.7	139.5	136.7	113.6	111.5	112.9	117.3	112.4	115.9	112.7	106.2	
Third quarter-year	116.2	130.2	244.9	143.2	148.6	141.2	143.9	135.7	116.5	113.1	114.1	114.6	109.8	114.7	111	104.6	
Fourth quarter-year	130.6	148.9	232.7	146.2	142.9	139.3	135.6	126	111.6	111.2	112.8	109.2	110.9	115	108.9	102.8	
First half-year	103.2	150.8	172.8	169.9	136.1	136.2	139.6	135.3	115.7	111.3	111.4	115.7	112.2	115.1	113.1	105.9	
Second half-year	121.4	139.6	233.8	144.7	143.2	140.3	139.8	130.8	114	121.1	113.4	111.9	110.3	114.8	109.9	103.7	
Calendar year	113.3	145.2	203.3	157.3	140.9	138.2	139.7	133	114.9	111.7	112.4	113.8	111.2	114.9	111.5	104.3	
Fiscal year ending June 30		137.1	156.2	201.9	140.4	141	139.9	137.5	123.3	112.7	111.8	114.6	112	112.7	113.9	107.9	

GOLD VALUE OF CURRENCY.

Table showing the value in gold of one hundred dollars in currency in the New York market, by months, quarter-years, half-years, calendar years, and fiscal years, from January 1, 1862, to February 28, 1878, both inclusive.

[Prepared by E. B. Elliott, United States Treasury.]

Periods.	1862.	1863.	1864.	1865.	1866.	1867.	1868.	1869.	1870.	1871.	1872.	1873.	1874.	1875.	1876.	1877.	1878.
January	97.6	68.9	64.3	46.3	71.4	74.3	72.2	73.7	82.4	90.3	91.7	88.7	89.7	88.9	88.6	94	97.9
February	96.6	69.3	63.1	48.7	72.3	72.8	70.7	74.4	83.7	89.7	90.7	87.6	89.1	87.3	88.2	94.8	96
March	96.2	64.7	61.4	57.5	78.6	74.1	71.7	76.2	86.8	90.1	90.8	86.6	89.2	86.6	87.5	95.4	
April	98.5	66	57.9	67.3	78.6	73.7	72.1	75.2	86.4	90.4	90	84.9	86.2	87.1	86.5	94.2	
May	96.8	67.2	56.7	73.7	72.9	73	71.6	71.8	87.2	88.7	88	85	89.9	86.3	88.8	93.5	
June	93.9	69.2	47.5	71.4	67.2	72.7	70.4	72.4	86.6	89	87.8	85.8	90	85.4	88.9	94.9	
July	88.6	76.6	38.7	70.4	66	71.7	70.1	73.5	85.6	89	8.5	86.7	91	87.2	89.4	94.9	
August	87.3	79.5	39.4	71.4	67.2	71	68.7	73.1	84.8	89	87.4	86.4	91.2	86.1	89.9	95.2	
September	84.4	74.5	44.9	68.7	68.7	68.7	69.6	73.1	87.1	87.3	87.1	86.7	91.2	86.4	90.9	96.8	
October	77.8	67.7	48.3	68.7	67.4	69.7	72.9	76.8	88.7	88.3	87.3	87.7	91.2	85.9	91.2	97.3	
November	76.3	67.6	42.8	68	69.5	71.6	71.4	76.9	88.9	88.9	88.6	91.6	90.2	87.2	91.7	97.3	
December	73.6	65.2	44	68.4	73.2	74.2	74	83.3	90.3	91.5	87.1	90.9	89.6	87.8	92.6	97.3	
First quarter-year	97.5	65.2	62.9	50.4	73.3	73.7	71.5	74.7	84.9	90	91	87.6	89.3	87.6	88.1	94.8	
Second quarter-year	96.3	67.4	53.6	70.7	73.6	73.2	71.7	73.7	88	89.7	88.6	85.3	89	86.3	88.7	94.2	
Third quarter-year	86.1	76.8	40.8	69.8	67.2	70.8	69.5	73.7	85.8	88.4	87.6	87.3	91.1	87.2	90.1	95.6	
Fourth quarter-year	76.6	67.2	44.9	68.4	70	71.8	73.7	79.4	88.9	90	88.7	91.6	90.2	86.9	91.8	97.3	
First half-year	96.9	66.3	57.9	58.9	73.5	73.4	71.6	73.9	86.4	89.8	89.8	86.4	89.2	86.9	88.4	94.1	
Second half-year	81	71.6	42.8	69.1	68.6	71.3	71.5	76.5	87.7	89.2	88.2	89.4	90.7	87.1	90.9	96.4	
Calendar year	88.3	68.9	49.2	63.6	71	72.4	71.6	75.2	87	89.5	89	87.9	89.9	87	89.8	95.4	
Fiscal year ended June 30		72.9	64	49.5	71.2	70.9	71.5	72.7	81.1	88.7	89.4	87.3	89.3	68.8	87.8	92.7	

Dates of maturity and amounts of 5-20 called bonds.

AGAINST 4½ PER CENTS.

1876, Dec. 1, 32d call	$10,000,000	
Dec. 6, 33d call	10,000,000	
Dec. 12, 34th call	10,000,000	
Dec. 21, 35th call	10,000,000	
1877, Jan. 6, 36th call	10,000,000	
Apr. 10, 37th call	10,000,000	
Apr. 24, 38th call	10,000,000	
May 12, 39th call	10,000,000	
May 28, 40th call	10,000,000	
June 3, 41st call	10,000,000	
June 10, 42d call	10,000,000	
June 15, 43d call	10,000,000	
June 27, 44th call	10,000,000	
July 5, 45th call	10,000,000	
Aug. 5, 46th call	10,114,550	
Aug. 21, 47th call	10,000,000	
Aug. 28, 48th call	10,000,000	
Sept. 11, 49th call	15,000,000	
		$185,114,550

AGAINST 4 PER CENTS.

1877, Oct. 5, 50th call	10,000,000	
Oct. 16, 51st call	10,000,000	
Oct. 19, 52d call	10,000,000	
Oct. 27, 53d call	10,000,000	
Nov. 3, 54th call	10,000,000	
1878, Mar. 6, 55th call	10,000,000	
		60,000,000
Total		245,114,550

TREASURY DEPARTMENT, UNITED STATES OF AMERICA,
BUREAU OF STATISTICS,
Washington, D. C., March 18, 1878.

Information asked for by the honorable Secretary.

Compare exports and imports for three years, and show aggregate excess of exports.

Reply by the Chief of the Bureau of Statistics.

Statements showing the imports and exports into and from the United States during the three fiscal years 1875, 1876, and 1877, with a classified statement of the exports of domestic products; also of the trade during the three calendar years ended December 31, 1877, are appended hereto.

The latter statement shows that the balance in favor of the United States during the three years indicated is as follows:

	Merchandise only.
In the calendar year 1875	$64,201,852
In the calendar year 1876	185,202,605
In the calendar year 1877	164,630,209
Making an aggregate of gold values	414,034,666

Excess of exports over imports.

	During the calendar year ended December 31.	
	1876.	1877.
Merchandise	$163,319,464	$140,088,657
Coin and bullion	21,883,141	24,541,552
Total excess	185,202,605	164,630,209

E. YOUNG, *Chief of Bureau.*

BUREAU OF STATISTICS, *March 16, 1878.*

Trade of the United States during the three years ended December 31, 1877.

GOLD VALUE.

	Year ended December 31—		
	1877.	1876.	1875.
Total domestic imports	$644,996,156	$623,709,566	$567,372,580
Total foreign exports	23,618,923	23,311,538	22,878,347
Total exports	668,615,079	647,021,104	590,250,936
Total imports	503,984,870	461,818,499	526,049,084
Balance in favor of the United States	164,630,209	185,202,605	64,201,852
SPECIE AND BULLION.			
Exports, domestic	37,429,661	47,973,762	70,108,852
Exports, foreign	10,883,006	8,380,713	9,194,662
Total exports	48,312,667	56,354,475	79,303,514
Total imports	23,771,115	34,471,334	22,896,148
Excess of specie exported	24,541,552	21,883,141	56,407,366

EDWARD YOUNG,
Chief of Bureau.

BUREAU OF STATISTICS, *March* 18, 1878.

RESUMPTION OF SPECIE PAYMENTS.

NOTES OF A CONFERENCE

BETWEEN THE

COMMITTEE ON BANKING AND CURRENCY

OF THE

HOUSE OF REPRESENTATIVES

AND THE

HON. JOHN SHERMAN, SECRETARY OF THE TREASURY,

April 1st and 4th, 1878.

MEMBERS OF THE COMMITTEE:

Hon. A. H. BUCKNER, *Chairman.*

Messrs. THOMAS EWING, AUGUSTUS A. HARDENBERGH, JESSE J. YEATES, WILLIAM HARTZELL, HIRAM P. BELL, E. KIRKE HART, BENJ. T. EAMES, S. B. CHITTENDEN, GREENBURY L. FORT, AND WILLIAM A. PHILLIPS.

WASHINGTON:
GOVERNMENT PRINTING OFFICE.
April, 1878.

COMMITTEE ON BANKING AND CURRENCY,
HOUSE OF REPRESENTATIVES,
Washington, April 1, 1878.

Present, Mr. Buckner, chairman;
Messrs. Ewing, Hardenbergh, Hartzell, Bell, Eames, Chittenden, Fort, and Phillips;
The Hon. John Sherman, Secretary of the Treasury.

The chairman read to the Secretary a copy of the letter sent to him on the 28th ultimo, in which were stated the several points upon which the committee wished to be informed at the conference set for to-day. The first was a statement showing the actual amount of gold and silver coin and bullion belonging to or in the custody of the Treasury Department on the 28th of March, where located, and what deductions were to be made from it on account of actual existing demands against it.

Secretary SHERMAN. I can give you a statement up to the 28th of February, 1878. I am not able now to give you the statement for the month of March, but can do it to-morrow or next day, and I will probably attach it to my answer. This, however, is the general result of the statement. We have at the Treasury, the different subtreasuries, assay-offices, and depositories:

In gold coin	$118,351,709
In gold bullion	7,937,300
In subsidiary silver coin	5,675,494
And in silver bullion	2,955,577

(See Appendix No. 3.)

I have also got the comparative debt statement, but I think I had better not put it in now, because I will have the complete statement made to-day. This being the first of the month, it could not be made up until to-day. (See Appendix No. 5.)

The CHAIRMAN. The next point called for by the committee is a statement of gold and silver coin and bullion in the Treasury, less the items deducted in your statement made before the Senate Finance Committee, from 1865 to 1877, inclusive.

Secretary SHERMAN. The Treasurer has tried to give that statement, as far as he can, but he could not give it complete, except as to the statement made on the 1st of February, 1877. In this statement he says this:

> The committee, in their inquiry No. 2, asked for a statement similar to the above, for each year from 1865. It has been found impracticable to comply, as to the years from 1865 to 1876, in the short time allowed, on account of the form in which reports from assistant treasurers and mints and assay offices were made prior to 1877. In fact, to make the statement as requested would necessitate correspondence with all the above offices.

I told him that as this statement gives you the items a year ago, and as you have also that statement for this year, that was all you would probably want. The amount of gold and silver available on the 1st of

February, 1877, was $11,936,771, after making the same deductions as were made in the table given to the Finance Committee, on page 4. This table (Appendix No. 2) contrasting with that table will show the condition of the Treasury as to gold and silver then and on the 1st of February of this year. The amount a year ago was $11,938,771, and the amount on the 1st of February this year was $71,775,860, making the increase of gold and silver available between the 1st of February, 1878 and the 1st of February, 1877, $59,839,089.

This statement (handing it to the committee) will give you the amount in silver coin, in silver bullion, in gold coin, &c.

There was another fact which I thought the committee would desire to have in this connection. I thought that the committee would want to know the distribution of this money on the 28th of March, 1878. We had in gold coin and standard silver dollars $114,666,958; in fractional silver coin $5,736,639; and in gold and silver bullion $13,664,914. The amount of silver standard dollars included in this is estimated at $454,711. (See Appendix No. 4.)

The CHAIRMAN. The third inquiry is the amount of bonds sold up to February 1, 1878, and not paid for.

Secretary SHERMAN. If that question means simply to inquire as to the amount of bonds not paid for at that date, my answer is that they are all paid for. There are no bonds issued unless they are paid for; but I suppose that what the committee means by this question is to ascertain the amount of bonds actually sold for resumption purposes, and also for refunding purpose. I have the distribution here; but in direct answer to the question it will be perhaps sufficient for me to say that there are no bonds which have not been paid for. We take subscriptions, but never issue the bonds until we get the money. An arrangement has been made with the Bank of Commerce, in New York, by which we allow that bank to collect currency and coin drafts for bonds, and when the coin is paid into the Treasury the bonds are sent to the person. The actual amount of bonds sold under the resumption act and under the refunding act is as follows:

Under the resumption act—

5 per cent. bonds of 1881	$17,494,350
4½ per cent. bonds of 1891	15,000,000
4 per cent. bonds of 1907	25,000,000
Total	57,494,350

The bonds issued on account of refunding are as follows:

5 per cent. bonds of 1881	$490,000,000
4½ per cent. bonds of 1891	185,000,000
4 per cent. bonds of 1907	55,000,000
Total	730,796,200

Which last sum added to the $57,494,350 on account of resumption makes the total $788,290,550.

I ought to say that the proceeds of all the bonds that were sold under the refunding act were applied to the payment of an equal amount of 5-20 bonds bearing 6 per cent. interest.

The CHAIRMAN. These bonds were sold at par, were they not?

Secretary SHERMAN. Yes, sir; par in coin. We paid out of the Treasury one-half of 1 per cent. for commissions and expenses.

The CHAIRMAN. The fourth inquiry is as to the usual amount of annual coin liabilities of the government, stating separately the liabilities for interest, sinking-fund, foreign service, &c.

RESUMPTION OF SPECIE PAYMENTS.   5

Secretary SHERMAN. I have this for last year. It is as follows:

Coin interest paid during fiscal year 1877	$92,883,431 27
Amount applied to the sinking-fund during fiscal year 1877	447,500 00
Amount paid for diplomatic service during fiscal year 1877	755,286 06
Amount paid for foreign naval service during fiscal year 1877	2,224,124 49
Amount of customs refunds during fiscal year 1877	5,247,800 65
Amount expended for refunding national debt, parting and refining bullion, &c., during fiscal year 1877	901,927 30
Total	102,460,069 77

You are aware that under the law importers very often deposit money in advance of their entries, and then, when their entries are liquidated, the excess is returned to them. That system is adopted in order to enable them to get their goods quickly. Also in some cases where disputes arise as to the amount of duties, if the duties are paid in excess, the excess is refunded. These refunds are in the ordinary current course of business.

The CHAIRMAN. This total of $102,460.69 is the coin payments for the last fiscal year?

Secretary SHERMAN. Yes, sir; divided up in the way I have stated.

The CHAIRMAN. The fifth question which the committee desired you to answer, is the amount of fractional currency redeemed and carried to the account of the sinking fund, and what applications of coin, if any, have been made on account of the sinking fund during the current fiscal year.

Secretary SHERMAN. The answer to that is:

The amount of fractional currency applied to the sinking fund in 1876 was $7,062,142.09, and in 1877, $14,043,458.05. So far in this fiscal year the redemptions of fractional currency amount to $3,382,621.45, making a total of $24,488,221.59 applied to that fund. No coin applications have been made to the sinking fund during the current fiscal year, except the redemptions of bonds heretofore called, amounting to $67,700.

Some cases occurred where bonds were sent on by parties by mistake, and we redeemed them; and they were put into the sinking fund. After that we adopted the habit of returning bonds that were sent by mistake.

The CHAIRMAN. The next question is, what is meant by balances in the sinking-fund accounts? Of what items are those balances made up?

Secretary SHERMAN. It is very natural for any person, lawyer or business man, to be misled by the use of the word "balance" in these sinking-fund accounts. A balance may not be a balance of money in hand; and, in this particular case, the word "balance" means either an amount of the sinking fund which has not been made good by the purchase of bonds, or an excess of the amount required by law. These are called balances, and this table on page 18 of the Finance Report shows very fully how the sinking fund is made up, and of what items it is composed. This table goes back to 1869, and shows at the end of that fiscal year a balance to new account; that is, the balance to new account is a balance in this case of an amount paid—more than the law required—into the sinking fund, and therefore it is put to the credit of the sinking-fund for the next year.

Then, the next year, they had not bought quite as many bonds for the sinking fund as the sinking-fund law required, and so there was a balance of $1,254,000 which was carried to the credit of the sinking fund to be made up the next year, and so on. These balances continued, amounting to somewhere between half a million and a million and a half of dollars. Sometimes they would be on the one side and sometimes on the other, and they were carried forward until 1873 or 1874, when, after the panic, the revenues fell off, and they failed to make good the sinking fund. The amount of deficit in making good the sinking fund in 1874 was stated at $16,305,000. Mr. Bristow, I am told, declined to carry forward this balance to the next year because it was apparent that, from the condition of the finances, he would not be able to make good that balance in addition to the sinking fund for the next year, and therefore the balance was dropped. It represents simply the amount which the government failed to apply to the sinking fund. Instead of carrying it forward in his accounts, the Secretary dropped it. That is what I did last year, and what Mr. Morrill had done. We did not undertake to carry forward the deficiency in one year to swell the sinking fund for the next year.

Mr. BELL. Then this term "balance" applied to the sinking fund indicates either the excess or the deficit in the sinking fund for the year?

Secretary SHERMAN. That is all. At first the balances were carried forward and were made good the next year, because they did not amount to much; but when the deficit became so great, and when it became apparent that it could not be made good, the Secretary just dropped it. Now, last year we were deficient in the sinking fund $9,235,000, simply because we could not, out of the surplus revenue, make good that fund.

The CHAIRMAN. On the whole, have not the deficiencies in the sinking-fund account been more than made good since the passage of the act?

Secretary SHERMAN. Yes. You will find a statement of that in Mr. Morrill's report. The sinking fund was never kept as an account in the Treasury Department until after the refunding act of 1870. A section in the refunding act provided for the stating of the account of the sinking fund, and then it was first commenced. Up to that time a statement was made showing how far the sinking fund had been kept under the act of February, 1862, and it was found that by the application of the surplus revenue to the payment of the debt, the stipulations of the sinking-fund act had been largely exceeded, to the amount of $200,000,000. Now the sinking-fund account is regularly kept, and the exact statement of it is shown by Mr. Morrill's reports and also by my annual reports.

The CHAIRMAN. Have you the report of the examiners at the sub-treasury office, New York, as to the coin there?

Secretary SHERMAN. Yes, sir; I have the preliminary report of Mr. E. O. Graves, which is as follows:

TREASURY OF THE UNITED STATES,
Washington, March 29, 1878.

SIR: I have the honor to submit a preliminary report upon the examination of the office of the assistant treasurer of the United States in New York, recently made under my direction in pursuance of the instructions given in your letter of the 11th instant. The funds found in the possession of that office at the close of business on the 12th instant, at which time I took charge (exclusive of currency and coupons in process of redemption and not charged to the cash), were as follows, the coin being verified by weight and the notes, currency, and securities by actual count and examination of each individual obligation:

Gold coin	$100,051,280 00
Gold bars	3,367,713 26
Coin checks, paid on March 12, 1878, but not charged up	1,069,114 78
Silver coin	1,396,436 28
Coin certificates	3,197,900 00
United States notes	32,614,479 00
National currency	428,711 00
Fractional currency and minor coin	194,088 92

RESUMPTION OF SPECIE PAYMENTS. 7

Redeemed legal-tender certificates of deposit, June 8, 1872	$3,335,000 00
Coin coupons	8,368 10
Coupons of District of Columbia bonds	110 41
Treasurer's checks for registered interest on District of Columbia bonds	273 75
Redeemed call bonds and interest	2,013 48
Treasurer's coin quarterly-interest checks:	
Funded loan of 1881	48,168 03
Funded loan of 1891	832,383 02
Funded loan of 1907	3,603 50
Receipts for advances on salaries of employés	2,421 00
Cash for petty expenses in cashier's hands	15 00
Seven-thirty notes purchased, being balance of amount of counterfeit 7-30 notes purchased, and for which judgment has been obtained in favor of the United States	8,750 31
Total	146,560,829 84
Total as shown by assistant treasurer'r report of March 12, 1878	146,566,996 35
Deficit	6,166 51

Only $1,777.51 of the deficit arose in the seven and one-half years during which the present incumbent has held the office of assistant treasurer, and of that amount $1,500 is due to a single shortage discovered in a package of notes received from a bank in payment of a draft, but which the bank refused to make good. This leaves a deficit from all other causes during the present assistant treasurer's incumbency of but $277.51; a most remarkable record considering the vast amount of money which has passed through his hands. The items composing the entire deficit will be explained in full in my final report.

Very respectfully, your obedient servant,

E. O. GRAVES.

To Hon. JOHN SHERMAN,
   Secretary of the Treasury.

The items of this deficit had been reported and known at the department, so that there was no actual variation between the statement as made by the assistant treasurer and the actual count. Perhaps I ought to say that this count occurred also here in Washington in July last, at the time that Mr. Gilfillan took possession of the Treasurer's Office. Every item and paper was counted before he gave his receipt for the money, and everything was found to be correct, except a small item of $1,831, of which we have a full account.

Mr. CHITTENDEN. I have prepared four questions in the interest of those whom I represent, to which I should like to have your answer:

First. With silver dollars and silver certificates full legal tender for all debts, including the customs and the public debt, is not gold practically demonetized; and how will you renew your supplies, or prevent its exclusive use as merchandise in foreign commerce?

Second. Is there no danger that the national banks, in taking care of themselves, will hoard greenbacks enough to exhaust your gold reserves when the day for resumption comes?

Third. Is it not probable that, before you have coined 100,000,000 of the new silver dollars, with greater activity in foreign trade, they will be exported at their bullion value to settle trade balances, and with what effect upon the price of silver bullion?

Fourth. Does not your success in resuming coin payments with our so-called double standard depend absolutely upon an advance in the price of silver bullion in London to about 59 pence sterling per ounce?

I have not spoken with any member of the committee in framing these questions. They were framed at my own table, and I am influenced only by my correspondence and by questions asked of me by those whom I represent.

Secretary SHERMAN. I would a great deal rather, in this conference give the committee the facts and let the committee draw its own infer ences, than attempt to give my own opinions. But I have no objections to answering any of those questions. I think that a certain amount of silver dollars issued will not have the effect which Mr. Chittenden thinks. I believe we can maintain at par in gold a certain amount of silver dollars; precisely what amount I would not like to say, because that is a question of opinion. But I have the idea that we can maintain at par in gold no less than $50,000,000; perhaps more—say from $50,000,000 to $100,000,000; but whenever those silver dollars become so abundant and so burdensome that the people would not have them and would not take them, and that they would not circulate, then undoubtedly they would gradually sink to the value of the bullion in them. That is my opinion, but I do not think it wise for either this committee or myself to discuss this question much, because the silver bill is a law, and, whatever we may think of its effects, the public mind will not be satisfied until that law is fairly tried. The effect of the silver bill is not going to be very rapid, nor will the fall in silver be anything like so rapid as is probably feared, and long before the silver dollar can sink to the value of silver bullion, Congress will undoubtedly correct the law if it were to have that effect. If, on the other hand, it should have the effect, which is anticipated, of raising the mass of silver up to the standard of gold, then Mr. Chittenden need not be afraid. Therefore, I say that I do not think I ought to give my opinion further on that subject. I have not changed my mind about the silver bill, although the newspapers say that I have. I think that (as a matter of policy) the silver bill, which makes silver available to pay bonds issued by the United States either before or after the refunding or resumption acts, is not good policy. I have stated that over and over again publicly, and I do not deny it. But the silver bill is the law. We are not infallible. It cannot operate quickly in that way, and therefore we had better give it the full benefit of an experiment, in the certainty that, if Congress finds that it has the effect which is now anticipated, Congress can at any moment stop the issue of silver dollars. I think that that is as far as I ought to answer these questions.

Mr. CHITTENDEN. It is not my object to embarrass the Secretary in any way in these questions.

The CHAIRMAN. The Secretary is of the opinion that "Sufficient to the day is the evil thereof;" that we will take care of the present, and let the future take care of itself.

Secretary SHERMAN. If you allow me, I can now, in connection with your question in regard to my opinion as to the practicability of resumption, and especially in regard to an interview published in the newspapers between Mr. Ewing and bankers in New York, give you my opinion. I have read that interview with a great deal of attention, because I know many of the gentlemen who took part in it.

The CHAIRMAN. It is proper for me on the part of the committee to say that it was not intended that that interview should be made public; but the report of it was surreptitiously obtained in some way.

Secretary SHERMAN. I do not think there was the slightest objection to publishing it.

The CHAIRMAN. Only probably on account of confidential relations.

Mr. EWING. We told those gentlemen at the conference that we had our secretary for the purpose of taking down their statements, not with a view to publishing them, but merely for the information of the committee, and the committee feels exceedingly annoyed about the publication, because it seems like a violation of that understanding; but the paper was surreptitiously obtained, and the committee does not feel at fault about it.

Mr. CHITTENDEN. Special pains were taken at New York to exclude newspaper reporters.

Secretary SHERMAN. It is pretty hard to exclude newspaper reporters; but I think it was right enough to have that conference published. It presents the opinions of very intelligent gentlemen, whose business it is to be familiar with the subject, and their opinions are entitled to full weight. I can only give you my general reply to them.

My reply would be about this: These gentlemen assume three propositions. First, that we cannot sell enough 4 per cent. bonds to prepare for resumption; second, that the national banks can throw upon the government the burden of resumption of bank-notes as well as of United States notes; third, that resumption requires the resumption and cancellation, without power of reissue, of United States notes below $300,000,000. To these I answer, that I believe that, with such auxiliary legislation as is pending in both houses, we can sell enough 4 per cent. bonds to prepare for resumption; but, if I am mistaken in this, we can sell either 4½ or 5 per cent. bonds, which they admit will command gold, silver, and bank-notes, to maintain resumption. Some of these gentlemen have proposed to me that, if I sell them 4½ per cent. bonds at par in coin, they will guarantee enough coin for resumption; and I have some better offers from other banks and bankers, so that, on this point, it is only a question of rate of interest on bonds. When it becomes clear that money cannot be had for 4 per cent., it is time enough to pay 4½. The silver bill has crippled my power to sell 4 per cent. bonds, but a wise savings bill, that will enable me to deal directly with the people, would go far to repair this. Upon the second point: It may as well be understood that the national banks cannot throw upon the government the burden of redeeming their notes. The attempt would be suicide. They are bound to redeem their notes on demand at the Treasury with United States notes or coin, and to maintain in their vaults very large reserves of United States notes. Any effort of theirs to force the redemption of their reserves of United States notes in coin would at once cause the government to withdraw all government deposits from them, to present all bank-notes held or received by the government for redemption, and, if need be, to exchange United States notes for bank-notes.

Such a struggle as these gentlemen contemplate would end in their losing their power to issue circulating notes at all. Their talk about forming a line to break the government is not discreet and is not dangerous. I am more concerned about what you will do than about what they will do. The United States Government already holds a larger cash reserve for the redemption of its notes in proportion to demand liabilities than any bank represented by these gentlemen, and it has power to increase it. Our certificates of deposit—the most dangerous form of liabilities—are secured, dollar for dollar, by coin or United States notes actually in hand, while the banks owe over $600,000,000 to depositors, the great body of which is represented by notes and bills discounted. The only demand liability we owe not covered by actual cash on hand is the United States notes, and of these $70,000,000 are in our vaults, and $70,000,000 more the banks are bound to retain in their reserves. With a coin reserve of $100,000,000 to $150,000,000, the redemption of $300,000,000 of United States notes would be easy, and that reserve could not be diminished to any considerable extent by the banks, or any combination of banks, without a continuous draft upon the banks to make it good. We can rely upon the intelligent self-interest of the banks to prevent such a struggle. Nothing could provoke it more quickly than threats by bank officers, and if such a struggle comes, the government, with its reserve, with ample revenue, and the power to sell bonds, can easily maintain resumption, without fear of a line of bank cashiers anxious to break the Treasury or to force high rates of interest.

On the last point: The power to reissue is plainly given by section 3579, Revised Statutes, and is not cut off any more by the notes coming into the Treasury in exchange for coin than in payment of a tax. Even if the Supreme Court hold them as no longer a full legal tender, they are as much so as a bank-note. If the choice must be made between the two, the common interest would decide in favor of the United States note. I believe they both ought to circulate and both be at par with coin. But nothing is so discouraging in the progress of resumption as for national banks to shrink from their share of the burden, or to make threats such as are stated by some of these gentlemen; and nothing is so injurious to the banking system, or will precipitate its overthrow more certainly, than a popular conviction that the banks are endeavoring to embarrass the government in maintaining resumption.

Mr. CHITTENDEN. I did not hear anything on the part of those gentlemen with whom we conversed at the sub-treasury in the form of a threat, and I appeal to Mr. Ewing to confirm my impression. There was nothing of that kind intended, I am sure. These gentlemen simply expressed the opinion that in an attempt to resume with any stock of gold that you were likely to have, the gold would be transferred to the banks naturally.

Mr. EWING. That was it.

Mr. CHITTENDEN. There was nothing like a threat?

Mr. EWING. No; on the contrary, there was a great desire manifested on the part of the bankers to make resumption safe.

Secretary SHERMAN. I have written propositions from these gentlemen, and from Mr. Coe himself, that if I will give them $4\frac{1}{2}$ per cent. bonds instead of 4 per cents., they will guarantee resumption. The trouble is this, that when I am trying to sell bonds at 4 per cent., they say I am acting both as a politician and as a financier. I suppose they mean that as a politician I am desirous to have the interest low, and that as a financier I am indifferent to the rate. I simply say that as soon as I cannot sell 4 per cent. bonds to the people, I know I can sell $4\frac{1}{2}$ per cents. to the banks; and in that way, if in no other, we can get enough gold to insure and to maintain resumption. To that I pledge my opinion and my earnest conviction.

Now, in regard to the reserve that is necessary, there is a difference of opinion. I would like to have so strong a reserve that there would be no question of our ability to resume, and I think (as I stated to the Committee on Finance of the Senate) that if I can have a reserve of one hundred and thirty millions; or, in other words, if I can increase my present reserve about fifty millions, I do not see how it is possible to prevent us from resuming. If it were known to-day that it was certain, I should have such a reserve by the first of January, and if it were certain that Congress would be willing to stand by the experiment of resumption, we would have resumption at once.

Mr. EWING. Neither of which can be made certain.

Secretary SHERMAN. Yes; if I could sell the bonds and get the reserve, the thing would be made certain in 24 hours.

Mr. EWING. Where do you suppose you could get so large a sum of metal?

Secretary SHERMAN. We produce bullion enough in this country. If I had this year's production of gold and silver (and I could very easily get it by selling bonds) I would have reserve enough.

Mr. EWING. Would you get any part of it abroad?

Secretary SHERMAN. Yes; some from abroad.

Mr. PHILLIPS. In your statement to the Senate committee as published, I understand you to say that there has been no increase of coin in the Treasury during the most of this year. Am I correct that you have not increased your coin through the months of January, February or March?

Secretary SHERMAN. No, sir. That is, we have not increased the coin belonging to the government, but the banks have increased on their deposits.

Mr. PHILLIPS. Is not the depreciated price of gold owing to the fact that the banks have taken it?

Secretary SHERMAN. No, sir; but simply because we went out of the market for the gold.

Mr. PHILLIPS. You have stated that you have not increased the volume of gold in the Treasury during this year.

Secretary SHERMAN. No, sir; because we have not sold any bonds.

Mr. PHILLIPS. Was the attempt made to sell bonds, and were you unable to do so?

Secretary SHERMAN. I have tried very hard to sell them and I could sell at a higher rate of interest. Let me explain that. The reason why I cannot sell bonds, is because they have got the impression in Europe that this silver bill is going to derange matters, and that belief brought back upon us (as these gentlemen say) seventy-five millions of bonds. As a matter of course, they came into competition with the Secretary in selling bonds; and as long as they had their bonds to sell, under a scaring market, I could not sell bonds unless the rate of interest was raised.

Mr. PHILLIPS. Then you cannot resume safely unless you can sell bonds at a higher rate of interest?

Secretary SHERMAN. I do not say that. I think 1 can. If you pass a bill to enable me to sell directly to the people I think I can sell 4 per cent. bonds.

Mr. PHILLIPS. How about 3.65 bonds?

Secretary SHERMAN. I cannot sell them.

The CHAIRMAN. I do not see how that is to aid you in resumption; because in selling bonds to the people you must sell them for greenbacks.

Secretary SHERMAN. Yes, sir.

The CHAIRMAN. The effect of all that is to equalize greenbacks with gold. Is that the theory?

Secretary SHERMAN. Partly that, and partly because with greenbacks we can buy gold or anything else. The law authorizes me to buy or to sell gold, and as a matter of course I can buy gold at the market price.

The CHAIRMAN. If the people paid greenbacks for 4 per cent. bonds, then you could sell these greenbacks for gold.

Secretary Sherman. Yes, sir.

Mr. BELL. You mentioned that the interest paid in coin was about ninety-two millions a year; have you any means of ascertaining what proportion of that amount is paid abroad.

Secretary SHERMAN. It is very difficult to state that. The interest.

is all paid to agents here, and we cannot distinguish the amount of interest that is paid to bondholders here, from the amount that is paid abroad. The best estimate that I can form is that the amount of bonds held abroad is about six hundred million dollars; but there is a difference of opinion about that. I think that that is pretty near the thing.

Mr. EAMES. I desire to present to the committee, in the presence of the Secretary of the Treasury, a consideration which, I think, is important in determining the question whether the government can resume or not in January, 1879. There is now outstanding about three hundred and forty-seven millions of greenbacks and three hundred and sixteen millions of national-bank notes, amounting together to some six hundred and sixty millions of paper currency. That is now used for the purpose of the business transactions of the country. The point to which I wish to direct the attention of the committee and of the Secretary of the Treasury is, whether the three hundred millions of legal tenders are not absolutely requisite for the business purposes of the country, and whether, therefore, there will be any very great desire to exchange them for gold.

Secretary SHERMAN. I do not think we have a great excess of currency now. These bankers say that there is not enough of currency. So long as there is a want of confidence in our ability to resume, it is likely that the greenbacks will be presented for redemption to some extent; but if we were so strong that the public mind was satisfied of our ability to resume, there would be no motive to present notes for redemption (especially when they may be redeemed in silver). Then, I agree that these notes will not be presented.

Mr. FORT. Would not a premium of 1 per cent. run these notes in for redemption, even with confidence restored?

Secretary SHERMAN. O, yes; but we must abolish the 1 per cent. difference.

Mr. PHILLIPS. Can you state any distinction between legal-tender notes and national-bank notes in regard to the obligation of redemption?

Secretary SHERMAN. Certainly, sir. We have nothing to do with the redemption of the national-bank notes. The banks can take care of that themselves, and they are doing it now. They have an enormous reserve.

Mr. PHILLIPS. It is stated in the papers of Saturday that you ordered the retirement of $767,000 of legal-tender notes for last month.

Secretary SHERMAN. Certainly. The law explicitly required that.

Mr. PHILLIPS. I thought that the law left it to your discretion.

Secretary SHERMAN. Not at all. The Treasurer of the United States, at the end of each month, on the report of the Comptroller of the Currency that such an amount of national-bank notes has been issued, retires and redeems from his currency reserves 80 per cent. of greenbacks. I have nothing to do with it.

Mr. FORT. Do you think that good policy?

Secretary SHERMAN. I do. That must be continued until the amount of greenbacks is reduced to $300,000,000.

Mr. PHILLIPS. Do you think it safe to reduce the volume of greenbacks to $300,000,000?

Secretary SHERMAN. I think $300,000,000 is enough.

Mr. PHILLIPS. Can you not safely resume unless you reduce the amount of greenbacks to $300,000,000?

Secretary SHERMAN. I cannot say that. The law provides a mode by which the currency can be reduced to $300,000,000.

Mr. HARDENBERGH. If Congress should adjourn, with the state of

RESUMPTION OF SPECIE PAYMENTS. 13

the finances as they are now, and without additional legislation, and with resumption fixed to take place on the 1st of January next, do you not suppose that the national banks will have to buy from thirty to fifty millions of gold to make themselves strong enough to meet resumption?

Secretary SHERMAN. Certainly; they are doing it largely now.

Mr. FORT. Do you still desire to cancel the forty-seven millions of legal tenders now outstanding in excess of the three hundred millions.

Secretary SHERMAN. I think it wise to stand by the present law.

The CHAIRMAN. Do you actually destroy this eighty per cent, of greenbacks?

Secretary SHERMAN. We reduce it monthly. The amount is stated in every debt-statement. It is an actual destruction of the greenbacks. The idea was that $300,000,000 of greenbacks can be easily and surely maintained at par in coin.

Mr. BELL. Is it your judgment that the volume of currency at $300,000,000 will be adequate to the business wants of the country?

Secretary SHERMAN. No; in my judgment the currency will be increased from time to time by the free action of the national banks, and I believe that the amount of circulation in this country, where we are accustomed to paper money, will be always largely in excess of what it would be in old countries where they hoard coin.

Mr. EWING. And in excess of what it is now?

Secretary SHERMAN. I am inclined to think that we can maintain the present volume of circulation—six hundred millions—but that is a larger paper circulation than was ever maintained by any other country. That is a question for the banks to decide for themselves.

Mr. PHILLIPS. Has not the volume of national-bank notes been steadily reduced since the passage of the resumption act?

Secretary SHERMAN. Certainly; because the banks chose to retire them. They have a right to do that, and they chose to retire them; I cannot control that. The Secretary of the Treasury has no more to do with the process of reducing the currency or of increasing it than any of you gentlemen—not near so much, because you can stop it and I cannot; I simply execute the law.

Mr. EWING. In your statement to the Senate Finance Committee I find the following:

TREASURY OF THE UNITED STATES,
Washington, March 18, 1878.

SIR: In accordance with your request, I have the honor to state the amount of gold and silver in the Treasury on the 28th ultimo, the date of the last debt-statement, which is as follows, viz:

Gold coin	$117,151,455 62	
Gold bullion	7,937,300 21	
		$125,088,755 93
Less amount to credit of disbursing-officers and outstanding checks	6,189,626 60	
Gold-certificates actually outstanding	44,498,500 00	
Called bonds and interest	6,818,677 29	
Interest due and unpaid	4,909,705 21	
		62,416,509 10
Available gold coin and bullion		62,672,246 83
Available silver coin, fractional		5,972,895 42
Available silver bullion		3,130,718 31
Total available gold and silver		71,775,860 56

According to this statement, the amount of gold and silver coin and bullion applicable to resumption, belonging to the United States on the last day of February, 1878, was $71,775,000. You then say that you have practically, for business purposes, $20,000,000 more of coin applicable to resumption, because you have deducted from the gold in the Treasury four items, making an aggregate of about $62,000,000, part of which you assume that you can use.

Secretary SHERMAN. Yes, sir.

Mr. EWING. Now, I ask you which of those items so deducted are practically available for resumption?

Secretary SHERMAN. The amount to the credit of disbursing-officers and outstanding checks varies but very little, because it rarely, if ever, gets below $5,000,000, and it varies from that up (the amount in process of disbursement), so that you can very fairly anticipate that fact (it is a business fact), just as a merchant can anticipate the coming in of his bills receivable.

Mr. EWING. Is not that banking?

Secretary SHERMAN. Every man does banking in that sense.

Mr. EWING. Would the Treasury be justified in disregarding outstanding existing interest obligations by applying the coin which was set apart to meet those obligations to the redemption of legal-tender notes?

Secretary SHERMAN. The Treasury will do just what any prudent individual will do; it will anticipate the demands upon it, and always have money to meet those demands. It is sufficient for me to say that the law authorizes the use in anticipation of coin-certificates. The amount of coin-certificates that may be issued can be 20 per cent. in excess of actual coin. The Secretary of the Treasury, from the known certainty that these coin-certificates will not be and cannot be presented all at once, and are not likely to be diminished in amount, can issue 20 per cent. in excess of the actual coin on deposit.

Mr. EWING. Yes, the law gives you that authority. What would 20 per cent. of the coin-certificates amount to?

Secretary SHERMAN. Nearly $9,000,000.

Mr. EWING. So that you might at this time issue coin-certificates to the amount of $9,000,000 beyond the amount of coin now in the Treasury?

Secretary SHERMAN. Yes, sir. The law authorizes that. I will say, however, that it has not been done. As to the next item, "Called bonds and interest"—$6,818,677—that amount is in the Treasury, and is always there. There is interest due and carried on the debt-statement for twenty or thirty years; but we count it as a demand that we must provide for, and it is covered by this deduction.

Mr. EWING. How much of that amount is for called bonds and interest on such bonds?

Secretary SHERMAN. The whole of it. We have now in the Treasury over $7,000,000 due to "called bonds and interest"—that is, bonds that are due and not bearing interest, but that are not presented for payment. Sometimes bonds come in three or four years after they are due, and they are then paid.

Mr. EWING. Can anything approaching that amount have gone beyond the ninety days when the payment of interest stops?

Secretary SHERMAN. Every dollar of that has gone beyond the ninety days. Whether that amount will be continuously in the Treasury is only to be told by a comparison of the statements of "called bonds and interest." I have no doubt that some of that amount will never be called for. You will find by reference to the monthly statements that the amount varies from month to month, but it is an item which can be counted on with almost as much certainty as any other item.

Mr. EWING. I notice from the Treasury report that the whole "slack" from the beginning of the government to August, 1877, is less than $2,000,000 out of the $7,000,000 of aggregate of called bonds and interest unpaid to date. I don't think you can very safely assume that the $5,000,000 of bonds under recent calls will not be presented.

Secretary SHERMAN. On the contrary, under the last call—which is charged up and included in this last statement (a call of $10,000,000, made on the 6th of December last and maturing on the 6th of March)—but $7,000,000 of bonds had been presented on the day before yesterday, leaving $3,000,000 not presented. That leaves two or three millions of that particular call. I do not say that you can rely upon it with absolute certainty.

Mr. EWING. This inquiry is to ascertain how much gold and silver can be certainly relied upon to redeem legal-tender notes.

Secretary SHERMAN. Well, I think you can fairly count on at least one-half of this $6,818,677 of "called bonds and interest." In all human probability there will be three or four millions of that amount that will not be called for.

Mr. EWING. Within what time?

Secretary SHERMAN. There will be that balance on that account all the time, because we are going on to make calls all the time.

Mr. EWING. But if you are pushed to get coin enough to redeem legal-tender notes you are certainly not going to continue the call of bonds; so that probably that item will disappear from your resources.

Secretary SHERMAN. In my judgment, we will go on and make those calls. Last year we accumulated $60,000,000 of actual gold in the Treasury, while at the same time we were making calls at the rate of $1,000,000 a day; and therefore your conclusion does not follow. If we had this question of resumption fixed beyond doubt, and if the people understood that it was to come, the bonds would be taken promptly and the calls would be rapid; because accumulation for resumption accompanies and is increased by refunding. The actual experiment shows it. Whenever we have made calls we have accumulated coin, until last December, when, by the agitation created here in Congress, it ceased. My calls were outstanding, but the bonds did not sell.

Mr. EWING. We are trying to ascertain the amount of coin which you can certainly use in redeeming legal-tender notes; and you say that in an exigency you can use that item of $6,818,677 of "called bonds and interest," or a portion of it. It seems to me that if the exigency arises you will be in such a condition that you will not be calling bonds and increasing your coin demand; and, therefore, that that fund is not available, and that you cannot safely draw upon it to redeem legal-tender notes; or if you do so in an extremity, you may not only fail of resumption, but also fail of paying the interest and principal of the debt.

Secretary SHERMAN. I say that having $62,000,000 of coin in our possession subject to demand liabilities (an aggregate sum), which by the experience of nine years is rarely diminished to the amount of ten or fifteen per cent. (never falling below $50,000,000, and sometimes going up as high as $80,000,000), we can fairly count that, in any probable state of circumstances at least $18,000,000 of that amount will be in the Treasury—not to be used (because I do not anticipate that our reserve will ever be drawn down to that), but that we may fairly count upon it as in the Treasury.

Mr. EWING. This accumulation has been during the period when legal-tender notes were not redeemable, but you certainly cannot assume that, because you have had that accumulation of coin in the Treasury heretofore when there was no redemption of legal-tender notes, you will continue to have it after redemption begins?

Secretary SHERMAN. I think we can assume if, when gold was not in circulation, there was a gold balance in the Treasury subject to demand without much variation, that, when all transactions are based on coin or paper redeemable in coin, this coin will remain in the Treasury. I believe that one of the first effects of resumption will be to increase the deposit of coin in the Treasury, because paper will be so much more convenient in all the transactions of life that paper will be used and the coin will be deposited with us. The subtreasury in New York will be, like the Bank of England, the place of deposit for all the coin of the country; and coin-certificates or greenbacks will be used for all current transactions, leaving the coin only to be drawn to meet the demands of foreign trade or the mutations and changes of supply and demand.

The CHAIRMAN. That would depend entirely upon the balance of trade?

Secretary SHERMAN. Very much.

The CHAIRMAN. That would be the key of the situation?

Secretary SHERMAN. Yes, sir.

Mr. EWING. You say, then, that at least $3,000,000 of this $6,818,677 for "called bonds and interest" might be used, if necessary, in the redemption of legal-tender notes?

Secretary SHERMAN. Practically. I would say that at least one-third of the amount, $2,000,000, might be so used. The next item of $4,909,705, "interest due and unpaid," stands in about the same position; in fact, it is more stable than the other.

Mr. EWING. You think that $2,000,000 of that could be used?

Secretary SHERMAN. Yes, and perhaps more. Here (showing a debt statement) are the items of this "interest due and unpaid;" much of it is on old loans. Very often people do not collect their coupons, but leave the interest to accumulate, so that this interest item is even more stable than the other item. This is the "interest due and unpaid" on outstanding bonds; the other is "the interest and principal of called bonds."

Mr. EWING. I see that this "interest due and unpaid" is made up chiefly on bonds not yet due. It therefore cannot run away.

Secretary SHERMAN. That always follows. Suppose a man who owns $10,000 of bonds neglects to cut off the coupons when they are due and lets them run for two or three months without collecting the interest, he is likely to do the same thing the next time.

Mr. EWING. But suppose it were understood that the Treasury was short of gold, would it not be likely that these overdue coupons would be run in for collection? In other words, could you safely use that fund to redeem legal-tender notes if you are pushed to that point?

Secretary SHERMAN. I do not think I would have occasion to use that fund, but I simply say (as I have said to the Senate committee) that while we can only surely count upon the actual coin on hand over and above our coin liabilities, we can yet, as business men, fairly understand that all of these demands, of which I have given the items, will not be presented at the same time, and that there will always be a balance of at least eighteen millions of them.

Mr. EWING. Do you count any of the coin-certificates in that category?

Secretary SHERMAN. Yes; I count 20 per cent. on coin-certificates.

Mr. EWING. You propose to issue 20 per cent. of new certificates beyond the amount of gold on hand?

Secretary SHERMAN. Yes, we could.

Mr. EWING. Which you may use for the redemption of legal-tender notes?

Secretary SHERMAN. I do not think I ever would, except in case of necessity, but the law authorizes it.

Mr. PHILLIPS. Have not our revenues, both from internal revenue and imports, been decreasing of late?

Secretary SHERMAN. Yes, but we have more gold revenue than we have gold expenditures.

Mr. PHILLIPS. But have not the revenues been decreasing this year as compared with the past year?

Secretary SHERMAN. Very largely this winter—especially in the whisky tax.

Mr. PHILLIPS. And will not the recent law in regard to whisky still further decrease the revenue?

Secretary SHERMAN. That gets me into legislative grounds, and I think you had better settle that question among yourselves. There is no doubt but that we will have a surplus revenue to the extent of a portion of the sinking-fund. I do not think that a deficiency can equal the sinking-fund.

Mr. PHILLIPS. The sale of bonds has been stopped?

Secretary SHERMAN. Yes, but we can renew their sale if we pay a higher rate of interest—if we issue $4\frac{1}{2}$ per cent. bonds. The time was (ever since I have been in public life) that it would have been looked upon as very remarkable to sell bonds at less than $4\frac{1}{2}$ per cent., and we are getting very strong when we refuse to sell bonds at $4\frac{1}{2}$ per cent. Never before in the history of the government have bonds been issued and sold at par at so low a rate of interest as four per cent.

Mr. PHILLIPS. You state that we have coin interest to pay to the amount of ninety millions a year. Do you think it would be safe to undertake resumption with that burden resting upon us?

Secretary SHERMAN. Clearly. If we have the power to reissue legal-tender notes at par, and the power to sell bonds, if necessary, we can undoubtedly keep the notes at par. Redemption would not go far before legal-tender notes would become scarce. I have stated that there were $70,000,000 of those legal-tender notes in our vaults, and there are also $70,000,000 of them in the custody of the national banks, whose interest it would be to keep them in their vaults.

Mr. PHILLIPS. Would it not be more to their interest to have the coin?

Secretary SHERMAN. These legal-tender notes are scattered all over the country.

Mr. PHILLIPS. The interest of the banks to get the gold might prompt them to send in these greenbacks for redemption.

Secretary SHERMAN. If you ask me whether 347 millions of legal-tender notes can be all paid with a hundred millions of coin if they are all presented on the same day, I will say no; but, with 600 millions of currency, you cannot purchase all the wheat and corn in the country in the same day.

Mr. PHILLIPS. Will not the mere act of resumption create a demand for gold which does not now exist?

Secretary SHERMAN. On the contrary, I think it will diminish the demand for gold. What would they want gold for?

Mr. PHILLIPS. These banks may wish to resume.

Secretary SHERMAN. They would rather resume in greenbacks. They deposit their gold with us for safe-keeping.

Mr. FORT. Would there not be a temptation for the banks to exchange their greenbacks for gold?

Secretary SHERMAN. I do not see what object they would have in doing it.

Mr. FORT. They would do it merely for the premium.

Secretary SHERMAN. But there would not be any premium.

Mr. EWING. How much of this item of "interest due and unpaid," $4,909,705, do you say may be counted as applicable to resumption?

Secretary SHERMAN. I would say about one-third of it.

Mr. EWING. That will be one million three hundred thousand.

Secretary SHERMAN. I never went into the division of this thing.

Mr. EWING. Then the item of "amount to credit of disbursing officers and outstanding checks," $6,189,626. How much of that can be used for resumption?

Secretary SHERMAN. You may count on the whole of it if you choose; because it is really only money in the course of disbursement. We always have in the hands of disbursing officers large sums of money, and every disbursing officer has a balance on hand, and we can reduce those balances to a large extent, or cut them off entirely.

Mr. EWING. You include "outstanding checks"; do you think you could count the whole sum they represent as part of the funds that could be used?

Secretary SHERMAN. No, sir.

Mr. EWING. How much of it?

Secretary SHERMAN. I cannot tell; because I cannot tell how much of this item is for "outstanding checks" and how much to the credit of disbursing officers.

Mr. EWING. Exclusive of those items you would only have on your theory $12,300,000 which you could add to the $62,000,000.

Secretary SHERMAN. It is totally immaterial whether you count that in or count it out. As I said before, my reliance would be on the actual coin reserve—to be increased as I have stated. I do not propose to resume on seventy-one millions of coin.

Mr. EWING. It strikes me that the addition of seventeen or eighteen millions, drawn from these four items, is not safe in calculating the resources for resumption.

Secretary SHERMAN. I think that if you ask any banker in New York how much of that fund is available for resumption purposes, he will put it higher than I do.

Mr. EWING. As a banker?

Secretary SHERMAN. As long as we are issuing United States notes, redeemable on demand, we are in the banking business.

Mr. EWING. And take the bankers' chances?

Secretary SHERMAN. We do it as a matter of course. We save the interest and have to do as bankers do.

Mr. EWING. You have got here under the item of "called bonds and interest" only $6,818,677. Has there not been a call of $10,000,000 since?

Secretary SHERMAN. No; there has been no call since. The last statement which you get to-day will include these "called bonds." The last call was made on the 6th of December, 1877, and matured on the 6th of March, 1878. It has been covered—about half of the amount—by the sale of bonds since the call issued.

Mr. EWING. Does this statement include all of the called bonds unpaid on the first of February, 1878?

Secretary SHERMAN. Yes, sir; all the called bonds that matured at that date.

Mr. FORT. What is the cost of selling bonds, including the expenses of the syndicate?

Secretary SHERMAN. One half of one per cent. is the limit under the law and our contract with the syndicate. The syndicate pays all the cost, including engraving, &c., out of the half of one per cent. Under the popular loan we pay one-fourth of one per cent. commission and pay the expenses out of the other fourth.

Mr. EWING. Going back to your statement before the Finance Committee, you add to the sixty-two millions of gold five millions nine hundred and seventy-two thousand dollars of fractional silver coin; do you regard that as available for resumption?

Secretary SHERMAN. Undoubtedly. We can issue that silver coin in exchange for United States notes to the full extent of the outstanding fractional currency; but, in my judgment, Congress ought to pass a law enlarging the limit of subsidiary silver to fifty million dollars.

Mr. EWING. Such an exchange would be a voluntary exchange on the part of the holder of legal-tender notes. I am not speaking of what you can buy with the subsidiary silver coin, but as to whether it is available for the *redemption* of legal-tender notes when presented.

Secretary SHERMAN. Yes; in my judgment that five millions of dollars will be all absorbed before the first of January.

Mr. EWING. But we are speaking of this as a redemption fund for the legal-tender notes after the first of January.

Secretary SHERMAN. If the five millions of subsidiary silver coin be paid out in exchange for United States notes or in current expenses, there will be left in the Treasury just so much the more current revenue which will be in gold.

Mr. EWING. But after resumption day you do not regard fractional silver as available for the purposes of redemption?

Secretary SHERMAN. Only to a small amount. We will still exchange silver coin for United States notes. But I think the whole amount now on hand will be paid out and gold will take its place.

Mr. EWING. The resumption law provides that the redemption of legal-tender notes shall be in sums of $50 and upward, and fractional silver currency is not a legal tender above $5. How, then, can it be counted upon as part of the *redemption* fund?

Secretary SHERMAN. Simply because it can be, and will be, probably, exchanged, as needed, for United States notes.

Mr. EWING. But after the first of January can it be used as part of the redemption fund?

Secretary SHERMAN. Yes, I think so; if it is used for the redemption of United States notes.

Mr. EWING. It is not a legal tender?

Secretary SHERMAN. That makes no difference. People come to us every day with United States notes for silver currency.

Mr. EWING. But I am speaking of using this fractional silver currency for the redemption contemplated by the law.

Secretary SHERMAN. I regard redemption as simply meaning paying, according to law, the United States notes in the coin which the holder has a right to demand. Any holder of a United States note may now come to the Treasury and ask to be paid in subsidiary silver coin. After the first of January we will pay him in silver dollars or in gold coin, just as he prefers. If we should redeem United States notes between now and the first of January to the extent of five millions of dollars, we have in place of it the revenue which comes into Treasury—probably in gold.

Mr. EWING. My point is this: that fractional silver coin cannot be counted as a fund with which to redeem, after the first of January, United States notes, because it is not a legal tender for as much as $50, and because, under the law, the presentation of legal-tender notes must be in sums of $50 and upward.

Secretary SHERMAN. I do not think it material for us to discuss that question, because that five millions of subsidiary silver coin will be used in exchange for United States notes precisely as the silver dollars will be.

The CHAIRMAN. You regard it as an asset in the Treasury for all the purposes of the resumption bill?

Secretary SHERMAN. Certainly. If you really want to drive me into the position, I can simply say that we can convert subsidiary silver coin into silver dollars and then we can pay it out. It is money there in the Treasury available for the payment of United States notes.

Mr. EWING. Might you not as well put in United States notes as money available for redemption?

Secretary SHERMAN. No; I think not. This subsidiary currency would, in the ordinary course of business, be paid out in lieu of other revenue, and would be replaced by gold or silver.

Mr. EWING. In the statement made on the 26th of February to this committee by the Treasurer, he says: "I am informed by the Director of the Mint that the amount of unpaid deposits belonging to private individuals and held by the mints and assay-offices on January 1, 1878, amounted to $2,114,000." Is that a proper deduction from the coin on hand?

Secretary SHERMAN. No, sir; that is a mint account.

Mr. EWING. But the amount in the mints is credited in your table.

Secretary SHERMAN. Only the amount belonging to the United States. There are private deposits of bullion under the law. That is a private deposit for trade-dollars. It is not a liability.

Mr. EWING. That is, the gold and silver are not counted in the statement of the amount in the mints?

Secretary SHERMAN. No, sir; that debit is for gold and silver deposited by private individuals for their own use.

Mr. EWING. In this statement you have got the available sum on hand at $71,000,000, without any deduction for accruing interest?

Secretary SHERMAN. Yes, sir.

Mr. EWING. Now, the interest which is accruing on bonds is to be paid by gold which has been accruing from customs, *pari passu?*

Secretary SHERMAN. Yes, sir.

Mr. EWING. You count all the gold thus coming in from customs as applicable to resumption, and yet here is a charge upon it of $17,277,000, up to the last of February, for accruing interest?

Secretary SHERMAN. The answer to that is that the interest is not due. If the interest is accruing, we have also revenue accruing. We have goods deposited with us and bonds issued for customs duties, but we do not count this as revenue, although the revenue is accruing with absolute certainty of payment, and will be paid within a year.

Mr. EWING. It is not fixed in amount?

Secretary SHERMAN. O, yes. The entries are liquidated and ascertained, and we hold the goods in bond; but we do not call that revenue, because it is not paid; and so it is with accruing interest. Interest, as it accrues, we count as such, but interest accruing will be met before it becomes due by revenue accruing.

Mr. EWING. But you have already credited your whole accruing revenue to your resumption fund?

Secretary SHERMAN. No; we have credited our accrued revenue. We do not in either case credit the accruing or prospective revenue or the accruing or prospective interest.

Mr. EWING. That is *retrospective* interest. It has accumulated to the extent of over seventeen millions to the date of your statement.

Secretary SHERMAN. It is no more fixed than the revenue which is accruing. This question of whether, in our liabilities, interest not yet due shall be counted has been variously discussed, and many take a different view of it; but I take it that the point is this: Can that interest be demanded on the 1st of March or on the 1st of April? Certainly not. There is accruing interest from the 1st of January to the 1st of July; but it is not due until the 1st of July, and cannot be counted, therefore, as a demand liability until the 1st of July; and in the mean time our ample coin revenues come in, and a great deal more than cover the accruing interest.

Mr. EWING. But as a matter of fact, if you take out that seventeen millions of accruing interest and say that you put that apart as a resumption fund, you will be short of revenue to pay your interest and to create the sinking fund, as the law requires.

Secretary SHERMAN. If we are bound not only to get gold enough to pay what is due, but bound to get gold enough also to pay what may be due in six months, as a matter of course we can never resume.

Mr. EWING. I think it fair enough to say that whatever you have on hand now which has no ascertainable charge against it may be counted as a redemption fund for the greenbacks, trusting to future revenue to meet the future accruing interest and liabilities. But the difficulty about this statement is, that you have taken all the gold in hand now, and have not counted the accruing interest, which amounts to the very large sum of $17,227,000 up to the date of your statement, while the law expressly sets apart the gold that has been accruing from the customs to meet the interest which has been accruing during the same time.

Secretary SHERMAN. No; but to meet the interest which has accrued.

Mr. EWING. The statement, I think, makes an incorrect impression on the public mind as to the amount of gold actually on hand for resumption purposes.

Secretary SHERMAN. But, according to your idea, you would have us accumulate seventeen millions of gold more to-day to meet an obligation that is not to fall due until July.

Mr. EWING. No; but my idea is that in your statement you should have deducted the $17,227,000 of interest accruing up to date from the amount of gold on hand, because that gold is pledged and set apart by the law as a special fund to pay this interest, and is not applicable to resumption.

Secretary SHERMAN. But we have other gold as sure to come in as the 1st of July will come, to meet that interest.

Mr. EWING. Yes; and you have other obligations to meet to the amount of all the gold hereafter coming in.

Secretary SHERMAN. We cannot be expected to pay a debt before it is due.

Mr. EWING. The receipts from customs for the fiscal year 1877 were $130,956,000. The receipts this year will be less, as the imports have fallen off. The interest on the public debt last year was $97,124,000. That interest this year will be a little less. The sinking-fund this year, according to the statement of the Treasurer, is $35,424,000, and the law sets apart customs as expressly to the sinking-fund as it does to the interest on the public debt. Section 3694 of the Revised Statutes provides that "the coin paid for duties on imported goods shall be set apart as a special fund, and shall be applied as follows: 1st. To the payment in coin of the interest on the bonds and notes of the United States. 2d. To the purchase or payment of one per centum of the entire debt of the United States, to be made within each fiscal year, which is to be set apart as a sinking-fund, and the interest of which shall be in like manner applied to the purchase or payment of the public debt. 3d. The residue to be paid into the Treasury."

Now, here is a special appropriation by law of the receipts from customs to the extent of the sinking-fund and of the interest on the debt, and these two items will this year, evidently, amount to the whole receipts from customs.

Secretary SHERMAN. I have already explained the operation of the sinking-fund. If we should undertake to do what you say we ought to do—set aside that $35,000,000 and apply it for sinking-fund purposes—as a matter of course, there would be at once a deficiency in the payment of your own salaries, and of all the other expenses of the government. Now, this sinking-fund is a well-known technical fund, and has been known from the foundation of the government. It is really nothing but a pledge by Congress that it will provide revenues enough, not only to pay the expenses of the government, but to pay, in addition, the sinking-fund of one per cent. upon the debt. Therefore the sinking-fund has been always used simply as a representative of the balance of revenues over expenditures. The current expenditures are always taken from the amount of revenues, and the balance is applied to the sinking-fund. If there is a deficiency in the revenue, so that there is no balance to be applied to the sinking-fund, of course that is the fault of Congress in failing to provide revenues sufficient to cover the appropriations, and the amount to be applied to the sinking-fund. That has been the established custom of this and other countries.

Mr. EWING. I am not speaking about the custom, but the law. The law says that the coin paid for duties shall be set apart as a special fund, first, for the payment of coin-interest on the public debt; and, second, for the purchase of one per cent. of the debt each year, and for payment of interest upon the accumulated sinking-fund. Now, I do not see how any custom or usage of the department, or usage of other countries, can change the obligation of the statute.

Secretary SHERMAN. Let me look at the resumption act, if you have it there, and I will show you that not only does it do that in express terms, but it has been held to do it by every administration. (Referring to the law.) This clause has always been held to apply to the sinking-fund in the form of surplus revenue: "And to enable the Secretary of the Treasury to prepare and provide for the redemption by this act authorized and required, he is authorized to use any surplus revenue from time to time in the Treasury not otherwise appropriated, and to sell, issue, and dispose of, at not less than par in coin, either of the description of bonds, &c." This passed January 14, 1875. It has been held, under this appropriation made in 1875, of the surplus revenue, that the excess of revenue over expenditures could be applied under it without regard to the sinking-fund; and that has been the construction put upon these words.

Mr. EWING. That is, by yourself, and Mr. Morrill, and Mr. Bristow, the only three Secretaries of the Treasury who administered that law.

Secretary SHERMAN. Yes, sir. That appropriation of surplus revenue has been held *pro tanto* to be an amendment of the act of 1870.

Mr. EWING. The words are "any surplus revenue from time to time in the Treasury not otherwise appropriated." Now in addition to section 3694 of the Revised Statutes which I have cited, there are, in sections 3688 and 3689, under the head of permanent annual appropriations, appropriations of the sums required for the sinking-fund. These provisions of law setting apart the customs as a special fund and permanently appropriating them to the sinking-fund, certainly are not affected by this provision of the resumption law, appropriating "any money in the Treasury not otherwise appropriated."

Secretary SHERMAN. I think it is; the words "surplus revenue" are not in it. That has been always construed to mean that sum of money which has been left after paying current expenses.

Mr. EWING. You mean always since the passage of the resumption law?

Secretary SHERMAN. I never saw that questioned. At all events it was so held, and acted upon when Mr. Bristow failed to make good the $16,305,421 of the sinking fund.

Mr. EWING. It was so held by the Secretary?

Secretary SHERMAN. Yes, sir; and was never questioned by Congress.

Mr. EWING. The subject may not have been looked into.

Secretary SHERMAN. That may be. As a matter of course, if Congress was to say that we should invest the sinking fund prior to and as against all appropriations made by Congress, it would leave a deficiency at once.

Mr. EWING. Congress has said it.

Secretary SHERMAN. I do not think that the fair construction. Still, that is a question for Congress and not for the Secretary.

Mr. EWING. The section from the Revised Statutes, which I have read, sets apart the duties on imported goods as a special fund for those two objects. A certain and permanent appropriation of the customs as a special fund, cannot reasonably be held to have been repealed or modified by this clause, which is usual to all laws—"out of any money in the Treasury not otherwise appropriated"—that is a common phrase in all statutes making appropriations.

Secretary SHERMAN. Look at the practical question. Would you have had Secretary Bristow, who met this difficulty in the first instance, refuse to pay the ordinary drafts for the expenses of the government to the extent of $16,000,000?

Mr. EWING. I would have had him execute the law, and most certainly and most especially I would not consent to the proposition that the resumption act overrides all the laws that preceded it, nor that the importance of resumption is so exigent and overwhelming, as that the permanent appropriations may be disregarded by the Executive in order to carry it into effect.

Secretary SHERMAN. All this you speak of occurred before the resumption law was passed. This very question about the application of the sinking-fund occurred June 30, 1874, and the resumption act was passed in 1875.

Mr. EWING. You are speaking of Mr. Bristow's interpretation?

Secretary SHERMAN. And Mr. Morrill's.

Mr. EWING. Not Mr. Morrill's. The resumption law passed before Mr. Morrill became Secretary.

Secretary SHERMAN. Yes; but, at all events, that question was determined by the department and was acquiesced in certainly by Congress, and rightly acquiesced in. I certainly take my share of the fault, if there is anything wrong in it, for I was then in Congress, of acquiescing in the construction that the ordinary expenses of the government must be paid before the sinking fund is attended to, and that if there is any deficiency it must fall on the sinking-fund.

Mr. EWING. But what warrant can there be for a ruling that this general power to provide for resumption by using "any money in the Treasury not otherwise appropriated" shall override the permanent appropriation of receipts from customs as a special fund to pay interest on the public debt and to keep up the sinking-fund.

Secretary SHERMAN. The answer to that is, that the resumption act expressly authorizes the use of the surplus revenue and the proceeds of bonds to carry the resumption act into effect; and you will see that the resumption act has been carried into effect thus far by the sale of bonds, even in the purchase of the silver bullion in the first instance. Mr. Bristow sold $15,000,000 of five per cent. bonds and used the proceeds of those bonds in the purchase of silver bullion, and so all that I did under the resumption act was done by the sale of bonds.

Mr. EWING. There has been this year applied to the sinking fund $3,000,000 of fractional currency?

Secretary SHERMAN. Yes; and I do not know how many United States notes. We have redeemed largely United States notes. Last month we redeemed $700,000. All that goes into the sinking fund.

Mr. EWING. Why?

Secretary SHERMAN. Because it is a part of the debt which is redeemed under the operation of law.

Mr. EWING. The sinking-fund section (3694), which I have cited, contemplates the purchase of bonds.

Secretary SHERMAN. Not necessarily.

Mr. EWING. I think it does.

Secretary SHERMAN. United States notes are a portion of the public debt.

Mr. EWING. I think that the sinking-fund act clearly contemplates the purchase of bonds only. The expression "one per cent. of the entire debt," simply means the mode of ascertaining the amount to be purchased. It further provides, "and interest on the debt so purchased."

Secretary SHERMAN. That is the computation of interest on the amount of debt as paid.

Mr. EWING. How do you compute interest on legal-tender notes?

Secretary SHERMAN. Probably at the current rate at which bonds are sold. I would not be able to tell you the exact rate last year, but the rule, I think, has been to compute the interest at the rate at which bonds were sold. Here is the computation. [Referring to it.] Page 18, Finance Report. I see that it is computed at 6 per cent.

Mr. EWING. Was there no redemption of bonds in 1876 for the sinking fund?

Secretary SHERMAN. Yes, a small amount.

Mr. EWING. This resumption law does not expressly provide that the legal-tender notes redeemed under it (80 per cent. of the issue of bank notes) shall be destroyed. They may be hereafter authorized to be reissued.

Secretary SHERMAN. These words in the act "until the amount outstanding shall be $300,000,000 of such legal-tender notes and no more," were held to mean a permanent retirement of notes in excess of that amount. If I ever had any doubt about that it was removed by the passage of the Revised Statutes, which re-enacts the old law about the reissue of United States notes. From that, taken with the resumption act, it seems plain that after the reduction of greenbacks to $300,000,000 had been reached, they may be reissued. The act provides that the reduction shall go on until the amount is reduced to $300,000,000 and no more.

Mr. EWING. I find according to the finance report of 1877, a deficiency in the sinking fund for that year of $9,225,000.

Secretary SHERMAN. That is correct.

Mr. EWING. And for 1876 a deficiency of $1,143,000; for 1875 a deficiency of $5,596,000; and for 1874 a deficiency of $16,305,000, making the total deficiency $32,670,000.

Secretary SHERMAN. I suppose that is correct.

Mr. EWING. If the gold received from the revenue had been applied, as this permanent appropriation requires, your stock of gold would be pretty largely reduced.

Secretary SHERMAN. Yes, and if the amount of money which had been applied to the sinking fund before the panic of 1873, in excess of the amount required by law, had been set apart for a resumption fund, we would have been at specie payments long ago, and that is what ought to have been done, in my judgment; but there is no use in "crying over spilled milk."

Mr. EWING. I understand that you feel at liberty under the usage to neglect any application to the sinking fund at all, if the purposes of the resumption law require it.

Secretary SHERMAN. No; I feel bound to do this, to apply the actual surplus revenue to the sinking fund; and that has been done. But when there is not sufficient surplus revenue to pay the sinking-fund I would let the deficit fall on the sinking fund. That is the way we have done.

Mr. EWING. And it has made a deficit in four years of $32,000,000.

Secretary SHERMAN. That is, the Government of the United States has failed to keep up the sinking-fund to that amount for the last four years.

Mr. EWING. And you do not feel required to apply any gold received from customs to the purchase of bonds for the sinking-fund?

Secretary SHERMAN. Except to the extent of the surplus revenue.

Mr. EWING. Even then you feel justified in paying the sinking fund in legal-tenders instead of in bonds.

Secretary SHERMAN. Yes; that is the construction put upon the law. We have a right to count the legal tenders and fractional currency returned under the operations of the law as so much debt paid. We do not retire any legal-tenders under any circumstances except in consequence of the issue of the national bank notes; but when legal-tender notes are retired in that way, we count them as so much debt paid and we credit them to the sinking fund.

Mr. EWING. And your construction of the statute is that the debt canceled must not necessarily be a bonded debt.

Secretary SHERMAN. That is the construction.

Mr. EWING. But that it may be a debt bearing no interest?

Secretary SHERMAN. Yes, sir.

Mr. EWING. And the Secretary of the Treasury is at liberty to fix the rate of interest on it?

Secretary SHERMAN. No; I do not wish to answer that in the affirmative, because my impression was that the interest was counted at the current rate. I have never had occasion yet to fix the interest.

Mr. EWING. In your statement to the Finance Committee of the Senate, as to the preparation the national banks have made for resumption, you have given the banks' statement showing the amount of gold held by them on December 28, 1877, as $5,506,556.

Secretary SHERMAN. That is the amount held by the New York City banks alone.

Mr. EWING. No; that is the amount held by all the national banks. All the national banks of the United States held $5,500,000 of gold coin on the 28th of December last.

Secretary SHERMAN. The banks have gold certificates, however. They own that gold in the Treasury and we do not count it as ours at all.

Mr. EWING. Is it counted in the $125,000,000?

Secretary SHERMAN. Yes. The amount of the specie of the banks, including gold-certificates, was, on the 28th of December, 1877, $32,907,750. That was the amount of coin and gold-certificates held by the national banks; but that amount is largely increased now. (See Appendix No. 6.)

Mr. EWING. Outside of the Treasury there is, it appears, $5,506,556 of gold in the banks. Do you think the actual gold coin in the banks has largely increased since then?

Secretary SHERMAN. I do not know about that; I think it has. There is an increase in the commercial cities; but I do not like to speak positively upon that point, because in a day or two you will have the actual returns from all those banks.

Mr. EWING. Adding the certificates held by the banks, $23,000,000, to the $5,000,000 of gold coin, you get the extent of their preparation for resumption.

Secretary SHERMAN. Yes, sir.

Mr. EWING. Unless you count the fractional silver coin as a redemption fund, which it seems to me it is not.

Secretary SHERMAN. The amount of gold held by the New York banks alone, including gold certificates, is $5,000,000 more to-day than the whole gold and silver coin in all the banks of the United States in December last.

Mr. EWING. Including gold-certificates?

Secretary SHERMAN. Yes, including certificates. The amount is $37,432,000, or $5,000,000 more than the whole amount in all the banks in the United States in December last. Now, as to how much gold has increased in the other banks I cannot say, but we will have the returns in a day or two, and perhaps in time to attach to this statement.

Mr. EWING. Probably $40,000,000 of gold coin and certificates together will represent the preparation of the national banks for resumption.

Secretary SHERMAN. It is more than that. The increase in the New York national banks alone from December to March was $13,000,000. All the great body of these coin-certificates is held by banks and bankers.

Mr. EWING. Do you think the aggregate of gold coin and certificates in the hands of the national banks would run up to $45,000,000?

Secretary SHERMAN. I should think so.

Mr. EWING. That $45,000,000, assumed to be held by the national banks and whatever amount you have in the Treasury belonging to the United States applicable to resumption, represents the whole preparation for the redemption of the $647,000,000 of paper money?

Secretary SHERMAN. So far as the national banks are concerned they have enormous resources. They are only bound to redeem their notes in United States notes, of which they have $70,000,000 on hand; they have also cash resources of various kinds as shown by this table, and very large ones. They have surplus profits to the amount of $173,000,000 over and above their capital stock. They have resources which will enable them to redeem in United States notes with great facility.

Mr. EWING. Their surplus profits are invested largely in buildings.

Secretary SHERMAN. They have invested largely in United States bonds. They have United States bonds on hand to the amount of nearly four hundred millions of dollars. They have $343,000,000 to secure their currency. Then they have bonds to secure deposits; and they have other United States bonds on hand; and they have very large cash funds. As a matter of course they have also very large loans and discounts, and they are liable to their depositors to a very large sum. But they have ample cash resources.

Mr. EWING. But I am speaking of the amount of gold and silver they have for resumption.

Secretary SHERMAN. The banks do not have to redeem any notes in gold; they redeem in United States notes.

Mr. EWING. After all, the problem is to float $647,000,000 of paper money redeemable in coin.

Secretary SHERMAN. Yes.

Mr. EWING. Now, is not the draft upon the government practically the same to the extent of the aggregate of the greenback circulation ($348,000,000), as though the entire circulation were money?

Secretary SHERMAN. I say no, emphatically; and all experience in other systems of banks would also say no. The truth is, the Government of the United States has nothing to do with the banks any more than it has to do with the other corporations and merchants of the country. The banks are as separate and distinct corporations as they can possibly be made. The United States have got to redeem $348,000,000 of legal tender notes, or to make them at par with coin. You recollect what I said before, that we have seventy millions undisputed money in coin.

Mr. EWING. I beg leave to say that I regard the statement as incorrect.

Secretary SHERMAN. Let me go on. We have seventy millions of coin and then we have seventy millions of currency in our possession, some of which at least belongs to us, and none of which is likely to be called for, unless it may be a portion of the certificates of deposit, amounting together to $26,000,000. Then we have these obligations on the part of the banks, which are not fictitious persons but strong corporations. They hold at least seventy millions in our notes and forty millions of gold or gold certificates in their vaults as a reserve at all times. Their notes are absolutely secured by United States bonds, so that if you take that into consideration it is very easy for us to resume. And then you must remember that the body of our notes is in circulation all over this broad country, scattered everywhere from one end of the land to the other. Now, is it likely that these notes are going to be rushed in for payment of them in coin?

Mr. EWING. I think it is.

Secretary SHERMAN. I say no; you have no confidence.

Mr. EWING. I have met very few who have confidence.

Secretary SHERMAN. I say that if you strengthen this reserve from seventy millions to from one hundred and twenty millions to one hundred and fifty millions, with power in the Secretary of the Treasury to sell bonds if necessary, and with power to reissue greenbacks, there is no danger of breaking the government. I do not think that anybody desires that. Everybody will be glad that the contest is over. Let us look out for ourselves and let the banks look out for themselves. The banks are not interested in running in our notes to get coin for them to embarrass us. On the contrary, these legal-tender notes are their money, and as long as they have them, they cannot be broken. Their notes are payable in our notes, and if they keep a strong reserve of our notes (and they will be interested in keeping a strong reserve), they give us aid practically by giving employment to our notes. There is no motive for them (unless there be a fear that we are not able to pay) to rush in and demand payment of our notes in coin. Now I can see very well that if we had a reserve of $130,000,000 of coin, with no demand liabilities whatever except for those legal-tender notes, we can maintain those notes at par in coin—scattered as they are over this country. It seems to me that there is no difficulty about it.

Mr. EWING. My question was this: Whether the general government, to the extent of its whole paper circulation outstanding, must not respond to the demands of the holders of the $647,000,000 of paper currency for conversion into coin?

Secretary SHERMAN. The government is bound to respond, to the extent of the amount of United States notes outstanding, but not one step farther.

Mr. EWING. Of course not.

Secretary SHERMAN. Very well. That is only $300,000,000. It is just as if Great Britain was behind that $300,000,000 of bank-notes—a separate and distinct power. We are under no obligation to redeem the national bank notes. On the contrary the banks are under obligation to redeem their own notes in our notes and we hold ample security for that. Anybody can present a national bank note at the Treasury, and the Treasury is ready to redeem it, having a deposit of 5 per cent. which the banks must keep good to redeem national bank notes. The banks are obliged to redeem their own notes in our notes, and they are therefore desirous to get our notes.

Mr. EWING. Suppose that through lack of confidence in your ability to maintain resumption, with the small accumulation of gold that you can obtain, there should be a demand for fifty millions of coin in any one month in New York. It makes no difference whether the demand is made on the banks for legal tenders, and then the legal tenders be sent to the Treasury for redemption, or whether the demand is directly on the Treasury, you have got to respond to the whole of that demand, and the gold has got to come out of the Treasury, because the banks have practically none in their vaults.

Secretary SHERMAN. It is scarcely a supposable proposition that you put to me that they could gather together in one mass an amount of legal-tender notes to break the Treasury if this reserve is anything like what I say. You can see as a matter of course that there are times when the Bank of England could not meet a demand for 25,000,000 pounds sterling in gold for bank notes. Perhaps at times the demand for half that amount would break it. But actual experiment shows that such a thing is practically impossible. The idea of accumulating $75,000,000 or $100,000,000 of United States notes and carrying them to the Treasury in the course of a month is practically impossible. The commencement of such a scheme as that would make legal-tender notes so scarce that it would be impossible to get them, and the very scarcity would increase their value so that they would be equal to coin.

Mr. EWING. They could very readily present at least their coin-certificates for redemption.

Secretary SHERMAN. Where are they? Scattered all over the country. The whole amount of money, including currency certificates in the city of New York, which is the great commercial deposit of the country, is only twenty million dollars, and they never get more than that. That is the amount of the aggregate. If they gathered every note and every certificate in all the national banks of New York, they would amount to twenty millions of dollars; and is it to be supposed that they would do that? Unless you maintain that we require to have as much gold on hand as there is paper money outstanding before we can have resumption, I do not see any difficulty about it.

Mr. EWING. Did I understand you to say that a demand for half of twenty five million pounds sterling on the Bank of England would break the bank?

Secretary SHERMAN. I do not know how much the reserve of the Bank of England is now, but the Bank of England, like all banks owe vast amounts of demand liabilities besides their notes. It holds the deposits of England. Every banking house in England almost, has an account in the Bank of England; and, therefore the danger which threatens the Bank of England would be the calling in of the deposits, and if notes to the amount of ten million pounds sterling were presented, in addition to the call of depositors, there would be such a draft upon the resources of the bank that the bank would have to suspend. But the advantage of our government now is that we have no demand liabilities not covered by actual money on hand. These national banks have six hundred million dollars due to depositors on call, but they have facilities to meet that liability. The strength of the United States Government is so much the greater from the fact that it owes nothing but these notes.

Mr. EWING. The gold coin and bullion of the Bank of England was, in December, 1877, one hundred and twenty-seven million dollars, and its entire circulation one hundred and thirty-three millions, so that it could pay its notes almost dollar for dollar.

Secretary SHERMAN. Yes; but add one hundred and twenty millions more that the bank is liable to be drawn upon for its deposits. How much does the bank owe its depositors?

Mr. EWING. One hundred and thirty-one million dollars.

Secretary SHERMAN. There is the danger. The call on the deposits might break it down.

Mr. EWING. Yet you do not seem afraid of the call of over six hundred millions of deposits of the national banks.

Secretary SHERMAN. I say that the national banks have ample resources in currency and United States bonds.

Mr. EWING. To pay the six hundred millions of deposits and to keep afloat three hundred and twenty millions of currency?

Secretary SHERMAN. They can not do it in a day, because it is not possible for the depositors to draw out their deposits in a day.

Mr. EWING. But contrast their situation with the situation of the Bank of England. The Bank of England has in circulation and deposits combined two hundred and sixty-six millions of dollars, and it has one hundred and twenty millions of coin against its circulation and deposits. Our national banks would have nine hundred and twenty millions of deposits and circulation, and have probably forty-five millions of coin to meet that; and yet you think that our national banks are in first-rate condition as compared with the Bank of England.

Secretary SHERMAN. You do not draw the distinction between our national banks and the Bank of England. The Bank of England occupies somewhat the position of our national government. But compare our situation with the Bank of England, and we are better off to-day.

Mr. EWING. You mean the Government of the United States?

Secretary SHERMAN. Yes. Let me give you the reason why. We have on hand one hundred and thirty-four millions of gold and silver; we have got seventy millions of paper money; which makes two hundred and four millions cash on hand in our Treasury.

Mr. EWING. You include money belonging to other people?

Secretary SHERMAN. So do you in your statement of the Bank of England.

Mr. EWING. This gold belongs to the bank.

Secretary SHERMAN. Take the full amount of the demand liabilities upon us and add them together, and then take the money which we have on hand, and we are in as good a condition as the Bank of England.

Mr. EWING. You are counting in the Treasury gold and legal-tenders which do not belong to the Treasury.

Secretary SHERMAN. No, that is a mistake.

Mr. EWING. The law expressly sets apart the gold on which certificates are issued as a special fund to redeem the certificates, so that it is not applicable to the redemption of legal-tender notes.

Secretary SHERMAN. But take the demand liabilities upon the United States and add them all together and then take all the money that we have got in the Treasury, and, I repeat, we are in a better condition than the Bank of England is.

Mr. BELL. Then your idea is that the question of sustaining resumption would depend, to a greater or less extent, on the amount of preparation on the day of resumption?

Secretary SHERMAN. Yes, sir; and after. I think we ought to be so strong that we can meet any reasonable demand made upon us.

Mr. EWING. The Bank of England has on hand in gold coin and bullion $120,000,000, and in the banking department $59,000,000 of notes.

Secretary SHERMAN. According to that the Bank of England has got $175,000,000 with which to pay $266,000,000. The total amount of demand liabilities on us is $407,000,000, and the total amount of coin and currency on hand $208,000,000. Add to that such an additional reserve as I propose to accumulate of $50,000,000, and it would make it $258,000,000 to meet $407,000,000, which is just about the proportion, according to the figures you give me, of $179,000,000, held by the Bank of England to meet its liabilities of $266,000,000. The disparity is not so great.

Mr. EWING. That is a statement of very little value, because you include gold and currency, which do not belong to us, and you lump it all in together; but if you put down your state of coin preparation for the obligations, which would be a coin demand after the 1st of January, 1879, you do not stand as favorably as the Bank of England.

Secretary SHERMAN. Considering that we have no demand liabilities except legal-tender notes, which have a pretty general circulation, I think that our condition on these figures is better than that of the Bank of England. Its liabilities are demand liabilities.

Mr. EWING. Will the reissue of legal-tender notes help you to maintain resumption?

Secretary SHERMAN. Yes; to have the power to reissue them; for if the greenbacks can be retained at par, and we can reissue them, it will save us from issuing bonds. We would only reissue greenbacks in exchange for coin or its equivalent. We would reissue them in payment of coin interest, but, as a matter of course, we could not reissue them unless they were equal to coin, just as the Bank of England would not issue a single note unless it was worth gold. We go on the supposition that the legal-tenders are on par with gold.

Mr. EWING. You have just now indicated a possibility of their not being at par with gold.

Secretary SHERMAN. No, sir.

Mr. EWING. You threw in the "if."

Secretary SHERMAN. The very moment you diminish the supply of greenbacks you bring them up to par again.

Mr. EWING. And your idea of reissuing greenbacks would be only to reissue them in exchange for coin?

Secretary SHERMAN. Or as a substitute for coin—to reissue them when they are at par with coin.

Mr. EWING. And you would reissue them for the purpose of increasing your coin supply?

Secretary SHERMAN. Yes, sir; practically. The public would be very willing to take the greenbacks if they were at par with coin, and as a matter of course they would be substitutes for coin.

The CHAIRMAN. Do you not think we could make them so if they were made receivable for four per cent. bonds?

Secretary SHERMAN. That is to be tried. I want to sell four per cent. bonds if I can. Whether, on actual experiment, four per cent. interest is enough in this country to induce the sale of bonds, Mr. Low and Mr. Chittenden can judge better than I.

Adjourned to Thursday morning, April 4, 1878, at half past ten o'clock.

THURSDAY, *April* 4, 1878.

Present, Mr. Buckner, chairman, Messrs. Ewing, Hardenbergh, Hartzell, Bell, Eames, Chittenden, Fort, and Phillips; the Hon. John Sherman, Secretary of the Treasury.

Mr. EWING. I ask your attention to a comparison of the condition of the Treasury for resumption with the condition of the Bank of England in 1819 and now, with the Bank of France this year, and with the banks of the United States in 1857 and 1861.

Secretary SHERMAN. When I said the other day that I thought the condition of the Treasury on the 1st of January next would be as good as the Bank of England, I had not then before me the actual figures or tables, but only spoke from a general knowledge of the facts. Since then I have given the matter a good deal of attention, and I have got some carefully-prepared tables, founded upon late information, giving the exact comparison of the condition of the Bank of England, the Bank of France, the Bank of Germany, the Bank of Belgium, the national banks, and the Treasury. These tables will show that pretty accurately.

[Secretary Sherman handed the tables to the committee, and they are printed in the appendix. The latest statement of the condition of these banks is found in the London Economist of February 23, 1878, and the older statements are found in McCulloch's Dictionary, a standard authority on the subject, on page 117.]

32   RESUMPTION OF SPECIE PAYMENTS.

Mr. EWING. I see you have given the figures of the Bank of France in pounds sterling.

Secretary SHERMAN. Yes; they are reduced to pounds sterling. I ought to say, explanatory of the statement which I have submitted, that there are two modes of making up the accounts of the Bank of England; one by dividing them into the bank department and the issue department, while the other is the consolidated statement.

Mr. EWING. How does this statement give it?

Secretary SHERMAN. It gives the consolidated statement—what is called the old form. The consolidated statement is but a combination of the two departments.

Mr. EWING. Still the consolidated statement charges to the bank the reserve on hand, does it not?

Secretary SHERMAN. If there is any material difference; perhaps I had better put it in both forms, because the Economist gives it in both ways. I will give here the table from the Economist:

ISSUE DEPARTMENT.

Notes issued	£38,698,020	Government debt	£11,015,100
		Other securities	3,984,900
		Gold coin and bullion	23,698,020
	38,698,020		38,698,020

BANKING DEPARTMENT.

Proprietors' capital	£14,553,000	Government securities	£15,203,201
Rest	3,414,161	Other securities	17,672,338
Public deposits, including exchequer, savings banks, commissioners of national debt, and dividend accounts	6,524,776	Notes	12,368,965
		Gold and silver coin	1,032,773
Other deposits	21,529,721		
Seven-day and other bills	255,619		
	46,277,277		46,277,277

Dated February 21, 1878.

F. MAY,
Chief Cashier.

THE OLD FORM.

The above bank-accounts would, if made out in the old form, present the following results:

Liabilities.		*Assets.*	
Circulation (including bank post-bills)	£26,584,674	Securities	£33,322,539
Public deposits	6,524,776	Gold and bullion	24,730,793
Private deposits	21,529,721		
	54,639,171		58,053,332

The balance of assets above liabilities being £3,414,161, as stated in the above account under the head "Rest."

Now, in regard to the United States, I have a statement here showing the apparent and probable condition of the United States Treasury on April 1, 1878, and on the 1st of January next. The only difference in these statements is that I add to the present condition of the Treasury the proposed accumulation of fifty millions of coin and a substantial payment before that of the fractional currency. I think it will be practically redeemed before that time. The actual results show the amount of demand liabilities on April 1, 1878, against the United States as

RESUMPTION OF SPECIE PAYMENTS. 33

$460,527,374, and they show the demand resources, including coin and currency, at $174,324,459, making the percentage of resources to liabilities 37. To show the probable condition of the Treasury on the first of January, 1879, I add the fifty millions of coin and I take off the fractional currency, and deduct estimated United States notes lost and destroyed, leaving the other items about the same. That would show an aggregate of probable liabilities of $435,098,400 and probable cash resources of $224,324,459, making 51 per cent. of the demand liabilities. The ratio of the Bank of England, at this time, is 45 per cent.; the ratio of the Bank of France is 65 per cent.; the ratio of the Bank of Germany is 58 per cent.; and the ratio of the Bank of Belgium is 25 per cent., all based upon the same figures. (See Appendices 7 and 8.)

Mr. EWING. Does not this statement charge to the Bank of England the unissued notes?

Secretary SHERMAN. No, sir; not at all. The notes on hand in the banking department are deducted from the notes issued, so that the circulation in the consolidated statement shows an aggregate of £26,584,674.

Mr. EWING. Does that include the amount of notes unissued?

Secretary SHERMAN. No, sir; the total amount of circulation, as shown by the issue department, is £38,698,020; but there is in the banking department some twelve millions of pounds. This statement deducts the notes on hand from the notes issued (which is proper), and gives the actual notes to be provided for at £26,584,674.

Mr. EWING. Is there not some error about that?

Secretary SHERMAN. Neither you nor I want to fall into any error about this; but my understanding is, that the whole amount of notes of the Bank of England issued by the issue department is £38,698,020; but the banking department has on hand £12,363,965, and in stating the amount of notes outstanding, they deduct that twelve millions from the thirty-eight millions, which ought to be done, because the twelve millions really belong to the Bank of England. Now, in stating ours we have done it differently. We have given the full aggregate without deducting the notes on hand, so that the account is more favorable to the Bank of England as thus stated than it is to us. If I am mistaken about this, I shall be very glad indeed to have you point it out, but I think I am not, because I have looked very carefully into it.

In regard to the national banks, here are some statements which are interesting to me and which were prepared in consequence of our interview the other day. I think they will be interesting to the committee. The first paper contains the circulation and deposits and specie of the State banks in 1857 and 1860, as compiled from statements in the finance report of 1876, pages 204 and 205. The next paper contains the circulation, deposits, and cash reserve of the national banks on the 28th day of December, 1877. The latest statement of the banks I cannot give you, because it is not yet made up. It was made in March last, and the returns are not fully in. This statement shows a general demand liability of $960,816,052, and it shows a total cash reserve of $145,019,338. The ratio of legal-tender funds to the amount of circulation is 48.4 per cent. The ratio of legal-tender funds to circulation and deposits is 15.1 per cent. The next paper exhibits the circulation, deposits, and cash resources of the national banks on December 28, 1877, on a different basis, counting the amount of national bonds owned by the banks and deposited with the Treasurer as money. This other table excludes them entirely. This gives the same figures, but counting the bonds at their nominal par as money, it shows this result: Total amount of liabilities $960,816.052, and total amount of cash resources

H. MIS. 48——3

(including four hundred and five millions of bonds) at $550,201.055. The ratio of cash resources to circulation is 183 per cent. and the ratio of cash resources to circulation and deposits is 57 per cent. (See Appendix No. 6.)

Mr. EWING. Do you think that the bonds can be counted as cash?

Secretary SHERMAN. Yes; the bonds are all worth par or above in gold.

The CHAIRMAN. The other cash held by the banks is legal-tender notes?

Secretary SHERMAN. Yes, and coin.

Mr. EWING. Do you think it safe to count these bonds as gold? Is it possible to convert them into gold?

Secretary SHERMAN. O, yes.

Mr. EWING. That is, the banks can sell over four hundred millions of bonds and get gold for them?

Secretary SHERMAN. Probably not to-day or in a moment.

Mr. EWING. At any time can the national banks accumulate four hundred millions of gold by sale of their bonds?

Secretary SHERMAN. Not in a day.

Mr. EWING. Or in a year?

Secretary SHERMAN. O, yes. I sold last year (within the year) of 4½ per cent. and 4 per cent. bonds two hundred and seventy-five million dollars.

Mr. EWING. How much gold did you get for them?

Secretary SHERMAN. Sixty or seventy millions of gold and the balance I paid for six per cent. bonds.

Mr. EWING. They were practically funded in other bonds. But I want to know now if you make up that table on the theory that these four hundred millions of bonds can be turned into gold for the purpose of resumption?

Secretary SHERMAN. I make up my statement on the theory that four hundred millions of bonds will more than pay four hundred millions of bank-notes at any time, such bonds as the banks hold, and that, if that is not so, we are bankrupt. I just give you this statement. Here also is an abstract of reports made to the Comptroller of the Currency, because these tables are taken from it. (See appendix No. 6.)

Mr. EWING. Here is a consolidated statement which I have prepared, and to which I wish to call your attention.

RESUMPTION OF SPECIE PAYMENTS.

MR. EWING'S TABLE.
THIS TABLE RELATES TO NO OTHER BANKS THAN BANKS OF ISSUE.

	Currency outstanding.	Deposits.	Total circulation and deposits.	Coin and bullion in the banks.	Estimated specie in the country.	Authority.
Bank of England, December, 1877	$133,950,000	$131,000,000	$265,550,000	$120,150,000	$772,000,000	London Economist's "Commercial History and Review of 1877." The specie deposits of the English country banks are unknown. The estimate as to the coin and bullion in Great Britain in 1875 was made by the deputy master of the British mint. (See Spofford's American Almanac, 326.)
English country banks, 1877	25,000,000					
Scotch and Irish banks	67,500,000					
Bank of England, 1818	130,000,000	32,000,000	162,000,000			Tooke's History of Prices, and Mushet's Inquiry into the Effects of Bank of England Issues. Palgrave's Notes on Banking says the amount of coin in England in 1819 was £10,000,000. The Bank paid out in 1821–'22 £12,000,000, and increased its stock from £3,400,000 in August, 1819, to £10,000,000 in August, 1822. Probable stock, $150,000,000.
English country banks, 1818	102,000,000					
Bank of England, 1822	87,925,000	18,000,000	105,925,000		50,000,000	
English country banks, 1822	40,350,000				150,000,000	
American banks, 1837	149,185,890	127,397,000	276,582,890	37,915,300	60,000,000	Report of Comptroller of the Currency, 1876. Mr. Webster's Speeches on the Currency, 1836. The excess of specie imported over that exported, between 1837 and 1843, was $30,000,000.
American banks, 1843	58,563,608	56,168,000	114,731,608	33,515,800	94,000,000	
American banks, 1857	214,351,000	230,350,000	444,701,000	58,349,006	240,000,000	Report of Comptroller of the Currency, 1876. Fawcett's Gold and Debt.
American banks, 1858	155,208,000	185,932,000	341,145,000	74,412,800		
American banks, 1861	202,000,000	257,229,000	459,229,000	87,674,000		
Bank of France, December, 1877	487,100,000	134,200,000	621,300,000	417,400,000	235,000,000	Report of Comptroller of the Currency, 1876. Amasa Walker. London Economist. Victor Bonnet's "Two Essays." French custom-house returns.
Imperial Bank of Germany, December, 1877	161,650,000	3,990,000	*236,000,000	120,850,000	1,400,000,000	London Economist. Fawcett's Gold and Debt. Official reports. Dr. Linderman's estimate (appendix to this volume, No. 9).
American banks and Treasury, 1878	643,000,000	614,822,900	1,257,822,900	†147,000,000	700,000,000	
					284,990,000	

* In this total of $236,000,000 are *not* included the deposits either of the Imperial or the other issuing banks of the Empire, of which latter there are thirty-two, but the average aggregate note circulation of all the banks, Imperial and local.
† This aggregate of $147,000,000 includes the coin held by the banks and bankers east of the Rocky Mountains, but does not include the subsidiary silver in the banks.

Secretary SHERMAN [examining the paper]. Your currency outstanding of the Bank of England is about what I have got it, about twenty-six million pounds; but yours is made up only to December, 1877, and mine is made up to February. I have no doubt that you have got this correct. There is no trouble about these figures, although we may sometimes look at them a little differently.

Mr. EWING. I cannot get the deposits in the English country banks.

Secretary SHERMAN. The great liability of the Bank of England is the deposits. I have no doubt that this table is substantially taken from the same authority, and I should like to have it go into the report of the conference as yours.

Mr. EWING. I wish you to state the probable amount of gold and silver, not including subsidiary coin, in the United States, outside of national banks and of the Treasury, and where it is or supposed to be.

Secretary SHERMAN. I am like you and like everybody else as to my knowledge on that subject. I have to depend upon the information from the Director of the Mint for it, and I can only give it to you as he gives it. This table here [handing it to the committee] gives that information from the best lights I can get, and I am inclined to think on the whole that it is about right, but I give it as the statement of the Director of the Mint, for I have no knowledge outside of that which I get from him and from the official documents.

[The paper, being an estimate of the amount of gold and silver bullion and coin in the United States on April 1, 1878, is published in the appendix No. 9, giving the total at $199,490,753 of gold and $65,500,000 of silver, making an aggregate in gold and silver of $264,000,000.]

Secretary SHERMAN. That statement is not only concurred in by Dr. Linderman, who has mainly prepared it, but it has been carefully examined by other officers of the Treasury Department who are familiar with the matter.

Mr. EWING. Have you with you the report of the sinking fund?

Secretary SHERMAN. In my report I refer to the sinking fund. I say:

"In the last annual report my predecessor stated that had the resources of the Treasury during each fiscal year, commencing with 1862, been sufficient to make a literal compliance with the conditions of the sinking-fund law practicable, a total of $433,848,215 would have been applied to that fund July 1, 1876; whereas the actual reduction of the debt, including accrued interest, less cash in the Treasury at that date, amounted to $658,992,226," or $220,954,459 in excess of the amount required by law to be provided for that fund. The details of the fund are given on pages 19–20 of my report.

Here is a table showing the excess or deficiency placed each year in the sinking fund since 1869:

Excess or deficiency placed each year in sinking fund, since 1869.

	Excess.	Deficiency.	Difference.
1869	$672,020 23		
1870		$744,711 80	
1871		257,474 32	
1872	2,823,891 46		
1873	1,451,588 95		
1874		16,305,421 96	
1875		5,996,039 62	
1876		1,143,769 82	
1877		9,225,146 63	
	4,947,500 64	33,672,564 15	
			$28,725,063 51

RESUMPTION OF SPECIE PAYMENTS. 37

Here is also a table showing the

Monthly redemptions of legal-tenders and fractional currency during the current fiscal year, to be applied to the sinking fund.

	Legal-tenders.	Fractional currency.
July, 1877	$670,112	$618,801 45
August, 1877	1,118,056	612,221 50
September, 1877	1,061,232	385,472 12
October, 1877	2,424,040	434,067 61
November, 1877	3,150,604	309,554 14
December, 1877	1,396,512	278,911 62
January, 1878	833,352	292,189 18
February, 1878	492,400	281,221 58
March, 1878	769,312	240,582 52
Total for 1878	11,915,620	3,453,021 72
Amount applied to the sinking fund during the fiscal year 1876	5,999,296	7,062,142 09
Amount applied to the sinking fund during the fiscal year 1877	10,007,952	14,043,458 05
Total	27,922,868	24,558,621 86

Now I want to show you also that the surplus revenue has not been equal to the sinking fund since 1874; but actually there has been more applied to the sinking fund than the surplus revenue during those years.

My report of December 3, 1877, will show the exact application of the amount. The amount of the surplus revenue is stated there at $30,340,577, which was applied as follows:

To the redemption of United States notes, &c	$10,071,617
To the redemption of fractional currency	14,043,458
To the redemption of 6 per cent. bonds for the sinking fund	447,500
To increase of cash balance in the Treasury	5,778,002
	30,340,577

That $5,778,002 has never been applied.

Mr. EWING. Is that thirty millions the sum of the sinking fund?

Secretary SHERMAN. It is the sum of the surplus revenue, the total revenue over expenditures. So that that five millions has not been applied.

Mr. EWING. Where do you expect to get the additional fifty millions of gold by January 1, 1879?

Secretary SHERMAN. You must see that for me to state too closely what I propose to do might prevent me from doing what I expect to do, and therefore I will answer your question just as far as I think you will say I ought to go. I answer, mainly from the sale of bonds. Indeed, in the present condition of the revenue, we cannot expect much help from surplus revenue, except so far as that surplus revenue may be applied to the payment of greenbacks and to the redemption of fractional currency in aid of the sinking fund. To that extent I think we can rely upon revenue enough to retire the United States notes redeemed under the resumption act; so that I would say that we can get the $50,000,000 of gold additional by the sale of bonds. As to the kind of bonds that I would sell, and as to how I would sell them, &c., I ought not to say anything on that subject at present, because you ought to allow me as an executive officer, in the exercise of a very delicate discretion, free power to act as I think right at the moment, holding me responsible for my action afterward. As to what bonds I will sell, or where I will sell them, or how I will sell them, as that is a discretionary power left with the Secretary, I ought not to decide that now, but to decide it as the case arises.

Mr. EWING. I understood you to say in your interview with the Senate committee that you would have to rely upon the natural currents of trade to bring gold from abroad; that is, that there cannot be a large sale of bonds for coin abroad. Is it on a foreign sale that you are relying?

Secretary SHERMAN. Not at all, but on a sale at home. Perhaps I might as well say that if I can get two-thirds of this year's supply of gold and silver, it will amount to a good deal more than $50,000,000, so that I do not have to go abroad for gold. If we can keep our own gold and silver from going abroad, it is more than I want.

The CHAIRMAN. For this $50,000,000 additional I suppose you rely to some extent on the coinage of silver?

Secretary SHERMAN. To some extent; silver and gold we consider the same under the law.

Mr. EWING. Do you expect to pay out the silver dollar coined by you for current expenses, or only for coin liabilities, or to hoard it for resumption?

Secretary SHERMAN. I expect to pay it out now only in exchange for gold coin or for silver bullion. I am perfectly free to answer the question fully, because on that point, after consulting with many members of both houses, I have made up my mind what the law requires me to do. I propose to issue all the silver dollars that are demanded in exchange for gold coin. That has been going on to some extent; how far I cannot tell. Then I propose to use the silver in payment for silver bullion, which I can do at par in gold. I then propose to buy all the rest of the silver bullion which I need under the law with silver coin. As a matter of course, in the current course of business, some of that silver coin will go into circulation; how much, I do not know. The more, the better for us. But most of it, I take it, will be transferred to the Treasury for silver-certificates (that seems to be the idea of the bill), and those silver-certificates will come into the Treasury in payment of duties, and in that way, practically, the silver will belong to the government again.

Until silver is so abundant that it becomes the acknowledged basis of coin transactions, we cannot pay out that silver for the ordinary expenses of the government, because we have not enough to pay all the expenditures in silver; and if the silver is maintained at par with gold, and if the United States notes are below par with gold, we cannot discriminate in favor of any class of creditors; we would, therefore, have to hold silver at par with gold until we either have enough to pay everything with it or until the legal-tender notes are practically at par with gold and silver. That is a matter over which I have no more control than any other citizen. The silver dollars being receivable for duties—the law allowing them to be converted into certificates which are receivable for customs—I must receive them; and I could not prevent, if I tried, the silver from coming into the Treasury, either for silver certificates or payment of duties. As to when I shall commence paying them out for the current expenditures of the government or in payment of the interest or principal of the debt I cannot tell, because that would depend upon the equality of the three kinds of currency—gold, silver, and paper. I do not know whether I make myself understood, but that is the general idea I have in my mind. As a matter of course, it being a great discretionary power which you have invested in the office of Secretary of the Treasury, while I hold the office I will be very careful to exercise that power so as to carry out in good faith the law as Congress has passed it, and that law, I think, contemplates that gold, silver, and paper shall be all brought on an equivalency.

Mr. EWING. Please state in detail the fund in the Treasury, other than gold and silver, applicable to resumption, and not covered by appropriations.

Secretary SHERMAN. It is very small. In round numbers, the $70,000,000 of currency in the Treasury, which is less than the average amount so held for the last five years, is subject to the following, viz:

Special fund for redemption of fractional currency	$10,000,000
Redemption of notes of national banks "failed," in "liquidation," and "reducing circulation"	12,000,000
Five per cent. redemption fund	9,000,000
Disbursing officers' balances	13,000,000
Certificates of deposit issued under act June 8, 1872	26,000,000

So that, you may say, some of those items are ours. First, the item of $10,000,000 for the redemption of fractional currency is ours; then the item of $13,000,000, held by disbursing officers, is ours. The two redemption funds, one of national banks that have failed, and the other in present redemption of national-bank notes (together $21,000,000), belong to the banks. We have to hold it, but the amount does not vary much. The certificates of deposit are less now than usual; they are only $26,000,000. I think that answers your question fully. (See Appendix No. 11 as to distribution of currency in the Treasury.)

Mr. EWING. No; what I desire to know is the funds in the Treasury other than gold and silver applicable to resumption, and not covered by appropriations.

Secretary SHERMAN. I do not count any of these as applicable to resumption.

Mr. EWING. You spoke the other day about $70,000,000 in the Treasury with which to maintain resumption.

Mr. SHERMAN. Not to redeem notes. That $70,000,000 is so much money that is almost constantly in our hands, and which cannot be presented for redemption. In that view only I spoke of it.

Mr. EWING. You did not speak of it, then, as a fund available for use in maintaining resumption?

Secretary SHERMAN. O, not at all; but as so much money which cannot be presented for redemption.

Mr. EWING. Cannot the $26,000,000 of certificates of deposit be presented for redemption?

Secretary SHERMAN. Yes; that much can be; but it is not likely to be. We have got the money to pay for it if it is presented, but it is not likely to be.

Mr. EWING. That depends upon the preferences of the holders of the certificates.

Secretary SHERMAN. Still, I can tell you that it is a great comfort to have $70,000,000, where it is not likely to be disturbed.

The CHAIRMAN. You are not liable to be called for it at any day?

Secretary SHERMAN. No, sir.

Mr. EWING. Then I understand that you have no right to use the special fund for the redemption of fractional currency?

Secretary SHERMAN. I do not think that we have any right to use any of that to redeem notes with, because we must redeem notes with coin; but, having this $10,000,000 on hand, it is ours.

Mr. EWING. Is it subject to use?

Secretary SHERMAN. It is pledged in law to redeem the fractional currency which is really lost or destroyed. If I have $1,000 belonging to a man who died without heirs I am pretty likely to fall heir to it; and that is the case with this special fund for the redemption of fractional currency.

Mr. EWING. What I desire to know is, not what the Treasury might be authorized by additional legislation to do for the purpose of resumption, but the resources of the Treasury under existing laws in legal-tender notes or bank notes that may be used in facilitating resumption. What are the items?

Secretary SHERMAN. I think that practically none of this fractional-currency money and none of this money on hand is available for resumption in the sense in which you use the term. It only lessens the burden of resumption to have the notes where they are not likely to be presented.

Mr. EWING. You certainly spoke the other day of this $70,000,000 as being a resource.

Secretary SHERMAN. I think it is, in this way: It is a resource, because it is like the notes of the Bank of England that are in the issue department. They do not have to be redeemed, or they are not likely to be redeemed, although they may have been issued. They diminish—to the extent that we hold these greenbacks in the Treasury—the amount of greenbacks outstanding among the people.

Mr. EWING. What has been the amount of sales of bonds per month since the last sales to the syndicate?

Secretary SHERMAN. Here it is:

Subscriptions received for four per cent. bonds per month since the last sales to syndicate

January, 1878	$2,846,550
February, 1878	744,200
March, 1878	1,445,450
	5,036,200

Mr. EWING. Then it would take four or five months of sales of bonds to meet outstanding called bonds?

Secretary SHERMAN. We will probably sell enough this month to meet the outstanding called bonds. I think we will be able to sell enough to cover the deficiency in the last call. I hope within this month to make an arrangement to sell, unless Congress should repeal the resumption act. I would like Congress to determine that. If it is not repealed I would undoubtedly sell, during the present month, a good deal more bonds. I would sell all the bonds that I wanted to sell.

Mr. EWING. Four per cent. bonds?

Secretary SHERMAN. That I cannot say. I will do the best I can. I would rather sell four per cent. bonds, and hope to do so; but if I sell any other bonds they will be sold at a premium. I can sell them in the market at above par.

Mr. EWING. Do you think that under existing law the legal-tender notes redeemed will be subject to be paid out as other funds returned to the Treasury?

Secretary SHERMAN. I think that the law is very clear that the amount of legal-tender notes redeemed in excess of $300,000,000 cannot be paid out. That is my construction of the law.

Mr. EWING. I am speaking of the others, and not those redeemed by the increase of bank currency.

Secretary SHERMAN. I do not think they can be issued. I think that those which are redeemed after the 1st of January, in excess of

$300,000,000, cannot be reissued under existing laws. I am not certain about it. It is a mooted queston; I would rather have your opinion on that than my own. It is a question which I would like very well to have Congress settle. The law proposes and provides for no mode of redeeming United States notes, except as bank-notes are issued (when eighty per cent. of United States notes must be redeemed). As the law provides for no other mode of canceling and destroying United States notes, it would seem to follow that all notes redeemed in any other way than under that law can be reissued, because the section of the Revised Statutes I mentioned provides that all notes which come into the Treasury may be reissued. But then, on the other hand, there is a provision in the resumption law which seems to contemplate that the amount outstanding on the 1st of January shall not exceed $300,000,000.

Mr. EWING. Provided the increase of bank currency is such as to bring down the legal-tender notes to $300,000,000.

Secretary SHERMAN. There is the question. That question I have never determined in my own mind. It may be that all the notes now outstanding, and which are not redeemed under the provisions of the resumption act, can be reissued.

Mr. EWING. If any can be they all can be, I think.

Secretary SHERMAN. That is a question I have not determined in my own mind. I have no doubt of my power to reissue all below $300,000,000. The law expressly provides for that; there is no provision of law which authorizes the reducing of them below $300,000,000. But the resumption act does contemplate the reduction of United States notes to $300,000,000.

Mr. EWING. Provided the bank currency is increased to such an extent as, under the provisions of that law, will reduce the greenback currency to $300,000,000.

Secretary SHERMAN. I frankly say that I wish and hope that that is the proper construction; for I do not want to retire greenbacks except as they are retired by the issue of bank notes, because I believe that that process will reduce them in time. I do not desire to hasten the process. But, as a matter of course, I would be very glad indeed if Congress would solve that question for me, just as I would like to have Congress solve the doubt which rests on the reissue of the $300,000,000.

Mr. PHILLIPS. You cancel legal-tender notes to the extent of eighty per cent. of the amount of national bank notes issued, but when these national bank notes are retired (as they have been to a far greater extent than they have been reissued) there is no means in law of reissuing legal-tender notes to that extent.

Secretary SHERMAN. The authority to reissue extends to every dollar of United States notes outstanding. Any of the United States notes that come into the Treasury in the ordinary course of business, either for redemption or in payment of taxes, I have the right to reissue.

Mr. PHILLIPS. That I understand.

Secretary SHERMAN. Then the question is whether that provision of the resumption act which contemplates the reduction of the volume of United States notes to $300,000,000 is a mandate to the executive officer not to reissue them until they fall below that amount. That is a question which I ought not to answer, because I have not made up my mind upon it.

Mr. EWING. But as to the legal-tender notes under $300,000,000, redeemed under the resumption law, you hold that you have the right to pay them out the same as any other fund in the Treasury.

Secretary SHERMAN. I do.

Mr. EWING. You have no more discretion respecting their reissue than you have respecting the reissue of notes received from taxes?

Secretary SHERMAN. No, sir; I issue them according to the exigencies of the public service. Still, you know that that is a disputed proposition. I know a very able Senator, for whose opinion I have great respect, who thinks differently. I think, therefore, that that is a question which Congress ought to settle.

Mr. EWING. Did any law-officer of the government, or any Secretary of the Treasury, give a written opinion to the effect that the authority given to the Secretary of the Treasury by the resumption law to use any surplus revenue from time to time in the Treasury, not otherwise appropriated, to prepare and provide for the resumption of legal-tenders, affects in any way the obligation imposed by that section of the Revised Statutes which declares that the coin paid for customs shall be set apart as a special fund, and applied, first, to the interest on the public debt, and, second to the sinking fund?

Secretary SHERMAN. No; I think that no law-officer of the government, or no Secretary of the Treasury, has yet authoritatively decided that question, as you put it now. The question which the Secretary of the Treasury did decide was, that United States notes and fractional notes, being a part of the public debt, may be included in the sinking-fund; and practically we have paid the full amount of the surplus revenue in that way and applied it to the sinking fund until last year. In one year, in Mr. Bristow's time, there was a deficiency of $5,000,000; and this last year I did not buy bonds to the extent of $5,000,000 of the surplus fund, so that the question which you now present, although it is presented to my mind very often, has not been decided, either by myself or by any Secretary of the Treasury or by any law, for the question has really never been presented in a way which made it necessary to decide it. My annual report will show the exact application of the amount of the surplus revenue. As, under the provisions of existing law, I was actually selling bonds under the resumption act, I did not see my way clear to go into the market and buy these bonds for the sinking fund, just as, during the whole of the war, the sinking-fund provision was held to be inoperative. While we were actually selling bonds, it was absurd for us to go into the market and buy bonds. The money lies in the treasury, subject to the order of Congress. If Congress directs that that $5,000,000 be applied to the sinking fund, it can do so, but it will only involve us in the same absurdity that the English were involved in when they undertook to carry out Sir William Pitt's sinking-fund law during their war.

Mr. EWING. But you can buy 6 per cent. bonds with it, and you can sell 4 per cent. bonds.

Secretary SHERMAN. I know that. We can sell 4 per cent. bonds, but what is the use of doing so?

Mr. EWING. What is the balance for the sinking fund?

Secretary SHERMAN. Five million seven hundred and seventy-eight thousand dollars.

Mr. EWING. Where is that—in the Treasury?

Secretary SHERMAN. It is in the general cash balance. It is in the coin accumulated. Mr. Bristow, in his report in 1875, mentions this very matter, and says that, in his opinion, the law requires him to call in bonds, and to invest this money; but Congress took no action upon it, and the result was that that year, or the preceding year, the balance over the surplus revenue, some $16,000,000, was not applied at all; and so, ever since the panic of 1873, there has been a balance not applied.

Mr. EWING. I don't think the surplus revenue has anything to do with it; what I wanted to know was whether any law-officer of the government, or any Secretary of the Treasury, had given a written opinion that the sinking fund was to be composed merely of surplus revenue under that section of the Revised Statutes which says that the income from customs shall be applied, first to the interest on the public debt, and second to the sinking fund.

Secretary SHERMAN. I can only say to you that established custom, as well as the theory of our government, would seem to require that any sinking fund provided for the extinguishment of the debt cannot be applied until after all current demands upon the Treasury are paid. Otherwise, the Treasury would be bankrupt whenever there was a temporary falling off in the revenue. For instance, the law which you read to me and which I helped to frame (the law of 1862), providing for the sinking fund, sets aside the receipts from customs to pay 1 per cent. of the debt. Now, although that was the law, just as mandatory as you have read it (requiring the sinking fund to be maintained at 1 per cent.), the sinking fund was never opened, nor could it be, during the war. The pledge was never carried out until the old floating debt was mainly refunded.

Mr. EWING. That was covered by the blanket of war necessity.

Secretary SHERMAN. Not at all. That matter was presented to Congress frequently on the ground that it was impossible to maintain a sinking fund until there was an excess of revenue over expenditure, and so it continued until I myself complained of it, after the war was over, insisting that while that was right during the war, it should not apply after peace, and we, therefore, carried through Congress a provision for the sinking fund, so that the money might be applied, so much every year, in pursuance of the old act of February, 1862, and so it continued to be carried out until the revenues fell below the expenditures, so as to make it impossible to pay the current expenses of the government, and to pay the sinking fund at the same time. Thus, from the necessity of the case, any Secretary of the Treasury was compelled to pay the current demands on the revenue before he paid the sinking fund, just as the manager of a railroad would be bound to pay his hands and furnish the fuel to run his locomotives before he would pay the interest on the first bonded debt.

Mr. EWING. Was not the public debt being reduced all that time?

Secretary SHERMAN. Up to the panic of 1873 it was being reduced all the time, and we paid more during all those years than the law required on what we call the sinking fund—that is, the redemption of the debt.

Mr. PHILLIPS. From what source did the payments come?

Secretary SHERMAN. From surplus revenues. And so it continued until 1873. Then, all at once, there was a deficiency of $16,000,000. Well, the Secretary of the Treasury, as a matter of course, would go on and pay the ordinary expenses first; and if there was any deficiency, he would report that deficiency to Congress, and if there was any fault about it, it was with Congress, for Congress should either provide additional revenues to keep up the sinking fund or else should reduce appropriations. Mr. Richardson was Secretary of the Treasury when the first trouble took place. The exact condition of the Treasury was given two months after the panic, and so on by every Secretary, and as Congress did not feel disposed (and I think rightfully—I was in Congress myself at the time, and take my share of the responsibility) to levy new taxes upon the people in a time of great distress, this deficiency in the sinking fund was allowed to continue from year to year until now, and I presume that it will be allowed to continue, although if Congress can see its way clear to levy a tax upon tea and coffee, to make good the sinking fund, I would like it very much. But I do not think Congress will do so.

Mr. EWING. I guess not.

Secretary SHERMAN. Because I do not think that the people would sustain Congress in it. So I do not think there can be any just criticism in throwing ou the sinking fund the actual deficiency in revenue, because any Secretary of the Treasury who would undertake to refuse to pay the current expenses of the government, and who would at the same time pay the whole amount of this technical sinking fund in the purchase and payment of the debt, would be overhauled very quickly.

Mr. EWING. I understood you to say on Monday that this appropriation in the resumption law, of any surplus revenue, authorized you to use any of the funds which would otherwise go to the sinking fund.

Secretary SHERMAN. Yes, for the redemption of United States notes and fractional currency, but not beyond that; I never claimed that.

Mr. EWING. For the redemption of the United States notes after the 1st of January.

Secretary SHERMAN. No, sir; we did not discuss that. The point you were putting to me was that we ought not to have used this money (which should go into the sinking fund) for the purpose of redeeming the United States notes and fractional currency, but that we ought to have applied it to the redemption of bonds; and I said in reply that the plain mandate of the resumption act requiring us to pay and cancel and retire the greenback notes was just as mandatory as the appropriations for your salary and mine.

Mr. EWING. Do I understand you now that the appropriation of "any surplus funds in the Treasury not otherwise appropriated," contained in the resumption law, will authorize you, after the 1st of January, 1879, to use funds which would otherwise go to the sinking fund in redemption of United States notes?

Secretary SHERMAN. My impression is that, under the resumption act, after the 1st of January, I can use all surplus revenue to pay any lawful demands on the Treasury of the United States.

Mr. EWING. That is, it gives you the command of the sinking fund for that purpose?

Secretary SHERMAN. Yes. If Congress fails to make enough appropriation for paying the current expenses, including any demand that may grow out of resumption, I would have a right, to the extent of the surplus revenue, to command those moneys, in order to carry out the resumption act, just as I would have a right to use it under any other act of Congress.

Mr. EWING. So that the sinking fund is not only subordinated to any subsequent appropriations by Congress, but is subordinated to this appropriation in the resumption law of the surplus funds, and is really the last thing which is to be looked after or provided for?

Secretary SHERMAN. Yes; for this reason: if I should fail to have money enough to meet the demands upon me for resumption purposes I am invested with the power to sell bonds; I would have the authority to go into the market and sell bonds. It would be idle for me to go into the market to sell bonds while I was actually buying bonds for the sinking fund. I would regard a demand made upon the Treasury for United States notes after the 1st of January next just like any other demand for a liability which I was bound to pay, and I can use all the means at my command, including the proceeds of the sale of bonds.

Mr. EWING. And the sinking fund?

Secretary SHERMAN. O, yes. The sinking fund, in my view, is nothing but the surplus of revenue over the expenditures. The nature of the sinking fund has been debated to an extent in folios greater than the folios you have got in this room. It was debated in the English Parliament in the famous Dr. Price controversy, which extended for thirty years, and that was the generally recognized idea of a sinking fund—that it was nothing but an agreement on the part of the law-making power to apply surplus revenues to a certain amount to the reduction of the public debt.

Mr. EWING. Has any law-officer of the government, or the Secretary of the Treasury, given a written opinion to the effect either that the sinking fund is subordinated to the special appropriations or to this general appropriation of surplus funds made in the resumption act?

Secretary SHERMAN. No; I do not think so. I know of none.

Mr. EWING. Has any law-officer of the government, or any Secretary of the Treasury, given a written opinion to the effect that the United States notes or fractional currency redeemed may be charged to the sinking fund?

Secretary SHERMAN. No; because I think that that is so clear that I would not ask for such an opinion. The United States notes and fractional currency have been regarded as a part of the public debt ever since their first issue, and in every statement of the public debt it has been always classified as a part of the public debt. In making up the statement of the sinking fund, you will find that we always included the whole aggregate of United States notes and fractional currency.

Mr. EWING. The law unquestionably requires that; but the law also requires that a sum equal to the interest of the sinking fund shall be applied annually.

Secretary SHERMAN. Yes; that has been done.

Mr. EWING. And if you put into the sinking fund notes that bear no interest, it is impossible to execute that provision for paying interest on the sinking fund?

Secretary SHERMAN. What is the sinking fund? The sinking fund is not the identical bonds that are canceled, destroyed, and burned. The sinking fund is neither the bonds paid and destroyed, nor the notes paid and destroyed. The sinking fund is like many other book accounts that are kept upon our books. It is a certain amount of money, and it is accumulated at the rate of 6 per cent. interest. It does not make any difference from what source the sinking fund comes.

Mr. EWING. If there were 5 per cent. bonds in the sinking fund, would you count interest on them at 6 per cent.?

Secretary SHERMAN. But there are no 5 per cent. bonds in the sinking fund. I fell into the same error the other day. I told you the other day that I thought that the interest was computed as at the rate of the bonds purchased; but, on inquiry, I find that I was mistaken, and that the habit has always been to redeem only the 6 per cent. bonds and to compute uniformly 6 per cent. interest on the whole amount of the sinking fund. The sinking fund heretofore has been always composed either of 6 per cent. bonds, United States notes, or fractional currency redeemed.

Mr. EWING. If you had 7.30 bonds in the sinking fund would you not compute the interest at 7.30, and if you had 4 per cent. bonds would you not compute the interest only at 4 per cent.?

Secretary SHERMAN. No, sir. The identity of the particular security is lost the moment that it is redeemed; and the sinking fund is computed at the rate of 6 per cent., because the 6 per cent. bonds are now available and can be paid off.

Mr. PHILLIPS. In case of the falling off of revenue, do you think that you would probably have to sell gold in hand to meet the current expenses of the government?

Secretary SHERMAN. If so, Congress would be in a very sorry predicament.

Mr. PHILLIPS. I am speaking of your power to resume.

Secretary SHERMAN. If Congress fails to give us money enough to meet its appropriations, we are broke. That is all that there is about it.

Mr. PHILLIPS. You would avail yourself then of the coin in your hands to meet the current expenditures of the government?

Secretary SHERMAN. Undoubtedly; but I cannot presume that our government is going to do that.

Mr. PHILLIPS. I observe that the currency balance on the 1st of April, 1877, was eight millions; a little over half a million on the 1st of this April.

Secretary SHERMAN. The balance now is greater than it was then. After I came into the office I established this fund of ten millions for the redemption of fractional currency. That fund had not been established until after I came in. The actual balance is $10,751,851, including that fund of $10,000,000. Formerly that fund had not been stated according to law.

Mr. PHILLIPS. But that fund had all accrued before this year?

Secretary SHERMAN. No, sir; it had not. It was never stated until after I came into office. It was required to be done under the act, and I thought that its not being done was a failure to comply with the act. I therefore directed it to be done.

Mr. PHILLIPS. That is held in legal tenders, is it not?

Secretary SHERMAN. Yes, sir.

Mr. PHILLIPS. But you stated a little while ago that, of your coin balance in hand, there was five millions that had come from the sinking fund.

Secretary SHERMAN. Here is the law under which that ten-million fund is required to be kept. It is the first section of the joint resolution for the issue of silver coin approved July 22, 1876.

It is as follows:

That the Secretary of the Treasury, under such limits and regulations as will best secure a just and fair distribution of the same through the country, may issue the silver coin at any time in the Treasury to an amount not exceeding ten million dollars, in exchange for an equal amount of legal-tender notes; and the notes so received in exchange shall be kept as a special fund separate and apart from all other money in the Treasury, and be reissued only upon the retirement and destruction of a like sum of fractional currency received at the Treasury in payment of dues to the United States; and said fractional currency, when so substituted, shall be destroyed and held as part of the sinking fund, as provided in the act approved April seventeen, eighteen hundred and seventy-six.

Now there is the answer, "Shall be held as a part of the sinking fund."

Mr. EWING. The answer makes against your construction, because *there* is a special provision of law that this non-interest-bearing security, when redeemed, *shall* go into the sinking fund. Why should that be put in the law if it was the law already?

Secretary SHERMAN. It had been done before that and afterward. This simply carries out the same thought and the same idea.

Mr. EWING. That is put in to accomplish a purpose.

Secretary SHERMAN. It is a negative pregnant.

Mr. EWING. It was an entirely unnecessary provision, if those notes so destroyed would necessarily go into the sinking fund.

Now, let me ask your attention again to the table you have given us of the items composing the seventy millions of currency in the Treasury.

That ten millions of a special fund for redemption of fractional currency cannot be used by the Secretary, nor the twelve millions for the redemption of the national-bank notes in liquidation, nor the 5 per cent. redemption fund of nine million dollars, nor the funds for which certificates of deposit are issued to the amount of twenty-six millions. None of those items are in the control of the Secretary for use.

Secretary SHERMAN. The ten millions and the thirteen millions are practically as absolutely paid off as if the amount of the United States notes outstanding were reduced to the amount of twenty-three millions.

Mr. EWING. But that fund of ten millions is not under your control under existing law.

Secretary SHERMAN. It is practically redeemed; it is in the Treasury; it is ours.

Mr. EWING. I am speaking of it as a resource. That cannot be used.

Secretary SHERMAN. I explained that before. It cannot be used to pay notes or anything of that kind, but it is none the less currency, which we do not need to provide for; that is all.

Mr. EWING. And the $12,000,000 held for redemption of national-bank notes in liquidation, that can't be used?

Secretary SHERMAN. No; but that is dead while the bank-notes do not come in. As they come in, they are redeemed.

Mr. EWING. Still, it cannot be used by the Secretary?

Secretary SHERMAN. No, sir; nor need it be redeemed.

Mr. EWING. Nor the 5 per cent. redemption fund nor the certificates of deposit?

Secretary SHERMAN. No, sir.

Mr. EWING. Then, of this $70,000,000, there would be only the $13,000,000 to the credit of disbursing officers, which the Secretary is at liberty to use?

Secretary SHERMAN. I would have to make the same explanation which I made in the beginning—that I do not regard the $70,000,000 as a fund on hand with which to redeem anything; but that it is $70,000,000 in hand which is not likely to be called for in coin, and that it lessens, to that extent precisely, the burden of resumption.

Mr. EWING. I understand that perfectly; but I want to bring out this fact definitely—that of that $70,000,000 there is but $13,000,000 that may be used (the balance in the hands of disbursing officers), and that the $57,000,000 cannot be used by the Secretary.

Secretary SHERMAN. No; but it is so much money that is locked up in the Treasury not to be redeemed. Therefore, instead of counting $340,000,000 of legal-tender notes liable to redemption, you may deduct the great body of this $70,000,000, just as in the statement of the Bank of England, which deducts from the total amount of notes issued all the notes held in the banking department.

Mr. EWING. I understand that; and with that explanation you admit my statement—that of the $70,000,000 only $13,000,000 can be issued and used by the Secretary of the Treasury under existing law.

Secretary SHERMAN. For the purposes of resumption.

Mr. EWING. For any purpose.

Secretary SHERMAN. We use it for the redemption of outstanding certificates and for the redemption of bank-notes. We pay it out every day. This money is the most active money that we have in the Treasury. We pay it out and receive it every day.

Mr. EWING. But not for any other purpose than that for which it is specially appropriated?

Secretary SHERMAN. It can only be paid for these particular purposes, but it is being paid out every day, and other money coming in its place.

Mr. EWING. Now, you make the amount of bank-notes of banks in liquidation by your statement to the Senate committee $21,000,000 or $22,000,000.

Secretary SHERMAN. I think that that includes not only notes of banks in voluntary liquidation, but of broken banks.

Mr. EWING. I read from your statement before the Senate committee:

On December 31, 1875, the amount was $346,479,756; on December 31, 1877, $321,672,505, and on February 28, 1878, the amount of bank-notes outstanding was $321,989,991; but the amount of bank-notes of banks in existence, not in process of liquidation, was $299,240,475; and the difference between these two sums being the notes of banks in process of liquidation, although the notes are in circulation, yet an equal amount of greenbacks are in the Treasury as a special deposit to redeem them.

That makes the difference between $321,672,505 and $299,240,475— about $22,000,000.

Secretary SHERMAN. I can tell you the explanation of that. I was correct in my statement before the Finance Committee. There are $21,000,000 or $22,000,000 of notes of outstanding banks in process of liquidation, of which $13,000,000 in United States notes is held in the Treasury, and for the balance we hold the bonds of banks that failed as security. The discrepancy, no doubt, is represented by the fact that we have not sold those bonds. I am surprised that we hold as much as $13,000,000 of notes, for we do not usually sell bonds until the proceeds are needed to redeem the outstanding notes of those bonds.

Mr. EWING. When a bank goes into liquidation it deposits greenbacks to redeem its notes.

Secretary SHERMAN. Yes; but failed banks do not. When banks fail we take possession of their bonds and we sell them only as we need the proceeds to meet their notes. I have no doubt that the great body of this $13,000,000 on hand is money deposited by banks which have voluntarily retired. They have to deposit greenbacks before they get their bonds. But in the case of banks that fail, we sell the bonds as we need the proceeds from time to time. That will doubtless explain the discrepancy.

Mr. EWING. That explains why the item is not $22,000,000 instead of $12,000,000.

Secretary SHERMAN. Yes; we can, if we desire, sell all the bonds that we hold as security for those broken banks, but the usual course is not to do so, but to give the stockholders the benefit of their circulation, and only to sell the bonds as money is needed to redeem the bank-circulation.

Mr. EWING. There is a fraction under $300,000,000 of national-bank notes outstanding, but the five per cent. redemption fund is only put down at nine millions; it should be fifteen millions.

Secretary SHERMAN. No; the explanation of that is this: As the notes of banks in operation come in we redeem them, and at the end of ten days, or oftener if the Treasury sees proper, these notes are returned to the banks issuing them, and are replaced by the banks with greenbacks. This redemption of bank-notes for the time diminishes the $15,000,000 or five per cent. fund to some extent, but at the end of ten

RESUMPTION OF SPECIE PAYMENTS.

days the redeemed bank-notes are sent back to the banks and replaced by other United States notes. In other words, there is a little leeway given there in the ordinary course of business.

Mr. EWING. That is only $500 to every bank. That would scarcely make the difference between $9,000,000 and $15,000,000.

Secretary SHERMAN. It will make it. Ten days' redemption makes about $5,000,000.

Mr. EWING. That explains the discrepancy, therefore.

Secretary SHERMAN. Yes; it is always so. Mr. Gilfillan has been of late very strict with the banks.

Mr. EWING. In case of a drain of gold from the Treasury, what measure would you resort to to check it—I mean after resumption?

Secretary SHERMAN. The Treasury ought to be so strong that the thing would check itself. You can scarcely imagine, in the probabilities of business, that, with no outstanding liabilities that are not covered by actual cash on hand except the $300,000,000 of legal-tender notes, the drain upon the government would be so great as to exhaust the reserve of $120,000,000. That proposition is all based, not upon the fact that $120,000,000 would pay $300,000,000—we all know that is not so—but upon the fact that it is impossible to gather together United States notes and to present them in such a mass and in such a continuous stream, and that the very effort to do so would raise the value of United States notes. Their convenience is so great, and the necessity for them so apparent, that such an effort would at once bring them up to par in gold. I think that a drain of five, ten, fifteen, or twenty millions would at once tend to bring up the value of greenbacks until they were at par in gold, and then there would be no object at all in drawing them out.

Mr. EWING. After resumption the greenback must remain at par in gold as long as the Treasury maintains resumption?

Secretary SHERMAN. Certainly; and while they are at par in gold they will not be presented to any considerable extent.

Mr. EWING. Of course, if there was an established difference of 1 per cent., or one-half of 1 per cent., between gold and greenbacks, the Treasury would be broken pretty quick?

Secretary SHERMAN. Yes, sir, or a quarter of 1 per cent.; there is no doubt about that.

Mr. EWING. Therefore, after resumption, greenbacks must necessarily be at par with gold so long as the Secretary is able to maintain resumption? Now, I am supposing a case of a drain of gold from the action of foreign creditors, or from any other cause, and want to know what means you would resort to to check it?

Secretary SHERMAN. I do not think that it would be necessary to resort to any means; but if it were necessary to devise some means, I would resort to such as have been adopted in other countries—the temporary suspension of specie payment. That is a question for Congress. The British bank act, which is so often quoted as the standard, makes no provision for suspension; there is no legal suspension of payment in England, nor does our law make any provision for it. If the government should meet such an adverse state of circumstances as to make suspension absolutely necessary, the government would necessarily have to take the responsibility of it, leaving Congress to determine whether the circumstances justified it. That has always been so.

Mr. PHILLIPS. Then do you think that the Secretary of the Treasury has the power to suspend specie payment?

Secretary SHERMAN. No, sir; but if demands were made upon the Treasury, which the Secretary could not pay unless he was to pay them out of his own pocket, he would have to stop paying. That is all there is about it.

Mr. EWING. When, short of the point of your actual inability to go further, would you feel at liberty to stop?

Secretary SHERMAN. That I cannot state. That will not occur in my time if you give me now such a reserve as I mention, and it will not occur at all, in your time or in my time, in my judgment. But we cannot anticipate what the future will bring forth. We do not know but that we may be involved in war, which would compel a suspension of payment, and we do not know what might be the effect of war in Europe.

Mr. PHILLIPS. I was going to ask you on that very point. Would not a general war in Europe result in raising the price of gold?

Secretary SHERMAN. Wise men differ very much upon that. I think that a general war in Europe would give such a demand for our agricultural products, and for everything that we produce and sell, that it would probably inspire confidence, and there would be less danger.

Mr. PHILLIPS. Might it not raise the price of gold as compared with currency?

The CHAIRMAN. Or might it not have the effect of sending our bonds here?

Secretary SHERMAN. We are not bound to pay for our bonds unless they are due.

Mr. EWING. But banks and others that hold gold would be tempted to buy bonds, and the gold would go out.

Secretary SHERMAN. I do not think so. I have shown you now in these figures that, with such a reserve as I have mentioned, the government of the United States is stronger for resumption than the Bank of England.

Mr. EWING. Is now?

Secretary SHERMAN. No; I say will be, if you give us the reserve I mention. It will then be stronger than the Bank of England.

Mr. EWING. You said on Monday that it is now stronger.

Secretary SHERMAN. I do not think that it is now, but I say that before the 1st of January, with an additional reserve of $50,000,000, and if you will provide enough means to carry on the current expenses of the government, with or without regard to the sinking fund, we will be stronger than the Bank of England. If you make good the sinking fund, we would be better off; but if you do not make it good, it does not affect the question of resumption. With that $50,000,000 additional (making our reserve $130,000,000 or $140,000,000), with the fact that our notes are of universal credit and are distributed throughout this great extent of country and among 40,000,000 of people, with the fact that $70,000,000 of our notes are now in the treasury not likely to be called upon, and with the fact that the banks have to take care of $70,000,000 more, which they cannot run in upon us without subjecting themselves to the violation of the law of their creation, with their notes absolutely secured by United States notes—if we cannot maintain specie payment, then it is impossible to maintain specie payment on a paper circulation.

The CHAIRMAN. That is on the theory all the time that paper and gold are equivalent?

Secretary SHERMAN. Certainly. Specie payment means the equivalency of gold and paper. It is on the theory that the 1 per cent. difference between gold and silver will disappear before the 1st of January that I propose to commence specie payments; but suppose that I am mistaken; suppose that your fears are well grounded and that I am over sanguine, as some people say I am, still, Congress will meet in December, and then the question will be so apparent to every man that, if the resumption act cannot be carried out, I shall come to Congress and say that I have been unable to accumulate this reserve, or that an adverse state of circumstances has arisen, and that I am unable to do what the resumption act requires of me.

Mr. EWING. But in the mean time the country is on the rack and torture of preparation for impracticable resumption.

Secretary SHERMAN. There you are mistaken. The process toward resumption is not a harsh process. What is harsh, and what has been of great weight upon the people, has been the effect of extreme paper inflation, resulting in the panic of 1873, sixteen or eighteen months before the passage of the resumption act. Last summer, when I accumulated $60,000,000 of gold, and was going on refunding the debt, every sign of prosperity was increasing and business was getting better.

Mr. EWING. In your conference with the Senate committee, you spoke of "this long, weary agony and struggle toward resumption," and I think that the country will agree with you that there is enough of agony in it.

Secretary SHERMAN. Wherever there is an evil caused by inflated money, the instincts of human nature lead men back to specie payment, and the whole process from 1873 down to the present time is a process toward resumption.

Mr. EWING. If the resumption law had never been passed, the country would have revived from the panic of 1873 during the year 1875.

Secretary SHERMAN. You and I, no doubt, differ very honestly on that point.

Mr. HARTZELL. What would be the effect of this resumption act upon the national banks and their depositors?

Secretary SHERMAN. I cannot see that it will have any injurious effect. Wherein?

Mr. HARTZELL. I understand from your statement here last Monday, that the national banks hold $600,000,000 of deposits. Lack of confidence might induce the depositors to go to these national banks and demand on the 1st of January, or soon after the resumption act takes effect, a large amount of gold.

Secretary SHERMAN. No; United States notes.

Mr. PHILLIPS. Which would command gold.

Mr. HARTZELL. And if the banks did not have them, and the supposition is that they could not——

Secretary SHERMAN. All the national banks in the country have but $70,000,000 of greenbacks.

Mr. HARTZELL. The banks would have to furnish to the depositors either gold or greenbacks, but they could not furnish either to half the amount of their deposits?

Secretary SHERMAN. No, sir.

Mr. EWING. The aggregate of deposits in all the banks, national, State, private, and savings banks, as shown by the report of the Comptroller, is $2,120,000,000.

Secretary SHERMAN (to Mr. Hartzell). Your question is a very proper one. I can only give you my idea. All banking is based upon the idea that a larger amount of paper money can be maintained in circulation than the money in which it is to be redeemed. Otherwise there would be no object in banking. The Bank of England and the small banks of England maintain a cash reserve varying from 9 per cent. up to about 33 or 40 per cent. The Bank of France and the Bank of Germany, which are really government depositories, maintain a large reserve. A reserve of 40 per cent. would be considered a very large reserve. The only answer to your question is that experience has shown, to the satisfaction of the banks, that their deposits will not be all demanded. If they are demanded they will be paid by credits. Most of these depositors are debtors to the banks, as well as creditors of the banks. They are customers. The balance of credits would pay off a good deal of the deposits of the banks, and experience shows that a certain amount of money on hand and available, with a good line of discounts to support it, is sufficient. As to the notes of national banks, every dollar of them is secured by United States bonds to an amount of at least 10 per cent. greater than the amount of notes outstanding; and these bonds are of such universal credit and ready sale that in the ordinary course of business they can be very readily converted into any kind of money.

Mr. EWING. What about the $1,500,000,000 of deposits in other banks than national banks?

Secretary SHERMAN. They are private individual debts; the government has nothing to do with them.

Mr. EWING. The government has certainly to consider them in the plan of resumption?

Secretary SHERMAN. It has to consider them just as it has to consider any other public fact.

Mr. EWING. More than that; they have a direct bearing on the practicability of government redemption, for the legal-tender note is the only paper money redeemable in coin, and on the $348,000,000 of legal-tender notes rest $300,000,000 of national-bank notes and $2,120,000,000 of cash demand deposits. That is all to be considered.

Secretary SHERMAN. It is all to be considered, but $10 will pay $100 of deposits in the ordinary course of business.

Mr. HARTZELL. Does the mere fact that the government will, on the 1st of January, be able to redeem all its legal-tender notes, bring us of itself to specie resumption? Is that what we mean by specie resumption?

Secretary SHERMAN. I mean by specie resumption not the payment of all these debts in coin, but I mean the equivalency of these United States notes with coin, so that the people will take paper at par with coin, and if they want the coin they can get it. I do not suppose that $1 out of $100 of greenbacks will be presented for redemption.

Mr. HARTZELL. The national banks are close corporations, as I understand, and there is a general understanding between them on all questions affecting their interests, as we find by their unanimity in applying for a repeal of the bank-tax.

Secretary SHERMAN. Mr. Chittenden here can tell you that there are no people who have such diverse views as the national banks.

Mr. HARTZELL. If it should appear that the safety and security of these national banks demanded it, could they not unite and get together such securities and present them to the Treasury as would drain the Treasury of all the gold that it has, and thus absolutely prevent, by their combination, the Secretary from carrying out the provisions of the resumption law?

Secretary SHERMAN. I do not think, in the first place, that they would attempt to make such a combination against the government, and, in the second place, I think that if they did it would be very easily met. It is not possible, with the amount of legal-tender notes which they hold—admitted to be about $70,000,000—that they could take the whole of them and present them to the Treasury. Such a thing is not possible, because the banks could not be brought into anything like a co-operation of that kind, nor could they keep up a continuous stream of demand on the Treasury; and then, besides, the Treasury has ample power to make the banks redeem their notes.

Mr. EWING. In legal-tender notes?

Secretary SHERMAN. Yes, in legal-tender notes.

Mr. EWING. Or in silver and gold?

Secretary SHERMAN. Yes; that would throw the gold back on the Treasury. Some of the papers thought that in my remarks the other day I threatened the banks. I did not threaten them, but there is no doubt about it that the Treasury would be stronger than the banks in such a contest. There is no danger that the national banks are going to combine to present their legal-tender notes to the Treasury.

The CHAIRMAN. It would be much more reasonable to suppose that the banks would agree among themselves that their obligations and operations would be in currency, and that their checks would be paid in currency rather than in gold.

Mr. HARTZELL. Suppose that the depositors in the national banks should run in and demand payment of their deposits; would not the national banks be bound to go under?

Secretary SHERMAN. The banks can pay their depositors in greenbacks, because greenbacks are legal tender.

Mr. HARTZELL. How could they when there are only about $220,000,000 of them in circulation?

Secretary SHERMAN. Then, if they cannot get them, how can they present them to us for redemption?

Mr. EWING. They have $70,000,000 which they can present in a week.

Secretary SHERMAN. How can they bring $70,000,000? The national banks in New York, where the largest accumulation of greenbacks is, have only got $11,000,000. I think it is sufficient to say that Mr. Hartzell's supposition is an impracticable one; first, because the banks could have no desire to do such a thing; and, secondly, because it could not be done. It would have to be a very slow operation, and with a reserve of $130,000,000 or $140,000,000 even that extreme danger could be met.

Mr. EWING. In case of an apprehension that the Treasury would have to suspend specie payments, and, consequently, that gold would rise, would not the banks want to convert their reserves, and would they not certainly convert their coin-certificates into gold?

Secretary SHERMAN. It might be; but a suspension of specie payment, or a sudden panic, never comes at a time when people are expecting it or protecting themselves. It always comes like an earthquake, when it is wholly unexpected.

Mr. EWING. You intimated a probability of a suspension by the government, from the running down of the coin in the Treasury.

Secretary SHERMAN. I say that such a thing might be possible.

Mr. EWING. The state of the Treasury is known all the time to the banks and to the public, and certainly the fact that the Treasury was running short of gold would create alarm, and would naturally cause the banks and other holders to precipitate their seventy millions of legal-tender reserves and their fifty-eight millions of gold-certificates on the Treasury.

Secretary SHERMAN. I can only say that the Bank of England has frequently run its gold down—at one time to a million of pounds.

Mr. EWING. Yes, sir; and the bank ran short once and then found a lot of one-pound notes, and they saved it from bankruptcy when gold could not.

Secretary SHERMAN. If you would ever run the Treasury down, so as to redeem the $140,000,000 of the present outstanding legal-tender notes, greenbacks would be so scarce that they would be taken readily by everybody, just as in England, when the bank balance ran down under the panic to one million pounds sterling, every one was anxious to get Bank of England notes. Everybody was eager to get them and to hoard them; so that I do not think this is a danger to be regarded.

Mr. EWING. I want to ask further about your means of stopping a drain. Would you not naturally withhold the greenbacks as they come into the Treasury, in case you became apprehensive at all of a drain of gold?

Secretary SHERMAN. I think I would. If it should so happen that there was a run upon the Treasury for greenbacks, I would not issue them until the run was over.

Mr. EWING. And until the Treasury felt as strong as usual?

Secretary SHERMAN. Yes, sir; and in that event I do not like to say what I would do. I would sell 5 per cent. bonds, if necessary, in an extreme case.

Mr. EWING. In such a contingency the banks would naturally contract their currency also.

Secretary SHERMAN. In case of a panic which would threaten to break the government, or to break the banks, as a matter of course the instinct is one of self-preservation; but that is so whether you have coin payments or currency payments.

Mr. EWING. I am not speaking of a panic, but of the state of the Treasury from time to time. If you find your gold running out, would you not hoard the greenbacks?

Secretary SHERMAN. Naturally; if I found the greenbacks coming in, I would hold on to them until they are called out again in the natural course of business.

Mr. EWING. For the purpose of diminishing the drain on the Treasury of gold?

Secretary SHERMAN. I might temporarily, until that drain passed; but ordinarily I would use them to redeem 6 per cent. bonds.

Mr. EWING. After the drain passed, what would you do?

Secretary SHERMAN. I would pay them out again.

Mr. EWING. That is, you would do very much as the Bank of England does—you would stop the movement of the currency out of the Treasury, as far as practicable?

Secretary SHERMAN. Yes, sir; and, as a matter of course, Congress would be in session from time to time and could be applied to. It may be that Congress may, by future legislation, provide for that contingency.

Mr. EWING. Have you any apprehension that the banks, before resumption day, will present their gold-certificates?

Secretary SHERMAN. I wish they would.

Mr. EWING. That would put a stop to your power to issue certificates to the amount of 20 per cent. beyond the gold on hand.

Secretary SHERMAN. It might, but there is no prospect of that. The power to issue certificates to the extent of 20 per cent. is a power which, up to this time, has not been exercised, and which would not be exercised except in an extreme case. But what motive would the banks have to withdraw the money deposited with us? It is deposited with us for safe keeping, and they would only withdraw it from a fear that it was not safe.

Mr. EWING. Might not the fact that there is a contingency in which

RESUMPTION OF SPECIE PAYMENTS. 55

you might issue coin-certificates in excess of the coin in the Treasury lead the banks to feel that they had better get their gold?

Secretary SHERMAN. I do not think so; but at any rate it is safe to say that that thing has not been done, and probably would not be done, except in an extreme emergency, such as would justify the Bank of England in issuing notes when it would not pay gold.

Mr. EWING. Is there not a further reason why the banks would take possession of their gold, when you reach specie payments, which is that they must pay gold when the gold is asked for?

Secretary SHERMAN. No.

Mr. EWING. Otherwise they will receive no deposits in gold.

Secretary SHERMAN. The banks under the law can always redeem in legal-tender notes.

Mr. EWING. I know that, but if they are to receive deposits in gold they certainly must pay their depositors in gold where the depositors want it. They must treat gold and paper as equivalent exactly, and, therefore, they must have gold on hand to pay those who want gold, otherwise they will not receive a dollar in gold deposits except as special deposits.

Secretary SHERMAN. The fact is that but little gold is paid even on coin payments.

Mr. EWING. But, as a matter of fact, must not the banks have the gold to pay whenever it is demanded?

Secretary SHERMAN. Yes, sir; on deposits they agree to pay in gold. As a matter of fact, they have some gold to pay now. They have gold in all the city banks, and the reserve of gold in the New York banks is very large; but there is no gold needed in Lancaster or Mansfield, Ohio, where you and I live; what do they need it for?

Mr. EWING. When you get to specie payments plenty of people will want to hoard it.

Secretary SHERMAN. No; they will hoard silver dollars. The class of people who hoard money are those to whom small sums are great ones.

Mr. EWING. The amount of gold in the banks now is very small, because there is a very small amount of obligations payable in gold; but after resumption day, when you establish that paper and gold and silver are equivalents, a large body of the bank depositors may want gold, and the banks must give gold to their customers who want it. Do you think it necessary to get the amount of legal-tender notes down to $300,000,000 before the 1st of January, 1879, in order to resume with safety?

Secretary SHERMAN. I would like to have it so, but even if I do not succeed, I would not postpone resumption on that account.

Mr. EWING. In the three and a quarter years since the resumption law was enacted, $35,000,000 of legal-tenders have been drawn in and canceled; is there any probability that, in the time left between now and resumption day, the remaining $47,000,000 can be retired?

Secretary SHERMAN. No; I think not.

Mr. EWING. Do you anticipate any considerable reduction of legal-tender notes by the increase of bank currency by next January?

Secretary SHERMAN. Yes, sir; last month there was a reduction of $1,000,000. I think that the amount will depend very much on the degree of confidence in the future which prevails in banking circles.

Mr. EWING. That is as to maintaining resumption?

Secretary SHERMAN. Yes, sir; that estimate of the amount will be reduced, probably, $1,000,000 a month.

Mr. EWING. That would leave you with $340,000,000 of legal-tender notes outstanding.

Secretary SHERMAN. Then I think we can fairly state that this money in the Treasury (that is, the balances held by disbursing officers, the $10,000,000 fund for the redemption of fractional currency, and the money held for the redemption of bank-notes on failed banks) will probably reduce it to the neighborhood of $300,000,000, nominally.

Mr. EWING. Still that $16,000,000 to disbursing officers goes out.

Secretary SHERMAN. But there is always about that much on hand.

Mr. EWING. But I understand that you want to reduce the total volume of legal-tender currency to $300,000,000.

Secretary SHERMAN. I do.

Mr. EWING. It is obvious that it cannot be reduced to $300,000,000 on the 1st of January, 1879.

Secretary SHERMAN. I say it would be better if it could be done; but if it cannot, I would not postpone resumption for that reason, because I think that with this large reserve which I mention we can maintain resumption on the full amount—with the advantage we have of having thirty or forty millions locked up in the Treasury not likely to be used.

Mr. EWING. Do you think that the balance of trade can be kept in our favor for the next few years?

Secretary SHERMAN. That is an uncertain problem.

Mr. EWING. You say, in your Senate interview, that the balance of trade brings us gold and silver and bonds. Has it brought us, in the past few years, gold and silver in excess of the gold and silver exported?

Secretary SHERMAN. No; you see heretofore silver has been largely exported as bullion, but we received gold, last season, in pretty large sums in this country—precisely how much, I am not prepared to say.

Mr. EWING. I have here, from the Bureau of Statistics, a statement of the imports and exports of coin and bullion, from 1865 to 1877, which shows a total, for the 13 years, of exports over imports of $692,000,000. (See appendix No. 10.)

Secretary SHERMAN. Yes, sir; that is so.

Mr. EWING. That is an average of exports over imports of gold and silver of $53,264,000 a year.

Secretary SHERMAN. That was at a time when paper money was in universal use, and there was no demand here for silver or gold; but now that we are to have specie payments, that course of things will be naturally expected to cease. You will find it easier to send off the products of our soil than the products of our mines, if we give the same use to the precious metals that is given in other countries.

Mr. EWING. For the past three years the average excess of the exports of gold and silver, over the imports (the balance of trade being in our favor) has been $42,396,000 a year; and that average is still continuing?

Secretary SHERMAN. Yes, sir. At this season of the year gold is shipped abroad, and at other seasons of the year it comes back. Sometimes the same gold will flow backward and forward two or three times in the year. After the cotton crop is marketed, and before June, when the canals are open, and products can be moved on the canals, is the time when gold naturally flows abroad, and it comes back in the fall.

Mr. EWING. Have you any reason to expect that the average exports of bullion, over imports, will not be in excess for the next two or three years as it has been for 17 years past?

Secretary SHERMAN. I would expect more exports, because of our home products of gold and silver, which may be stated, in round numbers, at $85,000,000. If we can hold two-thirds of it in this country, it is as much as we can expect. That would leave a balance of thirty or forty millions to go abroad. And suppose it does go abroad? We can stand the drain of thirty or forty millions a year, and still have a large amount of gold and silver in this country. (See Appendix No. 12.)

Mr. EWING. Do you not anticipate that drain?

Secretary SHERMAN. I would expect it. Our production of gold and silver is greater than is necessary to maintain resumption in this country, and it will go to help other countries.

Mr. EWING. Will it not go abroad irrespective of our demand for it here?

Secretary SHERMAN. It depends upon whichever demand is the greatest.

Mr. EWING. And upon whoever has the most ability to keep it?

Secretary SHERMAN. Yes, sir.

Mr. EWING. We being the debtor nation, and the people of Europe holding our debts, can they not attract gold from us at present?

Secretary SHERMAN. If we are a debtor nation we are also a nation which the European nations like to have for a debtor. Our nation has been a productive, active nation, and foreign capital seeks a favorite investment here.

Mr. EWING. Still, in case of a want of gold abroad they have it in their power to get it at any time by the sale of our securities.

Secretary SHERMAN. Yes; they can recall it if they want to do so, but the chances are that they will be more likely to invest in our securities in the future than they have been in the past, because this country is a stable country. It has gone through a great civil war, and it has elements of strength and stability which no European country possesses.

Mr. EWING. Our ability to keep gold practically depends upon this, whether our creditors abroad prefer to hold our bonds or to take our gold?

Secretary SHERMAN. Certainly.

Mr. EWING. If they prefer to take our gold they can get it by sending their bonds here and selling them.

Secretary SHERMAN. Yes.

Mr. EWING. And in the past three years, with the balance of trade largely in our favor, the excess of exports of specie over imports has been forty-two millions a year.

Secretary SHERMAN. That is because until last year we have never shown a determination to accumulate coin.

Mr. EWING. Our determination to accumulate coin was as strong in the month of January last as it ever has been, and yet the balance against us in that month was over two million dollars.

Secretary SHERMAN. The cause of the bonds flowing back was the fear of unfriendly legislation. The truth is, that (whether the fear was well or ill founded) a very large amount of our bonds came back which had to be paid in gold or silver because of pending legislation, but that movement has ceased. I got a letter yesterday from the highest authority, stating that that movement of bonds has gradually diminished.

Mr. EWING. Still the export of gold last Saturday was a million and a half of dollars.

Secretary SHERMAN. It always is large at this season of the year. This same gentleman tells me that he does not think that the export of gold this year will be greater than in former years, but that it commenced earlier, caused by the exportation of these bonds from abroad.

Mr. EWING. But the indications are that the excess of shipment of coin will be kept up as compared with the last three years.

Secretary SHERMAN. I hope not at anything like the same rate.

Mr. PHILLIPS. You have stated that you have not been able to accumulate gold at all this year.

Secretary SHERMAN. Yes; because I would not come into competition with the bonds which came back from abroad—caused by the agitation of the silver question.

Mr. PHILLIPS. Can you get coin from 4 per cent. bonds?

Secretary SHERMAN. Not just now to any great extent, but I hope that it will be better, and that I will be able to sell 4 per cent. bonds.

Mr. CHITTENDEN. Will not the mixed condition of the national bank currency be an element of strength in facilitating resumption? For example, if you were to present national bank currency to a bank for redemption, you must separate the notes. If you take any given amount of national bank currency which you find on deposit anywhere, you will be surprised to find how it represents banks from all sections of the country. I take it that no bank can be called upon to redeem any but its own issue.

Secretary SHERMAN. That is so; it is almost impossible to sort national bank bills.

Mr. CHITTENDEN. Will that be for you an element of strength or of weakness?

Secretary SHERMAN. It will be an element of strength. The difficulty of sorting national bank bills is very great. When they come to sort them in the Treasury the bills have to pass through four or five skilled hands. First, they are sorted into States, then into denominations, and then into banks. If you were to try and make a run on any particular bank in this country, as they used to do twenty or thirty years ago, it would be impossible to do so from the difficulty of assorting notes of different banks.

Mr. EWING. The balance of trade in our favor in the past three years has been due not so much to our largely increased exports as to our diminished imports, resulting from diminishing purchasing power.

The total exports for the three years ending June 30, 1874, were....	$1,550,939,000
The total exports for the three years ending June 30, 1877, were....	1,656,201,000
Excess of latter over former period...	105,362,000
The total imports for three years ending June 30, 1874, were.........	$1,836,137,000
The total imports for three years ending June 30, 1877, were.........	1,445,069,000
Excess of former over latter period...	391,068,000

Now I wish to ask you whether with the removal of the pressure from the country of the threat and preparation for resumption on the 1st of January, 1879, we may not expect that the imports will increase, and that we will go back to the old condition of importing more than we export, and in that way increase this drain of gold and silver?

Secretary SHERMAN. I think that the excessive imports for several years before the panic were evidence of the greatest extravagance and disregard of expenditure. People went into debt recklessly. That state of mind is always induced by a superabundance of paper money. I think that one of the best results of the panic (which was bad enough in depressing industry) was in stopping this extravagant and reckless importation of foreign goods. That is an element of real good which has come out of the evil which we have suffered from the past.

Mr. EWING. But you expect to maintain the same volume of paper money, and you expect to add to that volume a considerable amount of specie. That is, you expect to increase the currency as a result of resumption. Certainly, if this condition of extravagance arises from a superabundance of money, that extravagance will be increased very largely after resumption, if your theory be correct.

Secretary SHERMAN. There is a great deal of difference between irredeemable paper money, which fluctuates in value day by day, and redeemable money which always has a coin standard, and is measured by the values of the world. It is not a question of abundance of money so much as it is a question of fluctuations of value. A paper which is irredeemable and fluctuating always induces speculation. For instance, if a man sees that his neighbor has bought a piece of land on which he has made a large profit, he goes into speculation himself; and one man embarks in a hazardous enterprise because another man has done so and has succeeded. Now a redeemable paper money which is always at a fixed standard is less likely to produce that kind of speculative feverish adventure, even although it may be larger in volume.

Mr. EWING. So you understand that with inflation of currency after the 1st of January, 1879, there will not be inflation of values?

Secretary SHERMAN. No; values will be more stable.

Mr. EWING. As a matter of fact, did the greenback currency vary so greatly in purchasing power for the three years before the passage of the act of 1873?

Secretary SHERMAN. O, yes. The purchasing power of the greenback to-day is at least 60 per cent. more than it was before the panic.

Mr. EWING. Undoubtedly, because of the threatened contraction under the operation of the resumption law.

Secretary SHERMAN. No; but because of our getting back to a coin standard.

Mr. EWING. It is because the opinion of the country is that we must submit to an enormous contraction of our paper money, which is the currency with which business is done, in order to reach and maintain resumption.

Secretary SHERMAN. You and I differ about that. I have given you my view. I tell you that I think the falling off of importations is not an unfavorable sign. Every man knows now that money is money, and that he has to earn it. It is an evidence of more stable and economical management of affairs.

Mr. EWING. Do you expect the business of the country to revive after resumption?

Secretary SHERMAN. I think so.

Mr. EWING. Will not the imports increase largely as a necessary result of that revival, and will not, therefore, the balance of trade more likely turn against us by the increase of imports, the present favorable balance being due chiefly to the falling off of imports?

Secretary SHERMAN. I doubt very much whether the importations to this country for many years will equal what they were for the three or four years before the panic. The whole course of our industry has changed within the last three or four years. We are manufacturing now a great many things which we did not manufacture then. We are embarking in a great many industries which did not exist here before the panic. Prices have been reduced so that we can almost compete with any nation, and we export now many articles which we did not think of making until the last few years. When we manufacture upon the basis of a coin standard, like Great Britain and France, we can compete with those nations, because we have over them the great ad-

vantage of raw products. To be sure we have the disadvantage of higher-priced labor. Our labor is more intelligent and higher-priced.
The CHAIRMAN. And the disadvantage of higher priced money.
Secretary SHERMAN. Yes; but when we get down to compete with them on the same money, our natural advantages would countervalue the difference in wages and the difference in interest of money. We are now manufacturing a great variety of articles which were never manufactured in this country before. Values now—even gold values—are lower than they were before the panic all over the country. The same amount of money represents now a greater amount of either imports or exports than it did then, because nothing is truer than the fact than that that general revulsion which overcame us like a cloud extends all over the civilized world.
Mr. EWING. My belief is that on any revival, any letting up of the pressure caused by the resumption law, the imports will increase relatively to exports, and the old balance of trade will be re-established against us, and the drain of gold will return in its full force. (See Appendix No. 13.)
Mr. PHILLIPS. Will not the coin-certificates become a part of the currency, when specie payment comes, and so fill up the void made by the retirement of the legal-tenders, and probably neutralize the effect of the retirement of the legal-tenders?
Secretary SHERMAN. I think they will; but these coin-certificates are now represented by actual money on hand.
Mr. PHILLIPS. They increase the responsibility of the Treasury just in proportion. They will go into circulation, will they not?
Secretary SHERMAN. Yes. It does not make any difference whether currency is represented by coin-certificates or by actual coin. If they draw out coin, that coin goes into a general circulation, and if they leave it with us, then the certificates go into circulation.
Mr. PHILLIPS. But these coin-certificates will then go into general circulation as they do not go now.
Secretary SHERMAN. Coin-certificates do go into the general circulation for coin purposes now. They are largely used.
Mr. PHILLIPS. But will they not go in for general purposes as circulation?
Secretary SHERMAN. Perhaps they will.
Mr. PHILLIPS. There has been $35,000,000 of legal-tender notes retired under the resumption act?
Secretary SHERMAN. Yes.
Mr. PHILLIPS. Of that amount I have been informed that $15,000,000 has been in small notes; what rule have you to govern the Treasury in that respect?
Secretary SHERMAN. I am glad you mentioned that, because I would like to correct a misapprehension on that point. We always give to every man who makes a demand upon the Treasury any kind of bills he wants. We do not seek to force one-dollar, two-dollar, five-dollar, twenty-dollar, or one hundred-dollar bills. Every person who presents a draft at the Treasury gets the paper money he wants.
Mr. PHILLIPS. But the practical result is that some $15,000,000 of small bills have been retired, to the detriment of small change.
Secretary SHERMAN. Our impression is that that is a mistake.
Mr. PHILLIPS. It has been so stated to me.
Secretary SHERMAN. I can give you the fact exactly. I suppose it is because the banks, to whom the great body of the paper money is paid out, do not wish to handle small bills, and require large ones; but any-

body who wants the small bills can have them. I will give the exact amount at different dates, so that you will see how much the circulation of small bills has fallen off. *

Mr. PHILLIPS. Do you think that the proportion of small bills retired has not been much greater than the proportion of large bills retired?

Secretary SHERMAN. I do not know. I would rather give you the exact figures. General Butler talked to me yesterday about it, and I told him what I say to you. We never have attempted to withdraw the ones and twos from circulation.

Mr. PHILLIPS. But have they not gone out of circulation under the resumption act?

Secretary SHERMAN. Not to any very great extent. They do not go out simply because the banks and others who draw large amounts do not take them as freely as the people wish to have them. The banks do not wish to handle them.

The CHAIRMAN. It seems to me that upon your theory, on resumption, it would be very important that greenbacks should be used for our four per cent. bonds?

Secretary SHERMAN. Yes, sir.

The CHAIRMAN. And that if they can be also received for duties at the custom-house it would help you in resumption.

Secretary SHERMAN. Yes. As soon as we resume, or are ready to resume, we ought to receive greenbacks for customs-duties.

The CHAIRMAN. And bring them on a par with gold also by making them exchangeable for bonds.

Secretary SHERMAN. Yes; or redeem such as are presented in coin.

The CHAIRMAN. On that theory of resumption you would resume already, in order to have practical resumption.

Secretary SHERMAN. Yes; that is resumption, and we would not know about it. Within a year we have seen a decline of nine per cent. between greenbacks and gold. In December, 1876, gold was 110 per cent., and we have since had that decline and nobody has been hurt by it.

Mr. BELL. Suppose the greenbacks were to obtain an equality in value with gold, how would the repeal of the resumption act then affect resumption?

Secretary SHERMAN. The repeal of the resumption act would prevent me from maintaining resumption by the sale of bonds. That would be the first thing. Then the resumption act is the only provision of law which requires me to redeem United States notes in coin.

Mr. EWING. But you are at liberty to do so. If the resumption act were repealed, you might maintain an equivalency of paper and coin?

Secretary SHERMAN. No. It is perfectly clear that I have no right to exchange one form of money for another.

Mr. EWING. But you could pay out gold and silver.

Secretary SHERMAN. Yes.

Mr. EWING. And you could thus maintain an equality of coin and

---

* *Statement of one and two dollar United States notes outstanding at the dates mentioned.*

Date.	Ones.	Twos.	Totals.
June 30, 1873	28,911,309	34,210,856	63,122,165
June 30, 1874	26,571,512	28,117,438	54,688,950
June 30, 1875	27,416,863	26,345,326	53,762,189
June 30, 1866	28,007,504	27,480,479	55,487,983
June 30, 1877	25,160,297	25,369,825	50,530,122
April 1, 1878	22,744,288	22,707,443	45,451,731

paper upon your theory, which is, that as soon as paper and coin are equal nothing will be likely to occur to disturb the equilibrium?

Secretary SHERMAN. There will be more or less fluctuation, and we must be prepared to meet those fluctuations, so that if greenbacks become superabundant we can get gold for them; or if, on the other hand, gold becomes a drug, as it may, it will be deposited for greenbacks.

Mr. EWING. But if greenbacks become superabundant, and are presented to the Treasury for redemption, you will have to pay them out again?

Secretary SHERMAN. Yes, as soon as the equivalency is restored.

Mr. EWING. That is, you will hold whatever greenbacks come in until there is an equivalency?

Secretary SHERMAN. Yes; that is the effect of it.

Mr. PHILLIPS. Would it not be safer, by legislation and by taking greenbacks for customs-duties, to secure and maintain an equalization of values in that way rather than by resumption to authorize the combination of bankers to drain away the only credit resources in the Treasury?

Secretary SHERMAN. I think not; unless you maintain this equivalency you have no right, under your law, without violating your promise, to receive anything but coin in payment of customs-duties.

Mr. PHILLIPS. There may be various means of bringing up greenbacks by equalizing values. Would it not be safer for us to legislate so as to preserve an equality in values rather than to have forced resumption?

Secretary SHERMAN. No; because legislation is not powerful enough to do what can only be done by the actual redemption of the notes on presentation. No law can make two things equal to each other in values.

Mr. PHILLIPS. Can the law force you to resume if you have not the coin to do it?

Secretary SHERMAN. No; but we have the coin. As a matter of course, if we had not the coin we could not resume, but if we have the coin we can resume.

Mr. EWING. I understand that your idea is to exercise about the same power which is exercised by the Bank of England, in regard to these legal-tender notes.

Secretary SHERMAN. No; because the Bank of England loans out its notes for profit. That is its business.

Mr. EWING. The Bank of England, when a drain sets in, interrupts the movement of circulation by taking in its notes and not paying them out until the drain is checked. In that respect your idea of maintaining resumption is the same.

Secretary SHERMAN. Yes. When the notes are presented, the Secretary of the Treasury pays them in coin, silver or gold, at his discretion. When, in his judgment, it is wise to pay out these notes, either on the public debt or on the interest of the public debt, to those who are willing to take them, or any current expenses, he does it.

Mr. EWING. But he would not pay them out——

Secretary SHERMAN. Unless they were equivalent to coin.

Mr. EWING. And he would judge of their equivalency by the drain upon the Treasury?

Secretary SHERMAN. He would never be likely to pay out these greenbacks if they were to come back again on him for coin; and he would not be wise if he did it.

Mr. EWING. In that respect, he maintains resumption by exercising the same power and control over the paper currency as the Bank of England does?

Secretary SHERMAN. Yes, sir. Practically, that is done by the assistant treasurer in New York. I know, every day, how much coin-certificates are outstanding, and how much coin there is in the subtreasury. Every day these certificates are presented for redemption and somebody else deposits coin for other certificates, and thus the thing goes on, in ebb and flow, sometimes to the amount of a million or two a day. I see nothing of it, but I see the subtreasury reports every day. One man brings gold to the subtreasury and gets certificates, and another man brings the certificates and draws out the gold.

Mr. EWING. I think I have your idea pretty clearly that your control in putting out legal-tenders or withholding them is the lever by which their convertibility is to be maintained?

Secretary SHERMAN. Yes; and then there is, too, the fact that the Secretary is under the constant eye of Congress if he abuses his powers, because a great power is less liable to be abused than a small one. The eye of the public is on the Secretary in the exercise of power of this kind, and it is not likely to be abused. If there is any sign of his abusing it Congress is always present to prevent it. The Secretary would not dare to sell bonds to raise gold for resumption while he has any notes on hand unless there is a drain for the gold. All these powers will be exercised under the eye of Congress.

Mr. EWING. If there is a drain of gold you would sell bonds?

Secretary SHERMAN. The Secretary might sell bonds, and, again, when greenbacks were abundant in the Treasury he might make a call for six per cent. bonds, as I have done. I exercised my discretion in the matter last December, and I made a mistake in making a call for $10,000,000 of bonds which had better not have been made. I underestimated the effect of pending legislation. I did it under my discretion; but I did not sell enough bonds to redeem that call. So, the Secretary of the Treasury, administering under this law, if he found coin or greenbacks accumulating in his hands, would make a call of six per cent. bonds and would pay them off and sell four per cent. or four and a half per cent. bonds—whichever was the current bond in the market—and thus make good his money. That operation would go on without difficulty. That is the way, at least, that I would conduct it if I were in charge.

Mr. HARTZELL. I understood you to say that in order to complete your preparations for resumption additional bonds to the amount of, perhaps, fifty millions would have to be sold between now and the 1st of January.

Secretay SHERMAN. Yes; I think so.

Mr. HARTZELL. Is it your expectation that, after resumption day, you will have to continue the sale of bonds at different periods for the purpose of maintaining the specie reserve?

Secretary SHERMAN. Not at all. If I would sell any bonds at all after that, I would sell them merely for the purpose of refunding. It might be that, to meet a sudden drain, I would sell bonds in order to accumulate coin; but the very moment the drain ceased I would use the coin or the greenbacks which I had received in calling in 6 per cent bonds. Under that the whole of the public debt might be reduced to 4 per cents., if that should prove to be the ultimate rate of interest in this country.

Mr. HARTZELL. But the interest-bearing debt of the country has to be increased in order to bring about this result.

Secretary SHERMAN. Yes, in the absence of surplus revenue. There is no other way except by the increase of the public debt temporarily. We would have the coin to represent the bonds. That is all.

The conference here ended.

APPENDIX.

APPENDIX No. 1.

Statement of gold and silver in the Treasury on the 1st of February, 1877.

Gold coin	$71,944,129 47		
Gold bullion	8,720,150 25		
		$80,664,279 72	
Less amount to credit of disbursing-officers, and outstanding checks	3,074,445 45		
Less gold certificates actually outstanding	50,791,240 00		
Less called bonds and interest	10,117,672 63		
Less interest due and unpaid	9,993,750 26		
		73,977,108 34	
Available gold coin and bullion			$6,687,171 38
Silver coin	2,228,898 02		
Silver bullion	3,211,796 21		
		5,440,694 23	
Less outstanding checks		191,194 52	
Available silver coin and bullion			5,249,599 71
Available gold and silver coin and bullion			11,936,771 09

APPENDIX No. 2.

Statement of coin and bullion in the Treasury February 1, 1878.

Held by—	Gold coin.	Gold bullion.	Silver coin.	Silver bullion.
Treasurer United States, Washington	$397,628 39		$201,679 74	
Assistant treasurer United States, New York	92,024,604 20	$3,367,713 26	1,171,368 14	
Assistant treasurer United States, Boston	659,618 47		392,540 55	
Assistant treasurer United States, Philadelphia	454,884 35		809,674 75	
Assistant treasurer United States, Saint Louis	274,722 64		273,045 33	
Assistant treasurer United States, San Francisco	1,854,963 38		146,608 35	
Assistant treasurer United States, New Orleans	1,120,121 66		224,170 16	
Assistant treasurer United States, Baltimore	509,154 30		166,450 22	
Assistant treasurer United States, Cincinnati	230,064 83		217,877 33	
Assistant treasurer United States, Chicago	528,326 04		253,549 38	
Mint, Philadelphia	1,403,416 24	637,557 34	748,546 67	$671,116 55
Mint, San Francisco	978,757 74	5,039,352 92	41,327 65	893,651 51
Mint, Carson City	224,154 54	73,693 61	427,894 76	214,462 31
Mint, Denver	3,000 00		100 00	
United States assay-office, New York	3,672,671 37	2,079,834 24	21,148 22	1,048,137 70
United States assay-office, Boise City			500 00	
United States assay-office, Charlotte			200 00	
United States assay-office, Helena			500 00	
First National Bank, Milwaukee, Wis	28,078 19			
First National Bank, Portland, Oreg	165 00			
Totals	104,414,331 34	11,198,151 37	5,097,181 25	2,827,368 07

* The items to be deducted are the following, taken from page 4 of Senate interview:

Amount to credit of disbursing-officers and outstanding checks	$6,189,626 66
Gold-certificates actually outstanding	44,498,500 00
Called bonds and interest	6,818,677 29
Interest due and unpaid	4,909,705 21
	62,416,509 16

APPENDIX No. 3.

[In reply to inquiry No. 1. Letter of March 28, from Hon. A. H. Buckner.]

Statement of coin and bullion in Treasury at close of business February 28, 1878.

Held by—	Gold coin.	Gold bullion.	Silver coin.	Silver bullion.
Treasurer United States, Washington	$675,899 51	....	$170,377 97	....
Assistant treasurer United States, New York	99,699,528 09	$3,387,713 26	1,407,992 53	....
Assistant treasurer United States, Boston	663,577 50	....	379,903 05	....
Assistant treasurer United States, Philadelphia	467,415 70	....	797,294 75	....
Assistant treasurer United States, Saint Louis	276,031 00	....	263,694 98	....
Assistant treasurer United States, San Francisco	2,453,100 00	....	149,260 81	....
Assistant treasurer United States, New Orleans	1,168,719 00	....	217,573 95	....
Assistant treasurer United States, Baltimore	519,391 50	....	157,218 52	....
Assistant treasurer United States, Cincinnati	251,636 00	....	211,828 16	....
Assistant treasurer United States, Chicago	665,527 50	....	248,319 12	....
Mint, Philadelphia	2,829,834 32	556,035 45	887,057 86	1,244,000 00
Mint, San Francisco	4,045,079 73	1,887,305 36	72,920 54	904,861 65
Mint, Carson City	655,147 80	46,412 00	225,145 33	175,974 98
Mint, Denver	3,000 00	....	100 00	....
United States assay-office, New York	3,672,671 37	2,079,834 24	21,148 22	630,741 02
United States assay-office, Boise City	....	....	500 00	....
United States assay-office, Charlotte	....	....	200 00	....
United States assay-office, Helena	....	....	500 00	....
National banks and depositaries	300,150 03	....	456 45	....
In transit	....	....	455,000 00	....
Total	118,351,709 05	7,937,300 31	5,675,494 24	2,955,577 65

TREASURY UNITED STATES,
Washington, D. C., March 30, 1878.

APPENDIX No. 4.

Statement of coin and bullion in the Treasury March 28, 1878.

Date.	Offices, &c.	Gold coin and standard silver dollars.	Fractional silver coin.	Gold and silver bullion.
1878.				
March 27	Treasury of United States, Washington	$676,282 68	$958,165 65	....
27	Assistant treasury, Baltimore	511,648 09	149,093 52	....
27	Assistant treasury, New York	100,198,068 09	1,374,628 52	$3,367,713 26
27	Assistant treasury, Philadelphia	271,109 97	791,004 75	....
25	Assistant treasury, Boston	975,607 50	370,333 46	....
25	Assistant treasury, Cincinnati	233,659 50	207,141 33	....
25	Assistant treasury, Chicago	623,807 00	247,819 89	....
25	Assistant treasury, Saint Louis	279,373 00	251,208 84	....
23	Assistant treasury, New Orleans	1,139,747 00	213,706 76	....
19	Assistant treasury, San Francisco	2,803,900 00	150,646 66	....
23	National bank depositories	2,936,010 93	....	....
23	Mint United States, Philadelphia	1,245,220 75	642,114 97	1,633,609 46
16	Mint United States, San Francisco	1,903,552 50	79,260 86	4,927,353 92
0	Mint United States, Carson	933,032 05	279,260 09	65,387 97
	Mint United States, Denver	3,000 00	100 00	....
23	United States assay-office, New York	....	20,951 89	3,670,849 85
	Other small assay-offices	....	1,290 00	....
	Totals	114,666,958 97	5,736,630 19	13,664,914 46

NOTE.—Standard silver dollars included above, 454,711.

RESUMPTION OF SPECIE PAYMENTS. 67

APPENDIX No. 5.

Comparison of condition of the Treasury April 1, 1877, and April 1, 1878.

Balances.	1877.	1878.
Currency	$8,184,863 58	$751,851 35
Special fund for the redemption of fractional currency		10,000,000 00
Special deposit of legal-tenders for redemption of certificates of deposit	35,155,000 00	25,215,000 00
Coin	66,818,285 26	138,357,608 14
Coin-certificates	48,279,400 00	57,883,400 00
Coin, less coin-certificates	38,538,885 26	80,474,208 14
Outstanding called bonds	5,262,900 00	7,305,200 00
Other outstanding coin liabilities	6,786,028 00	4,643,276 28
Outstanding legal-tenders	362,656,204 00	347,848,712 00
Outstanding fractional currency	23,440,512 08	16,950,115 62
Outstanding silver coin	29,937,001 43	38,662,487 02
Total debt, less cash in Treasury	2,074,674,126 63	2,039,723,514 31
Reduction of debt for March	*14,107,016 41	2,313,614 77
Reduction of debt since July 1	*24,765,218 36	20,434,708 95
Market value of gold	105 00	101 25
Imports (12 months ending February 28)	420,199,831 00	475,638,634 00
Exports (12 months ending February 28)	603,631,538 00	637,757,892 00

* This reduction includes $9,553,800 Geneva award bonds canceled.

TREASURY DEPARTMENT, WARRANT DIVISION.

APPENDIX No. 6.

Circulation and deposits, and specie of the State banks, 1857 and 1860.

Years.	Circulation.	Deposits and bank balances.	Total.	Specie.	Ratios of specie to—	
					Circulation.	Circulation and deposits.
					Per cent.	Per cent.
1857	$214,778,822	$230,351,352	$445,130,174	$58,349,838	27.2	13.1
1860	207,102,477	253,802,129	460,904,606	83,594,537	40.4	18.1

Compiled from statement in Finance Report, 1876, pages 204, 205.

Circulation, deposits, and cash reserve of the national banks, December 28, 1877.

LIABILITIES.

Circulation	$299,240,475
Deposits	661,575,577
Total	960,816,052

CASH RESERVE HELD.

Gold coin	$5,506,556	
Silver coin	4,300,274	
United States gold-certificates	23,100,920	
Total specie		32,907,750
Legal-tender notes	$70,568,248	
United States certificates for legal-tenders	26,515,000	
Total legal-tenders		97,083,248
Five per cent. redemption fund		15,026,340
Total cash reserve		145,019,338
Ratio of legal-tender funds to circulation		48.4 per cent.
Ratio of legal-tender funds to circulation and deposits		15.1 per cent

RESUMPTION OF SPECIE PAYMENTS.

Circulation, deposits, and cash resources of the national banks December 28, 1877.

LIABILITIES.

Circulation	$299,240,475
Deposits	661,575,577
Total	960,816,052

CASH RESOURCES.

Gold coin	$5,506,556	
Silver coin	4,300,274	
United States gold-certificates	23,100,920	
Total specie		32,907,750
Legal tender-notes	$70,568,248	
United States certificates for legal-tenders	26,515,000	
Total legal-tenders		97,083,248
Five per cent. redemption fund		15,028,340
United States bonds, par value, $285,887,350; currency value, $405,181,717		405,181,717
Total cash resources		550,201,055
Ratio of cash resources to circulation		183 + per cent.
Ratio of cash resources to circulation and deposits		57.3 per cent

Abstract of reports made to the Comptroller of the Currency, showing the condition of the national banks in the United States, including national gold banks, at the close of business on Friday, the 28th day of December, 1877.

Resources.		Liabilities.	
Loans and discounts	$878,055,305 95	Capital stock paid in	$447,128,771 00
Overdrafts	3,801,438 92		
United States bonds to secure circulation	343,869,550 00	Surplus fund	121,618,455 32
United States bonds to secure deposits	13,538,000 00	Other undivided profits	51,530,910 18
United States bonds on hand	28,479,800 00		
Other stocks, bonds, and mortgages	32,169,491 03	National bank notes outstanding*	299,240,475 00
Due from approved reserve agents	75,960,087 27		
Due from other national banks	44,193,924 97	State bank notes outstanding	470,540 00
Due from State banks and bankers	11,479,945 65		
Real estate, furniture, and fixtures	45,511,932 25		
Current expenses	8,958,903 60	Dividends unpaid	1,404,178 34
Premiums paid	8,841,930 09		
Checks and other cash items	10,265,059 49	Individual deposits	604,512,514 52
Exchanges for clearing-house	64,664,415 01	United States deposits	6,529,031 09
Bills of other national banks	20,312,692 00	Deposits of United States disbursing officers	3,780,759 43
Fractional currency	779,084 78		
Specie, viz:		Due to other national banks	115,773,660 58
Gold coin $5,506,556.39			
Silver coin 4,300,274.31	32,907,750 70		
U. S. gold certificates 23,100,920.00		Due to State banks and bankers	44,807,958 79
Legal-tender notes	70,568,248 00		
United States certificates of deposit for legal-tender notes	26,515,000 00	Notes and bills rediscounted	4,654,784 51
Five per cent. redemption fund with Treasurer	15,028,340 14	Bills payable	5,843,107 03
Due from Treasurer other than redemption fund	1,465,236 94		
Aggregate	1,737,295,145 79	Aggregate	1,737,295,145 79

*The amount of circulation outstanding at the date named, as shown by the books of this office, was $321,672,505; which amount includes the notes of insolvent banks, of those in voluntary liquidation, and of those which have deposited legal-tender notes under the act of June 20, 1874, for the purpose of retiring their circulation.

JNO. JAY KNOX,
Comptroller of the Currency.

TREASURY DEPARTMENT,
  OFFICE COMPTROLLER OF THE CURRENCY,
    Washington, February 16, 1878.

RESUMPTION OF SPECIE PAYMENTS. 69

APPENDIX No. 7.

Statement showing the apparent and probable condition of the United States Treasury, including the proposed accumulation of $50,000,000 coin.

	Apparent.	Probable.
Demand liabilities, April 1, 1878:		
Legal-tender notes	$347,848,712 00	$340,000,000 00
Coin-certificates	57,883,400 00	57,883,400 00
Interest overdue	4,121,146 77	4,000,000 00
Debt, matured and interest	8,439,391 04	8,000,000 00
Currency-certificates	25,215,000 00	25,215,000 00
Fractional currency	16,950,115 62	
Demand notes	62,342 50	
Unclaimed Pacific Railroad interest	7,267 03	
Totals	460,527,374 96	435,098,400 00
Demand resources, April 1, 1878:		
Coin	138,357,608 14	188,357,608 14
Currency	35,966,851 35	35,966,851 35
Totals	174,324,459 49	224,324,459 49
Percentage of resources to liabilities	.37	.51

APPENDIX No. 8.

Statement showing resources and liabilities of certain European banks at dates mentioned below.

Bank.	Date.	Demand liabilities.		Total.	Demand resources.	Percentage of resources to liabilities.	Average depreciation, per cent.
		Circulation	Deposits.		Bullion.		
Bank of England	1818	26,202,000	7,928,000	34,130,000	6,363,000	.18+	2.13.2.
Do	1820	24,299,000	4,421,000	28,720,000	8,211,000	.28+	2.12.0.
Do	1822	17,465,000	6,399,000	23,864,000	10,098,000	.42+	Nil.
Do	1824	20,132,000	9,680,000	29,812,000	11,787,000	.39+	Nil.
Do	1826	21,564,000	7,200,000	28,764,000	6,754,000	.21+	Nil.
Do	1828	21,358,000	10,201,000	31,559,000	10,499,000	.33+	Nil.
Do	1830	21,465,000	11,621,000	33,086,000	11,150,000	.33	Nil.
Do	1832	18,320,000	10,278,000	28,598,000	7,514,000	.26+	Nil.
Do	1834	19,195,000	13,300,000	32,495,000	7,303,000	.22+	Nil.
Do	1836	18,018,000	12,040,000	30,058,000	5,250,000	.17+	Nil.
Do	1838	19,488,000	8,922,000	28,410,000	9,540,000	.33+	Nil.
Do	1840	17,170,000	6,254,000	23,424,000	4,299,000	.18+	Nil.
Do	1842	20,332,000	8,690,000	29,022,000	9,729,000	.33+	Nil.
Do	1844	21,485,000	12,138,000	33,623,000	15,315,000	.45+	Nil.
Do	1846	21,390,000	16,322,000	37,712,000	16,388,000	.43+	Nil.
Do	1878. Feb. 20	26,584,674	28,054,497	54,639,171	24,730,793	.45+	Nil.
Bank of France	Feb. 14	99,350,000	21,193,000	120,543,000	78,896,000	.65+	
Bank of Germany	Feb. 7	30,987,000	10,311,000	41,298,000	24,759,000	.58+	
National Bank of Belgium	Feb. 7	13,170,000	2,330,000	15,500,000	3,991,000	.25+	

APPENDIX No. 9.

An estimate of the amount of gold and silver bullion and coin in the United States April 1, 1878.

Gold.

In United States Treasury (including bullion fund of mints and assay office) October 31, 1877	$125,122,843 94
In national banks (exclusive of coin-certificates) October 1, 1877	4,867,909 18
In California banks	18,000,000 00
Private banks (Pacific coast)	2,000,000 00
State and county treasuries (Pacific coast)	4,000,000 00

Merchants and individuals (Pacific coast)	$4,000,000 00
Unpaid deposits, United States mints	500,000 00
Smelters and private refiners (exclusive of the Pacific coast)	500,000 00
Gold bullion in California	1,500,000 00
In private hands, including bullion dealers, savings-banks, and private bankers east of the Rocky Mountains	15,000,000 00
In State banks	2,000,000 00
	177,490,753 12
Production from October 31 to April 1	20,000,000 00
Approximate excess of imports over exports	2,000,000 00
	199,490,753 12

Silver.

Fractional coin in States east of the Rocky Mountains, including trade-dollars and Mexican coin, October 31, 1877	$42,000,000
California banks	2,000,000
Private banks (Pacific coast)	500,000
State and county treasuries (Pacific coast)	500,000
Merchants and individuals (Pacific coast)	500,000
Silver bullion (Pacific coast)	2,000,000
Silver bullion in hands of smelters and refiners east of the Rocky Mountains	1,000,000
	48,500,000
Silver bullion in mints	2,000,000
Production from mines to April 1	15,000,000
	65,500,000

I have not the data necessary to ascertain to which of the foregoing items should be credited the gain of gold and silver since October 31, 1877. It may be stated, however, that the Treasury stock has been increased, and the amount of trade and Mexican dollars which have gone into circulation may be set down at not less than 4,000,000, exclusive of about 1,200,000 trade-dollars in the mints.

According to the above estimate the amount of gold coin and bullion now in the country is	$199,490,753 12
And silver coin and bullion	65,500,000 00
Total	264,990,753 12

Allowing for gold and silver used in the arts and for manufacturing purposes and possible overestimation, say $15,000,000, the total amount of gold and silver in the country may be set down at about two hundred and fifty millions of dollars, of which about fifty millions are in the form of fractional silver, trade dollars, and Mexican coin, and $1,200,000 in standard silver dollars.

THE PRESENT AVERAGE PRODUCTION OF GOLD AND SILVER FROM THE MINES OF THE UNITED STATES.

I have availed myself of every facility to procure full information in relation to the product of the gold and silver mines of the United States, for the purpose of estimating approximately the present annual yield, with the following results, based upon the production for the first six months of the year and the average monthly out-turn since, so far as it was possible to ascertain the same:

State or Territory.	Gold.	Silver.	Total.
California	$15,000,000	$1,000,000	$16,000,000
Nevada	18,000,000	26,000,000	44,000,000
Montana	3,200,000	750,000	3,950,000
Idaho	1,500,000	250,000	1,750,000
Utah	350,000	5,075,000	5,425,000
Colorado	3,000,000	4,500,000	7,500,000
Arizona	300,000	500,000	800,000
New Mexico	175,000	500,000	675,000
Oregon	1,000,000	100,000	1,100,000
Washington	300,000	50,000	350,000
Dakota	2,000,000	....	2,000,000
Lake Superior	....	200,000	200,000
Virginia	50,000	....	50,000
North Carolina	100,000	....	100,000
Georgia	100,000	....	100,000
Other sources	25,000	25,000	50,000
Total	45,100,000	38,950,000	84,050,000

It is impossible to state with any degree of accuracy how long this large rate of production will be maintained. A gradual increase may be expected in Montana and Arizona, and there is nothing to indicate a decrease in any bullion-producing State or Territory, except in the State of Nevada, and that depends upon contingencies which to a great extent must be a matter of conjecture only. Several mines in different localities in that State have within the last year or two been opened and are producing considerable bullion, but whether they, and others which in the mean time may be discovered, will yield sufficient to make up the decrease, which, unless other ore-bodies on the Comstock shall be found, must sooner or later take place, is somewhat doubtful.

The superintendent of the mint at San Francisco has furnished, at my request, a statement, embraced in the appendix, of the yield of about thirty different mines, the bullion from which finds a market in San Francisco.

The yield of bullion from the two mines which embrace the great ore-chimney discovered in 1874 in the Comstock lode has, according to the official statement of the managers, amounted, up to October 31, 1877, to $78,852,918.48, of which $36,736,347.91 was gold. These mines are now producing at the rate of nearly three million dollars per month.

H. R. LINDERMAN,
Director of the Mint.

TREASURY DEPARTMENT, *April* 3, 1878.

APPENDIX No. 10.

Statement of imports and exports of specie (coin and bullion) during the fiscal years ended June 30, 1865, to 1877, inclusive, and the seven months ended January 31, 1878.

Fiscal years ended June 30—	Coin and bullion.					
	Exports.			Imports.	Excess of—	
	Domestic.	Foreign.	Total.		Imports.	Exports.
1865	$64,618,124	$3,025,102	$67,643,226	$9,810,072		$57,833,154
1866	82,643,374	3,400,697	86,044,071	10,700,092		75,343,979
1867	54,976,196	5,892,176	60,868,372	22,070,475		38,797,897
1868	83,745,975	10,038,127	93,784,102	14,188,368		79,595,734
1869	42,915,966	14,222,414	57,138,380	19,807,876		37,330,504
1870	43,883,802	14,271,864	58,155,666	26,419,179		31,736,487
1871	84,403,359	14,038,629	98,441,988	21,270,024		77,171,964
1872	72,796,240	7,078,294	79,877,534	13,743,689		66,133,845
1873	73,905,546	10,703,028	84,608,574	21,480,937		63,127,637
1874	59,599,686	6,930,719	66,630,405	28,454,906		38,175,499
1875	83,857,129	8,275,013	92,132,142	20,900,717		71,231,425
1876	50,038,691	6,467,611	56,506,302	15,936,681		40,569,621
1877	43,134,738	13,027,499	56,162,237	40,774,414		15,387,823
1877.						
July	4,197,923	285,641	4,483,564	1,107,814		3,375,750
August	1,665,357	388,526	2,053,883	1,612,143		411,740
September	2,239,416	844,195	3,083,611	3,846,382	$756,771	
October	1,693,583	317,379	2,010,962	1,717,793		293,169
November	1,197,733	367,121	1,564,854	2,266,083	701,229	
December	1,539,446	380,451	1,919,897	1,670,265		249,632
1878.						
January	3,230,996	522,758	3,753,754	1,790,964		1,962,790

Total for years 1865 to 1877, inclusive $692,435,569
Average 53,264,000
Average for last three years 42,396,000
Average gold and silver product of the United States, 1870 to 1876, inclusive 71,000,000
Average excess of production over net export, 1874, 1875, and 1876, $29,000,000; deduct $7,000,000 used in arts; leaving 22,000,000

EDWARD YOUNG,
Chief of Bureau.

BUREAU OF STATISTICS, *March 29, 1878.*
Hon. THOMAS EWING, *M. C.*

APPENDIX No. 11.

Distribution of currency in the Treasury of the United States, March 28, 1878.

Date.	Office, &c.	United States notes.	National-bank notes.	Currency.
1878.				
March 27	Treasurer United States, Washington	$6,432,588 20	$122,261 50	
27	Assistant treasurer United States, New York	32,107,136 84	458,066 92	
27	Assistant treasurer United States, Baltimore	3,481,053 00	44,478 00	
27	Assistant treasurer United States, Philadelphia	4,730,620 00	38,800 00	
25	Assistant treasurer United States, Boston	3,608,000 00	206,836 00	
25	Assistant treasurer United States, Cincinnati	1,322,089 00	356,000 00	
25	Assistant treasurer United States, Chicago	3,629,500 00	356,785 00	
25	Assistant treasurer United States, Saint Louis	2,270,094 00		
23	Assistant treasurer United States, New Orleans	1,560,000 00	163,000 00	
19	Assistant treasurer United States, San Francisco	1,127,300 00	470,000 00	
9	Depositary United States, Tucson	370,610 00		
	National-bank depositaries			6,065,059 69
23	Mint United States, Philadelphia	90,538 00		
	Total	60,729,529 04	2,246,227 42	6,065,059 69

APPENDIX No. 12.

[From Dr. Linderman's official report.]

Annual product of gold and silver from the American mines.

Year.	Gold.	Silver.	Total.
1870	$50,000,000	$16,000,000	$66,000,000
1871	43,500,000	23,000,000	66,500,000
1872	36,000,000	28,750,000	64,750,000
1873	36,000,000	35,750,000	71,750,000
1874	40,000,000	32,000,000	72,000,000
1875	40,000,000	32,000,000	72,000,000
1876	44,300,000	41,500,000	85,700,000
1877 (Wells, Fargo & Co.'s estimate)			100,000,000

Exports of specie in the fiscal years 1872, 1873, and 1874, in excess of imports for same years	$167,436,981
Average for each year	55,812,000
Excess of exports for the years 1875, 1876, and 1877	127,188,797
Average for each year	42,396,000
Excess since July 1, 1877, to January 31, 1878, inclusive	4,815,081

INDEX.

	Page.
Coin in the Treasury on February 28, 1878	3, 13
Bonds sold under resumption act and refunding act	4
Annual coin liabilities	5
Fractional currency redeemed	5
Report of coin at subtreasury, New York	6
Statement of the Bank of England	32
Statement of foreign banks and of American banks at different periods	35
Gold and silver bullion and coin in the United States on April 1, 1878	36
Sinking-fund balances from 1869 to 1877	36
Monthly redemptions of legal-tenders and fractional currency	37
Application of the surplus revenue of 1877	37
Existing demands upon fund in the Treasury	39
Sales of bonds in January, February, and March, 1878	40
Exports and imports from 1874 to 1877	58
Outstanding $1 and $2 bills from 1873 to 1878	61
Statement of gold and silver in the Treasury on February 1, 1877	65
Statement of coin and bullion in the Treasury February 1, 1878	65
February 28, 1878	66
March 28, 1878	66
Condition of national banks December 28, 1877	67
Comparison of condition of the Treasury April 1, 1877, and April 1, 1878	67
Circulation, deposits, and specie of State banks, 1857 and 1860	67
Circulation, deposits, and cash resources of national banks December 28, 1877	68
Apparent and probable condition of Treasury April, 1878	69
Resources and liabilities of certain European banks	69
Estimate of gold and silver bullion and coin in United States April 1, 1878	69
Imports and exports of specie from 1865 to January 31, 1878	72
Distribution of currency in Treasury March 28, 1878	72
Annual American product of gold and silver	73

EXCESSIVE TAXATION OF BANK SHARES

IN THE

STATE OF NEW YORK:

ITS INJUSTICE AND OPPRESSION.

SPEECH

OF

Hon. ELLIOT C. COWDIN,

OF NEW YORK,

IN THE ASSEMBLY,

APRIL 11, 1877.

The Assembly of the State of New York having under consideration the subject of the excessive taxation of bank shares —

Mr. COWDIN said :

Mr. SPEAKER — The national banks of the State appeal to the Legislature for justice. They simply ask that bank shares shall be assessed at no higher rate than other capital.

An impression has long prevailed on the part of those who are not familiar with the operations of national banks, that they are pets of the federal government, and that State and municipal authorities were, therefore, justified in laying upon them exceptionably heavy burdens. There could hardly be a grosser delusion—a graver mistake. A few facts will dispel the one and rectify the other.

Mr. Knox, the National Comptroller of the Currency, in his last report, declared that the tax on national banks is much greater than that upon any other capital in the country. They are subjected to two classes of taxes—federal and state. The taxes imposed by the law of 1863, which they pay to the federal government, are of three kinds, namely : One per cent annually upon the average amount of notes in circulation, one-half of one per cent upon deposits, and one-half of one per cent upon their capital stock, not invested in United States bonds. Moreover, the law requires the banks to keep a *reserve* of their deposits of 25 per cent in cities, and 15 per cent in the county, and prohibits them from using it in any way whatever; yet it does not relieve them from taxation on this portion of their deposits so kept on hand idle. Thus, on the one hand, while forced to keep themselves strong, on the other they are fined for so doing.

Besides these burdens, the national banks are also assessed by State, county and local authorities; and, as will be seen hereafter, they are, as a general rule, subjected to rates of taxation far in excess of those levied upon any other species of property.

Before entering into the details of the subject, allow me to correct the popular error that a portion of the property of the national banks is exempt from State taxation. I refer to United States bonds—the basis whereon the national banks rest. These bonds are subject to taxation by State authorities, like any other property, though exempt from taxation when held by all other parties. It is vain to urge that this is a palpable evasion of the laws of Congress. The State and city collector, with his warrant in his hand, will listen to no such plea in abatement of his tax.

Now, let us measure the burden of the National, State and municipal taxes upon our banks, and then we shall be prepared to compare it with the weight placed on other kinds of property.

Comptroller Knox's recent report shows that, by statistics gathered from upward of 2,000 national banks, located in all parts of the country, the federal tax on their capital in the year 1875 averaged from one to three per cent, the lowest rate being in Rhode Island and Arkansas, and the highest in the city of Albany; while the State and local taxes run from one-tenth of one per cent to three and three-tenths per cent, being 10 cents on $100 in the District of Columbia, and $3.60 on $100 in the city of Albany, making an aggregate of both kinds of from one and six-tenths per cent to six and six-tenths; that is, from $1.60 to $6.60 total tax on each $100 of banking capital. Now, where do these taxes fall most heavily? It is in the State where the banking interest is immensely larger than in any other, and where the interests of commerce generally most require that banking capital should be left free to perform its functions untrammeled by unjust burdens.

In this State more than one-third of the total amount of the personal property assessed is national bank stock. Does anybody imagine that this is relatively on a fair valuation, or that it has in it a single element of justice? One of the reasons of this excessive valuation is, that the amount of the capital of banks is easily ascertained, as is also the market value of the shares; and in the chief cities they are compelled to publish such statements from time to time as shall lay open to public inspection all their property, their deposits, circulation, surplus, discounts — every thing. It follows, therefore, that all that the local assessors have to do is to look at these figures. But in respect to all other descriptions of personal property, especially such as are analogous in its character to banks, the assessors are left very much in the dark.

The State assessors of New York, in their annual report of 1874, say that they are satisfied that not over fifteen per cent of the taxable personal property of the State finds its way to the assessment rolls at all, and of bonds and mortgages not over five per cent.

All that the banks ask is that measures shall be taken to place all personal property on the assessment rolls, that it and all other property be assessed at the same rates in proportion to the real value thereof; and that no discrimination shall be made against banks. In other words, the banks simply ask that if their property is to be assessed at its actual value, the like rule be applied to the assessment of all other property in the State, real and personal.

Is not this just? Indeed, is not any other rule of taxation manifestly unfair? Does it militate against the fairness of this rule that, if all property in the State was assessed at its full value (as our banks are), this would so reduce the rate of taxation that the banks would cheerfully pay taxes on the actual value of their property?

Let us look at the national banks in this State and compare their burdens with those imposed on national banks in other States. We now refer only to State, municipal and local taxes.

The average rate of these taxes on all the national banks in this State is within a fraction of three per cent on their capital. This is higher than in any other State in the Union except South Carolina and Kansas — and very much higher than in most of them.

Let us compare the taxes of this kind levied on the national banks in the city of New York with those levied on banks in some other cities. In New York city this tax is 3 1-10 per cent on the capital, while in Philadelphia — our greatest financial rival — it is only 8-10ths of one per cent; in Pittsburgh, 1-2 of one per cent; in Washington, 3-10ths of one per cent; in Boston, 1 9-10 per cent; in Baltimore, 2 per cent; in Chicago, 2 1-2 per cent; in Cincinnati, 2 6-10 per cent.

Let us now make comparisons between national banks in New York city and those in several other cities in respect to their entire tax, federal, State and local. For the year 1875 the total of the combined rates on the capital of the banks in New York city was 5 1-10 per cent, while in Philadelphia it was only 2 8-10; in Baltimore, 3 3-10; in Boston, 3 3-10; in Washington, 1 7-10; in St. Louis, 4 per cent; in Cincinnati, 4 6-10; in Chicago, 4 8-10 per cent. But worse than all is the unjust burden of taxation inflicted on some of the banks in the interior of this State. For example, in Syracuse they are taxed 6 56-100 per cent, and in Albany 6 6-10 per cent; and this, too, at a period when money was being loaned, on call, at an average of 3 per cent, and commercial paper was being readily discounted at from 4 to 6 per cent per annum, according to its grade.

Thus we see that the tax in the State of New York is by far more oppressive than that in any other State in the Union. And by whom has it been imposed? By her own representatives assembled in her own legislative halls. Yes, by them, Albany has been subjected to State and local taxes of 3 6-10 per cent, while the Legislature of Pennsylvania imposed State and local taxes upon the banks of Pittsburg of only one-half of one per cent.

The injustice heaped upon the national banks of New York is shown in the inequality of the local valuation on which taxes are levied. Last year the whole valuation of personal property in

New York city was $218,626,178, and of this sum, $85,145,116 was bank stock—thus rating the bank stock in the city at nearly 40 per cent of the personal property. Does not every body know that this is grossly unjust towards the city banks?

Compare the banks with some other kinds of corporate property in the city, and the injustice with which they are treated is equally apparent.

The national banks have to pay State and municipal taxes on their personal property at its full value. The capital, scrip and surplus of the fire and marine insurance companies in the State amount in round numbers to about $60,000,000; and yet they pay taxes on less than $7,000,000. A single national bank—the Bank of Commerce—pays one-third more State and municipal taxes than all the fire and marine insurance companies of the State. But there is no end to illustrations of the unjust discrimination against the national banks of our State. How can they bear up under the burdens thus heaped upon them by the State and local authorities, in addition to the federal taxes? Though the Legislature has nothing directly to do with the national burdens, it should regard their weight when fixing the further burdens which are laid upon the banks by its authority.

Let us bear in mind that when the national banks were organized in 1863, and were subjected to taxes by the general government, these taxes were regarded as necessary war contributions and temporary in their character.

Here, let it not be forgotten that in the dark and dreary hour, when hostilities commenced in the late war, and when the credit of the nation was at its lowest ebb, the associated banks of New York and other cities nobly came to the aid of the government by promptly taking $100,000,000 of treasury notes at par in coin; and in addition they took 6 per cent bonds to the amount of $50,000,000, and paid for them also in gold; and all this within a period of four months, the subscription amounting to more than their aggregate capital. But for these $150,000,000 so speedily advanced by the banks in coin, at that critical moment, who can tell what would have been the fate of the nation? But we well know what was the fate of the banks.

Senator Conkling, then a representative in congress, justly said:

"The banks were never stronger than when the Secretary of the Treasury appealed to them for loans. They allowed the Secretary to carry off their specie, their capital from their vaults, and they had to suspend."

Previous to the war the banks had been liable to taxation only by State authority, for home purposes, but when forced to become national banks they were compelled to pay national taxes. Peace came nearly twelve years ago, bringing in her train relief to other interests from special war burdens, including the repeal of the income tax, but the war taxes on the banks still remain, side by side with those on whisky and tobacco.

Mr. Speaker, the national banks ask no special favors of the State on account of their services to the government, or of these Federal exactions; but they do think that these facts add vigor to the demand for equal and exact justice at the hands of the State in the imposition of taxes by its authority. If the severe burdens under which our banks are now struggling are to be continued, serious results will follow. Many of our banks are now greatly reducing their capital; others will be forced to do the same thing. Still others may give up their charters and invest their capital in business on which the government lays a lighter hand; while that large class of stockholders who reside outside of the State of New York may find it to their interest to withdraw their funds to localities where the exactions are less exorbitant.

In consequence of these oppressive taxes the bank capital in the city of New York alone has been reduced, and is in process of reduction, to the amount of about $22,000,000. The reduced value of bank shares in the city, mainly caused by excessive taxation, amounts to nearly $10,000,000. The effect upon the city assessment rolls is obvious. It strikes from them $32,000,000. Can the tax payers of the city, who are not owners of bank stock, but who are now struggling under the weight of a city debt of $150,000,000, afford this reduction? Are the tax payers in other parts of the State ready to make up this deficieny?

Are the farmers prepared to do their share of it? Are the manufacturers and mechanics willing to come to the rescue?

Mr. Speaker, for myself I have an abiding faith in the future achievements of our country. In the two immense industries of Iron and Cotton we have already surpassed the world; and the great exhibition has shown the enormous progress we are making in every department of human industry. With peace assured throughout the Union, we are entering upon a decade which is likely to be the most prosperous in its history.

Business in our midst is liable to be cramped for lack of bank facilities. Every industrial interest which relies upon banks for assistance will be endangered, and the taxes which they could pay in, were they prosperous, will be lost to the State. The country, in its efforts soon to return to a sound currency, will require the utmost aid which organized capital can supply. Is the legislature of the State of New York prepared to see its chief city, hitherto the undisputed commercial and financial metropolis of the nation, surrender its supremacy? It is at this hour in serious jeopardy. New York has rivals who are jealous of her prosperity and greatness, and who are eager to pluck from her brow the crown of superiority she has so long worn. They boast of their lighter taxes, and of their greater advantages for carrying on trade, commerce, manufactures and banking. They predict the decline of the great metropolis. Shall the legislature of the empire State give aid and comfort to those who watch and wail for the decadence of the empire city?

When the growth and prosperity of the city are blighted, will its citizens alone feel the shock? To show how closely the interests of the people of other parts of the State are connected with those of its chief city, I need but refer to the fact that of the $85,000,000 of bank capital in the city, upwards of $6,000,000 are owned by persons dwelling in the interior counties. Will not the State suffer to its remotest borders when its great financial heart beats feebly and slowly?

The policy of severe and unequal taxation inflicted upon the banks of this State opens the door for capitalists from other States and countries to transact this business in modes which entirely escape taxation here. The banks of rival cities have established agencies among us; but having no property here they evade the tax gatherer, for their business does not come within the law. Foreigners are now doing the same thing on a large scale. Four Canadian banks alone, with an aggregate capital of $33,000,000, have agencies in the city of New York, who do a large proportion of the commercial business, and having none of their capital actually in the city they avoid taxation.

Is it wise to drive out of the State by unjust rates of taxation, our own native banking capital, which is willing to pay fair and even liberal rates, and to supply its place with foreign capital that pays no tax at all, and is in no wise identified with the welfare of our great commercial and industrial interests? Take, by way of illustration, the case of a few of our leading banks. The National Bank of Commerce of New York, with a capital stock paid in of $10,000,000, paid, in 1876, national, State and local taxes amounting to $407,892.90, equal to $1,333 for every working day in the year. The American Exchange National Bank, New York, with a capital stock paid in of $5,000,000, last year paid a total tax of $227,203.99, or $742 per day. The Metropolitan National Bank, New York, with a capital stock paid in of $4,000,000, paid last year taxes amounting to $202,197.30, or $660 per day.

The smaller banks bear even a greater burden in proportion to their strength. The Fallkill National Bank of Poughkeepsie, with a capital stock paid in of $400,000, last year, paid national, State, and local taxes amounting to $26,490. The First National Bank of Troy, with a capital stock paid in of $300,000, last year paid national, State and city taxes amounting to $16,058.56, leaving a net profit for the stockholders of only $9,714.44 — thus compelling the bank to draw $14,285.56 on previous earnings to pay its dividends. And I have the best authority for stating that at least two-thirds of the banks in the city of New York did not earn the dividends which last year they were compelled by the poverty and importunity of the shareholders to pay, but drew the deficiency from their reserves.

But, Mr. Speaker, I will not weary this House by multiplying special examples. The question before us is plain and simple. Shall our bank taxes be modified, or shall bank capital, as a controlling element in affairs, be driven from the State?

In my judgment, sir, it is far wiser and better to tax banks fairly and honestly, and thereby to check a further reduction of bank capital, rather than by legislative oppression and injustice to diminish the chief source of the revenue of the State, and thus increase the taxation upon our agricultural and other business interests.

In over-taxing the banking interest a serious wound is necessarily inflicted upon all industrial pursuits, and the losses of the capital whereon the State may levy taxes are multiplied in all directions.

I have stated that the reduction in and depreciation of bank capital in New York city alone, the past year, amount to some $32,000,000. The loss of tax on that sum must necessarily be made up by the State. It cannot be made up by the city, because the assessed valuation of all its real and personal property, exclusive of bank shares, the past year has been reduced $1,643,481. This burden, therefore, must fall on the property in the other portions of the State.

Now, Mr. Speaker, are the representatives on the floor of this house mindful of this fact ? Are they quite willing to pay their share of this excessive taxation, in addition to the amount they have been accustomed to pay ? No, sir, this cannot be.

Banks are the nutriment whereon all kinds of business feed, and from which they become vigorous and healthy. Show me a country, or even a large community, where banks do not exist, and I will show you a place where enterprise is stagnant. Banks, by their machinery, furnish the circulating medium for carrying on all branches of industry. The ordinary pursuits of civilized society depend upon the monetary operations of the banks to give them activity and prosperity, as the body relies upon the circulation of the blood to give it vigor and health.

Banks, when properly understood, will not be regarded as the favorites and instruments of capitalists and millionaires, so much as the agents of the industrial classes, and the servants of those enjoying credit but possessing moderate means. They not only deal in money, but they provide it for all. The capital they send out they first gather in small sums from many individuals, and thus benefit the State by bringing the aggregate of these minor contributions within the reach of the assessors, which, otherwise would escape taxation; for money, whatever be the amount, in the pockets of individuals, is exempt from taxation.

The banks, being institutions of discount and deposit, are to a certain extent the accountants of the business community, while at the same time they are needful instruments of the government for conducting its great financial transactions. The defenseless, necessarily resort to them for the safe investment of their savings and inheritances. Of the 360 stockholders of one of the national banks of Newark, New Jersey, more than 200 are women. The bank of Pittsburg, Pennsylvania, has 295 female shareholders. Bank shares, it is well known, are held in trust for invalids and helpless children. They are largely used as permanent investments by widows, orphans and executors, and also by the industrial classes. Of the 208,486 shareholders in the national banks throughout the country, one-half of them hold stock for an amount not exceeding $1,000 each. There are 104,976 holding only ten shares or less; 39,206 holding over ten and not more than twenty shares; 9,941 holding over thirty, and not more than forty shares. In the State of New York the average amount owned by each stockholder is about $2,000.

These figures show conclusively the high estimation in which national banks are held by the mass of the people, and that they are essentially popular, and not aristocratic institutions.

In Europe banking is done to a considerable extent by large capitalists like the Rothschilds and the Barings. In the United States it is done chiefly by gathering smaller sums into larger, and these consolidations of capital enable us to engage in enterprises which otherwise could not be undertaken.

Banks enjoy no privileges which are not open to all who will comply with the conditions whereon they are established, for the banking system is free to all who choose to engage in it. Then are they not entitled to fair and reasonable treatment from the people and the law-makers of the people?

Many banks in our chief cities—and the same is doubtless true to a considerable extent in all parts of the State—cannot, under the weight of the present taxation, earn legal interest on their capital. During the war they made money by handling heavy sums for the government, and by aiding to carry on large enterprises for individuals growing out of the war. Moreover the premium on the gold received for interest on their bonds added largely to their earnings. But all this is changed. During the year or two past, when the taxation of bank shares in the city was only on their par value, many of the banks did not earn their dividends, as I have already stated. What then can be expected of them now, when the shares are taxed at their full market value? while money in large sums is readily obtained on undoubted security at rates at least one-third less than the amount of taxes imposed, and while good commercial paper has been freely discounted for the past three years at an average rate of less than five per cent.

In view of these facts, Mr. Speaker, need I add that the struggle is one for existence. At such a crisis how is it possible for banks to stand a rate of taxation running up to 5 1-10, 6, and even 6 6-10 per cent, whose chief vocation in even prosperous times is to loan money at a rate limited by law to seven per cent per annum? The simple question is, whether this Legislature will allow the banks of the State, by means of unjust and oppressive laws, to be taxed out of existence?

What, then, are some of the remedies for the evils I have depicted? They lie partly in legislation and partly in the courts. Some of the remedies must be sought in Congress and in the federal courts. With these we have no concern now. We are dealing only with our own State authorities.

1. There should be legislation providing that banking property of whatever kind shall not be assessed at any higher rate in proportion to its actual value, than other property in the same locality is assessed in proportion to its actual value.

2. It should be made the duty of the local assessors, and especially of the State assessors, to see that this provision is carried into effect, and they should be clothed with ample power to do it.

3. That in making assessments of bank property, the amount of untaxable United States securities held by the bank shall be deducted from the amount of the assessment, and the tax levied on the balance only. This is in accordance with the judicial opinion of Mr. Chase, pronounced as Chief Justice of the United States, who, when Secretary of the Treasury, was the author of the National Banking Law.

4. That banks should be allowed to deduct the legal reserve which they are compelled by law to keep on hand, and which they are prohibited from using.

5. That the shareholder of bank capital shall be allowed to deduct, as with other personal property, from the amount of his shares, the amount of his actual indebtedness.

6. That the State assessors shall devise ways and means for carrying all these provisions into effect.

7. That the courts be empowered to bring assessors and assessment rolls before them by summary process, with authority to rectify inequalities in the rolls. By these just and simple expedients our banks may be preserved.

Mr. Speaker, I cannot believe that there is any desire on the part of the members of this House to destroy this great and indispensable part of our material fabric, or by undue legislative severity to drive any portion of the banking capital of New York beyond the borders of the State.

The statistics of the New York Clearing House show that ninety-six per cent of all the exchanges of commercial commodities are made by the banks without the use of money of any kind. They are a necessity of our times — an important part of the machinery that moves the products of agriculture, that turns the wheels of manufactures, and that floats the commerce of the world. Nay, more, they are the vehicles of material aid for giving remunerative employment to the toiling masses.

I know how difficult it is to convince those who regard banks merely as great reservoirs for the surplus money of the rich, that the people have any special concern in the subject I have discussed. There is abroad a mistaken and harmful impression, or prejudice, that banks are favored, powerful and selfish corporations, amply able to take care of themselves, and do take care of themselves.

I trust there is no member of this House who is thus deluded, or who does not see how the great aggregates of capital that appear so strong and prosperous are made up of the contributions of the frugal farmers and mechanics, of the careful workers on small salaries, of widows and orphans, of professional men of small means, of all classes of industrious toilers. And as the money that goes into these reservoirs of capital comes trickling from tens of thousands of humble rivulets, so the money that goes out of them is not only sent forth in large streams to fructify vast areas of enterprise, but in driblets, through thousands of little channels, doing good and creating good wherever it goes.

The hands and the feet might as well expect to receive the benefit of a free and vigorous circulation of the blood, while the heart was constricted, as for laboring men of this State to expect that employment would be ample and business lively, while they consented to the constriction of the very heart of the commerce and industry of the State by such legislation as has already begun to paralyze and has long since crippled the banks.

The people always are ready to do justice, when they know what it is. They are always ready to remedy wrong when they see it; and I will not so insult the good sense of the majority of the voters of the rural districts as to suppose that they cannot see and understand the gross, wanton, wicked injustice that has been perpetrated on the banks, when they read the plain, unanswerable evidence now presented. They will tell the legislators who aid in perpetuating such suicidal folly, that they have greatly underestimated the intelligence of their constituency. To that constituency, and to its representatives here assembled, I appeal with confidence.

THIRD REPORT

ON

Bank Taxation.

REGULATIONS

AS TO THE

New Internal Revenue Law,

OF MARCH 1, 1879,

EXEMPTING SAVINGS DEPOSITS FROM TAXATION.

CORRESPONDENCE WITH THE HON. GREEN B. RAUM, COMMISSIONER OF INTERNAL REVENUE.

New York:
AMERICAN BANKERS' ASSOCIATION, 247 BROADWAY.
1879.

AMERICAN BANKERS' ASSOCIATION, 1878-79.

President,
ALEX. MITCHELL, President Marine & Fire Ins. Bank, Milwaukee, Wis.

First Vice-President.
JACOB D. VERMILYE, President Merchants' National Bank, New York City.

Vice-Presidents.

ALABAMA.—William H. Pratt, President Bank of Mobile, *Mobile*.
ARKANSAS.—Logan H. Roots, President Merchants' National Bank, *Little Rock*.
CALIFORNIA.—Louis McLane, President Nevada Bank, *San Francisco*.
COLORADO.—Jerome B. Chaffee, President First National Bank of *Denver*.
CONNECTICUT.—Rowland Swift, President American National Bank, *Hartford*.
DAKOTA.—James C. McVay, President First National Bank, of *Yankton*.
DELAWARE.—Edward Betts, President First National Bank, *Wilmington*.
DISTRICT OF COLUMBIA.—John A. J. Creswell, President Citizens' National Bank of *Washington City*.
FLORIDA.—James M. Shoemaker, Cashier First National Bank, *Jacksonville*.
GEORGIA.—William H. Patterson, Cashier Citizens' Bank of Georgia, *Atlanta*.
IDAHO.—James H. McCarty, President First National Bank of *Boise City*.
ILLINOIS.—Chauncey B. Blair, President Merchants' National Bank, *Chicago*.
INDIANA.—F. A. W. Davis, Cashier Indiana Banking Co. of *Indianapolis*.
IOWA.—F. H. Griggs, President Citizens' National Bank, *Davenport*.
KANSAS.—John R. Mulvane, President Topeka Bank, *Topeka*.
KENTUCKY.—John W. Proctor, Cashier Central National Bank, *Danville*.
LOUISIANA.—A. Luria, Cashier Louisiana National Bank, *New Orleans*.
MAINE.—William E. Gould, Cashier First National Bank, *Portland*.
MARYLAND.—Henry A. Thompson, President National Bank of Baltimore, *Baltimore*.
MASSACHUSETTS.—William H. Foster, Cashier Asiatic National Bank, *Salem*.
MICHIGAN.—Henry P. Baldwin, President Second National Bank, *Detroit*.
MINNESOTA.—Horace Thompson, President First National Bank, *St. Paul*.
MISSISSIPPI.—George M. Klein, Cashier Mississippi Valley Bank, *Vicksburgh*.
MISSOURI.—Rufus J. Lackland, President Boatmen's Saving Bank, *St. Louis*.
MONTANA.—Samuel T. Hauser, President First National Bank of *Helena*.
NEVADA.—George Tufly, President Carson City Savings Bank, *Carson City*.
NEBRASKA.—H. Kountze, President First National Bank of Omaha, *Omaha*.
NEW HAMPSHIRE.—John A. Spalding, Cashier First National Bank of *Nashua*.
NEW JERSEY.—Alex. H. Wallis, President First National Bank of *Jersey City*.
NEW MEXICO.—S. B. Elkins, President First National Bank of *Santa Fe*.
NEW YORK.—Jacob D. Vermilye, President Merchants' National Bank, *New York*.
NORTH CAROLINA.—William E. Anderson, President Citizens' National Bank, *Raleigh*.
OHIO.—Daniel J. Fallis, President Merchants' National Bank of *Cincinnati*.
OREGON.—Henry W. Corbett, ex-Senator U. S. and Vice-Pres. First Nat'l Bk., *Portland*.
PENNSYLVANIA.—Joseph Patterson, President Western National Bank, *Philadelphia*.
RHODE ISLAND.—Edward A. Greene, President National Bank of Commerce, *Providence*.
SOUTH CAROLINA.—William C. Bresse, Cashier First National Bank, *Charleston*.
TENNESSEE.—H. E. Garth, President German National Bank, *Memphis*.
TEXAS.—A. F. Hardie, President City Bank of *Dallas*.
UTAH.—William H. Hooper, President Deseret National Bank, *Salt Lake City*.
VERMONT.—Henry P. Hickok, President Merchants' National Bank, *Burlington*.
VIRGINIA.—George M. Bain, Jr., Cashier Exchange National Bank, *Norfolk*.
WEST VIRGINIA.—J. Nelson Vance, President Exchange Bank, *Wheeling*.
WISCONSIN.—N. B. Van Slyke, President First National Bank, *Madison*.
WYOMING.—Edward Ivinson, President Wyoming National Bank, *Laramie City*.
WASHINGTON.—Dexter Horton, of Horton & Co., *Seattle*.

Executive Council.

GEORGE S. COE, President American Exchange National Bank of New York, Chairman.
JAMES BUELL, President Importers' and Traders' National Bank of New York.
MORTON MCMICHAEL, Jr., Cashier First National Bank of Philadelphia, Pa.
ENOCH PRATT, President National Farmers' and Planters' Bank of Baltimore, Md.
EDWARD TYLER, Cashier Suffolk National Bank of Boston, Mass.
J. W. LOCEWOOD, Cashier National Bank of Virginia, Richmond.
J. D. HAYES, Vice-President Merchants' and Manufacturers' National Bank, Detroit, Mich.
L. J. GAGE, Cashier First National Bank of Chicago, Ill.
WILLIAM G. DESHLER, President National Exchange Bank, Columbus, Ohio.
EDWARD B. JUDSON, President First National Bank, Syracuse, N. Y.
EX-Gov. SAMUEL MERRILL, President Citizens National Bank, Des Moines, Iowa.
M. KOPPERL, President National Bank of Texas, Galveston, Texas.
CHARLES PARSONS, President State Savings Association, St. Louis, Mo.
HOEL H. CAMP, Cashier First National Bank, Milwaukee, Wisconsin.
WILLIAM H. RHAWN, President National Bank of the Republic, Philadelphia, Pa.
OSCAR L. BALDWIN, Cashier Mechanics' National Bank, Newark, N. J.
LOGAN C. MURRAY, Cashier Kentucky National Bank, Louisville, Kentucky.
W. H. MORRISON, President First National Bank, Indianapolis, Ind.
J. B. MCMILLAN, Cashier Mobile Savings Bank, Mobile, Ala.
AUGUSTUS H. MOSS, President First National Bank Sandusky, Ohio.
J. H. MILLARD, Cashier Omaha National Bank, Omaha, Neb.

Treasurer.
GEORGE F. BAKER, President First National Bank, New York.

Secretary.
JAMES BUELL, President Importers' and Traders' National Bank, New York.

Assistant Secretary.
GEORGE MARSLAND, Editor, 247 Broadway, New York.

THIRD REPORT ON BANK TAXATION.

To Banks and Bank Officers.

Considerable uncertainty has prevailed as to the interpretation of the law of March 1st, 1879, exempting savings deposits, under certain conditions, from Federal taxation. Since the passage of the law we have had an active correspondence with banks and bank officers, with inquiries or applications for information, and we have obtained from the Internal Revenue Bureau at Washington the following papers, which contain all the regulations that the Commissioner, General Raum is at present prepared to announce. We shall be pleased to hear further from you on the subject.

The only part of the new law which affects the banks is the 22d section, which is as follows in the official copy sent to us:

SEC. 22. That whenever and after any bank has ceased to do business by reason of insolvency or bankruptcy, no tax shall be assessed or collected, or paid into the Treasury of the United States, on account of such bank, which shall diminish the assets thereof necessary for the full payment of all its depositors; and such tax shall be abated from such national banks as are found by the Comptroller of the Currency to be insolvent; and the Commissioner of Internal Revenue, when the facts shall so appear to him, is authorized to remit so much of said tax against insolvent State and savings banks as shall be found to affect the claims of their depositors.

That in making further collections of internal revenue taxes on bank deposits, no savings bank, recognized as such by the laws of its State, and having no capital stock, shall, on account of mercantile or business deposits heretofore received, upon which no interest has been allowed to the parties making such deposits, be denied the exemptions allowed to savings banks having no capital stock, and doing no other business than receiving deposits to be loaned or invested for the sole benefit of the parties making such deposits, without profit or compensation to the banks, if such bank has paid the lawful tax upon the entire average amount of such business or mercantile deposits. But nothing in this section shall be construed to extend said exemptions to deposits hereafter made, or in any way to affect the liability of such deposits to taxation.

That section thirty-four hundred and eight of the Revised Statutes be amended by striking out all after the thirtieth line, and inserting the following:

"The deposits in associations or companies known as provident institutions, savings banks, savings funds, or savings institutions, doing no other business than receiving and loaning or investing savings deposits, shall be exempt from tax on so much of such deposits as they have invested in securities of the United States, and on two thousand dollars of savings deposits and nothing in excess thereof made in the name of and belonging to any one person or firm. That all laws and parts of laws inconsistent with the provisions of this section be, and the same are hereby, repealed."

The next paper we received from the Commissioner is marked 106 a, and is as follows. It is the blank form for the returns of savings banks *without capital*:

Instructions for Savings Banks without Capital,

Issued by the Commissioner of Internal Revenue, in accordance with the New Law of March 1, 1879.

[*Form 106 a.*]

Semi-Annual Returns by Savings Banks of Deposits, &c.,

FOR THE SIX MONTHS ENDING MAY 31, 1879.

The semi-annual returns required under the provisions of Section 3414, U. S. Revised Statutes, and Section 21, Act of February 8, 1875, will be rendered on the following prescribed forms, viz:

First.—Those associations or companies known as provident institutions, savings banks, savings funds, or savings institutions, having no capital stock, and, prior to March 1, 1879, doing no other business than receiving deposits to be loaned or invested for the sole benefit of the parties making such deposits, without profit or compensation to the association or company; also, on and after March 1, 1879, those doing no other business than receiving and loaning or investing savings deposits—Form 106 a.

Second.—Those institutions of the character described in the last paragraph, except that they have a capital stock; also those which were in existence on the 18th day of June, 1874, and do business only as savings banks, and are recognized as such by the laws of their respective States or by Congress, although they have a capital stock or bond for the additional security of their depositors, and pay dividends thereon: *Provided*, That all the profits of such savings banks, less the aforementioned dividends on stock, not exceeding at the rate of eight per cent. per annum, are divided among the depositors, and that the capital stock is invested only in the same class of securities as is used for investing the deposits, and that interest at the rate of not less than four and one-half per cent. be paid in all cases to their depositors, to be made good if necessary from from the capital stock—Form 106 a.

Third.—All other returns required under the provisions of Section 3414, U. S. Revised Statutes, and Section 21 of the Act of February 8, 1875—Form 67.

The following instructions are issued for guidance in the preparation of the annexed returns on Form 106 b:

1. The return must be made in duplicate, by the President or Cashier (or Secretary or Treasurer, where authorized by law to perform the duties of Cashier), on the first day of June and the first day of December.

2. The return must be sworn to before the Collector, or a Deputy Collector, of the District in which the bank is situated, or before an officer with a seal, duly authorized to administer oaths.

3. One copy of the return will be delivered to the Collector, or his Deputy, and one mailed to the Commissioner of Internal Revenue.

4. The particulars relating to each subject of taxation must be stated for each month, under the heading for that month.

5. If there is nothing to report, the officer must indicate the fact by writing "0" in the proper place.

6. Where a bank or banker commences or discontinues business during the period covered by the return, the date of such commencement or discontinuance must be stated in red ink across the face of the return.

7. In case of discontinuance, the last return rendered will cover a taxable period ending on the day on which the business of the bank or banker ceased. Liability continues as long as any business described in Section 3407, Revised Statutes, is done. If the discontinuance in the case of a bank is in consequence of its insolvency or bankruptcy, and it is claimed that the collection of the tax shown to be due by the return will diminish the assets of the bank

necessary for the full payment of all its depositors, the return should be accompanied by a sworn statement of the President, Cashier, Receiver or Assignee, as to its assets and liabilities, in such form or manner as will clearly show what portion of the tax, if any, could be paid without diminishing the assets necessary for the full payment of the depositors.

8. In determining what shall be considered as taxable deposits, reference will be had to Section 3408, U. S. Revised Statutes. The term "United States Securities" includes only interest bearing obligations of the United States owned and held by the bank as an investment. The average of monthly deposits, subject to tax, must be made up from the "daily balances" of deposits by adding the daily balance of each day in the month during which business is done, and dividing the aggregate by the number of days in said month during which business is done. The "balance" of deposits of each day, which is thus first to be ascertained, is the entire amount of deposits remaining to the credit of depositors at the close of business for the day. But the balance of deposits of each day, in the case of savings banks, subject to tax, is the entire amount of deposits remaining to the credit of depositors at the close of business each day, less—1st, the amount of such *deposits* invested in securities of the United States; 2d, amounts of $2,000. or *under*, in the name of any one person.

9. In estimating the taxable deposits, deductions of amounts redeposited and of amounts overdrawn are not allowable. Attention is called to this matter from the fact that certain banks have heretofore made such deductions rendering assessments of additional tax with penalty necessary.

10. In the case of savings banks, when sums amounting to over $2,000 are deposited in the name of any one person, the whole amount, including the $2,000, is taxable up to March 1st, 1879; but, on and after March 1, 1879, not only will deposits of $2,000 and under, in the name of and belonging to any one person, be exempt, but from each deposit in excess of that amount, in the name of and belonging to any one person, the sum of $2,000 will be deducted as exempt.

11. All banks, except such institutions (savings banks) as are entitled to return on Form 106 *a* or Form 106 *b*, are liable to be taxed upon the entire amount of their average deposits. And those institutions which are entitled to return on Form 106 *a* or Form 106 *b* are liable upon the entire amount of such deposits, less the deductions authorized by Section 3408, Revised Statutes, as amended. (See instruction No. 8, above.)

EXTRACTS FROM INTERNAL REVENUE LAWS

RELATING TO SAVINGS BANKS.

Definition of a Bank or Banker.—Section 3407, U. S. Revised Statutes, provides that "Every incorporated or other bank, and every person, firm, or company having a place of business where credits are opened by the deposit or collection of money or currency, subject to be paid or remitted upon draft, check, or order, or where money is advanced or loaned on stocks, bonds, bullion, bills of exchange, or promissory notes, or where stocks, bonds, bullion, bills of exchange, or promissory notes are received for discount or for sale, shall be regarded as a bank or as a banker."

Tax on Deposits.—Section 3408, Revised Statutes, provides that "There shall be levied, collected, and paid * * A tax of one twenty-fourth of one per centum each month upon the average amount of the deposits of money, subject to payment by check or draft, or represented by certificates of deposit or otherwise, whether payable on demand or at some future day, with any person, bank, association, company, or corporation, engaged in the business of banking."

Deposits Exempt from Tax.—Section 3408, Revised Statutes, as amended by an Act approved March 1, 1879, provides that "Associations or companies known as provident institutions, savings banks, savings funds, or savings institutions doing no other business than receiving and loaning or investing savings deposits shall be exempt from tax on so much of such ' .. ' . ' . ' . ' .es of the United States, and on TWO THOUSAND

DOLLARS of savings deposits and nothing in excess thereof, made in the name of and belonging to any one person."

Section 22 of the internal revenue act approved March 1, 1879, provides "That in making further collections of internal revenue taxes on bank deposits, no savings bank, recognized as such by the laws of its State, and having no capital stock, shall, on account of mercantile or business deposits heretofore received, upon which no interest has been allowed to the parties making such deposits, be denied the exemptions allowed to savings books having no capital stock, and doing no other business than receiving deposits to be loaned or invested for the sole benefit of the parties making such deposits, without profit or compensation to the banks, if such bank has paid the lawful tax upon the entire average amount of such business or mercantile deposits; but nothing in this section shall be construed to extend said exemptions to deposits hereafter made, or in any way to affect the liability of such deposits to taxation."

Additional Tax on Notes used for Circulation, and paid out.—Section 3412, Revised Statutes, provides that "Every national banking association, State bank, or State banking association, shall pay a tax of ten per centum on the amount of notes of any person, or of any State bank or State banking association, used for circulation or paid out by them."

Section 3413, Revised Statutes, provides that "Every national banking association, State bank, or banker, or association, shall pay a tax of ten per centum on the amount of notes of any town, city, or municipal corporation, paid out by them."

Section 19 of the Act of February 8, 1875, provides "That every person, firm, association, other than national bank associations, and every corporation, State bank, or State banking association, shall pay a tax of ten per centum on the amount of their own notes used for circulation and paid out by them."

Section 20 of the same Act provides "That every such person, firm, association, corporation, State bank, or State banking association, and also every national banking association, shall pay a like tax of ten per centum on the amount of notes of any person, firm, association other than a national banking association, or of any corporation, State bank, or State banking association, or of any town, city, or municipal corporation, used for circulation and paid out by them."

Return to be made Semi-annually, Verified by Oath.—Section 3414, Revised Statutes, provides that "A true and complete return of the monthly amount of * * * deposits * * * as aforesaid, and of the monthly amount of notes of persons, town, city, or municipal corporation, State banks or State banking associations, paid out as aforesaid for the previous six months, shall be made and rendered in duplicate on the first day of December and the first day of June, by each of such banks, associations, corporations, companies, or persons, with a declaration annexed thereto, under the oath of such person, or the president or cashier of such bank, association, corporation, or company, in such form and manner as may be prescribed by the Commissioner of Internal Revenue, that the same contains a true and faithful statement of the amounts subject to tax, as aforesaid; and one copy shall be transmitted to the Collector of the district in which any such bank, association, corporation, or company is situated, or in which such person has his place of business, and one copy to the Commissioner of Internal Revenue."

Section 21 of the Act of February 8, 1875, provides. as to the ten per cent. tax on notes used for circulation and paid out, "That the amount of such circulating notes, and of the tax due thereon, shall be returned, and the tax paid at the same time, and in the same manner, and with like penalties for failure to return and pay the same, as provided by law for the return and payment of taxes on deposits, capital, and circulation, imposed by the existing provisions of internal revenue law."

Penalty for Neglect.—Section 3415, Revised Statutes, provides that, in default of the returns above required, the amount of deposits, and of notes subject to a tax of ten per cent. as aforesaid, shall be estimated by the Commissioner of Internal Revenue, upon the best information he can obtain, "And for any refusal or neglect to make return and payment, any such bank, association, corporation, company or person so in default shall pay a penalty of two hundred dollars, besides the additional penalty and forfeitures provided in other cases."

Tax to be paid Semi-annually.—Section 3409, Revised Statutes, and Section 21 of the Act of February 8, 1875, provide, in effect, that the taxes above referred to shall be paid semi-annually, on the first day of January and the first day of July; but the same shall be calculated at the rate per month as prescribed by Section 3408, so that the tax for six months shall not be less than the aggregate would be if such taxes were collected monthly.

Section 22 of an Act entitled "An Act to amend the laws relating to internal revenue," approved March 1, 1879, provides "That, whenever and after any bank has ceased to do business by reason of insolvency or bankruptcy, no tax shall be assessed or collected, or paid into the Treasury of the United States, on account of such bank, which shall diminish the assets thereof necessary for the full payment of all its depositors."

UNITED STATES INTERNAL REVENUE.

SEMI-ANNUAL RETURN BY SAVINGS BANKS, OF DEPOSITS, &c.

Return of Provident Institutions, Savings Banks, Savings Funds, or Savings Institutions, having no Capital Stock, and doing no other business than Receiving Deposits, to be Loaned or Invested for the sole benefit of Parties making such Deposits, without Profit or Compensation to the Association or Company; also, of Parties making Deposits, 1879, all such as are entitled to exemptions under Section 3408 R. S., as amended by Section 22 of the Act approved March 1, 1879.

[To be made in duplicate on the first day of December and the first day of June—one copy to be transmitted (by the party making the return) to the Collector, and one copy to the Commissioner of Internal Revenue.—Section 3414 Revised Statutes, and Section VII of the Act of February 8, 1875]

Account of Deposits, and of such Deposits less sums of $2,000 or under, deposited in the name of, and, on and after March 1, 1879, also belonging to, any one person in, and of Notes liable to a tax of ten per cent. paid out by _____, located at _____, in the Collection District of the State of _____, for the Six Months ending * May 31, 1879, liable to a Tax under the Internal Revenue Laws.

	*Dec., 1878.		*Jan., 1879.		*Feb., 1879.		*Mar., 1879.		*Apl., 1879.		*May, 1879.		†Total amount for six months		Rate.	Tax.	
	Dollars.	Cts.	Dollars.	Cts.	Dollars.	Cts.	Dollars.	Cts.	Dollars.	Cts.	Dollars.	Cts.	Dollars.	Cts.		Dollars.	Cts.
1. Average amount of deposits held during......																	
2. Less average amount of Deposits invested in U. S. Securities held during.....																	
3. Remainder......																	
4. Less average amount of Deposits of sums of $2,000, or under, made in the name of one person, held during [See instruction 10]......																	
5. Net Balance subject to Tax......															¼ of 1 p. ct. per month.		
6. Amount of own notes and notes of any person, firm, association (other than National Banking Association); also notes of any corporation, State Bank, or State Banking Association, used for circulation and paid out since last previous return; also amount of notes of any town, city, or municipal corporation so paid out....															10 per cent.		

Total Amount of Tax..

I, _____, do swear that this account contains, to the best of my knowledge and belief, a true and faithful statement of the average amount of Deposits, the average amount of Deposits of sums of $2,000, and under, in the name of, and, on and after March 1, 1879, also belonging to, any one person, held by this Bank during the time specified, and of the average amount of Deposit of this Bank invested in United States Securities as above set forth; and of the amount of notes of the character above specified paid out since the last previous return; also, that this Bank has no capital stock, and ,prior to March 1, 1879, did no other business than receiving Deposits to be loaned or invested for the sole benefit of the parties making such Deposits, without profit or compensation to the association or company; and on and after March 1, 1879, did no other business than loaning or investing savings deposits.

Sworn to and subscribed before me, this _____ day of _____, 1879.

‡ _____

* These dates are printed for the convenience of those using this Form for the period ending May 31, 1879.
† Found by adding together the amounts reported for each month.
‡ "President," "Cashier," "Treasurer," or "Secretary," as the case may be.

The second paper we received from the Commissioner is marked 106 b, and is the blank form for the returns of savings banks *with capital*. It is as follows:

Instructions for Savings Banks having a Capital Stock as Bond,

Issued by the Commissioner of Internal Revenue, in accordance with the New Law of March 1, 1879.

(*Form 106 b.*)

Semi-Annual Returns by Savings Banks of Deposits, &c.,

FOR THE SIX MONTHS' ENDING MAY 31, 1879.

The semi-annual returns required under the provisions of Section 3414, U. S. Revised Statutes, and Section 21, Act of February 8, 1875, will be rendered on the following prescribed forms, viz.:

First.—Those associations or companys known as provident institutions, savings banks, savings funds, or savings institutions, having no capital stock, and, prior to March 1, 1879, doing no other business than receiving deposits to be loaned or invested for the sole benefit of the parties making such deposits, without profit or compensation to the association or company; also, on and after March 1, 1879, those doing no other business than receiving and loaning or investing savings deposits—Form 106 *a.*

Second.—Those institutions of the character described in the last paragraph, except that they have a capital stock; also those which were in existence on the 18th day of June, 1874, and do business only as savings banks, and are recognized as such by the laws of their respective States or by Congress, although they have a capital stock or bond for the additional security of their depositors, and pay dividends thereon: *Provided*, That all the profits of such savings banks, less the aforementioned dividends on stock, not exceeding at the rate of eight per cent. per annum, are divided among the depositors, and that the capital stock is invested only in the same class of securities as is used for investing the deposits, and that interest at the rate of not less than four and one-half per cent. be paid in all cases to their depositors, to be made good if necessary from the capital stock—Form 106 *b.*

Third.—All other returns required under the provisions of Section 3418 U. S. Revised Statutes, and Section 21 of the Act of February 8, 1875—Form 67.

The following instructions are issued for guidance in the preparation of the annexed return on Form 106 *b*:

1. The return must be made in duplicate, by the President or Cashier (or Secretary or Treasurer, where authorized by law to perform the duties of Cashier), on the first day of June and the first day of December.

2. The return must be sworn to before the Collector, or a Deputy Collector, of the District in which the Bank is situated, or before an officer with a seal, duly authorized to administer oaths.

3. One copy of the return will be delivered to the Collector, or his Deputy, and one mailed to the Commissioner of Internal Revenue.

4. The particulars relating to each subject of taxation must be stated for each month under the heading for that month.

5. If there is nothing to report, the officer must indicate the fact by writing "0" in the proper place.

6. *Where a bank or banker commences or discontinues during the period covered by the return, the date of such commencement or discontinuance must be stated in red ink across the face of the return.*

7. In case of discontinuance, the last return rendered will cover a taxable period ending on the day on which the business of the bank or banker ceased. Liability continues as long as any business described in Section 3407, Revised Statutes, is done. If the discontinuance in the case of a bank is in consequence of its insolvency or bankruptcy, and it is claimed that

the collection of the tax shown to be due by the return will diminish the assets of the bank necessary for the full payment of all its depositors, the return should be accompanied by a sworn statement of the President, Cashier, Receiver, or Assignee, as to its assets and liabilities, in such form or manner as will clearly show what portion of the tax, if any, could be paid without diminishing the assets necessary for the full payment of the depositors.

8. The items of capital and deposits must be stated separately on the appropriate lines, and in no case must they be aggregated as capital and deposits.

9. In determining what shall be considered as taxable deposits, reference will be had to Section 3408, U. S. Revised Statutes, as amended. The term "United States Securities" includes only interest-bearing obligations of the United States owned and held by the bank as as an investment. The average of monthly deposits, subject to tax, must be made up from the "daily balances" of deposits by adding the daily balances of each day in the month during which business is done, and dividing the aggregate by the number of days in each month during which business is done. The "balance" of deposits of each day, which is thus first to be ascertained, is the entire amount of deposits remaining to the credit of depositors at the close of business for the day. But the balance of deposits of each day, in the case of savings banks, subject to tax, is the entire amount of deposits remaining to the credit of depositors at the close of business each day, less, 1st, the amount of *deposits* at that time held as an investment in United States Securities; 2d, amounts of $2,000, *or under*, in the name of any one person. (See instruction No. 11, and the affidavit on this form, and the foot-note as to liability of certain savings banks under Act of March 1, 1879.)

10. In estimating the taxable deposits, deductions of amounts redeposited and of amounts overdrawn are not allowable. Attention is called to this matter from the fact that certain banks have heretofore made such deductions rendering assessments of additional tax with penalty necessary.

11. In the case of savings banks, when sums amounting to over $2,000 are deposited in the name of any one person, the whole amount, including the $2,000, is taxable up to March 1, 1879; but on and after March 1, 1879, not only will deposits of $2,000 and under, in the name and belonging to any one person, be exempt, but from each deposit in excess of that amount, in the name of and belonging to any one person, the sum of $2,000 will be deducted as exempt.

12. All banks, except such institutions (savings banks) are entitled to return on Form 106 *a* or Form 106 *b*, are liable to be taxed upon the entire amount of their average deposits. All those institutions which are entitled to return on Form 106 *a* or Form 106 *b*, are liable upon the entire amount of such deposits, less the deductions authorized by Section 3408, Revised Statutes, as amended. (See instructions Nos. 9 and 11 above.)

EXTRACTS FROM INTERNAL REVENUE LAWS
RELATING TO BANKS.

Definition of a Bank or Banker.—Section 3407, U. S. Revised Statutes, provides that "Every incorporated or other bank, and every person, firm, or company having a place of business where credits are opened by the deposit or collection of money or currency, subject to be paid or remitted upon draft, check, or order, or where money is advanced or loaned on stocks, bonds, bullion, bills of exchange, or promissory notes, or where stocks, bonds, bullion, bills of exchange, or promissory notes are received for discount or for sale, shall be regarded as a bank or as a banker."

Tax on Deposits and Capital.—Section 3408, Revised Statutes, provides that "There shall be levied, collected, and paid, as hereafter provided: First. A tax of one twenty-fourth of one per centum each month upon the average amount of the deposits of money, subject to payment by check or draft, or represented by certificates of deposit or otherwise, whether payable on demand or at some future day, with any person, bank, association, company, or corporation, engaged in the business of banking; Second. A tax of one twenty-fourth of one per centum each month upon the capital of any bank, association, company, corporation, and on the capi-

Deposits Exempt from Tax.—Section 3,408, Revised Statutes, as amended by Section 22 of the Act of March 1st, 1879, provides that "Associations or companies known as provident institutions, savings banks, savings funds or savings institutions, doing no other business than receiving and loaning or investing savings deposits, shall be exempt from tax on so much of such deposits as they have invested in securities of the United States, and on TWO THOUSAND DOLLARS of savings deposits, and nothing in excess thereof, made in the name of and belonging to any one person." And the Act of June 18th, 1874, provides "That all deposits made in institutions now" (June 18th, 1874) "existing which do business only as savings banks, and are recognized as such by the laws of their respective States, or by Congress, are hereby declared to be exempt from taxation the same as deposits in savings institutions having no capital although they have a capital stock or bond for the additional security of their depositors, and pay dividends thereon; and no tax shall be assessed upon the deposits made in such institutions, or collected of them on said deposits, otherwise than as herein provided: *Provided*, That all the profits of such savings banks, less the aforementioned dividends on stock, not exceeding at the rate of eight per cent. per annum, are divided among the depositors, and that the capital stock is invested only in the same class of securities as is used for investing the deposits, and that interest at the rate of not less than four and one-half per cent. be paid in all cases to their depositors, to be made good if necessary from the capital stock."

Additional Tax on Notes used for Circulation, and paid out.—Section 3412, Revised Statutes, provides that "Every national banking association, State bank, or State banking association, shall pay a tax of ten per centum on the amount of notes of any person, or of any State bank or State banking association, used for circulation and paid out by them."

Section 3413, Revised Statutes, provides that "Every national banking association, State bank, or banker, or association, shall pay a tax of ten per centum on the amount of notes of any town, city or municipal corporation, paid out by them."

Section 19 of the Act of February 8, 1878, provides "That every person, firm, association, other than national bank associations, and every corporation, State bank, or State banking association, shall pay a tax of ten per centum on the amount of their own notes used for circulation and paid out by them."

Section 20 of the same Act provides "That every such person, firm, association, corporation, State bank, or State banking association, and also every national banking association, shall pay a like tax of ten per centum on the amount of notes of any person, firm, association other than a national banking association, or of any corporation, State bank, or State banking association, or of any town, city, or municipal corporation, used for circulation and paid out by them."

Returns to be made semi-annually, verified by oath—Section 3414, Revised Statutes, provides that "A true and complete return of the monthly amount * * of deposits, and of capital, as aforesaid, and of the monthly amount of notes of persons, town, city, or municipal corporation, State banks, or State banking associations paid out as aforesaid for the previous six months, shall be made and rendered in duplicate on the first day of December and the first day of June, by each of such banks, associations, corporations, companies, or persons, with a declaration annexed thereto, under the oath of such person, or of the president or cashier of such bank, association, corporation, or company, in such form and manner as may be prescribed by the Commissioner of Internal Revenue, that the same contains a true and faithful statement of the amounts subject to tax as aforesaid; and one copy shall be transmitted to the Collector of the district in which any such bank, association, corporation, or company is situated, or in which such person has his place of business, and one copy to the Commissioner of Internal Revenue."

Section 21 of the Act of February 8, 1875, provides as to the ten-per-cent. tax on notes used for circulation and paid out, "That the amount of such circulating notes, and of the tax due thereon, shall be returned, and the tax paid at the same time, and in the same manner, and with like penalties for failure to return and pay the same, as provided by law for the return and payment of taxes on deposits, capital, and circulation, imposed by the existing provisions of internal revenue law."

Penalty for Neglect.—Section 3415, Revised Statutes, provides that, in default of the returns above required, the amount of deposits, capital, and of notes subject to a tax of ten per cent. as aforesaid, shall be estimated by the Commissioner of Internal Revenue, upon the best information he can obtain, "And for any refusal or neglect to make return and payment, any such bank, association, corporation, company, or person so in default shall pay a penalty of two hundred dollars, besides the additional penalty and forfeitures provided in other

UNITED STATES INTERNAL REVENUE.

Annual Return of the Monthly Average Amount of Capital and Deposits of, and of Notes liable to a tax of ten per cent, paid out by, the Savings Bank having a Capital Stock, and doing no other business than receiving and loaning or investing Savings Deposits,) located at the .... , in the District of the State of .... , for the Six Months ending *May 31, 1879.

made in duplicate on the first day of December and the 31st day of June—one copy to be transmitted (by the party making the return) to the Collector, and one copy the Commissioner of Internal Revenue.—Section 3414, Revised Statutes, and Section 21 of the Act of February 8, 1875.]

	*Dec., 1878.		*Jan., 1879.		*Feb., 1879.		*Mar., 1879.		*Apl., 1879.		*May, 1879.		†Total amount for six months.		Rate.	Tax.
	Dollars.	Cts.	Dollars.	Cts.	Dollars.	Cts.	Dollars.	Cts.	Dollars.	Cts.	Dollars.	Cts.	Dollars.	Cts.		Dollars. Cts.
Average Capital........................																
Less average amount of Capital invested in United States Bonds........																
Average Taxable Capital..............																¹⁄₂₄ of 1 per ct. per month.	
Average amount of deposits held........																
Less average amount of Deposits invested to U. S. Securities held during............																
Remainder........................																
Less average amount of Deposits exceeding $2,000, made in the name of one person, held during [See Instructions].........																
Net Balance of Deposits subject to tax......																¹⁄₂₄ of 1 p. ct. per month.	
Amount of own notes and notes of person, firm, association (other than National Banking Association); also of any corporation, State Bank, or Banking Association, used for circulation and paid out since last previous return; also amount of notes of any town, city or municipal corporation so paid out.......																10 per cent.	

Total Amount of Tax........................

I, ... , do swear that the above account is, to the best of my knowledge and belief, a true and faithful statement of the average amount of Capital and Deposits, the average amount of Deposits, not exceeding $2,000, in the name of any one person, held by this Bank during the time specified, and of the average amount of Deposits of this Bank invested in Government Securities as above set forth; and of the amount of notes of the character above specified paid out since the last preceding return; I also, that this Bank was in existence on the 8th day of June, 1874, and does business only as a Savings Bank, doing no other business than receiving deposits to be loaned or invested for the sole benefit of the parties making such Deposits, except as hereinafter stated, and is recognized as such by the laws of the State of .... , and does not pay dividends on its paid-up capital stock or bond at a rate exceeding eight per cent. per annum, and divides all the profits, and said dividends on stock, among its depositors, and that the capital stock is invested only in the same class of securities as is used for investing the deposits, and pays to its depositors interest at the rate of not less than four and one-half per cent., to be made good from its capital stock or bond.

Sworn to and subscribed before me, this ....
day of .... 1879. }

These dates are printed for the convenience of those using this Form for the period ending May 31, 1879.   † Found by adding together the amount required for each month.   ‡ If the bank is a savings bank doing no other business than receiving and loaning or investing savings deposits, but was not in existence June 18, 1874, or pays dividends to its stockholders in excess of the rate of eight per cent. per annum, or pays interest to its depositors at a less rate than four and one-half per cent. per annum, the return it should be modified accordingly; and no deductions from deposits can be made on lines 5 and 7 for the months of December, 1878, and January and February, 1879.

§ Use "Cashier," "Treasurer," or "Secretary," as the case may be.

On the receipt of these papers we had several interviews in Washington with the Commissioner of Internal Revenue, and the following letter was addressed to that officer:

THE AMERICAN BANKERS' ASSOCIATION,
No. 247 Broadway.
NEW YORK, May 6th, 1879.

Hon. GREEN B. RAUM, *Commissioner of Internal Revenue, Washington, D. C.:*

Dear Sir,—The subjoined questions have been put to us relative to the Internal Revenue Law of 1st March, 1879, which, in section 22, confers certain privileges of exemption from the bank deposit tax upon savings institutions "doing no other business than receiving and loaning or investing savings deposits."

1. Have any general regulations been prepared by the Department for the guidance of the banks in making their returns in addition to those in blank forms 106 a, 106 b ?

2. Can the privileges of exemption under the new law be claimed by such savings banks as have a capital stock which is loaned, or otherwise used in the ordinary business of the respective institutions?

3. Can the said privileges be claimed by such institutions as are commonly called savings banks, though they discount commercial paper, make call loans, receive deposits subject to check at sight, and carry on generally a business like the ordinary business of commercial banks ?

These questions are respectfully submitted for the consideration of the Department, and we shall be much obliged by an early reply.

Yours truly,
(Signed) GEORGE MARSLAND,
Assistant Secretary.

A few days later we addressed a second letter to the Commissioner, in order that we might obtain as early as possible the information desired by our correspondents:

THE AMERICAN BANKERS' ASSOCIATION,
NEW YORK, 16th May, 1879.

Hon. GREEN B. RAUM, *Commissioner of Internal Revenue, Washington, D. C.:*

Dear Sir,—We are anxious to send to our constituents throughout the United States all the information we can on the subjects referred to in our letter to you of 6th May. For obvious reasons, our communication must be sent off in a few days at the latest. Anything you may favor us with will be appreciated. We are anxious to save, as far as possible, to you and to our constituents, trouble of correspondence and uncertainty in regard to your new regulations. In the multiplicity of your pressing avocations, we think that you may have overlooked our letter of 6th inst. above referred to. We shall be pleased to hear from you at your convenience.

Yours truly,
GEORGE MARSLAND,
Assistant Secretary.

The Commissioner, in reply, sent us promptly the following full and complete details:

TREASURY DEPARTMENT,
OFFICE OF INTERNAL REVENUE,
WASHINGTON, May 17th, 1879.

GEORGE MARSLAND, Esq.,

Ass't. Sec. A. B. Association, No. 247 Broadway, New York City:

Sir,—In your letter of 6th inst. you proposed the following questions relative to the Internal Revenue Act of March 1, 1879, which, in Section 22, confers certain privileges of exemption from the bank deposit tax upon savings institutions "doing no other business than receiving and loaning or investing savings deposits," viz.:

1st. Have any regulations been prepared

ance of the banks in making their returns in addition to those in blank forms 106 A and 106 B?

2d. Can the privileges of exemption under the new law be claimed by such savings banks as have a capital stock which is loaned or otherwise used in the ordinary business of the respective institutions?

3d. Can the said privileges be claimed by such institutions as are commonly called savings banks, though they discount commercial paper, make call loans, receive deposits subject to check at sight, and carry on, generally, a business like the ordinary business of commercial banks?

1st. In reply to your first question, you are informed that, as to savings banks, no general instructions other than those on forms 106A and 106B have been issued which have construed Section 22 of the Act of March 1st, 1879.

2d. In reply to your second question, you are informed that, in the opinion of this office, the privileges of exemption under Section 3408, R. S., as amended by said Section 22, cannot be extended to any banks doing any other banking business than receiving and loaning or investing savings deposits, and that, therefore, such privileges cannot be enjoyed by a savings bank having a capital stock when such capital stock is loaned or otherwise used in the ordinary business of the bank.

3d. That inasmuch as the law requires that the bank entitled to exemption shall not only be known as a provident institution, but also requires that it shall do no other business than receiving and loaning or investing savings deposits, such institutions as receive commercial deposits or deposits subject to check at sight, discount commercial paper, make call loans, or carry on, generally, a business like the ordinary business of commercial banks, are not entitled to the privileges of exemption named therein.

Very respectfully,
(Signed)   GREEN B. RAUM,
Commissioner.

These details are so important that we wrote to the Commissioner to ask whether we were authorized to print them as part of the official regulations of the Treasury Department relative to tax returns. The following is the reply:

TREASURY DEPARTMENT,
OFFICE OF INTERNAL REVENUE,
WASHINGTON, May 20th, 1879.

GEORGE MARSLAND, Esq.,
Ass't. Secretary of the American Bankers' Association, New York:

Sir,—In reply to you letter of 16th inst., I have to say that the desired permission to print for circulation my reply to your inquiries of the 6th inst., as to exemptions from taxation under Internal Revenue Act of March 1st, 1879, is granted.

Very respectfully,
(Signed)   GREEN B. RAUM,
Commissioner.

A full report on the subject embraced in this paper will be prepared for the Annual Convention. And, meanwhile, any further information that we may receive on the tax repeal movement we will endeavor to communi-

CONSTITUTION
OF THE
AMERICAN BANKERS' ASSOCIATION.

DECLARATION.

In order to promote the general welfare and usefulness of banks and banking institutions, and to secure uniformity of action, together with the practical benefits to be derived from personal acquaintance, and from the discussion of subjects of importance to the banking and commercial interests of the country; and especially in order to secure the proper consideration of questions regarding the financial and commercial usages, customs, and laws which affect the banking interests of the entire country, we have to submit the following Constitution and By-Laws for "The American Bankers' Association."

CONSTITUTION.

ARTICLE I.

Section 1. This Association shall be called "THE AMERICAN BANKERS' ASSOCIATION."

ARTICLE II.

Section 1. Any National or State bank, or trust company, or savings bank, may become a member of this Association, and also any banker upon a majority vote, upon payment of ten dollars ($10), and may send one delegate to the annual meetings of the Association; and any member may be expelled from the Association upon a vote of two-thirds of those present at any regular meeting.

Section 2. Delegates shall be an officer, or director, or trustee of the institutions they represent, or a member of a banking firm, or an individual doing business as a bank.

Section 3. Delegates shall vote in person; no voting by proxy shall be allowed.

Section 4. All votes shall be *vivâ voce*, unless otherwise ordered; any delegate may demand a division of the house.

ARTICLE III.

Section 1. The administration of the affairs of this Association shall be vested in the President of this Association and one Vice-President for each State and Territory which may be represented in this Association, and in an Executive Council, composed of twenty-one of the members of this Association, who shall be elected at the annual meetings and who shall serve until their successors are chosen or appointed.

Section 2. The Vice-Presidents shall have the supervision of the business of the Association in the States and Territories where they reside, and may call meetings when they may deem the same necessary; and in case of absence or disability of the President of the Association to preside, they may designate one of their number to act as President *pro tem.;* and said President *pro tem.* shall, in case of death or other disability of the President, be invested with all the power of President until a successor shall be duly elected or appointed.

Section 3. The Executive Council of twenty-one shall take charge of the general business of the Association, receive communications, arrange for holding meetings, procure and arrange subjects for discussion in the order in which they may come before the Convention, provide for speakers, and carry out the resolutions passed. They shall also act as a financial committee for raising and disbursing moneys. The attendance of five members of the Executive Council shall constitute a quorum for the transaction of business.

Section 4. The Executive Council of twenty-one may appoint and discharge the Secretary and Treasurer, or other employees of the Association at their discretion.

Section 5. Special meetings of the Executive Council may be called by request of three of its own members, giving two weeks' notice to the Secretary desiring him to call such special meeting. The Council shall have power to fill vacancies that may occur in their own body.

Section 6. The Executive Council shall provide—1st, for keeping the records of the proceedings of their own meetings, as well as that of the Association's annual or special meetings; 2d, they shall submit to each annual meeting a report, covering their own official acts as well as a statement of any new or unfinished business requiring attention; 3d, they shall make full statements of the financial condition of the Association; and, 4th, submit an estimate of the amount required to carry on the affairs of the Association according to their judgment of the business to be done, and recommend means for raising money to carry out such plans as may be resolved upon by the Association.

Section 7. The Secretary shall make and have charge of the records of the Association, as well as those of the Council and of the correspondence of the Executive Council. Such records shall be the property of this Association, and be held subject at all times to the order of the Executive Council.

Section 8. The Treasurer shall receive and account for all moneys belonging to the Association, and collect assessments, but shall pay out moneys only upon vouchers countersigned and approved by the President of the Association, or by the Secretary appointed by the Executive Council.

ARTICLE IV.

Section 1. Annual meetings of the Association shall be held at such times and places as shall be determined by the Executive Council. Special meetings may be called by the Council, if in their opinion circumstances require them, giving *two weeks*' notice of the time and place of meeting, together with the subject matter of business to come before such special meeting. The Executive Council shall meet to arrange the order of business on the first day preceding any general meeting of the Association.

ARTICLE V.

Section 1. The expenses of the Executive Council of the Association, in carrying out the business to be done by them, shall be provided for by assessment upon the members of the Association; provided, however, that no assessment above ten dollars be made in any current year upon each member of the Association; and the Executive Council shall have no authority to incur or contract on behalf of this Association any liability whatever beyond the ten dollars hereby authorized, and only that for the purposes hereby designated.

ARTICLE VI.

Section 1. Resolutions or subjects for discussion (except those referring to points of order or matters of courtesy) must be submitted to the Executive Council in writing at least *thirty days* before any general meeting of the Association, but any person desiring to submit any resolution or business in open convention can do so upon a two-thirds vote of the delegates present, referring the resolution to the Executive Council or Committee on Resolutions to report upon immediately.

ARTICLE VII.

Any one failing to pay within three months the assessment made for carrying on the business of the Association shall be considered as having withdrawn from membership, but may be reinstated upon application to the Treasurer and paying the assessment in arrears, with consent of the President.

ARTICLE VIII.

This Constitution may be altered or amended at any annual meeting by a vote of two-thirds of the members present, notice of the proposed amendment having been first submitted to the Secretary at least thirty days before the annual meeting, to be placed by him before the Executive Council, that they may arrange for bringing it before the Convention under the regular order of business.

BY-LAWS
OF THE AMERICAN BANKERS' ASSOCIATION.

1st. The following shall be the order of business at the annual or special general meetings of the Association:
1. Call of the Roll.
2. Reading of the reports of the Executive Council and the Treasurer.
3. The election of officers.

The consideration of subjects submitted in the report of the Executive Council, in the order in which they are submitted, unless changed by a suspension of the rules by a two-thirds vote.

2d. Any resolution or new business not upon the official programme or recommended by the Executive Council (excepting those relating to points of order or matters of courtesy) shall be referred to the Executive Council or Committee on Resolutions to report upon to the Convention.

3d. No member shall speak more than ten minutes upon one question without consent of the Convention.

4th. The rules of the House of Representatives of the United States shall govern the deliberations of the Association, so far as they may be applicable and in harmony with the Constitution and By-Laws.

5th. The annual assessment made by the Association shall be considered due at the beginning of the year, which year shall commence with the regular annual meeting, it being understood that absent members from such annual meetings shall not forfeit their membership nor the right to become members, provided they comply with the Constitution and By-Laws, and remit the amount of the assessment to the Treasurer within three months after such annual meeting.

6th. These By-Laws may be amended at any annual meeting, upon a vote of two-thirds of the members present.

Supreme Court of the United States.

G. CLARENCE CHURCHILL and others,
PLAINTIFFS IN ERROR,
vs.
THE CITY OF UTICA,
DEFENDANT IN ERROR.

No. 286.

ARGUMENT OF WM. M. EVARTS.

MAY IT PLEASE THE COURT:

I cannot think that the learned counsel, on the one side or the other, who have addressed the Court in this discussion, which it is permitted to me now to close, have at all over-rated the importance of the subject presented to your Honors. As a pecuniary interest, it is probably as large as ever came under your cognizance; LARGER THAN, IN THE COURSE OF JURISPRUDENCE, HAS EVER BEEN SUBMITTED TO ANY OTHER COURT; for, if looked at only in the measure of an annual tax to be laid by the various States upon the whole mass of the property of these national banks, it comes to an enormous value; and, regarded as a rule, not for a year, but for the continual course of taxation, the proportions swell to still larger dimensions. So, too, in the extent of the application of your rule to be laid down in this case, which, though coming from the State of New York, yet, since that State is under the Constitution and under the laws of the United States, must be substantially of the same character and have the same effects in all the States of the

Union, the magnitude of the interests is again presented as most serious.

But while I thus agree in the gravity of the issues from the pecuniary interests at stake, I must think that some of the topics, insisted upon by our learned opponents as great elements in the importance of this question, were misconceived. The question whether such a great mass of property should be withdrawn from the funds accessible to the taxation of the States, which presented itself to the learned court that decided this cause in the State of New York, so that, somewhat beyond the bounds of ordinary judicial decorum, the learned Judge spoke of of it as "frightful," and which, in the arguments of my learned opponents, has been brought to your notice in various tones of alarm and lament, is really not a topic for insisting upon the importance of this question. Whatever there is to disturb the equanimity of a court in that subject has already been disposed of by your Honors in the previous decisions; which have withdrawn absolutely, and under any form of property or ownership, the securities of the Federal Government known as the public debt. This matter of the three or four hundred millions of bank stock, which we are considering, is not the cause or the occasion of the subtraction of these funds from State taxation. It is as investments in the securities of the Federal Government, that these stocks are presented to your Honors as entitled to the immunity which belongs to these securities; and it is under decisions of this Court, which have made $3,000,000,000 of Federal debt not subject to State taxation, that this derangement of the funds, of the property, which, on one side or the other, is to bear the burdens of our double government, is effected.

For the like reason, there is as little foundation, on an accurate attention to the subject, for the suggestion of the impropriety of the want of uniformity which would be produced among citizens and in respect to property, if these investments, these bank capitals, these bank operations, should be withdrawn from the whole support of the State Governments under which they are protected in common with the whole mass of property of the same description, that is, the mass of personal property, and for the statement that this gives great magnitude to the interests presented to you; as if it were a question whether this mass of property, now before you, should escape taxation or not. That is not the question. It has been suggested to you already by my learned associates that, under the taxation of the National Government, as prescribed in the frame and as a part of the bill creating these banks, they are made to pay, in the support of our common burdens, a very large measure of taxation, amounting from two and a half to three per cent. in the average upon their whole capital, and that they thus pay from ten to twelve millions of dollars annually towards the support of the Federal Government.

At a time when practically we paid no taxes to the Federal Government, and the States had, undisturbed, the whole area of the real and personal property of the citizens of the United States by which to support their own institutions, a subtraction from the State Governments of a fund of taxation was equivalent to a withdrawal of it from contribution to the public burdens in any direct form. But now that we bear the burdens of taxation in our property in support of both the Federal Government and our State Governments, it is apparent that the suggestion, that the withdrawal of property from the legitimate exercise of the power of taxation by the States is relieving it from the payment of taxes, no longer has support in the fact. It becomes, therefore, as respects the burdens which the citizens of the United States and the citizens of the States, both being the same persons, are to bear, a question merely of the prudence, wisdom, and policy of the adjustment of taxes; for just so far as these banks contribute to Federal taxation, just so far they relieve all the other property of the citizens of the different States from their contributions to the burden of Federal taxation. If it be true that they no longer are computed in the mass of property that shares the burdens of State taxation, nevertheless the citizens of the States, in their other property, feel the contribution of these national banks to the needs of the National Government, just as distinctly and just as directly as they would, if they contributed to the support of the State Governments.

We are, therefore, relieved from both of these elements of difficulty and these disturbances in respect to the judgment of the court, so loudly insisted upon. If the present rate of taxation does not exact from this kind of property its full share of the burdens which it should be called upon to bear, then the Federal Government, the common master of all of these institutions in all portions of the country, acting in the general interest, but regarding also the private interest of the citizens of all the States, may increase the taxation; so that, instead of contributing ten or twelve millions of dollars as they now do, by enlarged rates they may be made to contribute twenty or twenty-four millions of dollars. That is wholly a question of policy and wisdom in the taxing power.

Your Honors will thus see that all these considerations really do not touch the burdens of the citizens, but only the question what, in the complex system of our government, which now is required, both in its general control and in its separate State jurisdiction, to demand taxes from the citizens, is the proper and beneficial adjustment for us, in our capacity of citizens of the State and citizens of the United States.

Nor am I at all disposed to dissemble or disguise the difficulties of the discussion. If they seem to me less formidable than the zeal and ability of my learned opponents, in the interest of their clients, have represented in urging them upon the Court, yet the respect due to the unanimous, adverse opinion of the highest court of the State of New York, expressed in the judgment of one of the most distinguished Judges that the State has produced, who now, by voluntary retirement, has closed one of the most honorable judicial careers that our history can show; the great *dictum* (as it is called) of Chief Justice Marshall, and the carefully weighed opinion of Mr. Webster, speaking always as one having authority, would admonish me of the rashness of my judgment. After all the difficulties, I apprehend that a thorough examination of the case will show, that, though the question comes here under the appellate jurisdiction of this Court, under the 25th section of the Judiciary Act, and though the subjects of discussion here, and the decision appealed from and to be reviewed here, do touch the construction of the Constitution and the laws of the United States, and the great constitutional conflict between the powers of the General Government on the one hand, and the rights and jurisdiction of the States on the other hand, yet all these questions, belonging to that high region of jurisprudence, have been really disposed of by the previous judgments of this Court; and the limit of the discussion, which, on the presentation of the case and your Honors' scrutiny of it, will prove to be needed for its determination, will be found to fall quite short of this elevated region, and really will turn upon questions of corporation law, as to what the relations of shareholders are, in the just idea of the constitution of a corporation, to the property and franchise, which, as an aggregate, are undoubtedly represented by the corporation itself. Since, then, it turns upon this question, what the relations of shareholders are to the property and franchise of a corporation, I shall consider whether or not the previous decisions of this Court have disposed of the question already, by its adjudications on the capital and the franchises of corporations; or whether, not having thus been absolutely covered by the previous decisions, the relation of shareholders to a corporation is such as to require their inclusion within the principles that this Court has already laid down, in regard to the aggregate property and franchise; or, if this is not the case, whether a discrimination can be made, which shall find a place for it as new and separate property in the hands of shareholders, to be unaffected by the rules established in reference to the aggregate property.

Now, if the Court please, I have but a word to say in regard to the particular circumstances of the case in which I especially speak; for the question to be discussed in it is the same as in the other cases, and is substantially the same question, I imagine, that must come up from the different States, whenever attempts shall be made to exercise the right of State taxation on this subject matter.

This Bank of Utica was constituted as a National Bank under the Act of 1863, and its capital was wholly invested in public securities of the United States that were issued before the 1st day of June, 1864,—a date only important, since it distinguishes those securities as being previous to the Banking Act of 1864 ; in which latter Banking Act, for the first time, appears the clause cited from the 41st section, which gives a license or permission for the taxation of shares. Whatever, then, there may be in any differences in this respect, as has been hinted at in the judgment of the Court below, this Bank occupies the most favorable position ; for its securities were taken by it, as investments, while there was the open and general pledge of the public faith, that they, protected by the National arm, were wholly free from State taxation. And the bank, organizing and acquiring these securities under such circumstances, if there be much for judicial consideration in what has been adverted to more or less in the argument, (to wit, the question of a breach of faith in the Government, in allowing taxation by permission of section 41 of the Act of 1864,) is within the most favorable consideration in that respect. But, I confess, I cannot see that the correction of the alleged breach of faith on the part of the Government, if it has been shown in any degree—I do not think it has been—could be made by a judicial determination of this Court. Undoubtedly we do press it, and properly, as an argument of much force, tending to the proper construction of section 41 and the license there given, that, in the view contended for by our learned opponents, a breach of faith might be involved ; whereas, in the construction which we suppose it properly bears, no such imputation is admissible.

If the Court please, this plaintiff in error, owning fifty shares in this bank, of the par value of $5,000, has been rated thereon as a tax-payer under the laws of the State of New York ; and is compelled thus far, by the judgment of the Courts of our State, and, unless your Honors shall reverse their decision, will be finally compelled to pay a tax, at whatever the rate of taxation is in the local community where this bank is placed, upon the par value of those shares. All the other stockholders are exposed to the same application of law ; and, under this decision, the united stockholders are to pay a rate of taxation under the jurisdiction of the State, upon what is equivalent, in their shares taken together, to the capital of the bank. In other words, $200,000 being the capital of this bank,—a National Bank—and being wholly invested in Federal securities, that capital is, by the form of assessing and collecting a due proportion of the tax on it from each shareholder, made to produce to the State of New York precisely the same amount of taxation, as if the same rate had been laid upon the capital of the bank ; and it is made to affect the actual beneficial value of the shares, and the receipts and profits of the shareholders, precisely in the same manner, and to the same effect and measure, as if the tax had been laid upon the aggregate capital. I think, in the whole course of this discussion, your Honors have not heard from our learned opponents any contradiction of that proposition : that this form and manner of taxation produces, as its fruit to the State, precisely the same amount, as the same rate of taxation upon the aggregate capital in the hands of the bank ; and that it produces the same effect in diminishing the value of the capital stock, by diminishing the profits of that capital stock, laid in the form now proposed, that it would produce, if it were laid upon the aggregate capital, and upon the corporation as the taxable person.

These matters of fact being thus clearly ascertained, free from dispute, we need next to look accurately and attentively to what are the premises concerning the taxability of the corporations themselves, having their capital in such investments ; from which we are to start upon the only inquiry left for discussion in this Court, whether the stock, as an aggregate, and the franchise, as a part of the value in the hands of the corporation, and the corporation, as a person subject to taxation, being exempt from this tax, this rate, this payment to the State of New York, the shareholders are subject to all from which the corporation itself is free.

I think that, on the second page of my brief, I have accurately stated the result of the determinations of this Court, both on this topic, as it relates to the investment in United States securities, and to the corporation, as a national institution within the protection of the Constitution, operating as an agency and means employed by the Government; and I say that it is settled by adjudged cases in this Court, that no tax can be imposed, by the laws or authority of a State, upon the securities in which the capital of this bank was invested, nor upon any person or corporation standing in the relation of owner of such securities, nor by any measure of his or its property as including such securities. The cases are familiar to your Honors, and I will only read a word or two from the former bank-tax case in the Court of Appeals, to show that the principle is as thoroughly recognized by that Court—obeying the decision of this Court, which had corrected its former errors—as it is by this Court itself. In that case, which is not reported as yet in any volume of our reports, but is the case which came up to this Court, and is reported here in 2 *Wallace*, Chief Judge DENIO said:

"It must be considered a settled point, that the power of taxation residing in the State Governments does not embrace, as a possible subject, the securities of the public debt of the United States."

Upon that clear recognition that the subject, the *res*, the investment, was absolutely protected against State taxation, his Honor, giving the opinion of the Court of Appeals in that case, went on to hold that, whenever the tax was laid, not upon the capital of the bank at its value to be ascertained by assessors, but upon the nominal or original capital of the bank, it was not a tax upon the Federal securities, although the whole of that capital was invested in those securities. That error this Court corrected by the decision in 2 *Wallace*; and now, more than ever, the Court of Appeals admits this principle, and submits to that application of the principle, but has found a means, in a decision and opinion in these cases, to say that, although Federal securities are not a possible subject of State taxation, yet that Federal securities, under the form of ownership which their relation to the shareholders of a national bank exhibits, can be made to pay precisely the same tax that they would, if they were a possible or real subject of State taxation.

The other immunity which we claim here, and concerning which it is important to know to what the determination, up to this point, of this Court has brought us, is the immunity of these banks in capital, in operations, and in franchises, from State taxation, not because of any form of investment of their property in Federal securities, but, in the absence of that investment, because of their mere character of Federal institutions. What, from this point of view, is their situation in regard to State taxation? Upon that point I apprehend this is a just postulate, not to be contested and not really contested by the arguments of the learned counsel:—that it is settled by adjudged cases in this Court, that this Bank, in its corporate capacity, is not subject to State taxation by the laws or under the authority of a State, upon its franchise, operations, or capital, (aside from the question of investments in Federal securities,) but that it is wholly exempt from such taxation, by reason of its relation to the Federal Government, as an agency or instrument of that Government in the exercise of its constitutional power. Without adverting or recalling your Honors' attention to the cases in your own Court, insisted upon so frequently and so familiar to you, I will, upon this point, only call your attention to the complete recognition of this proposition by the Court of Appeals. In the first Bank tax case—the one which was decided on appeal by this Court in 2 *Black*—a case reported in 23 *New York Reports*, Judge DENIO gives this as the clear judgment of that Court upon the proposition:

"But when it had once been settled that the bank was a constitutional agency and instrument for the moneyed operations of the Government, it followed necessarily, as it seems to us, that it could no more be taxed by State authority, than the Treasury Department, the Mint, the Post Office, or the Army or Navy; and it was upon this ground that the Maryland Statute was held to be unconstitutional."

And his Honor, Judge Comstock, in giving a dissenting opinion in that case, in which he obtained the concurrence of this learned Court on the appeal to it, made these observations:

"As to all subjects over which the taxing power of a State extends, there are no limitations dependent on the power of its exercise. If we admit the right to tax this credit in any mode and to any extent, we must admit it in a different mode and to a greater extent. There is no limit to the principle. The acknowledgment of the right in any degree involves a conflict between the Federal Union and the parts of which it is composed; but, as the Union is supreme in the exercise of all its powers, including the vital one of borrowing money, no authority can be constitutionally opposed to it, which confines the exercise of those powers. This is a principle which requires the absolute exemption of the National credit from State taxation."

Has the last proposition that I have mentioned been questioned, that this Bank, in its capital, its operations and its franchise, was wholly exempt from State taxation? Has that been questioned in the decision of the Court below, or in the arguments here? I must say that, in the decision of the Court below, I do not think it is questioned, although there are some observations that go to support the point, that the decision with regard to the United States Bank stood upon surer grounds, in respect to the character of that institution, than the argument about these National Banks, in respect to their character, could stand; but, nevertheless, I understand that learned Court to place its decision wholly upon the proposition that this tax, not being constitutional if laid upon the capital of the Bank and its franchise in bulk, by reason of an exemption of both as an accredited agent of the Federal Government within its constitutional power, can, nevertheless, be assessed upon the shareholders. But one of the learned counsel who last addressed the Court in favor of the defendants, Judge Parker, in his brief, and orally, has somewhat questioned the fact that these Banks, in their aggregate and corporate interests, are exempt from State taxation. He has presented an analysis of the power of the United States Bank, as we call it, and the powers and duties of these banks, and has intimated that the discrimination is wholly unfavorable to the position of these banks; yet, if your Honors please, it can hardly come to this, that he here contends that these banks are not within the exemption which the principles laid down by this Court extended to the United States Bank; for to say that would be to say that these National Banks were not constitutional creations; because, as Chief Justice Marshall said in the discussions in the case of *McCulloch* vs. *The State of Maryland*, if the bank is not one of the means and agencies of the Federal Government, which, by mere force of that relation, comes to be protected from State taxation, then it has no lawful existence; "for who," says he, "can point out the right of the Government of the United States to establish a banking corporation, unless it be as a means, an agency, and performing some of the functions of Government attributed to the National authority by the Federal Constitution?"

So I think we may start with this proposition; that these banks, both in respect to the investment and in respect to their corporate immunities, are absolutely protected against this very rating and assessment and taxation which has been enforced against the shareholders. The law of the State of New York, under which, during the last year, these taxes have been laid, and under which it is proposed to lay them in the future, to wit, the Enabling Act, as it is called, which has been placed before your Honors, assumes to levy taxes "on all the shares" of the banks in the assessment of taxes "in the town or ward where such banking association is located and not elsewhere, whether the holder thereof reside in such town or ward or not;" and then it provides that, for the purpose of collecting such taxes, it shall be the duty of every banking association, organized under the Act of Congress, "to retain so much of any dividend or dividends, belonging to any shareholders, as shall be necessary to pay any taxes hereby authorized." Under that law, transferring taxation from the body corporate and its aggregate investments to the owners of proportionate shares of its corporate franchise, of its corporate investment, it has been held by the Court of Appeals that, notwithstanding the principles which exempt the bank and which the Court of Appeals itself recognizes, the shareholders can be made to pay what comes to the same in regard to the State, and comes to the same in regard to their own pockets. This is supported by that Court upon one of two grounds or perhaps upon both: first, by the mere authority of the State, without asking leave or allowance from this Government; and, secondly, by the authority communicated or permitted by the proviso of the 41st section of the National Currency Act of June 3d, 1864.

Is it not, then, entirely true that there is but one question for discussion here, having, if you please, a twofold application, one, to the question of investment in Federal securities, and one to the corporate aggregate known as the National Bank ; and that question is, whether what cannot be done to the bank as a whole, can be done, from the peculiar form of organization, to the property held by the shareholders ; so that what the State loses by the immunity that this Court has thrown over the investment in the aggregate, is recovered by the State, with the full power of taxation over the same *res*, in a different form of approach and attack ; that what this Court has decided is necessary, is essential, is vital to the public credit, in respect of the investment, that what this Court has decided is necessary, is essential, is vital to the corporate existence, for the public purposes of the Government of the United States, and so must be protected by the power of interpreting the Constitution lodged in this Court and the authority of its mandate to be executed by the power of the nation, is, nevertheless, to be wrested from Federal control to the destruction and ruin of institutions, created to be preserved ; to the injury and burden of the public credit, intended to be advanced ; simply by the form of saying to the tax rater and the tax collector, "Lay the tax, that you would have exacted from the corporation, distributively upon the shareholders, and we escape from the Federal Constitution and the Supreme Court of the United States, by the form and manner of assessing and collecting ; since there is, in the practice of the States, a well-known habit of levying taxes indifferently upon the aggregate or upon the shareholders, as convenience dictates ; always recognizing that, whichever form they adopt, they tax the same thing, acquire their returns from the same persons, and receive into the Treasury the same results. Certainly there never was such a discomfiture of fact and substance, of constitutional power, and of the firm, strong reasoning of this Court, as would result, if this ingenious combination between the Legislature of a State and its officers for the assessment and collection of taxes can effect this result, and destroy what this Court has undertaken to preserve.

I will first consider, as most briefly and satisfactorily to be attended to, the question whether the State, in the taxation it insists upon against these shareholders, derives any authority from the 41st section of the Act of Congress of June 3, 1864, and I say unquestionably that it does not; and without any discussion of whether that section be, as Mr. Webster imagined it would not be, unconstitutional, and without examining the particular construction of that section, whether it be such as to allow these stocks, thus invested in Federal securities, to be taxed or not, irrespective of that, but supposing that the section communicates a license according to its terms, and that, if its terms were observed, this tax would be protected and allowable under it, I say that there is no credit nor power given to the State in this taxation from that section, simply for the reason that it has not observed the conditions. The conditions are, that, if the State taxes the shares of the national banks, it shall impose upon them no other nor higher rate of taxation than it imposes upon the general investment of personal property of the State; and, secondly, observing that, that it shall also tax them at no other rate than it imposes specifically upon the shares of State banking institutions. It is undisputed here, that, under the laws of the State of New York, no rate nor tax whatever is laid upon the shares of State banking institutions. The statutes of the State of New York say that the shares of State banking institutions shall not be taxed to the shareholders, and they are not taxed. What, then, is the taxation upon a State banking institution in the State of New York? It is a tax upon the aggregate capital of the bank, exacted from the Corporation itself. Now, will my learned friends tell me that, although the State of New York does not lay any tax upon the shareholders of State banks, and so does not observe the condition of the 41st section of the Act of Congress, it does lay the same rate upon the capital of the bank in the hands of the corporation, and that that is equivalent to laying it on the shareholders? If they will only do that, they will relieve me from the need of any argument; for, if laying a tax on the capital is the same as laying it on the shares for the purposes of a

State corporation, then laying it on the shares is the same as laying it on the capital of the National Banks, and that is all that I have undertaken to prove. But even if they thus surrender the practical question to escape from a special difficulty, the actual state of the system of taxation and its enforcement in the State of New York would not relieve them, because, in regard to the tax rated and collected from the corporations created by State laws as the persons taxed, and taxed upon their aggregate capital, under the decisions of this Court, controlling and acted upon in the State of New York, it is required, that, before the capital of the State bank presents its aggregate for the rating of the tax and its payment, there should be a deduction from it of every dollar that is invested in Federal securities; so that, as a matter of fact, if, side by side with this National Bank in the city of Utica, there were a State bank, of the same capital of $200,000, having that capital invested precisely as the capital of this National Bank is invested, in Federal securities, while, under the form of taxation laid and enforced by the State upon the banks which I represent, there would be paid a full rate upon the $200,000, distributed upon the shares, there would not be one dollar of tax laid or claimed against the State institution, that carried on business in the same street, under the authority of the State of New York. Therefore, put it on matter of form or put it on matter of substance, your State authority lays no taxation on State institutions situated precisely as this National institution is situated; and hence, when you seek authority by permission and license of the Act of Congress, the limitations and the conditions must of course be observed, and they wholly fail. I ask your Honors' attention to a very intelligent and well-considered opinion, given in our State, in which it has been held by a branch of the Supreme Court, that, conceding that the shares may be taxable for aught that the authority of the United States gives under the permission of the 41st section of the National Banking Act, yet, for the want of the observance of its conditions, the law against which we are now remonstrating and arguing is wholly invalid, because the State does not lay a tax. That learned Court say:

" The system of taxation adopted by the State, under the provision of th
Revised Statutes, is, that the laws of the State provide for the taxing the cap
ital of a State bank, and the stockholder is not to be taxed, as an individua
upon his shares. Therefore there is no State law, making provision in an
case for taxing the shareholders in State banks for their shares. Conse
quently the shareholders of National banks, or State banks, are not liable t
taxation in such shares."—*The People* vs. *The Town of Barton*, 29 Howard
New York Practice Reports, 371.

This your Honors will rest upon, as satisfactory proof tha
the system of taxation is such as I have stated ; and the au
thority of that Court—indeed, I think no authority is neede
for it—is, that, if the permission to tax by the State rests upo
the 41st section, this tax cannot be sustained, for the reason tha
the conditions are not observed. I shall, therefore, for the res
confine myself to asking what is the great and principal questio
of the case presented to the Court, to wit, the assumed power c
the State of New York to levy taxes upon this fund and capita
by the form and means of taxing shareholders, when it canno
do it in any other way ;—a power against the will of the Govern
ment, against the decisions of this Court, against any construc
tion of the Constitution of the United States that would see
to inhibit it. But I ask attention, for one moment, to what
assume will be regarded, when a case shall properly arise fc
it, as the proper construction of this proviso. Your Honors wi
notice, that the 41st section provides for the taxation of thes
institutions by the National Government, and then goes o
to say :

"*Provided*, That nothing in this act shall be construed to prevent all th
shares in any of the said associations, held by any person or body corporat
from being included in the valuation of the personal property of such perso
or body corporate, (from being included in the valuation of the personal pro
erty of such person or corporation) in the assessment of taxes, imposed by, c
under State authority, at the place where such bank is located, and not els
where; but not at a greater rate than is assessed upon any other moneye
capital in the hands of individual citizens of such State: *Provided furthe*
That the tax so imposed, under the laws of any State, upon the shares of an
of the associations authorized by this act, shall not exceed the rate impose
upon the shares in any of the banks organized under authority of the Stat
where such association is located."

I apprehend that no one can claim, that there is anything in this act that had relation to exemptions, except such as grew out of its creating these public institutions agencies of the Government. In other words, the exemption, created or inferrible from this act, would be the exemption that belonged to these banks as agencies; and there is nothing in this act that has any connection with the exemption of United States securities. When, therefore, you are construing this proviso, which is intended to save from the operation of an inferential exemption from this act, you must not carry your proviso or saving clause beyond the principal provision, which it is designed to define, not to avoid. It means, then, that nothing in the nature of these institutions, as agencies or instruments of the authority of the United States under the Constitution, shall save them from taxation on their property, in the same way as other moneyed capital may be taxed by States; but it was under other laws of the United States that the immunity of the investment in Federal securities was claimable, and was created. The Congress of the United States, adopting and following the judgment of this Court, enacted, in the statute of February 25, 1862, that the Federal securities, whether held by individuals, corporations, or associations, should be exempt from all taxation under State or municipal authority. It is, then, under that and similar statutes, that this form and application of immunity is derived; and this saving clause does not operate on that act. It merely means, " You may tax the investments in the corporate property made by these corporations, as you might do, if the immunity of Federal agency was not over them." When you come to the question, whether, under cover of this saving clause against a particular effect of the statute, you have opened to the States taxation upon Federal securities owned by these corporations, when you have closed it against taxation in any and every other form of ownership, you are proposing to give to this section a force which it never, in legislative intent, could have been designed to have, and which, on any sound principle of construction, it cannot bear. Its meaning, so far as the question of these investments by these banks in the Federal securities goes, would be to put them, in that respect, on the same footing with an individual having his moneyed capital invested in that manner; and on the same footing in which a State corporation having its capital invested in these securities, would stand. Is it to be said, that, when all the moneyed capital in the hands of individuals and State corporations, that is invested in the United States securities, is protected against taxation by the State, as soon as one of the National banks invests in United States securities, it has opened and exposed to taxation those very securities, which are exempt by the law of 1862, by force of a proviso which says that the *banking* act shall not be construed to exempt the National banks from State taxation ?

I think, therefore, that, on any construction of that section (even if, by conformity of the State to the rate of taxation on State bank shares that it has laid on national bank shares, the permission of that section could be invoked in favor of this tax) these three banks would be still exempt from the payment of any tax on that portion of their capital which was invested in the United States securities, for the reason that I have stated to the Court. But if this proviso is not before the Court for adjudication because it has not been followed by the State, it will be for your Honors to consider how far that point can be disposed of in your judgment.

It seems really as if we were reduced to but a very narrow region of reasoning, if we are so far advanced successfully. It must come to this, that the State, having no power (for this law gives none) to pass the act which it has actually passed, no power derived from the Federal government, assumes a right to tax these investments and tax this capital in the form of shares, although it cannot tax them, as has been so often urged, in the aggregate or corporate capacity. The argument can rest upon nothing but this: it asserts a distinction between the capital stock of the corporation in the aggregate, and all the shares of such capital stock as subjects of taxation ; such a distinction between these two descriptions of property, (I say two descriptions of the same thing,) that a tax levied upon the shares is constitutional, although a tax levied upon the aggregate is unconstitutional. It asserts another distinction, a distinction between the corporation and the shareholders or members of the corporation ; for are not shareholders members of the corporation ? Is not the corporation composed of members ? When all the members of a corporation cease to exist does not the corporation cease ? It asserts a distinction between the corporation and the shareholders or members of the corporation, as taxable persons, to the effect that a tax upon, or in respect of, the same property, distributed upon the corporate members, is constitutional, though, laid upon the corporate body, it is unconstitutional. I have looked in vain through the briefs and listened in vain to the arguments of my learned friends, to find any other ground for them to discriminate for the constitutionality of the tax on the shareholders, admitting the unconstitutionality of the tax on the corporation and its property, except in the one or the other of these two forms.

I will take up first the question of investments. I say that the proposition, that the investments of a corporation in Federal securities of the whole or a part of its capital stock cannot be made subject to State taxation, laid upon its capital stock, and yet that the same investments may be subjected to State taxation, laid upon the divisions or parts of its capital stock known as shares, cannot be maintained. The first reason I assign for this is, because the attempted distinction overlooks the legal character and grounds of the exemption. The exemption is of the *res*, of the subject of the securities. It has no relation to any form of enjoyment or ownership of them. It says that this subject of property shall not yield a tax ; and the exemption is laid for the sake of the investment, and not from partiality to any owner, or any form of ownership. It is that the thing itself may be better, that it may be worthier, that it may be more valuable, the occasions and the duties of the Federal Government requiring that it should be made so and kept so ; and it has no more concern with any form of ownership, as matter of policy or as matter of personal protection, than it has with the remotest considerations from the topic. It is that this thing shall have the virtue in it of being worthier than other property, because it is exempted from State taxation.

When you are talking about the different relations which the shareholder and the corporation have to the corporate property, and the different relations that the corporation and the shareholders have to what are called shares, you are talking of what is interesting and important in some views of the law ; but you are talking of a subject that has no relation to this question, whether, for the purposes of maintaining the exemption of this investment from taxation, the exemption is to attend it in every form of substantial ownership ; for it is only through forms of substantial ownership that the worthiness of the thing is to be preserved. There is no such separation possible as leaving the securities as worthy as before, but disparaging their purchase, because in a certain form they cannot be owned without being taxable.

But it also overlooks the legal ground, and character of taxation. Taxation pertains to the subject, the *res*, and has nothing to do with ownership and cares nothing about it. It is wholly immaterial to the taxing power what the form of ownership may be ; it is the value that it is after. In whatever owner it finds that value, the taxing power will extract it by proceeding *in rem*, if you please, and not care who is the owner; or, if convenient, it collects the tax through the medium of the owner, and the coercion is only to make him pay it. The taxing power, in pursuing its method of taxing, is no respecter of persons or forms or title. It is the thing it looks to; and when land is the subject of taxation, as we all know, the exaction of the tax or enforcement of it is wholly unconcerned with titles, incumbrances, liens, divisions of equity and at law in the enjoyment of the owner. It taxes the property, and sells it by an absolute and paramount title, dealing with the thing itself. The relation is the same towards personal property, although there may not be occasion or opportunity to apply practically the same effect. I say, then, you overlook the nature of the distinction, when you say that the same thing is to be extracted from taxation in one form of enjoyment and not in another.

Now, suppose that a government, wishing to invite population or to improve the domestic habits of its people, establishes an arrangement promising freedom from taxation to all dwelling houses that should be built. The dwelling houses are built, the law being that dwelling houses shall be exempt from taxation. Can you tax the owner of a dwelling house on the rent he gets from his tenant ? Is not that taxing his dwelling house ? Is the promise performed, is the faith kept, when you say, "We do not tax your dwelling house, we do not tax you on the fee of your dwelling house, we tax you on the *rent* of your dwelling house" ? You tax the dwelling house in one of the forms of its owner's enjoyment of it as property. Can you tax the tenant and say, "We tax you in proportion to the rent that you pay to your landlord" ? That is taxing the dwelling house ; that is taxing the house ; the thing which has been procured by the public interests, upon the promise that it should not bear taxation. Is not the taxation of the occupation of the house, whether it be imposed upon the landlord or upon the tenant, a tax upon the house ? Certainly it is.

And this shows us that taxation and exemption, correlative terms, touch and adhere to the subject, and have no concern with ownership, title, property, or enjoyment. All title, ownership, property, enjoyment, is lesser than, and is included in, the matter that is the subject of property, and that swallows up title, interests, legal and beneficial relations ; and when, in the sense of taxation and the sense of exemption, the subject has been rescued from burdens, nobody can feel them. Has, the subject been rescued, if anybody can feel the burden in consequence of the subject ? Has the subject been saved from contribution, if anybody, in consequence of connection with the subject, has to contribute ? Certainly not. You must find some other relation than that of ownership, whether it be legal or equitable, that you tax, or else you tax the property itself.

This, too, exalts the forms and phrases of the law above the law itself. The United States Government have thought it necessary to give to their securities this credit, and thus to send them out into the whole nation and to the world. They have not broken their faith by any legislation. They have not broken their faith by any construction of legislation. They have not broken their faith by any adjudication of this court up to this time, whatever the Court of New York may have thought. Twice corrected by this Court on these subjects, now, with legal effrontery, not personal, that learned court comes here and says: "You have told us over and over again that we cannot tax United States securities; cannot tax them in the measure of anybody's property; cannot tax them in the form of valuing property at a nominal, and not a real, standard; but we have found one shape in which we can tax them in spite of you; if a national bank owns them, we can make the shareholders pay the tax." This, I say, stultifies the acts of Congress and nullifies the decisions of this Court on that subject.

How do you get a tax on these securities and make a shareholder in a bank pay it? The whole capital of the bank is free. That is admitted. It is free by its own nature, by its being invested in these securities. It is free, because it has been decided that the States cannot tax this capital. This is all admitted. But it is said, "We tax the shareholders." They must tax these shareholders upon this property, this value, either because they do not own it, or because they do. You may tax it because they do not own it, as you would tax A on property of B, and tell him that, since B is not able to pay your tax, you tax A on his property. That, however, is not to be imputed. Then you tax the shareholders because they do own this property, because they have some ownership in this investment; and yet the brief of my learned opponents admits that the owner of United States securities cannot be taxed by the States for them.

Let us look at that a little more closely. Suppose that A holds, as trustee, $100,000 worth of the securities of the United States, and is asked to give an account of his taxable property in his relation as trustee, and he states that the trust fund is all invested in United States securities. That exempts him from taxation. Then the tax-gatherer hunts up the *cestui que* trust and says, "What have you?" The answer is, "My only income is from a trust fund in the hands of A, my trustee; he is the man to pay the tax." "Oh, we cannot tax that, because he holds United States securities; what is your beneficial property?" "It is $100,000." "Then we will tax you." "Well, but," the *cestui que* trust says, "I do not own the property; A is the legal owner, my trustee; why not tax him, if anybody is to be taxed? I do not own the property; if anybody is to pay the tax, the owner, the trustee, is to pay." "No," says the tax-gatherer, "we cannot tax the owner; he is exempt on account of the investment; but we tax you, as the *cestui que* trust, because you are the beneficial owner and not the legal owner, and you shall pay the tax." I imagine that, if the State should pursue that method, this Court would correct it and say, "that this $100,000, in its legal estate, in its equitable estate, in its legal control, in its beneficial enjoyment, is free from taxation." Yet no man can distinguish between a legal ownership in United States securities, and an ownership in those same securities, lodged in a form and organization by which twenty people part with their legal control over them, and turn themselves into the enjoyment of them as beneficial or equitable owners. Take the case: twenty men meet together, with $5,000 in Federal securities each, as private property, and put them in bodily and make the capital of $100,000, invested in them, of a bank organized under this act, and come out what? Organized into a bank, with their Federal securities owned by the bank, of which they are the owners, of which they are the members, of which they are the stockholders, the legal institution holding the legal property. Has that transmutation made the securities taxable that were not taxable before, when the exemption adheres to the securities, and not, by name, to any form of ownership?

But, if your Honors please, the proposition that the corporations, created and performing their public functions as agencies of the Federal Government, cannot be taxed by the State on their capital, franchise, or operations, and yet that the shareholders, in respect of their membership and ownership of the corporate body, franchise, and capital, can be taxed, is self-repugnant and illusory; and, in connection with this point, let me look for a moment and briefly, though a subject inviting for illustration, upon the frame and scheme of the National Bank system, one of the most remarkable creations in the progress of this nation, one of the most essential means of carrying this nation through its late trials, and saving it from the disasters and convulsions which attend a restoration of peace in the financial circumstances of the nation and its citizens. What is it, and what is the whole idea of it ? What is the whole service of it ? What is the whole genius of it ? It is this ; it is to call into the fiscal operations of the Government, in the execution of its powers and duties under the Constitution, the capital, the resources, the processes of private interest and business, and employ them as agencies and means in the public service. It is the connection of the special duty and function of the General Government with the living circulation of the great body of the nation, over which it is the Government. Government might have loan offices, loan agencies, sub-Treasuries, and multiply them in every village, and they would be a dead organization of the Government, mere functionaries ; but, by this system, by a happy improvement upon everything we had ventured or imagined in our financial experience, the Government seized upon the living energies of the American people and made them, by their voluntary organizations, agents in the public service of the country, just as distinctly, just as usefully, as, in calling upon the citizens to enroll their persons in the military service of the country, you have, instead of a dead organization, a living body of citizen soldiers. That is what the bill did, and what it wanted to do, and what it has successfully and wonderfully accomplished. That was the thing ; it was the private persons, and the private interests, and the private processes, and the private energy of the people, that it wanted to unite in this public service. That was the substance, and the rest was nothing but form. It was to combine or organize the collective private capital and resources of the nation under the well-known form of legal incorporation, as the most convenient, if not the necessary form of accomplishing public objects. Now, as I have said of an army, it is the array that constitutes the army. It is the power, it is the array, that you want ; and the rest of organization, of articles of war, of arrangement of ranks and grades, and all the machinery of control, is for the array, and not the array for it; and so it is the array under this organized banking system that is useful. It is the array of the private enterprise, capital, and business, that is wanted; and the corporate form, a well-known arrangement for managing property, is adopted, because it is suitable for this, just as it is for the purely private operations and affairs of life.

Upon this mere statement, which cannot be contravened, it is apparent that the instrumentality adopted by Congress for executing these powers of the Government, has for its essential element this associated capital and these personal exertions; and that the corporation is but the form of wielding and operating the capital. Then, as I have said, it is not the artificial person that is the object of Government's care, or that is the principle or substance of its object. That is but a form, and, as a form alone, is it to be allowed to operate and to have its consequences: If immunity from State taxation be the prerogative and the necessity of these legal organizations, it is the immunity of the contributed capital and of the contributors that is needed. If the immunity is essential for the Government's purpose to maintain the corporation, it is essential for the Government's purpose that this immunity should rest upon those who are to contribute their capital and find their inducements to volunteer in this service of the Government; and any protection or immunity, that shall occupy itself and confine itself to the protection of the corporate capacity, and leave the individuals, the members, unprotected, would soon exhibit the fact that it is the members who make up the corporation, and not the corporation which secures its own masters and members.

All the arguments which we have heard about the bank and the shareholders, that the bank holds its property by its own title, and that no shareholder has any title in it; that all the shareholders together cannot assign nor transfer nor convey any of its property, but that a share in a corporation is a new form of property; and that it belongs to the shareholder, and that the corporation does not own that, and the corporation cannot sell that, cannot convey that—perfectly sound, as familiar as any other of the first elements of the law—insisted upon here to carry certain consequences, have no effect whatever on those consequences. As to the subject matter of this controversy, they can have no effect. Various definitions have been given about the relation of a shareholder to a corporation. My friends seemed to prefer that loosest connection, which makes the shareholder the holder of a *chose* in action or right of action against a corporation, the same as a creditor ; and they pushed it so far as to say that they think, on the whole, that a creditor has a nearer and closer right to the property of a corporation than a shareholder has, because he will have to be first paid when the affairs of the corporation are closed ; and the learned Court below has adopted that idea to some extent. These familiar doctrines are not in dispute here. It is for the very reason that a corporate organization has these consequences, that a corporate organization has been selected by Congress, as the means of wielding this public operation that is essential to the service of the Government. It is for the very reason of these effects, that it has adopted it, to wit : that a form is provided in our law, whereby the various owners of property may combine to manage it in a common agency, having this great principle, that its identity shall be preserved, although individual owners may dispose of their interests ; and that the public will, or major voice, or administrative delegation, shall govern the common property for the common good, instead of having it stand always on the individual right of every man to have his own will carried out. That is all there is to a corporation. You may talk about it forever ; it is wholly a form, known in our law, whereby men may put their property together and keep it in that form of ownership and organization for purposes of convenience and nothing else ; and nobody owns it but they, after they have done that. It is purely a short, elliptical expression to say that the corporation owns it. It is owned by the shareholders ; it is owned by the owners of the property. As against each other, they have committed it and themselves to a form of organization, which permits of the disposition of the property and the maintenance of the title, with the advantages that I have named. But to say that there are two properties, to wit, $200,000 of investment that belongs to the corporation, and another $200,000 that belongs to the shareholders, is perfectly absurd. To say that this united ownership in a subject of property, when the subject of property is free from taxation, leaves the individual shareholders subject to taxation on their shares,—I mean when it is exempt from taxation by an authority stronger than that which undertakes to divert the form of taxation,—is simply saying that the paramount government is master of the question of the taxation of the property, and the State government is yet final master of the question, by being master of form and device. This Government is no master of the question whether this property shall be taxed, if the State Government is master of the question of any form or contrivance, which—by paltering about corporations and shareholders, and shares being personal property, individual property, and the corporation being aggregate property—can exact a tax from the property. Therefore I say, that no rule of law has ever asserted, and no refinements of argument can ever maintain, that the corporation has its capital invested in certain property, and the shareholders have their shares represented by other and different property. When the *res* cannot be taxed, I want you to find some other *res* than the shareholders, which can be taxed. Can the property of the corporation perish, and that of the shareholder survive? The rule of law is "*res perit domino;*" the owner loses property when it is destroyed. The shareholders lose their property when the capital of the corporation is sunk. That we all know, and some of us have felt; and we never heard of such a distinction, as that the corporation had one property and we had another property; that the corporation could not be taxed on its, but we might on ours.

Now, put this question: suppose, as may be done unless there be some distinction in our States,—and there is not in the constitution of New York or in the constitution of most of the States,—that the ordinary rate of taxation is 3 per cent.; that is the rate in New York city on capital; 3 per cent. is laid on the aggregate capital of a bank, and 3 per cent. upon the shareholders, on the par value of their shares; in that case are two values taxed, or is it one value that is taxed twice? Does that property pay the usual rate of single taxation, 3 per cent., or does it pay 6 per cent.? It pays $12,000; $6,000 exacted from the corporation, and $6,000 from the shareholders. Is that 3 per cent. on $400,000, or is it 6 per cent. on $200,000? It is a question of one value, as a subject of taxation. However they may be distributed on interests, they are really the different forms of owning the same thing. Suppose that a Government, interested to invite capital in favor of manufactures, declares that it will not tax the capital of manufacturing companies that shall be formed under it; and, having got them formed, it taxes the shareholders on their shares. It says, " We cannot tax the capital; we promised not to tax the capital; but we tax your shares." Would that be allowable? All of this illustrates, that it is form and arrangement of ownership in the same thing, that is meant to be taxed in one form and cannot be taxed in another form, but still is the same thing; and that the exemption is not formal and modal, but is of the thing itself.

We are prepared now for a further proposition of general reasoning, which I am able to support also by the distinctest and most explicit authority. If one of the States issues a charter to a corporation, with a clause in it exempting the capital stock from taxation for a limited term, and within that term lays a tax upon the shareholders, will not this Court correct that legislation as a breach of the clause of the Constitution against impairing the obligation of contracts? I submit that the premises of that question are the premises of this question. We have a provision of the Constitution of the United States that the obligation of contracts shall not be violated by the States; we have a State making an obligatory contract that it will not tax the bank, and it afterwards taxes the shareholders. Does it not thereby violate that contract? What are the premises of this question? The premises of this question are, that the Constitution of the United States protects this aggregate investment and the aggregate capital, franchise, and operations of these banks from State taxation, and the State taxes the shares; does that violate, or not, the constitutional protection? I submit that, to a legal mind, this question carries its own answer; and it is only from the peculiarity of the jurisdiction of this Court, under the Constitution of the United States, in relation to sovereign communities, that we are enabled to have, in the form of a law suit and a legal decision, a question that would usually be left to the discussions of public faith and the maintenance of the honor of a State. In the third volume of *Howard's Reports*, this whole subject is disposed of by the unanimous judgment of this Court. Having handed that case to my learned opponents before their arguments, Judge Parker ventured to make some remark upon it by saying that it turned upon contract; and they conceded that, under this clause of the Constitution, if the State had bound itself not to tax the bank, it could not tax the shares. Now, with great respect to my learned friend, conceding that, he might as well concede, that, if the State of New York, under the Constitution, cannot tax the bank, it cannot tax the shares; and no lawyer can draw a discrimination between the two cases. Now let us be sure that this case, of so grave consequences to the discussion before us, is as applicable as I have stated it. It is the case of *Gordon* vs. *The Appeal Tax Court*, 3 *Howard*, 133, an appeal from the Court of Appeals of the State of Maryland. I will read the section of exemption of the Maryland statute:

"That upon any of the aforesaid banks accepting of, and complying with, the terms and conditions of this act, the faith of the State is hereby pledged not to impose any further tax or burden upon them."

This is the phrase of the exemption; the State is pledged "not to impose any further tax or burden upon them, during the continuance of their charters under this act," and that is all; there is not a word about stockholders there. The bank accepted this law, complied with its provisions, and some years afterwards a law was passed taxing the shareholders for their shares, as component parts of their general personal property. Let us see how counsel stated the question. On page 139 the counsel for the shareholder stated it thus:

"The tax of 1841 clashes with the exemption. It is laid on everything which constitutes the property of the bank, because, in a schedule, everything, even the franchise, goes to make up the aggregate value of the stock; and the tax is laid on the cash value of the stock. By the 17th section, the assessors are directed to value it at the market price. But the market price is governed by the value of all the different species of property held by the bank, including even the franchise, because a purchaser looks at all these when about to invest. It is impossible to separate that portion of the tax which falls upon the franchise, and, as the legislature has covered the whole, the entire tax must fall."

The counter proposition, at pages 141, 2, 3, is precisely what is laid down here, that the bank could not be taxed; but this is not a taxation of the bank; this is a taxation of the shares, as component parts of the property of the individual, in common with the other taxable property of the State, against which it has not precluded itself by a correlative obligation not to tax the bank. It was insisted upon there, as here, that the difference of title made the difference of substance; that the stock was personal property, transferable by and belonging to its owner; and that the stockholders do not own the property of the bank and cannot convey any title to it. In other words, we had the same indisputable facts and law about the relations of stockholders and stock, capital and shares, that are insisted upon here as regards the modal administration of the *res* owned; and that was urged upon the Court as a reason for saying that a tax on the shareholders was not a violation of the contract not to tax the bank; but the answer of the Court was, "That is not the way to keep the contract you have made; the subject matter, the purpose, the object, the promise, the result, all make your promise cover the property in its beneficial, and not its formal ownership, and the promise is broken when you tax the shares of the bank;" and his Honor, Judge Wayne, delivering the unanimous opinion of the Court, put the subject on the same grounds; nay, its reasons and its phrases will answer for a decision of this cause. After that, a similar case arose before a very learned court in New Jersey, which is reported in 3 *Zabriskie*, 484. Chief Justice Green, a judicial authority well known to this Court, in giving the opinion of the Supreme Court of New Jersey, said:

"When an incorporated company is, by its charter, exempt from taxation, the stock of the company, in the hands of the stockholders, cannot be taxed. It represents, and is, the title to the property of the company, and is therefore included in the exemption of the charter."

There the exemption of the charter was in regard to the railroads of New Jersey. The form of it, I think, was this: Fish was taxed upon his shares in the railroads, as a part of his personal property in the aggregate; it was put down at its value with all the other items of his property, and he contested the valuation, insisting that that portion of his property, which was represented by the shares, was not taxable. The exemption of the stock was found in the charter of the company, which provided that it should pay 10 cents to the State on each passenger, "and that no other tax or impost shall be levied or assessed upon said company." The State did not assess the company, but assessed the shareholders. The Supreme Court of New Jersey said that could not be done, and your Honors were not troubled with that case because you had disposed of the Maryland case. This also confirms, by judicial authority, what I insist upon, that taxation upon the bank, and again upon the shares, is nothing but double taxation. In the same opinion the New Jersey court say :

"The stock of incorporated banks, although the bank pays a tax on its capital, may be taxed in the hands of stockholders if authorized by the legislature, although it is a second tax on the same property. Double taxation may be unequal, oppressive, and unjust; but it is not prohibited by any constitutional provision, and it is in the discretion of the legislature, and courts cannot declare void a statute, within the constitutional power of the legislature, because its operation may appear unjust and oppressive."

Of course this topic had relation to another item of taxation, not coming within the protection of the promise of the charter and the Constitution of the United States. The Chief Justice says that we cannot strike down a tax that our Legislature has put upon shares, because it has also put it on the stock; it is two taxations of the same thing ; but, as our Legislature can put a double rate upon one thing and a single rate upon another, however oppressive it may be, it is not for us to interfere.

There seems then, if your Honors please, to be very little
reason for regretting the absence of judicial authorities, upon
what must be considered the principal question of the case.
The solution is very simple. The relation of the corporation
and of the stockholders, in respect to the property which constitutes but one subject of ownership and of taxation, is a twofold relation to a single capital or value. The relation of legal
and equitable title in the same land is the best analogy. So
long as a tax is laid upon property, no variety, diversity, nor
complexity of title can increase the property or the tax. You
cannot make the subject of taxation any larger by reason of
these different titles that are carved out of it, or these different
arrangements for its management. If Congress means to protect
this capital under the Constitution, and this Court has held that
it has authority so to do, then it means to do it in a way that
practically saves it from the tax ; and, so long as the exemption
is applied to the property, it will exempt every form and every
title in that property.

The statutes of our State, in an unbroken course of legislation, have recognized this fact ; that stock in the aggregate, and
the corporation as a person to be taxed, represent the same
property as the shares of stock and the shareholders as
persons to be taxed ; and they have varied, as his Honor
Judge Nelson well knows, in the course of years, their forms of
applying taxation to corporations, as seemed to them most convenient. Under the statute of 1813, and until the change by
the Revised Statutes, all the interests of corporations in the
State of New York were taxed upon the shareholders in respect
of their shares, as included in the bulk of their property. From
the period of the Revised Statutes, a change was made by collecting the bulk of the tax from the bulk of the property ; and,
as a part of the same system of assessing and collecting the tax,
it was in so many words enacted, that no shares of stockholders,
in corporations that were taxed by the State, should themselves
pay any tax. When the stockholders paid the tax, under the
old system, there was no tax on the corporation ; when the corporation paid the tax, under the new system, there was none on

the stockholders, by the arrangement of the law which treated the form clearly as *modal*, for the convenience of the State, for the security of the collection of the tax, and for the considerations of policy which prefer secondary rather than direct taxation, which latter our systems have avoided as much as possible.

There is no reason to hold, that, in the State of New York or anywhere else, there are any principles of law, by which these propositions that are established can possibly be disturbed. I have referred in my brief to a couple of cases in the Massachusetts Reports, where this question is well considered and presented ; that it is all one subject of taxation, and is taxable, under the system of the laws, either to the persons or to the corporation, as may be found convenient.

If the Court please, the exemption from taxation, enjoyed by the National Banks under the Constitution and Laws of the United States, is of the capital by reason of its investment in Federal securities ; and again of its capital, its franchise, and its operations, all that it is in character, in property, and in faculty, by reason of its being an instrument of the General Government in the exercise of its constitutional powers. As the learned Judge Comstock says in the case in 23 *New York Reports*, "no corporation aggregate that the world ever saw ever owned anything but its capital, property, and its franchise." Nothing is added, by the creation of a corporation, to the property that the contributors put in by way of capital, except the franchise; that is added, making the artificial person a creature of law; but the franchise is all that has been added. Here we have these bodies, that are in their capital exempt, and in their franchise exempt. What is there about them that can be taxed? This left nothing that constitutes an element of value, or of possession, or of property, to be taxed. If the franchise had come from the State, if the franchise were taxable by the State, as the creature of the State, you might find something in the constitution of the corporation, (although its capital be exempted if invested in United States securities,) that would endure State taxation. They might tax the franchise inordinately, or moderately ; they made the franchise, and they may tax it ;

and the investment of the capital in United States securities does not exempt the taxation of the franchise from the power of the State; and that was the distinction which was made by some observations of Mr. Justice Nelson in the first bank tax case in 2 *Black*, referring to the state of the law in New York. Franchise may bear a tax, he said. The Legislature changed their law, but did not come up to the point of taxing the franchise, which was taxing for the right to be, and with reference to nothing else. The right to be a bank, the right to continue from year to year to be a bank, may be taxed. That was all that was open under the observation of this Court. They did not put the tax on the franchise, but they put the tax on the capital, on a valuation that did not make it necessary to find what it was really worth, but took a nominal value for it; and thought they had avoided the judgment of this Court by that contrivance. They had not taxed the right of the corporation to be; they had taxed its capital upon a nominal, instead of a real, value. The Court said, "You may have any form of valuation you choose; but, whatever your form of valuation, you must exempt United States securities from it." That is the case in 2 *Wallace*. Now the contrivance here is, that of having a bank, with its franchise from the Federal Government, with its property protected under Federal law, with its operations and its capital protected as agents and instruments of the Government, incapable of taxation, withdrawn from the taxable property of the State; and they pursue all these into the divided shares, and exact the tax upon them distributively.

What is a stockholder in a corporation? He is nothing, and has nothing, in a corporation, except by his proportion in the capital stock, and his participation in the franchise. It is to the stockholders by name that the franchise is given, they being natural persons, that they should have the franchise to be an artificial person. Is not that a form in which the natural persons are, in the purpose and apparatus of the law, used as one? There is neither fragment nor figment for a tax to rest upon, when there is that extent of exemption.

Now, if the Court please, on the general question, as something has been said, so inconsiderately, about the comparative magnitude or connections of the interest with the government of the old United States Bank, and of this many-headed institution, distributed all through the country, let me call your Honors' attention to the importance of the relations of these banks, even in the single subject of the distribution of the public debt. There was issued in one year the whole bulk, in three series, of the Seven-thirty currency notes, 830 millions in twelve months ; and, of that issue of the Federal debt, these National Banks took and distributed 736 millions, leaving to the Government, in its official organizations of treasury, sub-treasury and special agencies, only 66 millions out of 830 millions to be so disposed of ; illustrating thus what I have ventured to suggest was the genius of this institution. Now, to say of these two great governments, Federal and State, standing against one another, under the Constitution, with their relations adjudicated by this Court, that all these relations are suddenly changed by the intervention of this corporate form of a National Bank ; and that the State becomes the master of the two governments, by taking away from the Federal Government what it had reserved to itself, by giving back to the State Governments what they had lost under the legislation of the country, this is to make the corporation, the mere form, the master of the substance, and controller of those political and public relations. It is like the Genie of the bottle ; when the seal is up, he becomes the master of the servants. This contrivance of the National Banks, instituted for other and additional public purposes, and serving these great public needs, immediately takes in its hands hundreds of millions of Federal stocks with which to serve the Government, and in its hands, and in the hands of nobody else in this country, they can be taxed through the medium of shareholders! At this moment these banks hold 622 millions of dollars of the Federal securities of the United States,—a third of the debt that is out in any other shape than that of mere currency, perhaps more than a third, for I have not the statistics in my mind ; and yet that mass of public debt, free by impression on its face from taxation by the States, free in the hands of every individual, of every corporation, of every association, must contribute such taxes as the States may choose to impose, discriminating or destructive or otherwise, simply because one agency of the Government is helping it in the advancement of its interests in another public matter, to wit, the debt !

If the Court please, it will not avail anything to meet these propositions by the argument that the States, by their natural authority, have dominion for taxation over every subject of property and every person within their jurisdiction. This right and this power, as necessary parts of the State sovereignty, are conceded ; for it is idle to talk of taxation as being a special prerogative of sovereignty. It is sovereignty. It is the sovereign that taxes. It is as universal as the sovereign. "The decree went out that all the world should be taxed," because the Roman empire extended over what was then called the world. Taxation takes all you have. Put taxation and conscription together, and it is the sovereignty over the person and the property, to the extent of the jurisdiction of the State. But taxation goes no further than sovereignty ; and whatever impedes or qualifies or displaces the sovereignty of the States, impedes, qualifies, displaces, taxation by the States. What power there is in taxation to destroy, is shown by the recent Act of Congress inimical to the continuance of the State banks, which taxes their circulation, after a certain prospective period, ten per cent. If a State has power to tax, there is no limit. That you have decided over and over again. It can tax these shares discriminately, if it chooses ; hostilely, destructively, fatally, if you concede the power. You say, with jealous preservation of the Constitution, " There is no such power ; " and the State says, " True, but we will tax the shares or parts hostilely, destructively, fatally ; " and you are called upon to say that they can ; you are called upon to surrender, as I say, to this dominant fiction in law, the personality of a corporation. As by the decisions is expressly stated, whenever the Government have called the property of the citizens into the service of the United States, in the performance of a public duty under the Constitution as an instrument and an agency, that becomes an instrument of the United States, and exempted from State taxation ; unless it be compatible with the public interests that the Government of the United States should concede it.

There are but two methods to deal with this subject. One is that which the State of New York has always avowed, and, I believe, honestly intended to conform to. Looking at it from the side of the State, it may differ from the view that is taken on the side of the Federal Government, but still the principles laid down in 23 *New York Reports* by Chief Judge Denio are, that, when there is a conflict, the adjudications of the Supreme Court of the United States are final as to the supremacy of the Federal power ; and that the only question for a State Court, as new circumstances one after another present new cases, is to see whether there is a conflict, and to yield. There is but one other method ; and that is the method of South Carolina, in the decisions that are cited on the brief. The argument of Mr. Grimké for the United States, than which none abler was ever made on this question, was never answered by Mr. Legaré, nor was it ever answered by the Court. The decision was put upon the ground, that, if there was a conflict, the State of South Carolina could not help it, but it governed what was within its own dominions. That was the proposition, that the reasoning of the Supreme Court, by the mouth of the great Chief Justice, was vicious, unsound, dangerous. Its only viciousness was, that the supremacy of the Union over the States was asserted ; its only unsoundness was, that the supremacy of the Union over the States was asserted ; its only danger was, that the supremacy of the Union over the States was asserted ; and this, the South Carolina, method of dealing with the conflict, as we all know at last, is WAR.*

EXECUTIVE COMMITTEE OF NATIONAL BANKS.

EXECUTIVE COMMITTEE.

THOMAS COLEMAN, President First National Bank, Troy, N. Y.
JOSEPH U. ORVIS, President Ninth National Bank, New York.
P. C. CALHOUN, President Fourth National Bank, New York.
E. B. JUDSON, President First National Bank, Syracuse, N. Y.
CALEB SAGER, President First National Bank, Trenton, N. J.
W. H. AINEY, President Second National Bank, Allentown, Pa.
C. H. CLARK, President First National Bank, Philadelphia.
ADAM REINEMAN, President Third National Bank, Pittsburg, Pa.
THOMAS SWANN, President First National Bank, Baltimore, Md.
GEORGE STETSON, President First National Bank, Bangor, Me.
G. L. TREADWELL, President Nat. Mechanics and Traders' Bank, Portsmouth, N. H.
E. D. TIFFANY, President First National Bank, Hartford, Conn.
JOSEPH GRINNELL, President First National Bank, New Bedford, Mass.
C. B. HALL, Cashier Boston National Bank, Boston, Mass.
EDWARD BETTS, President First National Bank, Wilmington, Del.
GEORGE ADAMS, Cashier First National Bank, Wheeling, Va.
G. WORTHINGTON, President First National Bank, Cleveland, Ohio.
B. T. STONE, President Fourth National Bank, Cincinnati.
J. S. THOMAS, President First National Bank, Cadiz, Ohio.
M. L. PIERCE, President First National Bank, Lafayette, Ind.
E. AIKEN, President First National Bank, Chicago, Ill.
H. P. BALDWIN, President Second National Bank, Detroit, Mich.
F. W. CRONENBOLD, President First National Bank, St. Louis, Mo.
AUSTIN CORBIN, President First National Bank, Davenport, Iowa.
JAMES E. THOMPSON, President First National Bank, St. Paul, Minn.
NATHAN T. SPRAGUE, JR., Vice-President First National Bank, Brandon, Vt.
CHARLES H. CHILDS, JR., Cashier Third National Bank, Providence, R. I.

SUB-COMMITTEE.

E. B. JUDSON, President.
THOMAS COLEMAN, Vice-President.
JOSEPH U. ORVIS, Sec'y and Treasurer.
C. H. CLARK, of Philadelphia.
B. T. STONE, of Cincinnati.
F. W. CRONENBOLD, of St. Louis.
CHARLES B. HALL, Boston.

NEW YORK, *March* 24, 1866.

On the 12th of February last, this Committee forwarded the "Brief and Points of Messrs. Evarts and Sedgwick," of Counsel for the Committee in this very important case, involving pecuniary interests "larger than in the course of jurisprudence has ever been submitted to any other court." Whatever the decision may be, the Committee feel sure that everything has been done to put the matter before the highest tribunal of the country in an appropriate manner.

The argument of Mr. Evarts was then promised, and is now forwarded ; and to its careful perusal, the Committee invite all interested in National Banks.

JOSEPH U. ORVIS,
Sec. and Treas. Ex. Committee.

NEW YORK, *March* 24, 1866.

SUPREME COURT OF THE UNITED STATES.

No. 289.—DECEMBER TERM, 1865.

ADAM VAN ALLEN, in behalf of himself and all other Stockholders in the First National Bank of Albany, Plaintiffs in Error,

vs.

MICHAEL A. NOLAN, et al., as the Board of Assessors of the City of Albany . . . . . .

In error to the Court o Appeals of the State of New York.

Mr. Justice NELSON delivered the opinion of the Court.

This is a writ of error to the Court of Appeals of the State of New York. The case presented is this: The plaintiffs in error are stockholders in the First National bank in the city of Albany, and the defendants constitute a board of assessors of taxes in the same city. The whole of the capital stock of the bank consisted in stocks and bonds issued by the United States under various acts of Congress; and it was insisted before the board that the shares of the bank held by the plaintiffs as stockholders, were not subject to assessment and taxation under State authority; which position was denied by the board, and the assessment made and tax enforced. The case was carried to the Supreme Court of the State, and thence to the Court of Appeals, which court affirmed the authority of the board of assessors to levy the tax.

The case is now before us under the 25th section of the judiciary act. The decree of the Court of Appeals must be reversed, on the ground that the enabling act of the State, passed March 9th, 1865, (Sess. 1, ch. 97), does not conform to the limitations by the act of Congress passed June 3, 1864, organizing the national banks, and providing for their taxation. (§ 41.) The defect is this : one of the limitations in the act of Congress is, "that the tax so imposed under the laws of any State upon the shares of the associations authorized by this act, shall not exceed the rate imposed upon the shares of any of the banks organized under the authority of the State where such association is located." The enabling act of the State contains no such limitation. The banks of the State are taxed upon their capital, and although the act provides that the tax on the shares of the national banks shall not exceed the par value, yet, inasmuch as the capital of the state banks may consist of the bonds of the United States, which are exempt from state taxation, it is easy to see that this tax on the capital is not an equivalent for a tax on the shares of the stockholders. This is an unimportant question, however, as the defect may be readily remedied by the State legislature. The main and important question involved, and the one which has been argued at great length and with eminent ability, is, whether the State possesses the power to authorize the taxation of the shares of these national banks in the hands of Stockholders, whose capital is wholly vested in stock and bonds of the United States ? The court are of opinion that this power is possessed by the State, and that it is due to the several cases that have been so fully and satisfactorily argued before us at this term, as well as to the public interest involved, the question should be finally disposed of ; and we shall proceed, therefore, to state, as briefly as practicable, the grounds and reasons that have led to their judgment in the case.

The first act providing for the organization of these national banks, passed 25th February, 1863, contained no provision concerning State taxation of these shares ; but Congress reserved the right, by the last section, at any time, "to amend, alter, or repeal the act." The present act of 1864 is a re-enactment of the prior statute, with some material amendments, of which the section concerning State taxation is one.

In organizing these banks under this act, it is made the duty of the association to deliver to the treasurer of the United States, registered bonds, bearing interest, to an amount not less than thirty thousand dollars, nor less than one-third of the capital stock paid in ; which bonds shall be deposited with the treasurer, and by him safely kept, &c. This provision fixes the minimum limit of the amount of the bonds to be deposited with the treasurer, but no maximum is fixed, and the whole amount of the capital may be invested in them. On the deposit of these bonds with the treasurer, the association is entitled to receive from the comptroller of the currency circulating notes of different denominations, registered and countersigned, equal in amount to ninety per centum of the current market value of the bonds so deposited. (§ 21.) There is a limit to the amount of the circulating currency to be issued to these associations, not to exceed, in the aggregate, three hundred millions of dollars. This sum was to be apportioned among the several banks organized under the act. (§ 22.) These notes, after being signed by the president and cashier, are authorized to be issued and to circulate as money, and are to be received at par in all parts of the United States, in payment of taxes, excises, public lands, and all other dues to the United States, except for duties on imports ; also, for all salaries and other debts and demands owing by the United States, except interest on the public debt, and in redemption of the national currency. (§ 23.)

These associations also possess all the powers necessary for carrying on the business of banking, by discounting and negotiating promissory notes, drafts, bills of exchange, and other evidences of debt ; by receiving deposits, buying and selling exchange, coin, and bullion ; by loaning money on personal security ; by obtaining, issuing, and circulating notes according to the provisions of this act, &c. The duration of the charter is twenty years.

They are also made depositories of public moneys, when designated by the Secretary of the Treasury, and may be employed as fiscal agents of the government.

Now, these are very great powers and privileges conferred by the act upon these associations, and which are founded upon a new use and application of these government bonds, especially the privilege of issuing notes to circulate in the community as money, to the amount of ninety per centum of the bonds deposited with the treasurer, thereby nearly doubling their amount for all the operations and business purposes of the bank. This currency furnishes means and facilities for conducting the operations of the associations, which, if used wisely and skilfully, cannot but result in great advantages and profits to all the members of the association—the shareholders of the bank.

In the granting of chartered rights and privileges by government, especially if of great value to the corporators, certain burthens are usually, if not generally, imposed as conditions of the grant. Accordingly we find them in this charter. They are very few, but distinctly stated.

They are, first, a duty of one-half of one per centum each half year, upon the average amount of its notes in circulation; second, a duty of one-quarter of one per centum each half year, upon the average amount of its deposits; third, a duty of one-quarter of one per centum each half year, on the average amount of its capital stock beyond the amount invested in United States bonds; and fourth, a State tax upon the shares of the association held by the stockholders, not greater than assessed on other moneyed capital in the state, nor to exceed the rate on shares of stock of State banks.

These are the only burthens annexed to the enjoyment of the great chartered rights and privileges that we find in this act of Congress; and no objection is made to either of them except the last—the limited State taxation.

Although it has been suggested, yet it can hardly be said to have been argued, that the provision in the act of Congress concerning the taxation of the shares by the State, is unconstitutional. The suggestion is, that it is a tax by the State upon the bonds of the government which constitute the capital of the bank, and which this court has heretofore decided to be illegal. But this suggestion is scarcely well founded; for were we to admit, for the sake of the argument, this to be a tax of the bonds or capital stock of the bank, it is but a tax upon the new uses and new privileges conferred by the charter of the association—it is but a condition annexed to the enjoyment of this new use and new application of the bonds ; and if Congress possessed the power to grant these new rights and new privileges, which none of the learned counsel has denied, and which the whole argument assumes, then we do not see but the power to annex the conditions is equally clear and indisputable. The question involved is altogether a different one from that decided in the previous bank cases, and stands upon different considerations. The State tax under this act of Congress involves no question as to the pledged faith of the government. The tax is the condition for the new rights and privileges conferred upon these associations.

But, in addition to this view, the tax on the shares is not a tax on the capital of the bank. The corporation is the legal owner of all the property of the bank, real and personal ; and within the powers conferred upon it by the charter, and for the purposes for which it was created, can deal with the corporate property as absolutely as a private individual can deal with his own. This is familiar law, and will be found in every work that may be opened on the subject of corporations. A striking exemplification may be seen in the case of the Queen vs. Arnold, (9 Adolp. & Ellis N. S. P., 806.) The question related to the registry of a ship owned by a corporation. Lord Denman observed : " It appears to me that the British corporation is, as such, the sole owner of the ship. The individual members of the corporation are no doubt interested in one sense in the property of the corporation, as they may derive individual benefits from its increase, or loss from its decrease ; but in no legal sense are the individual members the owners."

The interest of the shareholder entitles him to participate in the net profits earned by the bank in the employment of its capital, during the existence of its charter, in proportion to the number of his shares ; and, upon its dissolution, or termination, to his proportion of the property that may remain of the corporation after the payment of its debts. This is a distinct independent interest or property, held by the shareholder like any other property that may belong to him. Now, it is this interest which the act of Congress has left subject to taxation by the States, under the limitations prescribed, as will be seen on referring to it.

That act provides as follows :

"That nothing in this act shall be construed to prevent all the shares of any of the said associations, held by any person or body corporate, from being included in the valuation of personal property of such person or corporation in the assessment of taxes imposed by and under State authority, at the place where such bank is located, and not elsewhere, but not *at a greater rate than is assessed upon other moneyed capital in the hands of individual citizens of such State : Provided further, that the tax so imposed under the laws of any State, upon the shares of the associations, authorized by this act, shall not exceed the rate imposed upon the shares of any of the banks organized under the authority of the State where such association is located :* Provided also, that nothing in this act shall exempt the real estate of associations from either State, county, or municipal taxes to the same extent according to its value as other real estate is taxed."—(§ 41.)

It is said that Congress possesses no power to confer upon a State authority to be exercised which has been exclusively delegated to that body by the Constitution, and, consequently, that it cannot confer upon a State the sovereign right of taxation ; nor is a State competent to receive a grant of any such power from Congress. We agree to this.

But, as it respects a subject-matter over which Congress and the States may exercise a concurrent power, but from the exercise of which Congress, by reason of its paramount authority, may exclude the States, there is no doubt Congress may withhold the exercise of that authority and leave the States free to act. An example of this relation existing between the Federal and State governments is found in the pilot-laws of the States, and the health and quarantine laws.

The power of taxation under the Constitution as a general rule, and as has been repeatedly recognized in adjudged cases in this Court, is a concurrent power. The qualifications of the rule are the exclusion of the States from the taxation of the means and instruments employed in the exercise of the functions of the Federal government.

The remaining question is, has Congress legislated in respect to these associations, so as to leave the shares of the stockholders subject to State taxation ?

We have already referred to the main provision of the act of Congress on this subject, and it will be seen it declares "that nothing in this act shall be construed to prevent *all the shares* in any of the said associations, held by any person, or body corporate, from being included in the valuation of the personal property of such person or corporation in the assessment of taxes imposed by or under State authority, at the place where such bank is located : "—and in another section of the act (§ 40) it is declared "that the president and cashier of every such association shall cause to be kept, at all times, a full and correct list of the names and residences of all the shareholders in the association, and the number of shares held by each, in the office where its business is transacted, and such list shall be subject to the inspection of all shareholders and creditors of the association, *and the officers authorized to assess taxes under State authority*, during business hours of each day," &c.

These two provisions—the one declaring that nothing in the act shall be construed to prevent the shares from being included in the valuation of the personal property, &c., in the assessment of taxes imposed by State authority ; and the other providing for the keeping of the list of the names and residences of the shoreholders, among other things, for the inspection of the officers authorized to assess the State taxes—not only recognize, in express terms, the sovereign right of the State to tax, but prescribes regulations and duties to these associations, with a view to disembarrass the officers of the State engaged in the exercise of this right. Nothing, it would seem, could be made plainer, or more direct and comprehensive on the subject. The language of the several provisions are so explicit and positive as scarcely to call for judicial construction.

Then, as to the shares, and what is intended by the use of

the term? The language of the act is equally explicit and decisive.

The persons forming an association are required to make a certificate, which shall specify, among other things, the amount of its capital stock, and the number of shares into which the same shall be divided, the names and places of residence of the shareholders, and the number of shares held by each.—(§ 6.)

The capital stock shall be divided into shares of one hundred dollars each, and shall be deemed personal property. The shareholders of the association shall be held individually responsible, equally and ratably, and not one for another, for all contracts, debts, and engagements of such association to the extent of the amount of their stock therein at the par value, in addition to the amount invested in such shares.—(§ 12.)

In the election of directors, and in deciding all questions at meetings of shareholders, each shareholder shall be entitled to one vote on each share of stock held by him.—(§ 11.) Fifty per centum of the capital stock of every association shall be paid in before it shall commence business, and the remainder in instalments of at least ten per centum per month till the whole amount is paid ; and if any shareholder, or his assignee, shall fail to make the payment, or any instalment on his stock, the directors may sell the stock at public auction.—(§ 14, 15.) No association shall make any loan or discount on the security of the shares of its own capital.—(§ 35.)

We have already referred to the list of the names and residences of the shareholders, and the number of shares, to be kept for the inspection of the State assessors.

Now, in view of these several provisions in which the term shares, and shareholders, are mentioned, and the clear and obvious meaning of the term in the connexion in which it is found, namely, the whole of the interest in the shares and of the shareholders ; when the statute provides, that nothing in this act shall be construed to prevent *all the shares* in any of the said associations, &c., from being included in the valuation of the personal property of any person or corporation in the assessment of taxes imposed by State authority, &c., can there be a doubt, but that the term "shares," as used in this connexion, means the same interest as when used in the other portions of the act. Take, for examples, the use of the term in the certificate of the numbers of shares in the articles of association :—In the division of the capital stock into shares of one hundred dollars each ; in the personal liability clause, which subjects the shareholder to an amount, and, in addition, to the amount invested in such shares; in the election of directors, and in deciding all questions at meetings of the stockholders, each share is entitled to one vote ; in regulations of the payments of the shares subscribed ; and, finally, in the list of shares kept for the inspection of the State assessors. In all these instances, it is manifest that the term as used means the entire interest of the shareholder ; and it would be singular, if in the use of the term in the connexion of State taxation, Congress intended a totally different meaning, without any indication of such intent.

This is an answer to the argument that the *term*, as used here, means only the interest of the shareholder as representing the portion of the capital, if any, not invested in the bonds of the Government, and that the State assessors must institute an enquiry into the investment of the capital of the bank, and ascertain what portion is invested in these bonds, and make a discrimination in the assessment of the shares. If Congress had intended any such discrimination, it would have been an easy matter to have said so. Certainly, so grave and important a change in the use of this term, if so intended, would not have been left to judicial construction.

Upon the whole, after the maturest consideration we have been able to give to this case, we are satisfied that the States possess the power to tax the whole of the interest of the shareholder in the shares held by him in these associations, within the limit prescribed by the act authorizing their organization.

But, for the reasons stated in the fore part of the opinion, the judgment must be reversed and the case remitted to the Court of Appeals of the State of New York, with directions to enter judgment for the plaintiffs in error, with costs.

No. 286.

G. CLARENCE CHURCHILL, impleaded with EDWARD S. BRAYTON *et al.*, Plaintiffs in Error,
vs.
The City of Utica.

} In error to the Court of Appeals of the State of New York.

Churchill is the only party against whom judgment was rendered in the court below, and the party who has brought a writ of error to this court.

The judgment is reversed, and the case remitted to the court below for proceedings there as directed in the case of Van Allen and others *vs.* Nolan and others. We refer to the opinion in that case as governing this one.

S. N.

No. 288.

CHAUNCY P. WILLIAMS, in behalf of himself and all other stockholders in the National Albany Exchange Bank, Plaintiffs in Error,
vs.
MICHAEL A. NOLAN *et al.*, as the Board of Assessors of the City of Albany.

} In error to the Court of Appeals of the State of New York.

The opinion in the case of Van Allen and others *vs.* Nolan and others, governs this case, and the same judgment must be entered.

Judgment reversed and case remitted.

S. N.

True copy,
D. W. MIDDLETON, C. S. C. U. S.

www.ingramcontent.com/pod-product-compliance
Lightning Source LLC
Chambersburg PA
CBHW022100300426
44117CB00007B/523